Globalization and Poverty
Volume I

The Globalization of the World Economy

Series Editor: Mark Casson
Professor of Economics
University of Reading, UK

1. Transforming International Organizations
   William G. Egelhoff
2. Strategic Alliances
   Paul W. Beamish
3. Structural Change, Industrial Location
   and Competitiveness
   Joanne E. Oxley and Bernard Yeung
4. Developing and Newly Industrializing
   Countries (Volumes I and II)
   Chris Milner
5. Historical Foundations of Globalization
   James Foreman-Peck
6. Trade and Investment Policy
   (Volumes I and II)
   Thomas L. Brewer
7. The Globalization of Financial Services
   Mervyn K. Lewis
8. Foreign Direct Investment and
   Technological Change (Volumes I and II)
   John Cantwell
9. The Globalization of Business Firms
   from Emerging Economies
   (Volumes I and II)
   Henry Wai-chung Yeung
10. Globalization and Labour Markets
    (Volumes I and II)
    David Greenaway and Douglas R. Nelson

11. Financial Market Integration and
    International Capital Flows
    Gregor Irwin and David Vines
12. Governing the Global Environment
    Carlo Carraro
13. SMEs in the Age of Globalization
    David B. Audretsch
14. Privatization and Globalization: The
    Changing Role of the State in Business
    Ram Mudambi
15. Globalization and the Location of Firms
    John Cantwell
16. Globalization and Economic and
    Financial Stability
    H. Peter Gray and John R. Dilyard
17. Critical Perspectives on Globalization
    *Marina Della Giusta, Uma S.
    Kambhampati and Robert Hunter Wade*
18. Global Supply Chain Management
    (Volumes I and II)
    Masaaki Kotabe and Michael J. Mol
19. Globalization and Poverty
    (Volumes I, II and III)
    Paul Collier and Jan Willem Gunning

Future titles will include:

Globalization and Productivity
*David Greenaway, Holger Görg and
Richard Kneller*

Multinational Firms and the Local Economy
Klaus Meyer

Radical Economic Perspectives on
Globalization
Gerald A. Epstein

Wherever possible, the articles in these volumes have been reproduced as originally published using facsimile reproduction, inclusive of footnotes and pagination to facilitate ease of reference.

For a list of all Edward Elgar published titles visit our site on the World Wide Web at
www.e-elgar.com

Globalization and Poverty Volume I
What Has Happened?

Edited by

Paul Collier

Professor of Economics
Oxford University, UK

and

Jan Willem Gunning

Professor of Development Economics
The Free University, Amsterdam, The Netherlands

THE GLOBALIZATION OF THE WORLD ECONOMY

An Elgar Reference Collection
Cheltenham, UK • Northampton, MA, USA

Published by
Edward Elgar Publishing Limited
Glensanda House
Montpellier Parade
Cheltenham
Glos GL50 1UA
UK

Edward Elgar Publishing, Inc.
William Pratt House
9 Dewey Court
Northampton
Massachusetts 01060
USA

A catalogue record for this book is available from the British Library

Library of Congress Control Number: 2007935149

ISBN 978 1 84542 769 6 (3 volume set)

Printed and bound in Great Britain by MPG Books Ltd, Bodmin, Cornwall.

Contents

Acknowledgements   vii

Introduction   Paul Collier and Jan Willem Gunning   ix

PART I   HISTORY OF GLOBALIZATION

1.   Robert E. Lucas, Jr. (2003), 'The Industrial Revolution: Past and
     Future', *Federal Reserve Bank of Minneapolis 2003 Annual Report*,
     5–20   3
2.   Jeffrey G. Williamson (2005), 'Winners and Losers Over Two
     Centuries of Globalization', in *Wider Perspectives on Global
     Development*, Chapter 6, Hampshire, UK: Palgrave Macmillan,
     136–74   19
3.   Paul Collier and David Dollar (2002), 'The New Wave of
     Globalization and its Economic Effects', in *Globalization, Growth
     and Poverty*, Chapter 1, Oxford, UK: Oxford University Press for
     the World Bank, 23–51   58

PART II   IMPACT ON POVERTY AND INEQUALITY

4.   Ravi Kanbur (2001), 'Economic Policy, Distribution and Poverty:
     The Nature of Disagreements', *World Development*, **29** (6), 1083–94   93

A   Global Poverty

5.   François Bourguignon and Christian Morrisson (2002), 'Inequality
     Among World Citizens: 1820–1992', *American Economic Review*,
     92 (4), September, 727–44   107
6.   Martin Ravallion (2004), 'Competing Concepts of Inequality in the
     Globalization Debate', *Brookings Trade Forum 2004*, Washington,
     DC: Brookings Institution Press, 1–38   125
7.   Shaohua Chen and Martin Ravallion (2004), 'How Have the World's
     Poorest Fared Since the Early 1980s?', *World Bank Research
     Observer*, **19** (2), Fall, 141–69   163

B   International Convergence or Divergence?

8.   Lant Pritchett (1997), 'Divergence, Big Time', *Journal of Economic
     Perspectives*, **11** (3), Summer, 3–17   195
9.   Branko Milanovic (2002), 'True World Income Distribution, 1988
     and 1993: First Calculation Based on Household Surveys Alone',
     Economic Journal, **112** (476), January, 51–92   210

C   Regional Convergence or Divergence?

10. Dan Ben-David (1993), 'Equalizing Exchange: Trade Liberalization
     and Income Convergence', *Quarterly Journal of Economics*, **108** (3),
     August, 653–79   255
11. Anthony J. Venables (2003), 'Winners and Losers from Regional
     Integration Agreements', *Economic Journal*, **113** (490), October,
     747–61   282

D   Domestic Inequality and Poverty

12. David Dollar and Aart Kraay (2002), 'Growth is Good for the Poor',
     Journal of Economic Growth, **7**, 195–225   299
13. Martin Ravallion (2001), 'Growth, Inequality and Poverty: Looking
     Beyond Averages', *World Development*, **29** (11), 1803–15   330
14. Howard L.M. Nye and Sanjay G. Reddy (2002), 'Dollar and Kraay
     on "Trade, Growth and Poverty": A Critique', 1–11, unpublished   343
15. Edward Anderson (2005), 'Openness and Inequality in Developing
     Countries: A Review of Theory and Recent Evidence', *World
     Development*, **33** (7), 1045–63   354

E   Country Perspectives

16. Ravi Kanbur and Xiaobo Zhang (2005), 'Fifty Years of Regional
     Inequality in China: A Journey Through Central Planning, Reform,
     and Openness', *Review of Development Economics*, **9** (1), 87–106   375
17. Arvind Panagariya (2004), 'India's Trade Reform', *India Policy
     Forum 2004*, **1**, 1–68   395
18. Norman Loayza, Pablo Fajnzylber and César Calderón (2005),
     'The Experience of Economic Growth in Latin America and the
     Caribbean', Washington, DC: World Bank, 1–51, abridged   463
19. Paul Collier and Jan Willem Gunning (1999), 'Why Has Africa
     Grown Slowly?', *Journal of Economic Perspectives*, **13** (3),
     Summer, 3–22   514

Name Index   535

Acknowledgements

The editors and publishers wish to thank the authors and the following publishers who have kindly given permission for the use of copyright material.

American Economic Association for articles: Lant Pritchett (1997), 'Divergence, Big Time', *Journal of Economic Perspectives*, **11** (3), Summer, 3–17; Paul Collier and Jan Willem Gunning (1999), 'Why Has Africa Grown Slowly?', *Journal of Economic Perspectives*, **13** (3), Summer, 3–22; François Bourguignon and Christian Morrisson (2002), 'Inequality Among World Citizens: 1820–1992', *American Economic Review*, **92** (4), September, 727–44.

Blackwell Publishing Ltd for articles: Branko Milanovic (2002), 'True World Income Distribution, 1988 and 1993: First Calculation Based on Household Surveys Alone', *Economic Journal*, **112** (476), January, 51–92; Anthony J. Venables (2003), 'Winners and Losers from Regional Integration Agreements', *Economic Journal*, **113** (490), October, 747–61; Ravi Kanbur and Xiaobo Zhang (2005), 'Fifty Years of Regional Inequality in China: A Journey Through Central Planning, Reform, and Openness', *Review of Development Economics*, **9** (1), 87–106.

Brookings Institution for excerpts: Martin Ravallion (2004), 'Competing Concepts of Inequality in the Globalization Debate', *Brookings Trade Forum 2004*, 1–38; Arvind Panagariya (2004), 'India's Trade Reform', *India Policy Forum 2004*, **1**, 1–68.

Elsevier for articles: Ravi Kanbur (2001), 'Economic Policy, Distribution and Poverty: The Nature of Disagreements', *World Development*, **29** (6), 1083–94; Martin Ravallion (2001), 'Growth, Inequality and Poverty: Looking Beyond Averages', *World Development*, **29** (11), 1803–15; Edward Anderson (2005), 'Openness and Inequality in Developing Countries: A Review of Theory and Recent Evidence', *World Development*, **33** (7), 1045–63.

Federal Reserve Bank of Minneapolis for excerpt: Robert E. Lucas, Jr. (2003), 'The Industrial Revolution: Past and Future', *Federal Reserve Bank of Minneapolis 2003 Annual Report*, 5–20.

MIT Press Journals for article: Dan Ben-David (1993), 'Equalizing Exchange: Trade Liberalization and Income Convergence', *Quarterly Journal of Economics*, **108** (3), August, 653–79.

Oxford University Press for excerpt and article: Paul Collier and David Dollar (2002), 'The New Wave of Globalization and its Economic Effects', in *Globalization, Growth and Poverty*, Chapter 1, 23–51; Shaohua Chen and Martin Ravallion (2004), 'How Have the

World's Poorest Fared Since the Early 1980s?', *World Bank Research Observer*, **19** (2), Fall, 141–69.

Palgrave Macmillan for excerpt: Jeffrey G. Williamson (2005), 'Winners and Losers Over Two Centuries of Globalization', in *Wider Perspectives on Global Development*, Chapter 6, 136–74.

Sanjay G. Reddy for his own article: Howard L.M. Nye and Sanjay G. Reddy (2002), 'Dollar and Kraay on "Trade, Growth and Poverty": A Critique', 1–11, unpublished.

Springer Science and Business Media for article: David Dollar and Aart Kraay (2002), 'Growth is Good for the Poor', *Journal of Economic Growth*, **7**, 195–225.

World Bank for excerpt: Norman Loayza, Pablo Fajnzylber and César Calderón (2005), 'The Experience of Economic Growth in Latin America and the Caribbean', 1–51, abridged.

Every effort has been made to trace all the copyright holders but if any have been inadvertently overlooked the publishers will be pleased to make the necessary arrangement at the first opportunity.

In addition the publishers wish to thank the Library of Indiana University at Bloomington, USA, for their assistance in obtaining these articles.

Introduction

Paul Collier and Jan Willem Gunning

Introduction

Globalization is a highly charged subject, arousing both excitement and fear. These are reflected in much of the popular debate, which is polarized by political ideology. These volumes focus on a core issue of contention in this debate since the subject is the implications of globalization for poverty and inequality. However, we are concerned only with the contributions of academic economics. Even with this limitation, there is plenty of scope for disagreement.

Economic theory, notably the simple trade models of Ricardo and Heckscher-Ohlin, suggests beneficial effects of globalization. The huge differences in incomes and endowments around the globe imply the opportunity for mutual benefits as factor returns are equalized through trade and factor movements, and raised through technological exchange. Globalization is seen as the realization of these opportunities through the removal of barriers to the flows of goods, services, factors and knowledge.

The economic critiques of this vision basically introduce distributional effects. Many of the distributional effects indeed map into popular fears of globalization. Unskilled workers in developed countries fear that the outsourcing of jobs to low-income countries and immigration will reduce their wages. Whether outsourcing and immigration have such effects once allowance is made for multiple channels of causation is an empirical matter, but the possibility is theoretically unimpeachable. Farmers fear the loss of protection under WTO rules. In developing countries workers in protected industries stand to lose from trade liberalization, leading to job losses. Again, while these groups might be compensated through other mechanisms, one direct effect of liberalization will be to lower their incomes. The growing mobility of capital arouses fears in trade unions of the loss of power relative to capital, leading to declining wages, and in governments of the loss of tax revenue through tax competition leading to an erosion of social provision.

Whereas in the Ricardian model a government acts unilaterally, in game theoretic approaches governments react to each other and this may indeed generate a race to the bottom. Finally, governments of small, low-income countries fear the loss of sovereignty as international institutions in which they have little influence restrict their scope for policy choice: international rules may be designed to favor international corporations at their expense. The theory of intellectual property rights indeed suggests that such countries could be net losers from the global extension of these rights. The above critiques qualify but do not destroy the basic Ricardian vision. Many of the papers collected here quantify the net effect either of a particular causal channel, such as migration, or of all the channels for a particular type of country during a particular period. Other papers explore specific distributional effects.

In the present work the first volume is predominantly descriptive, the second is organized around the various channels of transmission and the third focuses on policy.

Volume I: What Has Happened?

Volume I opens with a broad historical sweep. Robert E. Lucas, Jr. (2003; Chapter 1) considers the period since the Industrial Revolution as a guide to growth opportunities for developing countries. He argues that openness to global markets is central to rapid growth. While autarkic strategies have occasionally succeeded, this has only been for brief periods. He forecasts that those countries that are currently poor will benefit most from globalization, and so become the fastest growers of the twenty-first century. This claim of global convergence is considered in the next two papers. Jeffrey G. Williamson (2005; Chapter 2) shows that over the past two centuries the distributional impact of globalization has varied: some spurts of globalization saw convergence between countries, others divergence. Paul Collier and David Dollar (2002; Chapter 3) argue that the post-1980 burst of globalization is itself distinctive, with a large group of developing countries catching up on developed countries through penetration of global markets in manufactures, leaving a residual group of poor countries in both relative and absolute decline. One important lesson is that globalization is not inevitable, as is often claimed.

There have been periods during which both particular countries and sometimes the world as a whole have retreated towards autarky. The notable such period was 1914–45 during which all the indices of globalization went into reverse. However, while these episodes demonstrate that globalization is reversible, they do not generally demonstrate that such a reversal is desirable. While the reversals have usually had unambiguously adverse effects, globalization may well leave some very poor countries behind.

We then turn to more in-depth studies of changes in poverty and inequality. Ravi Kanbur (2001; Chapter 4) sets the scene for these papers, noting that disagreements are often due to differences in aggregation levels: broad aggregates of winners conceal sub-groups of losers. Disagreements can also be due to the use of different measures. Several different measures of global inequality are defensible. Martin Ravallion (2004; Chapter 6) discusses them and shows how they lead to very different conclusions.

We then turn to actual applications of these measures. Until the work of Angus Maddison, the time series of global poverty and inequality did not usually go back before 1900. Maddison carefully constructed estimates of income, country by country, that provide some basis for much longer-term analysis. This is potentially important for the study of globalization which started well before 1900. François Bourguignon and Christian Morrisson (2002; Chapter 5) use Maddison's data to construct a long times series on global poverty and inter-country inequality. They show that until around 1980 global poverty had been rising massively since 1800. Shaohua Chen and Martin Ravallion (2004; Chapter 7) show that since then global poverty has fallen dramatically. Just as there are many defensible measures of inequality, so there are many measures of poverty. The rise and decline in poverty simply uses the headcount measure. In principle, the data underlying the headcount measure could equally be used to generate a poverty gap measure. Potentially, the trends in global poverty would look different on more sophisticated measures but, to date, this has not been done.

We then address distributional effects of economic integration at the global, regional and national levels. The papers by Lant Pritchett (1997; Chapter 8) and Branko Milanovic (2002; Chapter 9) debate recent international inequality, and specifically whether countries are converging or diverging. As the papers show, choices of data and of weighting procedures can make a large difference to the results. The next two papers address convergence versus divergence at the level of a region, with implications for regional trade policies. Dan Ben-David (1993; Chapter 10) shows how as Europe integrated the poorer countries tended rapidly to converge on the richer: integration was a powerfully equalizing force. Most regional trade agreements are among developing countries and it might be hoped that the same convergence process would be at work. However, Anthony J. Venables (2003; Chapter 11) shows that economic theory predicts that integration among developing countries would have the opposite effect from integration among developed countries, generating divergence. An implication is that the proliferation of regional trade blocs in the context of continuing high external protection may have contributed to global inequality. This does not mean that developing countries should abandon regional integration. Rather, that the effects of regional integration become more benign the more open members are to the global economy.

The distributional implications of globalization at the national level are addressed by David Dollar and Aart Kraay (2002; Chapter 12), in a paper that provoked much controversy. They find that the distribution of income is not systematically affected by the growth process, with the implication that the poor are not left behind. The three following papers comment on this result, qualifying it and challenging it. One conclusion from the critiques is that while Dollar and Kraay are right on average, there are also large groups of people who have been left behind by the growth process in particular countries. Edward Anderson (2005; Chapter 15) points to the divergent results of time-series and cross-section studies. While the former show that openness has increased wage inequalities, the cross-section results find little overall effect. He suggests other effects of openness may be offsetting that on wage differentials. Overall, these results suggest that the growth process is not intrinsically problematic, but that its effects differ radically according to context, part of which may well be policy choices.

Finally, we include some salient country experiences. It is often noted that the fall in global poverty since 1980 is entirely accounted for by China, elsewhere gains were offset by losses. When the data are disaggregated by geographic region, there are indeed remarkable differences. China's massive reduction in poverty coincided with its remarkable expansion of its manufactured exports. While the opening of the Chinese economy was surely important for poverty reduction, Ravi Kanbur and Xiaobo Zhang (2005; Chapter 16) show that its impact was uneven, leading to a sharp increase in regional inequalities. India has combined accelerating growth with globalization, but in very different manner, breaking into the global market in services. Latin America contrasts with China and India: since 1980 it has very substantially reduced its barriers to the world economy, but apparently without much effect on growth. Similarly, despite substantial liberalization, Africa has experienced accelerating divergence from the rest of the world: during 1980–2000, the region was on average in absolute decline. While these geographic differences in performance are striking, evidently underlying them must be some analytic distinctions: for example, China might be distinctive because of its policies, or Africa because of its climate. We therefore turn in Volume II to channels of transmission.

Volume II: What are the Channels of Transmission?

Traditional growth theory poses a puzzle (Howard Pack (1994; Chapter 1)): it implies that the marginal productivity of capital should be radically higher in the most capital-scarce countries.

Pack makes this point. In principle, the response to this massive disequilibrium would be some combination of three distinct adjustment mechanisms. Capital would flow to poor countries, labor would migrate to richer countries and trade in goods would be driven by their relative factor content. Between them these three mechanisms would restore an equilibrium in which the returns to each factor would be equalized across countries. This would not only be globally beneficial, but in particular it would bring both prosperity and equity to developing countries: overall living standards would rise but workers would gain at the expense of the owners of capital. Mancur Olson Jr. (1996; Chapter 2) accepts this model but argues that the three adjustment mechanisms work very imperfectly, so that big discrepancies can persist. Applied to globalization, this would imply that its effects were favorable but too limited: more globalization would be better. The subsequent papers are chosen to investigate each of the three adjustment mechanisms in turn.

We begin with trade in goods. Paul Krugman and Anthony J. Venables (1995; Chapter 3) present a model in which trade in goods need not be beneficial for poor countries. The central mechanism in their model is agglomeration externalities, which confer scale economies on locations where production is already concentrated. This advantage for the established producers prevents trade from being driven by factor proportions. As a result, trade can merely reinforce this advantage rather than eliminating it. Another implication of their model is that if wage differentials widen sufficiently to induce production to begin in a new, low-wage location, the subsequent growth of production in that location will be explosive as its agglomeration economies accrue. This provides a plausible account of how Asia has succeeded in penetrating global markets in manufacturing with such success. In contrast to this model in which scale economies are central, Adrian Wood and Kersti Berge (1997; Chapter 4) provide an alternative account of trade flows within the framework of the standard, constant-returns-to-scale Heckscher–Ohlin model, simply by augmenting its customary specification of endowments as labor and capital, with endowments of human capital and natural resources. Both papers provide possible explanations as to why Africa and Latin America have failed to emulate the Asian success in manufactured exports. Krugman and Venables would stress that once agglomerations built up in Asia other regions may have permanently missed the boat, the world having sufficient industrial locations to meet demand. Wood and Berge would stress that Africa and Latin America both have much larger resource endowments than Asia. Because of the Dutch disease induced by this resource wealth they do not have a comparative advantage in manufactures. Whether the Heckscher–Ohlin or the Krugman–Venables model offers the better description of reality is an empirical question: presumably both endowments and agglomeration economies matter to some extent.

Two papers offer different interpretations of the empirical literature on the effect of trade on growth. Andrew Berg and Anne Krueger (2003; Chapter 6) show that the preponderance of applied studies find that trade promotes growth, while Francisco Rodríguez and Dani Rodrik (2000; Chapter 5) are skeptical and offer detailed critiques of the econometric evidence. However, while they offer reasonable grounds for doubting that trade has been shown to be beneficial for growth, they do not argue that the effect of trade has been negative. L. Alan Winters, Neil McCulloch and Andrew McKay (2004; Chapter 7) provide the most comprehensive survey and also directly addresses the links through to poverty. Their survey shows that evidence of the poverty-reducing effects of growth is robust, while the link from trade to growth is generally positive but less firmly established.

While the bulk of the evidence on the effect of growth has been macro, there is a growing literature based on firm-level and household evidence. One route by which globalization might raise growth is if manufacturing firms learn from exporting. Clearly, since the more productive firms are more likely to export, this has to be controlled in order to investigate the possibility of reverse causality. Kraay (1999; Chapter 8) finds that for China exporting has no effect on firm productivity. By contrast, Arne Bigsten *et al.* (2004; Chapter 9) find that for Africa exporting strongly raises productivity. The differing results may reflect the massive contrast between domestic markets. To the extent that productivity growth is driven by competition, the internal Chinese market may be sufficient to provide a stimulus, whereas the internal market of the typical African country may be too small and protected, so that exporting makes a major difference.

The above papers all consider the effect of trade on developing countries. Robert C. Feenstra and Gordon H. Hanson (1999; Chapter 10) consider the claim that globalization has resulted in lower wages for unskilled workers in developed countries. They conclude that, while wages have indeed fallen, this cannot credibly be attributed to globalization.

We next turn to migration. Globalization may induce both permanent and temporary migration. Williamson (2004; Chapter 11) shows that the mass migrations of the nineteenth century, both from Europe to America and within Asia, were powerfully equalizing and much more important than trade in goods. During the twentieth century, restrictions on immigration radically reduced this equalizing force. Winters *et al.* (2003; Chapter 12) propose a way of restoring the beneficial effects of migration without the need for permanent migration. They show that were unskilled workers in low-income countries to be permitted to work in rich countries temporarily, there would be enormous mutual gains. At present, migrants are typically highly skilled. The analysis of the consequences of this emigration for low-income countries has been through three phases. A literature pioneered by Bhagwati analyzed its detrimental effects and proposed compensation mechanisms. An influential counter-revolution challenged this, proposing that there were benefits because the opportunity of emigration raised the incentive for education and so augmented supply. Maurice Schiff (2005; Chapter 13) shows that this counter-argument is seriously flawed: the brain drain is indeed likely to have adverse effects on the country from which the skilled emigrate.

The third mechanism is capital mobility. As Lucas noted, the capital scarcity of developing countries should, in principle, attract a massive inflow of capital. In fact, however, capital inflows, both through portfolio flows and direct investment, have been concentrated in a few countries. Lemma W. Senbet (2001; Chapter 14) shows that the share of US portfolios held in emerging markets is far lower than can be accounted for by considerations of risk. Portfolio flows have been volatile and sometimes even apparently perverse. When portfolio finance attempts to leave a country, it can trigger or amplify a financial crisis.

The Asian crisis of 1997 is a dramatic illustration that exposure to international finance can deepen problems. Coordinated withdrawals of portfolio finance might be responses to different types of internal weakness: fiscal deficits, low foreign exchange reserves or weak banks. Barry Eichengreen, Ricardo Hausmann and Ugo Panizza (2003; Chapter 15) consider the problem of 'original sin', that is when a country accumulates liabilities in foreign currency but assets in domestic currency. They argue that the problem arises because of the lack of international markets in bonds denominated in domestic currency and propose that the World Bank could pump-prime the emergence of such a market through issuing bonds diversified in a range of emerging market currencies.

Although Africa is the most capital-scarce region, Paul Collier, Anke Hoeffler and Catherine Pattillo (2001; Chapter 16) show that it has had exceptionally large outflows of capital exacerbating the initial capital scarcity. They account for this in terms of the high-risk and poor investment climate that have characterized much of Africa. Real investment is often highly irreversible and runs the risk of confiscation and policy change. In the poorest countries it is largely confined to the extractive industries. E. Borensztein, J. De Gregorio and J.-W. Lee (1998; Chapter 17) show that FDI is an important mechanism for the transfer of technology but that it requires a minimum stock of human capital in the host country. Thus, whereas for the typical recipient country this component of capital mobility augments productivity, the poorest countries do not get these benefits.

Volume III: Policy Responses

In Volume III we turn to policy issues. We consider the implications of globalization for the size of government, for labor and environmental standards, for aid, for the role of the IMF, for intellectual property rights and global public goods.

A major concern about globalization is that it may emasculate government efforts to redistribute income to lower-income groups. Commonly, high-income groups derive their incomes from factors which are internationally mobile, notably capital and skilled labor, whereas low-income groups depend upon immobile factors, notably unskilled labor. In this situation, if some governments attempt to redistribute income, then the high-income groups can protect themselves by moving factors to those countries that do not redistribute. This will frustrate the redistribution attempt and may cause a race to the bottom. It might appear from this that globalization would lead to a diminished role for government. Rodrik (1998; Chapter 1) shows that in fact the opposite is the case: the more open a economy, the larger is its government as a share of GDP. His explanation is that openness exposes the economy to greater volatility which increases the need for public safety nets. Large government is a response to this need, and indeed maintains the policy choice of openness from pressures that would otherwise arise to retreat into protectionism.

Trade can be a source of tension when the trading partners have different social or moral norms or when they apply different standards (Rodrik, 1997). This tension is the source of much of the heat in the globalization debate. We consider three types of standards: for labor, products and firms.

In the case of labour standards, the key question is whether differences in national norms (e.g. with regard to child labor) justify trade restrictions. Bhagwati (2004) stresses that where trade restrictions do not reflect protectionism (which, of course, they often do), but moral objections, it is important to establish whether or not the concern is with the welfare of workers in the exporting countries. In some cases, consumers in rich countries are *not* concerned with labor standards in the exporting country, but exclusively with their own conscience. They may, for example, object to consuming goods produced with child labor, irrespective of the impact of their actions on the welfare of the children concerned. This is legitimate but would call for labelling rather than trade restrictions. Labelling would enable the consumer to choose goods produced in a way he/she considers morally acceptable.

More commonly, however, consumers claim that they do wish to promote the welfare of working children in poor countries. T.N. Srinivasan (1996; Chapter 2) argues that, if this is the objective, then trade policy is an inefficient instrument. His paper can be seen as an application to labor standards of Corden's (1974) argument that where a restrictive trade policy is welfare enhancing, it is dominated by policies which directly address the distortion causing the welfare increase. This has become a common theme in the contributions by economists to the debate on globalization. For example, Bhagwati (2004) argues at great length that many of the concerns of the anti-globalization activists are legitimate but that they do not affect the case for free trade.

The empirical literature on child labor tries to explain why parents would keep their children out of school in spite of high returns to education. One possibility is that they face credit constraints. Kathleen Beegle, Rajeev H. Dehejia and Roberta Gatti (2006; Chapter 3) present evidence that in Tanzania credit-constrained households heavily relied on child labor in response to negative shocks, whereas for other households much of the effect of such shocks was mitigated through borrowing. Clearly, credit market imperfections can also explain a failure to invest in education, as in Galor and Zeira (1993). Credit market imperfections can therefore explain both 'permanent' and temporary use of child labor. In either case, an import ban would not solve the problem and might well make it worse.

For product standards the debate has focused on the implications for trade policy of differences in environmental and safety standards. As in the case of child labor, this is best analyzed as the effect of trade in the presence of a domestic distortion. In the case of product standards, the distortion could be the absence of an environmental policy in the exporting country. Clearly, by exacerbating the distortion trade can then be immiserizing for the exporting country. Globalization might, for example, offer timber firms an additional incentive for using undervalued forest resources. In such a situation there is, of course, a case for intervention (by the domestic government, unless the environmental externality operates cross-border), but not for trade restrictions. Bhagwati and Srinivasan (1996; Chapter 5) argue this case. While their argument is much more general, it is particularly relevant in the context of globalization.

Labor and product standards are very controversial in policy debates. There is, however, considerable consensus on these issues in academic papers. This is not true for the case of standards for firms: here there exists considerable disagreement (Rodrik, 1997). Non-academic critics of globalization have argued that globalization has increased the power of multinational corporations and that this has led to lower wages and worse working conditions in poor countries. The econometric evidence on this is reviewed by Drusilla K. Brown, Alan V. Deardorff and Robert M. Stern (2003; Chapter 4): typically, the evidence is that multinational firms pay a wage premium. Much more controversial is the possible effect of lobbying by multinational corporations on international standards, including trade law. Here the issue is not whether corporations are adequately constrained by domestic or international standards, but rather whether such standards are influenced by these corporations in a way which is harmful to poor countries (Bhagwati, 2004, ch. 12). On this there is very little academic research. The TRIPS initiative has come to be seen in many poor countries as evidence of the very selective commitment of OECD countries to free trade and protection of property rights.

In Volume II we noted that for the poorest countries private capital flows were modest or even perverse. This provides one rationale for public capital flows in the form of aid. The effectiveness of such aid flows has been an active and controversial area of research. Results appear to be highly sensitive to specification: different authors have obtained sharply different results with virtually the same data. Some results appear to show that aid is unconditionally effective in raising growth and others that it is unconditionally ineffective, and some that it is effective conditional upon policy. Collier and Dollar (2002; Chapter 6) pose the question if the purpose of aid is to reduce poverty how best should it be allocated between countries? First, they estimate country by country the number of people permanently lifted out of poverty by the growth induced by a given amount of aid. For an allocation of aid to be 'poverty-efficient' this number should be the same in all aid-receiving countries. They show that actual allocations of aid are a long way from poverty efficiency, mainly because so much aid goes to middle-income countries.

Debt relief is a public resource transfer analytically very similar to aid, and indeed commonly financed from the same pool of resources. Debt relief is distinctive partly in its different criteria for allocation. However, the main focus of academic interest is on whether debt relief provides a boost to growth over and above an equivalent aid flow. This can arise if the stock of debt raises doubts about the ability of the country to service new debt. In that case, the access of the country to credit is effectively reduced and this is restored by debt relief. Additionally, investment might be deterred by a large debt stock since it signals that investors face a future tax liability. While such a 'debt overhang' is a theoretical possibility, there has been little empirical analysis of its practical importance. One such study is that by Catherine Pattillo, Hélène Poisson and Luca Ricci (2004; Chapter 7), who find that high indebtedness indeed has a strong adverse effect on growth. According to their estimates, doubling external debt reduces the growth of per capita physical capital and that of total factor productivity both by about one percentage point. While debt forgiveness resolves the debt-overhang problem *ex post*, it would be better to avoid it by preventive measures. Seema Jayachandran and Michael Kremer (2006; Chapter 8) propose that an international body should have the power to declare governments as unfit to borrow: any debt which they incurred would be 'odious' and its repayment would be unenforceable.

The IMF has two distinct roles in globalization. It is a 'policeman' of economic policies in developing countries, controlled predominantly by the governments of the North. It is also an insurer, providing financial assistance to governments at times of crisis. Both of these roles have attracted critical attention. In its policeman role the IMF was central to the design of stabilization and structural adjustment programs. These programs have come in for considerable popular criticism since they often coincided with sharp reductions in public spending and acute increases in poverty. Because they were often introduced in conditions of crisis brought about by unsustainable public spending, a reasonable counterfactual is that even without the programs poverty would have increased. The analysis by David E. Sahn and Stephen D. Younger (2004; Chapter 9) suggests that while much of the popular criticism is indeed unjustified, the programs largely failed to have much impact on poverty reduction. Their favored explanation in poor human resource development echoes the finding of Borenstzein *et al.* noted above. In our *Economic Journal* article we provide a critique of IMF programs that is not based merely on an observed increase in poverty (Collier and Gunning (1999; Chapter 10)). We argue that while the programs may have been better than nothing, they were frequently poorly designed, notably in terms of sequencing, which in turn had avoidable consequences in terms of poverty. Hausmann *et al.* (n.d.) criticize the sequencing common in structural adjustment programs. Their argument is that since liberalization inevitably involves a sequence, the appropriate sequence is that which tackles successively whichever of the potential policy constraints upon growth happen to be currently binding. They see structural adjustment programs as poorly designed, with their content guided only by a vision of a desirable end-state of complete liberalization rather than by an efficient path toward such a state.

Whereas our focus was on low-income countries, Joseph E. Stiglitz (1999; Chapter 11) presents a critique of the role of the IMF in middle-income countries hit by financial crisis. His argument is that the IMF tends to diagnose financial crisis as due to fiscal irresponsibility and to prescribe deflation when the real culprit was excessively risky international private lending. In turn, the reason for this excessive lending was that the international banks that lent the money knew that they would not bear the full cost of their risk exposure because the IMF would provide a bailout financed by the taxpayers of the governments that capitalize the IMF. Given the high costs that financial crises inflict, it has been questioned whether international capital mobility provides a net benefit to emerging market countries. A sensible strategy might seem to be for the central bank to hold large foreign exchange reserves. However, given the considerable wedge between the interest rate charged by international banks and the rate paid on reserves, such a strategy is costly. Given that safe capital mobility is costly, it is potentially preferable to limit capital account convertibility. This is the argument of Rodrik (1998; Chapter 12).

Like the IMF, the WTO has attracted considerable critical attention. While it is an expansion of the GATT, its progress toward negotiated global trade liberalization has been considerably more fraught than its predecessor organization. Collier (2006; Chapter 13) attempts to explain these greater difficulties in terms of structural differences from the GATT. It is extraordinarily difficult to estimate the impact of a global trade agreement such as the Doha Round. The estimates which are commonly used are generated by computable general equilibrium models. While this is the only feasible approach, such results must be interpreted with caution since the empirical basis for the models is inevitably weak. However, the effects of one important component of the WTO do not need to be estimated by a computable general equilibrium model since they can be derived unambiguously from the first principles of economic theory. This is the effect of adding intellectual property rights into the WTO. Such rights are unusual, in that they convert a public good, knowledge, into a private good. The justification for this is that without it there is little incentive to generate the knowledge. This can provide a sound rationale for the creation of intellectual property rights for new knowledge, although there is trade-off as the normal benefits that come from being a public good are lost. However, the introduction of intellectual property rights into the WTO amounted to a sudden global extension of property rights for existing knowledge. It thereby created rents without having any incentive effect. Since these property rights were overwhelmingly owned by the high-income countries while they were extended to the markets of developing countries, the resulting transfer through rents was highly regressive. In the case of pharmaceuticals, there is an important ongoing debate on the effect of patent protection on the poor. Michael Kremer (2002; Chapter 14) and others have argued that for diseases specific to poor countries, such as malaria, patent protection cannot work and other incentives must be offered for research.

Our final policy theme is on international public goods and their financing. Governments supply those public goods that are useful at the national level, but there is no equivalent for the supply of those public goods that are regional or global. Consequently, they are liable to be radically under-supplied. Since it is likely that public goods are potentially disproportionately important for those people with low consumption of private goods, the under-provision of global public goods may matter most for the poor, although the distributional impact will vary good by good. We consider one particular good, namely disease eradication: Scott Barrett (2003; Chapter 15) applies game theory to show that even if global benefits exceed costs, coordination between nations is not enough: active cooperation is required. Often, a critical problem in the provision of global public goods is the lack of finance for them due to free-riding. Anthony B. Atkinson (2007; Chapter 16) discusses a range of possible options for raising finance through global taxation.

References

Bhagwati, J. (2004), *In Defense of Globalization*. New York: Oxford University Press.

Corden, W.M. (1974), *Trade Policy and Economic Welfare*. Oxford: Oxford University Press.

Galor, O. and J. Zeira (1993), 'Income Distribution and Macroeconomics', *Review of Economic Studies*, **60**, 35–52.

Hausmann, R., D. Rodrik and A. Velasco (n.d.) *Growth Diagnostics*, Kennedy School of Government, Harvard, Cambridge, MA; mimeo.

Rodrik, D. (1997), *Has Globalization Gone Too Far?* Washington, DC: Institute for International Economics.

Part I
History of Globalization

[1]

The Region

The Industrial Revolution
Past and Future

Robert E. Lucas Jr.
John Dewey Distinguished Service Professor of
Economics, University of Chicago
Adviser, Federal Reserve Bank of Minneapolis

We live in a world of staggering and unprecedented income inequality. Production per person in the wealthiest economy, the United States, is something like 15 times production per person in the poorest economies of Africa and South Asia. Since the end of the European colonial age, in the 1950s and '60s, the economies of South Korea, Singapore, Taiwan and Hong Kong have been transformed from among the very poorest in the world to middle-income societies with a living standard about one-third of America's or higher. In other economies, many of them no worse off in 1960 than these East Asian "miracle" economies were, large fractions of the population still live in feudal sectors with incomes only slightly above subsistence levels. How are we to interpret these successes and failures?

Economists, today, are divided on many aspects of this question, but I think that if we look at the right evidence, organized in the right way, we can get very close to a coherent and reliable view of the changes in the wealth of

nations that have occurred in the last two centuries and those that are likely to occur in this one. The Asian miracles are only one chapter in the larger story of the world economy since World War II, and that story in turn is only one chapter in the history of the industrial revolution. I will set out what I see as the main facts of the economic history of the recent past, with a minimum of theoretical interpretation, and try to see what they suggest about the future of the world economy. I do not think we can understand the contemporary world without understanding the events that have given rise to it.

I will begin and end with numbers, starting with an attempt to give a quantitative picture of the world economy in the postwar period, of the growth of population and production since 1950. Next, I will turn to the economic history of the world up to about 1750 or 1800, in other words, the economic history known to Adam Smith, David Ricardo and the other thinkers who have helped us form our vision of how the world works. Third, I will sketch what I see as the main features of the initial phase of the industrial revolution, the years from 1800 to the end of the colonial age in 1950. Following these historical reviews, I will outline a theoretical structure roughly consistent with the facts. If I succeed in doing this well, it may be possible to conclude with some useful generalizations and some assessments of the world's future economic prospects.

The world economy in the postwar period

Today, most economies enjoy sustained growth in average real incomes as a matter of course. Living standards in all economies in the world 300 years ago were more or less equal to one another and more or less constant over time. Following common practice, I use the term *industrial revolution* to refer to this change in the human condition, although the modifier *industrial* is slightly outmoded, and I do not intend to single out iron and steel or other heavy industry, or even manufacturing in general, as being of special importance. By a country's average real income, I mean simply its gross domestic product (GDP) in constant dollars divided by its population. Although I will touch on other aspects of society, my focus will be on economic success, as measured by population and production.

Our knowledge of production and living standards at various places and times has grown enormously in the past few decades. The most recent empirical contribution, one of the very first importance, is the Penn World Table project conducted by Robert Summers and Alan Heston.[1] This readily available, conveniently organized data set contains population and production data on every country in the world from about 1950 or 1960 (depending on the country) to the present. The availability of this marvelous body of data has given the recent revival of mathematical growth theory an explicitly empirical character that is quite different from the more purely theoretical investigations of the 1960s. It has also stimulated a more universal, ambitious style of theorizing aimed at providing a unified account of the behavior of rich and poor societies alike.

As a result of the Penn project, we now have a reliable picture of production in the entire world, both rich and poor countries. Let us review the main features of this picture, beginning with population estimates. Over the 40-year period from 1960 through 2000, world population grew from about 3 billion to 6.1 billion, or at an annual rate of 1.7 percent. These numbers are often cited with alarm, and obviously the number of people in the world cannot possibly grow at 2 percent per year forever. But

many exponents of what a friend of mine calls the "economics of gloom" go beyond this truism to suggest that population growth is outstripping available resources, that the human race is blindly multiplying itself toward poverty and starvation. This is simply nonsense.

There is, to be sure, much poverty and starvation in the world, but nothing could be further from the truth than the idea that poverty is increasing. Over the same period during which population has grown from 3 billion to 6.1 billion, total world production has grown much faster than population, from \$6.5 trillion in 1960 to \$31 trillion in 2000. (All the dollar magnitudes I cite, from the Penn World Table or any other source, will be in units of 1985 U.S. dollars.) That is, world production was nearly multiplied by five over this 40-year period, growing at an annual rate of 4 percent. Production per person—real income—thus grew at 2.3 percent per year, which is to say that the living standard of the average world citizen more than doubled. Please understand: I am not quoting figures for the advanced economies or for a handful of economic miracles. I am not excluding Africa or the communist countries. These are numbers for the world as a whole. The entire human race is getting rich, at historically unprecedented rates. The economic miracles of East Asia are, of course, atypical in their magnitudes, but economic growth is not the exception in the world today: It is the rule.

Average figures like these mask diversity, of course. Figure 1 shows one way to use the information in the Penn World Table to summarize the distribution of the levels and growth rates of population and per capita incomes in the postwar world. It contains two bar graphs of per capita incomes, one for 1960 and the other for 1990 (not 2000). The horizontal axis is GDP per capita, in thousands of dollars. The vertical axis is population. The height of each bar is proportional to the number of people in the world with average incomes in the indicated range, based on the assumption (though, of course, it is false) that everyone in a country has that country's average income. The figure shows that the number of people (not just the fraction) in countries with mean

---

[1] A good description is available in: Robert Summers and Alan Heston, "The Penn World Table (Mark 5): An Expanded Set of International Comparisons, 1950–1988." *Quarterly Journal of Economics*, 105 (1991): 327–368. The latest versions of the tables are available at pwt.econ.upenn.edu.

incomes below $1,100 has declined between 1960 and 1990. The entire world income distribution has shifted to the right, without much change in the degree of income inequality, since 1960. At the end of the period, as at the beginning, the degree of inequality is enormous. The poorest countries in 1990 have per capita incomes of around $1,000 per year compared to the U.S. average of $18,000: a factor of 18. This degree of inequality between the richest and poorest societies is without precedent in human history, as is the growth in population and living standards in the postwar period.

A great deal of recent empirical work focuses on the question of whether per capita incomes are converging to a common (growing) level, or possibly diverging. From Figure 1 it is evident that this is a fairly subtle question. In any case, it seems obvious that we are not going to learn much about the economic future of the world by simple statistical extrapolation of events from 1960 to 1990, however it is carried out. Extrapolating the 2 percent population growth rate backward from 1960, one would conclude that Adam and Eve were expelled from the garden in about the year 1000. Extrapolating the 2.2 rate of per capita income growth backward, one would infer that people in 1800 subsisted on less than $100 per year. Extrapolating forward leads to predictions that the earth's water supply (or supply of anything else) will be exhausted in a finite period. Such exercises make it clear that the years since 1960 are part of a period of transition, but from what to what? Let us turn to history for half the answer to this question.

Comparison to earlier centuries

The striking thing about postwar economic growth is how recent such growth is. I have said that total world production has been growing at over 4 percent since 1960. Compare this to annual growth rates of 2.4 percent for the first 60 years of the 20th century, of 1 percent for the entire 19th century, of one-third of 1 percent for the 18th century.[2] For these years, the growth in both population and production was far lower than in modern times.

[2] The sources for these and many other figures cited in this section are given in Chapter 5 of my *Lectures on Economic Growth* (Cambridge: Harvard University Press), 2002.

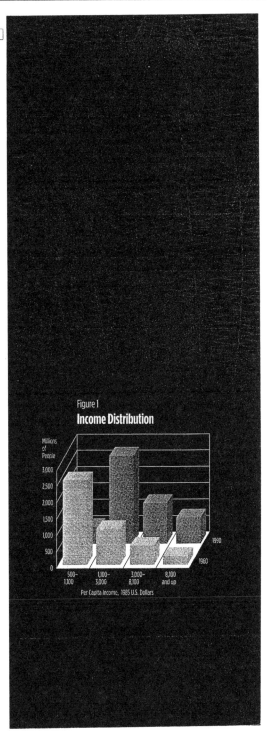

Figure 1

Income Distribution

Millions of People

Per Capita Income, 1985 U.S. Dollars

Moreover, it is fairly clear that up to 1800 or maybe 1750, no society had experienced sustained growth in per capita income. (Eighteenth century population growth also averaged one-third of 1 percent, the same as production growth.) That is, up to about two centuries ago, per capita incomes in all societies were stagnated at around $400 to $800 per year. But how do we know this? After all, the Penn World Tables don't cover the Roman Empire or the Han Dynasty. But there are many other sources of information.

In the front hall of my apartment in Chicago there is a painting of an agricultural scene, a gift from a Korean student of mine. In the painting, a farmer is plowing his field behind an ox. Fruit trees are flowering, and mountains rise in the background. The scene is peaceful, inspiring nostalgia for the old days (though I do not know when the painting was done or what time period it depicts). There is also much information for an economist in this picture. It is not difficult to estimate the income of this farmer, for we know about how much land one farmer and his ox can care for, about how much can be grown on this land, how much fruit the little orchard will yield and how much the production would be worth in 1985 U.S. dollar prices. This farmer's income is about $2,000 per year. Moreover, we know that up until recent decades, almost all of the Korean workforce (well over 90 percent) was engaged in traditional agriculture, so this figure of $2,000 ($500 per capita) for the farmer, his wife and his two children must be pretty close to the per capita income for the country as a whole. True, we do not have sophisticated national income and product accounts for Korea 100 years ago, but we don't need them to arrive at fairly good estimates of living standards that prevailed back then. Traditional agricultural societies are very like one another, all over the world, and the standard of living they yield is not hard to estimate reliably.

Other, more systematic, information is also available. For poor societies—all societies before about 1800—we can reliably estimate income per capita using the idea that average living standards of most historical societies must have been very near the estimated per capita production figures of the poorest contemporary societies. Incomes in, say, ancient China cannot have been much lower than incomes in 1960 China and still sustained stable or growing populations. And if incomes in any part of the world in any time period had been much larger than the levels of the poor countries of today—a factor of two, say—we would have heard about it. If such enormous percentage differences had ever existed, they would have made some kind of appearance in the available accounts of the historically curious, from Herodotus to Marco Polo to Adam Smith.

To say that traditional agricultural societies did not undergo growth in the living standards of masses of people is not to say that such societies were stagnant or uninteresting. Any schoolchild can list economically important advances in technology that occurred well before the industrial revolution, and our increasing mastery of our environment is reflected in accelerating population growth over the centuries. Between year 0 and year 1750, world population grew from around 160 million to perhaps

700 million (an increase of a factor of four in 1,750 years). In the assumed absence of growth in income per person, this means a factor of four increase in total production as well, which obviously could not have taken place without important technological changes. But in contrast to a modern society, a traditional agricultural society responds to technological change by increasing population, not living standards. Population dynamics in such a society obey a Malthusian law that maintains product per capita at $600 per year, independent of changes in productivity.

How then did these traditional societies support the vast accomplishments of the ancient civilizations of Greece and Rome, of China and India? Obviously, not everyone in these societies was living on $600 per year. The answer lies in the role and wealth of landowners, who receive about 30 percent to 40 percent of agricultural income. A nation of 10

[I]n contrast to a modern society, a traditional agricultural society responds to technological change by increasing population, not living standards.

million people with a per capita production of $600 per year has a total income of $6 billion. Thirty percent of $6 billion is $1.8 billion. In the hands of a small elite, this kind of money can support a fairly lavish lifestyle or build impressive temples or subsidize many artists and intellectuals. As we know from many historical examples, traditional agricultural society can support an impressive civilization. What it cannot do is generate improvement in the living standards of masses of people. The Korean farmer plowing his field in the painting in my hallway could be in any century in the last 1,000 years. Nothing in the picture would need to be changed to register the passage of the centuries.

If the living standard in traditional economies was low, it was at least fairly equally low across various societies. Even at the beginning of the age of European colonialism, the dominance of Europe was military, not economic. When the conquistadors of Spain took control of the societies of the Incas and the Aztecs, it was not a confrontation between a rich society and a poor one. In the 16th century, living standards in Europe and the Americas were about the same. Indeed, Spanish observers of the time marveled at the variety and quality of goods that were offered for sale in the markets of Mexico. Smith, Ricardo and their contemporaries argued about differences in living standards, and perhaps their discussions can be taken to refer to income differences as large as a factor of two. But nothing remotely like the income differences of our current world, differences on the order of a factor of 25, existed in 1800 or at any earlier time. Such inequality is a product of the industrial revolution.

The beginnings of the industrial revolution

Traditional society was characterized by stable per capita income. Our own world is one of accelerating income growth. The course of the industrial revolution, our term for the transition from stable to accelerating growth, is illustrated in Figure 2, which plots total world population and production from the year 1000 up to the present. I use a logarithmic scale rather than natural units, so that a constant rate of growth would imply a straight line. One can see from the figure that the growth rates of both population and production are increasing over time. The vertical scale is millions of persons (for population)

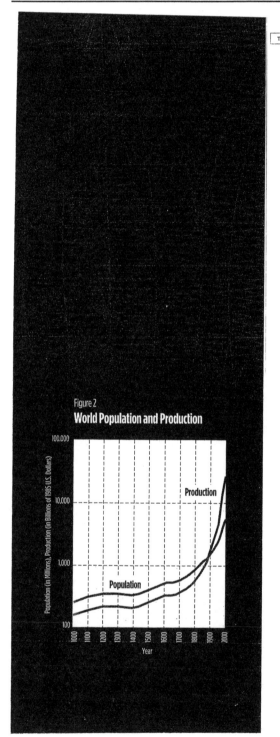

Figure 2

World Population and Production

The Region

and billions of 1985 U.S. dollars (for production). The difference between the two curves is about constant up until 1800, reflecting the assumption that production per person was roughly constant prior to that date. Then in the 19th century, growth in both series accelerates dramatically, and production growth accelerates more. By 1900 the two curves cross, at which time world income per capita was $1,000 per year. The growth and indeed the acceleration of both population and production continue to the present.

Of course, the industrial revolution did not affect all parts of the world uniformly, nor is it doing so today. Figure 3, based on per capita income data estimated as I have discussed, is one way of illustrating the origins and the diffusion of the industrial revolution. To construct the figure, the countries (or regions) of the world were organized into five groups, ordered by their current per capita income levels. Group I—basically, the English-speaking countries—are those in which per capita incomes first exhibited sustained growth. Group II is Japan, isolated only because I want to highlight its remarkable economic history. Group III consists of northwest Europe, the countries that began sustained growth somewhat later than Group I. Group IV is the rest of Europe, together with European-dominated economies in Latin America. Group V contains the rest of Asia and Africa.

As shown in Figure 3, per capita incomes were approximately constant, over space and time, over the period 1750–1800, at a level of something like $600 to $700. Here and below, the modifier "approximately" must be taken to mean plus or minus $200. Following the reasoning I have advanced above, $600 is taken as an estimate of living standards in all societies prior to 1750, so there would be no interest in extending Figure 3 to the left. The numbers at the right of Figure 3 indicate the 1990 populations, in millions of people, for the five groups of countries. About two-thirds of the world's people live in Group V, which contains all of Africa and Asia except Japan.

Reading Figure 3 from left to right, we can see the emergence over the last two centuries of the inequality displayed in Figure 1. By 1850 there was something like a factor of two difference between the English-speaking countries and the poor countries of Africa and Asia. By 1900, a difference of per-

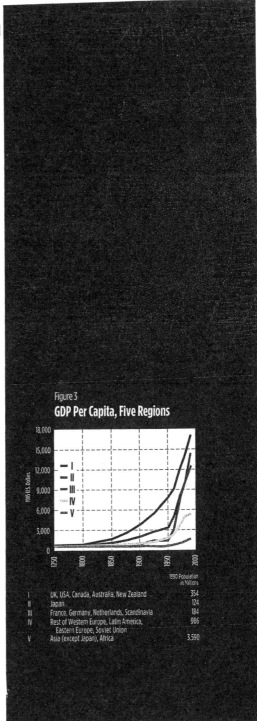

Figure 3
GDP Per Capita, Five Regions

		1990 Population in Millions
I	UK, USA, Canada, Australia, New Zealand	354
II	Japan	124
III	France, Germany, Netherlands, Scandinavia	184
IV	Rest of Western Europe, Latin America, Eastern Europe, Soviet Union	986
V	Asia (except Japan), Africa	3,590

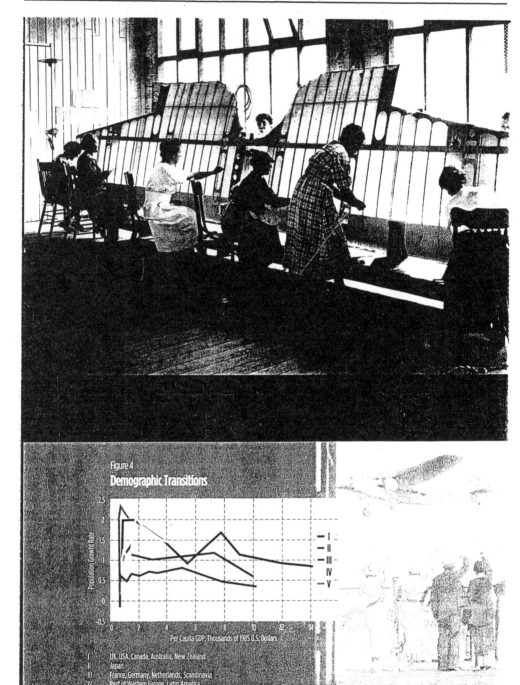

Figure 4

Demographic Transitions

I   UK, USA, Canada, Australia, New Zealand
II   Japan
III France, Germany, Netherlands, Scandinavia
IV   Rest of Western Europe, Latin America,
      Eastern Europe, Soviet Union
V   Asia (except Japan), Africa

The Region

haps a factor of six had emerged. At that time, the rest of Europe was still far behind England and America, and Japanese incomes were scarcely distinguishable from incomes in the rest of Asia. In the first half of the 20th century, the inequality present in 1900 was simply magnified. The English-speaking countries gained relative to northern Europe, which in turn gained on the rest of Europe and Asia. Notice, too, that per capita income in what I have called Group V, the African and Asian countries, remained constant at around $600 up to 1950. The entire colonial era was a period of stagnation in the living standards of masses of people. European imperialism brought advances in technology to much of the colonized world, and these advances led to increases in production that could, as in British India, be impressive. But the outcome of colonial economic growth was larger populations, not higher living standards.

In the period since 1950, the pattern of world growth has begun to change character, as well as to

accelerate dramatically. What was at first thought to be the postwar recovery of continental Europe and of Japan turned out to be the European and Japanese miracles, taking these countries far beyond their prewar living standards to levels comparable to the United States. (There are some miracles in my Group IV, too—Italy and Spain—that are not seen on the figure because they are averaged in with Latin America and the communist world.) The second major change in the postwar world is the beginning of per capita income growth in Africa and Asia, entirely a post-colonial phenomenon. The industrial revolution has begun to diffuse to the non-European world, and this, of course, is the main reason that postwar growth rates for the world as a whole have attained such unprecedented levels.

If we use growth in per capita income as the defining characteristic of the industrial revolution, then it is clear from Figure 3 that the revolution did not begin before the late 18th century. If we use growth

in total product, reflecting improvements in technology, as the defining characteristic, then Figure 2 makes it clear that the beginnings of the revolution must have been centuries earlier (or, that there must have been important, earlier revolutions). What occurred around 1800 that is new, that differentiates the modern age from all previous periods, is not technological change by itself but the fact that sometime after that date fertility increases ceased to translate improvements in technology into increases in population. That is, the industrial revolution is invariably associated with the reduction in fertility known as the *demographic transition*.

Figure 4 provides a rough description of the demographic transitions since 1750 that have occurred and are still occurring. The figure exhibits five plotted curves, one for each country group. Each curve connects 10 points, corresponding to the time periods beginning in 1750 and ending in 1990, as indicated at the bottom of Figure 3. (Note that the periods are not of equal length.) Each point plots the group's average rate of population growth for that period against its per capita income at the beginning of the period. The per capita GDP figures in 1750 can just be read off Figure 3, from which it is clear that they are about $600 for all five groups. Population growth rates in 1750 average about 0.4 percent and are well below 1 percent for all five groups. For each group, one can see a nearly vertical increase in population growth rates with little increase in GDP per capita, corresponding to the onset of industrialization. This, of course, is precisely the response to technological advance that Malthus and Ricardo told us to expect. Then, in groups I to IV a maximum is reached, and as incomes continue to rise, population growth rates decline. In group V—most of Asia and Africa—the curve has only leveled off, but does anyone doubt that these regions will follow the path that the rest of the world has already worn?

Theoretical responses

I have brought the story of the industrial revolution up to the present. Where are we going from here? For this, we need a theory of growth, a system of equations that makes economic sense and that fits the facts I have just reviewed. There is a tremendous amount of very promising research now occurring in economics, trying to construct such a system, and in a few years we will be able to run these equations into the future and see how it will look. Now, though, I think it is accurate to say that we have not one but two theories of production: one consistent with the main features of the world economy prior to the industrial revolution and another roughly consistent with the behavior of the advanced economies today. What we need is an understanding of the transition.

One of these successful theories is the product of Smith, Ricardo, Malthus and the other classical economists. The world they undertook to explain was the world on the eve of the industrial revolution, and it could not have occurred to them that economic theory should seek to explain sustained, exponential growth in living standards. Their theory is consistent with the following stylized view of economic history up to around 1800. Labor and resources combine to produce goods—largely food, in poor societies—that sustain life and reproduction. Over time, providence and human ingenuity make it possible for given amounts of labor and resources to produce more goods than they could before. The resulting increases in production per person stimulate fertility and increases in population, up to the point where the original standard of living is restored. Such dynamics, operating over the centuries, account for the gradually accelerating increase in the human population and the distribution of that population over the regions of the earth in a way that is consistent with the approximate constancy of living standards everywhere. The model predicts that the living standards of working people are maintained at a roughly constant, "subsistence" level, but with realistic shares of income going to landowners, the theory is consistent as well with high civilization based on large concentrations of wealth.

This classical theory is not inconsistent with the enormous improvements in knowledge relevant to productivity that occurred long before the 18th century, improvements that supported huge population increases and vast wealth for owners of land and other resources. Increases in knowledge over the centuries also stimulated a large-scale accumulation of productive capital: shipbuilding, road and harbor construction, draining of swamps, and breeding and raising of animal herds for food and

power. Capital accumulation, too, played a role in supporting ever larger populations. Yet under the Malthusian theory of fertility, neither new knowledge nor the capital accumulation it makes profitable is enough to induce the sustained growth in living standards of masses of people that modern economists take as the defining characteristic of the industrial revolution.

The modern theory of sustained income growth, stemming from the work of Robert Solow in the 1950s, was designed to fit the behavior of the economies that had passed through the demographic transition.[3] This theory deals with the problem posed by Malthusian fertility by simply ignoring the economics of the problem and assuming a fixed rate of population growth. In such a context, the accumulation of physical capital is not, in itself, sufficient to account for sustained income growth. With a fixed rate of labor force growth, the law of diminishing returns puts a limit on the income increase that capital accumulation can generate. To account for sustained growth, the modern theory needs to postulate continuous improvements in technology or in knowledge or in human capital (I think these are all just different terms for the same thing) as an "engine of growth." Since such a postulate is consistent with the evidence we have from the modern (and the ancient) world, this does not seem to be a liability of the theory.

The modern theory, based on fixed fertility, and the classical theory, based on fertility that increases with increases in income, are obviously not mutually consistent. Nor can we simply say that the modern theory fits the modern world and the classical theory the ancient world, because we can see traditional societies exhibiting Malthusian behavior in the world today. Increases since 1960 in total production in Africa, for example, have been almost entirely absorbed by increases in population, with negligible increases in income per capita. Understanding the progress of the industrial revolution as it continues today necessarily entails understanding why it is that Malthusian dynamics have ceased to hold in much of the contemporary world. Country after country has gone through a demographic transition, involving increases in the rate of population growth followed by decreases, as

[3] Robert M. Solow, "A Contribution to the Theory of Economic Growth." *Quarterly Journal of Economics*, 70 (1956): 65–94.

The Region

income continues to rise. Some of the wealthiest countries—Japan and parts of Europe—are just about maintaining their populations at current levels. People in these wealthy economies are better able to afford large families than people in poor economies, yet they choose not to do so.

If these two inconsistent theories are to be reconciled, with each other and with the facts of the demographic transition, a second factor needs to work to decrease fertility as income grows, operating alongside the Malthusian force that works to increase it. Gary Becker proposed long ago that this second factor be identified with the *quality* of children: As family income rises, spending on children increases, as assumed in Malthusian theory, but these increases can take the form of a greater number of children or of a larger allocation of parental time and other resources to each child. Parents are assumed to value increases both in the quantity of children and in the quality of each child's life.[4]

Of course, both the quality-quantity trade-off in Becker's sense and the importance of human capital are visible well before the industrial revolution. In any society with established property rights, a class of landowners will be subject to different population dynamics due to the effect their fertility has on inheritances and the quality of lives their children enjoy. Such families can accumulate vast wealth and enjoy living standards far above subsistence. For the histories of what we call civilization, this deviation from a pure Malthusian subsistence model is everything. For the history of living standards of masses of people, however, it is but a minor qualification.

[4] Gary S. Becker, "An Economic Analysis of Fertility." In Richard Easterlin, ed., *Demographic and Economic Change in Developed Countries.* Princeton: Princeton University Press, 1960. See also Robert J. Barro and Gary S. Becker, "Fertility Choice in a Model of Economic Growth." *Econometrica.* 57 (1989): 481–501.

Whatever the importance of human capital accumulation in the original industrial revolution, there is no doubt that rapid improvement in skills is characteristic of its diffusion in the modern world economy.

Similarly, in any society of any complexity, some individuals can, by virtue of talent and education, formal or informal, acquire skills that yield high income, and as the Bachs and the Mozarts can testify, such exceptions can run in families. For most societies, though, income increases due to what a modern economist calls *human capital* are exceptional and often derivative, economically, from landowner wealth.

For a landless family in a traditional agricultural economy, the possibilities for affecting the quality of children's lives are pretty slight. If there is no property to pass on, an additional child does not dilute the inheritance of siblings. Parents could spend time and resources on the child's education in the attempt to leave a bequest of human capital. All parents do this to some degree, but the incentives to do so obviously depend on the return to human capital offered by the society the parents live in. Where this return is low, adding the quality dimension to the fertility decision may be only a

minor twist on Malthusian dynamics. In short, neither the possibility of using inheritable capital to improve the quality of children's lives nor the possibility of accumulating human capital needs to result in fundamental departures from the predictions of the classical model.

But these additional features do offer the possibility of non-Malthusian dynamics, and the possibility has promise because the process of industrialization seems to involve a dramatic increase in the returns to human capital. People are moving out of traditional agriculture, where the necessary adult skills can be acquired through on-the-job child labor. More and more people are entering occupations different from their parents' occupations that require skills learned in school as well as those learned at home. New kinds of capital goods require workers with the training to operate and to improve upon them. In such a world a parent can do many things with time and resources that will give a child advantages in a changing economy, and the fewer children a parent has, the more such advantages can be given to each child.

It is a unique feature of human capital that it yields returns that cannot be captured entirely by its "owner." Bach and Mozart were well paid (though neither as well as he thought he deserved), but both of them provided enormous stimulation and inspiration to others for which they were paid nothing, just as both of them also gained from others. Such *external effects*, as economists call them, are the subject matter of intellectual and artistic history and should be the main subject of industrial and commercial history as well. These pervasive external effects introduce a kind of feedback into human capital theory: Something that increases the return on human capital will stimulate greater accumulation, in turn stimulating higher returns, stimulating still greater accumulation and so on.

On this general view of economic growth, then, what began in England in the 18th century and continues to diffuse throughout the world today is something like the following. Technological advances occurred that increased the wages of those with the skills needed to make economic use of these advances. These wage effects stimulated others to accumulate skills and stimulated many families to decide against having a large number of unskilled children and in favor of having fewer children, with more time and resources invested in each. The presence of a higher-skilled workforce increased still further the return to acquiring skills, keeping the process going. Wouldn't such a process bog down due to diminishing returns to skill-intensive goods? Someone has to dig potatoes, after all. It might, and I imagine that many incipient industrial revolutions died prematurely due to such diminishing returns. But international trade undoubtedly helped England attain critical mass by letting English workers specialize in skill-demanding production while potatoes were imported from somewhere else.

Whatever the importance of human capital accumulation in the original industrial revolution, there is no doubt that rapid improvement in skills is characteristic of its diffusion in the modern world economy. Nancy Stokey estimates that the major stimulus of the North American Free Trade

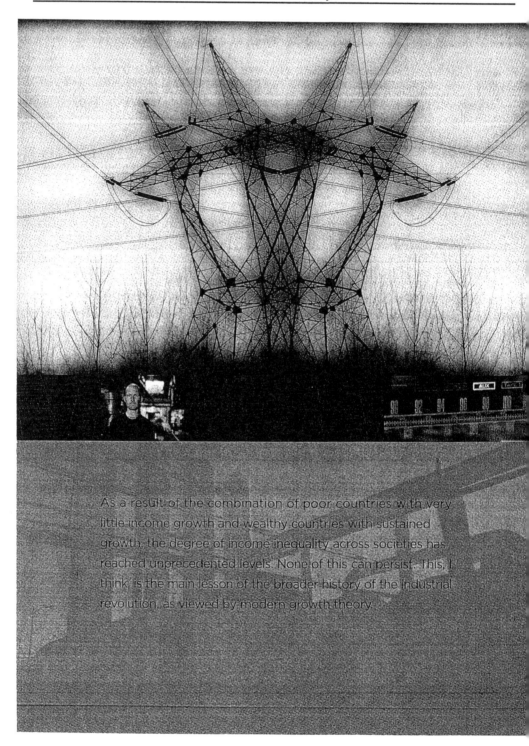

As a result of the combination of poor countries with very little income growth and wealthy countries with sustained growth, the degree of income inequality across societies has reached unprecedented levels. None of this can persist. This, I think, is the main lesson of the broader history of the industrial revolution, as viewed by modern growth theory.

Agreement to economic growth in Mexico will be not the inflow of physical capital (though that is considerable), but the increased accumulation of human capital that will be stimulated by the higher rate of return the new physical capital will induce.[5] Post-NAFTA Mexico is increasingly an economy that assigns high rewards to training and technological skills.

Generalizations from experience

Economically, the 60 years since the end of World War II have been an extraordinary period. The growth rates of world population, production and incomes per capita have reached unprecedented heights. As a result of the combination of poor countries with very little income growth and wealthy countries with sustained growth, the degree of income inequality across societies has reached unprecedented levels. None of this can persist. This, I think, is the main lesson of the broader history of the industrial revolution, as viewed by modern growth theory.

I have interpreted this period as the beginning of the phase of the diffusion of the sustained economic growth that characterizes the European industrial revolution to the former colonies of the non-European world. The rapid growth of non-European nations (and some of the poorer European ones) is mainly responsible for the extraordinarily rapid growth of world production in the postwar era. But enough other societies have been largely left out of this process of diffusion that the degree of inequality among nations remained about the same in 1990 as it was in 1960. As those economies that have joined the modern world catch up to the income levels of the wealthiest countries, their growth rates of both population and income will slow down to rates that are close to those that now prevail in Europe. We have seen these events occur in Japan; they will follow in country after country.

At the same time, countries that have been kept out of this process of diffusion by socialist planning or simply by corruption and lawlessness will, one after another, join the industrial revolution and become the miracle economies of the future. The income growth rates in these catch-up economies

[5] Nancy L. Stokey. "Free Trade, Factor Returns, and Factor Accumulation." *Journal of Economic Growth*, 1 (1996): 421–448.

may be very high, but as fewer and fewer countries remain in this category, the effect on world averages will shrink. If so, then world population growth will attain a peak and begin shrinking toward less than 1 percent, and world production growth will similarly cease to rise and will fall back toward 3 percent. In other words, we will see a

About the Author

In this essay, Robert E. Lucas Jr. continues a discussion featured in his 2002 book *Lectures on Economic Growth*, published by Harvard University Press.

In 1995 Lucas received the Nobel Memorial Prize in Economic Sciences. He is a past president of the Econometric Society and the American Economic Association, a fellow of the American Academy of Arts and Sciences and the American Philosophical Society and a member of the National Academy of Sciences.

Go to minneapolisfed.org for:

- An excerpt from *Lectures on Economic Growth*, December 2001 *Region*

- Observations on Lucas' rational expectations paper, December 1995 *Region*

- *Region* interview with Robert Lucas, June 1993

world that, economically, looks more and more like the United States.

What do history and economic theory have to say about factors that will accelerate this process of catching up? What policies for Pakistan or Nigeria would materially affect the likelihood of an economic miracle? For backward economies, dealing on a day-to-day basis with more advanced economies is the central element in success. No successes have been observed for autarchic, produce-everything-ourselves strategies (though such strategies can possibly work well for a few years: think of Russia in the 1920s or India in the 1950s). Trade has the benefit of letting a smaller country's industries attain efficient scale, but I think an even more important factor is the need to get up to world standards, to learn to play in the big leagues. The only way learning and technology transfer can take place is for producers to compete seriously internationally. Learning-by-doing is perhaps the most important form of human capital accumulation.

Macroeconomic policy, however, does not appear to be of central importance to growth. Korea, Brazil and Indonesia have all enjoyed rapid growth under inflationary policies (though others—Argentina, Chile and, again, Brazil—have had the opposite experience). Of course, in all these cases, inflation has arisen from monetary expansion to cover fiscal deficits. Certainly, I do not want to endorse inflation—it is an unnecessary waste of resources with no positive side effects—but this seems to be a largely separate issue from growth. It is always a mistake to think of everything as interconnected (though, of course, everything is, in some sense): I think it is more fruitful to break a problem down into manageable pieces and address the pieces one at a time.

Of the tendencies that are harmful to sound economics, the most seductive, and in my opinion the most poisonous, is to focus on questions of distribution. In this very minute, a child is being born to an American family and another child, equally valued by God, is being born to a family in India. The resources of all kinds that will be at the disposal of this new American will be on the order of 15 times the resources available to his Indian brother. This seems to us a terrible wrong, justifying direct corrective action, and perhaps some actions of this kind can and should be taken. But of the vast increase in the well-being of hundreds of millions of people that has occurred in the 200-year course of the industrial revolution to date, virtually none of it can be attributed to the direct redistribution of resources from rich to poor. The potential for improving the lives of poor people by finding different ways of distributing current production is *nothing* compared to the apparently limitless potential of increasing production. ◼

Recommendations for Further Reading

For a good introduction to the way economists today are using theory to measure the importance of different sources of economic growth, see Stephen L. Parente and Edward C. Prescott, *Barriers to Riches* (Cambridge: MIT Press), 2000. I've used this book in class at Chicago, with good success. My students also enjoyed the more anecdotal treatment in William Easterly, *The Elusive Quest for Growth: Economists' Adventures and Misadventures in the Tropics* (Cambridge: MIT Press), 2002. [See review in the September 2003 *Region*.]

Michael Kremer's 1993 paper "Population Growth and Technological Change: One Million B.C. to 1990," *Quarterly Journal of Economics* (107: 681-716) stimulated everyone who thinks about economic growth. So did Lant Pritchett's "Divergence, Big Time" in the 1997 *Journal of Economic Perspectives* (11: 3-18) and Jeffrey D. Sachs and Andrew Warner, "Economic Reform and the Process of Global Integration," *Brookings Papers on Economic Activity*, (1995): 1-118. Though published in professional journals, all of these papers have much to offer the nontechnical reader.

—*Robert Lucas*

[2]

Winners and Losers over Two Centuries of Globalization

Jeffrey G. Williamson

Introduction

The world has seen two globalization booms over the past two centuries, and one bust. The first global century ended with the First World War and the second started at the end of Second World War, while the years in between were ones of anti-global backlash. This chapter reports what we know about the winners and losers during the two global centuries, including aspects almost always ignored in modern debate – how prices of consumption goods on the expenditure side are affected, and how the economic position of the poor is influenced. It also reports two responses of the winners to the losers' complaints. Some concessions to the losers took the form of anti-global policy manifested by immigration restriction in the high-wage countries and trade restriction pretty much everywhere. Some concessions to the losers were also manifested by a 'race towards the top' whereby legislation strengthened losers' safety nets and increased their sense of political participation. The chapter concludes with four lessons of history and an agenda for international economists, including more attention to the impact of globalization on commodity price structure, the causes of protection, the impact of world migration on poverty eradication and the role of political participation in the whole process.

Globalization and world inequality

Globalization in world commodity and factor markets has evolved in fits and starts since Columbus and da Gama sailed from Europe more than 500 years ago. We begin with a survey of this history so as to place contemporary events in better perspective, and then ask whether globalization raised world inequality. This question can be split into two more: what happened to income gaps between nations? What happened to income gaps within nations? Collaborative work with Peter Lindert stresses the question about world inequality (Lindert and Williamson, 2002a, 2002b), but this chapter concentrates on the second two questions, the reason being that answers to these have more relevance for policy and for the ability of a globally integrated world to survive. Indeed, at various points in the chapter, I ask when there has been global backlash in the past – driven by complaints of the losers – and whether and how the complaints of the losers were accommodated by the winners. Finally, this chapter also stresses the contribution of world migration to poverty eradication.

Recent scholarship has documented a dramatic divergence in incomes around the globe over the past two centuries. Furthermore, all of this work shows that the divergence was driven overwhelmingly by the rise of between-nation inequality, not by the rise of inequality within nations (Berry, Bourguignon and Morrisson, 1991; Maddison, 1995; Pritchett, 1997; Bourguignon and Morrisson, 2000; Dowrick and DeLong, 2002). Figure 6.1 uses the work of Bourguignon and Morrisson to summarize these trends and confirms that changing income gaps between countries explain changing world inequality. However, the fact that the rise of inequality within nations has not driven the secular rise in global inequality hardly implies that it has been irrelevant, and for two reasons. First, policy is formed at the country level, and it is changing income distribution within borders that usually triggers political complaint and policy responses; and, second, it is the political

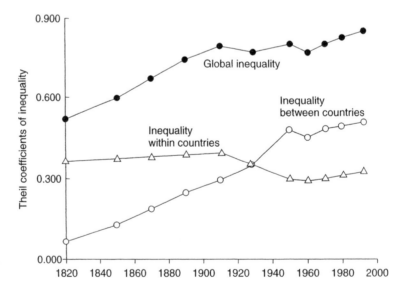

Figure 6.1   Global inequality of individual incomes, 1820–1992

Source: Adapted from Bourguignon and Morrisson (2000). The 'countries' here consist of fifteen single countries with abundant data and large populations plus eighteen other country groups. The eighteen groups were aggregates of geographical neighbours having similar levels of GDP *per capita*, as estimated by Maddison (1995).

voice of the losers that matters, and they can be at the top, the bottom, or the middle of that distribution. Furthermore, the absence of a net secular change in within-country inequality at the global level may simply reveal an equilibrium process whereby rising within-country inequality breeds policy responses that force the distribution back to some culturally acceptable steady state. That level may be far higher for the United States than for Japan, to take two modern economic giants as examples. I start by decomposing the centuries since 1492 into four distinct globalization epochs. Two of these were pro-global, and two were anti-global. I then explore whether the two pro-global epochs made the world more unequal, and whether it produced a backlash.

Making a world economy

Epoch I: anti-global mercantilist restriction, 1492–1820

The voyages of discovery induced a transfer of technology, plants, animals and diseases on an enormous scale, never seen before and maybe since. But the impact of Columbus and da Gama on trade, factor migration and globalization was a different matter entirely. For globalization to have an impact on relative factor prices, absolute living standards and GDP *per capita*, domestic relative commodity prices and/or relative endowments must be altered. True, there was a world trade boom after 1492, and the share of trade in world GDP increased markedly (O'Rourke and Williamson, 2002a). But was that trade boom explained by declining trade barriers and global integration? A pro-global decline in trade barriers should have left a trail marked by falling commodity price gaps between exporting and importing trading centres, but there is absolutely no such evidence (O'Rourke and Williamson, 2002b). Thus, 'discoveries' and transport productivity improvements must have been offset by trading monopoly mark-ups, tariffs, non-tariff restrictions, wars and pirates, all of which served in combination to choke off trade.

Since there is so much confusion in the globalization debate about its measurement, it might pay to elaborate on this point. Figure 6.2 presents a stylized view of post-Colombian trade between Europe and the rest of the world (the latter denoted by an asterisk). *MM* is the European import demand function (that is, domestic demand minus domestic supply), with import demand declining as the home market price (p) increases. *SS* is the foreign export supply function (foreign supply minus foreign demand), with export supply rising as the price abroad (p^*) increases. In the absence of transport costs, monopolies, wars, pirates and other trade barriers, international commodity markets would be perfectly integrated: prices would be the same at home and abroad, determined by the intersection of the two schedules. Transport costs, protection, war, pirates, and monopoly drive a wedge (t) between export and import prices: higher tariffs, transport costs, war embargoes and monopoly rents increase the wedge while lower barriers reduce it. Global commodity market integration is represented in Figure 6.2 by a decline in the wedge: falling transport costs, falling trading monopoly rents, falling tariffs, the suppression of pirates, or a return to peace all lead to falling import prices in both places, rising export prices in both places, an erosion of price gaps between them and an increase in trade volumes connecting them.

The fact that trade should rise as trade barriers fall is, of course, the rationale behind using trade volumes or the share of trade in GDP as a proxy for international commodity market integration. Indeed, several authors have used Maddison's (1995) data to trace out long-run trends in commodity market integration since the early nineteenth century, or even earlier (e.g. Hirst and Thompson, 1996; Findlay and O'Rourke, 2002). However, Figure 6.2 makes it clear that global commodity market integration is not the only reason why the volume of trade, or trade's share in GDP, might increase over time. Just because we see a trade boom does not necessarily mean that more liberal trade policies or transport revolutions are at work. After all, outward shifts in either import demand (to *MM'*) or export supply (to *SS'*) could also lead to trade expansion, and such shifts could occur as a result of population growth, the settlement of previously unexploited frontiers, capital accumulation, technological change, a shift in post-Colombian income distribution favouring those who consume imported 'exotic' luxuries and a variety of

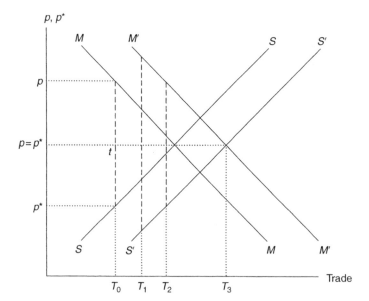

Figure 6.2   Explaining the European trade boom, 1500–1800

Source: Adapted from O'Rourke and Williamson (2002a: Figure 3).

other factors. Figure 6.2 thus argues that the *only* irrefutable evidence that global commodity market integration is taking place is a decline in the international dispersion of commodity prices, or what I call commodity price convergence. However, we cannot find it (O'Rourke and Williamson, 2002b).

If declining trade barriers do not explain the world trade boom after Columbus, what was it? Just like world experience from the 1950s to the 1980s (Baier and Bergstrand, 2001), it appears that European income growth – or growth of incomes of the landed rich – might have explained as much as two-thirds of the trade boom over the three centuries as a whole (O'Rourke and Williamson 2002a).[1] The world trade boom after Columbus would have been a lot bigger without those anti-global interventions. And labour migration and capital flows were, of course, only a trickle.

Epoch II: the first global century, 1820–1913

The 1820s were a watershed in the evolution of the world economy. International commodity price convergence did not start until then. Powerful and epochal shifts towards liberal policy (e.g. dismantling mercantilism) were manifested during that decade. In addition, the 1820s coincide with the peacetime recovery from the Napoleonic wars on the continent, launching a century of global *pax Britannica*.[2] In short, the 1820s mark the start of a world regime of globalization.

Transport costs dropped very fast in the century prior to the First World War. These globalization forces were powerful in the Atlantic economy, but they were partially offset by a rising tide of protection. Declining transport costs accounted for two-thirds of the integration of world commodity markets over the century following 1820, and for *all* of world commodity market integration in the four decades after 1870, when globalization backlash offset some of it (Lindert and Williamson, 2002a). The political backlash of the late nineteenth century and interwar period was absent in Asia and Africa – partly because these regions contained colonies of free-trading European countries, partly because of the power of gunboat diplomacy and partly because of the political influence wielded by natives who controlled the natural resources that were the base of their exports. As a result, the globalization-induced domestic relative price shocks were even bigger and more ubiquitous in Asia and Africa than those in the Atlantic economy (Williamson, 2002). Put another way, commodity price convergence between the European industrial core and the periphery was even more dramatic than it was within the Atlantic economy. In short, the liberal dismantling of mercantilism and the worldwide transport revolution worked together to produce truly global commodity markets across the nineteenth century. The persistent decline in transport costs worldwide allowed competitive winds to blow hard where they had never blown before. True, there was an anti-global policy reaction after 1870 in the European centre but it was nowhere near big enough to cause a return to the pre-1820 levels of economic isolation. On the other hand, these globalization events were met with rising levels of protection in Latin America, the United States and the European periphery, and to very high levels, as Figure 6.3 documents. However, I postpone until the end of this chapter the question as to whether it was a globalization backlash that triggered protection in the periphery or whether it was something else. If history is to offer any lessons for the present, we had better get the causes of the backlash straight.

Factor markets also became more integrated worldwide. As European investors came to believe in strong growth prospects overseas, global capital markets became steadily more integrated, reaching levels in 1913 that may not have been regained even today (Clemens and Williamson, 2001b; Obstfeld and Taylor, 2002). International migration soared in response to unrestrictive immigration policies and falling steerage costs (Hatton and Williamson, 1998; Chiswick and Hatton, 2002), but not without some backlash: New World immigrant subsidies began to evaporate towards the end of the century, political debate over immigrant restriction became very intense and, finally, quotas were imposed. In this case, it is clear that the retreat from open immigration policies to quotas was driven by complaints from the losers at the bottom of the income pyramid, the unskilled native-born (Goldin, 1994; Timmer and Williamson, 1998; Williamson, 1998; Chiswick and Hatton, 2002).

Epoch III: beating an anti-global retreat, 1913–50

The globalized world started to fall apart after 1913, and it was completely dismantled between the wars. New policy barriers were imposed restricting

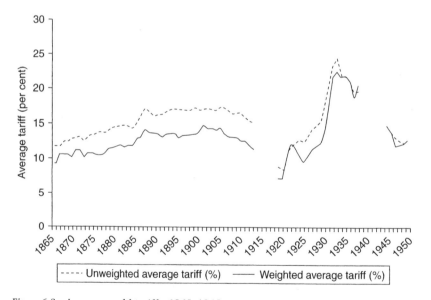

Figure 6.3   Average world tariffs, 1865–1945

Source: Adapted from Coatsworth and Williamson (2002: Figure 1).

the ability of poor populations to flee miserable conditions for something better, barriers that still exist today, a century later. Thus, the foreign-born share in the US population fell from a pre-1913 figure of 14.6 per cent to an interwar figure of 6.9 per cent. Higher tariffs and other non-tariff barriers (NTBs) choked off the gains from trade. Barrier-ridden price gaps between Atlantic economy trading partners doubled, returning those gaps to 1870 levels (Lindert and Williamson, 2002a: Table 1; Findlay and O'Rourke, 2002). The appearance of new disincentives reduced investment in the diffusion of new technologies around the world, and the share of foreign capital flows in GDP dropped from 3.3 to 1.2 per cent (Obstfeld and Taylor, 1998: 359). In short, the interwar retreat from globalization was carried entirely by anti-global economic policies.

Epoch IV: the second global century, 1950–2002

Globalization by any definition resumed after the Second World War. It has differed from pre-1914 globalization in several ways (Baldwin and Martin, 1999). Most important by far, factor migrations are less impressive: the foreign-born are a much smaller share in labour-scarce economies than they were in 1913, and capital exports are a smaller percentage of GDP in the post-war United States (0.5 per cent in 1960–73 and 1.2 per cent 1989–96: Obstfeld and Taylor, 1998: Table 11.1) than they were in pre-war Britain (4.6 per cent in 1890–1913). On the other hand, trade barriers are probably lower today than they were in 1913. These differences are tied to policy changes in one dominant nation, the United States, which has switched from a protectionist welcoming immigrants to a free trader restricting their entrance.

Ever since Eli Heckscher and Bertil Ohlin wrote almost a century ago (Flam and Flanders, 1991), their theory has taught that trade can be a substitute for factor migration. While modern theory is much more ambiguous on this point, history is not. In the first global century, before quotas and restrictions, factor mobility had a *much* bigger impact on factor prices, inequality, and poverty than did trade (Taylor and Williamson, 1997). Perhaps this explains why the second global century has been much more enthusiastic about commodity trade than about migration. In any case, I start with the more recent globalization experience, the second global century.

Did the second global century make the world more unequal?

International income gaps: a post-war epochal turning point?

The Bourguignon and Morrisson evidence in Figure 6.1 documents what looks like a mid-twentieth-century turning point in their between-country inequality index, since its rise slows down after 1950. However, the

Bourguignon and Morrisson long-period database contains only fifteen countries. Using post-war purchasing power parity (PPP) data for a much bigger sample of 115, Melchior, Telle and Wiig (2000) actually document a *decline* in their between-country inequality index in the second half of the twentieth century, and Sala-í-Martin (2002) shows the same when focusing on poverty.[3] The first three authors document stability in between-country inequality up to the late 1970s, followed by convergence. Four other studies find the same fall in between-country inequality after the early 1960s (Schultz, 1998; Firebaugh, 1999; Boltho and Toniolo, 1999; Radetzki and Jonsson, 2000).[4] Among these studies, perhaps the most useful in identifying an epochal regime switch is that of Boltho and Toniolo (1999), who show a rise in between-country inequality in the 1940s, rough stability over the next three decades, and a significant fall after 1980, significant enough to make their between-country inequality index drop well below its 1950 level. Did the post-war switch from autarky to global integration contribute to this epochal change in the evolution of international gaps in average incomes?

Trade policy and international income gaps: late twentieth-century conventional wisdom

Conventional (static) theory argues that trade liberalization should have benefited Third World countries more than it benefited leading industrial countries. After all, trade liberalization should have a bigger effect on the terms of trade of countries joining the larger integrated world economy than on countries already members.[5] And the bigger the terms of trade gain, the bigger the GDP *per capita* gain.

So much for theory: reality suggests the contrary. The post-war trade that was liberalized the most was in fact intra-OECD trade, not trade between the OECD and the rest. From the very beginning in the 1940s, the GATT explicitly excused low-income countries from the need to dismantle their import barriers and exchange controls. This GATT permission served to lower GDP in low-income countries below what it might have been, but the permission was consistent with the anti-global ideology prevailing in previously colonial Asia and Africa, in Latin America where the great depression hit so hard, and in Eastern Europe, dominated as it was by the state-directed USSR. Thus the succeeding rounds of liberalization over the first two decades or so of GATT brought freer trade and gains from trade mainly to OECD members. However, these facts do *not* suggest that late twentieth-century globalization favoured rich countries. Rather, they suggest that globalization favoured all (rich industrial) countries who liberalized and penalized those (poor pre-industrial) countries who did not. There is, of course, an abundant empirical literature showing that liberalizing Third World countries gained from freer trade after the OECD leaders set the liberal tone, after the 1960s.

First, the authors of a large National Bureau of Economic Research (NBER) project assessed trade and exchange control regimes in the 1960s and 1970s by making classic partial-equilibrium calculations of deadweight losses (Bhagwati and Krueger, 1973–76). They concluded that the barriers imposed significant costs in all but one case. However, these welfare calculations came from standard models which did not allow protection a chance to lower long-run cost curves as would be true of the traditional infant industry case, or to foster industrialization and thus growth, as would be true of those modern growth models where industry is the carrier of technological change and capital deepening. Thus, economists have looked for more late twentieth-century proof to support the 'openness-fosters-growth' hypothesis.

Second, analysts have contrasted the growth performance of relatively open with relatively closed economies. The World Bank has conducted such studies for forty-one Third World countries going back before the first oil shock (1973). The correlation between trade openness and growth is abundantly clear in these studies, as illustrated in Table 6.1. Yet, such analysis is vulnerable to the criticism that the effect of trade policies alone cannot be isolated since other policies usually change at the same time. Thus, countries that liberalized their trade also liberalized their domestic factor markets, liberalized their domestic commodity markets and set up better property rights enforcement. The appearance of these domestic policies may deserve more credit for raising income while the simultaneous appearance of more liberal trade policies may deserve less.

Third, there are country event studies where the focus is on periods when Third World trade policy regimes change dramatically enough to see their effect on growth. For example, Krueger (1983, 1984) looked at trade opening

Table 6.1   Trade policy orientation and growth rates in the Third World, 1963–92

	Average annual rates growth of GDP per capita (%)		
Trade policy orientation	1963–73	1973–85	1980–92
Strongly open to trade	6.9	5.9	6.4
Moderately open	4.9	1.6	2.3
Moderately anti-trade	4.0	1.7	−0.2
Strongly anti-trade	1.6	−0.1	−0.4

Notes: In all periods the three strongly open economies were Hong Kong, Singapore and South Korea. The identities of the strongly anti-trade countries changed over time. In 1963–73, they were Argentina, Bangladesh, Burundi, Chile, Dominican Republic, Ethiopia, Ghana, India, Pakistan, Peru, Sri Lanka, Sudan, Tanzania, Turkey, Uruguay and Zambia. For the two overlapping later periods, the strongly anti-trade countries were the previous sixteen, *plus* Bolivia, Madagascar and Nigeria, *minus* Chile, Pakistan, Sri Lanka, Turkey and Uruguay.

Sources: Adapted from Lindert and Williamson (2002a: Table 3) based on World Bank data.

moments in South Korea around 1960, Brazil and Colombia around 1965 and Tunisia around 1970. Growth improved after liberalization in all four cases. More recently, Dollar and Kraay (2000a) examined the reforms and trade liberalizations of sixteen countries in the 1980s and 1990s finding, once again, the positive correlation between freer trade and faster growth. Of course, these reform episodes may have changed more than just global participation, so that an independent trade effect may not have been isolated.

Fourth, macroeconometric analysis has been used in an attempt to resolve the doubts left by simpler historical correlations revealed by the other three kinds of studies. This macroeconometric literature shows that free-trade policies had a positive effect on growth in the late twentieth century, especially with many other relevant influences held constant. The most famous of these is by Sachs and Warner (1995), but many others have also confirmed the 'openness-fosters-growth' hypothesis for the late twentieth century (e.g. Dollar, 1992; Edwards, 1993; Dollar and Kraay, 2000a).[6] In spite of this evidence, it must be said that there are still some sceptics who doubt that support for the 'openness-fosters-growth' hypothesis is unambiguous, of which more later.

When the twentieth-century leader went open: the United States

The American surge in wage and income inequality generated an intense search for its sources. First, there were the globalization sources. These included the rise in unskilled worker immigration rates, due to rising foreign immigrant supplies and to a liberalization of US immigration policy. Increasing competition from imports that used unskilled labour intensively was added to the globalization impact, a rising competition due to foreign supply improvements (aided by US outsourcing), international transportation improvements and trade liberalizing policies. Second, there were sources apparently unrelated to globalization, such as a slowdown in the growth of per worker skill supply and biased technological change that cut the demand for unskilled workers relative to skilled workers.

The debate evolved into a 'trade versus technology' contest, although it might have learned far more by greater attention to immigration and skills (or schooling) supply, and by attention to the century *before* the 1970s. Some contestants agree with Wood (1994, 1998) that trade was to blame for much of the wage widening. Others contestants reject this conclusion, arguing that most or all of the widening was due to a shift in technology that has been strongly biased in favour of skills. Most estimates tend to resemble the guess by Feenstra and Hanson (1999) that perhaps 15–33 per cent of the rising inequality was due to trade competition. Still, everyone seems to agree that going open in the late twentieth century was hardly egalitarian for America.

William Cline offers the boldest attempt at an overall quantitative accounting of these potential sources. Cline blames globalization less· than do Feenstra, Hanson and most other writers, and concludes that skill-biased technological change is bigger than any globalization effect (Cline, 1997: Table 5.1). Cline's interpretation of his own estimates is, however, very different from mine, and perhaps my longer historical perspective accounts for the difference. The proper question, it seems to me, is left unasked by Cline and other economists in the debate, namely: 'how did the period 1973–93 differ from the one that preceded it, 1953–73?' If the other sources added up to pretty much the same impact in the first post-war period, then it would be the *change* in globalization forces between the two periods that mattered. Thus, it seems to me that Cline's study illustrates how economists throw away information by confining their analysis to the recent widening of wage gaps. When the world economy became increasingly integrated in the two centuries before 1980, technology also had its factor bias, and the mismatch between technological bias and skills growth kept shifting, with inequality implications (Williamson and Lindert, 1980; Goldin and Katz, 1999, 2000; Lindert, 2000; Lindert and Williamson, 2002a). Why ignore this history?

Globalization, inequality and the OECD

The United States was not the only OECD country to undergo a rise in inequality. The trend toward wider wage gaps has also been unmistakable in Britain. Although there was less widening in *full-time labour earnings* for France or Japan, and none at all for Germany or Italy, income measures that take work hours and unemployment into account reveal some widening even in those last four cases. Burniaux *et al.*'s (1998) study surveyed the inequality of disposable household income in the OECD since from the mid-1970s. Up to the mid-1980s, the Americans and British were alone in having a clear rise in inequality. From the mid-1980s to the mid-1990s, however, twenty out of twenty-one OECD countries had a noticeable rise in inequality. Furthermore, the main source of rising income inequality after the mid-1980s was the widening of labour earnings. The fact that labour earnings became more unequal in most OECD countries, when *full-time* labour earnings did not, suggests that many countries took their inequality in the form of more unemployment and hours' reduction, rather than in wage rates.

Globalization, inequality and the Third World

The sparse literature on the wage inequality and trade liberalization connection in developing countries is mixed in its findings and narrow in its focus. Until recently, it concentrated on six Latins (Argentina, Chile, Colombia, Costa Rica, Mexico and Uruguay) and three East Asians (Korea, Singapore and Taiwan), and the assessment diverged sharply between regions and epochs. Wage gaps seemed to fall when the three 'Asian tigers' liberalized in the 1960s and early 1970s. Yet wage gaps generally widened when the six Latin American countries liberalized after the late 1970s (Wood, 1994, 1997, 1998; Robbins, 1997; Hanson and Harrison, 1999; Robbins and Gindling, 1999). Why the difference?

As Wood (1997) has rightly pointed out, historical context was important, since other things were not equal during these liberalizations. The clearest example where a Latin wage widening appears to refute the egalitarian Stolper–Samuelson prediction was the Mexican liberalization under Salinas in 1985–90. Yet this pro-global liberalization move coincided with the major entry of China and other Asian exporters into world markets. Thus Mexico faced intense new competition from less skill-intensive manufactures in all export markets. Historical context could also explain why trade liberalization coincided with wage widening in the five other Latin countries, and why it coincided with wage narrowing in East Asia in the 1960s and early 1970s. Again, timing matters. Competition from other low-wage countries was far less intense when the 'Asian tigers' pulled down their barriers in the 1960s and early 1970s compared with the late 1970s and early 1980s when the Latin Americans opened up.

But even if these findings were not mixed, they could not have had a very big impact on global inequalities. After all, the literature has focused on nine countries that together had less than 200 million people in 1980, while China by itself had 980 million, India 687 million, Indonesia 148 million and Russia 139 million. All four of these giants recorded widening income gaps after their economies went global. The widening did not start in China until after 1984, because the initial reforms were rural and agricultural and therefore had an egalitarian effect. When the reforms reached the urban industrial sector, China's income gaps began to widen (Griffin and Zhao, 1993: 61; especially Atinc, 1997). India's inequality has risen since liberalization started in the early 1990s. Indonesian incomes became increasingly concentrated in the top decile from the 1970s to the 1990s, though this probably owed more to the Suharto regime's ownership of the new oil wealth than to any conventional trade-liberalization effect. Russian inequalities soared after the collapse of the Soviet regime in 1991, and this owed much to the handing over of trading prerogatives and assets to a few oligarchs (Flemming and Micklewright, 2000).

Border effects, limited access and the Third World

Income widening in these four giants dominates global trends in within-country inequality,[7] but how much was due to liberal trade policy and globalization? Probably very little. Indeed, much of the inequality surge during their liberalization experiments seems linked to the fact that the opening to trade and foreign investment was incomplete and selective. That is, the rise in inequality appears to have been based on the exclusion of much of the population from the benefits of globalization. The question is: what accounts for the exclusion? China, where the gains since 1984 have been so heavily concentrated in the coastal cities and provinces (Griffin and Zhao, 1993; Atinc, 1997) offers a good example. Those that were able to participate in the new, globally linked economy prospered faster than ever before, while the rest in the hinterland were left behind,[8] or at least enjoyed less economic success. China's inequality had risen to American levels by 1995 (a Gini of 0.406), but the pronounced surge in inequality from 1984 to 1995 was dominated by the rise in urban–rural and coastal–hinterland gaps, not by widening gaps within any given locale. This pattern suggests that China's inequality – like that of Indonesia, Russia and other giants – has been raised by differential access to the benefits of the new economy, not by widening gaps among those who participate in it, or among those who do not. But why have the globalization-induced growth shocks favoured China's coastal provinces? How much is due to policy, and how much to border effects associated with external trade, effects that have favoured the coastal provinces for centuries?

Consider another example. In the aftermath of GATT-related liberalization in 1986 and of NAFTA-related liberalization in 1994, Mexico has undergone rising inequality, not falling inequality as most observers predicted. However, Hanson (2002) has shown that much of this result can be traced to an uneven regional stimulus and, in particular, to the boom along the US border. Is it only a matter of waiting for these 'border effects' to spread? Apparently, since Robertson (2001) has shown that the Stolper–Samuelson predictions work just fine for Mexico after 1994, if one allows for a reasonable three- to five-year lag.

Did the first global century make the world more unequal?

Global divergence without globalization

Figure 6.1 (p. 137) documents the rise of income gaps between nations since 1820. While the evidence may not be as precise, we also know that global income divergence started long before 1820. Indeed, international income gaps almost certainly widened after 1600 or even earlier. Real wages, living standards, health and (especially) output *per capita* indicators all point to an early modern 'great divergence' which took place in three dimensions – between European nations, within European nations and between Europe and Asia. Real wages in England and Holland pulled away from the rest of the world in the late seventeenth century (van Zanden, 1999; Pomeranz, 2000; Allen, 2001; Pamuk and Ozmucur, 2002; Allen *et al.*, 2002). Furthermore, between the sixteenth and the eighteenth centuries the landed and merchant classes in England, Holland, along with France, pulled far ahead of everyone – their compatriots, the rest of Europe, and probably any other region on earth. This divergence was even greater in real than in nominal terms, because luxuries became much cheaper relative to necessities (Allen *et al.*, 2002; Hoffman *et al.*, 2002), an issue with powerful contemporary analogies, as we shall see below. While we will never have firm estimates of the world income gaps between 1500 and 1820, what we do have suggest unambiguously that global inequality rose long before the first industrial revolution. Thus, industrial revolutions were never a necessary condition for widening world income gaps. It happened with industrial revolutions and it happened without them.[9]

Despite the popular rhetoric about an early modern world system, there was no true globalization move after the 1490s and the voyages of da Gama and Columbus. As I argued previously using Figure 6.2 (p. 139), intercontinental trade was monopolized, and huge price mark-ups between exporting and importing ports were maintained even in the face of improving transport technology and European 'discovery'. Furthermore, most of the traded commodities were non-competing: that is, they were not produced at home and thus did not displace some competing domestic industry. In addition, these traded consumption goods were luxuries out of reach of the vast majority of each trading country's population. In short, pre-1820 trade had only a trivial impact on the living standards of anyone but the very rich. Finally, and as I mentioned above, the migration of people and capital was only a trickle before the 1820s; true globalization began only after the 1820s.

Thus, while global income divergence has been with us for more than four centuries, globalization has been with us for fewer than two. This conflict raises serious doubts about the premise that rising world integration is responsible for rising world inequality. According to history, globalization has never been a necessary condition for widening world income gaps. It happened with globalization and it happened without it.

When the nineteenth-century leader went open: Britain

Britain's nineteenth-century free-trade leadership, especially its famous Corn Law repeal in 1846, offers a good illustration of how the effects of global liberalization depend on the leader, and how the effects of going open can be egalitarian for both the world and for the liberalizing leader. The big gainers from nineteenth-century British trade liberalization were British labour – especially unskilled labour – and the rest of Europe and its New World offshoots, while the clear losers were British landlords, the world's richest individuals (Williamson, 1990). How much the rest of the world gained (and whether British capitalists gained at all) depended on foreign trade elasticities and induced terms of trade effects. But since these terms of trade effects were probably quite significant for what was then called 'the workshop of the world', Britain must have distributed considerable gains to the rest of the world as well as to her own workers. Workers – especially unskilled workers – gained because Britain was a food importing country[10] and because labour was used much less intensively in import-competing agriculture than was land (Irwin, 1988; Williamson, 1990). Whether and how much the periphery gained also must have depended on deindustrialization there, a long-run force I explore later. History offers two enormously important cases where the world leader going open had completely different effects: pro-global liberalization in nineteenth-century Britain was unambiguously egalitarian at the national and, in the short run at least, the world level – American liberalization in the late twentieth century was not.

European followers and the New World

What about the globalization and inequality connection for the rest of Europe and its New World offshoots? Two kinds of (admittedly imperfect) evidence document distributional trends within countries participating in the global economy. One relies on trends in the ratio of unskilled wages to farm rents per acre, a relative factor price whose movements launched inequality changes in a world where the agricultural sector was big and where land was a critical component of total wealth.[11] It tells us how the typical unskilled (landless) worker near the bottom of the income pyramid did relative to the typical landlord at the top (w/r). The other piece of inequality evidence relies on trends in the ratio of the unskilled wage to GDP per worker (w/y). These trends tell us whether the typical unskilled worker near the bottom was catching up with or falling behind the income recipient in the middle.

When w/r and w/y trends are plotted for the Atlantic economy against initial labour scarcity between 1870 and the First World War (Williamson, 1997), they conform to the conventional globalization prediction (Figure 6.4). Inequality fell and equality rose in land-scarce and labour-abundant Europe due either to trade boom, or to mass emigration, or to both, as incomes of the abundant factor (unskilled labour) rose relative to the scarce factor (land). In addition, those European countries which faced the onslaught of cheap foreign grain after 1870, but chose not to impose high tariffs on grain imports (such as Britain, Ireland and Sweden), recorded the biggest loss for landlords and the biggest gain for workers. Those who protected their landlords and farmers against cheap foreign grain (such as France, Germany and Spain) generally recorded a smaller decline in land rents relative to unskilled wages. To the extent that globalization was the dominant force, inequality should have fallen in labour-abundant and land-scarce Europe. And fall it did. However, these egalitarian effects were far more modest for the European industrial leaders who, after all, had smaller agricultural sectors. Land was a smaller component of total wealth in the European industrial core where improved returns on industrial capital, whose owners were located near the top of the income distribution, at least partially offset the diminished incomes from land, whose owners tended to occupy the very top of the income distribution.

Globalization had a powerful inegalitarian effect in the land-abundant and labour-scarce New World, and for symmetric reasons. Not surprisingly,

Figure 6.4   Initial real wage versus subsequent inequality trends, 1870–1913

Source: Adapted from O'Rourke and Williamson (1999: Figure 9.2).

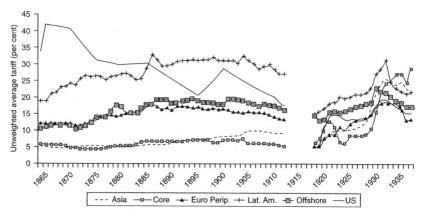

Figure 6.5   Unweighted average of regional tariffs, 1865–1939

Source: Adapted from Coatsworth and Williamson (2002: Figure 2a).

Latin America, the United States, Australia, Canada and Russia all raised tariffs to defend themselves against an invasion of European manufactures and the deindustrialization it would have caused (Blattman, Clemens and Williamson, 2002; Coatsworth and Williamson, 2002). Indeed, the levels of protection in the United States, Canada, Australia, Latin America and the European periphery were *huge* compared to continental Europe. Figure 6.5

reports that in the 1880s the United States and Latin America had tariffs *five–six* times higher than Western Europe, and the European periphery had levels *three* times higher! It is absolutely essential to know *why* tariffs were so much higher in the periphery than in the European core up to the 1930s, but we save this discussion for the end of the chapter.

Terms of trade gains in the periphery before 1913

Terms of trade movements might signal who gains the most from trade, and a literature at least two centuries old has offered opinions about whose terms of trade should improve most and why (Diakosavvas and Scandizzo, 1991; Hadass and Williamson, 2003). Classical economists thought the relative price of primary products should rise given an inelastic supply of land and natural resources. This conventional wisdom took a revisionist U-turn in the 1950s when Hans Singer and Raúl Prebisch argued that since 1870 the terms of trade had deteriorated for poor countries in the periphery – exporting primary products – while they had improved for rich countries in the centre – exporting industrial products.

The terms of trade can be influenced by changes in transport costs and changes in policy. It can also be influenced by other events, such as world productivity growth differentials across sectors, demand elasticities, and factor supply responses. But since transport costs declined so dramatically in the first global century (O'Rourke and Williamson, 1999; Findlay and O'Rourke, 2002; Williamson, 2002), this is one likely source that served to raise *everybody's* terms of trade. Furthermore, and as we have seen, rich countries such as Britain took a terms of trade hit when they switched to free trade by the mid-century, an event that must have raised the terms of trade in the poor, non-industrial periphery even more. But in some parts of the periphery, especially before the 1870s, other factors were at work that mattered even more, and they greatly reinforced these pro-global forces.

Probably the most powerful nineteenth-century globalization shock did not involve transport revolutions at all. It happened in Asia, and it happened mid-century. Under the persuasion of American gun ships, Japan switched from virtual autarky to free trade in 1858. In the fifteen years following 1858, Japan's foreign trade rose 70 times, from virtually 0 per cent to 7 per cent of national income (Huber, 1971). The prices of exportables soared in home markets, rising towards world market levels. The prices of importables slumped in home markets, falling towards world market levels. One researcher estimates that, as a consequence, Japan's terms of trade rose by a factor of 4.9 over those fifteen years (Yasuba, 1996). Thus, the combination of declining transport costs worldwide and a dramatic switch from autarky to free trade unleashed a powerful terms of trade gain for Japan.

Other Asian nations followed this liberal path, most forced to do so by colonial dominance or gunboat diplomacy. Thus, China signed a treaty in 1842 opening her ports to trade and adopting a 5 per cent *ad valorem* tariff limit. Siam adopted a 3 per cent tariff limit in 1855. Korea emerged from its autarkic 'hermit kingdom' a little later (with the Treaty of Kangwha in 1876), undergoing market integration with Japan long before colonial status became formalized in 1910. India went the way of British free trade in 1846, and Indonesia mimicked Dutch liberalism. In short, and whether they liked it or not, Asia underwent tremendous improvements in their terms of trade by this policy switch, and it was reinforced by declining transport costs worldwide.

For the years after 1870, there is better evidence documenting terms of trade movements the world around, country by country (Williamson, 2002; Hadass and Williamson, 2003). Contrary to the assertions which Prebisch and Singer made half a century ago, not only did the terms of trade improve for a good share of the non-Latin American poor periphery[12] up to the First World War, but they improved a lot more than they did in Europe. Over the four decades prior to the First World War, the terms of trade rose by only 2 per cent in the European centre, by almost 10 per cent in East Asia and by more than 21 per cent in the Southern Cone, Egypt and India combined.

Why am I able to report such different historical findings than did Prebisch and Singer, or than did W. Arthur Lewis a little later? One reason is that Prebisch and his followers were motivated by deteriorating terms of trade in Latin America, while I am casting a wider net. Another is that I have reported the terms of trade performance only during the first global century (up to 1913), not during the anti-global interlude that followed. A third reason is that the peripheral terms of trade reported here are those which prevailed in each home market (e.g. Alexandria, Bangkok or Montevideo), not the inverse of those prevailing in London or New York. In a world where transport costs plunged steeply, everybody could have found their terms of trade improving, but some primary producers in the periphery actually enjoyed the biggest pre-war improvements. If other members of the periphery did not enjoy the same big gains, it was not the fault of globalization induced by transport revolutions and liberal policy. Rather, the fault lay with the characteristics of those primary products themselves.

This pre-1913 terms of trade experience seems to imply that globalization favoured some parts of the poor periphery even more than it did the rich centre, and to that extent it must have been a force for more equal world incomes. That inference is probably false. Over the short run, positive and quasi-permanent terms of trade shocks of foreign origin will always raise a nation's purchasing power, and the issue is only how much. Over the long run a positive terms of trade shock in primary product producing countries should reinforce comparative advantage and pull resources into the export sector, thus causing deindustrialization. To the extent that industrialization is the prime carrier of capital-deepening and technological change, then economists like Singer were right to caution that positive external price shocks for primary producers might actually *lower* growth rates in the long run. Of course, small-scale, rural cottage industry is not the same as large-scale, urban factories, so industry may not have been quite the carrier of growth in the 1870 periphery that it might be in the Third World today. In any case, while nobody has yet tried to decompose the short-run and long-run components of quasi-permanent terms of trade shocks like these, there has been a recent effort to explore the possibility that positive terms of trade shocks had a negative effect around the periphery (Hadass and Williamson, 2003). Adding terms of trade variables to a now-standard empirical growth model and estimating that model for a nineteen-country sample between 1870 and 1940 confirms that an improving terms of trade augmented long-run growth in the centre. However, the same terms of trade improvement was *growth-reducing* in the periphery. It appears that the short-run gain from an improving terms of trade was overwhelmed by a long-run loss attributed to deindustrialization in the periphery; in contrast, the short-run gain was reinforced by a long-run gain attributed to industrialization in the centre.

These results imply that globalization-induced (positive) terms of trade shocks before the First World War were serving to augment the growing gap between rich and poor nations. Did the same happen after 1950 when Prebisch, Singer and other critics of conventional policy were so vocal? Maybe. Is the same true today, fifty years later? Probably not. After all, manufactures have been a rapidly rising share of developing country output and exports since the 1970s. The share of manufactures in the total commodity exports in developing countries rose spectacularly from around 30 per cent in 1970 to more than 75 per cent in 2002 (Hertel, Hoekman and Martin, 2002: Figure 2). To put it the other way around, agricultural and mineral primary product exports as a share in total exports fell from 70 to 25 per cent over the past thirty years in the Third World. Enough of the Third World is now sufficiently labour-abundant and natural resource-scarce so that their comparative advantage lies with (simple, labour-intensive) manufactures, implying that the growth of trade has helped it industrialize. The classic image of Third World specialization in primary products has almost evaporated, leaving a contracting vestige mainly just in Africa.

Rising inequality in the primary product-exporting periphery

There were powerful global forces at work before 1913 and the Third World was very much a part of it. There was commodity price convergence within and between Europe, the newly settled non-Latin countries, Latin America and Asia, and the price convergence was bigger in the periphery than it was in the core. The convergence was driven by a transport revolution that was more dramatic in the Asian periphery where, in addition, it was not offset by tariff intervention. It also appears that relative factor prices converged world-wide at the same time that average living standards and income *per capita* diverged sharply between centre and periphery.[13] The relative factor price convergence was manifested by falling wage–rental ratios in land-abundant and labour-scarce countries, and rising wage–rental ratios in land-scarce and labour-abundant countries. The convergence took place everywhere around the globe. These events set in motion powerful inequality forces in land and resource abundant areas, *especially* around the pre-industrial periphery, as in Southeast Asia and the Southern Cone. Quite the opposite forces were at work in land- and resource-scarce areas, such as East Asia.

These distributional events in the periphery were ubiquitous and powerful (Williamson, 2002). They must have had important implications for political developments which probably persisted well in to the late twentieth century, just as W. Arthur Lewis' research agenda always implied.

North–North and South–South mass migrations, with segmentation in between

North–North migrations between Europe and the New World involved the movement of something like 60 million individuals. We know a great deal about the determinants and impact of these mass migrations. South–South migration within the periphery was probably even greater, but we know very little about its impact on sending regions (such as China and India), on receiving regions (such as East Africa, Manchuria and Southeast Asia), or on the incomes of the 60 million or so who moved. As Lewis (1978) pointed out long ago, the South–North migrations were only a trickle – like today, poor

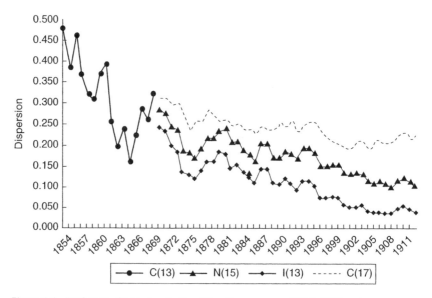

Figure 6.6   Real wage dispersion in the Atlantic economy, 1854–1913
Source: Adapted from O'Rourke and Williamson (1999: Figure 2.2).

migrants from the periphery were kept out of the high-wage centre by restrictive policy, by the high cost of the move and by their lack of education. World labour markets were segmented then, just as they are now. Real wages and living standards converged among the currently industrialized countries between 1850 and the First World War (Figure 6.6).[14] The convergence was driven primarily by the erosion of the gap between the New World and Europe. In addition, many poor European countries were catching up with the industrial leaders. How much of this convergence in the Atlantic economy was due to North–North mass migration?

The labour force impact of these migrations on each member of the Atlantic economy in 1910 varied greatly (Taylor and Williamson, 1997). Among receiving countries, Argentina's labour force was augmented most by immigration (86 per cent), Brazil's the least (4 per cent), with the United States in between (24 per cent). Among sending countries, Ireland's labour force was diminished most by emigration (45 per cent), France the least (1 per cent), with Britain in between (11 per cent). At the same time, the economic gaps between rich and poor countries diminished: real wage dispersion in the Atlantic economy declined between 1870 and 1910 by 28 per cent, GDP *per capita* dispersion declined by 18 per cent and GDP per worker dispersion declined by 29 per cent (Taylor and Williamson, 1997; Hatton and Williamson, 1998). What contribution did the mass migration make to that convergence?

Migration affects equilibrium output, wages and living standards by influencing aggregate labour supply, and these effects have also been estimated. In the absence of the mass migrations, wages and labour productivity would have been a lot higher in the New World and a lot lower in Europe. The biggest impact, of course, was on those countries that experienced the biggest migrations. Emigration is estimated to have raised Irish wages by 32 per cent, Italian by 28 per cent and Norwegian by 10 per cent. Immigration is estimated to have lowered Argentine wages by 22 per cent, Australian by 15 per cent, Canadian by 16 per cent and American by 8 per cent.

This partial-equilibrium assessment of migration's impact is higher than a general-equilibrium assessment would be since it ignores trade and output mix adjustments, as well as domestic and global capital market responses, all of which would have muted the impact of migration. In any case, the assessment certainly lends strong support to the hypothesis that mass migration made an important contribution to late nineteenth-century convergence in the North. In the absence of the mass migrations, real wage dispersion between members of the Atlantic economy would have *increased* by something like 7 per cent, rather than decrease by 28 per cent, as it in fact did. In the absence of mass migration, wage gaps between Europe and the New World would have *risen* from 108 to something like 128 per cent, when in fact they declined to 85 per cent. These results have been used to conclude that migration was responsible for *all* of the real wage convergence before the First World War and about two-thirds of the GDP per worker convergence.

There was an additional and even more powerful effect of North–North mass migrations on 'northern' income distribution. So far I have discussed only the effect of migration on convergence in per-worker averages between countries; I have not discussed the impact of migration on income distribution within the Atlantic economy as a whole. To do so, I would need to add on the large income gains accruing to the millions of poor Europeans who moved overseas. Typically, these migrants came from countries whose average real wages and average GDP per worker were perhaps only half of those in the receiving countries. These migrant gains were a very important part of the net equalizing effect on 'northern' incomes of the mass migrations.

North–North mass migrations had a strong levelling influence in the North up to 1913. They made it possible for poor migrants to improve the living standards for themselves and their children. It also lowered the scarcity of resident New World labour which competed with the immigrants, while it raised the scarcity of the poor European labour that stayed home (whose incomes were augmented still further by emigrant remittances). South–South and North–North migrations were about the same size. Until new research tells us otherwise,[15] I think it is safe to assume that South–South migrations put powerful downward pressure on real wages and labour productivity in Burma, Ceylon, East Africa, Manchuria, and other labour-scarce regions that received so many Indian and Chinese immigrants. Since the sending labour-surplus areas were so huge, it seems less likely that the emigrations significantly served to raise labour scarcity there.

The unimportance of global capital markets

Using *ceteris paribus* assumptions, I have just concluded that mass migration accounted for *all* of the real wage convergence observed in the Atlantic economy during the first global century. But *ceteris* was not *paribus*, since there were other powerful forces at work, capital accumulation responses being one of them. Capital accumulation was rapid in the New World, so much so that the rate of capital deepening was faster in the United States than in any of its European competitors, and the same was probably true of other rich New World countries. Thus, the mass migrations may have been at least partially offset by capital accumulation, and a large part of that accumulation was being financed by international capital flows which reached magnitudes unsurpassed since. One study has made exactly this kind of adjustment (Taylor and Williamson, 1997) by implementing the zero-migration counterfactual in a model where the labour supply shocks generate capital flow responses that maintain a constant rate of return on capital (e.g. perfect global capital market integration).[16] The assumed capital-chasing-labour offsets are certainly large in this experiment, but mass migration *still* explains about 70 per cent of the convergence, leaving only about 30 per cent to other forces.

Capital market responses were simply not big enough to deflate significantly the powerful income-levelling effects of mass migration within what we now call the OECD. Indeed, while it is true that global capital markets were at least as well integrated prior to the First World War as they are today (Obstfeld and Taylor, 1998, 2002), capital flows were mainly an *anti-convergence* force. This statement is, of course, inconsistent with simple two-factor theory prediction that capital should flow from rich to poor countries. It never did. As Lucas (1990) made famous, Table 6.2 shows that British capital inflows and GDP *per capita* were *positively*, not negatively, correlated just before the First World War, and that the same was true for all private capital inflows in the 1990s (Clemens and Williamson, 2001b; see also Obstfeld and Taylor, 2002). The wealth bias that Lucas and others have noticed was just as powerful a century ago, and it is explained by the fact that capital chased after abundant natural resources, youthful populations and human capital abundance. It did *not* chase after cheap labour.

International capital flows were never a pro-convergence force. They drifted towards rich, not poor, countries; they raised wages and labour productivity in the labour-scarce and resource-abundant New World, not the labour-abundant Third World. And what was true of the first global century has also been true of the second. But this does not imply that the Third World has been losing capital by export.[17] Rather, it implies that there has

Table 6.2   Wealth bias during the two global centuries

Time period	1907–13	1992–98
Dependent variable	Annual average gross British capital received (flow, in 1990 US$)	Annual average change in stock of private capital liabilities (flow, in 1990 US$)
GDP, 1990 US$	0.000208 (3.32)*** [0.534]	0.00467 (8.68)*** [0.624]
GDP *per capita*, 1990 US$	10,700 (2.43)** [0.965]	97,900 (2.20)** [0.410]
Constant	−11,100,000 (−1.06)	−44,700,000 (−0.11)
Estimator	OLS	OLS
N	34	155
R^2	0.414	0.463

Notes: *t*-statistics are in parentheses, elasticities (at average regressor values) are in square brackets. *** Significant at the 1 per cent level. ** Significant at the 5 per cent level.

Source: Adapted from Clemens and Williamson (2001b: Table 2).

always been a churning of capital among richer countries outside of Asia and Africa. Nor does it imply that global capital markets have been at fault for failing to redistribute world capital towards poor countries. Instead, it implies that, for other reasons, the poor countries have never been the best place to make investments.

Trade policy and international income gaps: why the big regime switch?

In 1972, Paul Bairoch argued that protectionist countries grew *faster* in the nineteenth century, not slower as every economist has found for the late twentieth century. Bairoch's sample was mainly from the European industrial core, it looked at pre-1914 experience only and it invoked unconditional analysis, controlling for no other factors. Like some modern studies (see Table 6.1, p. 144), Bairoch simply compared growth rates of major European countries in protectionist and free-trade episodes. More recently, O'Rourke (2000) got the Bairoch finding again, this time using macroeconometric conditional analysis on a ten-country sample drawn from the pre-1914 Atlantic economy (Australia, Canada, Denmark, France, Germany, Italy, Norway, Sweden, the United Kingdom, the United States). In short, these two scholars were not able to find *any* evidence before the First World War supporting the 'openness-fosters-growth' hypothesis.[18]

These pioneering historical studies suggest that there was a fundamental tariff–growth regime switch somewhere between the start of the First World War and the end of Second World War: before the switch, protection was associated with fast growth; after the switch, protection was associated with slow growth.[19] Clemens and Williamson (2001a) think the best explanation for the tariff–growth paradox is the fact that during the interwar years, and led by the industrial powers, tariff barriers facing the average exporting countries rose to very high levels; and since the Second World War, again led by the industrial powers, tariff barriers facing the average exporting country fell to their lowest levels in a century and a half. A well developed theoretical literature on strategic trade policy[20] predicts that nations have an incentive to inflate their own terms of trade by tariffs, but thereby to lower global welfare – a classic prisoner's dilemma. Inasmuch as favourable terms of trade translate into better growth performance and tariffs are non-prohibitive, we might expect the association between own tariffs and growth to depend at least in part on the external tariff environment faced by the country in question. After accounting for changes in world policy environment, Clemens and Williamson (2001a) show that there is no incompatibility between the positive tariff–growth correlation before 1914 and the negative tariff–growth correlation since 1970.

It has not always been true that open countries finish first, and it need not be true in the future either. There is growing evidence suggesting that the benefits of openness are neither inherent nor irreversible but rather depend upon the state of the world. When considering the move to openness, heads of state are facing a game, not an isolated decision. The low-level equilibrium of mutually high tariffs is only as far away as some big world event that persuades influential leader countries to switch to anti-global policies. Feedback ensures that the rest must follow in order to survive. Thus, today's low-tariff equilibrium was only as far away as Western coordination in the early post-war years, and the creation of transnational public institutions whose express purpose was to impede a return to interwar anti-global autarky.

But what sparks such shifts from one equilibrium to another? Why did it happen in the 1920s and 1950s? Could it happen again?

Trade policy and international income gaps: what about the pre-1940 periphery?

Were Latin America, Eastern Europe and the rest of the periphery part of this paradox, or was it only an attribute of the industrial core? While the work cited above has shown that protection fostered growth in the industrial core before the Second World War, it also shows that it did *not* do so in most of the periphery (Clemens and Williamson, 2001a; Coatsworth and Williamson, 2002). Table 6.3 reports this result, where the model estimated is of the convergence variety, but it is conditioned only by the country's own tariff rate and regional dummies. The tariff rate and GDP *per capita* level are both measured at year *t*, while the subsequent GDP *per capita* growth rate is measured over the half-decade following.[21] The two world wars are ignored.

The tariff–growth paradox is stunningly clear in Table 6.3. In columns (1) and (3), the estimated coefficient on log of the tariff rate is 0.14 for 1875–1908 and 0.36 for 1924–34. Thus, and in contrast with late twentieth-century evidence, tariffs were associated with *fast* growth before 1939. But was this true for all regions, or was there instead an asymmetry between industrial economies in the core and primary producers in the periphery? Presumably, the protecting country has to have a big domestic market, and has to be ready for industrialization, accumulation and human capital deepening if the long-run tariff-induced dynamic effects are to offset the short-run gains from trade given up. Table 6.3 tests for asymmetry in columns (2) and (4), and the asymmetry hypothesis wins. That is, protection was associated with faster growth in the European core and their English-speaking offshoots (the coefficient on own tariff 1875–1908 is 0.56 and highly significant), but it was *not* associated with fast growth in the European or Latin American periphery, nor was it associated with fast growth in interwar Asia (when tariffs rose even in the colonies: see Figure 6.5, p. 151). Indeed, before the First World War, protection in Latin America was associated significantly and powerfully with *slow* growth. The moral of the story is while policy makers in Latin America, Eastern Europe and the Mediterranean may, after the 1860s, have been very aware of the pro-protectionist infant-industry argument[22] offered for a newly integrated (*Zollverein*) Germany by Frederich

Table 6.3   Tariff impact of GDP *per capita* growth, by region

Dependent variable	5-year overlapping average growth rate			
	(1)	(2)	(3)	(4)
Included countries	All	All	All	All
Years per period	1	1	· 1	1
Time interval	1875–1908	1875–1908	1924–34	1924–34
ln GDP *per capita*	0.15	0.10	−0.73	−0.89
	1.14	*0.75*	*−1.77*	*−2.13*
ln own tariff	0.14	0.56	0.36	1.65
	1.64	*3.35*	*1.27*	*2.83*
(European periphery		−0.72		−2.45
dummy) × (ln tariff rate)		*−3.32*		*−3.18*
(Latin America dummy) 7×		−0.97		0.58
(ln tariff rate)		*−3.15*		*0.49*
(Asia dummy) × (ln tariff		−0.19		−1.47
rate)		*−0.84*		*−2.02*
European periphery dummy	−0.21	1.58	−0.04	6.15
	−1.24	*2.77*	*−0.08*	*3.10*
Latin America dummy	0.19	3.01	−0.73	−3.31
	0.94	*3.13*	*−1.31*	*−0.96*
Asia dummy	−0.26	0.30	−1.17	2.39
	−1.09	*0.55*	*−1.52*	*1.24*
Constant	−0.12	−0.76	5.92	3.99
	−0.11	*−0.68*	*1.55*	*1.05*
Country dummies?	No	No	No	No
Time dummies?	No	No	No	No
N	1,190	1,190	372	372
R^2	0.0357	0.0498	0.0227	0.0605
Adj. R^2	0.0317	0.0433	0.0094	0.0398

Note: *t*-statistics are in italics.

Source: Adapted from Coatsworth and Williamson (2002: Table 1).

List or for a newly independent (economically federated) United States by Alexander Hamilton, there is absolutely no evidence which would have supported those arguments in the periphery. We must look elsewhere for plausible explanations for the exceptionally high tariffs in Latin America and the European periphery during the first global century.

Lessons of history I: will there be South–North mass migration in our future?

It may be useful to repeat what we have learned about the mass European emigration: almost all of the observed income convergence in the Atlantic economy, or what we are now calling the North, was due to this North–North mass migration, and that same movement also generated more

162   *Winners and Losers in Globalization*

equal incomes in the labour-abundant sending regions. It is important to remember this fact when dealing today with the second global century.

Although the migrations were immense during the age of mass North–North and South–South migration prior to the First World War, there was hardly any South–North migration to speak of. Thus, while the mass migration to labour-scarce parts of the North played a big role in erasing poverty in the labour-surplus parts of the North, it did not help much to erase poverty in the South. The same is true today. Will this world labour market segmentation break down in the near future? It all depends on policy. Certainly demographic and educational forces are contributing to the breakdown of world labour market segmentation along South–North lines. As young adult shares shrink in the elderly OECD, and while they swell in the young Third World going through demographic transitions, perhaps the pressure will become too great to resist the move to a more liberal OECD immigration policy, especially in Europe and Japan. The educational revolution in the Third World (Easterlin, 1981; Schultz, 1987) has helped augment this pressure, as potential emigrants from poor countries are better equipped to gain jobs in the OECD (Clark, Hatton and Williamson, 2002; Hatton and Williamson, 2002).

The two underlying fundamentals that drove European emigration in the late nineteenth century were the size of real wage gaps between sending and receiving regions – gaps that gave migrants the incentive to move – and demographic booms in the low-wage sending regions – a force that served to augment the supply of potential movers (Hatton and Williamson, 1998). These two fundamentals are even more prominent in Africa today, and recent work suggests that Africans seem to be just as responsive to them as were Europeans a century ago (Hatton and Williamson, 2001, 2002). Although this is no longer an age of unrestricted intercontinental migration, new estimates of net migration for the SSA countries suggest that exactly the same forces are at work driving African cross-border migration today. Rapid growth in the cohort of young potential migrants, population pressure on the resource base and poor economic performance are the main forces driving African emigration. In Europe a century ago, more modest demographic increases were accompanied by strong catching-up economic growth in low-wage emigrant regions. Furthermore, the sending regions of Europe eventually underwent a slowdown in demographic growth, serving to choke off some of the mass migration. Yet, migrations were still mass. Africa today offers a contrast: economic growth has faltered, its economies have fallen further behind the leaders and there will be a demographic speed-up in the near future. The pressure on African emigration is likely to intensify, including a growing demand for entrance into the high-wage labour markets of the developed world. Indeed, if European doors were swung open, there is an excellent chance that by 2025 Africa would record far greater mass migrations than did nineteenth-century Europe.

The demographic unknown in this equation is, of course, African success in controlling the spread of the HIV/AIDS. If it is controlled early, then these emigration predictions are more likely to prevail.

This analysis for African emigration has been recently extended to US immigration by source from 1971 to 1998 (Clark, Hatton and Williamson, 2002; Hatton and Williamson, 2002). Here again, the economic and demographic fundamentals that determine immigration rates across source countries are estimated – income, education, demographic composition and inequality. The analysis also allows for persistence in these patterns as they arise from the impact of the existing immigrant foreign-born stocks, implying strong 'friends and neighbours' effects. Most of these Third World fundamentals will be serving to increase the demand for high-wage jobs in the OECD. How will the OECD respond to this challenge? If it opens its doors wider, the mass migrations will almost certainly have the same influence on levelling world incomes and eradicating poverty that it did in the first global century. It will help erode between-country North–South income gaps, and it will improve the lives of the millions of poor Asians and Africans allowed to make the move. And it will help eradicate poverty among those who will not move, making their labour more scarce at home and augmenting their incomes by remittances, forces that were powerful in pre-quota Europe a century ago.

Inequality will rise among OECD residents, of course, just as it did in the immigrant-absorbing New World a century ago.[23] Perhaps not as much, since the unskilled with whom the immigrants compete are a much smaller share of the OECD labour force today, but inequality will rise just the same. Are we ready to pay that price? Perhaps not. Indeed, we have seen how rising inequality created an anti-global backlash a century ago, a backlash that included a retreat into immigrant restriction that *still* characterizes the high-wage OECD today.

Lessons of history II: absolute or relative income? Nominal or real income?

The debate over the impact of globalization on world inequality almost always measures performance in relative terms. The questions posed are: Have international income gaps between poor and rich countries widened with globalization? Has inequality within countries widened with globalization? Something is very wrong with these questions and the measures they imply. Here are better questions: If gaps between rich and poor countries have widened, and if globalization is the cause, is it because poor countries have not gained from going global, or is it because they have actually lost? If the gaps between rich and poor within countries have widened, and if globalization is the cause, is it because poor citizens have not gained by their country going global, or is it because they have actually lost? To the extent that policy is driven by the *absolute* losses to vocal citizens and/or vocal nations, rather than relative losses, it is all the more amazing that so many contemporary economists insist on using relative inequality measures. Economic historians know better. I offer two examples.

Example 1

During the great British political debates over a move to free trade in the decades before the 1846 Repeal of the Corn Laws, predicted impact was *always* assessed by reference to *both* nominal incomes on the employment side *and* to consumption goods prices on the expenditure side. Indeed, free-traders called the high duties on agricultural imports 'bread taxes' (Williamson, 1990), and thought that the relative price of this wage good (grain) was central to working-class living standards. And they were absolutely right. Since grain – and its derivative, bread – made up such an enormous share of working-class budgets, the falling relative price of this importable made a fundamental contribution to the rise in real wages and the living standards of the poor.

Example 2

During the great rise in European inequality between 1500 and 1800, when Malthusian forces dominated the closed European economy (O'Rourke and Williamson, 2002a, 2002c), staple food and fuels became more expensive, while luxury goods, like imported exotics and domestic servants, became cheaper (Hoffman *et al.*, 2002). These relative price changes served to aug-ment rising nominal inequality – and, indeed, to reduce living standards of the working poor. What happened in the nineteenth century when Europe went open? The price of imported food fell, contributing to the absolute real wage gains associated with the industrial revolution, and to an absolute decline in land rents. What had been a pre-globalization inegalitarian price effect was converted into a post-globalization egalitarian price effect. And since the poor devote such a large share of their budget to food, the poorest gained the most.

   Economic historians cannot take all the credit for asking the right questions, since one can also find a few rare examples in the huge literature on the current globalization–inequality connection. Dollar and Kraay (2000b) report from late twentieth-century country cases and cross-country analysis that globalization leads to poverty reduction in poor countries, and that trade openness benefits the poor as much as it benefits all others.[24] Of course, it may not be the poor who vote, and thus the impact of going open on their economic performance may be unimportant to policy formation in poor countries and thus to the survival of global liberalism there.

   The two historical examples from the first global century suggest an agenda for the second. If 'going global' has had a real impact on participating economies over the past three decades, then we should see its impact on relative commodity prices in home markets: the price of importables should have fallen relative to the price of exportables and perhaps even relative to the price of non-tradables. What do the rich and poor consume in these countries? What happened to the cost of their consumption market baskets when their country went open? Did the price movements on the expenditure side serve to reinforce or offset income movements on the employment side? The answers to these questions are very hard to find in the literature on the second global century. True, some time ago William Cline (1980) asked whether world commodity price shocks had much to do with within-country nominal income inequality, concluding 'not much' while, as I pointed out above, Robertson (2001) asked the same question of Mexico since NAFTA, concluding a 'great deal'.[25] But do global-induced relative commodity changes induce uneven *real income changes on the expenditure side* to the extent that the poor consume a very different market basket than the rich? They certainly did for Vietnam in the 1990s. According to Edmonds and Pavcnik (2002), during the liberal period between 1993 and 1998 the price of rice rose by 29 per cent relative to the Vietnamese consumer price index (CPI), and this relative price change must have had important inegalitarian effects on the expenditure side since the budget of the poor in that country is so dominated by rice.

It seems to me that economists should be searching for contemporary cases where the expenditure budgets of the rich and poor are very different, and where the rich consume in large proportions skill- and capital-intensive importables plus the services of the poor, and where the poor consume in large proportions land-intensive food and housing. They should also search for countries that have a recent history of switching from anti-global to pro-global policies. The best places to find both conditions satisfied are, of course, poor countries in Asia and Africa.

Lessons of history III: accommodating the losers with safety nets and suffrage

Any force that creates more within–country inequality is automatically blunted today – at least in the OECD, a point that is sometimes overlooked in the inequality debate. That is, any rise in the inequality of households' net disposable post-fisc income will always be less than the rise in gross pre-fisc income inequality. Any damage to the earnings of low-skilled workers is partially offset by their lower tax payments and higher transfer receipts, such as unemployment compensation or family assistance. Broadening the income concept therefore serves to shrink any apparent impact of globalization on the inequality of living standards. And by muting their losses, such safety nets also, presumably, mute any political backlash.

So far, so good. But does globalization destroy these automatic stabilizers by undermining taxes and social transfer programmes? In a world where businesses and skilled personnel can flee taxes they don't like, there is the well-known danger that governments may compete for internationally mobile factors by cutting tax rates and thus social spending. As Rodrik (1997, 1998) and Agell (1999, 2000) have stressed, however, the relationship between a country's vulnerability to international markets and the size of its tax-based social programmes is *positive*, not negative as a 'race to the bottom' would imply. Thus, countries with greater global market vulnerability have higher taxes, more social spending and broader safety nets. Furthermore, 'vulnerability' to global market changes is in part an endogenous policy choice: there is a trade-off between going open and investing in safety nets. In any case, while there may be other reasons for the positive correlation between openness and social programmes, there is no apparent tendency for globalization to undermine the safety nets.

While these stabilizers certainly prevail in the OECD today, one might suppose they were not common during the first global century when such safety nets were not yet in place. One might also suppose that there was no trade-off between going open and investing in safety nets at that time in what we now call the OECD. If one were inclined to make those suppositions, one would be very wrong. Europe was globalized by 1913, and the increased market vulnerability created greater wage and employment instability. Huberman (2002) and Huberman and Lewchuk (2001) show that authorities responded to workers' complaints by establishing labour market regulations and social insurance programmes, and by giving them the vote. Empirical analysis of seventeen European countries shows that the legislation gave workers reason to support free trade. Thus, globalization was compatible with government intervention before 1913, just as it has been since 1950. And, to repeat, the first global century was also one during which the vote was extended increasingly to the previously disenfranchised (Acemoglu and Robinson, 2000; Huberman and Lewchuk, 2001). It also appears that the two were related. The interesting question is: how long it will take poor nations today to put the same modern safety nets in place and to empower all citizens in the debate over global policy choices?

Lessons of history IV: why do countries protect?

What better place to end this chapter than to ask: why do countries protect? I am aware that the 1990s generated a flourishing theoretical literature on endogenous tariffs. That literature is primarily motivated by recent OECD, and mainly US, experience, thus ignoring the enormous variance over time and across regions with very different endowments, institutions and histories.

Look again at Figure 6.5, where the enormous variance in levels of protection is documented for both the first global century and for the interwar years, and where three big facts are revealed. First, tariffs in the independent periphery (Latin America, the non-Latin European offshoots and the European periphery) were vastly higher than they were in the European core. Second, in an apparent – but maybe not real – globalization backlash, tariffs rose *much* more steeply in the periphery than in the European core during the first globalization century up to the First World War. Third, what made the interwar years so autarkic was not a move towards protection in the periphery – since tariffs in Latin America, the European periphery and the non-Latin offshoots were just about as high in the 1930s as they were before the First World War.[26] What made the interwar years so autarkic was the rise of protection in the European core and the United States.

Economists need to confront these facts and to offer explanations for them. When one does so for Latin America from 1820 to 1950, one finds that the motivations for protection were very complex and changed over time (Coatsworth and Williamson, 2002). Those exceptionally high Latin American tariffs were driven up by government revenue needs, strategic tariff reactions to trading partner policy (e.g. very high tariffs in the United States), Stolper–Samuelson lobbying forces and protection of the local manufacturing industry. Before we can be confident about what causes the globalization backlash today, we need to know what caused it in the past. Over the century 1820–1913,[27] only a (perhaps small) part of the anti-global policy in Latin America was driven by development goals, by deindustrialization fears, or by the complaints of the losers. Furthermore, these determinants changed over time: revenue goals diminished in importance as Latin America became better integrated with global capital markets, as *pax americana latina* diminished the need for and thus the financial burden of standing armies and as these young countries developed less distorting internal tax revenue sources. Economists need to make the same kind of assessment for the second global century if we are to understand the sources of the globalization backlash better.

Notes

Thanks are due to Michael Clemens, John Coatsworth, Tim Hatton, Peter Lindert and Kevin O'Rourke for collaboration, Barbara Fagerman and Tony Shorrocks of UNU-WIDER for organization and the support of the US National Science Foundation (SES-0001362).

1. The causality is worth stressing here. While the modern globalization–inequality debate chases the causation from globalization to within-country inequality, the period 1500–1800 was characterized by population pressure on the land which raised land rents and thus the incomes of Europe's rich. Rising inequality increased the demand for imported luxuries, causing a trade boom. It also caused a boom in all well-placed European ports around the Atlantic economy. It seems to me that a paper by Acemoglu, Johnson and Robinson (2002) has the causality wrong.
2. For an excellent survey, see Findlay and O'Rourke (2002).
3. This benign interpretation certainly has its critics, most recently from the World Bank itself (Milanovic, 2002).
4. They all use PPP data for which the fall is far clearer. Indeed, it disappears in studies that use income data in US dollars (Melchior, Telle and Wiig, 2000: 16).
5. For example, when Mexico joined NAFTA in 1994, its economy was only about 6 per cent the size of the United States. Furthermore, only about 9 per cent of US

trade was with Mexico, while about 75 per cent of Mexican imports and 84 per cent of Mexican exports involved the United States (Robertson, 2001: 1). These shares suggest that Mexico satisfied the 'small-country assumption' and took North American market prices as given, thus getting the full measure of terms of trade gains by going open.

6. For an excellent critical survey, see Dowrick and DeLong (2002).
7. The giants also dominate trends in between-country inequality. Much of the fall in the between-country inequality index offered by Melchior, Telle and Wiig (2000: 15) is due to the fact that the populations in Japan and the United States are getting relatively fewer and less rich, while those in China and India are getting richer and more populous.
8. Migration from the hinterland to the cities was pretty much prohibited before the mid-1990s.
9. Granted, nineteenth-century industrial revolutions greatly contributed to an acceleration in the growing gap between industrial core and pre-industrial periphery (e.g. Pritchett, 1997).
10. Labour would not have gained much from free trade on the continent since, among other things, agriculture was a far bigger employer, so big that the employment effects (the nominal wage) dominated the consumption effects (the cost of living). See O'Rourke (1997).
11. Agricultural output and land input shares are certainly smaller today even in the Third World, but to ignore them in the inequality debate is a big mistake. It is also a mistake to ignore self-employment income in the large service sector. Yet, economists studying the modern Third World seem to have an obsession with earnings distributions of hired labour.
12. In two of the studies cited (Williamson, 2002; Hadass and Williamson, 2003), the periphery sample is limited to nine – Argentina, Burma, Egypt, India, Japan, Korea, Taiwan, Thailand and Uruguay – which, of course, excludes non-Southern Cone Latin America where the terms of trade appear to have fallen most dramatically. This small sample from the periphery is augmented by twelve more countries in a third study: Brazil, Ceylon, Chile, China, Colombia, Cuba, Greece, Indonesia, Mexico, the Philippines, Peru and Turkey (Blattman, Clemens and Williamson, 2002).
13. These facts deserve stress. While there was income *per capita* and living standards divergence between centre and periphery in the first global century, there was powerful convergence in *relative* factor prices. One wonders whether the same has been true in the second global century – and, if so, why economists have not noticed it.
14. Figure 6.6 plots convergence in the Atlantic economy for sample sizes of 13, 15 and 17. The largest sample includes: Argentina, Australia, Brazil, Canada, the United States; Belgium, Denmark, France, Germany, Great Britain, Ireland, Italy, the Netherlands, Norway, Portugal, Spain, Sweden (Williamson, 1996; O'Rourke and Williamson, 1999).
15. Timothy J. Hatton and I are embarking on that South–South migration project, covering the years from about 1850 to the present.
16. Davis and Weinstein (2002) do the same for the United States today, agreeing that all factor inflows, capital and labour, should be looked at together.
17. Apparently, Africa has suffered significant capital flight in recent times. Indeed, as of 1990, Africans placed a huge 39 per cent of their wealth portfolios outside the region, a year when the figure was 3 per cent for South Asia, 6 per cent for East Asia and 10 per cent for Latin America (Collier and Gunning, 1999: 92). This is hardly surprising given that the region has suffered negative terms of trade shocks, civil war and confiscation.

18. There are two additional studies worth mentioning here. Capie (1983) found support for the Bairoch hypothesis using event analysis with a pre-1914 European sample of four (Germany, Italy, Russia and the United Kingdom). Vamvakidis (2002) could not find any interwar evidence supporting the 'openness-fosters-growth' hypothesis either, although it was (once again) based on a small, mostly OECD sample.

19. In an influential article, Rodriguez and Rodrik (2001) have argued that the late twentieth-century evidence allows us to say only that free trade was not harmful for growth.

20. Exemplified by Dixit (1987) and surveyed in Bagwell and Staiger (2000).

21. Thus, the last pre-Second World War observation is 1934, which relates to growth between 1934 and 1939, and the last pre-First World War observation is 1908, which relates to growth between 1908 and 1913.

22. Late nineteenth-century Latin American policy makers certainly were so aware (Bulmer-Thomas, 1994: 140). However, it is important to stress 'late' since the use of protection specifically and consciously to foster industry does not occur until the 1870s or 1890s: for example Argentina with the 1876 tariff; Mexico by the early 1890s; Chile with its new tariff in 1897; Brazil in the 1890s; and Colombia in early 1900s (influenced by the Mexican experience). So, the qualitative evidence suggests that domestic industry protection becomes a motivation for Latin American tariffs only in the late nineteenth century.

23. I stress 'residents' here, since the addition of low-wage immigrants (especially those without the vote) at the bottom of a country's income distribution has far less politically explosive implications than their presence may have on the wages of low-skilled 'residents' (who *do* have the vote). A look at the structure of wages will control for this important distinction in immigrant countries, but a look only at the country's income distribution may not.

24. A more recent study by Sala-í-Martin (2002) is more descriptive, asking only what happened from 1970 to 1998, assigning no blame or applause to causes. He shows that while poverty rates have fallen since 1970, within-country inequality has increased. See also Chen and Ravallion (2001).

25. To quote Robertson (2001: 3): 'When Mexico joined the GATT, it opened its borders to trade with an arguably labour-abundant world, which may explain why it protected less-skill-intensive industries. Joining NAFTA, however, deepened integration with [the] skill-abundant ... US and Canada. The relative price of skill-intensive goods reversed its rise. As suggested by the Stolper–Samuelson theorem, relative wages also reversed their trend.'

26. Figure 6.5 measures 'protection' by average tariff levels only, thus ignoring NTBs. NTBs were on the rise in the interwar years, so the indicator in Figure 6.5 understates the anti-global regime switch.

27. Blattman, Clemens and Williamson (2002) expand the historical analysis from Latin America to the rest of the world between 1870 and 1937.

References

Acemoglu, D. and J. Robinson (2000) 'Why Did the West Extend the Franchise? Democracy, Inequality, and Growth in Historical Perspective', *Quarterly Journal of Economics* 461: 1167–99.

Acemoglu, D., S. Johnson and J. Robinson (2002) 'The Rise of Europe: Atlantic Trade, Institutional Change and Economic Growth', paper presented to the Economic History Workshop, Harvard University, 5 April.

170   *Winners and Losers in Globalization*

Agell, J. (1999) 'On the Benefits from Rigid Labour Markets: Norms, Market Failures and Social Insurance', *Economic Journal* 108: F143–F164.

————— (2000) 'On the Determinants of Labour Market Institutions: Rent Sharing vs. Social Insurance', CESifo Working Paper 384, Munich: University of Munich.

Allen, R. C. (2001) 'The Great Divergence: Wages and Prices from the Middle Ages to the First World War', *Explorations in Economic History*, 38: 411–47.

Allen, R. C. *et al.* (2002) 'Preliminary Global Price Comparisons, 1500–1870', paper presented at the XIII Congress of the International Economic History Association, Buenos Aires, 22–26 July.

Atinc, T. M. (1997) *Sharing Rising Incomes: Disparities in China*, Washington, DC: World Bank.

Bagwell, K. and R. W. Staiger (2000) 'GATT-Think', NBER Working Paper 8005, Cambridge, MA: NBER.

Baier, S. J. and J. H. Bergstrand (2001) 'The Growth of World Trade: Tariffs, Transport Costs, and Income Similarity', *Journal of International Economics* 53: 1–27.

Bairoch, P. (1972) 'Free Trade and European Economic Development in the Nineteenth Century', *European Economic Review* 3: 211–45.

Baldwin, R. and P. Martin (1999) 'Two Waves of Globalization: Superficial Similarities, Fundamental Differences', NBER Working Paper 6904, Cambridge, MA: NBER.

Berry, A., F. Bourguignon and C. Morrisson (1991) 'Global Economic Inequality and Its Trends since 1950', in L. Osberg (ed.), *Economic Inequality and Poverty: International Perspectives*, Armonk, NY: M. E. Sharpe.

Bhagwati, J. and A. O. Krueger (eds) (1973–76) *Foreign Trade Regimes and Economic Development*, multiple volumes with varying authorship, New York: Columbia University Press, for the NBER.

Blattman, C., M. A. Clemens and J. G. Williamson (2002) 'Who Protected and Why? Tariffs the World Around 1870–1937', paper presented at the conference on The Political Economy of Globalization, Dublin, 29–31 August.

Boltho, A. and G. Toniolo (1999) 'The Assessment: The Twentieth Century – Achievements, Failures, Lessons', *Oxford Review of Economic Policy* 15(4): 1–17.

Bourguignon, F. and C. Morrisson (2000) 'The Size Distribution of Income among World Citizens: 1820–1990', Washington, DC: World Bank, mimeo.

Bulmer-Thomas, V. (1994) *The Economic History of Latin America Since Independence*, Cambridge: Cambridge University Press.

Burniaux, J.-M. *et al.* (1998) 'Income Distribution and Poverty in Selected OECD Countries', OECD Economics Department Working Paper 189, Paris OECD.

Capie, F. (1983) 'Tariff Protection and Economic Performance in the Nineteenth Century', in J. Black and L. A. Winters (eds), *Policy and Performance in International Trade*, London: Macmillan.

Chen, S. and M. Ravallion (2001) 'How Did the World's Poorest Fare in the 1990s?', *Review of Income and Wealth* 47: 283–300.

Chiswick, B. R. and T. J. Hatton (2002) 'International Migration and the Integration of Labor Markets', in M. D. Bordo, A. M. Taylor and J. G. Williamson (eds), *Globalization in Historical Perspective*, Chicago: University of Chicago Press.

Clark, X., T. J. Hatton and J. G. Williamson (2002) 'Where Do US Immigrants Come From, and Why?', NBER Working Paper 8998, Cambridge, MA: NBER.

Clemens, M. A. and J. G. Williamson (2001a) 'A Tariff-Growth Paradox? Protection's Impact the World Around 1875–1997', NBER Working Paper 8459, Cambridge, MA: NBER.

————— (2001b) 'Wealth Bias in the First Global Capital Market Boom, 1870–1913', unpublished manuscript.

Cline, W. R. (1980) 'Commodity Prices and the World Distribution of Income', *Journal of Policy Modeling* 2(1): 1–17.

———— (1997) *Trade and Income Distribution*, Washington, DC: Institute for International Economics.

Coatsworth, J. H. and J. G. Williamson (2002) 'The Roots of Latin American Protectionism: Looking Before the Great Depression', NBER Working Paper 8999, Cambridge, MA: NBER.

Collier, P. and J. W. Gunning (1999) 'Explaining African Economic Performance', *Journal of Economic Literature* 37: 64–111.

Davis, D. and D. Weinstein (2002) 'Technological Superiority and the Losses from Migration', Columbia University Department of Economics Discussion Paper 0102–60, New York: Columbia University.

Diakosavvas, D. and P. L. Scandizzo (1991) 'Trends in the Terms of Trade of Primary Commodities, 1900–1982: The Controversy and Its Origin', *Economic Development and Cultural Change* 39: 231–64.

Dixit, A. (1987) 'Strategic Aspects of Trade Policy', in T. F. Bewley (ed.), *Advances in Economic Theory: Fifth World Congress*, New York: Cambridge University Press.

Dollar, D. (1992) 'Outward-Oriented Developing Economies Really Do Grow More Rapidly: Evidence from 95 LDCs, 1976–1985', *Economic Development and Cultural Change* 40: 523–44.

Dollar, D. and A. Kraay (2000a) 'Trade, Growth, and Poverty', Washington, DC: World Bank, mimeo.

———— (2000b) 'Growth *is* Good for the Poor', Washington, DC: World Bank, mimeo; published in A. Shorrocks and R. van der Hoeven (eds), *Growth, Inequality and Poverty: Prospects for Pro-Poor Economic Development*, Oxford: Oxford University Press, for UNU-WIDER, 2004.

Dowrick, S. and J. B. DeLong (2002) 'Globalization and Covergence', in M. D. Bordo, A. M. Taylor and J. G. Williamson (eds), *Globalization in Historical Perspective*, Chicago: University of Chicago Press.

Easterlin, R. A. (1981) 'Why isn't the Whole World Developed?', *Journal of Economic History* 41: 1–19.

Edmonds, E. and N. Pavcnik (2002) 'Does Globalization Increase Child Labor? Evidence from Vietnam'; NBER Working Paper 8760, Cambridge, MA: NBER.

Edwards, S. (1993) 'Openness, Trade Liberalization, and Growth in Developing Countries', *Journal of Economic Literature* 31: 1358–94.

Feenstra, R. C. and G. H. Hanson (1999) 'The Impact of Outsourcing and High-Technology Capital on Wages: Estimates for the United States, 1979–1990', *Quarterly Journal of Economics* 114: 907–40.

Findlay, R. and K. H. O'Rourke (2002) 'Commodity Market Integration, 1500–2000', in M. D. Bordo, A. M. Taylor and J. G. Williamson (eds), *Globalization in Historical Perspective*, Chicago: University of Chicago Press.

Firebaugh, G. (1999) 'Empirics of World Income Inequality', *American Journal of Sociology* 104(6): 1597–630.

Flam, H. and M. J. Flanders (1991) *Heckscher–Ohlin Trade Theory*, Cambridge, MA: MIT Press.

Flemming, J. S. and J. Micklewright (2000) 'Income Distribution, Economic Systems, and Transition', in A. B. Atkinson and F. Bourguignon (eds), *Handbook of Income Distribution*, 1, Amsterdam: Elsevier Science.

Goldin, C. (1994) 'The Political Economy of Immigration Restriction in the United States, 1890 to 1921', in C. Goldin and G. D. Libecap (eds), *The Regulated Economy: A Historical Approach to Political Economy*, Chicago: University of Chicago Press.

Goldin, C. and L. F. Katz (1999) 'The Returns to Skill in the United States across the 20th Century', NBER Working Paper 7126, Cambridge, MA: NBER.

——— (2000) 'Decreasing (and Then Increasing) Inequality in America: A Tale of Two Half Centuries', in F. Welch (ed.), *Increasing Income Inequality in America*, Chicago: University of Chicago Press.

Griffin, K. and R. Zhao (eds) (1993) *The Distribution of Income in China*, New York: St Martin's Press.

Hadass, Y. S. and J. G. Williamson (2003) 'Terms of Trade Shocks and Economic Performance 1870–1940: Prebisch and Singer Revisited', *Economic Development and Cultural Change* 51: 629–56.

Hanson, G. (2002) 'Globalization and Wages in Mexico', paper presented at the IDB Conference on Prospects for Integration in the Americas, Cambridge, MA: Harvard University, 31 May–1 June.

Hanson, G. and A. Harrison (1999) 'Trade Liberalization and Wage Inequality in Mexico', *Industrial and Labor Relations Review* 52: 271–88.

Hatton, T. J. and J. G. Williamson (1998) *The Age of Mass Migration*, Oxford: Oxford University Press.

——— (2001) 'Demographic and Economic Pressure on African Emigration', NBER Working Paper 8124, Cambridge, MA: NBER.

——— (2002) 'What Fundamentals Drive World Migration?', paper presented at the WIDER Conference on Poverty, International Migration and Asylum, Helsinki, 27–28 September; published in G. J. Borjas and J. Crisp (eds), *Poverty, International Migration and Asylum*, Basingstoke: Palgrave Macmillan, for UNU-WIDER, 2005.

Hertel, T., B. M. Hoekman and W. Martin (2002) 'Developing Countries and a New Round of WTO Negotiations', *World Bank Research Observer* 17: 113–40.

Hirst, P. Q. and G. Thompson (1996) *Globalization in Question: The International Economy and the Possibilities of Governance*, Cambridge: Polity Press.

Hoffman, P. T., D. S. Jacks, P. A. Levin and P. H. Lindert (2002) 'Real Inequality in Europe since 1500', *Journal of Economic History* 62: 322–55.

Huber, J. R. (1971) 'Effects on Prices of Japan's Entry into World Commerce after 1858', *Journal of Political Economy* 79: 614–28.

Huberman, M. (2002) 'International Labor Standards and Market Integration Before 1913: A Race to the Top?', paper presented to the conference on the Political Economy of Globalization, Dublin, 29–31 August.

Huberman, M. and Wayne Lewchuk (2001) 'The Labor Compact, Openness and Small and Large States Before 1914', University of Montreal, mimeo.

Irwin, D. A. (1988) 'Welfare Effects of British Free Trade: Debate and Evidence from the 1840s', *Journal of Political Economy* 96: 1142–64.

Krueger, A. O. (1983) 'The Effects of Trade Strategies on Growth', *Finance and Development* 20: 6–8.

——— (1984) 'Trade Policies in Developing Countries', in R. Jones and P. Kenan (eds), *Handbook of International Economics*, 1, Amsterdam: North-Holland.

Lewis, W. A. (1978) *The Evolution of the International Economic Order*, Princeton, NJ: Princeton University Press.

Lindert, P. H. (2000) 'Three Centuries of Inequality in Britain and America', in A. B. Atkinson and F. Bourguignon (eds), *Handbook of Income Distribution*, 1, Amsterdam: Elsevier Science.

Lindert, P. H. and J. G. Williamson (2002a) 'Does Globalization Make the World More Unequal?', in M. D. Bordo, A. M. Taylor and J. G. Williamson (eds), *Globalization in Historical Perspective*, Chicago: University of Chicago Press.

———— (2002b) 'Mondialisation et inégalité: une longue histoire', *Revue d' économie du developpement*, 10(1–2): 7–51.

Lucas, R. (1990) 'Why Doesn't Capital Flow from Rich to Poor Countries?', *American Economic Review* 80: 92–6.

Maddison, A. (1995) *Monitoring the World Economy, 1820–1992*, Paris: OECD.

Melchior, A., K. Telle and H. Wiig (2000) 'Globalization and Inequality: World Income Distribution and Living Standards, 1960–1998', *Studies on Foreign Policy Issues* Report 6B, Oslo: Royal Norwegian Ministry of Foreign Affairs.

Milanovic, B. (2002) 'The Ricardian Vice: Why Sala-í-Martin's Calculations of World Income Inequality Cannot Be Right', Washington, DC: World Bank, mimeo.

Obstfeld, M. and A. M. Taylor (1998) 'The Great Depression as a Watershed: International Capital Mobility over the Long Run', in M. D. Bordo, C. Goldin and E. N. White (eds), *The Defining Moment: The Great Depression and the American Economy in the Twentieth Century*, Chicago: University of Chicago Press.

———— (2002) 'Globalization and Capital Markets', in M. D. Bordo, A. M. Taylor and J. G. Williamson (eds), *Globalization in Historical Perspective*, Chicago: University of Chicago Press.

O'Rourke, K. H. (1997) 'The European Grain Invasion, 1870–1913', *Journal of Economic History* 57: 775–801.

———— (2000) 'Tariffs and Growth in the Late 19th Century', *Economic Journal* 110: 456–83.

O'Rourke, K. H. and J. G. Williamson (1999) *Globalization and History*, Cambridge, MA: MIT Press.

———— (2002a) 'After Columbus: Explaining Europe's Overseas Trade Boom, 1500–1800', *Journal of Economic History* 62: 417–56.

———— (2002b) 'When Did Globalization Begin?', *European Review of Economic History* 6(1): 23–50.

———— (2002c) 'From Malthus to Ohlin: Trade, Growth and Distribution Since 1500', NBER Working Paper 8955, Cambridge, MA: NBER.

Pamuk, S. and S. Ozmucur (2002) 'Real Wages and Standards of Living in the Ottoman Empire, 1489–1914', *Journal of Economic History* 62: 293–321.

Pomeranz, K. (2000) *The Great Divergence: China, Europe, and the Making of the Modern World Economy*, Princeton, NJ: Princeton University Press.

Pritchett, L. (1997) 'Divergence, Big Time', *Journal of Economic Perspectives* 11: 3–18.

Radetzki, M. and B. Jonsson (2000) 'The 20th Century – the Century of Increasing Income Gaps. But How Reliable Are the Numbers?', *Ekonomisk Debatt* 1: 43–58.

Robbins, D. J. (1997) 'Trade and Wages in Colombia', *Estudios de Economia* 24: 47–83.

Robbins, D. J. and T. H. Gindling (1999) 'Trade Liberalization and the Relative Wages for More-Skilled Workers in Costa Rica', *Review of Development Economics* 3: 140–54.

Robertson, R. (2001) 'Relative Prices and Wage Inequality: Evidence from Mexico', St Paul, MN: Macalester College, mimeo.

Rodriguez, F. and D. Rodrik (2001) 'Trade Policy and Economic Growth: A Skeptic's Guide to the Cross-National Evidence', in B. S. Bernake and K. Rogoff (eds), *NBER Macroeconomics Annual 2000*, 15, Cambridge, MA: MIT Press.

Rodrik, D. (1997) *Has Globalization Gone Too Far?*, Washington, DC: Institute for International Economics.

———— (1998) 'Why Do More Open Economies Have Bigger Governments?', *Journal of Political Economy* 106: 997–1033.

Sachs, J. D. and A. Warner (1995) 'Economic Reform and the Process of Global Integration', *Brookings Papers on Economic Activity* 1: 1–53.

174   *Winners and Losers in Globalization*

Sala-í-Martin, X. (2002) 'The Disturbing "Rise" of Global Income Inequality', NBER Working Paper 8904, Cambridge, MA: NBER.

Schultz, T. P. (1987) 'School Expenditures and Enrollments, 1960–1980: The Effects of Income, Prices, and Population Growth', in D. G. Johnson and R. D. Lee (eds), *Population Growth and Economic Development: Issues and Evidence*, Madison: University of Wisconsin Press.

———— (1998) 'Inequality in the Distribution of Personal Income in the World: How Is It Changing and Why?', *Journal of Population Economics* 11: 307–44.

Taylor, A. M. and J. G. Williamson (1997) 'Convergence in the Age of Mass Migration', *European Review of Economic History* 1: 27–63.

Timmer, A. and J. G. Williamson (1998) 'Immigration Policy Prior to the 1930s: Labor Markets, Policy Interactions, and Globalization Backlash', *Population and Development Review* 24: 739–71.

Vamvakidis, A. (2002) 'How Robust Is the Growth–Openness Connection? Historical Evidence', *Journal of Economic Growth* 7: 57–80.

van Zanden, J. L. (1999) 'Wages and the Standard of Living in Europe, 1500–1800', *European Review of Economic History* 3: 175–98.

Williamson, J. G. (1990) 'The Impact of the Corn Laws Just Prior to Repeal', *Explorations in Economic History* 27: 123–56.

———— (1996) 'Globalization, Convergence, and History', *Journal of Economic History* 56: 277–306.

———— (1997) 'Globalization and Inequality: Past and Present', *World Bank Research Observer* 12: 117–35.

———— (1998) 'Globalization, Labor Markets and Policy Backlash in the Past', *Journal of Economic Perspectives* 12: 51–72.

———— (2002) 'Land, Labor, and Globalization in the Third World 1870–1940', *Journal of Economic History* 62: 55–85.

Williamson, J. G. and P. H. Lindert (1980) *American Inequality: A Macroeconomic History*, New York: Academic Press.

Wood, A. (1994) *North-South Trade, Employment and Inequality*, Oxford: Clarendon Press.

———— (1997) 'Openness and Wage Inequality in Developing Countries: The Latin American Challenge to East Asian Conventional Wisdom', *World Bank Economic Review* 11: 33–57.

———— (1998) 'Globalization and the Rise in Labour Market Inequalities', *Economic Journal* 108: 1463–82.

Yasuba, Y. (1996) 'Did Japan Ever Suffer from a Shortage of Natural Resources Before World War II?', *Journal of Economic History* 56: 543–60.

[3]
The New Wave of Globalization and Its Economic Effects

S
INCE ABOUT 1980 THERE HAS BEEN UNPRECEDENTED
global economic integration. Globalization has happened
before, but not like this. Economic integration occurs
through trade, migration, and capital flows. Figure 1.1
tracks these flows. World trade is measured relative to world
income. Capital flows are proxied by the stock of foreign
capital in developing countries relative to their GDP. Migration is proxied
by the number of immigrants to the United States. Historically, before
about 1870 none of these flows was sufficiently large to warrant the
term globalization.

Figure 1.1   Three waves of globalization

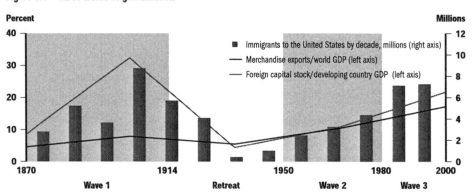

Source: Foreign capital stock/developing country GDP: Maddison (2001), table 3.3; Merchandise exports/world GDP: Maddison (2001), table F-5; Migration: Immigration and Naturalization Service (1998).

23

For about 45 years, starting around 1870, all these flows rapidly became substantial, driven by falling transport costs. What had been many separate national economies started to integrate: the world's economies globalized. However, globalization is not an inevitable process; this first wave was reversed by a retreat into nationalism. Between 1914 and 1945 transport costs continued to fall, but trade barriers rose as countries followed beggar-thy-neighbor policies. By the end of that period trade had collapsed back to around its 1870 level. After 1945 governments cooperated to rein in protectionism. As trade barriers came down, and transport costs continued to fall, trade revived. This second wave of globalization, which lasted until around 1980, was approximately a return to the patterns of the first wave.

Since 1980 many developing countries—the "new globalizers"— have broken into world markets for manufactured goods and services. There has been a dramatic rise in the share of manufactures in the exports of developing countries: from about 25 percent in 1980 to more than 80 percent today. There has also been a substantial increase in FDI. This marks an important change: low-income countries are now competing head-on with high-income countries while previously they specialized in primary commodities. During this new wave of global market integration, world trade has grown massively. Markets for merchandise are now much more integrated than ever before.

In this chapter we contrast this new third wave of globalization with the two previous waves. We analyze its main processes and show how it is affecting poverty and inequality.

Previous waves of globalization and reversals

MOST DEVELOPING COUNTRIES HAVE TWO POTENTIAL sources of comparative advantage in international markets: abundant labor and abundant land. Before about 1870 neither of these potentials was realized and international trade was negligible.

The first wave of globalization: 1870–1914

The first wave of global integration, from 1870 to 1914, was triggered by a combination of falling transport costs, such as the switch from sail to steamships, and reductions in tariff barriers, pioneered by an

Anglo-French agreement. Cheaper transport and the lifting of man-made barriers opened up the possibility of using abundant land. New technologies such as railways created huge opportunities for land-intensive commodity exports. The resulting pattern of trade was that land-intensive primary commodities were exchanged for manufactures. Exports as a share of world income nearly doubled to about 8 percent (Maddison 2001).

The production of primary commodities required people. Sixty million migrated from Europe to North America and Australia to work on newly available land. Because land was abundant in the newly settled areas, incomes were high and fairly equal, while the labor exodus from Europe tightened labor markets and raised wages both absolutely and relative to the returns on land. South-South labor flows were also extensive (though less well documented). Lindert and Williamson (2001b) speculate that the flows from densely populated China and India to less densely populated Sri Lanka, Burma, Thailand, the Philippines, and Vietnam were of the same order of magnitude as the movements from Europe to the Americas.[1] That would make the total labor flows during the first wave of globalization nearly 10 percent of the world's population.

The production of primary commodities for export required not just labor but large amounts of capital. As of 1870 the foreign capital stock in developing countries was only about 9 percent of their income (figure 1.1). However, institutions needed for financial markets were copied. These institutions, combined with the improvements in information permitted by the telegraph, enabled governments in developing countries to tap into the major capital markets. Indeed, during this period around half of all British savings were channeled abroad. By 1914 the foreign capital stock of developing countries had risen to 32 percent of their income.

Globally, growth accelerated sharply. Per capita incomes, which had risen by 0.5 percent per year in the previous 50 years, rose by an annual average of 1.3 percent. Did this lead to more or less equality? The countries that participated in it often took off economically, both the exporters of manufactures, people and capital, and the importers. Argentina, Australia, New Zealand, and the United States became among the richest countries in the world by exporting primary commodities while importing people, institutions, and capital. All these countries left the rest of the world behind.

Between the globalizing countries themselves there was convergence. Mass migration was a major force equalizing incomes between them. "Emigration is estimated to have raised Irish wages by 32 percent, Italian

25

GLOBALIZATION, GROWTH, AND POVERTY

by 28 percent and Norwegian by 10 percent. Immigration is estimated to have lowered Argentine wages by 22 percent, Australian by 15 percent, Canadian by 16 percent and American by 8 percent." Indeed, migration was probably more important than either trade or capital movements (Lindert and Williamson 2001b).

The impact of globalization on inequality *within* countries depended in part on the ownership of land. Exports from developing countries were land-intensive primary commodities. Within developing countries this benefited predominantly the people who owned the land. Since most were colonies, land ownership itself was subject to the power imbalance inherent in the colonial relationship. Where land ownership was concentrated, as in Latin America, increased trade could be associated with increased inequality. Where land was more equally owned, as in West Africa, the benefits of trade were spread more widely. Conversely, in Europe, the region importing land-intensive goods, globalization ruined landowners. For example, Cannadine (1990) describes the spectacular economic collapse of the English aristocracy between 1880 and 1914. In Europe the first wave of globalization also coincided with the establishment for the first time in history of the great legislative pillars of social protection—free mass education, worker insurance, and pensions (Gray 1998).

Ever since 1820—50 years before globalization—world income inequality as measured by the mean log deviation had started to increase drastically (figure 1.2).[2] This continued during the first wave of globalization. Despite widening world inequality, the unprecedented increase in growth reduced poverty as never before. In the 50 years before 1870, the incidence of poverty had been virtually constant, falling at the rate of just 0.3 percent per year. During the first globalization wave, the rate of decline more than doubled to 0.8 percent. Even this was insufficient to offset the increase in population growth, so that the absolute number of poor people increased.

Figure 1.2   Worldwide household inequality, 1820–1910

Mean log deviation

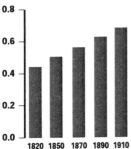

Source: Bourguignon and Morrisson (2001).

The retreat into nationalism: 1914–45

Technology continued to reduce transport costs: during the inter-war years sea freight costs fell by a third. However, trade policy went into reverse.

As Mundell (2000) puts it: "The twentieth century began with a highly efficient international monetary system that was destroyed in World War I, and its bungled recreation in the inter-war period brought on the great depression." In turn, governments responded to depression by protectionism: a vain attempt to divert demand into their domestic markets. The United States led the way into the abyss: the Smoot-Hawley tariff, which led to retaliation abroad, was the first: between 1929 and 1933 U.S. imports fell by 30 percent and, significantly, exports fell even more, by almost 40 percent.

Globally, rising protectionism drove international trade back down. By 1950 exports as a share of world income were down to around 5 percent—roughly back to where it had been in 1870. Protectionism had undone 80 years of technical progress in transport.

During the retreat into nationalism capital markets fared even worse than merchandise markets. Most high-income countries imposed controls preventing the export of capital, and many developing countries defaulted on their liabilities. By 1950 the foreign capital stock of developing countries was reduced to just 4 percent of income—far below even the modest level of 1870.

Unsurprisingly, the retreat into nationalism produced anti-immigrant sentiment and governments imposed drastic restrictions on newcomers. For example, immigration to the United States declined from 15 million during 1870–1914 to 6 million between 1914 and 1950.

The massive retreat from globalization did not reverse the trend to greater world inequality. By 1950 the world was far less equal than it had been in 1914 (figure 1.3). Average incomes were, however, substantially lower than had the previous trend been maintained: the world rate of growth fell by about a third. The world's experiment with reversing globalization showed that it was entirely possible but not attractive. The economic historian Angus Maddison summarizes it thus: "Between 1913 and 1950 the world economy grew much more slowly than in 1870–1913, world trade grew much less than world income, and the degree of inequality between regions increased substantially" (Maddison 2001, p. 22).

The combination of a slowdown in growth and a continued increase in inequality sharply reduced the decline in the incidence of poverty— approximately back to what it had been in the period from 1820 to 1870. The decline in the incidence was now well below the rate of population growth, so that the absolute number of poor people increased by about 25 percent. Despite the rise in poverty viewed in terms of income, this was the great period of advances in life expectancy, due to the global

Figure 1.3 Worldwide household inequality, 1910–50

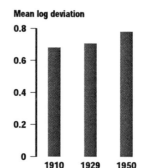

Mean log deviation

Source: Bourguignon and Morrisson (2001).

27

spread of improvements in public health. Poverty is multi-dimensional, and not all its aspects are determined by economic performance.

The second wave of globalization: 1945–80

The horrors of the retreat into nationalism gave an impetus to internationalism. The same sentiments that led to the founding of the United Nations persuaded governments to cooperate to reduce the trade barriers they had previously erected. However, trade liberalization was selective both in terms of which countries participated and which products were included. Broadly, by 1980 trade between developed countries in manufactured goods had been substantially freed of barriers, but barriers facing developing countries had been substantially removed only for those primary commodities that did not compete with agriculture in the developed countries. For agriculture and manufactures, developing countries faced severe barriers. Further, most developing countries erected barriers against each other and against developed countries.

The partial reduction in trade barriers was reinforced by continued reductions in transport costs: between 1950 and the late 1970s sea freight charges again fell by a third. Overall, trade doubled relative to world income, approximately recovering the level it had reached during the first wave of globalization. However, the resulting liberalization was very lopsided. For developing countries it restored the North-South pattern of trade—the exchange of manufactures for land-intensive primary commodities—but did not restore the international movements of capital and labor.

By contrast, for rich countries the second wave of globalization was spectacular. The lifting of barriers between them greatly expanded the exchange of manufactures. For the first time international specialization within manufacturing became important, allowing agglomeration and scale economies to be realized. This helped to drive up the incomes of the rich countries relative to the rest.

Economies of agglomeration. The second wave introduced a new type of trade: rich country specialization in manufacturing niches that gained productivity from agglomerated clusters. Most trade between developed countries became determined not by comparative advantage based on differences in factor endowments but by cost savings from agglomeration and scale. Because such cost savings are quite specific to each activity,

28

although each individual industry became more and more concentrated geographically, industry as a whole remained very widely dispersed to avoid costs of congestion.

Firms cluster together, some producing the same thing and others connected by vertical linkages (Fujita, Krugman, and Venables 1999). Japanese auto companies, for example, are well known for wanting certain of their parts suppliers to locate within a short distance of the main assembly plant. As Sutton (2000) describes it: "Two-thirds of manufacturing output consists of intermediate goods, sold by one firm to another. The presence of a rich network of manufacturing firms provides a positive externality to each firm in the system, allowing it to acquire inputs locally, thus reducing the costs of transport, of coordination, of monitoring and of contracting."

Clustering enables greater specialization and thus raises productivity. In turn, it depends upon the ability to trade internationally at low cost. The classic statement of this was indeed Adam Smith's: "The division of labor is limited only by the extent of the market" (*The Wealth of Nations*). Smith argued that a larger market permits a finer division of labor, which in turn facilitates innovation. For example, Sokoloff (1988) shows that as the Erie Canal progressed westward in the first half of the 19th century, patent registrations rose county by county as the canal reached them. This pattern suggests that ideas that were already in people's heads became economically viable through access to a larger market.

However, while agglomeration economies are good news for those in the clusters, they are bad news for those left out. A region may be uncompetitive simply because not enough firms have chosen to locate there. As a result "a 'divided world' may emerge, in which a network of manufacturing firms is clustered in some 'high wage' region, while wages in the remaining regions stay low" (Sutton 2000).

Firms will not shift to a new location until the gap in production costs becomes wide enough to compensate for the loss of agglomeration economies. Yet once firms start to relocate, the movement becomes a cascade: as firms re-base to the new location, it starts to benefit from agglomeration economies.

During the second globalization wave most developing countries did not participate in the growth of global manufacturing and services trade. The combination of persistent trade barriers in developed countries, and poor investment climates and anti-trade policies in developing countries, confined them to dependence on primary commodities. Even by

29

GLOBALIZATION, GROWTH, AND POVERTY

1980 only 25 percent of the merchandise exports of developing countries were manufactured goods.

Cascades of relocation did occur during the second wave, but they were
to low-wage areas within developed countries. For example, until 1950
the U.S. textile industry was clustered in the high-wage Northeast. The
cost pressure for it to relocate built up gradually as northern wages rose
and as institutions and infrastructure improved in southern states. Within
a short period in the 1950s the whole industry relocated to the Carolinas.

The effect on inequality and poverty. During globalization's second
wave there were effectively two trading systems: the old North-South
system, and the new intra-North system.

The intra-North system was quite powerfully equalizing: lower-income
industrial countries caught up with higher-income ones. Figure 1.4 shows
this pattern of long-term convergence among OECD economies.

Second wave globalization coincided with the growth of policies for
redistribution and social protection within developed societies. Not
only did inequalities reduce between countries—probably an effect of
globalization—but inequality was reduced within countries, probably
as a result of these social programs. Figure 1.5 shows the dramatic
reduction both in between-country and within-country inequality that
occurred in developed countries during the period. The second wave

Figure 1.4   Long-term convergence among OECD countries

Percent annual growth rate 1820–1990

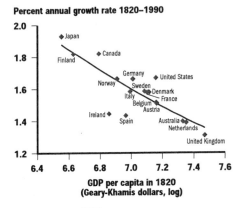

**GDP per capita in 1820
(Geary-Khamis dollars, log)**

Source: Maddison (1995).

30

of globalization was thus spectacularly successful in reducing poverty within the OECD countries. Rapid growth coincided with greater equity, both to an extent without precedent. For the industrial world it is often referred to as the "golden age."

Second wave globalization was not golden for developing countries. Although per capita income growth recovered from the inter-war slowdown, it was substantially slower than in the rich economies. The number of poor people continued to rise. Non-income dimensions of poverty improved—notably rising life expectancy and rising school enrollments. In terms of equity, within developing countries in aggregate there was little change either between countries or within them (figure 1.6). As a group, developing countries were being left behind by developed countries.

World inequality was thus the sum of three components: greater equity within developed countries, greater inequality between developed and developing countries, and little net change in developing countries. The net effect of these three very different components was broadly no change. World inequality was about the same in the late 1970s as it had been a quarter of a century earlier (figure 1.7).

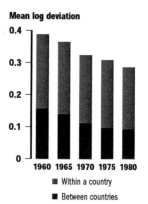

Figure 1.5   Household inequality in rich countries, 1960–80

Mean log deviation

- Within a country
- Between countries

Source: Clark, Dollar, and Kraay (2001).

The new wave of globalization

T HE NEW WAVE OF GLOBALIZATION, WHICH BEGAN ABOUT 1980, is distinctive. First, and most spectacularly, a large group of developing countries broke into global markets. Second, other developing countries became increasingly marginalized in the world economy and suffered declining incomes and rising poverty. Third, international migration and capital movements, which were negligible during second wave globalization, have again become substantial. We take these features of the new global economy in turn.

The changing structure of trade: the rise of the new globalizers

The most encouraging development in third wave globalization is that some developing countries, accounting for about 3 billion people, have succeeded for the first time in harnessing their labor abundance to give them a competitive advantage in labor-intensive manufactures and

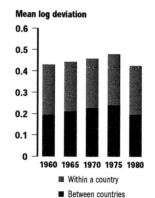

Figure 1.6   Household inequality in the developing world, 1960–80

Mean log deviation

- Within a country
- Between countries

Source: Clark, Dollar, and Kraay (2001).

31

GLOBALIZATION, GROWTH, AND POVERTY

Figure 1.7   Worldwide household inequality, 1960–79

Mean log deviation

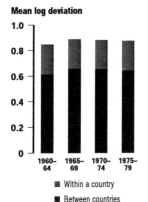

- Within a country
- Between countries

Source: Clark, Dollar, and Kraay (2001).

services. In 1980 only 25 percent of the exports of developing countries were manufactures; by 1998 this had risen to 80 percent (figure 1.8). Davis and Weinstein (forthcoming) show that developing country exports are indeed now labor-intensive.

This is an astonishing transformation over a very short period. The developing countries that have shifted into manufactures trade are quite diverse. Relatively low-income countries such as China, Bangladesh, and Sri Lanka have manufactures shares in their exports that are above the world average of 81 percent. Others, such as India, Turkey, Morocco, and Indonesia, have shares that are nearly as high as the world average. Another important change in the pattern of developing country exports has been their substantial increase in exports of services. In the early 1980s, commercial services made up 17 percent of the exports of rich countries but only 9 percent of the exports of developing countries. During the third wave of globalization the share of services in rich country exports increased slightly—to 20 percent—but for developing countries the share almost doubled to 17 percent.

What accounted for this shift? Partly it was changing economic policy. Tariffs on manufactured goods in developed countries continued to decline, and many developing countries undertook major trade liberalizations. At the same time many countries liberalized barriers to foreign investment and improved other aspects of their investment climate. Partly it was due to continuing technical progress in transport

Figure 1.8   Shares in merchandise exports in developing country exports

Percent

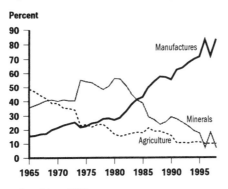

Source: Martin (2001).

32

and communications (Venables 2001). Containerization and airfreight brought a considerable speeding up of shipping, allowing countries to participate in international production networks. New information and communications technologies mean it is easier to manage and control geographically dispersed supply chains. And information based activities are "weightless" so their inputs and outputs (digitized information) can be shipped at virtually no cost.

Some analysts have suggested that new technologies lead to the "death of distance" (Cairncross 1997) undermining the advantage of agglomeration. This is likely true in a few activities, while for other activities distance seems to be becoming even more important—for example, the proximity requirements of "just-in time" technologies. The OECD agglomerations continue to have massive cost advantages and technological change may even be increasing these advantages. Even within well-located countries there will be clustering as long as agglomeration economies are important, and hence wage pressure to migrate to towns and cities. For example, within the United States, which has similar institutions across the country, there has been a clear trend for economic activity and labor to migrate away from the center of the country. One hundred years ago the Mississippi River and the Great Lakes provided reasonably good transport links. But recent increases in the scale of ocean-going ships and related declines in ocean shipping rates have increased the competitiveness of U.S. coastal locations compared to the center. It is cheaper to ship iron ore from Australia to Japan than the much shorter distance across the Great Lakes from Minnesota to the steel mills of Illinois and Indiana. For large countries such as China and India we can expect to see more migration toward coastal areas as development proceeds.

By the end of the millennium economic activity was highly concentrated geographically (map 1.1). This reflects differences in policies across countries, natural geographic advantages and disadvantages, and agglomeration and scale economy effects. As the map shows, Africa has a very low output density and this is unlikely to change through a uniform expansion of production in every location. Africa has the potential to develop a number of successful manufacturing/service agglomerations, but if its development is like that of any other large region, there will be several such locations around the continent and a need for labor to migrate to those places. Africa is much less densely populated than Europe, and the importance of migration to create agglomerations is therefore greater.

33

GLOBALIZATION, GROWTH, AND POVERTY

Map 1.1   GNP density

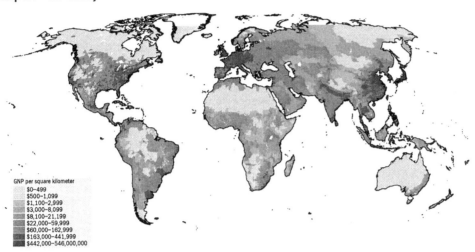

GNP per square kilometer
- $0–499
- $500–1,099
- $1,100–2,999
- $3,000–8,099
- $8,100–21,199
- $22,000–59,999
- $60,000–162,999
- $163,000–441,999
- $442,000–546,000,000

Source: Sachs, Mellinger, and Gallup (2001).

However, most countries are not just victims of their location. The newly globalizing developing countries helped their firms to break into industrial markets by improving the complementary infrastructure, skills and institutions that modern production needs. So, to some extent those developing countries that broke into world markets just happened to be well located, and to some extent they shaped events by their own actions. To get some understanding of this distinction it is useful to look at the characteristics of the post-1980 developing globalizers. We rank developing countries by the extent to which they increased trade relative to income over the period, and compare the top third with the remaining two-thirds. The one-third/two-thirds distinction is of course arbitrary. We label the top third "more globalized" without in any sense implying that they adopted pro-trade policies.[3] The rise in trade may have been due to other policies or even to pure chance. By construction, the "more globalized" had a large increase in trade relative to income: 104 percent, compared to 71 percent for the rich countries. The remaining two-thirds of developing countries have actually had a decline in trade to GDP over this period. The variation in export performance is illustrated in figure 1.9.

34

The more globalized were not drawn from the higher-income developing countries. Indeed, in 1980 they were poorer as a group.[4] The two groups had very similar educational attainment in 1980 (table 1.1). Since 1980, the more globalized have made very significant gains in basic education: the average years of primary schooling for adults increased from 2.4 years to 3.8 years. The less globalized made less progress and now lag behind in primary attainment. The spread of basic education tends to reduce inequality and raise health standards, as well as being complementary to the process of raising productivity. It can also be seen in table 1.1 that both groups reduced inflation to single digits over the past two decades. Finally, as of 1997 the more globalized fared moderately better on an index of property rights and the rule of law. [5] The same measure is not available for 1980, but clearly countries such as China and Hungary have strengthened property rights as they have reformed.

During third wave globalization, the new globalizers also cut import tariffs significantly, 34 points on average, compared to 11 points for the countries that are less globalized (figure 1.10). However, policy change was not exclusively or even primarily focused on trade. The list of post-1980 globalizers includes such well-known reformers as Argentina,

Figure 1.9   Change in trade/ GDP for selected countries, 1977–97

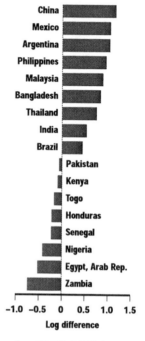

Source: World Bank (2001d).

Table 1.1   Characteristics of more globalized and less globalized developing economies

(population-weighted averages)

Socioeconomic characteristics	More globalized (24)	Less globalized (49)
Population, 1997 (billions)	2.9	1.1
Per capita GDP, 1980	$1,488	$1,947
Per capita GDP, 1997	$2,485	$2,133
Inflation, 1980 (percent)	16	17
Inflation, 1997 (percent)	6	9
Rule of law index, 1997 (world average = 0)	−0.04	−0.48
Average years primary schooling, 1980	2.4	2.5
Average years primary schooling, 1997	3.8	3.1
Average years secondary schooling, 1980	0.8	0.7
Average years secondary schooling, 1997	1.3	1.3
Average years tertiary schooling, 1980	0.08	0.09
Average years tertiary schooling, 1997	0.18	0.22

Source: Dollar (2001).

35

GLOBALIZATION, GROWTH, AND POVERTY

Figure 1.10   Decline in average import tariffs, mid-1980s to late-1990s

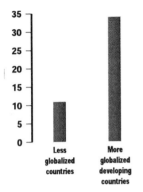

Source: Dollar and Kraay (2001b).

Figure 1.11   Results from a better rule of law

Percentage points of GDP

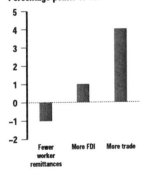

Source: Dollar and Zoido-Lobatón (2001).

36

China, Hungary, India, Malaysia, Mexico, the Philippines, and Thailand, which undertook reforms involving investment liberalization, stabilization, and property rights. The outcome of increased integration into the world economy need not be due to changes in trade policy. Dollar and Zoido-Lobatón (2001) find that reliable property rights, strong rule of law, and macroeconomic stability are all associated with more trade and FDI. A one standard deviation increase on an index of the rule of law (roughly the difference between Kenya and Uganda) is associated with 4 percentage points of GDP more in trade and 1 percentage point more FDI (figure 1.11). They also find that it is associated with lower emigration.

As they reformed and integrated with the world market, the "more globalized" developing countries started to grow rapidly, accelerating steadily from 2.9 percent in the 1970s to 5 percent through the 1990s (figure 1.12). They found themselves in a virtuous circle of rising growth and rising penetration of world markets. It seems likely that growth and trade reinforced each other, and that the policies of educational expansion, reduced trade barriers, and strategic sectoral reforms reinforced both growth and trade.

Whether there is a causal connection from opening up trade to faster growth is not the issue. In those low-income countries that have broken into global markets, more restricted access to those markets would be damaging to growth, regardless of whether industrialization was triggered by opening up. However, opening up integrates an economy into a larger market, and from Adam Smith on economists have suggested that the size of the market matters for growth. A larger market gives access to more ideas, allows for investment in large fixed-cost investments and enables a finer division of labor. A larger market also widens choice. Wider choice for high-income consumers is irrelevant for poverty reduction, but wider choice may have mattered more for firms than for consumers. For example, as India liberalized trade, companies were able to purchase better-quality machine tools. Similar effects have been found for the Chinese import liberalization. Finally, a larger market intensifies competition and this can spur innovation. There is some evidence that integration with the world economy is more important for small and poor economies than it is for large economies like India and China (Sachs and Warner 1995; Collier and Gunning 1999).

There is also a large amount of cross-country regression evidence on openness and growth (see box 1.1). This should be treated with caution but not dismissed altogether. Lindert and Williamson (2001a) summarize it:

The doubts that one can retain about each individual study threaten to block our view of the overall forest of evidence. Even though no one study can establish that openness to trade has unambiguously helped the representative Third World economy, the preponderance of evidence supports this conclusion. One way to see the whole forest more clearly is to consider two sets, one almost empty and one completely empty. The almost-empty set consists of all statistical studies showing that protection has helped Third World economic growth, and liberalization has harmed it. The second, and this time empty, set contains those countries that chose to be less open to trade and factor flows in the 1960s than in the 1960s and rose in the global living-standard ranks at the same time. As far as we can tell, there are no anti-global victories to report for the postwar Third World. We infer that this is because freer trade stimulates growth in Third World economies today, regardless of its effects before 1940. (pp. 29–30)

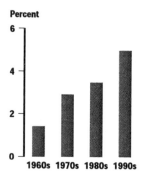

Figure 1.12   Per capita GDP growth rates: more globalized developing countries

Percent

Source: Dollar and Kraay (2001b).

Box 1.1   Openness and growth: Regression evidence

IT IS DIFFICULT TO ESTABLISH A LINK BETWEEN openness and growth in a rigorous manner. The specific trade liberalization actions that are important often include non-tariff measures such as eliminating licensing schemes or allowing access to foreign exchange for current account transactions, and it is difficult to quantify these policies. Further, countries tend to pursue a broad package of reforms at the same time so that identifying the separate effect of one reform may not be possible. Recognizing these limitations, what does the cross-country literature find? Sachs and Warner (1995) claim that liberal trade policies cause growth. They develop a measure of openness based on tariff rates for capital equipment, the extent of non-tariff barriers, and the degree of distortion in the foreign exchange market (proxied by the parallel market premium). Dollar (1992) creates

an index of the price level adjusted for factor endowments, arguing that high prices for tradable goods reflect high levels of import protection, and finds a significant effect on growth. Both measures have been criticized (by Rodriguez and Rodrik 1999, among others) on the grounds that they are more a measure of good institutions and policies in general than of trade policy narrowly defined. This points up an important identification problem: the countries with more open trade and investment policies tend to be ones with more reliable property rights and better economic institutions more generally. Frankel and Romer (1999) find that openness as measured by the share of trade in income is robustly related to long-term growth. They are able to rule out the possibility of reverse causation from growth to trade by "instrumenting" for trade with geography variables.

(box continues on following page)

GLOBALIZATION, GROWTH, AND POVERTY

Box 1.1 continued

While this is supportive of models in which access to markets accelerates growth, there is no easy way to rule out the possibility that geography matters for growth through other channels. A different approach to measuring openness is taken by Ades and Glaeser (1999) in their study of 19th century America. They focus on openness in the sense of access to seaports and rail services, and find that backward, open regions tend to grow fast and converge on more advanced regions. Specifically, they interact their openness measure with the initial level of development and find that the combination of openness and backwardness

is associated with especially rapid development. Finally, there are some recent studies that focus on changes in growth rates and changes in trade and FDI. This approach has the advantage that all of the variables that do not change over time drop out of the analysis (geography, ethnolinguistic fractionalization, institutional measures that show no time variation), reducing the multicollinearity problems. Dollar and Kraay (2001b) show that both increased trade and increased FDI are related to accelerated growth. They control for changes in other policies and address reverse causation with internal instruments.

To conclude, since 1980 the global integration of markets in merchandise has enabled those developing countries with reasonable locations, policies, institutions, and infrastructure to harness their abundant labor to give themselves a competitive advantage in some manufactures and services. The initial advantage provided by cheap labor has sometimes triggered a virtuous circle of other benefits from trade. For example, when Bangalore initially broke into the world software market, it did so by harnessing its comparative advantage in cheap, educated labor. As more firms gravitated to the city it began to reap economies of agglomeration. The increased export earnings financed more imports, thereby both intensifying competition and widening choice. There is some evidence that between them these four effects of trade raise not only the level of real income, but also its rate of growth. However, the growth process is complex. Trade is certainly not sufficient for growth.

Marginalization: Why has the experience of many poor countries been the opposite of the globalizers?

Countries with total populations of around 2 billion people have not integrated strongly into the global industrial economy. They include most of Africa and many of the economies of the FSU. These countries often suffered deteriorating and volatile terms of trade in the markets for their primary commodity exports. In aggregate their per capita income actually declined during the third wave. Why did these countries diverge so drastically from the globalizers? Can they belatedly emulate the globalizers in harnessing their comparative advantage in abundant labor, thereby diversifying their exports toward services and manufactures? There are three views:

The "Join the Club" view. This view argues that weak globalizers have failed to harness their comparative advantage in abundant labor because of poor economic policies. If, for example, infrastructure is poor, education is inadequate, corruption is rampant, and trade barriers are high, then the cost advantage from abundant labor might be more than offset by these disadvantages. According to this view, as and when policies, institutions, and infrastructure are improved, then countries will integrate into world markets for manufactures and services.

The "Geographic Disadvantage" view. This view argues that many of the countries that have failed to enter global manufacturing markets suffer from fundamental disadvantages of location. Even with good policies, institutions, and infrastructure, a landlocked, malaria-infested country simply will not be competitive in manufacturing or in services such as tourism. It is sometimes argued that it is precisely because the benefits of good policies, institutions, and infrastructure in such environments are so modest that they are not reformed.

For many developing countries, transport costs to OECD markets are higher than the tariffs on their goods, so that transport costs are even more of a barrier to integration than the trade policies of rich countries. Sometimes the explanation for high transport costs is indeed adverse geography. But transport costs are also heavily influenced by the quality of infrastructure as implied by the "Join the Club" view. Limão and Venables (2000) find that "African economies tend to trade less with the rest of the world and with themselves than would be predicted by a simple gravity model, and the reason for that is their poor infrastructure" (p. 25). That includes inefficient seaports, but even more importantly the internal infrastructure of roads, rail, and telecommunications. Collier and Gunning (1999, pp. 71–72) document these infrastructure deficiencies in Africa:

> There is less infrastructure than elsewhere. For example, the density of the rural road network is only 55 kilometers per thousand

square kilometers, compared to over 800 in India, and there are only one-tenth the telephones per capita of Asia. The quality of infrastructure is also lower. The telephone system has triple the level of faults to Asia's and the proportion of diesel trains in use is 40 percent lower. Prices of infrastructure use are much higher. Freight rates by rail are on average around double those in Asia. Port charges are higher (for example, a container costs $200 in Abidjan as opposed to $120 in Antwerp). Air transportation is four times more costly than in East Asia. Much of international transport is cartelized, reflecting the regulations of African governments intended to promote national shipping companies and airlines. As a result of these high costs, by 1991 freight and insurance payments on trade amounted to 15 percent of export earnings, whereas the average for developing countries is only 6 percent. Further, the trend has been rising for Africa whereas it has been falling elsewhere: the comparable figures for 1970 were 11 percent and 8 percent.

Thus, many of the weak globalizers have high transport costs to world markets partly due to intrinsically poor location and partly due to bad infrastructure. As a result they will have low wages, and even when trade is free of barriers it will not bring those wages into line with wages in more favored locations.

The "Missed the Boat" view. This view accepts the argument of the "Join the Club" view that, if any of these countries had had good policies it would have broken into world manufacturing and services, but it further argues that most of them have now missed the boat. World demand for manufactures is limited by world income, and because of agglomeration economies firms will locate in clusters. Although there is room for many clusters, firms already have satisfactory locations in labor-abundant countries and so the latecomers have nothing to offer.

Who's right?

Most plausibly, each view is right to some extent. It seems highly likely that there will be room for some new entrants to the market for global manufactures and services, and some well-located cities in countries that reform their policies, institutions, and infrastructure will surely develop successful clusters. Equally, it seems plausible that if all countries reformed, there would be more well-located sites than new clusters, so some would indeed have missed the boat. Finally, some countries are indeed badly located and will simply not industrialize. Such countries might become competitive in international services, but at present markets in services are far less integrated than markets in merchandise. This is partly because until very recently trade negotiations have focused on reducing barriers to merchandise trade.

Regardless of whether the disadvantages faced by the weak globalizers were intrinsic or could have been altered by better policy, their growth rates were even lower during third wave globalization than during the second wave. One reason is that many countries dependent on primary commodities suffered declining prices for their exports. This was probably related to the slowdown in growth in developed countries. Could globalization itself have contributed to the economic marginalization of some countries? One way it might have adversely affected the weak globalizers is through the growth of international capital markets. Most marginalized countries integrated into world capital markets not through attracting capital inflows but through capital flight. By 1990 Africa, the region where capital is most scarce, had about 40 percent of its private wealth held outside the continent, a higher proportion than any other region. This integration was not a policy choice: most African governments erected capital controls, but they were ineffective. The main drivers of capital flight have been exchange rate misalignment, poor risk-ratings, and high indebtedness (Collier, Hoeffler, and Patillo 2001). However, capital flight was probably eased by the growth of international banking, some of it offshore, with poor practices of disclosure. A second way that globalization may have affected the weak globalizers adversely is through a rising risk of civil war. The incidence of civil war has declined sharply in the globalizing developing regions, but has risen sharply in Africa. Dependence on primary commodity exports is a powerful risk factor in civil conflict, probably because it provides easy sources of finance for rebel groups. Whereas most regions have diversified their exports, Africa has remained heavily dependent on primary commodities. Furthermore, conflicts tend to last longer: the chances of reaching peace are much lower during third wave globalization than during the second wave.

41

GLOBALIZATION, GROWTH, AND POVERTY

The re-emergence of international capital flows

Controls on capital outflows from high-income countries were gradually lifted: for example, the United Kingdom removed capital controls in 1979. Governments in developing countries have also gradually adopted less hostile policies toward investors. Partly as a result of these policy changes and partly due to the oil shock of the 1970s, significant amounts of private capital again began to flow to developing countries.

Total capital flows to developing countries went from less than $28 billion in the 1970s to about $306 billion in 1997, in real terms (figure 1.13), when they peaked. In the process, their composition changed significantly. The importance of official flows of aid more than halved, while private capital flows became the major source of capital for a number of emerging economies. The composition of private capital flows also changed markedly. FDI grew continuously throughout the 1990s. Mergers and acquisitions were the most important source of this increase, especially those resulting from the privatization of public companies. Net portfolio flows grew from $0.01 billion in 1970 to $103 billion in 1996, in real terms. New international mutual funds and pension funds helped to channel the equity flows to developing countries. The importance of syndicated bank loans and other private flows decreased steadily in relative terms throughout this period, especially after the debt crises of the 1980s.

Even though net private capital flows to developing countries increased during the third wave of globalization, by one measure they remained

Figure 1.13   Net capital flows to developing countries by type of flow, 1970–98

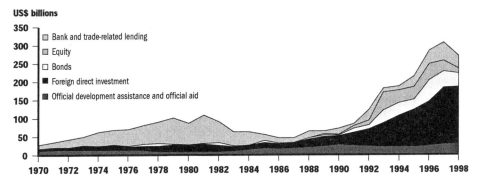

US$ billions

Source: Schmukler and Zoido-Lobatón (2001).

more modest than during the first wave. By 1998 the foreign capital stock was 22 percent of developing country GDP, roughly double what it had been in the mid-1970s but still well below the 32 percent reached in 1914 (Maddison 2001). Some countries receive large inflows, while other countries receive little. The top 12 emerging markets are receiving the overwhelming majority of the net inflows—countries such as Argentina, Brazil, China, India, Malaysia, Mexico, and Thailand. Much the most successful developing countries in attracting FDI were Malaysia and Chile, both with stocks of FDI of about $2,000 per capita.

FDI brings not just capital, but also advanced technology and access to international markets. It is critical for participating in international production networks. Dollar and Kraay (2001b) find that FDI has a powerful growth effect, whereas the overall level of investment by itself does not have a significant effect on growth—other factors are more important.

Capital flows to developing countries are just a tiny proportion of the global capital market. Because capital owners are concerned about risk, most global capital flows are between developed countries rather than from developed to developing countries. Even Malaysia and Chile have less FDI per capita than any of the major developed economies. FDI per capita in the United States is more than $3,200 per capita, while in Africa it is only $124 (Maddison 2001). This is despite the fact that differences in capital per member of the labor force between developed and developing countries are now far larger than they were during the first wave of globalization. World capital markets could clearly do more to raise growth in low-income countries. As we discuss in Chapter 3, there is evidence of systematic bias against Africa.

Migration pressures are building

The massive gaps in income that had built up by the end of globalization's second wave created intense economic pressures for people to migrate out of poor areas—both rural-urban migration within countries and international migration. These pressures were largely frustrated by immigration controls, but in some rich countries controls were somewhat relaxed during the third wave, with powerful effects on wages in poor countries.

Recall that in the first great wave of modern globalization, from 1870 to 1910, about 10 percent of the world's population relocated permanently. Much of this flow was driven by economic considerations, the

43

desire to find a better life in a more favorable location. The same forces operate today, though policies toward international migration are much more restrictive than in the past. About 120 million people (2 percent of the world's population) live in foreign countries (that is, not in the country of their citizenship). Roughly half of this stock of migrants is in the industrial countries and half in the developing world. However, because the population of developing countries is about five times greater than the population of the developed countries, migrants comprise a larger share of the population in rich countries (about 6 percent) than in poor countries (about 1 percent).

The main economic rationale for migration is that wages for the same skills differ vastly in different locations, especially between developing countries and rich ones. The average hourly labor compensation in manufacturing is about $30 per hour in Germany, and one one-hundredth of that level (30 cents) in China and India (figure 1.14). That gap is particularly extreme, but even between the United States and newly industrialized countries such as Thailand or Malaysia the compensation gap is ten-fold. Now, some of that difference results from the fact that the typical German worker has quite a bit more education and training than the typical Chinese or Indian. However, skill differences can only explain a small amount of the wage differential. A study following individual, legal immigrants found that on average they left jobs in Mexico paying $31 per week and on arrival in the United States could immediately earn $278 per week (a nine-fold increase). Similarly, Indonesian workers in Indonesia earn 28 cents per day, compared to $2 per day or more in next-door Malaysia. Clearly there are huge real gains to individual workers who migrate to more developed economies.

These large wage differentials across countries lead to mounting migration pressures, although the actual scale of migration depends upon the entry restrictions that migrants face. Hatton and Williamson (2001) study emigration from Africa. They find that both widening wage differentials and a demographic bulge of 15–29-year-olds are producing large and growing economic pressure for migration, although so far much of this has been bottled up by entry restrictions. Emigration from Mexico has been less restricted. There are about 7 million legal Mexican migrants living in the United States, and an additional estimated 3 million undocumented workers. This means that about 10

Figure 1.14   Hourly labor costs in manufacturing

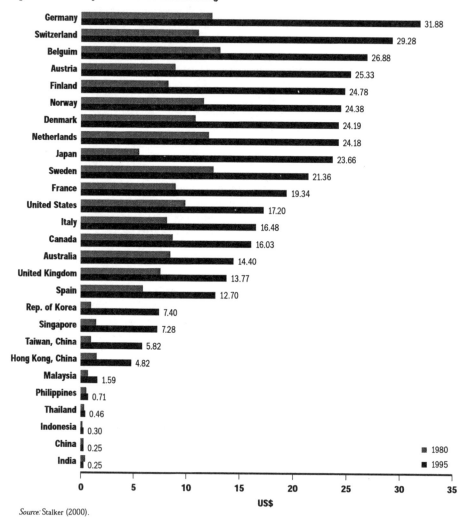

Source: Stalker (2000).

45

percent of Mexico's population is living and working in the United States. Emigration on this scale has a significant effect on developing country labor markets. Hatton and Williamson estimate the effect of out-migration from Africa on the wages of those who remain behind. They find that emigration powerfully raises the wages of remaining unskilled workers. It is likely that emigration from Mexico has substantially raised Mexican wages.

The benefits of migration to the sending region go beyond the higher wages for those who remain behind. Migrants send a large volume of remittances back to relatives and this is an important source of capital inflows (figure 1.15). India receives six times as much in remittances from its workers overseas every year as it gets in foreign aid.

Further, much trade and investment depends on personal and family networks. To take a significant historical example, a large number of Chinese have emigrated from China to other Asian countries (especially Thailand, Malaysia, Indonesia, and Singapore). The Chinese family networks play a significant role in trade and investment between these countries and China. It is inherently difficult to study and quantify this phenomenon, but there is more general evidence that language plays a large role in explaining trade and investment flows, and it makes sense that the stronger tie of family and kinship would have an even greater effect. The point here is that migration can facilitate the other flows of globalization—trade, capital, and ideas. Take, for example, the recent surge in Indian immigration to the United States. It happens that this immigration is particularly related to the high-tech sectors. It will support greater flows of technology and information between the United States and India, and also encourage more U.S. investment in India. Some successful Indian entrepreneurs in the United States may themselves open plants back in their home country, or U.S. companies may hire Indian engineers to work in India. And because much of manufacturing and services trade is associated with these kinds of networks, trade between the two countries is likely to increase.

What have been the effects of third wave globalization on income distribution and poverty?

The breakthrough of developing countries into global markets for manufactures and services, and the re-emergence of migration and capital flows,

46

Figure 1.15   Workers' remittances, 1999

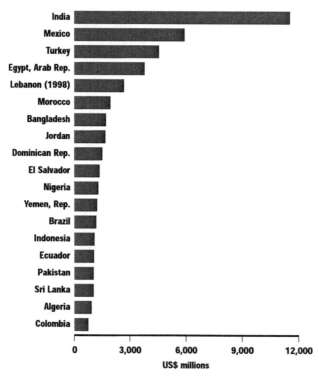

Source: World Bank (2001d).

have affected poverty and the distribution of income between and within countries. Domestic policy choices unrelated to globalization also affect income distribution.

Among developed countries globalization has continued to generate the convergence of the first and second waves. By 1995 inequality between countries was less than half what it had been in 1960 and substantially less than it had been in 1980. However, as figure 1.16 shows, there was a serious offsetting increase in inequality within individual countries, reversing the trend seen during the second wave. A part of this may have been due to immigration. However, it may also have been

47

GLOBALIZATION, GROWTH, AND POVERTY

Figure 1.16   Household inequality in rich countries, 1980–95

Mean log deviation

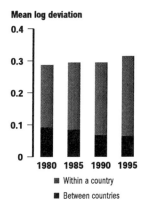

- ■ Within a country
- ■ Between countries

Source: Clark, Dollar, and Kraay (2001).

Figure 1.17   Household inequality in the globalizing world, 1975–95

Mean log deviation

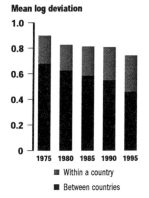

- ■ Within a country
- ■ Between countries

Source: Clark, Dollar, and Kraay (2001).

due to policy changes on taxation and social spending unconnected to globalization. Global economic integration is consistent with wide differences in domestic distributional policies: inequality differs massively between equally globalized economies. For the OECD economies taken as a whole, globalization has probably been equalizing as inequality between countries has radically decreased.

Among the new globalizers the same pattern of convergence has been evident as has occurred among the OECD economies over a longer period. Sachs and Warner (1995) find that this is indeed a general phenomenon among open economies. Treating the OECD and the new globalizers as a common group of integrated economies, overall inequality has declined (figure 1.17).

As in the OECD countries, within-country inequality has increased in the new globalizers. However, this is entirely due to the rise in inequality in China, which alone accounts for one-third of the population of the new globalizers. China started its modernization with an extremely equal distribution of income and extremely high poverty. Intra-rural inequality in China has actually decreased. The big growth in inequality has been between the rural areas and the rising urban agglomerations (figure 1.18), and between those provinces with agglomerations and those without them.

A closer investigation of the changes in inequality within countries is provided in Dollar and Kraay (2001a) and Ravallion (forthcoming). There are substantial difficulties in comparing income distribution data across countries. Countries differ in the concept measured (income versus consumption), the measure of income (gross versus net), the unit of observation (individuals versus households), and the coverage of the survey (national versus subnational). Dollar and Kraay restrict attention to distribution data based on nationally representative sources identified as high-quality by Deininger and Squire (1996), and perform some simple adjustments to control for differences in the types of surveys. These data cover a total of 137 countries. They focus on what has happened to the income of the poorest 20 percent of the population. They find that on average there is a one-to-one relationship between the growth rate of income of the poor and the growth rate of average income in society. However, there is much variation around that average relationship. They then investigate whether changes in trade account for any of this variation. They find no relationship between changes in openness and changes in

Figure 1.18   Increased inequality in China reflecting growing inequality among locations

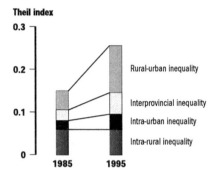

Source: Nehru (1997).

inequality, whether openness is measured by the share of trade in income, the Sachs-Warner measure of openness, average tariff rates, or capital controls. Ravallion qualifies this result. He finds that although *on average* openness does not affect inequality, in low-income countries it is associated with greater inequality. Regardless of its net effect, there are winners and losers from trade policies.

The combination of rapid growth with no systematic change in inequality has dramatically reduced absolute poverty in the new globalizing countries. Between 1993 and 1998 (the most recent period for which we have data) the number of people in absolute poverty declined by 14 percent to 762 million. For them, the third wave of globalization is indeed the golden age. Poverty is predominantly rural. As the new globalizers have broken into world markets their pace of industrialization and urbanization has increased. People have taken the opportunity to migrate from risky and impoverished rural livelihoods to less vulnerable and better paid jobs in towns and cities. Not only has poverty declined viewed in terms of income, but other dimensions of poverty have rapidly improved. Both average years of schooling and life expectancy have improved to levels close or equal to levels reached by the rich countries in 1960. Vietnam illustrates this experience. As it has integrated into the world economy, it has had a large increase in per capita income and no significant change in inequality. The income of the poor has

49

risen dramatically, and the level of absolute poverty has dropped sharply, from 75 percent of the population in 1988 to 37 percent in 1998. Poverty was cut in half in only 10 years. We can be unusually confident of this information because a representative household survey was conducted early in the reform process (1992–93), and the same 5,000 households were visited again six years later. Of the poorest 5 percent of households in 1992, 98 percent had higher incomes six years later. Vietnam was unusually successful in entering global markets for labor-intensive products such as footwear, and the increased employment might be expected to benefit poor households. Uganda had a similar experience: dramatic poverty reduction and no increase in inequality.

While the more globalized economies grew and converged, the less globalized developing economies declined and diverged. Their growth experience was worse than during the second wave, but their divergence has been longstanding. Ades and Glaeser (1999) find that at least since 1960, less globalized developing countries, defined by the share of trade in income, have tended to diverge. Decline and divergence had severe consequences for poverty in its various dimensions. Between 1993 and 1998 the number of people in absolute poverty in the less globalized developing countries rose by 4 percent to 437 million. Not only were per capita incomes falling, but in many countries life expectancy and school enrollments declined.

During the second wave of globalization the rich countries diverged from the poor countries, a trend that had persisted for a century. During the third wave the new globalizers have started to catch up with the rich countries, while the weak globalizers are falling further behind.

The change in the overall distribution of world income and the number of poor people are thus the net outcomes of offsetting effects. Among rich countries there has been convergence: the less rich countries have caught up with the richest, while within some rich countries there has been rising inequality. Among the new globalizers there has also been convergence and falling poverty. Within China there has also been rising inequality, but not on average elsewhere. Between the rich countries and the new globalizers there has been convergence. Between all these groups and the weak globalizers there has been divergence. The net effect is that the long trend of rising global inequality and rising numbers of people in absolute poverty has been halted and even reversed (figure 1.19). Bourguignon and Morrisson (2001) estimate that the number of people in absolute poverty fell by about 100 million between 1980 and 1992 (the endpoint of their analysis). Chen and Ravallion (2001) estimate that there was a further fall of about 100 million between 1993 (the closest date for comparison) and 1998.

Thus, globalization clearly can be a force for poverty reduction. In subsequent chapters we look at important factors at the global and local level that will determine whether it continues to be so. The next chapter takes up the global architecture for flows of goods, capital, and people, focusing on measures to strengthen integration and to enable locations currently left out of globalization to participate and benefit. Chapter 3 then turns to the national and local agenda in developing countries. Chapter 4 takes up issues of power, culture, and the environment. Chapter 5 brings together and summarizes the agenda for action to make globalization work better for poor countries and poor people.

Figure 1.19   Worldwide household inequality, 1975–99

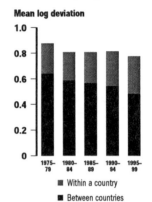

Source: Clark, Dollar, and Kraay (2001).

Notes

1. Much of the emigration from India was forced, rather than voluntary.

2. The mean log deviation has the advantage that it can be decomposed into inequality between locations and inequality within locations. It also has an intuitive interpretation. Income distributions everywhere are skewed in favor of the rich, so that the "typical" person (one chosen randomly from the population) has less income than the average for the whole group. Roughly speaking, the mean log deviation (times 100) is the percent gap between the typical person and the average income. The more skewed the distribution in favor of the rich, the larger is this gap. So, for example, if per capita income in the world is around $5,000 and the median person is living on $1,000 (80 percent less), the mean log deviation will be around 0.8.

3. For this calculation we separated out rich economies (the original members of the OECD plus Chile; Korea; Singapore; Taiwan,China; and Hong Kong, China). The "more globalized"—the top third of developing countries in terms of increased trade to GDP between the 1970s and the 1990s—are Argentina, Bangladesh, Brazil, China,

Colombia, Costa Rica, Côte d'Ivoire, the Dominican Republic, Haiti, Hungary, India, Jamaica, Jordan, Malaysia, Mali, Mexico, Nepal, Nicaragua, Paraguay, the Philippines, Rwanda, Thailand, Uruguay, and Zimbabwe. The "less globalized" are all other developing countries for which we have data. The less globalized group is a very diverse set of countries. It includes failed states whose economic performance has been extremely poor. It also includes some countries of the former Soviet Union that went through a difficult transition in the 1990s. Some of the less globalized countries have had stable but not increasing trade, and positive but slow growth.

4. The more globalized had per capita GDP, at purchasing power parity, of $1,488 in 1980, compared to $1,947 for other developing countries (table 1.1). These are population-weighted averages so that relatively poor China and India have a large weight. However, even a simple average of GDP per capita was significantly lower for the globalizers in 1980.

5. The rule of law index has a standard deviation of 1.0. The 0.44 advantage of the globalizers is roughly the same as Uganda's advantage over Zambia on this measure.

51

References

The word "processed" describes informally reproduced works that may not be commonly available through library systems.

Ades, A., and E. Glaeser. 1999. "Evidence on Growth, Increasing Returns, and the Extent of the Market." *Quarterly Journal of Economics* 114(3): 1025–46.

Bourguignon, F., and C. Morrisson. 2001. "Inequality among World Citizens: 1820–1992." Working Paper 2001–25, DELTA, Paris.

Cairncross, F. 1997. *The Death of Distance: How the Communications Revolution Will Change Our Lives*. Boston, MA: Harvard Business School Press.

Cannadine, David. 1990. *The Decline and Fall of the British Aristocracy*. New Haven, CT: Yale University Press.

Chen, S., and M. Ravallion. 2001. "How Did the World's Poorest Fare in the 1990s?" Development Research Group, World Bank, Washington, D.C. Processed.

Clark, X., D. Dollar, and A. Kraay. 2001. "Decomposing Global Inequality, 1960–99." World Bank, Washington, D.C. Processed.

Collier, P., and J. W. Gunning. 1999. "Explaining African Economic Performance." *Journal of Economic Literature* XXXVII (March): 64–111.

Collier, P., A. Hoeffler, and C. Pattillo. 2001. "Flight Capital as a Portfolio Choice." *The World Bank Economic Review* 15(1): 55–80.

Davis, D. R., and D. E. Weinstein. Forthcoming. "An Account of Global Factor Trade." *American Economic Review*.

Deininger, K., and L. Squire. 1996. "A New Data Set Measuring Income Inequality." *The World Bank Economic Review* 10(3): 565–91.

Dollar, D. 1992. "Outward-Oriented Developing Countries Really Do Grow More Rapidly: Evidence from 95 LDCs, 1976–85." *Economic Development and Cultural Change* 40(3): 523–44.

_____. 2001. "Globalization, Inequality, and Poverty since 1980." World Bank, Washington, D.C. http://www.worldbank.org/research/global.

Dollar, D., and A. Kraay. 2001a. "Growth Is Good for the Poor." Policy Research Working Paper No. 2587, World Bank, Washington, D.C.

_____. 2001b. "Trade, Growth, and Poverty." Policy Research Working Paper No. 2199, World Bank, Washington, D.C.

Dollar, D., and P. Zoido-Lobatón. 2001. "Patterns of Globalization." World Bank, Washington, D.C. Processed.

Frankel, J., and D. Romer. 1999. "Does Trade Cause Growth?" *The American Economic Review* 89(3): 379–99.

Fujita, M., P. Krugman, and A. J. Venables. 1990. *The Spatial Economy: Cities, Regions, and International Trade.* : Cambridge, MA: MIT Press.

Gray, J. 1998. *False Dawn: The Delusions of Global Capitalism.* London, Great Britain: Granta Books.

Hatton, T., and J. G. Williamson. 2001. "Demographic and Economic Pressure on Emigration Out of Africa." National Bureau of Economic Research Working Paper No. 8124, National Bureau of Economic Research, Cambridge, MA.

Limão, N., and A. J. Venables. 2000. "Infrastructure, Geographical Disadvantage, and Transport Costs." World Bank, Washington, D.C. Processed.

Lindert, P., and J. Williamson. 2001a. "Does Globalization Make the World More Unequal?" National Bureau of Economic Research Working Paper No. 8228, National Bureau of Economic Research, Cambridge, MA.

_____. 2001b. "Globalization: A Long History." Paper prepared for the Annual Bank Conference on Development Economics-Europe conference. World Bank, Europe—Barcelona. June 25–27.

Maddison, A. 1995. *Monitoring the World Economy, 1820–1992.* Paris: Organisation for Economic Co-operation and Development.

_____. 2001. *The World Economy: A Millennial Perspective.* Paris: Organisation for Economic Co-operation and Development.

Martin, W. 2001. "Trade Policies and Developing Countries." World Bank, Washington, D.C. Processed.

Mundell, R. 2000. "A Reconsideration of the Twentieth Century." *American Economic Review* 90(3): 327–40.

Nehru, V. 1997. *China 2020: Development Challenges in the New Century.* Washington, D.C.: World Bank.

Ravallion, M. Forthcoming. "Growth, Inequality, and Poverty: Looking Beyond Averages." *World Development.*

Rodriguez, F., and D. Rodrik. 1999. "Trade Policy and Economic Growth: A Skeptic's Guide to the Cross-national Evidence." National Bureau of Economic Research, Working Paper Series No. 7081: 1–[79], April.

Sachs, J. D., A. Mellinger, and J. L. Gallup. 2001. "The Geography of Poverty and Wealth." *Scientific American* 284(3): 70–75.

Sachs, J. D., and A. Warner. 1995. "Economic Reform and the Process of Global Integration." *Brookings Papers on Economic Activity* 1(96): 1–118.

Schmukler, S., and P. Zoido-Lobatón. 2001. "Financial Globalization: Opportunities and Challenges for Developing Countries." World Bank, Washington, D.C. Processed.

Sokoloff, K. 1988. "Inventive Activity in Early Industrial America: Evidence from Patent Records." *Journal of Economic History* XLVIII (4): 813–50.

Stalker, P. 2000. *Workers without Frontiers: The Impact of Globalization on International Migration.* Geneva, Switzerland: International Labour Organization.

Sutton, J. 2000. "Rich Trade, Scarce Capabilities: Industrial Development Revisited." Discussion Paper No. EI/28 (Sept.), London School of Economics and Political Science, London, United Kingdom.

Venables, A. J. 2001. "Geography and International Inequalities: The Impact of New Technologies." Presented at the 13th Annual Bank Conference on Development Economics, May 1–2, World Bank, Washington, D.C.

World Bank. 2001d. *World Development Indicators 2001*. Washington, D.C.

Part II
Impact on Poverty and Inequality

[4]

Pergamon

www.elsevier.com/locate/worlddev

World Development Vol. 29, No. 6, pp. 1083–1094, 2001
© 2001 Elsevier Science Ltd. All rights reserved
Printed in Great Britain
0305-750X/01/$ - see front matter

PII: S0305-750X(01)00017-1

Economic Policy, Distribution and Poverty: The Nature of Disagreements

RAVI KANBUR *

Cornell University, Ithaca, New York, USA

Summary. — The last 20 years have seen growing areas of agreement on poverty reduction strategies, but disagreements on economic policy, distribution and poverty seem to have intensified. This paper tries to identify the underlying nature of these disagreements, related to differences in perspective and framework between "Finance Ministry" and "Civil Society" tendencies. It is argued that the deep divisions one sees can be located in differences in the level of aggregation adopted, the time horizon considered, and assumptions made on market structure and power. Mutual understanding could be advanced by further exploration of these differences, and the adoption by both sides of the approach of dialogue rather than negotiation. © 2001 Elsevier Science Ltd. All rights reserved.

Key words — globalization, economic policy, poverty, inequality, Seattle, World Bank, disagreements

1. INTRODUCTION

The end of history lasted for such a short time. If the early 1990s raised hopes of a broad-based consensus on economic policy for growth, equity and poverty reduction, the late 1990s dashed them. The East Asian crisis and the Seattle debacle saw to that. In the year 2000, the Governors of the World Bank, whose mission it is to eradicate poverty, could meet only under police protection, besieged by those who believe instead that the institution and the policies it espouses cause poverty. The street demonstrations in Prague, Seattle and Washington, DC, are one end of a spectrum of disagreement, which includes vigorous debate in the pages of the leading newspapers, passionate involvement of faith-based organizations, and the genteel cut and thrust of academic discourse.

The last two years have seen my involvement in an extensive process of consultation on poverty reduction strategies. [1] The consultation reached out to most interested constituencies in the academic, policy making and advocacy communities. It covered the international

* This paper is based on an invited presentation to the Swedish Parliamentary Commission on Global Development (Globkom) on 22 September 2000. I am grateful to Mia Horn-af-Rantzien, Secretary of the Commission, for her encouragement to produce a written version of the presentation. These ideas have also been presented at meetings organized by the Canadian Ministry of Finance in Ottawa, the World Food Day Symposium at Cornell University, the PREM network of the World Bank, and the Faculty of Social Studies seminar at the University of Warwick. I am grateful to the participants in these meetings for their constructive comments. The observations in this paper are based on my operational experiences over the last few years. For more formal academic assessment of the literature on distribution, poverty and development see Kanbur, R. (2000). Income

distribution and development. In A. B. Atkinson, & F. Bourguignon (Eds.), *Handbook of income distribution* (Vol. I). Amsterdam: North Holland, and Kanbur, R. (1998). Poverty reduction strategies: five perennial questions. In R. Culpeper, & C. McAskie (Eds.), *Towards autonomous development in Africa*. Ottawa: The North–South Institute, Ottawa. For an assessment of the implications for development assistance, see Kanbur, R., Sandler, T., & Morrison, K. (1999). *The future of development assistance*. Washington, DC: Overseas Development Council, and for World Bank specific commentary see Kanbur, R., & Vines, D. (2000). The World Bank and poverty reduction: past, present and future. In C. Gilbert, & D. Vines (Eds.), *The World Bank: structure and policies*. Cambridge, UK: Cambridge University Press. Final revision accepted: 3 January 2001.

financial institutions (IFIs) and the myriad UN specialized agencies, Government Ministries in the North and the South, Northern aid agencies, academic analysts in rich and poor countries, Northern and Southern advocacy nongovernmental organizations (NGOs), and NGOs with ground-level operations working with the poor. It involved a global electronic consultation, as well as conventional written contributions, and scores of meetings. A particularly valuable exercise was the systematic attempt to elicit directly the "Voices of the Poor" through participatory assessments.

This paper presents an analysis of the broad themes of disagreement in these consultations and more generally among those concerned with poverty reduction. It has to be noted first of all that there are swathes of agreement in areas where there would not have been consensus two decades ago. Any discussion of disagreements has to start with an acknowledgement of these areas of agreement. But, clearly, there are deep divisions on economic policy, distribution and poverty. These divisions spilled out in the consultations, mostly politely but sometimes in vehement discourse, written and oral, harbingers of the street battles to come.

The paper tries to answer an obvious question: How can people with seemingly the same ends disagree so much about means, and how can seemingly the same objective reality be interpreted so differently? The simple answer, which the protagonists themselves often provide, is of course to question the motives or the analytical capacity of those one disagrees with. The suggestion that "the others" are either not truly interested in attacking poverty (quite the opposite, in fact), or that they make elementary errors of fact or interpretation, is never very far below the surface.

It is argued here, however, that at least some of the disagreement can be understood in terms of differences in perspective and framework. Understanding disagreements in these terms—rather than in terms of motives or intelligence—is more conducive to encouraging dialogue rather than confrontation. The object of this paper is to provide an account of some of the underlying reasons for deep disagreements on economic policy, distribution and poverty, and to couch these in an analytical rather than a rhetorical frame. But before doing this we need to say a little more about disagreements over what and disagreements between whom.

2. DISAGREEMENTS OVER WHAT AND BETWEEN WHOM?

Disagreements over what? The next section will review some broad areas of consensus on poverty reduction strategies. But the focus of this paper is on disagreements, and these have begun to coalesce around a seemingly irreduceable core of economic policy instruments. There are major disagreements on the pace and sequencing of fiscal adjustment, monetary and interest rate policy, exchange rate regimes, trade and openness, internal and external financial liberalization including deregulation of capital flows, the scale and methods of large scale privatization of state owned enterprises, etc. Perhaps trade and openness is the archetypal, emblematic, area around which there are deep divisions, and where certainly the rhetoric is fiercest.

Disagreements between whom? Any attempt at categorization and classification risks doing violence to a complex and richly textured reality. But the following grouping would be recognizable to many, and captures broad elements of policy disagreements. One group, call them Group A, could be labeled "Finance Ministry." In this group would obviously be some who worked in finance ministries in the North, and in the South. It would also include many economic analysts, economic policy managers and operational managers in the IFI's and the Regional Multilateral Banks. A key constituent would be the financial press, particularly in the North but also in the South. Finally, one would include many, though not all, academic economists trained in the Anglo-Saxon tradition. Another group, call them Group B, could be labeled "Civil Society." This group would obviously include analysts and advocates in the full range of advocacy and operational NGOs. There would also be people who worked in some of the UN specialized agencies, in aid ministries in the North and social sector ministries in the South. Among academics, noneconomists would tend to fall into this group.

To repeat, any such classification is bound to be too simple a reflection of reality. Although the terminology of "Group A" and "Group B" is easier to deploy, A and B are better thought of as tendencies rather than as defined and specific individuals. There are clearly people who work in the IFIs who are not "Finance Ministry types," just as there are academic economists trained in the Anglo-Saxon tradition who would, for example, caution strongly on capital account liberalization. The UN specialized agencies and Northern aid agencies are often a battle ground between Finance Ministry and Civil Society tendencies. As the next section makes clear, some NGO positions on specific policies would be approved of in Finance Ministries, and vice versa.

This being said, however, the proposed classification offers a sharp enough, and recognizable enough, characterization of divisions to help us understand the nature of disagreements. Group A types are those who tend to believe that the cause of poverty reduction is best served by more rapid adjustment to fiscal imbalances, rapid adjustment to lower inflation and external deficits and the use of high interest rates to achieve these ends, internal and external financial sector liberalization, deregulation of capital controls, deep and rapid privatization of state-owned enterprises and, perhaps the strongest unifying factor in this group—rapid and major opening up of an economy to trade and foreign direct investment. On each of these issues, Group B types tend to lean the other way.

The real question we face is why? Why is it that these two groups disagree so much across key areas of economic policy? The basic contention of this paper is that much of the reason lies in differences in perspective and framework on three key features characterizing assessments of economic policy, distribution and poverty: Aggregation, Time Horizon, and Market Structure. First, Group A tends to view the consequences of economic policy in much more aggregative terms than does Group B. Second, Group B's major concerns are with consequences over a time horizon which is both much shorter and much longer than the "medium-term" horizon which Group A typically adopts. Third, Group A instinctively approaches the distributional consequences of economic policy through a competitive market structure, while Group B instinctively thinks of a world in which market structure is characterized by pockets of market power, and economic policy feeds through this noncompetitive structure to the consequences for the poor.

The elaboration of Aggregation, Time Horizon and Market Structure, as providing a framework for understanding deep disagreements on economic policy, distribution and poverty, is the core task of this paper. But before elaborating on disagreement, let us consider areas of agreement.

3. SOME AREAS OF AGREEMENT

The consultations revealed wide areas of agreement—some old, some new, and some surprising.

There is no question that there is now broad agreement that education and health outcomes are on par with income in assessing poverty and the consequences of economic policy. This is now so commonplace that it is easy to forget it was not always the case, that 25 years ago great intellectual and policy battles were fought in the World Bank on broadening the conception of development and poverty reduction. Perhaps today's new proposals on conceptualizing poverty—for example, that empowerment and participation should in their turn be treated on par with education and health and income—will equally become tomorrow's foundations.

Another area in which the consultations revealed considerable agreement, at least at a certain level of generality, was on the role of international public goods in determining the well being of the poor. Whether couched in terms of crossborder spillovers of environmental externalities or financial instability, or in terms of the central role of basic research into tropical agriculture and tropical diseases, the recognition was clearly abroad that public intervention is needed in these areas. The emerging importance of this issue was instinctively grasped by most. It may well be that this happy state of affairs is due precisely to the fact that this is a relatively new issue in the policy arena, that once we get into the details, divisions will grow. Thus, for example, while there was overall broad support for the idea of a Vaccine Purchase Fund to bridge the gap between the costs of basic research and the purchasing power of the poorest countries, there was already some dissent on such funds being unwarranted subsidies to corporations, who should instead be directed to supply drugs they already have at prices the poorest can afford.

A third area where there is a surprising amount of agreement, or more accurately not as much disagreement as there was 20 or even 10 years ago, is on the old "Markets versus State" debate. There has definitely been some coming together on this. Particularly interesting were the positions of NGOs with actual ground-level operations working directly with poor. In the consultations, these organizations tended to be very pragmatic. The question for them was always what worked to improve the standard of living of the people they were helping, not about ideologies favoring state over market or the other way round.

Consider, for example, the work and philosophy of SEWA, the Self-Employed Women's Association, which operates in Gujarat State in India. [2] SEWA grew out of the long history of organizing textile workers in Ahmedabad, but applied and modified those lessons to organizing women in the informal sector. Starting from an urban base, it has now also expanded to organizing in rural areas (http://www.sewa.org). SEWA's ground-level campaigns, and their national advocacy work, reflects a pragmatism which eschews ideological positions on "state versus market." They have supported certain types of trade liberalization because they increase the demand for the output and labor of their members. But they have opposed other types of trade liberalization when they hurt, for example, the employment and incomes of the husbands and brothers and fathers of their members. They are strong supporters of deregulating the control of the Gujarat State Forestry Commission on the livelihoods of their members. But they oppose deregulation of the pharmaceutical industry because of the devastating impact of these on basic drug prices, and they support increased regulation in Export Processing Zones to ensure that labor standards are met. Is SEWA pro-state or pro-market? It is difficult to say. What is clear is that SEWA is pro-poor. One of their best known pamphlets is in fact entitled "Liberalizing for the Poor."

The more one moves away from ground-level operations, the more one moves to advocacy groups of any shade, pragmatism gives way to more defined *a priori* positions on state and market. But even here, the divides are not as great as they were at the height of the cold war, or at the zenith of post cold war triumphalism that heralded the "end of history." At the turn of the century the real questions are to do with the right balance of market and state, and how things actually work on the ground.

Alongside this lessened divide on markets versus state, there is broad agreement on the central importance of institutions in regulating markets, in regulating government, in determining the interaction between households in the market place, and thus in determining the outcomes for the poor. One of the striking findings from the Voices of the Poor exercise was how important institutions such as the police and the courts were to the reality of poor people's lives. At the macro level, the role of institutions in determining the investment climate was also agreed upon in the consultations. Of course, once again, this was at a certain level of generality. When detailed discussions started, and especially when they impinged on economic policies, divisions tended to appear.

So there is broad consensus in some areas and at a certain level of discourse, to set against the divisions that are the focus of this paper. But these very agreements throw into sharp relief the disagreements that remain. It is almost as if the battle is more intense because it is now focused more sharply on fewer and fewer remaining issues. Let us turn now to the nature of these disagreements.

4. THE NATURE OF DISAGREEMENTS I: AGGREGATION

In the current discourse on economic policy, distribution and poverty, there is a strong sense of people talking past each other, each side equally convinced that it has the truth, even when confronted with seemingly the same objective reality. How can that be? One key factor is that different people instinctively operate at different levels of aggregation when they talk about outcomes, or about the consequences of different economic policy interventions. This goes beyond the simple point about GDP versus poverty or other distribution indicators, which is the usual way in which this divide is portrayed. Many in Group A now work with poverty measures which calculate, for example, the fraction of people in a country who fall below a critical level of income or expenditure—the most commonly used threshold is the famous $1 per person per day poverty line. Even with something like this measure, the two groups have very different perspectives on poverty outcomes. Some of the differences are obvious, others less so.

The following personal experience illustrates the reaction that many analysts in Group A get when they present their formal poverty analysis to broader audiences. After doing detailed academic work on the Ghana Living Standards Survey (GLSS) in the 1980s and early 1990s, in 1992 I found myself as the head of the World Bank's Field Office in Ghana. Work on GLSS data by a range of analysts showed that the incidence of poverty in Ghana, defined as above but with a local poverty line, fell during 1987–91. The exact magnitude varied depending on the detailed calculations, but there was a three or four percentage point decline over these four years. This was pitifully small, but it was actually very good by African standards.

The analysis presented, in common with the best practice in this area, had made all the necessary adjustments and corrections to overcome the shortcomings of these sorts of data. For example, considerable effort was put into correcting for regional price variations, making imputations for dwellings, correcting for household size, etc., in arriving at the poverty measure. But when the analysis was presented in Ghana, very few people believed it. From academics in the universities, through foreign and local NGOs, to the trade unions and the Rotary Clubs—there was an astonishing degree of disbelief. This is not an uncommon reaction, at least in Africa, to such analysis which shows poverty decreasing. The natural reactions of Group A analysts to this disbelief usually go through the whole gamut— that people do not really understand the detailed statistical analysis, that those who criticize represent special interest groups, that some people will never admit that they are better off, etc. [3] But before dismissing disbelief in this way, it is as well to consider that there might be legitimate reasons for this response, understandable even within the standard framework of household survey based analysis.

There at least three reasons why the claim that poverty had gone down in Ghana, for example, could be questioned. The first of these is well recognized by household survey analysts. The income-expenditure based measurement of well being has improved a lot over the years—for example, production for home consumption is now routinely included, capturing of regional price variation is getting better, and imputing use value to dwellings is also becoming standard. But, one thing that these measures do not capture very well, or at all, is the value of public services. There are separate modules in these surveys with questions on education and health and infrastructure and so on, but these are rarely, almost never, integrated into the income/expenditure measure of well-being because of conceptual and data difficulties. It is this income/expenditure measure that is used in calculating the headline poverty ratios.

So, it is quite possible for public services to worsen considerably and yet for this effect to not show up in the income-expenditure based measures of poverty incidence. If the bus service that takes a woman from her village to her sister's village is cancelled, it will not show up in these measures. If the health post in the urban slum runs out of drugs, it will not show up. If the primary school text books disappear, or if the teacher does not turn up to teach, it will not show up. But those with ground-level operations and personnel will pick these up. To them, as well as to the poor, the claim that poverty has gone down will ring hollow. None of this is to say that it is not useful to calculate nationally representative, household survey based, income-expenditure poverty measures. It is simply to say that focusing on them solely misses out on disaggregated detail which others can help to fill in, and which influences the perceptions and assessments of these others.

The second reason for the disconnect one often finds between household survey based poverty measures used by Group A and the perceptions of Group B is that of regional or group disaggregation. Even accepting the income-expenditure based measures to be an accurate representation of well-being, quite often a national decrease in the poverty incidence can be composed of large movements in opposite directions. For example, in Ghana, during 1987–91, the drop in national poverty was composed of a drop in rural areas and a rise in urban areas. In Mexico during 1990–94, the decrease in national poverty was composed of a drop in urban areas, but an increase in some rural regions. It is important to realize that we are not talking here about the odd household or two getting worse off. The poverty index for entire regions increased. While the decrease in the national poverty index, and the drops in those regions which are driving this decrease at the national level, are clearly to be welcomed, just focusing on the aggregate picture is liable to miss out the increasing poverty in Accra, the capital of Ghana, or in the Chiapas region of Mexico. For an NGO working with street children in Accra, or for a local official coping with increased poverty among indigenous peoples in Chiapas, it is cold comfort to be told, "but national poverty has gone down." A similar story can be told about gender-based disaggregation, and other groupings based on ethnicity and race.

It should be clear that in the above type of disconnect neither view is "wrong." Different parts of the same objective reality are being seen and magnified. It is both true that the national poverty incidence has declined, and that major groups have been made worse off. The problem is that instead of attempting to understand the other perspective each side hunkers down to defend its view in increasingly strident terms. Group A analysts just keep repeating that poverty has gone down, and do not make any concessions to the complex group specific patterns, while Group B analysts and advocates become increasingly irritated and alienated from a discourse which does not match the reality they know.

Consider now a third and not frequently appreciated disconnect related to aggregation. The work horse poverty concept of Group A analysts is the incidence of poverty—the percentage of the total population below some poverty line, say one dollar per person per day. This is the concept they instinctively go for. For example, the leading International Development Target, broadly accepted by donor agencies, is to halve by 2015 the incidence of poverty. But analysts and especially advocates and operational types in Group B instinctively think of the absolute numbers of poor as the criterion. The potential for disconnect should be clear. In Ghana, for example, while the incidence of poverty was falling at around one percentage point per year over 1987–91, the total population was growing at almost twice that rate, with the result that the absolute number of poor, even using the standard income-expenditure based measure, grew sizably.

Think again of the local NGO with ground-level operations. If the number of people turning up at soup kitchens, the number of homeless indigents who have to be provided shelter, the number of street children, increases, then those who work in these organizations are, quite rightly from their perspective, going to argue that poverty has gone up. That the incidence of poverty has fallen is of little relevance to them, and to be told repeatedly and insistently that poverty has fallen is bound to lead to difficulties in communication and dialogue. One sees this also at the global level. The World Bank's figures show that over the 1990s the absolute numbers of the poor stayed roughly constant at around 1.2 billion. The incidence of poverty has fallen, since total world population is on the increase. Has global poverty fallen or stayed the same? One challenge often heard in the consultations was: "How can you say economic growth helps the poor? Look, there has been all this growth in the 1990s, and yet the total number of poor has not changed at all!" Leaving to one side the growth issue, to which a whole section is devoted later in the paper, it is easy to see how communication can be derailed

by different groups meaning different things by the same word—poverty. In this case a good start would be clarity and comprehension, but even that might not help because the issue of whether the criterion is the incidence of poverty or the absolute numbers of the poor is still left open.

Thus, instinctive adoption of different levels of aggregation in describing and evaluating the distributional and poverty consequences of economic policies explain at least some of the disconnect one observes. The above arguments and characterizations would all be present for each of the economic policies in dispute—for example, the impact of trade policy reform on distribution and poverty. Understanding these differences is the first step in more fruitful dialogue between those who primarily rely on national poverty incidence measures derived from household surveys to assess the evolution of poverty, and those who have a much more finely disaggregated view of the outcomes of economic policy. Unfortunately, at the moment the lack of mutual comprehension is leading to polarization, with Group A often retreating into the formal technical bunker, and simply repeating their findings without trying to understand what Group B is trying to say, and Group B dismissing Group A analysis as either out of touch with reality or, even worse, actively manipulated to get certain answers. Neither of these positions is healthy, and bridging the aggregation divide is essential if we are to move forward.

5. THE NATURE OF DISAGREEMENTS II: TIME HORIZON

Implicit or explicit differences in the time horizon over which the consequences of policy are assessed explain some of the deep disagreements on economic policy, distribution and poverty.

The "medium term" is the instinctive time horizon that Group A uses when thinking about the consequences of trade policy, for example. This is implicit in the equilibrium theory which underlies much of the reasoning behind the impact of policy on growth and distribution. It is also implicit in the way empirical analysts interpret their crosscountry econometric relationships between growth, equity or poverty on one side and measures of openness on the other. There is, of course, no simple way to link the short or medium or long-term of economic theory and modeling to actual calendar time. But by and large, when Group A talks about the consequences of policies for distribution and growth they have in mind a 5–10 year time horizon.

Group B has concerns that are both more short term and more long term. Those who work with the daily reality of poor people's lives, are extremely concerned, like the poor themselves, about short-term consequences of economic policy which can drive a family into starvation, to sell its assets at fire sale prices, or to pull its children out of school. For them it is no use to be told that over a 5–10 year horizon things will pick up again. In fact, it is not even good enough to be told that in the medium term things will be better than they would have been without the shock of this policy change because without the policy change things were in decline anyway. All this is true, but short-run survival trumps medium-run benefits every time, if the family is actually on the edge of survival. As Keynes might have said, in the short run they could all be dead.

Increasingly, Group A accepts the issue of short-term vulnerability and shocks as being an important one, not only because it affects well-being in the short term, but because behavioral responses to this vulnerability may themselves lead to inefficiencies which affect the prospects for growth and poverty reduction in the medium term. Moreover, the issue of safety nets is back on the table, after its banishment in the 1980s, the banishment itself being a reaction to their inefficiencies and misuse in the 1960s and 1970s. But safety nets are sometimes thought of by Group A as being an add on, to address the negative short-term consequences of trade opening, for example. They tend to be cautious about them as a systematic part of an insurance and redistribution mechanism, and they certainly would not want to see trade opening to be halted or slowed down because these safety nets and compensation mechanisms, however temporary, were not in place. This last point is central, and an acid test. In the absence of safety nets, Group B would be cautious or downright hostile to trade openness. Group A would want to press ahead, often dismissing those who argue for caution as either not understanding that openness would actually lead to greater equity and poverty reduction, or as special interest groups with protection on their minds. Not facing up to the implicit difference in time horizon accounts for at least some of the vehement disagreements on this score.

There are also those who have what they see as a much longer time horizon than a decade. Environmental groups, including some with religious perspectives on stewardship of the earth's resources, fall into this category. For them, it is the 50 or the 100-year perspective that is important. They do not see how economic growth can be sustained given limits on the earth's carrying capacity, and they see both immediate and long-term negative consequences of resource depletion. An important corollary of this line of thinking is that implicit or explicit redistribution from rich countries to poor countries will have to substitute for economic growth as the foundation for global poverty reduction. Group A are essentially techno-optimists. They refer back to the gloomy scenarios painted by the Club of Rome in the 1970s and point out that none of these came to be true. While there are clearly some market distortions which lead to an inefficiently high level of resource depletion, and crossborder spillover effects which lead to their own coordination problems, their answer is to fix these distortions rather than forcibly hold down investment and growth. In any event, they do not see it as a politically feasible option over the 5–10 year horizon to ask the rich countries to undertake massive redistribution in favor of the poor countries, and they have a strong sense that technological change will come to the rescue over a 50 or 100-year horizon, as it always has in the past.

In the consultations, therefore, Group A was fending off both shorter term and longer term perspectives. But the real point is that oftentimes it was not clear that it was this difference in perspective, rather than the specifics of trade policy or privatization policy or whatever, which was driving the difference. Clarity is not resolution, but it is a start.

6. THE NATURE OF DISAGREEMENTS III: MARKET STRUCTURE AND POWER

Undoubtedly the most potent difference in framework and perspective centers on market structure and power. The implicit framework of Group A in thinking through the consequences of economic policy on distribution and poverty is that of a competitive market structure of a large number of small agents interacting without market power over each other. The instinctive picture that Group B has of market structure is one riddled with market power wielded by agents in the large and in the small. This is true whether they are talking about the power of big corporations in the market place or in negotiating with governments, or of the power of the local moneylender in determining usurious rates of interest in the village economy. They see the formulation and implementation of economic policy as being influenced by agents with market power, and they see policy feeding through to consequences through a market structure which is not competitive.

The immediate response of Group A to the suggestion that openness in trade, for example, might hurt the poor in poor countries is to (implicitly or explicitly) invoke the basic theorems of trade theory. Opening up an economy to trade will benefit the more abundant factor because this factor will be relatively cheap and opening up will increase demand for this factor overall. Since unskilled labor is the factor abundant in poor countries, opening up will benefit unskilled labor and hence the poor. Leaving aside the fact that this is a theory of medium-term equilibrium, and thus subject to the disagreements discussed in the previous section, it is also a theory based on competitive product and factor markets. In particular, if local product and factor markets are segmented, because of poor infrastructure or because of the local monopoly power of middlemen and moneylenders, the simple theory will not go through quite so simply. But it is precisely such situations (as well as the disaggregated and the short term consequences discussed earlier) that are highlighted repeatedly in discussions about the possible negative consequences of openness. The tendency among Group A is to dismiss these claims, and to revert again to stating the conclusion that openness is good for equity.

Another example is capital mobility. Leaving to one side the question of portfolio capital, where Group A has itself moved to a more cautious stance since the financial crises of the late 1990s, there is the issue of mobility of investment capital. A very strong belief in Group B is that increased mobility of investment capital makes workers in both receiving and sending countries worse off. Such a view is derided by Group A analysts as being incoherent— "How can you say that when capital leaves the US it hurts US workers, and when it gets to Mexico it hurts Mexican workers as well?!"

Of course, in a framework with perfectly competitive markets, it is indeed incoherent to suggest that increased capital mobility makes workers worse off everywhere. At most, it will make workers in only one country worse off. Moreover, since with mobility capital will move to the highest return, this is more efficient so the gainers could more than afford to compensate the loser, if such a mechanism existed. But consider the following set up. Capital and labor markets are not perfectly competitive. Rather, capital and labor bargain in each country over wages and employment. Now make capital mobile. It can be seen that this is akin to increasing the bargaining power of capital relative to labor, so that increasing capital mobility, whatever its effects on efficiency, could end up making workers in both countries worse off relative to capital. This is the implicit framework Group B used over and again in the consultations, with added emphasis on the political power of big multinational corporations to influence economic policy on such issues as capital controls or regulation of Foreign Direct Investment. The answer of Group A was to reply with the findings of the (implicit or explicit) competitive framework, and cycle of nondialogue would go on from there.

The above are examples from trade and openness, but the same divide is present in discussions of the consequences of other economic policies such as privatization of state owned enterprises. The implicit framework of those supporting rapid and large scale privatization is one where state monopoly is replaced by a competitive structure of firms without monopoly power. The implicit framework of those more cautious in this regard is one of a state monopoly, which might be at least somewhat responsive to the needs of consumer through political pressure, being replaced by a private monopoly with no such restraints.

The point of the above discussion is to highlight differences in basic frameworks used instinctively in thinking through the distributional and poverty consequences of economic policies. Of course, many in Group A are aware of how noncompetitive elements can affect their predictions (for example, trade theory has made great strides in recent years in incorporating elements of monopolistic competition), but in policy discourse it seems as though Group A has by and large plumped for the competitive market structure framework. But thinking through the distributional consequences of economic policies when market structures are not competitive, in the small or in the large, will be needed before the framework of Group A can be made to speak to the concerns of Group B. For example, whether the capital-labor bargaining framework discussed above is valid is an empirical question that can be tested for different countries and industries. But until such models are worked out commensurately with the now standard competitive framework models, there can be no basis for comparison and assessment. Until that is done, it will be a standoff between two very different perspectives on market power.

7. A SEEMING DISAGREEMENT: THE "GROWTH" RED HERRING

The word "growth" was immediately divisive in the consultations, with Group A accusing Group B of being "anti-growth," and Group B characterizing Group A as holding the view that "growth is everything." In fact, there is more agreement here than meets the eye, and the rhetoric of both groups stands in the way of seeing the degree of agreement that does exist. Unfortunately, the word "growth" is used in both in its technical sense of "an increase in real national per capita income," and also to connote a particular policy package, disagreements over key elements of which has been the focus of this paper. This package is "growth-oriented policies" as seen by Group A and "economic policies which hurt the poor" as seen by Group B. If used in the technical sense, one would probably find less disagreement on whether growth so defined could help poverty reduction. Or rather, the discussion could then focus on economic policies and on Aggregation, Time Horizon and Market Structure as discussed in this paper, which is where the true nature of disagreements is to be found.

Consider the claim by some that others are "anti-growth," usually followed by empirical demonstrations that growth (increase in real per national per capita income) is strongly correlated across countries and over time with reductions in national-level measures of income poverty. There is no question that these correlations are very strong indeed. But that is not the point. In all of the consultations over the two years, not one person from Group B in Eastern Europe, for example, claimed that the disastrous increase poverty and worsening of social indicators in Eastern Europe in the 1990s had nothing to do with the precipitous decline in real national per capita income during this period. Nobody made the claim that had the

decline in per capita income been even greater, the poor would have somehow been better. The claim that they did make, however, was that the policy package that the transition economies were advised (or forced) to adopt was what led to the decline in per capita income and to the increase in poverty.

As another example, not one person from Group B in East Asia claimed that the tremendous improvement in poverty and social indicators in East Asia, over the 30 years prior to 1997, had nothing to do with the fact that per capita income in these countries multiplied several fold over this period. Nobody made the claim that the position of the poor would have been better had this growth been negative. But what they did claim was that the policy package put in place by these countries over these years differed in key elements from the policy package currently being recommended by the IFI's and some Northern Finance Ministries. Finally, coming to 1997, not one person from Group B in East Asia claimed that the sharp increases in poverty registered in East Asia during the crisis had nothing to do with the fact that per capita income collapsed. They did not make the claim that had the per capita income decline been greater, the poor would have been better off. What they did claim was that the policy package these countries were encouraged to adopt in the mid 1990s, especially rapid capital account and financial sector liberalizations, caused the crisis and the attendant decline in per capita income and the increase in poverty.

To characterize these positions of Group B as claims that growth does not help the poor, and to then refute them by showing the undoubted negative correlation between per capita income and poverty, not only misses the point—it does the debate a disservice as well. The real debate to be engaged is on the policy package and the consequences of different elements of it for distribution and poverty. Correlations between per capita income and poverty are beside the point because the real dispute is about the consequences of alternative policies.

Now in fact, in written and oral contributions from Group B in the consultations, very often one would indeed find statements of the type "growth is not the answer to poverty" or "the IFI's are obsessed with growth as the answer to poverty." But an effort must be made to understand what the true meaning of such statements is, from their context and from extended dialogue. Statements such as the ones above often captured intent much better if "growth" were replaced by something like "Washington consensus policies" or "the standard IFI package." It might be argued that one should take the words for what they are, but one also finds very often that Group A uses "growth" as shorthand for "growth-oriented policies" by which they would mean a certain type of policy package, the contents of which we have been discussing. If Group A slips into this usage, it is understandable that in responding, Group B does the same. Thus part of the problem is that the word "growth" is used to mean both an increase in per capita income, and to refer to a policy package, and this is true of Group A and Group B.

None of the above is to minimize in any way the deep disagreements that do exist on Aggregation, Time Horizon and Market Structure. Even with growth defined as increase in per capita income, Section 5 has already discussed how some in Group B argue that this is not the answer over a 50 or a 100-year time horizon. Moreover, Section 4 discussed how any given increase in per capita income could be associated with myriad disaggregated patterns of distributional and poverty change, even when national poverty falls. But the vehemence of the "growth" debate, on both sides, is somewhat misplaced if by growth one means simply an increase in real national per capita income. The current growth debate, certainly as presented by some elements of Group A, misses the point, and derails dialogue on the real issues of poverty reduction strategies.

8. ON POLICY MESSAGING: NEGOTIATION VERSUS DIALOGUE

Faced with such deep divisions based on legitimate differences in perspective and framework, what should one do? The answer is clearly to develop dialogue based on an attempt at mutual understanding of the different frameworks, how they can lead to different interpretations and conclusions, what sort of evidence might help to resolve some of the differences, and to come out with measured and nuanced positions. Unfortunately, quite the opposite seems to be happening. Over the past few years, the divide has grown and a polarization has set in. For the IFI's, the siege of their biannual meetings is proving a traumatic experience. More generally, Seattle both symbolized and crystallized the vehemence of the disagreements. The stance everywhere is one of confrontation and negotiation, rather than understanding and dialogue.

My focus here is on Group A, especially when it presents policy messages that synthesize analytical work. Here again, a negotiating stance seems to be in play, especially among some parts of the IFI's and the G7 Treasuries. Even when, intellectually and analytically, Group A accepts the complications, qualifications and nuances brought about by considerations of disaggregation, differences in time horizon, and noncompetitive market structures, the tendency is for the policy messaging—for example on trade and openness—to be sharp and hard, for fear that to do otherwise would be read as a sign of weakness by "the other side." Especially since Seattle, a "line in the sand," "this far, no further," mentality seems to have gripped elements of Group A—in the IFI's, in the G7 Treasuries, in the Financial Press and some in academia. "Give them an inch of nuance and they'll take a mile of protection" is the mindset. Paradoxically, the growing areas of agreement noted at the outset—for example on education and health, and on institutions—tend to lead to a sharper stance being taken on the remaining areas of dispute on core economic policies.

This is unfortunate. At least twice before, elements of Group A have taken such a hard stance, with a negotiating mindset, and both times have had to retreat after considerable conflict which negatively affected the prospects for future dialogue. The first example of this is capital account convertibility, on which the IFI's, with the broad support of G7 Treasuries, took a bold stand in the early and mid-1990s, and dismissed those who were skeptical of the benefits and fearful of the consequences. Since the 1997 crisis the tune has changed, but the earlier intransigence did not help the dialogue when the need for a nuanced position was finally recognized.

The second example is debt relief for the poorest countries. Prior to 1995 the IFI's, again with broad backing from many G7 Treasuries, stood very firm against debt relief. The policy messaging of the time was sharp and hard, for fear that any opening would be the "thin end of the wedge" through which large-scale debt write downs would break open the IFI's. In 1995, the policy messaging changed and indeed began to call for debt relief.[4] It is hard to believe that analysis and evidence suddenly revealed the truth in 1995. Rather, the G7

Treasuries and the IFI's recognized political pressure from the growing global coalition for debt relief. But the negotiating stance adopted before 1995 sowed seeds of mutual suspicion that affect the dialogue on debt relief today, even under very different circumstances.

There is a second strand of argument in play on the simplicity or complexity of policy messages, this time directed at the IFI's and Aid agencies by some elements of Group A, particularly some in the Financial Press and in the G7 Treasuries. This is that these agencies should keep their policy messages simple, for fear that any complications and nuances will lead them into ever more complicated activities. Keeping their messages simple, in this view, will save the aid agencies from themselves, or at least from their tendency to take on a broader and broader development agenda. This point is made in the context of economic policies, but also in fear that the agreement on the importance of institutions, for example, may lead aid agencies to intervene where they cannot and should not.

Some clear thinking is needed here. It is perfectly coherent to hold simultaneously the view that the consequences of economic policy for distribution and poverty are complex and nuanced, and that aid agencies and donors cannot and should not attempt too complex a set of interventions in developing countries. Indeed, there is an argument to be made for outside intervention to be highly cautious precisely because of the complexity of the situation on the ground. This is certainly true of institutional reform, but it is also true of economic policy. What is problematic, however, is to present a falsely simple view of the world in the policy messaging emerging from aid agency analysis, as a device to restrain complex and unproductive expansionism by aid agencies. The latter problem must be faced on its own terms, and must not be allowed to influence the synthesis of analysis.

If the world is complex, or if the evidence is uncertain, or if legitimate differences in perspective and framework explain differences in conclusions, analysis must take these on board.

Moreover, the policy messaging that comes from such analysis must reflect the nature of those complexities. Inappropriate simplifying and hardening of policy messages, either as a way of constraining the operations of an aid agency, or as a negotiating device because of the fear that nuancing will be seen as a sign of weakness in policy debate, will only serve to polarize the debate further and will not be conducive to broad-based dialogue.

9. CONCLUSION

When the institution whose self-stated mission it is to eradicate poverty can only hold its Annual Meetings under siege from those who believe its mission is to further the cause of the rich and powerful, there is clearly a gap to be bridged. Moreover, the gap is not just between the IFI's and their critics. There is a growing divide on key areas of economic policy, even as agreement broadens in other areas. Indeed, the conflict over economic policy gets more intense as the areas of disagreement shrink to what seem to be an irreduceable core.

This paper has argued that underlying the seemingly intractable differences are key differences of perspective and framework on Aggregation, Time Horizon and Market Structure. Simply recognizing and understanding the underlying nature of the disagreements in these terms would be one step in bridging the gap. But more is needed. More is needed from both sides, but my focus here is on Group A. For those at the more academic end of that spectrum, the message is that explicitly taking into account these complications is more likely to shift the intellectual frontier than falling back yet again on conventional analysis. [5] For those at the more operational and policy end of the spectrum, especially those in policy-making and policy-implementing institutions, the message is that recognizing and trying to understand legitimate alternative views on economic policy, being open and nuanced in messages rather than being closed and hard, is not only good analytics, it is good politics as well.

NOTES

1. Most of this consultation was under the auspices of the World Bank's World Development Report on Poverty, of which I was Director until I resigned in May 2000.

2. In July 1999 I was involved in an immersion exercise organized by SEWA and the German Institute for North-South Dialogue. Officials from aid agencies and parliaments were taken by SEWA to experience for a

few days the lives of the women SEWA works for and with.

3. I include myself among those who have had such reactions.

4. As the World Bank's Chief Economist for Africa, in 1995–96 I was a member of the joint World Bank/IMF Task Force which put together the first proposal for debt relief to the Heavily Indebted Poor Countries (HIPC).

5. An equally interesting set of further analytical issues is opened up when interactions between Aggregation, Time Horizon and Market Structure are considered.

A
Global Poverty

[5]

Inequality Among World Citizens: 1820–1992

By FRANÇOIS BOURGUIGNON AND CHRISTIAN MORRISSON*

This paper investigates the distribution of well being among world citizens during the last two centuries. The estimates show that inequality of world distribution of income worsened from the beginning of the 19th century to World War II and after that seems to have stabilized or to have grown more slowly. In the early 19th century most inequality was due to differences within countries; later, it was due to differences between countries. Inequality in longevity, also increased during the 19th century, but then was reversed in the second half of the 20th century, perhaps mitigating the failure of income inequality to improve in the last decades. (JEL D31, F0, N0, O0)

The revival of interest in empirical growth economics during the 1990's brought with it a revival of interest in the world distribution of income. Indeed, most of the recent literature on convergence of GDP per capita across countries goes beyond theoretical issues of the determinants of the economic growth of nations. It deals with the world distribution of income and with whether the distribution between rich and poor is likely to equalize or to become more polarized in the long run.[1]

This treatment of world inequality is oversimplified because it considers all citizens in a given country as perfectly identical. By ignoring income disparities within countries, the recent empirical growth literature gives a biased view of the evolution of world inequality over time, clearly underestimating it. This line of work focuses on "international" rather than "world" inequality. By 1820, for instance, this paper estimates that the Gini coefficient for world distribution of income was 0.50 whereas

it would have been only 0.16 if individual incomes had been equal within each country.

A possible justification for focusing on international differences in GDP per capita is that they tend to change more quickly and more dramatically than national differences. Therefore, the dynamics of the world distribution of income would derive mainly from the component of world inequality that arises from the evolution of differences between countries rather than within countries. Indeed, this paper shows that inequality among countries is a key factor in explaining world inequality. But it also shows that world inequality is not well approximated by the hypothesis that all citizens within a country have the same income.

Many attempts have been made to estimate changes in world inequality of personal incomes.[2] This paper, by updating previous work from the 1950's to the 1980's and extending it back to the beginning of the 19th century, is the first to take a broad historical view. This view of world inequality over almost two centuries differs substantially from the literature on world economic inequality in the post-World War II

* Bourguignon: Delta, 48 Boulevard Jourdan, 75014 Paris, France (e-mail: bourg@delta.ens.fr) and World Bank; Morrisson: University Paris I and Delta, 36 Chemin Desvallières, 92410 Ville d'Avray, France. We thank Anthony Atkinson, Gary Fields, Branko Milanovic, and two anonymous referees for helpful comments on earlier drafts of this paper. We also thank participants at seminars sponsored by the World Bank and the International Labour Organization. Assistance by Bénédicte Sabatier is gratefully acknowledged. Any errors remain the authors' responsibility.

[1] See the 1997 symposium of the *Journal of Economic Perspectives* on the "Distribution of World Income," which deals with convergence issues, especially the articles by Charles I. Jones (1997) and Lant Pritchett (1997). See also Danny T. Quah (1996a, b).

[2] Studies on the postwar period until the 1980's include Alan P. Kirman and Luigi M. Tomasini (1969), John Whalley (1979), Albert Berry et al. (1983a, b, 1991), Irma Adelman (1984), Robert Summers et al. (1984), Margaret E. Grosh and E. Wayne Nafziger (1986), Henri Theil (1989), Pan A. Yotopoulos (1989), Martin Ravallion et al. (1991), Ronald V. A. Sprout and James H. Weaver (1992), Theil and James L. Seale, Jr. (1994), and T. Paul Schultz (1998). For recent estimates directly based on available national household surveys see Shaohua Chen and Ravallion (2000) and Branko Milanovic (2002).

era. It also differs from the limited, historically oriented literature (William J. Baumol et al., 1994; Pritchett, 1997) because it provides a quantitative rather than a qualitative picture of the evolution of world income inequality.

This paper shows that world income inequality was already high in the early 19th century (a Gini coefficient of 0.50), when the industrial revolution was under way in Britain and beginning in France. Then, with the spreading of the industrial revolution to Western Europe and to European-populated countries in the Americas and the Pacific—referred to, following Angus Maddison (1995), as the "European offshoots"—and increasing inequality within these booming countries, world inequality soared. From 1820 to the eve of World War I, inequality rose almost continuously. The Gini coefficient went from 0.50 to 0.61, and the Theil index from 0.52 to 0.79. The increase in inequality decelerated somewhat between the wars and slowed even more after 1950. By then, however, the world Gini coefficient had reached 0.64, a level of inequality unknown in most contemporary societies (even today's more inegalitarian countries have Gini coefficients less than 0.60). Roughly speaking, world inequality peaked in the middle of the 20th century after more than a century of continuous divergence. Changes during the last 50 years look minor compared with that dramatic evolution, and the situation appears to be stabilizing.[3]

This overall evolution of world inequality hides complex mechanisms and changes in the nationality of individuals at various levels in the world income hierarchy. For instance, during the initial period of world divergence, strong convergence was taking place among European countries and their offshoots in America and the Pacific after 1890, whereas income disparities between this group of countries and the rest of the world were growing. Likewise, the apparent stabilization of world income distribution since 1950 reflects a relative slowing of economic growth among European countries and their offshoots, a catching up by Japan and East Asia, and the take-off of China beginning in the 1980's. However, differences in growth in GDP

per capita among countries are insufficient to explain this complex evolution in the 19th or 20th century. For instance, China's growth performance has been important in shaping the evolution of the world distribution of income because of China's exceptionally large demographic weight and its dramatic changes in income distribution. Similarly, the increased world disparities observed in the 19th century as a consequence of the industrial revolution had much to do with initial population size in Western Europe and its growth rate. This paper's main contribution is a detailed description of the evolution of world income distribution over the last two centuries. Moreover, the paper quantifies the importance of aggregate economic growth, population growth, and the structure of domestic income inequalities in this process.

Income is only one dimension of economic well being. Any analysis of the evolution of world inequality should also take other dimensions into account. Unfortunately, finding historical data for these other dimensions is even more difficult than finding data for income. This paper considers the evolution of inequality in longevity around the world, using national estimates of life expectancy at various points in time. That evolution parallels the evolution of income for about a century, after which it reversed, unlike the evolution of income inequality. If life expectancy is taken as a proxy for the health of a population, then evidence suggests that health disparities are probably not much larger today than they were in the early 19th century. Whether this should be interpreted as mitigating the failure of world income inequality to decline is a difficult conceptual question and is not tackled here. However, it is worth noting that the evolution of world inequality may not be the same along income and nonincome dimensions of well being.

In Section I, the paper first looks at the data and the methodology used to reconstitute the world distribution of income while taking domestic income disparities into account rather than assuming no heterogeneity within countries, as most of the recent literature does. Section II presents the findings on the overall evolution of world income distribution since 1820 and the results of sensitivity analysis for several assumptions made in constructing the data base. It also compares this evolution with and without accounting for domestic income

---

[3] Note that the estimates obtained by Milanovic (2002) would not suggest such a deceleration in the increase of world inequality. This is discussed in more detail later in this paper.

inequality. Section III provides a partial explanation of changes in world income distribution by decomposing the changes into the contribution of three components: the evolution of the world structure of GDP per capita, the structure of population, and domestic income inequality. It also analyzes the movement of countries and world citizens along the world income scale. Section IV focuses on changes in world disparities in life expectancy. The main findings are summarized in the concluding section.

I. Methodology and Data for the World Distribution of Income

Estimation of the distribution of income relies on three types of data for each country (denoted by i) included in the analysis: real GDP per capita, Y_i, expressed in constant purchasing power parity (PPP) dollars; population, N_i; and the distribution of income summarized by nine decile income shares, D_{ij}, $j = 1, ..., 9$ and the top two vintile shares, D_{ij}, $j = 10, 11$. The world distribution is then obtained by assuming that each quantile in a country is made up of individuals with identical incomes. For each country, nine groups are defined of $0.1N_i$ people with income $y_{ij} = 10Y_i^* \times D_{ij}$, for $j = 1, ..., 9$ and two groups of $0.05N_i$ people with income $y_{ii} = 20Y_i \times D_{ij}$, for $j = 10, 11$. These groups are pooled and ranged by income and then the cumulative function and Lorenz curve of the world distribution of income are computed. With n countries, these two functions are thus described by $11n$ points. Income inequality measures are computed on these $11n$ groups. It is also possible to follow the country composition of the various quantiles of the world distribution (what share of the top centile of the world belongs to country X?) and the world rank of the various quantiles of a given country (what share of the population of country X is in the top world decile, or any other quantile, of the world distribution?)

Data on GDP per capita and population are from Maddison (1995), the first to construct a consistent historical series starting as early as 1820 for some countries and ending in 1992. Because the data series for many Eastern European and non-European countries did not start until some time between 1870 and 1913, the original series needed to be extended back to 1820. To fill in the gaps, growth rates observed

for comparable neighboring countries over the same period were used. Countries were also grouped in a slightly more aggregated way than in Maddison (1995) to avoid dealing with countries that were too small to affect world income distribution and to minimize problems of missing income distribution data (see the Appendix for groupings). The groupings were based on considerations of historical consistency and homogeneity. For instance, Austria, Hungary, and Czechoslovakia were grouped because they share obvious common characteristics over the 1820–1992 period, not just the post-World War II period. Similarly, Germany was kept united throughout the whole period. Argentina and Chile, two Latin American countries with recent European immigration, were also considered jointly, as were Taiwan and the Republic of Korea, two economies that shared a similar evolution over the last 40 years and similar histories of economic growth and income distribution during the previous hundred years or so.

Data were assembled for 33 countries or groups of countries. Each country or county group represents at least 1 percent of world population or world GDP in 1950. None of them can thus be thought of as negligible in the world economy. Countries like China,[4] India, Italy, and the United States, whose weight in the world is significant, are considered individually. The groups include small groups of comparable, medium-size countries and large groups of very small countries that came into existence only relatively recently and so could not be followed over a much longer period. For instance, Sub-Saharan Africa is broken down into four countries or groups: Nigeria, the largest country in the region; South Africa; Cote d'Ivoire, Ghana, and Kenya, three countries with a similar economic evolution; and the remaining 46 countries. Data are available, though very imperfectly, for the first three groups, whereas for the countries in the last group data are limited to the recent past.

To permit a simpler analysis of the evolution of the distribution of world income, the 33

---

[4] There has been some discussion on the recent growth performance of China. The calculations used here correspond to Maddison's (1995) "fast growth" scenario. Calculations assuming more modest growth performance were also made. They are not reported here for lack of space; however, they do not lead to fundamentally different conclusions.

groups were also aggregated into six blocks, defined geographically, economically, or historically: Africa; Asia excluding the "dragons" (Japan, Korea, and Taiwan); the Asian dragons; Latin America excluding Argentina and Chile; Eastern Europe (Bulgaria, Greece, Poland, Romania, Russia, Turkey, and Yugoslavia); and Western Europe and offshoots (all of Western Europe, including Austria, Hungary, and Czechoslovakia, and its offshoots in America, including Argentina and Chile, and in the Pacific).

Because of the obvious discrepancy between household purchasing power and GDP per capita, using GDP per capita in place of mean personal income may bias the estimation of the evolution of world inequality. Correcting for the share of nonhousehold income in GDP or the share of nonconsumption expenditures or taking into account the effects of changes in the terms of trade on the purchasing power of national agents proved impossible for the historical period. For comparability reasons, the GDP per capita convention was retained even after 1950, though a better approximation of international differences in mean living standards would have been possible.

Data sources for income distribution in the 33 country groups differ by period under analysis. Data are generally size-weighted disposable household income per capita.[5] For the post-World War II period, the data are updated from Berry et al. (1983a, b). For the pre-World War II period, data for today's developed countries are from existing historical series and adapted to fit the decile/vintile definition. Data for the United States and the United Kingdom are from Peter Lindert (2000). Data for continental Europe are from Morrisson (2000). Distribution data are available or can be guessed from available historical evidence for a few other countries for a few dates prior to 1950. For the remaining countries and country groups, distribution was arbitrarily assumed to be the same as in a similar country for which some evidence was available for the appropriate period. (The data, data sources, and assumptions behind

them are available at: ⟨http://www.delta.ens. fr/XIX⟩.)

In view of these assumptions, it would be unwise to take the resulting estimates of national income distribution at face value. This also holds for GDP per capita estimates for the distant past. To gauge the resulting imprecision in world distribution estimates, measurement errors were generated randomly on Y_i and D_{ij}, and Monte Carlo experiments were conducted to determine plausible confidence intervals for world inequality measures.

Multiplicative measurement errors on GDP per capita are assumed to be distributed normally with mean unity and a standard deviation of 10 percent during the 19th century, 5 percent for the first half of the 20th century, 2.5 percent after 1950, and 0 in 1992. These seemed reasonable orders of magnitude. For distribution data, stochastic deviations from central estimates, D_{il}^0 were specified as:

$$(1) \quad D_{ij} = D_{ij}^0 + u_i \cdot (D_j^M - D_{ij}) + v_i \cdot (D_j^m - D_{ij})$$

where u_i and v_i are two independent, normally distributed, zero-mean random variables with identical standard deviation, and D_j^M and D_j^m are two arbitrary reference distributions corresponding to the most and the least inegalitarian distributions among all directly observed distributions. The standard deviation of the measurement error terms, u_i and v_i, was calibrated so that the resulting standard deviation of the Gini coefficient averaged 2 percentage points in the 19th century and 1 percentage point in the 20th century. With the width of the 95-percent confidence interval approximately equal to double these values, these seemed reasonable orders of magnitude. Indeed, a Gini coefficient of 0.44 rather than 0.40 would today imply a very significant difference in our knowledge of the distribution. All these measurement errors are drawn independently for all countries for all dates, for GDP per capita, and for the distribution of income.

II. Evolution of World Distribution of Income Since 1820

Table 1 shows the shares of various income quantiles in world income and a set of standard inequality measures for selected years at 20- to 30-year intervals over the whole period. Stan-

---

[5] Distribution data in agreement with this definition are generally available for the recent period. For more distant periods, available distribution data have been corrected in an approximate way to fit the same definition.

TABLE 1—THE WORLD DISTRIBUTION OF INCOME AND LIFE EXPECTANCY:
INEQUALITY AND POVERTY INDICES FOR SELECTED YEARS

Index	1820		1850	1870	1890	1910	
	Estimate	SE[a]				Estimate	SE[a]
Income shares (percents)							
Bottom 20 percent	4.7	0.16	4.3	3.8	3.4	3.0	0.11
Bottom 40 percent	13.5	0.39	12.1	11.0	9.9	8.8	0.24
Bottom 60 percent	25.7	0.61	23.3	21.4	19.5	17.6	0.37
Bottom 80 percent	43.7	0.74	40.7	38.0	35.0	33.0	0.48
Top 10 percent	42.8	0.64	45.2	47.6	49.8	50.9	0.52
Top 5 percent	31.8	0.51	32.2	33.4	34.9	36.7	0.54
Summary inequality measures							
Coefficient of Gini	0.500	0.009	0.532	0.560	0.588	0.610	0.005
Theil index	0.522	0.018	0.598	0.672	0.745	0.797	0.017
Mean logarithmic deviation	0.422	0.016	0.485	0.544	0.610	0.668	0.015
Standard deviation of logarithm	0.826	0.016	0.873	0.919	0.971	1.027	0.015
Mean world income (PPP $ 1990)	658.7	23.2	735.7	890.0	1,113.8	1,459.9	24.1
World population (millions)	1,057.0		1,201.1	1,266.0	1,450.5	1,719.0	
Poverty							
Headcount (percents)							
Poverty	94.4	0.32	92.5	89.6	85.7	82.4	0.38
Extreme poverty	83.9	0.94	81.5	75.4	71.7	65.6	1.21
Headcount (millions)							
Poverty	997.8	3.4	1,110.5	1,134.3	1,243.6	1,416.5	8.2
Extreme poverty	886.8	9.9	978.8	954.0	1,040.5	1,127.7	24.1
Life expectancy							
Mean	26.5				29.9	32.8	
Theil index (between countries)	0.012				0.032	0.045	

[a] The computation of these standard errors is explained in the text.

dard errors of these inequality measures, computed in the Monte Carlo experiment described above, are reported for a few years. Figure 1 shows the evolution of density curves estimated using Kernel techniques on country decile observations. For the sake of clarity only four curves are shown, which delimitate in an obvious way the period under analysis.

The evolution shown by these indicators is unambiguous. World inequality worsened quickly and more or less continuously from 1820 to 1950, pausing only between 1910 and 1929. The rate of increase then decelerated considerably. On average, the Gini coefficient rose by 1 percentage point every decade from 1820 to 1950 and then almost leveled off between 1950 and 1992. On closer inspection, however, the indicators in Table 1 reveal a slightly more intricate picture for 1950–1992. Income distribution continued to worsen during the period, improving only between 1950 and 1960 and showing some signs of stability between 1970 and 1992. In particular, the share of the four bottom world deciles stopped falling between

1980 and 1992 for the first time since 1820, but that of the top decile increased again after a slight drop in the 1950's.

This finding is robust with respect to measurement errors. Since the distribution of all summary measures was close to normal, twice the standard error reported in Table 1 in each direction corresponds to a 95-percent confidence interval. With these confidence intervals, the overall imprecision in the change in the Gini coefficient during 1820–1950 does not exceed 2.5 percentage points, whereas the estimated increase is 14 percentage points. After 1950, however, measurement errors make the continuing increase in world income inequality ambiguous. Both conclusions apply to all summary inequality measures, including the ordinates of the Lorenz curve at the top of Table 1. All distributions observed in the 19th century Lorenz-dominate all distributions observed in the 20th century, even when measurement errors are taken into account. At the other end of the period, the distribution in 1992 is Lorenz-dominated by all distributions observed before

TABLE 1—*Continued*

	1950					1992	
1929	Estimate	SE[a]	1960	1970	1980	Estimate	SE[a]
2.9	2.4	0.04	2.4	2.2	2.0	2.2	0.03
8.2	6.8	0.10	6.8	6.1	5.7	6.4	0.07
16.7	14.2	0.17	14.1	12.8	12.5	13.5	0.10
32.3	31.1	0.23	31.9	30.4	29.5	28.2	0.13
49.8	51.3	0.31	50.0	50.8	51.6	53.4	0.14
35.0	35.5	0.31	34.1	34.2	35.0	36.0	0.19
0.616	0.640	0.002	0.635	0.650	0.657	0.657	0.001
0.777	0.805	0.009	0.776	0.808	0.829	0.855	0.005
0.690	0.775	0.008	0.766	0.823	0.850	0.827	0.005
1.064	1.154	0.007	1.161	1.210	1.234	1.184	0.005
1,817.1	2,145.5	16.1	2,798.6	3,773.8	4,544.0	4,962.0	—
2,042.1	2,511.3		3,024.7	3,664.5	4,414.0	5,459.1	
75.9	71.9	1.07	64.3	60.1	55.0	51.3	1.06
56.3	54.8	0.42	44.0	35.6	31.5	23.7	0.52
1,550.5	1,805.6	26.8	1,946.5	2,200.7	2,426.6	2,800.5	57.8
1,149.7	1,376.2	9.0	1,330.1	1,304.7	1,390.3	1,293.8	24.1
38.5	50.1			59.4		61.1	
0.046	0.025			0.012		0.013	

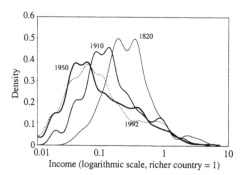

FIGURE 1. GAUSSIAN KERNEL ESTIMATE OF THE DENSITY
OF THE WORLD INCOME DISTRIBUTION:
1820, 1910, 1950, AND 1992

1950. However, comparison with the 1950, 1970, and 1980 distributions yields ambiguous results when confidence intervals are taken into account.[6]

The Lorenz-dominance criterion ignores gains in social welfare due to a higher mean income by focusing exclusively on the distribution of *relative* incomes. Changes in world social welfare may be gauged by using generalized Lorenz dominance, which compares the absolute income of successively poorer segments of the population.[7] Simple calculations made from the data in Table 1 show that this dominance criterion breaks down only once, between 1929 and 1950. Except for that interval, the mean income of all bottom quantiles of the world distribution increased continuously.

The change in the world distribution of income is dramatically illustrated by the evolution of the density curve, as shown in Figure 1. To

---

[6] Using estimates directly based on household surveys, Milanovic (2002) finds an unambiguous increase in world

inequality between 1987 and 1997. This does not necessarily contradict the results here. World inequality may have increased since 1992 or the use of GDP per capita rather than mean household income as directly estimated in household surveys may cause some discrepancy over a relatively short period of time.

[7] On this concept, see Anthony F. Shorrocks (1983).

make the curves comparable over time, income was normalized by the mean income of the richest country. The continuous and rapid increase in world inequality is noticeable with the leftward shift of the main modes of the distribution and the lengthening of its right-hand tail. In conformity with the results reported above, this shift stops after 1950. Another noticeable change is the shift of the secondary mode in the right-hand part of the curve. This mode, representing the distribution of income in the richest countries, tends to move leftward at an approximately constant distance from the first mode and to become more prominent over time. Between 1950 and 1992, however, this evolution seems to have been reversed.

In addition to the relative income scales explored in Figure 1 and through inequality measures, it is interesting to look at absolute scales. The poverty and extreme poverty ratios reported in Table 1 show the proportion of the world population below two absolute income thresholds. The poverty lines were calibrated so that poverty and extreme poverty headcounts in 1992 coincided roughly with estimates from other sources (see World Bank, 1990, 2001; Chen and Ravallion, 2000): 2.8 billion and 1.3 billion people, respectively.[8] The poverty lines are then taken to be constant over time.

With this definition of poverty, the worsening of the world distribution of income was not severe enough to cause the proportion of poor people to increase despite the growth in world mean income. In effect, world economic growth, though strongly inegalitarian, contributed to a steady decline in the headcount measure of poverty throughout the period under analysis. Over the 172 years considered here, the mean income of world inhabitants increased by a factor of 7.6. The mean income of the bottom 20 percent increased only by a factor of slightly more than 3, that of the bottom 60 percent by about 4, and that of the top decile by almost 10. At the same time, however, the extreme poverty headcount fell from 84 percent of the world population in 1820 to 24 percent in 1992. Even with the weaker definition of pov-

erty, the drop is substantial: from more than 90 percent in 1820 to 51.3 percent in 1992.

While the poor declined steadily as a proportion of the population during the last two centuries, the number of poor people continued to rise. The number of people in extreme poverty rose as well, although the increase seems to have stopped in the last 20 years or so. Both evolutions result from a complex combination of effects linked to growth in the mean income of the world population, changes in its distribution, and differential rates of population growth along the world income scale. But changes in world distribution of income played a major role. World economic growth since 1820 could have caused poverty to decline dramatically, despite population growth, had the world distribution of income remained unchanged—that is, had the growth rate of income been the same across and within countries. Had that been the case, the number of poor people would have been 650 million in 1992 rather than 2.8 billion and the number of extremely poor people 150 million instead of 1.3 billion. Likewise, the leveling off in the number of extremely poor people since 1970 can be attributed to the stabilization of their relative position since then.

Differences in country economic growth rates practically explain all of the increase in world inequality and in the number of poor people. Table 2 decomposes world inequality into that due to income disparities within a country or country group and that due to disparities between countries, using two inequality measures. The within-country component of inequality is obtained by difference and corresponds to average country inequality weighted by total income for the Theil index or total population for the mean logarithmic deviation (see Bourguignon, 1979; Shorrocks, 1980). The between-country component refers to the inequality that would be observed if incomes were identical within each country.

As expected, within-country inequality decreased as a share of world inequality over the 1820–1992 period, though it remained an essential part of total inequality throughout the period (see Table 2). It represented 80 percent and more of total inequality in the first half of the 19th century, a time when most countries were at about the same income level. Essentially, the United Kingdom, some continental European countries, and the United States were

---

[8] These definitions correspond to poverty lines equal to consumption per capita of $2 and $1 a day, expressed in 1985 PPP.

TABLE 2—DECOMPOSITION OF WORLD INCOME INEQUALITY INTO "WITHIN" AND "BETWEEN" INEQUALITY
(VARIOUS INEQUALITY MEASURES)

| | Theil index | | | Mean logarithmic deviation | | | Standard deviation of logarithm | |
Year	Inequality within country groups	Inequality between country groups	Total inequality	Inequality within country groups	Inequality between country groups	Total inequality	Inequality between country groups	Total inequality
1820	0.462	0.061	0.522	0.370	0.053	0.422	0.300	0.826
1850	0.470	0.128	0.598	0.374	0.111	0.485	0.432	0.873
1870	0.484	0.188	0.672	0.382	0.162	0.544	0.515	0.920
1890	0.495	0.250	0.745	0.393	0.217	0.610	0.592	0.971
1910	0.498	0.299	0.797	0.399	0.269	0.668	0.668	1.027
1929	0.412	0.365	0.777	0.356	0.334	0.690	0.747	1.064
1950	0.323	0.482	0.805	0.303	0.472	0.775	0.907	1.154
1960	0.318	0.458	0.776	0.300	0.466	0.766	0.920	1.161
1970	0.315	0.492	0.808	0.304	0.518	0.823	0.977	1.210
1980	0.330	0.499	0.829	0.321	0.528	0.850	0.994	1.234
1992	0.342	0.513	0.855	0.332	0.495	0.827	0.926	1.184

the only exceptions. GDP per capita in China or India was around $500 (in 1990 PPP); that of the United Kingdom was only three times larger. The gap between countries widened rapidly, however. By 1910 the differential between the United Kingdom and China had risen to 6:1 and by 1950 to 10:1. This widening gap plus the substantial decline in within-country inequality between 1910 and 1950 explain why, by 1950, within-country inequality accounted for only 40 percent of total world inequality—half its share in 1820. Thus the increase in between-country inequality was much larger than the increase in overall inequality—as measured by the Theil index or the mean logarithmic deviation—between 1820 and 1950. In the postwar period, the shares of the within-country and between-country components of inequality seem to have stabilized.[9]

The within-country component of world inequality is sufficiently important for the density function of the world distribution of income to be substantially different when country income decile information is used, as in Figure 1, and when they are not, as in Figure 2. The same is true of the evolution of density curves. Figure 2 shows Kernel estimates of the density func-

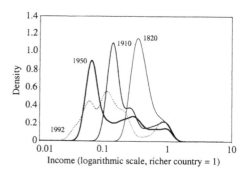

FIGURE 2. GAUSSIAN KERNEL ESTIMATE OF THE DENSITY OF THE WORLD INCOME DISTRIBUTION WHEN INEQUALITY WITHIN COUNTRIES IS IGNORED: 1820, 1910, 1950, AND 1992

tion using GDP per capita for the groups of countries in the analysis. The density curve for 1820 has a single mode and a small hump at the bottom right end of the curve. The corresponding curve in Figure 1 was flatter with a double-peaked main mode and a secondary mode on the right tail. Over time, the density curve shifts leftward, as in Figure 1, but two secondary modes appear in 1910 and become more prominent in 1950. This evolution is much less pronounced in Figure 1. Likewise, there is a dramatic flattening of the density curve between 1950 and 1992 and a double mode appears in the left half of the curve. No such dramatic

---

[9] The figures on the change in inequality between countries are consistent with the rough estimates by Pritchett (1997). He found that the standard deviation of the logarithm of income per capita might have doubled between 1870 and 1990, increasing from 0.5 to a little more than 1.

change is observed when inequality within countries is taken into account.

This comparison of Figures 1 and 2 points out the danger of interpreting changes in the distribution of GDP per capita across countries (Fig. 2) as true changes in the world distribution of income, as much of the recent literature does. Economic analysis tends to consider countries as the logical statistical unit for assessing international convergence or divergence of income and to ignore population size. However, if the intention is to analyze the world distribution of income and the degree of inequality or poverty among world citizens, ignoring income disparities within countries may be misleading. The effect of changes in the world hierarchy of GDP per capita may have very different impacts on the distribution of income among world citizens depending on the degree of inequality in countries where income variations are largest.

III. Sources of Changes in the World Distribution of Income

What effect have economic and population growth and changes in domestic income distribution in the countries and country groups had on the evolution of world inequality? The contribution of changes in domestic income distribution is easily computed using the same decomposable measures as above.

The contributions of economic and population growth are a little more difficult to assess. The effect of a country's economic growth is evaluated by computing what the change in world inequality would have been had income per capita in that country grown at the same rate as mean world income per capita during the period under analysis. This permits capturing the effect on world inequality of the differential rate of growth between a country and the rest of the world.

The resulting decomposition is exact for relatively small countries, which cannot significantly affect world averages. Things are different for larger countries and a fortiori for regions. For that reason, the decomposition methodology is approximate—the sum of national contributions may differ from the observed change in inequality.[10] But since the

objective is to identify the major sources of change rather than to quantify them precisely, this is not a problem. The same hypothetical scenario of a common growth rate is used for evaluating the contribution of the population growth of a country or a region to the change in world inequality. Table 3 shows the results of that decomposition when the 33 country groups are aggregated into six regions. For simplicity, the period was broken into four intervals of 40–50 years each.

Whether inequality is measured by the Theil index or the mean logarithmic deviation, the dominant disequalizing force throughout the 19th century and the first half of the 20th century was the relatively slow economic growth of the Asian region, the most populated area of the world. Between 1820 and 1950, income per capita in that region, which represented almost two-thirds of the global population in the early 19th century, grew at an average annual rate of 0.2 percent, some 4.5 times slower than the world average and 6 times slower than the average for the Western European regions, including offshoots. India, the slowest growing large country in the world in that period, and China, which did little better, accounted for most of Asia's slow growth. Maddison's (1995) data suggest that income per capita increased slightly more than 10 percent in India and about 17 percent in China between 1820 and 1950 while the increase in European countries in which the industrial revolution started was around 400 percent—and bigger yet in their offshoots. True, the terminal years of this period were among the worst growth years for India and China for the last two centuries. The picture is less dramatic for the subperiod 1820–1910. Even so, however, Asia underperformed all the other regions of the world by a wide margin.

The second major world disequalizing factor was the rapid enrichment of the European population. The first century and a half after the beginning of the industrial revolution witnessed a dramatic divergence in the world economy as the richest countries became ever richer and the

---

[10] This decomposition discrepancy is reported at the bottom of each panel of Table 3. Note that there is no

perfect decomposition formula available in the present case. Ours generalizes the well-known methodology introduced by Dilip Mookherjee and Shorrocks (1982) to noninfinitesimal changes—which was also used in the context of the world distribution of income by Berry et al. (1983a).

TABLE 3—DECOMPOSITION OF CHANGE IN INEQUALITY BY REGIONAL INCOME, POPULATION, AND INEQUALITY EFFECTS

Source of change in world inequality	Africa	Asia	Japan, Korea, and Taiwan	Latin America	Eastern Europe	Europe and European settlements	Total	Total observed change in inequality	Discrepancy
A. *Theil Index:*									
1820–1870									
Difference in income growth from world average	0.005	**0.050**	0.002	0.000	0.000	**0.039**	**0.095**		
Difference in population growth from world average	0.000	0.003	0.000	0.001	0.001	0.010	**0.015**		
Within-country group inequality	0.001	0.001	0.000	0.000	0.000	**0.013**	0.016		
Total							**0.126**	0.149	−0.023
1870–1910									
Difference in income growth from world average	0.008	**0.068**	0.000	0.000	0.002	**0.032**	**0.110**		
Difference in population growth from world average	0.000	0.003	0.000	0.000	−0.002	0.007	0.007		
Within-country group inequality	0.001	0.004	0.000	0.001	0.006	−0.001	**0.010**		
Total							**0.127**	0.125	0.002
1910–1950									
Difference in income growth from world average	0.005	**0.110**	0.001	−0.003	−0.004	**0.050**	**0.159**		
Difference in population growth from world average	−0.001	0.000	−0.003	−0.001	0.003	−0.002	−0.004		
Within-country group inequality	0.004	**−0.010**	−0.003	0.000	**−0.038**	**−0.093**	**−0.139**		
Total							**0.016**	0.008	0.009
1950–1992									
Difference in income growth from world average	**0.015**	**−0.064**	0.003	0.001	**0.011**	**0.072**	**0.038**		
Difference in population growth from world average	0.003	**0.009**	0.004	−0.003	**0.015**	−0.005	**0.023**		
Within-country group inequality	0.005	**0.010**	0.000	0.002	0.000	**−0.035**	**−0.018**		
Total							**0.043**	0.050	−0.007
B. *Mean Logarithmic Deviation*									
1820–1870									
Difference in income growth from world average	0.004	**0.042**	0.000	0.001	0.000	**0.030**	**0.077**		
Difference in population growth from world average	0.000	0.004	0.000	0.001	0.003	**0.009**	0.017		
Within-country group inequality	0.001	0.001	0.000	0.000	0.000	0.008	0.010		
Total							**0.103**	0.121	−0.018
1870–1910									
Difference in income growth from world average	0.007	**0.063**	0.000	0.000	0.000	**0.026**	**0.095**		
Difference in population growth from world average	0.001	0.005	0.000	0.000	0.000	**0.009**	0.014		
Within-country group inequality	0.001	0.004	0.000	0.001	0.004	0.002	0.011		
Total							**0.121**	0.124	−0.003
1910–1950									
Difference in income growth from world average	0.005	**0.123**	0.001	−0.002	0.000	**0.046**	**0.174**		
Difference in population growth from world average	−0.004	0.002	−0.003	−0.001	0.002	−0.004	**−0.008**		
Within-country group inequality	0.006	**−0.016**	−0.003	0.000	**−0.035**	**−0.020**	**−0.069**		
Total							**0.097**	0.107	−0.010
1950–1992									
Difference in income growth from world average	**0.020**	**−0.083**	**0.042**	0.000	−0.001	**0.077**	**0.055**		
Difference in population growth from world average	−0.003	0.000	0.005	−0.004	0.012	**−0.041**	**−0.031**		
Within-country group inequality	**0.012**	**0.030**	−0.001	0.001	−0.002	**−0.011**	0.029		
Total							**0.053**	0.053	0.000

Note: Entries in bold correspond to dominant sources of change.

poorest countries were virtually cut off from economic growth.[11] The income differential between Europe and its offshoots on the one hand and Asia or Africa on the other—between the richest 20 percent of the world and the poorest 60 percent—soared from 1:3 in 1820 to 1:5 in 1910 to 1:9 in 1950. This enrichment of Europe plus the growing relative impoverishment of Asia between 1820 and 1950 represented an increase in inequality nearly equivalent to the total increase in world inequality for the whole 1820–1992 period.

The disequalizing contribution of European economic growth to world inequality did not vanish after 1950. Growth in Europe and its offshoots remained systematically higher than the world average during that period too. At the other extreme, however, a big change was taking place. Slow economic growth in Africa was now significantly increasing world inequality, while Asia's improving growth performance was resulting in a substantial drop in world inequality. Driving the dramatic evolution in the Asia region was China's impressive growth, especially in the last 12 years of the period under analysis.[12] Although other countries in Asia also grew faster than the world average during the last 40 years or so (except India[13]), China's growth dominates because of its size.

In addition to Asia's economic growth, a second set of equalizing forces has been the evolution of inequality within regions and countries. The most important change was the decline in inequality in Western Europe during the first half of the 20th century. Two primary forces lay behind that drop. First was the redistribution that took place in most developed countries in the period from before World War I until after World War II. Its impact on the world distribution of income was substantial as measured by an inequality measure like the Theil index, which gives more weight to changes at the top of the distribution. Together with the equalizing effect of the Soviet revolu-

tion in Russia and the socialization of Eastern European countries, this equalization of incomes within Western Europe offset a large part of the increase in world inequality arising from divergences in national economic growth rates. This compensation is less important with the mean logarithmic deviation than with the Theil index because of the lower weight it gives to richer countries.

The second force behind the drop in inequality in the Western Europe region was the convergence of mean incomes among European countries and their offshoots during the 20th century. Overall inequality within this group of countries increased slightly between 1820 and 1870, remained stable until 1910, and then fell substantially, causing a drop in the world Theil index of more than 12 percentage points (Table 3). Approximately half of this fall was due to the equalization of national income distributions just mentioned. The rest was due to the evolution of inequality *across* European countries.[14] The increase in European inequality between 1820 and 1870 reflects the divergent evolution of the Anglo-Saxon countries (Australia, Canada, the United Kingdom, and the United States) and the rest of Europe. Income per capita in the United Kingdom was about 40 percent higher than in continental Europe at the beginning of the 19th century. By 1870, this difference had doubled. In the aggregate, inequality changed only slightly between 1870 and 1910. But there was much underlying mobility. The United States and the United Kingdom switched ranks in the world income distribution, Germany returned to its initial position in the group, and Spain and Portugal replaced Chile and Argentina at the bottom of the scale. Some true convergence took place among European countries at the beginning of the 20th century, even though the U.S. advantage over other countries was reinforced at the end of World War II. Europe began to catch up with the United States afterward. As a consequence, inequality between countries in the European group in 1992 dropped back to the level observed in 1820. This very strong convergence, which also included the effects of the

[11] This finding corroborates the intuition developed by Pritchett (1997).

[12] This conclusion would still hold if the lowest estimate of Chinese growth found in the literature were used.

[13] Of course, the equalizing effect of Asian growth would be still stronger if the analysis were extended by a few years to take into account India's recent acceleration of growth.

[14] Indeed, the within-country component of inequality in Table 3 is defined at the *regional* level. It thus includes inequality across countries of the same region.

economic recovery after the war, explains the drop in European inequality shown in Table 3 and its important equalizing effect on the world distribution of income during the 20th century. This effect is less pronounced with the mean logarithmic deviation than with the Theil index, which emphasizes the top of the distribution, which includes most of the European population.

A similar convergence might have been expected as a result of the contribution of the Asian dragons—Japan, Korea, and Taiwan—to the evolution of the world distribution. It is not surprising that this group had no effect on the level of world inequality before 1950, when their growth was like that of other nonindustrial countries. Between 1950 and 1992, however, they leaped over several rungs in the world hierarchy of income, multiplying their income per capita by approximately 10 and moving from slightly below the world mean to the mean of the richest group of countries. This contributed to a worsening of world inequality, although the effect is substantial only with the mean logarithmic deviation (see Table 3).[15]

In sum, both disequalizing and equalizing forces contributed to the change in the world distribution of income from 1820 to 1992. On the disequalizing side, the main forces were the consistently better economic performance of European countries and their offshoots, the relatively poor growth performances of China and India until late in the 20th century, the divergence between Anglo-Saxon and the other European countries in the first half of the 19th century, and the slow growth of Africa in the second half of the 20th century. On the equalizing side, the main forces were the equalizing of incomes within Western European countries, Russia, and Eastern Europe in the interwar period and after World War II; the European countries quick catch-up to the United States after World War II; and China's outstanding growth performance in the last decade or two of the period. While the rapid growth of the Asian dragons was another important phenomenon in this period, the effect on world income distribution was ambiguous and limited.

Two factors have been ignored in this discussion. First, nothing has been said of Latin America because its economic growth over the last two centuries has roughly coincided with the world average. In other words, it has always been midway between the high rates of growth of the European group and the relatively slow rates observed in Asia and Africa. Second, it is remarkable that population growth rates do not seem to be associated with any big change in the world distribution of income. One reason is that changes in the regional structure of world population have not been very big. Over 170 years, the major change has been that the less populated regions in 1820, Africa and Latin America, have grown more rapidly than the others— the growth of the North American, Australian, Argentine, and Chilean populations being amalgamated with that of old Europe. Overall, this has been equivalent to Asia losing some of its demographic importance in favor of Africa and Latin America—not a very significant change for the world distribution of income. It must also be stressed that pure demographic changes have ambiguous effects on the distribution of income when they affect one end of the distribution more than the other, which leads to crossing Lorenz curves. As an example of this ambiguity, the population effect for 1950–1992 is inegalitarian with the Theil index but egalitarian with the mean logarithmic deviation (see Table 3).

Another dimension of the changes in the world distribution of income is the mobility of world citizens within the world income scale. Country differences in GDP per capita, population growth, and income distribution are responsible for changes in the world distribution of income, as analyzed above, and for mobility within the world income scale.

Table 4 shows the regional composition of various quantiles of the world distribution for selected years. Mobility of regional groups of individuals within the world income scale is responsible for changes in that composition, and results from a complex combination of relative changes in countries' relative mean income, population, and domestic income distribution. For instance, the increasing share of European countries and their offshoots in the top world decile between 1820 and 1950 resulted from both their relative increase in population and mean income between 1820 and 1910 and from

---

[15] This difference between the Theil index and the mean logarithmic deviation suggests that the growth of Asian dragons produced an ambiguous shift in the world Lorenz curve.

TABLE 4—REGIONAL COMPOSITION OF SELECTED WORLD QUANTILES: SELECTED YEARS (PERCENTS)

World quantiles	Africa	Asia	Japan, Korea, and Taiwan	Latin America	Eastern Europe	European countries and offshoots	Total
1820							
Total	6.9	64.9	3.6	1.8	8.2	14.6	100
Bottom 60 percent	7.9	75.8	3.2	1.7	6.0	5.3	100
Mid 30 percent	5.8	55.3	4.4	1.4	12.5	20.5	100
Top 10 percent	4.1	32.5	3.5	3.0	8.0	48.9	100
1910							
Total	6.2	51.6	3.7	3.8	12.9	21.7	100
Bottom 60 percent	8.1	71.1	2.9	4.1	9.5	4.4	100
Mid 30 percent	4.6	25.0	5.6	4.1	21.2	39.6	100
Top 10 percent	0.9	25.0	1.8	1.9	6.3	64.1	100
1950							
Total	8.9	49.6	4.5	5.5	10.9	20.7	100
Bottom 60 percent	12.7	74.4	2.7	4.6	3.5	2.1	100
Mid 30 percent	4.2	18.2	8.7	8.3	25.8	34.8	100
Top 10 percent	1.2	4.4	2.1	3.0	8.3	81.1	100
1992							
Total	12.0	54.8	3.5	7.6	8.3	13.8	100
Bottom 60 percent	17.4	72.7	0.0	6.5	3.2	0.3	100
Mid 30 percent	5.0	36.2	5.3	11.1	19.7	22.6	100
Top 10 percent	1.4	6.1	18.2	3.8	4.1	66.4	100

the increase in their mean income 1910 and 1950. Their declining share between 1950 and 1992 was due to a slower rate of population growth than in the rest of the world and to the rapid economic growth of the Japan, Korea, and Taiwan group, which moved a substantial number of people in that country group into the top world decile. In other words, Europe's ascending supremacy from 1820 to 1950 was checked by the economic rise of the Asian dragons and the relative decline in the European population.

At the other end of the spectrum, the dominant change has been the continuously increasing share of Africa among the world poor, an evolution that accelerated sharply during the 20th century. Because of Africa's rapid population growth and its lower than average economic growth, this region's share among the world's poorest 60 percent increased from 8 percent at the end of the 19th century to 17.5 percent in 1992. This evolution would be even more pronounced with a more restrictive definition of poverty. In 1950, only 12 percent of world inhabitants with incomes of less than half the world median income lived in Africa. By 1992, 30 percent did. Poverty, largely an Asian problem until just after World War II, is fast becoming an African problem. Asia, after a sharp decline from 1820 to 1950, is catching up

with more developed regions. Its share in the three mid-deciles of world income doubled from 18 to 36 percent between 1950 and 1992. Finally, Latin America's shares in world income followed its increasing share of the world population, with an increasing concentration in the middle deciles.

Another way of looking at the dynamics of the world distribution of income is to consider how citizens within countries perform on an income scale defined at the world level, the approach taken in the recent literature on convergence and mobility (see, in particular, Quah, 1996a). The corresponding transition matrices are shown in Table 5, with four income bands defined (as in Quah, 1996a) as simple proportions of the world mean.

The dominant impression from Table 5 is of extremely low mobility of individuals throughout the period of analysis. Less than 30 percent of people changed income band during successive 40-year intervals, and less than 10 percent did in the two extreme bands, except between 1910 and 1950. Mobility increased over time, though, by approximately 15 percentage points overall—and it changed direction. Until 1910, mobility was predominantly downward, whereas it was more balanced after 1910. Finally, the implications of the transition matrices shown in

TABLE 5—RELATIVE INCOME MOBILITY MATRIX AND MOBILITY RATIOS:
SELECTED PAIRS OF YEARS

Income in final year relative to world mean income (wmi)	Income in initial year relative to world mean income (wmi)				Total (share in world population)	Mobility ratios
	Less than 1/2 wmi	From 1/2 to 1 wmi	From 1 to 2 wmi	More than 2 wmi		
1820–1870						
Less than 1/2 wmi	98.8	35.0	0.0	0.0	52.3	
From 1/2 to 1 wmi	1.2	63.2	10.9	0.0	26.8	
From 1 to 2 wmi	0.0	1.8	80.2	3.7	12.2	
More than 2 wmi	0.0	0.0	8.9	96.3	8.6	
Total	39.1	39.2	14.0	7.7	100.0	
(Immobility ratio)						84.6
(Upward mobility)						3.0
(Downward mobility)						12.4
1870–1910						
Less than 1/2 wmi	99.5	38.3	0.0	0.0	58.9	
From 1/2 to 1 wmi	0.5	60.1	32.6	0.0	20.9	
From 1 to 2 wmi	0.0	1.6	63.1	7.5	10.0	
More than 2 wmi	0.0	0.0	4.3	92.5	10.3	
Total	48.9	26.8	13.8	10.5	100.0	
(Immobility ratio)						78.8
(Upward mobility)						1.6
(Downward mobility)						19.6
1910–1950						
Less than 1/2 wmi	91.7	31.3	0.0	0.0	57.9	
From 1/2 to 1 wmi	8.3	47.5	6.1	0.0	15.5	
From 1 to 2 wmi	0.1	21.2	65.8	19.6	14.2	
More than 2 wmi	0.0	0.0	28.1	80.4	12.5	
Total	55.8	21.4	11.1	11.7	100.0	
(Immobility ratio)						71.4
(Upward mobility)						14.4
(Downward mobility)						14.2
1950–1992						
Less than 1/2 wmi	89.7	20.5	0.0	0.0	56.2	
From 1/2 to 1 wmi	7.8	49.5	20.2	0.0	14.9	
From 1 to 2 wmi	1.7	18.4	45.2	4.8	10.4	
More than 2 wmi	0.8	11.6	34.6	95.2	18.5	
Total	59.1	15.5	13.0	12.4	100.0	
(Immobility ratio)						78.3
(Upward mobility)						15.2
(Downward mobility)						11.4

Notes: The table entries are initial year's population in each income band by income in the final year (percentage). The immobility ratio is the share of world population not changing relative income band. Upward (downward) mobility is the share of world population moving up (down) one income band or more.

Table 5 for the evolution of the world distribution of income changed over time too. In particular, the "twin peaks effect" noted by Quah (1996b), in which mobility leads to a polarized distribution of world income, is noticeable in the 1950–1992 period and to a much lesser extent in 1820–1870. In the two middle periods, comparing the "total" rows and columns of Table 5 simply shows a straight increase in the inequality of the distribution of relative income between the initial and the terminal year.

It is important to note that the changes in the mobility matrices are due largely to the growth performance of a small number of countries or country groups. Thus, the drop in inequality within and across European countries and their offshoots between 1910 and 1950 explains most of the increase in upward mobility in that period. Likewise, the acceleration of growth in China and the Asian dragons is responsible for the upward mobility observed from 1950 to 1992. Both phenomena can be viewed as exceptional. Thus, to consider the transition matrices for recent periods as stationary, as is often done in the convergence literature, seems largely unjustified in a historical perspective.[16]

IV. Other Dimensions of World Inequality: Life Expectancy

The current income of individuals, even aside from the question of whether average income per capita is satisfactorily proxied by GDP per capita, is a restricted definition of welfare. A more comprehensive definition of economic well being would consider individuals over their lifetime, and inequality would be evaluated not just within the population alive at a point in time but within successive cohorts. To the extent that life expectancy is a summary of people's health conditions, it is another dimension of individual welfare, independent of income and comparable to, but easier to evaluate than other nonincome dimensions like safety, freedom, or access to justice or education. Thus, life expectancy could be another source of inequality, both within and across countries.

Estimates of life expectancy for the 33 countries and country groups considered here were gathered from the historical demography literature for the pre-1950 period and from the United Nations *Demographic Yearbook* for the 1950–1992 period. For countries or periods for which no direct estimate was available, life expectancy was set arbitrarily to that of a comparable neighboring country.[17] Note that all individuals within a country or group of countries are assumed to have the same life expectancy. Thus,

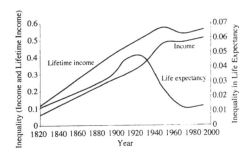

FIGURE 3. EVOLUTION OF INTERNATIONAL INEQUALITY IN INCOME, LIFETIME INCOME, AND LIFE EXPECTANCY (THEIL INDEX)

unlike for income, within-country inequality of life expectancy is assumed to be zero.

Average life expectancy in the world has more than doubled, rising from 26 years in 1820 to 60 years today (see bottom of Table 1). Progress was initially slow and deeply inegalitarian. Mean world life expectancy was only 33 years prior to World War II—an improvement of only seven years in more than a century. Underlying this evolution of the mean, however, was near stagnation in Asia and Africa, a seven-year increase in Latin America, and a nearly 17-year increase in European countries and their offshoots. As with income, inequality in life expectancy thus worsened considerably during the 19th century. Unlike income, however, world inequality in life expectancy fell considerably after 1930, as improvement in world mean life expectancy accelerated. Both trends were strongly influenced by the rapid catching up of countries left behind during the 19th century. Average life expectancy increased more than 20 years in several Asian countries between 1930 and 1992, but only 12 to 15 years in European countries. In relative terms, the difference is bigger still.

Thus the evolution of world inequality in life expectancy is quite different from that of GDP per capita (see Figure 3). Around 1930, divergence in life expectancy gave way to convergence.[18] There was no such turning point for income. At best, divergence decelerated after 1950, but it was not reversed.

---

[16] It is also worth noting that the mobility pattern in world distribution of income during the last 170 years seems far from Markovian, as is generally assumed in the convergence literature. For instance, multiplying the transition matrix of 1820–1870 by that of 1870–1910 results in a matrix that is substantially different from the one actually observed between 1820 and 1910.

[17] Statistical sources and data may be consulted at ⟨http://www.delta.ens.fr/XIX⟩.

[18] The burst of HIV in Africa might well reverse this trend in the future.

The evolution of life expectancy and of GDP per capita can be combined to determine the time path of world inequality of lifetime income. The upper curve in Figure 3 shows the evolution of world inequality of lifetime income, LY, defined in a standard way as (constant) current income (y) discounted over life expectancy (L):

$$(2) \qquad LY = y(1 - e^{-\delta L})/\delta.$$

The curve shown in Figure 3 is based on discount rate δ set to 2 percent per annum.[19]

As expected, the evolution of world inequality of lifetime income differs slightly from that of income alone. The initial divergence is reinforced since the increasing disparities in life expectancy compound the divergence in income. After 1950, however, the drop in world inequality in life expectancy combines with the deceleration of income divergence to produce a convergence of world lifetime income. However, the convergence of life expectancy seems to have stopped or slowed considerably during the last two decades of the period so that the evolution of world inequality of lifetime income parallels that of income. Simple simulation shows that this evolution is not very sensitive to changes in the discount rate within a reasonable range or, equivalently, to the inclusion of the growth rate of income in the equation. This combination of the two effects does not take into account the interaction between changes in life expectancy and changes in population growth rates. Life expectancy increased rapidly in developing countries after 1950, reducing the inequality that had built up in the 19th century. But population began to grow faster in these countries, with some nonneutral effects on the distribution of income.

V. Summary of Findings

Unlike the recent literature on income inequality, which focuses on the divergence of

GDP per capita across countries in the last 40 years, this paper focuses on a longer period and takes a more general perspective on world inequality. Because the analysis begins in 1820, it takes into account the major effects that the Industrial Revolution had on the world distribution of income. Because the analysis looks explicitly at the distribution of income within countries, it evaluates world inequality among individuals rather than countries. And because the analysis also takes into account the contribution of changes in world disparities in life expectancy, it incorporates a broader view of individual welfare.

To summarize, this analysis shows that world income inequality worsened dramatically over the past two centuries. The Gini coefficient increased 30 percent and the Theil index 60 percent between 1820 and 1992. This evolution was due mainly to a dramatic increase in inequality across countries or regions of the world. The "between" component of the Theil index went from 0.06 in 1820 to more than 0.50 in 1992. Changes in inequality within countries were important in some periods, most notably the drop in inequality within European countries and their offshoots in America and in the Pacific during the first half of the 20th century. In the long run, however, the increase in inequality across countries was the leading factor in the evolution of the world distribution of income. The burst of world income inequality now seems to be over. There is comparatively little difference between the world distribution today and in 1950. This does not mean that the distribution has become stable or that a convergence analogous to that witnessed among European countries and their offshoots in the early 20th century is beginning to take place on a world scale. On the contrary, the increasing concentration of world poverty in some regions of the world is worrying. When world inequality in lifetime income rather than current income is analyzed, 1950 seems to be an important turning point. World inequality seems to have fallen since 1950 as a result of the pronounced drop in international disparities in life expectancy. But now that disparities in life expectancy are back to the levels before the big divergence of the 19th century, this source of convergence has lost its influence.

---

[19] Note that equation (2) combines income and life expectancy in a very specific way. Another particular combination would be the equal-weight linear formula used by the United Nations Development Programme in computing the Human Development Index. For an in-depth discussion of the measurement of the resulting "multidimensional" inequality see Anthony B. Atkinson and Bourguignon (1982).

APPENDIX: LIST OF COUNTRIES AND COUNTRY GROUPS USED IN THE ANALYSIS

A) Africa

Côte d'Ivoire, Ghana, Kenya
Egypt
Nigeria
North Africa
South Africa
46 African countries

B) Asia

China
India
Indonesia
Bangladesh, Burma, Pakistan
Thailand, Philippines
45 Asian countries

C) Japan, Korea, Taiwan

Japan
Korea, Taiwan

D) Latin America

Brazil
México
Colombia, Peru, Venezuela
37 Latin American countries

E) Eastern Europe

Bulgaria, Greece, Romania, Yugoslavia
Poland
Russia
Turkey

F) Western Europe and European offshoots

Argentina, Chile
Australia, Canada, New Zealand
Austria, Czechoslovakia, Hungary
France
Germany
Italy
Scandinavian countries
Spain, Portugal
Switzerland, Benelux, and microstates
United Kingdom, Ireland
United States

REFERENCES

Adelman, Irma. "Development Strategies and the Size Distribution of World Income." *Middle East Technical University Studies in Development,* 1984, *11*(1–2), pp. 177–93.

Atkinson, Anthony B. and Bourguignon, François. "The Comparison of Multi-Dimensioned Distributions of Economic Status." *Review of Economic Studies,* April 1982, *49*(2), pp. 183–201.

Baumol, William J.; Nelson, Richard R. and Wolff, Edward N. "The Convergence of Productivity, Its Significance, and Its Varied Connotations," in William J. Baumol, Richard R. Nelson, and Edward N. Wolff, eds., *Convergence of productivity: Cross-national studies and historical evidence.* New York: Oxford University Press, 1994, pp. 3–19.

Berry, Albert; Bourguignon, François and Morrisson, Christian. "Changes in the World Distribution of Income between 1950 and 1977." *Economic Journal,* June 1983a, *93*(37), pp. 331–50.

_____. "The Level of World Inequality: How Much Can One Say?" *Review of Income and Wealth,* September 1983b, *29*(3), pp. 217–41.

_____. "Global Economic Inequality and Its Trends since 1950," in Lars Osberg, ed., *Economic inequality and poverty: International perspectives.* Armonk, NY: Sharpe, 1991, pp. 60–91.

Bourguignon, François. "Decomposable Income Inequality Measures." *Econometrica,* July 1979, *47*(4), pp. 901–20.

Chen, Shaohua and Ravallion, Martin. "How Did the World's Poorest Fare in the 1990s?" Mimeo, World Bank, 2000.

Grosh, Margaret E. and Nafziger, E. Wayne. "The Computation of World Income Distribution." *Economic Development and Cultural Change,* January 1986, *34*(2), pp. 347–59.

Jones, Charles I. "On the Evolution of the World Income Distribution." *Journal of Economic Perspectives,* Summer 1997, *11*(3), pp. 19–36.

Kirman, Alan P. and Tomasini, Luigi M. "A New Look at International Income Inequalities." *Economia Internazionale,* August 1969, *22*(3), pp. 437–61.

Lindert, Peter. "Three Centuries of Inequality in

Britain and America," in Anthony B. Atkinson and François Bourguignon, eds., *Handbook of income distribution.* Amsterdam: Elsevier, 2000.

Maddison, Angus. *Monitoring the world economy.* Paris: OECD, 1995.

Milanovic, Branko. "True World Income Distribution, 1988 and 1993: First Calculation Based on Household Surveys Alone." *Economic Journal,* January 2002, *112*(476), pp. 51–92.

Mookherjee, Dilip and Shorrocks, Anthony F. "A Decomposition Analysis of the Trend in UK Income Inequality." *Economic Journal,* December 1982, *92*(368), pp. 886–902.

Morrisson, Christian. "Historical Perspectives on Income Distribution: The Case of Europe," in Anthony B. Atkinson and François Bourguignon, eds., *Handbook of income distribution.* Amsterdam: Elsevier, 2000.

Pritchett, Lant. "Divergence, Big Time." *Journal of Economic Perspectives,* Summer 1997, *11*(3), pp. 3–17.

Quah, Danny T. "Empirics for Economic Growth and Convergence." *European Economic Review,* June 1996a, *40*(6), pp. 1353–75.

_____. "Twin Peaks: Growth and Convergence in Models of Distribution Dynamics." *Economic Journal,* July 1996b, *106*(437), pp. 1045–55.

Ravallion, Martin; Datt, Gaurav and van der Walle, Dominique. "Quantifying Absolute Poverty in the Developing World." *Review of Income and Wealth,* December 1991, *37*(4), pp. 345–61.

Schultz, T. Paul. "Inequality in the Distribution of Personal Income in the World: How it is Changing and Why." *Journal of Population Economics,* August 1998, *11*(3), pp. 307–44.

Shorrocks, Anthony F. "The Class of Additively Decomposable Inequality Measures." *Econometrica,* April 1980, *48*(3), pp. 613–25.

_____. "Ranking Income Distributions." *Economica,* February 1983, *50*(197), pp. 3–17.

Sprout, Ronald V. A. and Weaver, James H. "International Distribution of Income: 1960–1987." *Kyklos,* 1992, *45*(2), pp. 237–58.

Summers, Robert; Kravis, Irving B. and Heston, Alan. "Changes in the World Income Distribution." *Journal of Policy Modeling,* May 1984, *6*(2), pp. 237–69.

Theil, Henri. "The Development of International Inequality: 1960–1985." *Journal of Econometrics,* September 1989, *42*(1), pp. 145–55.

Theil, Henri and Seale, James L., Jr. "The Geographic Distribution of World Income, 1950–1990." *De Economist,* November 1994, *142*(4), pp. 387–419.

United Nations. *Demographic yearbook.* New York: United Nations Publications, various years.

Whalley, John. "The Worldwide Income Distribution: Some Speculative Calculations." *Review of Income and Wealth,* September 1979, *25*(3), pp. 261–76.

World Bank. *World development report 2000/2001: Attacking poverty.* Oxford, U.K.: Oxford University Press, 2001.

_____. *World development report, 1990.* Oxford, U.K.: Oxford University Press, 1990.

Yotopoulos, Pan A. "Distribution of Real Income: Within Countries and by World Income Classes." *Review of Income and Wealth,* December 1989, *35*(4), pp. 357–76.

[6]

MARTIN RAVALLION

World Bank

Competing Concepts of Inequality in the Globalization Debate

How much are the world's poor sharing in the gains from the economic growth fueled by greater economic integration? There are seemingly conflicting answers from the two sides of the ongoing debate on globalization and inequality. On one side, the website of a prominent nongovernmental organization (NGO) in the antiglobalization movement, the International Forum on Globalization, confidently claims that "globalization policies have . . . increased inequality between and within nations."[1] This stands in marked contrast to the claims made by those more favorable to globalization. For example, an article in the *Economist* magazine states with equal confidence that "globalization raises incomes, and the poor participate fully."[2]

Why do such different views persist? Surely the evidence would be conclusive one way or the other? I have heard it claimed by a prominent advocate for one side of this debate that the other side is simply "ignorant of the facts." But surely the facts would be clear enough by now?

It must be acknowledged that the available data on poverty and inequality are far from ideal, though neither side of this debate has paid much attention to the data problems.[3] There are also potentially important differences in the types of

Martin Ravallion is with the World Bank's Development Research Group. For comments the author is grateful to Abhijit Banerjee, Jean-Yves Duclos, Francisco Ferreira, Emanuela Galasso, Ravi Kanbur, Peter Lambert, Branko Milanovic, Berk Ozler, Lant Pritchett, Eric Thorbecke, Dominique van de Walle, Adam Wagstaff, and participants at the workshop for the Brookings Trade Forum, 2004. These are the views of the author and should not be attributed to the World Bank.

1. See "IFG Book Store for Publications and Tapes" (www.ifg.org/store.htm [August 2004]). Similarly, the policy director of Oxfam writes that "there is plenty of evidence that current patterns of growth and globalization are widening income disparities." See Justin Forsyth, letter to the *Economist*, June 20, 2000, p.6.

2. *Economist*, May 27, 2000, p. 94.

3. For a fuller discussion of the data and measurement issues underlying the globalization debate, see Ravallion (2003).

1

data used. The pro-globalization side has tended to prefer "hard" quantitative data while the other side has drawn more eclectically on various types of evidence, both systematic and anecdotal or subjective. Differences in the data used no doubt account in part for the differing positions taken. However, since both sides have had access to essentially the same data, it does not seem plausible that such large and persistent differences in the claims made about what is happening to inequality in the world stem entirely from one side's ignorance of the facts.

One reason why such different views persist is that it is difficult to separate out the effects of globalization from the many other factors impinging on how the distribution of income is evolving in the world. The processes of global economic integration are so pervasive that it is hard to say what the world would be like without them. These difficulties of attribution provide ample fuel for debate, though they also leave one suspicious of the confident claims made by both sides.

Conflicting assessments can also stem from hidden contextual factors. Diverse impacts of the same growth-promoting policies on inequality can be expected given the different initial conditions among countries. Policy reforms shift the distribution of income in different directions in different countries. Yet both sides make generalizations about distributional impacts without specifying the context. In a given national setting, there may well be much less to disagree about.

This paper looks into another possible reason for the continuing debate about the facts: the two sides in this debate do not share the same values about what constitutes a just distribution of the gains from globalization. The empirical facts in contention do not stem solely from objective data on incomes, prices, and so on but also depend on value judgments made in measurement—judgments that one may or may not accept. It can hardly be surprising that different people hold different normative views about inequality. And it is well understood in economics that those views affect how one defines and measures inequality— although it is ethics, not economics, that determines what trade-offs one accepts between the welfare of different people. A class of "ethical measures" of inequality is built on this realization.[4] What is more notable in the present context is that important differences in values have become embedded in the methodological details underlying statements about what is happening to inequality in the world. These differences are rarely brought to the surface and argued out properly in this debate.[5]

---

4. A seminal early contribution was made by Atkinson (1970). For an excellent survey of approaches to the measurement of inequality, see Cowell (2000).

5. More generally, economists have been reticent to debate values, preferring to focus on "facts." This has led some observers to argue that modern economics has become divorced from ethics, though that is a questionable characterization, as Dasgupta (2003) argues forcefully.

Martin Ravallion   3

This discussion points out three key differences in the value judgments made about distributive justice that underlie the globalization debate. The first concerns one of the favorite empirical claims of the critics of globalization, namely that inequality between countries has been rising during the period of globalization—suggesting that the gains have been unfairly distributed. The pro-globalization side disputes this, arguing instead that inequality between countries has been falling over the last twenty years or so. The value judgment here relates to whether one should weight *countries* equally or *people* equally when assessing distributional outcomes.

The second difference in concepts of inequality relates to how much weight one should attach to the way average gains from reform vary with income versus the differences in impacts found at a given level of income. The pro-globalization side has tended to focus on aggregate measures of inequality or poverty, while the antiglobalization side has pointed to the losers among the poor and those vulnerable to poverty—often, it seems, to the point of ignoring the aggregate outcomes. A value judgment underlying this difference in perspective relates to the weight one attaches to *horizontal* versus *vertical* inequality when assessing the distributional impacts of globalization.

The third issue concerns another distinction between two concepts of inequality: *relative* inequality, which depends solely on proportionate differences in incomes, versus *absolute* inequality, which depends on the absolute differences—the "income gap between rich and poor." Virtually all the research by economists on world inequality has used the former concept, which has then become embedded in more popular writings supporting globalization. By contrast, critics of globalization appear often to be more concerned with absolute inequality. Here again we will see that the difference in concepts of inequality carries weight for the position one takes in the globalization debate.

Some Stylized "Facts"

A common finding in the literature is that changes over time in the extent of income inequality at the country level are uncorrelated with rates of economic growth. In other words, growth is distribution neutral on average.[6] Figure 1 illustrates this lack of correlation found between changes in inequality and growth in average living standards. Each point in the figure represents two household surveys at different dates for the same country, and the figure provides about 120

6. Evidence on this point can be found in World Bank (1990, chap. 3; 2000, chap. 4); Ravallion and Chen (1997); Ravallion (2001); Dollar and Kraay (2002).

Figure 1. Relative Inequality and Growth in Mean Household Income per Capita

Change in relative Gini index (annualized)

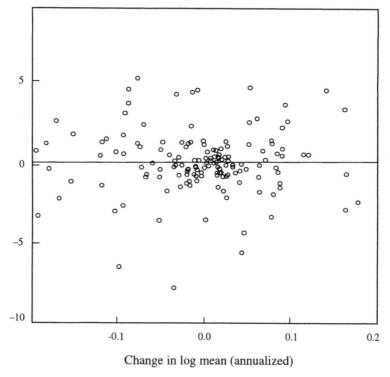

Change in log mean (annualized)

Source: Author's calculations based on data from World Bank, PovcalNet (http://iresearch.worldbank.org/povcalnet [November 2004]).

such "spells" spanning the 1990s. [7] The proportionate change in inequality between the two surveys is plotted against the growth rate in mean household income (or consumption) per person between the same two surveys. Inequality is measured by the usual Gini index. The simple correlation coefficient between changes in the log Gini index and the growth rates shown in Figure 1 is -.06. Among growing economies, inequality rises about half the time and falls half the time. This also holds for growing poor countries. Thus these data confirm other studies suggesting that the Kuznets hypothesis—the proposition that with growth in a low-income country, inequality first increases then starts to fall after a certain point—has generally not been borne out by experience in growing developing countries.[8]

7. This is an updated version of the data set described in Ravallion and Chen (1997).
8. Bruno, Ravallion, and Squire (1998); Fields (2001).

Martin Ravallion   5

The observation that changes in inequality tend to be uncorrelated with growth rates has an important implication. Since growth tends to leave income shares unchanged on average, absolute poverty measures (whereby the poverty line has fixed real value) will tend to fall with growth. The same share of a larger pie means of course a higher income. The expected negative correlation between rates of poverty reduction and rates of growth across countries has been borne out by a large body of empirical research using household-level survey data for many countries.[9] Granted, there have been cases in which growth has left the poor behind in absolute terms, but they are the exception rather than the rule.

Is the world becoming more unequal in the current period of globalization? Measuring inequality among people in the world as a whole, different studies and different time periods give different answers to this question. Bourguignon and Morrison find signs of slightly rising inequality from the 1970s to the early 1990s, Sala-i-Martin reports evidence suggesting a tendency for inequality to fall in the 1990s, and Milanovic reports rising inequality in some subperiods and falling inequality in others, with no clear trend.[10]

However, even if one takes the view that inequality has been rising, it has clearly not increased enough to choke off the gains to the poor from growth in the world economy. Figure 2 gives estimates of the poverty rate for the developing world over the period 1981–2001. Over this twenty-year period, the percentage of the population of the developing world living on less than $1 a day was almost halved, falling from 40 to 21 percent. The number of poor by this measure fell from 1.5 billion in 1981 to 1.1 billion in 2001.

Some of these "stylized facts" about what has been happening to poverty and inequality in the world have been questioned. The claims often heard from critics of globalization that the world is becoming more unequal appear to stem in part from the fact that many poor countries have not participated in the growth of the world economy. Indeed, looking back over the last 100 years or so, initially poorer countries have tended to experience lower subsequent growth rates.[11] Poor countries are not catching up with rich ones—indeed, it looks like the opposite has been happening. For example, an often quoted statistic is that the average income of the richest country in the world was about ten times that of the poorest around the end of the nineteenth century but is closer to sixty times higher today. Furthermore, on top of this long-term trend, there have been claims that inequality between countries has increased sharply since about 1980.[12]

9. Evidence on this point can be found in World Bank (1990, chap. 3; 2000, chap. 4); Ravallion (1995, 2001); Ravallion and Chen (1997); Fields (2001, chap. 5).
10. Bourguignon and Morrison (2002); Sala-i-Martin (2002a); Milanovic (2004).
11. Pritchett (1997).
12. Milanovic (2004). We will return to the issue of how inequality between countries should

6   *Brookings Trade Forum: 2004*

Figure 2. Poverty Incidence in the Developing World, 1981–2001[a]

Percent[b]

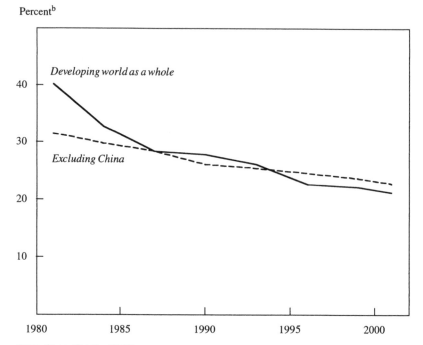

Source: Chen and Ravallion (2004b).
a. The figure gives the percentage of the population of low- and middle-income countries estimated to live in households with consumption or income per person less than $32.74 a month at 1993 purchasing power parity.
b. Percent of population of the developing world living on less than $1 a day.

Another issue that has sometimes been raised regards the fact that the above discussion relates only to absolute poverty, whereby the poverty line has fixed real value. Measures of relative poverty, in which the poverty line responds positively to the mean, naturally show less impact from growth. Indeed, in the extreme case in which the poverty line is directly proportional to the mean, a growth process that raises all incomes by an equal proportion will leave measured poverty unchanged. One can question whether such a poverty measure makes any sense: although relative deprivation may matter to welfare, it surely cannot be argued that absolute levels of living are irrelevant. When one compares poverty lines across countries with their average consumption levels, one finds higher poverty lines in richer countries, though the relationship tends to be quite inelastic among poor countries, consistent with the view that absolute deprivation dominates.[13] However, as developing countries grow, the idea of what

---

be measured.
13. Ravallion (1994, p. 41).

"poverty" means will undoubtedly evolve, too. Then a sole focus on absolute poverty will overstate the importance of growth to poverty reduction in the longer term.

As support for the view that globalization is good for poverty reduction, the pro-globalization side of the debate has often pointed to the developing world's overall success against absolute poverty since the early 1980s. It is argued that pro-globalization policies in developing countries are pro-poor because they generate higher economic growth, which does not come with higher inequality and so reduces absolute poverty.[14] However, a closer inspection of the aggregate poverty numbers, such as in figure 2, immediately raises some doubts about the role played by globalization versus other factors. China is hugely important in the world's overall success against extreme poverty; indeed, the total number of poor in the world (by the $1-a-day standard) excluding China has remained quite stable over this period, at around 850 million.[15] As is clear from figure 2, there was a dramatic decline in China's poverty incidence in the early 1980s; about 200 million people crossed the $1-a-day threshold between 1981 and 1984. Note, however, that this largely *preceded* the country's external trade reforms.[16] More plausibly, the sharp drop in poverty in China in the early 1980s was due to another kind of reform: the de-collectivization of agriculture after Premier Deng's reforms starting in 1978.[17]

Furthermore, while the evidence is compelling that growth tends to reduce absolute poverty, that does not imply that every policy that is good for growth will also reduce poverty. Specific growth-promoting policies in specific country contexts can have impacts on distribution that belie such generalizations. For example, Lundberg and Squire find evidence that trade openness tends to increase inequality.[18] There is also some evidence of an interaction effect with mean income, such that trade openness tends to be associated with *higher* inequality in poor countries but lower inequality in high-income countries.[19]

The aforementioned issues have received attention in the literature, although all of them are sufficiently important and sufficiently contentious to merit further research. The rest of this paper examines some issues that have received far less attention, related to what we mean by "inequality." It will be argued that differences between competing concepts of inequality influence the way empirical evidence is interpreted and hence the position one takes in the globalization debate.

14. See, for example, World Bank (2002, pp. 18 and 49).
15. Chen and Ravallion (2004b).
16. Ravallion and Chen (2004).
17. Ravallion and Chen (2004).
18. Lundberg and Squire (2003).
19. Barro (2000); Ravallion (2001).

Figure 3. Gini Indixes of Gross Domestic Product per Capita across Countries under Alternative Weighting Schemes

Gini index (percent)

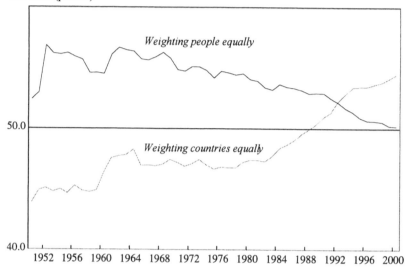

Source: Milanovic (2004).

Divergence versus Between-Country Inequality

Critics of globalization have pointed to data suggesting that inequality between countries has been rising since around 1980. The contribution of glob-alization per se to this trend is unclear.[20] However, putting the attribution prob-lem to one side, there is another important question about how inequality should be measured. The measures most widely quoted by the critics of globalization treat each country as one observation. The implicit value judgment here is that countries, not people, should get equal weight in assessing the fairness of the divi-sion of gains from globalization. An alternative approach is to give people equal weight. Estimates of the decomposition of world inequality into between-coun-try and within-country components have typically used population weights.[21] By this alternative concept, all individuals at a given real income level get equal weight in assessing between-country inequality, no matter where they live. A per-son in China does not count less than a person in Chad at the same real income.

20. For further discussion, see Williamson (1998) and O'Rourke (2002).
21. See, for example, Schultz (1998), Bourguignon and Morrison (2002), and Sala-i-Martin (2002a). For an overview of the theory of inequality decomposition, see Cowell (2000).

Martin Ravallion   9

The choice between these concepts of inequality matters greatly to the message conveyed on how fairly the benefits of aggregate growth are being shared. If instead of weighting countries equally one uses population weights, then the tendency for rising inequality between countries vanishes.[22] Indeed, with population weighting, there is evidence of a trend *decline* in the between-country component of inequality since roughly the mid-1970s. In marked contrast to the series in which countries are weighted equally, the population-weighted series in figure 3 suggests that inequality between countries is now the lowest it has been in half a century. The two weighting schemes deliver dramatically different messages.

What arguments can be made for choosing between the two series in figure 3? Some economists have seen this as a purely technical matter of what is "right" and "wrong." For example, Sala-i-Martin has argued that weighting countries equally is a "mistake that delivers a very misleading picture and one is led to conclude (wrongly) that there has been 'divergence big time'."[23] However, intelligent people can disagree about whether countries or people should be weighted equally. Consider the inequality between two equal-sized groups, A and B, in which each person in group A has an income of $1 a day while each person in B has an income of $10. (So we abstract from intragroup inequality.) Now imagine instead that group B is only one tenth the size of A. Is your assessment of the extent of inequality between A and B any different with this change? No doubt some readers will say "no" on the grounds that either way a typical person in group A has only one tenth of the income as one in B. Others will say "yes," on the grounds that with fewer people in group B, one's concern about the extent of intergroup inequality is diminished.

When assessing how rich countries are doing relative to poor countries, it is natural to take the country as the unit of observation. Knowing that the income per capita of a rich country is thirty times greater (even at purchasing power parity) than a poor country has a salience for our comprehension of the extent of the disparities in the world. The practice of weighting countries equally is almost universally followed in the large macroeconomic literature on growth and distributional empirics. Weighting countries equally is a close cousin of the method used to measure "sigma convergence" in the literature on growth empirics. The rise in between-country inequality over the last twenty years that is evident in figure 3 when countries are weighted equally is indicative of what is called in the growth literature (unconditional) divergence. Weighting countries equally makes sense

22. There have been a number of recent estimates of the time series of global inequality, including Schultz (1998), Bourguignon and Morrison (2002), Sala-i-Martin (2002a), and Milanovic (2004).

23. Sala-i-Martin (2002a, pp. 25–26); in the last phrase he quotes the title of Pritchett (1997).

in a regression that is being used to test theories about the causes of cross-country differences in growth rates. In that case, each country can be thought of as a draw from the universe of all the combinations of country policies, shocks, initial conditions, and outcomes.

It has been argued that countries are the relevant unit of observation for comparing policies and for drawing conclusions about what policies work best for reducing inequality between countries. Milanovic makes this argument in favor of weighting countries equally.[24] This view is more defensible for certain economy-wide policies than others, such as social sector policies, which are often developed and implemented at subnational (even local) levels. However, for the sake of argument, let us agree that policies are implemented at country level. Is this a compelling argument for weighting countries equally when assessing global inequality? It is the impacts of those policies on people that we care about. The lack of policy reform and growth in a small country surely cannot be deemed to cancel out the policy reforms that helped generate so much economic growth in China over the last twenty years or so. Yet that is what inequality measures that weight countries equally do. While it can be agreed that for purely descriptive purposes, and for testing the implications of certain growth models, one may not care about the population shares of countries when assessing inequality between them, weighting people unequally in such a seemingly arbitrary way can be questioned when—as is plainly the case in the globalization debate—one is attaching normative significance to measures of between-country inequality.

The practice of weighting countries equally when measuring inequality between countries also implies troubling inconsistencies in methodology. It is not clear why one would be happy to use population weights when measuring inequality *within* countries but not *between* them. Indeed, one would probably never question the need to weight by household size (or the number of adult equivalents) when calculating an inequality measure from a sample survey for a given country, and the same logic surely applies to the between-country component of total inequality. Weighting countries equally rather than people is also inconsistent with the way one would normally calculate the global mean income. A measure of inequality is a summary statistic of the information on how income is found to vary with the quantile (such as percentile) of the population ranked by income. One would probably not even think of using the unweighted overall mean income, so why would one use unweighted means at given percentiles of the distribution when measuring inequality?

Another defense of weighting countries equally starts by rejecting the implicit assumption in population weighting that individual welfare depends on "own

24. Milanovic (2004).

income," and allowing instead the possibility that welfare also depends on country of residence. Population weights can be questioned in all circumstances in which group membership has individual welfare significance independent of income. This can happen in a variety of ways. For example, the local political jurisdiction of residence can matter to one's access to local public goods. Group membership can also matter to one's ability to insure against income risk or to smooth consumption. Social norms of behavior or "culture" are also formed in groups and can influence welfare in important ways.[25] There are ample precedents for attaching significance to geographic identity in public policy. The constitutions of a number of federations (including Australia and the United States) give states political representation in the upper houses of parliament, independently of their population sizes. Those living in smaller states thus get higher weight. Similarly, it is "one country, one vote" at the United Nations and many other international organizations.

What is not clear in the present context is how persuasive such arguments are for weighting countries equally rather than people. Yes, one can allow that country identity matters. However, it would seem hard to imagine that this type of argument would justify weighting countries equally. That surely goes too far in the other direction. Some sort of hybrid weighting scheme may be called for, derived from an explicit assumption on the weight one attaches to country identity in assessing individual welfare. Suppose that the role of "country identity" can be captured by including a country-specific multiplicative factor in the underlying function of own income that one uses to assess individual welfare in a given country. Then the appropriate weights will be products of population weights and these country-specific factors. It would seem extremely unlikely that the appropriate country factors would be the inverse population shares.

A further issue concerns the robustness of the population-weighted inequality series shown in figure 3. China and India (the two most populous countries by far) naturally play an important role in the striking difference between the two series in figure 3. The high rates of growth in China and (more recently) India since the mid-1980s have been a major inequality-reducing force between people in the world. Take these countries out of the population-weighted series, and the decline in between-country inequality over the last two decades or so largely vanishes; the result is particularly sensitive to just one country, China.[26] By the same token, assessments of how (population-weighted) inequality is changing between countries can be quite sensitive to errors in measuring growth in China

25. For a model of economic behavior incorporating group identities, see Akerlof and Kranton (2000). Kanbur (2003) questions individualism in the context of a critique of the policy significance often attached to inequality decompositions.

26. This has been noted by Schultz (1998), Sala-i-Martin (2002a), and Milanovic (2004).

and India. For example, there are reasons to suspect biases in the official estimates of China's rate of growth, stemming in part from deficiencies in the underlying administrative data sources, particularly at the local level. (The practice of
setting growth rate targets for local governments has not helped!) China's
National Bureau of Statistics has gone a long way toward correcting these problems, but it still appears likely that the long-term growth rate in national income
per capita has been overestimated by 1 to 2 percentage points.[27] The rate of
decline in inequality evident in figure 3 when people are weighted equally is
almost certainly overstated.

The sensitivity of the population-weighted series to inclusion of the most
populous countries is clearly not a good reason for weighting countries equally.
Still, that sensitivity does speak to the need for statistical caution in inferring from
the population-weighted series in figure 3 that inequality is falling between countries. How confident can one be in claiming that inequality is falling when that
no longer holds if one eliminates just one country?

As demonstrated by the examples above, the implicit values in empirical work
matter greatly to the conclusions drawn about the distributive justice of current
globalization processes. And arguments can be made both ways.

Vertical versus Horizontal Inequalities

The empirical question at stake in the globalization debate is often posed in
terms of how mean gains from reforms vary by prereform income. Do the mean
proportionate gains rise or fall as income increases? Studies deemed to be favorable to the supporters of globalization are those that find that the mean proportionate gains are just as high for the poor as for the nonpoor.[28]

This perspective emphasizes what can be termed the vertical impacts of
reform, that is, the differences in mean impacts between people at different
income levels. Critics of globalization, by contrast, appear often to be more concerned about what we can call the horizontal impacts, such as when they point
to the fact that there are losers among the poor, even when the net gains to the
poor as a whole are positive. Borrowing from the literature on inequality and taxation, we can define the horizontal impacts as the differences in impact among
people who are equal ex ante in terms of welfare; such impacts indicate horizontal inequality in the reform.[29]

27. Maddison (1998); Wang and Meng (2001).
28. See, for example, Dollar and Kraay (2002).
29. For further elaboration of the various concepts of horizontal inequality found in the literature, see Jenkins and Lambert (1999).

A conventional poverty or inequality measure implicitly attaches weight to both horizontal and vertical inequality. To see how, imagine that each person receives an income gain from the reform (which could be positive, negative, or zero). Then calculate a prereform poverty and inequality measure (based on the distribution of incomes excluding these gains) and a postreform measure (including the gains). The difference between the two reveals the overall impact of the reform. One can then decompose the impact of a policy reform into vertical and horizontal components, as follows. Define the *conditional mean gain* as the mean of these gains at a given level of income. Imagine replacing each person's actual gain by the conditional mean corresponding to that person's income and calculating the impact on the poverty or inequality measure with this new synthetic distribution. This can be interpreted as the vertical component of the change in inequality or poverty. If there are no differences in the impacts by levels of income, then the vertical component is zero. However, when some people among those at approximately the same initial income level incur a net loss from reform while others enjoy a gain, this will add to inequality. To isolate this horizontal component, replace each person's actual gain by the deviation between that gain and the conditional mean, and again recalculate the summary statistic on this synthetic distribution. If the impact is predicted perfectly by prereform income, then this horizontal component is zero.[30] Ravallion and Lokshin derive such a decomposition for the impacts of trade reform on inequality and give an empirical example for a specific trade reform.[31]

The issue then is not whether horizontal inequality is reflected in current aggregate measures but whether it is *adequately* reflected. Observers can reasonably object to the horizontal inequalities of globalizing reforms—quite independent of the impacts that those reforms have on conventional inequality or poverty measures. One possible reason is that the initial distribution of income (as measured in practice) need not be horizontally equitable. This can stem from the inadequacies of income as a welfare indicator. There are conceptual and practical problems in measuring household income or consumption, and in making cost-of-living comparisons when prices and household characteristics vary (including the choice of equivalence scales for dealing with differences in family size and demographics).[32] Nor are standard measures (such as household

30. Note that the vertical and horizontal components need not add up exactly to the total change in measured poverty or inequality. A special case in which the decomposition is exact for proportionate gains (normalized by prereform income) is for the mean log deviation measure of inequality. For details, see Ravallion and Lokshin (2004).

31. Ravallion and Lokshin (2004).

32. A good overview of the issues and literature on welfare measurement can be found in Slesnick (1998). On the bearing that measurement choices can have on policy, see Ravallion (1994).

income per person) likely to reflect well the extent of inequality within households or differences in access to nonmarket goods. These concerns point to the importance of introducing supplementary indicators of welfare into distributional assessments.[33] If we think that certain types of households may in fact be poorer than measured incomes suggest, then our attention will naturally be drawn to impacts on those household types, even if they have similar (measured) incomes. Peoples' subjective assessments of economic welfare and the fairness of the outcomes from economic transactions have been found to depend on a variety of factors, including how much effort different people supplied as well as their initial income.[34] Reference-group effects on welfare—whereby the same income can yield different welfare for people in different reference groups, such as different neighborhoods—can also imply a concern for differences in impacts among people at the same ex ante income.

We can also care about horizontal inequalities even when we are happy with how economic welfare is measured. In the economics of public policy, there is precedent for concern over horizontal inequality, notably in the context of income tax changes—though the point would appear to apply with equal force to other types of policy reform. For example, Pigou wrote that horizontal inequality created "a sense of being unfairly treated . . . in itself an evil."[35] Auerbach and Hassett argue that one might want to give greater weight to horizontal inequities in a tax system on the grounds that "large differences [in tax rates] among similar individuals, regardless of their source, might be viewed as intrinsically arbitrary, and therefore more costly to the social fabric."[36]

Two recent studies of tax and transfer policies have shown how inequality or poverty measures can be re-defined to give higher weight to horizontal inequality. In the context of measuring the extent of horizontal inequality in a tax reform, Auerbach and Hassett show how an Atkinson index of social welfare can be decomposed into vertical and horizontal components that can differ in their inequality aversion parameters.[37] In a similar vein, Bibi and Duclos allow differential weights on the horizontal versus vertical components of the impacts of targeted transfers on the Foster-Greer-Thorbecke class of poverty measures.[38] The same ideas from the analysis of taxes and transfers have a bearing on other areas of public policy, including trade and other efficiency-oriented reforms.

33. Ravallion (1996).
34. For a survey of experimental evidence relevant to this point, see Konow (2003). Subjective assessments of economic welfare have also revealed a more complex set of factors than typically postulated by economists (Ravallion and Lokshin, 2002).
35. Pigou (1949, p. 50).
36. Auerbach and Hassett (2002, p. 1117).
37. See Atkinson (1970).
38. Bibi and Duclos (2004); Foster, Greer, and Thorbecke (1984).

In the context of reform, it may seem unfair that people at similar initial incomes are rewarded very differently. Such assessments will probably depend in part on whether people were aware of the risks they were exposed to and could have taken actions to protect themselves. Many of the welfare losses from globalization stem from factors for which the losers are essentially blameless. When the sole employer in a company town is driven out of business, the town's workers and residents can hardly be blamed for the losses they incur.

In the case of trade reform, the household characteristics that are likely to matter most to horizontal welfare impacts are those that influence net trading positions in relevant markets. Whether a household is a net demander or a net supplier of the specific goods and factors whose prices are changed by trade reform will depend on (among other things) its *assets* (for example, how much land a farm household controls will influence whether it is a net producer or net consumer of food), *demographics* (since this will naturally influence consumption patterns), and *location* (which will matter to both production and consumption opportunities). There is no obvious basis for thinking that these are characteristics that stem from choices for which one would fairly ask the households themselves to bear the adverse consequences of reform.

Such horizontal inequities can also interact powerfully with preexisting social tensions—such as those between different ethnic groups that vary in their production and consumption behaviors—thus fueling social conflict, even to the point of violence. Chua describes how social conflict in parts of Africa has emanated from the fact that different tribal groups have (for various, and contested, reasons) fared very differently under market-friendly regimes.[39] To some extent these conflicts can stem from historical vertical inequalities between groups. However, it can be conjectured that a large share of inequality is horizontal, in that ex-ante similar people in different groups fare very differently under the market-oriented reform. There is no reason to suppose that a conventional inequality measure would weight the consequent social conflicts appropriately. Extreme horizontal inequalities raise concerns about social and political stability. The protests from the losers can be loud, even when the aggregate net gains are positive.

Conventional measurement practices may well underweight horizontal inequality. Indeed, the measure will remain exactly the same if all the incomes in a society are simply reordered; this property is variously called the *anonymity axiom* or the *symmetry axiom* in the theory of poverty and inequality measurement. Thus if a policy change results in one person losing and another gaining, such that they swap places in the distribution, this will not have had any impact

39. Chua (2003, chap. 4).

whatsoever on standard measures. Yet this kind of churning in the distribution is unlikely to go unnoticed by the people involved. One should not be surprised if the losers in the process are unhappy about the outcome and that this fuels criticisms of the policies that led to it.

If it is agreed that these largely theoretical arguments suggest that the horizontal inequities of reform merit greater attention, the next question is whether horizontal inequalities are likely to be quantitatively important in the welfare outcomes of specific growth-promoting policy reforms, including trade reforms. Development experience has shown that many of the things that promote growth can have both winners and losers among the poor—and for other income groups, too. This arises from the heterogeneity in economic circumstances, such as differences in net trading positions in relevant markets for goods and factors. For example, some of the poor are net suppliers of food while others are net demanders, which means that changes in the relative price of food associated with trade reform benefit some but hurt others, with these diverse impacts found both vertically and horizontally in the distribution of income.[40] There can be heterogeneity in other dimensions of welfare at given incomes, such as in access to publicly provided goods and services. Greater openness to external trade often increases the demand for skills that can be quite inequitably distributed in poor countries. Whether the poor gain relatively more than the nonpoor from trade openness will depend crucially on antecedent inequalities in other dimensions, notably human capital.

Two examples illustrate the heterogeneity in impacts of trade reform. The first example relates to China's recent accession to the World Trade Organization (WTO). To provide a detailed picture of the welfare impacts of this trade reform, Chen and Ravallion use China's national rural and urban household surveys to measure and explain the welfare impacts of goods and factor price changes attributed to accession to the WTO. The price changes were estimated using a general equilibrium model to capture both direct and indirect effects of the initial tariff changes. The welfare impacts were estimated as first-order approximations of a money metric of utility, based on a household model incorporating own-production activities, calibrated to the household-level data imposing minimum aggregation. In the aggregate, Chen and Ravallion find a positive impact of WTO accession on mean household income but virtually no change in aggregate inequality and slightly lower aggregate poverty in the short term as a result of the reform.[41] (The estimated impact on the Gini index, for example, was so

40. See, for example, the results of Ravallion and van de Walle (1991) regarding the welfare effects of higher rice prices in Indonesia.
41. The results are documented fully in Chen and Ravallion (2004a).

small as to be almost undetectable.) However, there is still a sizable and at least partly explicable variance in impacts across household characteristics at a given income. Rural families tend to lose; urban households tend to gain. And there are larger impacts in some parts of the country than others. For example, one finds non-negligible welfare losses among agricultural households in the northeast—a region in which rural households are more dependent on feed grain production (for which falling relative prices are expected from WTO accession) than elsewhere in China. Vertical differences in preintervention incomes accounted for virtually none of the measured welfare impacts of this trade reform.

The second example comes from research on the likely impacts of agricultural trade reform in Morocco. Here the simulated trade reform entailed the deprotection of cereal producers through substantial reductions in tariffs on imported cereals. As in the China study, the price changes were estimated using a general equilibrium model, and the welfare impacts were estimated as first-order approximations of a money metric of utility using a household survey.[42] In this case, the results suggested that the trade reform would increase overall consumption inequality in Morocco. However, this was entirely due to the reform's impact on horizontal inequality; indeed, the vertical component—the contribution of the inequality in gains conditional on income—was inequality reducing. And, as in China, the horizontal welfare impacts are correlated with household demographics and location.

Simply averaging over such horizontal inequalities can miss a great deal of what matters to the debate on globalization, including social protection policies. Credible assessments of the likely welfare impacts (both horizontally and vertically) can clearly have implications for social protection—though it is probably little more than wishful thinking to imagine that full compensation is feasible, given the informational and incentive constraints on targeted policies.[43] It is important for policy discussions to recognize that diverse welfare impacts can underlie averaged impact calculations.[44] In this light, claims about the distributional impacts of trade or other reforms that use cross-country regressions are of questionable relevance for determining policy in any specific country; such regressions can readily hide the heterogeneity in impacts within countries as well as between them.[45]

42. Details can be found in Ravallion and Lokshin (2004).
43. For a fuller discussion of this point, see van de Walle (1998).
44. Kanbur (2001) provides a nice illustration of this point in the context of assessments of Ghana's performance in reducing absolute poverty.
45. For further discussion of the concerns about cross-country regressions in this context, see Ravallion (2001).

18   *Brookings Trade Forum: 2004*

Horizontal inequality is a long-established concept in the literature on inequal-ity measurement, although it has received less attention than vertical inequality in theoretical work.[46] Measures of horizontal inequality have typically been applied to studying tax reforms, but they can be adapted to a wider range of reforms and economic changes. (In the present context, the relevant horizontal inequalities are not confined to horizontal impacts that can be measured in mon-etary units.) Like absolute inequality, horizontal inequality has thus far taken a back seat in studies by economists related to inequality and globalization.

None of this denies the importance of knowing the implications for aggregate poverty and inequality. That is surely the first-order issue in this context. Even when horizontal inequity is a concern, one would presumably want to balance it against other policy objectives, such as reducing absolute poverty. If one follows the critics of globalization who focus solely on the losers among the poor, then one risks undermining the prospects for important poverty-reducing policy changes. At the same time, it must be recognized that undervaluing or even ignoring the horizontal heterogeneity in impacts can generate a seriously incom-plete picture and an unnecessarily narrow basis for policy.

Relative versus Absolute Inequality

Thus far the focus has been solely on what is known as *relative inequality* in the literature on inequality measurement. Relative inequality depends on the ratios of individual incomes to the mean. This property stems from the scale inde-pendence axiom in inequality measurement, whereby multiplying all incomes by a constant is deemed to leave inequality unchanged. The stylized fact that growth or greater openness in developing countries tends not to be systematically asso-ciated with rising (or falling) inequality rests on this specific concept of inequal-ity. However, it appears that many people do not think about inequality in relative terms. Careful surveys of university students asked which of two income distri-butions was more unequal; the answers suggest that about half of the students did not accept the scale independence axiom.[47]

An alternative concept, suggested by Kolm, is *absolute inequality*, which depends on the absolute rather than relative differences in levels of living.[48] A measure of absolute inequality is unchanged if all incomes increase by the same amount. Consider an economy with just two households with incomes: $1,000

46. For an overview of the theory and references, see Jenkins and Lambert (1999).
47. Amiel and Cowell (1999, chap. 4).
48. Kolm (1976). There are also intermediate measures, which contain the concepts of absolute and relative inequality as extreme cases; see, for example, Bossert and Pfingsten (1990).

and $10,000. If both incomes double in size, then relative inequality will remain the same: the richer household is still ten times richer. But the absolute difference in their incomes has doubled, from $9,000 to $18,000. Thus relative inequality is unchanged, but absolute inequality has risen.

While relative inequality has been the preferred concept in empirical work in development economics, perceptions that inequality is rising may well be based on absolute disparities in living standards. That is one interpretation of what people mean when they talk about the "gap between the rich and the poor" and the "widening economic divide."[49] Observers such as citizens and NGOs working in developing countries can easily see the increasing absolute gap in living standards between selected poor people (possibly those an NGO works with) and selected "rich" people. The fact that the proportionate gap may well be unchanged is less evident to the naked eye, if only because this requires knowledge of the overall mean. Furthermore, there is little obvious reason for assuming that it is the relative inequalities in incomes (rather than absolute inequalities) that matter instrumentally to valued social outcomes. Arguably inequalities in power relate more to absolute rather than relative inequality in income.

Here again, the value judgments made about what "inequality" means have considerable bearing on the position one takes in the globalization debate. Finding that the share of income going to the poor does not change on average with growth does not mean that "growth raises the incomes (of the poor) by about as much as it raises the incomes of everybody else."[50] Given existing inequality, the income gains to the rich from distribution-neutral growth will of course be greater than the gains to the poor. In the above example of two households, the income gain from growth is ten times greater for the high-income household. To say that this means that the poor "share fully" in the gains from growth is clearly a stretch. And the example is not far fetched. For the richest decile in India, the income gain from distribution-neutral growth will be about four times higher than the gain to the poorest quintile; it will be fifteen to twenty times higher in Brazil or South Africa.

The common empirical finding in the literature that changes in relative inequality have virtually zero correlation with rates of economic growth naturally carries little weight for those who are concerned instead about absolute inequality. In figure 4 the relative inequality index used in figure 1 has been replaced by an absolute Gini index, based on absolute differences in incomes (not normalized by the mean). In marked contrast to figure 1, a strong positive correlation emerges

49. International Forum on Globalization (2002, p. 8).
50. *Economist*, May 27, 2000, p. 94.

Figure 4. Absolute Inequality and Growth in Mean Household Income per Capita

Change in absolute Gini index (annualized)

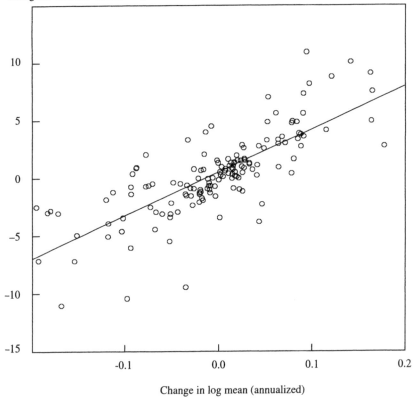

Change in log mean (annualized)

Source: Author's calculations based on data from World Bank, PovcalNet (http://iresearch.worldbank.org/povcalnet [November 2004]).

(a correlation coefficient of .64). The absolute gap between the rich and the poor tends to rise in growing economies and fall in contracting ones.

If one is a relativist, then one might conclude from figure 1 that there is no aggregate trade-off between economic growth and reducing inequality, though it should be noted that this is only true on average; there may well be a trade-off in specific country circumstances. If one is an absolutist, then an aggregate trade-off is implied by figure 4: in a typical developing country, someone who values lower absolute inequality must be willing to have less growth and higher absolute poverty.

The distinction between absolute and relative inequality also affects assessments of the prospects for reducing poverty through economic growth. Naturally, what happens to inequality during the growth process is relevant to its impact on poverty. A widely used benchmark for quantifying the impact of future growth on poverty is to assume that relative inequality does not change. For example, Chen and Ravallion find that for the developing world as a whole in 2001, the poverty gap index (for the "$1 per day" poverty line at 1993 purchasing power parity) has an elasticity with respect to the mean of –2.5 when relative inequality is held constant.[51] If all income levels grow at the same rate, then the aggregate poverty gap index will fall at a rate of 5 percent a year for a growth rate of 2 percent a year in mean household income per capita. However, what if *constant absolute inequality* is used as the distributional benchmark? When the Chen-Ravallion calculations are repeated holding absolute inequality constant instead, the elasticity rises sharply to -12. So instead of the poverty gap falling at a rate of 5 percent a year for a growth rate of 2 percent a year, the same growth rate keeping absolute inequality constant would see the poverty gap falling at a remarkable 24 percent a year. Of course, all such calculations are fanciful unless it can be established how one could achieve such a growth process in reality. However, these simple calculations serve to illustrate how sensitive our assessments of the impact on poverty of distribution-neutral growth can be to the concept of inequality used in defining what "distribution-neutral" means.

Economists specializing on income distribution are well aware of the distinction between absolute and relative inequality, though it is hardly ever mentioned in empirical work on growth and distribution.[52] Contributions to the globalization debate, in both popular and academic forums, have rarely been explicit about which concept is being used. Indeed, critics of globalization are often vague about what they mean by inequality, though what they have in mind appears to be closer to absolute inequality than relative inequality. Defenders of globalization invariably point to evidence on relative inequality without mentioning that it is not the only possible concept of inequality and that the results obtained, and their interpretation for country policy, are significantly affected by this choice.

Yet the evaluative judgments made about the distributional changes associated with globalization may depend crucially on whether one thinks about inequality in absolute or relative terms. There is no economic theory that tells us that inequality is relative, not absolute. It is not that one concept is right and the other wrong. Nor are they two ways of measuring the same thing. Rather, they are two different concepts. The revealed preferences for one concept over another reflect

51. Chen and Ravallion (2004b).

52. Fields (2001) notes that absolute inequality exists as a concept, though he quickly moves on to focus solely on relative inequality.

implicit value judgment about what constitutes a fair division of the gains from growth. Those judgments need to be brought into the open and given critical scrutiny before one can take a well-considered position in this debate.

Conclusions

Both sides of the globalization debate often use the term "inequality" as though we all agree on exactly what that means. But we almost certainly do not all agree—and that could well be the nub of the matter. This paper has demonstrated that the factual claims one hears about what is happening to inequality in the world depend critically on value judgments embedded in standard measurement practices. Three such issues have been highlighted: whether one weights people equally or countries equally when assessing what is happening to global inequality, what weight one attaches to horizontal inequalities, and whether one focuses on relative inequality or absolute inequality in assessing the welfare impacts of globalization.

Forming defensible value judgments on each of these issues is hardly straightforward, and this discussion has illustrated that arguments can be made both ways. Readers should form their own judgments as to what side they take on each of these issues. But this discussion points to some tentative conclusions. On the first issue, while it is simplistic to say that it is a purely technical "mistake" to not weight by population sizes, it can be agreed that there is something troubling about comparing inequality among countries while ignoring the (huge) differences in the size of their populations—thus giving higher weight to people living in smaller countries. Whether population weights are the right approach is still unclear, given that country identity can matter to welfare. Neither weighing method is ideal, but weighting countries equally would seem hard to defend when making judgments about inequality.

On the second issue, while knowing what is happening to aggregate inequality and poverty is clearly of first-order importance, horizontal inequalities need to get more attention than they typically do in assessments of the welfare impacts of policy reforms. Conventional inequality measures may well undervalue horizontal inequality. In this respect, the globalization debate takes on the character of two ships passing in the dark of night: one side says that inequality has been unchanged in the aggregate and (hence) that poverty has fallen; the other side points to the losers among the poor. Arguably both are right.

Martin Ravallion   23

On the third issue, both sides of the globalization debate need to be clearer about whether one is talking about absolute or relative inequality and to recognize that the other side may not share their concept. Relative inequality has been the more prominent concept in applied work by economists, though arguably it is absolute inequality that many people see in their daily lives and that motivates their concerns about distributive justice. Greater attention to absolute inequality would help inform important debates about development, including globalization. However, the trade-offs with other valued goals, including fighting absolute poverty, need to be confronted explicitly.

Both academic and popular contributions to the globalization debate have rarely acknowledged the differences in values that underlie the seemingly conflicting evidence on what has been happening to inequality and poverty. Most readers of the popular press and the web sites reporting on this topic do not see the embedded value judgments in the "facts" presented to them. It seems unlikely that most protagonists in this debate are deliberately duping the public; indeed, there appears to be some common ground of values, such as in the shared concern about absolute poverty. Hopefully, then, the debate can move on to address more directly the competing concepts of inequality that lie at the heart of the matter.

Comments
and Discussion

Erik Thorbecke: Over the years I have enjoyed reading Martin Ravallion's papers, and this one is no exception. It highlights some fundamental issues inherent to the concept of income inequality in a transparent way and provides a convincing explanation of the conflict between the two sides of the globalization debate. Since I agree pretty much with the content of the author's paper, I propose to raise a few issues extending his analysis. I have four comments: the first two are relatively minor points whereas the last two are substantive and go to the heart of measuring income inequality.

First, Ravallion correctly points out that "churning," that is, two individuals swapping places in the income distribution so that one person gains and another loses, would not be seen to have any impact on the inequality measure whatsoever. Yet he remarks that "one should not be surprised if the losers in the process are unhappy about the outcome and that this fuels criticisms of the policies that led to it." But the issue is deeper: any churning, assuming a convex utility function (reflecting declining marginal utility of income), will lead to a net reduction of utility. The loss of utility to the loser will be greater than the gain in utility to the gainer. Hence if enough churning takes place, it could be potentially destabilizing from a societal standpoint.

A second minor comment is that class conflicts could result from vertical inequality. For example, a structural adjustment and trade liberalization program could lead to higher food prices in a developing country, benefiting farmers who are net sellers of food, while agricultural workers (the landless) would be negatively affected by the reform.

Now I come to my more substantive comments. Ravallion is concerned about the robustness of population-weighted inequality series and the need for statis-

24

tical caution in inferring that inequality is falling when weighting people equally. I believe that this is a crucial issue that needs to be extended not just to the underlying data but also to the implicit and explicit assumptions and methodologies used in deriving world inequality measures. The fundamental question that needs to be asked is, how sensitive is the Gini coefficient (or any other inequality measure) to measurement errors and assumptions used in deriving it? Instead of reporting one unique scalar value for the Gini coefficient, could one derive a range of values depending on Bayesian and non-Bayesian estimates of the likely effects of measurement errors and underlying methodologies used to derive the worldwide income distribution? One advantage of this procedure would be that it would force the analyst to identify and confront the key assumptions and measurement errors to which the Gini coefficient is sensitive.

Let me illustrate with the help of some examples. In his derivation of the change in inequality in the worldwide income distribution, Sala-i-Martin made a number of assumptions.[1] For example, he left out the former Soviet Republics, Bulgaria, and Yugoslavia—countries that all underwent large increases in inequality in the 1990s. He also derived within-country distributions from quintile distributions, assuming zero variance within quintiles. This use of sparse and fragmentary data led Milanovic, paraphrasing Winston Churchill, to claim that "never was so much calculated with so little."[2]

The question I am raising is how far can one go in estimating the likely effects of such assumptions on the real Gini? It should certainly be possible to infer how much the Gini coefficient would be underestimated by ignoring the intraquintile variance (using six points of an income distribution rather than the whole distribution).

When it comes to measurement errors, we can distinguish between sampling errors—to the extent that much of the information comes from household surveys—and nonsampling errors. The latter clearly dwarf the former. One example given in Ravallion's paper is the systematic bias in computing growth rates for China: the long-term annual per capita growth rate is likely to have been overestimated by 1 to 2 percent. This kind of overestimation for a country constituting almost a sixth of the global population—particularly if various segments of the Chinese income pyramid were affected differentially—is bound to have a significant impact on the magnitude of the inequality measure. Obviously, expert judgment would be required in order to estimate a lower bound and an upper bound for the Gini coefficient. To repeat, the process of computing such a (confidence) interval would have the great advantage of pinpointing critical data,

1. Sala-i-Martin (2002a, 2002b).
2. Milanovic (2002).

procedures, and assumptions to which the magnitude of the Gini coefficient is sensitive and would thereby lead to more robust estimates.

My final question is whether income is an appropriate measure of welfare. Typically, the income distribution is approximated from the total consumption (total expenditures plus the imputed value of home consumption) of households as reported by household surveys. This is an incomplete measure of money-metric welfare because it ignores the imputed value of the benefit received by households from public services (in particular, education and health services) and public goods. Might it not be better to use outcome variables, such as health and educational status, instead of or in conjunction with income to measure welfare? Income is relatively unbounded upwardly. Much of the income inequality is driven by right-hand tails of national distributions. One example suffices to illustrate this point: the richest 10 percent of the U.S. population has an aggregate income equal to that of the poorest 43 percent of the people of the world, or alternatively, the total income of the richest 25 million Americans is equal to the total income of almost 2 billion people.[3] Measures of inequality are quite sensitive to these high incomes.

On the other hand, health and educational status are more bounded, as would be the case, for instance, if life expectancy were taken as the measure of health status. In any population the life expectancy of the oldest individual is rarely more than 50 percent above the average life expectancy. Worldwide inequality would be significantly lower if measured in terms of health or educational status than in terms of income and might reflect more accurately the actual welfare (happiness) enjoyed by different individuals in different settings. Of course, aside from the difficulty of obtaining reliable information on health status, there is the additional problem of the quality of health and quality of life for individuals who enjoy the same life expectancy. Does a Sri Lankan woman with the same health status as an American woman enjoy the same level of welfare? Making allowance for different levels of quality of life is most difficult and might only be assessed through subjective surveys. What appears clear, however, is that a Sri Lankan with the same life expectancy as an American and receiving an income one-tenth that of her middle-class American counterpart—which in her society might place her in the top income quintile—would, in all likelihood, enjoy a welfare level almost certainly greater than one-tenth that of her counterpart and perhaps even comparable. Welfare and happiness depend not just on material welfare but also on the various types of capital available to individuals, such as social capital and health capital. It is important to remind ourselves that income is a very inadequate measure of welfare—although at the present time we have to rely on it, faute de mieux.

3. Milanovic (2000).

Lant Pritchett: One of the difficulties of commenting on the work of Martin Ravallion is that he very rarely, if ever, makes mistakes. I know this from having had many, many debates with him, none of which I can claim to have won in his judgment, and actually few of which I can claim to have won by even my own judgment. As the title of the conference is "Globalization, Poverty, and Inequality" and the author talked mostly about inequality, I will discuss globalization and poverty. In that way I will not have to go head-to-head with anything he said about inequality.

I would like to make two points. First, current globalization talk is—and is almost bound to be—nonsense, for reasons that I will go into shortly. Second, I would argue that most economists should not buy into the commonly accepted low poverty lines as a basis for social objectives that economic policy should address.

First, regarding "globalization," we economists keep talking about it as if it was the central driving phenomenon of the period in which we live when, in fact, I would argue that the central driving phenomenon of the last century and even of the last fifty years is nearly the opposite: the division of the global economy into smaller and smaller units. These shrinking, proliferating units limit the mobility of persons, which is the key factor that matters most for inequality.

So while we argue whether "globalization" is good or bad for the poor or good or bad for inequality, we should be discussing whether the recent set of processes called X has this or that effect. Before naming X, we should determine what its central features are. I would argue that there have been four central processes over the last fifty years. First, there has been the proliferation of sovereigns.[1] This means that there are more borders, more legal jurisdictions and independent judiciaries, more monies, more flags, and more representatives in the United Nations. Second, technological innovations have caused the transport costs of many things, including information, money, and goods, to decline. Third, there is a set of processes in which some of the many nation-states pursue policies that are modestly more liberal regarding the movement of some items of economic relevance across the increasing numbers of national borders. Fourth, the movement of labor is, in general, completely excluded from liberalization policies.

There are two key points. First, I would argue that there is no particularly strong reason to call this set of four processes "globalization." Suppose that in 2004 the state of Idaho seceded from the United States and set up as a new sovereign entity with an army, borders, and a currency; disallowed all movement of persons from all other countries, including the United States; and imposed a tariff of 10 percent on all goods from the rest of the United States. Then suppose

---

1. Braun, Hausmann, and Pritchett (2004).

ten years later in 2014 Idaho lowers its tariff on USLI (that is, United State less Idaho) products to 3 percent. Wouldn't we think it odd if the literature on the impact of that policy change referred to the study of the process of integration when *dis*integration was the central phenomenon?

The second point is that whatever we call the process X, economists should have no strong preconceptions about the answer to that particular question about how X should have affected inequality. Let me quickly review some facts in support of such cautiousness.

First, the number of sovereigns in the world has increased. It has gone from something like 50 before World War II to approximately 200 today, and these sort of sovereign entities control borders and hence inhibit economic transactions across geographic space. This is an enormous antiglobalizing trend, and it has divided up the world economic base into smaller and smaller, not larger and larger, units. And even with something approaching full liberalization, there are studies that suggest that border effects per se are large even across highly liberalized environments. For instance, trade between the United States and Canada appears to be substantially lower because of a border, in spite of the fact that one can hardly imagine more trade liberalization between two countries in the absence of true integration.

One thing that has happened over the historical scale is that only around 10 percent of the total global inequality was cross-country variation in 1820—that is, economically, it was about the same to be a peasant in England as it was to be one in India. Today, something like 60 percent of the total global inequality across individuals is accounted for by differences in average income across countries. So for some reason, this process called X has been associated with a huge increase in the amount of inequality that is accounted for by differences across the borders of nation states.

The second thing is that the current era of X inhibits the mobility of persons across national boundaries. These barriers are huge, in that they prevent large amounts of movement. The differentials in the real, purchasing-power-adjusted wages of unskilled labor between the United States and countries that sent substantial fractions of their population to the United States around the turn of the century were between two-to-one and four-to-one. That is, the wage differentials that drove people out of Ireland, Italy, or Norway into Minnesota or New York were substantial but not astronomic.

The current wage differentials between potential sending and receiving countries are enormously higher—from six-to-one to ten-to-one.[2] Substantially higher wage differentials accompanied by substantially lower migration flows (as pro-

---

2. Pritchett (forthcoming).

portions of both sending and receiving country populations) suggest that the obvious is true: the guys with guns guarding the borders are a binding constraint on labor mobility.

Such barriers to labor mobility have implications for the dynamics of population and real wages. If the economic process generates large region-specific shocks to the desired population in a geographic region (say, as a result of changes in technology or agriculture, economies of scale, or urbanization), those shocks must be accommodated. If there is labor mobility, negative shocks are accommodated by people moving out of Kansas and into California. If there is no labor mobility, those geographic shocks are accommodated by people becoming poor but being trapped in their region, while those for whom the shock is positive get rich. When a region experiences a negative shock and people move out, it creates a ghost region, but when there are barriers to the mobility of labor, it produces zombies—and as everyone knows, a zombie is the living dead. A zombie is a country in which the real wage wants to go down dramatically because of a negative shock to the desired population, but the population cannot get out. So the only way to accommodate that shock is a huge fall in the real wage.

Comparing data on GDP per capita and population from regions within countries to data across countries leads to striking results. Within countries (particularly large countries), there are large differences in the growth of population with small differences in the growth of income per head. Across countries the opposite is true: there is enormous disparity in the growth rate of income per head and very little disparity in the growth rate of population less the rate of natural increase.

Thus I would argue that one of the things we have learned from the processes called X is that the world is not, in fact, globalized. The key market that is not globalized is the market for labor, and when one does not, in fact, have a liberal market for labor, one cannot, in theory, predict with any accuracy using existing models how other policies and the liberalizing of other markets will or will not affect inequality.

I close this discussion of what *is not* globalization with a question about why figure 1 is facetious. Figure 1 compares the welfare gains from removing restrictions on labor mobility, which estimates suggest would double world GDP, with the gains to be had from everything that is on the World Trade Organization agenda for the current round. Notice that the changes that are the focus of discussion in the literature generate welfare gains that are not even detectable compared to the huge gain that supposedly would be produced by full liberalization of labor markets. But, of course, this graph is facetious because, for some reason, we simply do not want to talk about liberalizing or globalization in the only market where it really matters: labor.

30   *Brookings Trade Forum:2004*

Figure 1. Estimated Welfare Gains from Removing Restrictions on Labor Mobility versus Removal of Other Restrictions, or Why Is this Graph Facetious?

Gains as percent of world GDP

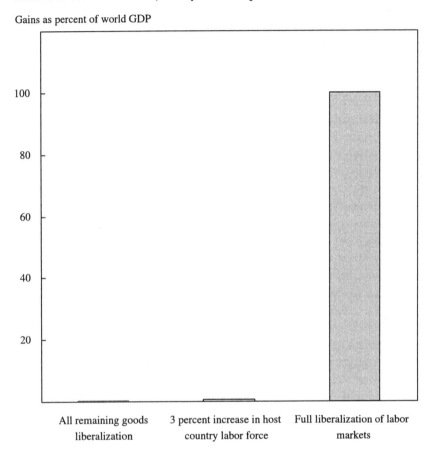

All remaining goods liberalization	3 percent increase in host country labor force	Full liberalization of labor markets

Now I will expand on my second point. The question often asked is, "Do the processes called X affect poverty?" Well, that requires a definition of poverty. Nearly all of the poverty numbers in the public domain are the Foster-Greer-Thorbecke (FGT) measures of poverty. When the World Bank, via Martin Ravallion, reports on the number of the poor, it is based on such a calculation. And these numbers all depend on there being a poverty line.

The thing about a poverty line is that income gains above it count zero toward the reduction of poverty. This is not about how much being below the poverty line counts. With the "poverty intensity" parameter of the FGT measures you can vary poverty intensity in a variety of semiplausible ways. But if you state that "poverty reduction is my objective," and you set a poverty line, every gain to income above that line counts for *zero* in your objective function.

Hence before we can ask, "How does X affect poverty?" we must draw a poverty line. It would seem that a reasonable poverty line, particularly an upper bound on poverty lines for global analysis, should be set where the analyst is comfortable that *zero* is a reasonable approximation to his or her true social welfare function.

A huge problem with nearly all of the literature to date is that it has bought into a monopoly of very low poverty lines for global absolute poverty—a monopoly of the "dollar a day" or "two dollars a day" poverty lines. But it is simply ludicrous, in my view, to set those as upper bound poverty lines. Zero is not a reasonable approximation to the appropriate weight in the social welfare function of any reasonable policymaker at a poverty line drawn through a dollar a day or two dollars a day, for the following three reasons.

First, people do not regard gains to their income as being anywhere near zero at two dollars a day, and I am a big believer that the social welfare function should be nonpaternalistic. In fact, if you examine the relationship between subjective well-being and income across nations from the World Values Survey, it is very difficult to argue that this flattens out at anything like two dollars a day.[3] It might flatten out at $20,000 a year, but it does not flatten out at $730 a year.

Second, "the rich" of poor countries have enormously lower incomes than "the poor" of rich countries. Dani Rodrik has calculated whether the "rich" (defined as the top 10 percent) in the bottom 10 percent of countries have higher income than the "poor" (defined as the bottom 10 percent) in a rich country. By his calculation, the purchasing power parity (PPP) income of a rich individual in a poor country is P$2,800—only P$7 a day—while the income of a poor individual in a rich country is three times higher, at P$8,640 or P$23 a day. If the bottom 10 percent of the rich-country population is poor, then so is the top 10 percent in poor countries. If you suspect PPP adjustments, I suspect you are wrong: the poor of rich countries are better off than the top quintile in nearly every poor country by every non-money-metric indicator of well-being—food share, child mortality, malnutrition, and schooling. In India, Nepal, and Nigeria, the malnutrition rate is 30 percent among the *top* 20 percent of households (as measured by the asset index).[4] It is ludicrous to think that "we" do not care about the impact of globalization on "the rich" in India when, in fact, 30 percent of the people who are rich have children who are malnourished. If the poor of rich countries are poor, then so are people in the upper tails of the income distribu-

3. See Pritchett (2004).
4. Pritchett (2004).

tion of poor countries. And even if you do not care about income and only think money should be instrumental toward some warm and cuddly goal such as schooling, there is still no reason to cut off poverty at a low line such as two dollars a day, since the increments of income to well-being at those low levels are still very high.

I think the word poverty should always have an adjective that makes it clear what the relevant standard is. The dollar-a-day standard should define "destitute poverty" while the two-dollars-a-day line should define "extreme poverty," and a poverty line of ten dollars a day (in 1993 PPP dollars) should define "global poverty." Then when we discuss things like what is the impact of processes called X (not globalization) on poverty, there is neither an unwarranted monopoly of a single standard nor confusion. After all, the dollar-a-day standard is sharply penurious—only 7 percent of people in Sri Lanka are "destitute poor." While it might be *one* interesting question about whether globalization benefits the destitute poor, certainly that is not the only question of interest. We might conceivably have non-zero concern for people in the tenth percentile in Sri Lanka, who are excluded from consideration under the dollar-a-day standard. Thus we can also ask, "Does process X that some call globalization benefit the ten-dollar-a-day poor?" If some policy changes produce large gains in aggregate incomes in India, and the gain is slightly larger for the thirty-fifth percentile— who by any reasonable *global* standard are very poor people—than for the fifteenth, this scenario would not be considered a case of "globalizing policy reform that did not benefit 'the poor.'"

What I am pleading for here is a bit more focus on economics, on how identifiable policy changes affect the distribution of income (both central tendency and dispersion), using validated theories and empirical evidence, and a bit less attention to questions in which one badly defined concept is related to another badly defined concept as, for instance, in the question, "Is globalization good or bad for poverty?"

Discussion: Roger Betancourt noted that the reason that one side of the debate was interested in absolute inequality and the other was interested in relative inequality is that the essential differences are in measures of economic power that can affect policy outcomes. Unless the discussion focuses on measures of economic power, arguments will center on the interpretation of axioms rather than on real problems. Betancourt felt that the most important question was the impact of particular measures on the poor.

Bill Easterly challenged Ravallion's focus on the heterogeneity of the effect of shocks, such as in the case of changes in trade policy and the large numbers of losers. The problem with this focus is that it can apply to almost any change in economic policy or, for that matter, technology. In the United States, every week hundreds of thousands of jobs (approximately) are destroyed and hundreds of thousands are created. Although the losers complain loudly, no one believes that we should stop technological change and use typewriters rather than computers. He felt that the focus on the heterogeneity of winners and losers is misguided unless the losers are concentrated politically and can contest changes. Yet in terms of overall welfare, almost any economic change has winners and losers. Ravallion responded that this missed his point—that there is no foundation for the way conventional measures weight the horizontal components of inequality.

Carol Graham noted that Ravallion's discussion of losers echoed the earlier discussion about the need to do better at anticipating losses and providing losers with better protection. She then asked if the answer to the question whether absolute or relative inequality mattered more would be different if there was better protection for those who fell behind.

Related to this, Susan Collins referenced a paper by Rodrik and Fernandez as very relevant to the points raised by Ravallion.[1] That paper finds that the support for trade reform in a particular country is more likely to be influenced by the share of the relevant population that *perceives* it is at risk of losing than by whether the actual benefits of the reform outweighed the costs.

Branko Milanovic commented that Ravallion's paper brought out the ambiguities and difficulties associated with the entire debate. These include not only the difference between relative and absolute inequality but also the difference between horizontal and vertical inequality. He noted that unweighted inequality between countries (Concept 1 inequality) has been rising over the last twenty or so years. Intercountry inequality is, of course, less important than inequality between individuals, but it is not irrelevant. Not only does it represent a de facto test of the income convergence hypothesis—a fact that is quite well known—but there are additional elements that may underscore widening intercountry disparities. One is stimulus to migration that comes with increasing differences in mean country incomes. Another is the realization that each country is not just a random assortment of individuals but is effectively a culture. That means that one cannot easily say that inequality between countries does not matter at all. One cannot say that Chad is so hopeless that everyone should move out. If there is a culture, then there is probably some value to that culture per se. Thus a hopeless falling behind of such countries represents, in a social Darwinian world, a destruction of that culture. The importance of Concept 1 inequality can also be

1. Rodrik and Fernandez (1991).

seen when applied to inequality between regions within a single country. If one notes that inequality between states in the United States is much lower than among the provinces in China, and is decreasing within the United States while it is increasing in China, then it reveals something very important about the way that labor and capital markets work in the United States versus in China.

Milanovic also noted that there are various sources of data driving the debate on global inequality and the important role of China therein. Maddison's data, for example, suggest that China's growth is still high, but instead of 9 percent per year over the period of last twenty years, it is closer to 5.5 percent on average.[2] That changes the story for global inequality, first because global inequality around 1978–80 is lower than if official Chinese numbers are used and then because its decline is also smaller. Finally, Milanovic noted that in a paper he wrote about Yugoslavia more than twenty years ago, he found that really poor republics did not mind becoming poorer as long as others who were richer were also becoming poorer. He called this a Verkhovensky improvement. Verkhovensky, a hero from Dostoyevsky's *The Possessed*, was a radical leveler. People, or countries, might like to be more equal *even* if that is not got going to make them better off in an absolute sense.

Abhijit Banerjee highlighted the determining role in the debate of the way in which India and China are weighted. If you believe that India and China are driving all the results, then there is really nothing else in the global poverty numbers. He then noted that the whole point of having a good theory of inequality was to be able target those who are likely to get hurt, for example, by trade or innovation.

Sylvia Ostry compared views about inequality in the United States and Europe using Hirschman's concepts of exit and voice, and suggested that there were advantages to the American focus on exit.[3] The concepts of voice and exit reflect the complex, systemic relationship of institutions and how they differ across countries.

A number of speakers also commented on the Pritchett discussion. Bill Easterly noted that the proliferation of sovereigns was a very clever point about globalization but one that needed qualifying. This is because even in the areas where sovereigns are proliferating, such as the former Soviet Union, there is no true free trade or factor mobility. In a similar vein, Susan Collins reiterated Pritchett's point about the many dimensions in which the world is more global. At the same time, there are many dimensions in which we are far from total globalization. The discussion often focuses too much on extremes, while reality is much closer to the middle and, in some places, to a scenario of small nation-states with very little interaction.

2. Maddison (1998).
3. Hirschman (1970).

Martin Ravallion   35

Carol Graham commented on Pritchett's point about the top 20 percent of people in Brazil having worse health indicators than the poorest people in the United States. She made the point that in this instance, the discussion is really about differences in social insurance, public health, and other public policies and not about income poverty. Finally, Ravallion took issue with Pritchett's suggestion to focus on $15 a day as a poverty number, which he thought would be worse than the current focus on $1 a day. He also noted that the World Bank had initially avoided highlighting a single indicator, publishing instead a range of numbers to show the distribution. But people very quickly focused on a single line with a headcount index, and he believes they will continue to do so.

References

Akerlof, George, and Rachel Kranton. 2000. "Economics and Identity." *Quarterly Journal of Economics* 115, no. 3: 715–53.

Amiel, Yoram, and Frank Cowell. 1999. *Thinking about Inequality: Personal Judgment and Income Distributions.* Cambridge University Press.

Atkinson, Anthony B. 1970. "On the Measurement of Inequality." *Journal of Economic Theory* 2, no.3: 244–63.

Auerbach, Alan J., and Kevin A. Hassett. 2002. "A New Measure of Horizontal Equity." *American Economic Review* 92, no. 4: 1116–25.

Barro, Robert. 2000. "Inequality and Growth in a Panel of Countries." *Journal of Economic Growth* 5, no.1: 5–32.

Bibi, Sami, and Jean-Yves Duclos. 2004. "Equity and Policy Effectiveness with Imperfect Targeting." Mimeo. Université Laval, Québec.

Bossert, Walter, and Andreas Pfingsten. 1990. "Intermediate Inequality: Concepts, Indices and Welfare Implications." *Mathematical Social Sciences* 19, no. 2: 117–34.

Bourguignon, Francois, and Christian Morrison. 2002. "Inequality among World Citizens: 1820–1992." *American Economic Review* 92, no. 4: 727–44.

Braun, Matias, Ricardo Hausmann, and Lant Pritchett. 2004. "Disintegration and the Proliferation of Sovereigns: Are There Lessons for Integration?" In *FTAA and Beyond: Prospects for Integration in the Americas*, edited by Antoni Estevadeordal and others. Harvard University Press.

Bruno, Michael, Martin Ravallion, and Lyn Squire. 1998. "Equity and Growth in Developing Countries: Old and New Perspectives on the Policy Issues." In *Income Distribution and High-Quality Growth*, edited by Vito Tanzi and Ke-young Chu, chap. 4. MIT Press.

Chen, Shaohua, and Martin Ravallion. 2004a. "Household Welfare Impacts of WTO Accession in China." *World Bank Economic Review* 18, no. 1: 29–58.

————. 2004b. "How Have the World's Poorest Fared Since the Early 1980s?" *World Bank Research Observer* 19, no. 2: 141–70.

Chua, Amy. 2003. *World on Fire.* New York: Anchor Books.

Cowell, Frank. 2000. "Measurement of Inequality." In *Handbook of Income Distribution*, edited by Anthony B. Atkinson and Francois Bourguignon, pp. 87–166. Amsterdam: North-Holland.

Dasgupta, Partha. 2003. "What Do Economists Analyze: Values or Facts?" Paper prepared for the Conference on the Place of Value in a World of Facts, London School of Economics, October 2003.

Dollar, David, and Aart Kraay. 2002. "Growth Is Good for the Poor." *Journal of Economic Growth* 7, no. 3: 195–225.

Fields, Gary S. 2001. *Distribution and Development.* New York: Russell Sage.

Foster, James, Joel Greer, and Erik Thorbecke. 1984. "A Class of Decomposable Poverty Measures." *Econometrica* 52, no. 3: 761–65.

Hirschman, Albert O. 1970. *Exit, Voice, and Loyalty: Responses to Decline in Firms, Organizations, and States.* Harvard University Press.

International Forum on Globalization. 2002. *Alternatives to Economic Globalization: A Better World is Possible.* San Francisco: Berrett-Koehler.

Jenkins, Stephen P., and Peter J. Lambert. 1999. "Horizontal Inequality Measurement: A Basic Reassessment." In *Handbook of Income Inequality Measurement*, edited by Jacques Silber. Boston, Mass.: Kluwer Academic Publishers.

Kanbur, Ravi. 2001. "Economic Policy, Distribution and Poverty: The Nature of Disagreements." *World Development* 29, no. 6: 1083–94.

_____. 2003. "The Policy Significance of Inequality Decompositions." Mimeo. Cornell University.

Kolm, Serge. 1976. "Unequal Inequalities, I." *Journal of Economic Theory* 12 (June): 416–42.

Konow, James. 2003. "Which is the Fairest One of All? A Positive Analysis of Justice Theories." *Journal of Economic Literature* 41, no. 4: 1188–1239.

Lundberg, Mattias, and Lyn Squire. 2003. "The Simultaneous Evolution of Growth and Inequality." *Economic Journal* 113 (April): 326–44.

Maddison, Angus. 1998. *Chinese Economic Performance in the Long Run.* Paris: Organization for Economic Cooperation and Development.

Milanovic, Branko. 2000. "The Median-Voter Hypothesis, Income Inequality and Income Redistribution: An Empirical Test with the Required Data." *European Journal of Political Economy* 16: 367–410.

_____. 2002. "The Ricardian Vice: Why Sala-i-Martin's Calculations of World Income Inequality Are Wrong." Mimeo. Washington: World Bank, Development Research Group.

_____. 2004 (forthcoming). *Worlds Apart: Global and International Inequality 1950–2000.* Princeton University Press.

O'Rourke, Kevin. 2002. "Globalization and Inequality: Historical Trends." *Aussenwirtschaft* 57, no. 1: 65–101.

Pigou, Arthur C. 1949. *A Study in Public Finance*, 3d ed. London: Macmillan.

Pritchett, Lant. 1997. "Divergence, Big Time." *Journal of Economic Perspectives* 11, no. 3: 3–17.

_____. 2004 (forthcoming). "Who Is *Not* Poor: Dreaming of a World Truly Free of Poverty." *World Bank Research Observer.*

_____. Forthcoming. "The Future of Migration: Irresistible Forces Meet Immovable Ideas." In *The Future of Globalization: Explorations in Light of the Recent Turbulence.*

Ravallion, Martin. 1994. *Poverty Comparisons.* Chur, Switzerland: Harwood Academic Books.

_____. 1995. "Growth and Poverty: Evidence for Developing Countries in the 1980s." *Economics Letters* 48, no. 3: 411–17.

_____. 1996. "Issues in Measuring and Modeling Poverty." *Economic Journal* 106 (September): 1328–44.

_____. 2001. "Growth, Inequality and Poverty: Looking Beyond Averages." *World Development* 29, no. 11: 1803–15.

_____. 2003. "The Debate on Globalization, Poverty and Inequality: Why Measurement Matters." *International Affairs* 79, no. 4: 739–54.

_____. 2004. "Pro-Poor Growth: A Primer." Working Paper 3242. Washington: World Bank.

Ravallion, Martin, and Shaohua Chen. 1997. "What Can New Survey Data Tell Us about Recent Changes in Distribution and Poverty?" *World Bank Economic Review* 11, no. 2: 357–82.

Ravallion, Martin, and Michael Lokshin. 2002. "Self-Rated Economic Welfare in Russia." *European Economic Review* 46, no. 8: 1453–73.

_____. 2004. "Gainers and Losers from Agricultural Trade Reform in Morocco." Working Paper 3368. Washington: World Bank.

Ravallion, Martin, and Dominique Van de Walle. 1991. "The Impact on Poverty of Food Pricing Reforms: A Welfare Analysis for Indonesia." *Journal of Policy Modeling* 13, no. 2: 281–99.

Rodrik, Dani, and Raquel Fernandez. 1991. "Resistance to Reform: Status Quo Bias in the Presence of Individual-Specific Uncertainty." *American Economic Review* 81, no. 5: 1146–55.

Sala-i-Martin, Xavier. 2002a. "The Disturbing 'Rise' of Global Income Inequality." Working Paper 8904. Cambridge, Mass.: National Bureau of Economic Research.

_____. 2002b. "The World Distribution of Income." Working Paper 8933. Cambridge, Mass.: National Bureau of Economic Research.

Schultz, T. Paul. 1998. "Inequality in the Distribution of Personal Income in the World: Changing and Why." *Journal of Population Economics* 11, no. 3: 307–44.

Slesnick, Daniel T. 1998. "Empirical Approaches to the Measurement of Welfare." *Journal of Economic Literature* 36, no. 4: 2108–65.

Van de Walle, Dominique. 1998. "Targeting Revisited." *World Bank Research Observer* 13, no. 2: 231–48.

Wang, Xiaolu, and Lian Meng. 2001. "A Re-evaluation of China's Economic Growth." *China Economic Review* 12, no. 4: 338–46.

Williamson, Jeffrey G. 1998. "Globalization and the Labor Market: Using History to Inform Policy." In *Growth, Inequality and Globalization*, edited by Philippe Aghion and Jeffrey C. Williamson, pp. 103–99. Cambridge University Press.

World Bank. 1990. *World Development Report: Poverty*. New York: Oxford University Press.

_____. 2000. *World Development Report: Attacking Poverty*. Oxford University Press.

_____. 2002. *Globalization, Growth and Poverty*. Washington.

[7]

How Have the World's Poorest Fared since the Early 1980s?

Shaohua Chen • Martin Ravallion

A new assessment is made of the developing world's progress against poverty. By the frugal $1 a day standard there were 1.1 billion poor people in 2001—almost 400 million fewer than 20 years earlier. During that period the number of poor people declined by more than 400 million in China, though half the decline was in the early 1980s and the number outside China rose slightly. At the same time the number of people in the world living on less than $2 a day rose, so that there has been a marked bunching up of people living between $1 and $2 a day. Sub-Saharan Africa has become the region with the highest incidence of extreme poverty and the greatest depth of poverty. If these trends continue, the 1990 aggregate $1 a day poverty rate will be halved by 2015, meeting the Millennium Development Goal, though only East and South Asia will reach this goal.

A cloud of doubt hangs over our knowledge about the extent of the world's progress against poverty. A widely cited World Bank (2002) estimate is that there were 200 million fewer poor people in the world in 1998 than in 1980. This figure has been contested and for good reasons. Deaton (2002b) contrasts this seemingly optimistic assessment with the estimate in *World Development Report 2000/2001: Attacking Poverty* (World Bank 2000), which appeared to show little or no progress. Deaton argues that the claim in World Bank (2002) was based on methodologically inconsistent estimates from two studies—Bourguignon and Morisson (2002) (up to 1992) and Chen and Ravallion (2000) (beyond that).[1] With reference to the relevant chart in World Bank (2002) Deaton writes:

> The historical data in this chart were assembled by François Bourguignon and Christian Morrisson.... They derive their estimates by applying (sometimes sketchy and outdated) distributional information to the consumption figures from national accounts data, a technique that is almost certainly the

The World Bank Research Observer, vol. 19, no. 2,
© The International Bank for Reconstruction and Development / THE WORLD BANK 2004; all rights reserved.
doi:10.1093/wbro/lkh020   19:141–169

only methodology that would allow the construction of data for a century and a half. . . . After 1993, when the Bourguignon and Morrisson data end, *Globalization* [World Bank 2002] uses the poverty estimates that were assembled by Shaohua Chen and Martin Ravallion. . . . But Chen and Ravallion's data from 1987 to 1993, which is when poverty increased, are dropped from the chart. In consequence, and without any new information, we go from an assessment that the number of poor people in the world was showing little or no decline from 1987 to 1998 in *Attacking Poverty* to an assessment, in *Globalization*, of a continuous and accelerating decline from 1980 to 1998. (see www.imf.org/external/pubs/ft/fandd/2002/06/deaton.htm)

These concerns are too important to ignore. The splicing of these different data sources is questionable. The only solution is to construct a new, internally consistent series over the 1980s and 1990s.

This article offers a new assessment of progress in reducing poverty over 1981–2001 using more consistent data and methods—closely following the methods underlying the *Attacking Poverty* (World Bank 2000) numbers, which had been based on Chen and Ravallion (2000). In common with our past estimates, we draw on nationally representative surveys as much as possible. The article reviews our methods of measuring poverty from those surveys and notes any changes from past estimates, though we refer readers to other sources for further discussion of our methods and alternatives.[2] The new estimates presented here supersede all our previous estimates in that we recalculate everything back in time on a consistent basis incorporating the new data.[3]

We summarize our results in a standard regional tabulation following previous work. However, we have also created a Web-based interactive tool, PovcalNet, that allows users to access the primary distributions and so estimate poverty measures for alternative country groupings or for a selected set of individual countries (http://iresearch.worldbank.org/povcalnet).

A notable feature of these new estimates is that they go back to the early 1980s, allowing an assessment of the validity of the poverty reduction claim in World Bank (2002). We have previously resisted going back this far because of concerns about the coverage and quality of the survey data available for the early 1980s. Our efforts to expand coverage have helped allay our fears about reliability of the data from this time period. However, it is clear that our estimates for the first year in our series, 1981, are not as reliable as those in the rest of the series.

The new estimates suggest that the World Bank (2002) figure of 200 million fewer poor people is probably an underestimate. Indeed, our best estimates suggest that the figure is almost twice that number. That is good news. However, closer inspection of the data leaves little room for complacency about the world's progress against poverty. Indeed, the picture that emerges is one of highly uneven progress, with serious setbacks in some regions and time periods. The number of people living on less than $2 a day has risen.

It should not be forgotten that there are limitations to our measures. There are continuing concerns about aspects of the underlying data, including the purchasing power parity (PPP) exchange rates, the accuracy and comparability of the surveys used, and intrinsic limitations of the welfare measures based on those surveys. Potentially important examples of the limitations of the welfare measures is that our definition of poverty does not directly reflect inequality within households or access to public goods.

The article first describes the coverage of the survey data. It then discusses the poverty line and exchange rates, followed by the measures of poverty, and then presents the main results.

Coverage of the Household Surveys

This is our first attempt to estimate global poverty measures back to the early 1980s. Our previous estimates started in 1987 (Chen and Ravallion 2000, 2001). In retrospect, starting the series in 1987 was an unfortunate choice, because the late 1980s and early 1990s were a difficult time for the world's poor, given sharply lower growth in both China and India. Going back further in time should give a clearer idea of the long-term trend.

We draw on 454 surveys covering 97 countries representing 93 percent of the population of all low- and middle-income countries (Part 2 member countries of the World Bank). Taking the most recent survey for each country, about 1.1 million households were interviewed. The surveys were mostly done by government statistics offices as part of their routine operations.

The poverty measures are estimated from the survey data. No secondary sources are used for measuring poverty at each survey round (unlike all other compilations of distributional data and global poverty measures that we know of), although other data sources are used for interpolation, given that the surveys of different countries do not coincide in time. Households are ranked by consumption or income per person. The distributions are weighted by household size and sample expansion factors, so that a given fractile (such as the poorest decile) has the same share of the country-specific population across the sample. Thus the poverty counts give the number of people living in households with per capita consumption or income below the poverty line. The data come in various forms, ranging from micro data to specially designed grouped tabulations from the raw data constructed following our guidelines. Datt and Ravallion (1992) and Chen and others (1994) describe our estimation methods for grouped data.

As in previous work we try to eliminate obvious comparability problems, either by reestimating the consumption or income aggregates or by dropping a survey. However, there are problems that we cannot deal with. Differences in survey methods (such as in questionnaire design) can create nonnegligible differences in the estimates for consumption or income. For example, although one-week recall for food consumption is common in surveys, some countries use a longer period, which is likely to give a lower estimate of consumption and hence higher measured poverty. An unusual case is China, in which households are surveyed frequently throughout the year, allowing an estimate of annual income, whereas other countries typically use recall data for a month or less, obtained from one or just a few interviews; there is evidence that China's practice yields lower inequality measures (Gibson and others 2001).

A specific data problem that has received attention in the recent literature concerns the 55th round of India's National Sample Survey (NSS) for 1999/2000, which has created a potentially serious comparability problem with previousNSS rounds (see Datt and Ravallion 2002; Deaton 2002a, 2003). For greater comparability with previous NSS rounds, we use Deaton's (2003) adjusted distributions. The official distributions from the 55th round give a lower poverty rate in 1999/2000 (32.3 percent below $1 a day compared with 34.8 percent using Deaton's corrections). (The distributions are, of course, the same in the previous large sample survey, for which we obtain a $1 a day poverty rate of 41.9 percent.) However, Deaton's correction requires an unchanging probability of being poor conditional on consumption of the goods that appear to have been unaffected by the change in survey design. Changes in relative prices can cast doubt on this assumption (Datt and Ravallion 2002; Sen and Himanshu 2003).

Possibly, Deaton's method overestimates the decline in poverty in India between the 55th and previous rounds. An alternative approach to comparing the surveys for 1999/2000 with the previous large sample survey of 1993 has been proposed by Sundaram and Tendulkar (2003). It entails comparing estimates over time based on a mixed recall period instead of the uniform recall period used by the official data and by Deaton (2003). The comparison is possible only between these two surveys. With the Sundaram and Tendulkar distributions, the $1 a day poverty rate for India falls from 38.7 percent in 1993 to 32.3 percent in 1999/2000—a 6.4-percentage-point drop rather than our 7.1-percentage-point drop estimate using the Deaton-adjusted distributions.

Appendix table A.1 lists the surveys used, their dates, and whether consumption or income data are used. Population coverage varies greatly by region, ranging from 74 percent of the population of the Middle East and North Africa to 98 percent of the population of South Asia. Not all available surveys are included. Surveys are excluded if essential data are missing (such as for the PPP exchange rates or consumer price indices used to update poverty lines over time) or if there are serious comparability problems with the rest of the data set.

Naturally, the further back one goes, the fewer the number of surveys. Coverage deteriorates in the last year or two of the series, given the lags in survey processing. A simple but useful guide to the reliability of our estimates is to count the number of surveys by year and to compare the number with the three-year moving total centered on each year—given that having a survey last year or next year can help greatly in estimating poverty this year (figure 1). By this measure, our estimates are the most reliable for the mid- to late 1990s and the least reliable for 1981. We have only 15 surveys up to 1983, though the number rises sharply to 32 surveys for the period up to 1985. By contrast, we have 86 surveys during 1986–90.

Most regions are still quite well covered, from at least the second half of the 1980s (East and South Asia being well covered from 1981 onward). Two exceptions stand out. Unsurprisingly, country coverage in Eastern Europe and Central Asia is weak for the 1980s, when most of these countries did not officially exist. More worrying is the lack of coverage for Sub-Saharan Africa in the 1980s. The estimates for the early 1980s rely heavily on projections based on distributions for the late 1980s, as a list of the average survey year by region for each reference year

Figure 1. Number of National Household Surveys by Year, 1979–2002

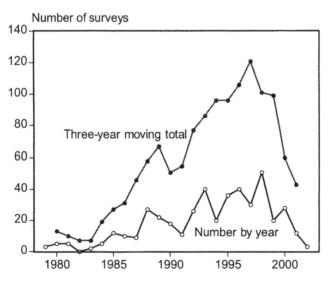

Source: National household surveys.

shows (table 1). Although survey coverage for Africa has improved considerably over our previous estimates (Chen and Ravallion 2001), the weakness of the coverage of Africa should be kept in mind when interpreting our results.

Even in regions with seemingly good survey coverage in the 1980s, there are questions about some of the data. The other side of the coin of improved household survey data for developing countries in the 1990s is the much weaker survey data in the 1980s. Consider China, the country with the largest population. The National Bureau of Statistics (NBS) has provided us with income distributions for China from surveys done in 1980 (rural areas) and 1981 (urban). However, the NBS was only beginning to resume doing national household surveys at that time (it had ceased doing surveys during the Cultural Revolution, 1966–76) and it can be conjectured that these early efforts were not as good (Chen and Ravallion 1996). The early NBS surveys (prior to 1985) did not include 30 percent of provinces. However, this does not appear to be a source of bias because the provincial coverage was uncorrelated with poverty; we could convincingly reject the null hypothesis that the first available estimates of all our poverty measures were the same for provinces omitted as for those included (Ravallion and Chen 2004). The sample sizes for these early surveys are also smaller than the other NBS surveys for China that we use, though the sample sizes are still adequate. For the 1980 survey in rural areas, 16,000 randomly sampled households were interviewed, and for the 1981 urban sample, about 9,000. By contrast, from 1985 onward the sample sizes were about 70,000 in rural areas and 30,000 in urban areas.

Table 1. Average Date of the Surveys Used for Each Reference Year, 1981–2001

Region	1981	1984	1987	1990	1993	1996	1999	2001
East Asia	1981.5	1984.6	1987.4	1990.4	1992.5	1996.1	1999.1	2000.4
Eastern Europe and Central Asia	1988.2	1988.1	1988.3	1989.6	1993.6	1995.7	1998.9	1999.7
Latin America and the Caribbean	1983.2	1984.7	1986.6	1990.4	1992.5	1996.1	1998.1	2000.1
Middle East and North Africa	1987.1	1987.8	1988.1	1990.0	1993.0	1996.0	1998.0	1998.2
South Asia	1980.9	1983.9	1987.2	1989.7	1993.0	1995.9	1999.0	1999.4
Sub-Saharan Africa	1988.6	1988.3	1989.6	1990.2	1993.0	1995.1	1996.6	1997.0
Total	**1982.8**	**1985.3**	**1987.7**	**1990.2**	**1992.8**	**1995.9**	**1998.5**	**1999.4**

Note: Population-weighted mean for all the surveys that were used to estimate the poverty measures for each reference year.

Source: National household surveys.

Exchange Rates and Poverty Lines

We use the same PPP estimates for consumption as Chen and Ravallion (2001), which were produced by the World Bank's Data Group (data sources and methods are described in Ahmad 2003). For 69 of the sample 97 countries, the PPPs are based on price and consumption basket data collected by the 1993 International Comparison Project (ICP). For almost all countries that did not participate in the 1993 ICP, the bank's PPPs are based on interpolations from the cross-country regressions described in Ahmad (2003). Two exceptions are China and India, for which the bank's PPPs are based on other sources—India's on an update of the country's 1985 PPP and China's on a credible independent study of prices levels in 10 cities (Ahmad 2003). As in Chen and Ravallion (2000), the Penn World Tables are used in preference to the World Bank's PPPs for five countries (Ghana, Mauritania, Nicaragua, the Philippines, and Uganda) for which the bank's PPPs give poverty rates that are implausibly low, whereas the PPPs for 1993 from the Penn World Tables (version 5.6) give more believable estimates.[4]

The international poverty line in our work prior to Chen and Ravallion (2001) was set at $1 a day at 1985 PPP (more precisely, at $31 a month or $1.02 a day; see Ravallion and others 1991). The original $1 a day poverty line was chosen as being representative of the poverty lines typical of low-income countries (Ravallion and others 1991). The same principle was applied by Chen and Ravallion (2001) in updating the poverty line using the new PPPs for 1993.

But the 1985 PPPs based on Penn World Tables are not comparable with the World Bank's PPPs at base 1993, either in primary data or method used. So one cannot update the poverty line simply by adjusting for inflation in the United States between 1985 and 1993. Indeed, that gives a poverty line that is well above those typical of low-income countries (Chen and Ravallion 2001).[5] To be consistent with the original aim of using a poverty line that is representative of the lines actually found in poor countries, we recalculate the dollar value of the original set of poverty lines using the new PPPs and compare this with mean consumption, also calculated by the new PPPs. Following Chen and Ravallion (2001), the resulting poverty line is $1.08 a day ($32.74 per month) in 1993 PPP prices. This is the median of the 10 lowest poverty lines in the set of countries used by Ravallion and others (1991). This is the main poverty line focused on here and is referred to as the "$1 a day" line or "extreme poverty."

However, the poverty rate on this basis must be deemed a conservative estimate, because aggregate poverty in the developing world is defined by perceptions of poverty rates in the poorest countries. (Not a new observation, this was argued explicitly in World Bank 1990 and Ravallion and others 1991.) Thus two broader definitions are also considered. In one the poor include all those who would be judged poor by standards more typical of middle-income countries. For this purpose the poverty line is set at twice the $1 a day line.

The second definition allows for "relative poverty." Chen and Ravallion (2001) proposed an operational approach for measuring relative poverty, building on Atkinson and Bourguignon (1999). By this measure of relative poverty people are deemed poor if they do not attain either the $1 a day consumption level (loosely interpretable as "physical needs") or a given proportion of mean consumption ("social needs"). The constant of proportionality was set at one-third, which gave the best fit to the data on poverty lines for developed and developing economies used in setting the $1.08 poverty line (Chen and Ravallion 2001). We fix the real value of the relative poverty line over time for each country. So these poverty lines are relative between countries but absolute over time. (Chen and Ravallion 2001 discuss this choice further.) Making the poverty lines relative over time would mean that for countries with mean consumption of greater than $3.23 a day the poverty measures will be independent of the absolute levels of consumption (and depend solely on the percentile of the population for which the Lorenz curve has a slope of 1/3).

Measuring Poverty from the Surveys

Three poverty measures are computed. The first measure is the *headcount index*, given by the percentage of the population living in households with consumption or income per person below the poverty line. This is the easiest measure to interpret, but it has the well-known deficiency that it says nothing about differences in the depth of poverty below the line. A second measure, the *number of poor people*, is obtained by applying the estimated headcount index to the population of each region (under the assumption that countries without surveys have the same headcount index on average as those with surveys). A third measure, the *poverty gap index*, gives mean distance below the poverty line as a proportion of the poverty line (where the mean is taken over the whole population, counting the nonpoor as having zero poverty gap). PovcalNet also gives estimates of the squared poverty gap, in which individual poverty gaps are weighted by the gaps themselves, to reflect inequality among the poor (Foster and others 1984).

In keeping with our previous work, we aim to measure poverty in terms of household consumption expenditure per capita. Of the 454 surveys used, 247 allow us to estimate the distribution of consumption expenditures; this is true of all the surveys used in the Middle East and North Africa, South Asia, and Sub-Saharan Africa. Whenever there is a choice consumption data are preferred to income data, because consumption is likely to be the better measure of current welfare. About one-quarter of the cases without consumption distributions do have survey-based estimates of mean consumption. For those cases the income mean is replaced by the consumption mean, leaving the Lorenz curve the same (all incomes are scaled up by the ratio of the consumption mean to the income mean). There is, however, no obvious basis for adjusting the Lorenz curve; one expects higher inequality in an income distribution than in a consumption distribution for the same place and data.

Our previous estimates for China (Chen and Ravallion 2001) relied on income Lorenz curves, but we used the survey means for household consumption expenditure per capita supplied by the NBS. For this update we obtained complete consumption distributions from the NBS back to 1990. To maintain consistency with our methods for other countries, we switch to consumption (for both the distribution and the mean) from 1990 onward, though we have no choice but to keep our old method for the 1980s. This raises a concern about comparability between our estimates for China for the 1990s and for the 1980s. To assess whether this is a problem, we also calculate our estimates for the 1990s using the old method. The two sets of estimates for the 1990s match up quite closely (table 2), so the comparisons over time do not appear to be of concern. Ravallion and Chen (2004) discuss this and other issues concerning China's poverty and inequality data in greater detail.

One important difference with Chen and Ravallion (2001) is that when only an income distribution is available, we do not follow our past practice of rescaling mean income by one minus the national savings rate. This practice was questioned by Deaton (2002a), and in Chen and Ravallion (2001) we noted the implications of

Table 2. Poverty Headcount Estimates for China by Old and New Methods, 1990–2001

		Headcount index (%)	
Year	Poverty line (1993 PPP$)	Old method: income distribution with adjustment to the mean (%)	New method: consumption distribution with consumption mean (%)
1981	1.08	63.76	
	2.15	88.12	
1984	1.08	40.99	
	2.15	78.49	
1987	1.08	28.45	
	2.15	67.41	
1990	1.08	31.53	33.01
	2.15	69.93	72.64
1993	1.08	29.46	28.36
	2.15	64.59	68.13
1996	1.08	16.91	17.38
	2.15	50.63	53.36
1999	1.08	16.42	17.77
	2.15	47.19	50.05
2001	1.08	16.51	16.64
	2.15	44.45	46.67

Source: Authors' calculations based on China's national household surveys.

dropping this rescaling. Since then we have assembled surveys for 27 countries for which we have both consumption and income distributions, to test this assumption in our past work by calculating the poverty measures using both consumption and income for the same country. There is only a small and statistically insignificant difference between the two sets of estimates: Consumption has a lower mean but also lower inequality, with the effect that poverty measures are quite close. For the $1 a day line the mean headcount index is 17.8 percent for consumption and 21.2 percent for income; the difference is not statistically significant ($t=0.73$; $n=27$). For the $2 a day line the mean headcount index is slightly higher for consumption (48.2 percent) than for income (44.8 percent) but, again the difference is not statistically significant ($t=0.49$). So we abandon our past practice of rescaling the mean for income surveys. The main implication is that our poverty measures for Latin America (where income surveys are more common than elsewhere) drop a few percentage points.

Having converted the international poverty line at PPP to local currency in 1993, we convert it to the prices prevailing at each survey date using the country-specific official consumer price index (CPI).[6] The weights in this index may or may not accord well with consumer budget shares at the poverty line. In periods of relative price shifts, this will bias our comparisons of the incidence of poverty over time, depending on the extent of utility-compensated substitution possibilities for people at the poverty line.

To estimate regional poverty at a given reference year (say, 1998) we "line up" the surveys in time using the same method as in our past work. We start the series in 1981 and make estimates at three yearly intervals, except for 2002, when there were too few surveys, so we estimate for 2001 instead. We thus make estimates for 1981, 1984, 1987, 1990, 1993, 1996, 1999, and 2001. These are called reference years, as distinct from survey years, which are spread over the interval 1979–2002 (see figure 1).

For the 97 countries, 9 have only one survey, 19 have two surveys, and 69 have three or more surveys over the period. If there is only one survey for a country, measures for each reference year are estimated by applying the growth rate in real private consumption per person from the national accounts to the survey mean—assuming that the Lorenz curve for that country does not change.[7] This seems the best option for dealing with this problem, though there can be no guarantee that the Lorenz curve would not have shifted or that a survey-based measure of consumption would have grown at the same rate as private consumption in the national accounts. For example, growth of private consumption in the national accounts might reflect growth in spending by nonprofit organizations— which are not separated from households in the national accounts for most developing economies—rather than growth in household spending (Ravallion 2003b).

When the reference date (say, 1993) is between two surveys (say, 1989 and 1995), one option is simply to interpolate between the two surveys. However, this could be problematic when there is a long time period between surveys, and it ignores the extra information available from the national accounts data. To bring the national accounts information into the picture, mean consumption is first estimated at the reference year using the national accounts growth rate between the survey year and the reference year. For the example here there are two means at the reference year based on two surveys, M93(89) and M93(95), where M93(t) is the estimated mean for 1993 using the survey for year t. Using the 1989 distribution and M93(89) yields headcount index H93(89). Similarly, using the 1995 distribution and the 1993 mean yields H93(95). Then the poverty headcount for 1993 is estimated as the weighted average of H93(89) and H93(95).[8]

Results

Estimates of the headcount indices for $1.08 at 1993 PPP for 1981–2001 show that the percentage of the population of the developing world living below $1 a day was almost halved over 1981–2001, falling from 40 percent to 21 percent (table 3). Expressed as a proportion of world population, the decline is from 33 percent to 18 percent. This assumes that nobody in developed areas lives below $1 a day.) The number of poor people fell by 390 million, from 1.5 billion in 1981 to 1.1 billion in 2001 (table 4).

There was clearly more progress in some periods than in others. As already noted, the late 1980s and early 1990s were a difficult period for the world's poor, with low growth in both China and India. Once growth was restored, the rate of poverty reduction by the $1 a day standard in the 1990s had returned to its long-term trend. The percentage below $1 a day fell from 28 percent to 21 percent over 1990–2001, about the same trend decline (in percentage points per year) as for 1984–2001 as a whole. The number of poor people fell by about 130 million in 1990s. The poverty measures for $2 a day follow a broadly similar pattern, though with a less dramatic decline in the early 1980s and even stronger signs of stagnation in the period around 1990 (see tables 3 and 4).

The new estimates suggest less progress in getting over the $2 a day line. By this higher standard the poverty rate has fallen from 67 percent in 1981 to 53 percent in 2001 (see table 3). This has not been sufficient to prevent a rise in the number of people living below $2 a day, from 2.4 billion to 2.7 billion (see table 4). Thus the number of people living between $1 and $2 has risen sharply over these two decades, from about 1 billion to 1.6 billion. This marked bunching up of people just above the $1 line suggests that a great many people in the world remain vulnerable to aggregate economic slowdowns.

Table 3. Headcount Indices of Poverty by Region for Two International Poverty Lines, 1981–2001 (%)

Poverty line and region	1981	1984	1987	1990	1993	1996	1999	2001
$1.08 a day (1993 PPP)								
East Asia	57.7	38.9	28.0	29.6	24.9	16.6	15.7	14.9
China	63.8	41.0	28.5	33.0	28.4	17.4	17.8	16.6
East Asia excluding China	42.0	33.5	27.0	21.1	16.7	14.7	11.0	10.8
Eastern Europe and Central Asia	0.7	0.5	0.4	0.5	3.7	4.3	6.3	3.6
Latin America and Caribbean	9.7	11.8	10.9	11.3	11.3	10.7	10.5	9.5
Middle East and North Africa	5.1	3.8	3.2	2.3	1.6	2.0	2.6	2.4
South Asia	51.5	46.8	45.0	41.3	40.1	36.6	32.2	31.3
India	54.4	49.8	46.3	42.1	42.3	42.2	35.3	34.7
South Asia excluding India	42.2	37.0	41.0	38.7	33.1	19.7	22.9	21.0
Sub-Saharan Africa	41.6	46.3	46.8	44.6	44.1	45.6	45.7	46.4
Total	40.4	32.8	28.4	27.9	26.3	22.8	21.8	21.1
Total excluding China	31.7	29.8	28.4	26.1	25.6	24.6	23.1	22.5
$2.15 a day (1993 PPP)								
East Asia	84.8	76.6	67.7	69.9	64.8	53.3	50.3	47.4
China	88.1	78.5	67.4	72.6	68.1	53.4	50.1	46.7
East Asia excluding China	76.2	72.0	68.4	63.2	56.7	53.2	50.8	49.2
Eastern Europe and Central Asia	4.7	4.1	3.2	4.9	17.3	20.7	23.8	19.7
Latin America and Caribbean	26.9	30.4	27.8	28.4	29.5	24.1	25.1	24.5
Middle East and North Africa	28.9	25.2	24.2	21.4	20.2	22.3	24.3	23.2
South Asia	89.1	87.2	86.7	85.5	84.5	81.7	78.1	77.2
India	89.6	88.2	87.3	86.1	85.7	85.2	80.6	79.9
South Asia excluding India	87.3	84.0	85.0	83.5	81.0	71.3	70.5	69.0
Sub-Saharan Africa	73.3	76.1	76.1	75.0	74.6	75.1	76.0	76.6
Total	66.7	63.7	60.1	60.8	60.2	55.5	54.4	52.9
Total excluding China	58.8	58.4	57.5	56.6	57.4	56.3	55.8	54.9

Source: Authors' calculations based on national household survey data.

Regional Differences

Performance in poverty reduction has been far from uniform across regions. Indeed, there have been notable changes in regional poverty rankings over this period. In 1981 East Asia had the highest incidence of extreme poverty in the world, with 58 percent of the population living below $1 a day. Next was South Asia, followed by Sub-Saharan Africa, Latin America, Middle East and North Africa, and Eastern Europe and Central Asia. Twenty years later, Sub-Saharan Africa had swapped places with East Asia, where the headcount index had fallen to 15 percent. South Asia remained in second place, but Eastern Europe and Central Asia had overtaken the Middle East and North Africa. The ordering of regions is not, however, robust to the choice of poverty line. At the $2 a day poverty line South Asia edges out East

Table 4. Number of Poor People by Region for Two International Poverty Lines, 1981–2001 (millions)

Poverty line and region	1981	1984	1987	1990	1993	1996	1999	2001
$1.08 a day (1993 PPP)								
East Asia	795.6	562.2	425.6	472.2	415.4	286.7	281.7	271.3
China	633.7	425.0	308.4	374.8	334.2	211.6	222.8	211.6
Eastern Europe and Central Asia	3.1	2.4	1.7	2.3	17.5	20.1	30.1	17.0
Latin America and Caribbean	35.6	46.0	45.1	49.3	52.0	52.2	53.6	49.8
Middle East and North Africa	9.1	7.6	6.9	5.5	4.0	5.5	7.7	7.1
South Asia	474.8	460.3	473.3	462.3	476.2	461.3	428.5	431.1
India	382.4	373.5	369.8	357.4	380.0	399.5	352.4	358.6
Sub-Saharan Africa	163.6	198.3	218.6	226.8	242.3	271.4	294.3	312.7
Total	1,481.8	1,276.8	1,171.2	1,218.5	1,207.5	1,097.2	1,095.7	1,089.0
$2.15 a day (1993 PPP)								
East Asia	1169.8	1108.6	1028.3	1116.3	1079.3	922.2	899.6	864.3
China	875.8	813.8	730.8	824.6	802.9	649.6	627.5	593.6
Eastern Europe and Central Asia	20.2	18.3	14.7	22.9	81.3	97.8	113.0	93.3
Latin America and Caribbean	98.9	118.9	115.4	124.6	136.1	117.2	127.4	128.2
Middle East and North Africa	51.9	49.8	52.5	50.9	51.8	60.9	70.4	69.8
South Asia	821.1	858.6	911.4	957.5	1004.8	1029.1	1039.0	1063.7
India	630.0	661.4	697.1	731.4	769.5	805.7	804.4	826.0
Sub-Saharan Africa	287.9	326.0	355.2	381.6	410.4	446.8	489.3	516.0
Total	2,450.0	2,480.1	2,477.5	2,653.8	2,763.6	2,674.1	2,738.8	2,735.4

Source: Authors' calculations based on national household survey data.

Asia for the highest headcount index in 1981, and it edges out Africa for the highest headcount index in 2001.

The dramatic progress in East Asia has meant that by 2001 the region had already reached the Millennium Development Goal of halving the 1990 $1 a day poverty rate by 2015. China's progress against absolute poverty was a key factor (given the country's population weight), though the rest of East Asia had the same proportionate decline in poverty over 1981–2001 as did China (see table 3). In 1981 China's incidence of poverty at the $1 a day measure was roughly twice that for the rest of the developing world; by the mid-1990s China's poverty rate had fallen well below the average. There were 400 million fewer people living under $1 a day in China in 2001 than 20 years earlier, though a staggering half of this decline was in the period 1981–84 (see table 4). This was enormous progress for China's (and the world's) poor people. The most plausible explanation would appear to be China's reforms, starting in the late 1970s, which decollectivized agriculture and, in the "household responsibility system," gave farmers considerably greater control over their land and output choices (Ravallion and Chen 2004 discuss this and other explanations for China's success against absolute poverty). This was a one-off reform, however, suggesting that the sharp drop in global poverty by the $1 a day standard in the early 1980s was also unusual. China experienced a further drop in the poverty count of 120 million between 1993 and 1996, which is generally attributed to the substantial but short-lived increases in 1994 and 1995 in the procurement prices for food grains paid by the government, which greatly reduced the burden on farmers of this form of taxation (World Bank 1997; Ravallion and Chen 2004).

The long-run trend decline in the global $1 a day poverty rate over 1981–2001 is 0.86 percentage point a year (table 5). For 1984–2001, which is more indicative of the overall trend given the unusual large decline in extreme poverty between 1981 and 1984 resulting from China's agrarian transition, the trend is 0.66 percentage point a year.[9] Focusing on the 1990s could also be deceptive, because the early 1990s had relatively high poverty as a result of the stalled growth in China and India.

For the developing world outside China, the headcount index for the $1 a day poverty line fell from 32 percent to 23 percent over 1981–2001. This was not sufficient to prevent an increase in the total number of poor people, which rose from 850 million to 880 million. The decline in the headcount index over time in the developing world excluding China was close to linear (figure 2), with a trend decline of 0.42 percentage point a year (with a standard error of 0.029).

The number of poor people has also fallen in South Asia, from 475 million in 1981 to about 430 million in 2001 (figure 3), and the poverty rate fell from 52 percent to 31 percent. The South Asia series suggests a remarkably robust trend rate of decline in the $1 a day headcount index of 1 percentage point a year (see table 5). (For South Asia a linear trend clearly fits better than an exponential trend.) If maintained, this will be sufficient to reach the Millennium Development Goal for poverty reduction. The critical value needed to reach the goal is −0.83 percentage point a year, which is outside the 95 percent confidence interval (−0.87, −1.09) for the estimate of South Asia's trend rate of poverty reduction.

The extent of bunching up that has occurred between the $1 and $2 a day poverty lines is particularly striking in East and South Asia, where the total number is 1.2 billion, roughly equally split between the two regions. Although this points again to the vulnerability of the poor, it also suggests that substantial further

Table 5. Trend Rates of Change by Region in the Headcount Index for the $1 a Day Poverty Line, 1981–2001 and 1984–2001 (percentage points per year)

Region	1981–2001	1984–2001	Critical rate for halving the 1990 headcount index
East Asia	−1.87*	−1.36*	−0.59
	(0.32)	(0.19)	
China	−1.99*	−1.37*	−0.66
	(0.40)	(0.26)	
Latin America and Caribbean	−0.03	−0.10	−0.23
	(0.04)	(0.03)	
South Asia	−0.98*	−0.95*	−0.83
	(0.05)	(0.05)	
India	−0.91*	−0.83*	−0.84
	(0.10)	(0.12)	
Sub-Saharan Africa	0.12	0.00	−0.89
	(0.09)	(0.08)	
Total	−0.86*	−0.66*	−0.56
	(0.12)	(0.06)	

*Significant at the 1 percent level.

Note: The numbers in parentheses are standard errors. Eastern Europe and Central Asia and the Middle East and North Africa regions are dropped from this table because there were so few people living below the $1 a day poverty line in 1990. Trends were estimated by linear regression on time. All regressions were tested for first-order serial correlation in the errors using the Lagrange multiplier tests. The null hypothesis of serial independence could not be rejected in any case.

Source: Authors' calculations based on national household survey data.

impacts on poverty can be expected from economic growth, provided that it does not come with higher inequality.

There is less sign of progress against poverty outside Asia. The number of poor people increased in Latin America, where the poverty rate has been roughly constant over time (10 percent for $1 a day and 25 percent for $2 a day, which is closer to the national poverty lines in that region). The Middle East and North Africa region experienced a marked downward trend in the poverty rate during the 1980s, but the rate stabilized in the 1990s at around 2 percent for the $1 a day poverty line and at a little more than 20 percent for the $2 a day line.

Both the incidence of poverty and the number of poor people rose in Eastern Europe and Central Asia in the 1990s compared with the 1980s. Although very few people live below $1 a day in this region, the poverty rate by the $2 a day standard rose from almost 2 percent in 1981 to 20 percent in 2001. However, the paucity of survey data for this region in the 1980s should not be forgotten. Thus the estimates are based heavily on interpolations, which do not allow for any changes in distribution. Distribution was probably better from the point of view of the poor in the

Figure 2. Headcount Indices of Poverty Incidence in the Developing World for the $1 a Day International Poverty Line, with and without China, 1981–2001

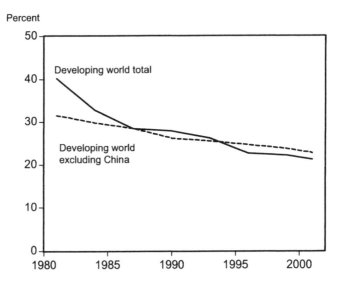

Note: The actual $1 a day poverty line is $1.08 (1993 PPP).
Source: Authors' calculations based on national household survey data.

1980s, in which case poverty would have been even lower than estimated here. There are also some signs of recent progress for the poorest in the region, though it is too early to say if this represents a change in trend.

The incidence of poverty in Sub-Saharan Africa has fluctuated around a mean of 45 percent for the $1 a day line (75 percent for the $2 a day line), with no significant trend in either direction (see table 5). The number of poor people almost doubled over 1981–2001, from 164 million to 316 million. By the $1 a day measure the share of the world's poor living in Africa has risen from 11 percent in 1981 to 29 percent in 2001.

The critical rates of decline in poverty needed to achieve the Millennium Development Goal by 2015 are given in table 5. The actual trend rates of decline in the aggregate $1 a day poverty rate will be sufficient to achieve the Millennium Development Goal if progress is maintained until 2015. However, the variations found over time point to a need for caution. For the full time period studied, the critical trend needed to reach the Millennium Development Goal is just outside the 95 percent confidence interval for the estimated trend, so it can be claimed with

Figure 3. Number of Poor People by Region for the $1 a Day International Poverty Line, 1981–2001

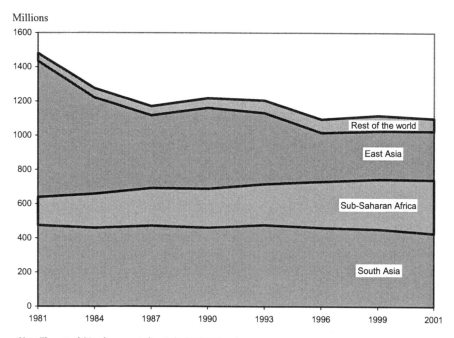

Millions

Note: The actual $1 a day poverty line is $1.08 (1993 PPP).

Source: Authors' calculations based on national household survey data.

95 percent confidence that the trend over 1981–2001 exceeds that needed to halve the 1990 headcount index for $1 a day. However, 1981–84 was an unusual subperiod, as we have noted. For the period 1984–2001 the critical trend for the Millennium Development Goal is within the 95 percent confidence interval. For the series starting in 1984, it can only be said with about 90 percent confidence that the aggregate trend exceeds the critical value needed to halve the 1990 poverty rate.

Poverty Gap Indices

The poverty gap index, PG, is related to the headcount index, H, as $PG=(1-MP)H$, where MP is the ratio of the mean income of the poor to the poverty line. Regional rankings for the poverty gap index (table 6) are the same as those for the headcount index (see table 3), and they follow the same change in patterns over time.

Table 6. Poverty Gap Indices by Region for Two International Poverty Lines, 1981–2001 (%)

Poverty line and region	1981	1984	1987	1990	1993	1996	1999	2001
$1.08 a day (1993 PPP)								
East Asia	20.58	11.11	7.69	7.65	6.13	3.52	3.57	3.35
China	23.41	11.82	8.17	8.87	7.34	3.82	4.18	3.94
Eastern Europe and Central Asia	0.18	0.14	0.11	0.11	0.84	1.25	1.86	0.75
Latin America and Caribbean	2.75	3.45	3.36	3.57	3.52	2.36	4.03	3.36
Middle East and North Africa	1.00	0.76	0.61	0.49	0.27	0.39	0.53	0.45
South Asia	16.06	13.86	12.35	11.00	10.21	8.97	6.63	6.37
India	17.27	14.99	12.68	11.09	10.86	10.55	7.22	7.08
Sub-Saharan Africa	17.03	19.65	20.10	19.07	19.24	19.80	20.10	20.53
Total	13.92	10.20	8.64	8.23	7.62	6.44	6.20	5.99
$2.15 a day (1993 PPP)								
East Asia	47.20	36.45	29.36	30.55	27.22	19.95	18.94	17.78
China	50.82	37.92	29.67	32.94	29.85	20.33	19.79	18.44
Eastern Europe and Central Asia	1.43	1.16	0.87	1.35	5.49	7.06	8.25	5.87
Latin America and Caribbean	10.66	12.44	11.48	11.81	12.04	9.25	10.97	10.20
Middle East and North Africa	8.81	7.36	6.80	5.69	5.05	5.74	6.54	6.14
South Asia	45.78	43.02	41.86	39.92	38.84	36.52	32.98	32.35
India	47.22	44.68	42.52	40.43	40.10	39.93	34.89	34.43
Sub-Saharan Africa	38.54	41.77	42.14	40.77	40.53	41.24	41.79	41.42
Total	35.02	30.79	27.86	27.80	26.82	23.76	23.05	22.20

Source: Authors' calculations based on national household survey data.

The most striking finding for the regional poverty gap indices is the depth of poverty in Africa, which has a $1 a day poverty gap index of 20 percent compared with 6 percent for the developing world as a whole. Furthermore, the mean income of Africa's poor has been falling over time, dropping from $0.64 per person per day in 1981 to $0.60 in 2001 for the $1 a day poverty line, though remaining roughly constant for the $2 a day line (table 7). In the rest of the world poverty became shallower. The mean income of the poor in the developing world as a whole rose for the $1 a day poverty line from about $0.70 in 1981 to $0.77 in 2001 and even more markedly for the $2 a day line, from $1.02 to $1.25.

The fact that the mean income of the poor is lowest in Africa implies that unless inequality falls sufficiently, it will take more growth in Africa than in other regions

Table 7. Mean Daily Income of the Poor by Region for Two International Poverty Lines, 1981–2001 (1993 PPP$)

Poverty line and region	1981	1984	1987	1990	1993	1996	1999	2001
$1.08 a day (1993 PPP)								
East Asia	0.69	0.77	0.78	0.80	0.81	0.85	0.83	0.83
China	0.68	0.77	0.77	0.79	0.80	0.84	0.82	0.82
Eastern Europe and Central Asia	0.81	0.80	0.76	0.85	0.83	0.76	0.76	0.91
Latin America and Caribbean	0.77	0.76	0.74	0.73	0.74	0.84	0.66	0.70
Middle East and North Africa	0.86	0.86	0.87	0.85	0.89	0.87	0.86	0.87
South Asia	0.74	0.76	0.78	0.79	0.80	0.81	0.85	0.86
India	0.73	0.75	0.78	0.79	0.80	0.81	0.86	0.86
Sub-Saharan Africa	0.64	0.62	0.61	0.62	0.61	0.61	0.60	0.60
Total	0.70	0.74	0.75	0.76	0.76	0.77	0.77	0.77
$2.15 a day (1993 PPP)								
East Asia	0.95	1.13	1.22	1.21	1.25	1.35	1.34	1.35
China	0.91	1.11	1.21	1.18	1.21	1.33	1.30	1.30
Eastern Europe and Central Asia	1.50	1.55	1.57	1.56	1.47	1.42	1.41	1.51
Latin America and Caribbean	1.30	1.27	1.26	1.26	1.27	1.33	1.21	1.26
Middle East and North Africa	1.50	1.52	1.55	1.58	1.61	1.60	1.57	1.58
South Asia	1.05	1.09	1.11	1.15	1.16	1.19	1.24	1.25
India	1.02	1.06	1.10	1.14	1.15	1.14	1.22	1.23
Sub-Saharan Africa	1.02	0.97	0.96	0.98	0.98	0.97	0.97	0.99
Total	1.02	1.11	1.15	1.17	1.19	1.23	1.24	1.25

Source: Authors' calculations based on national household survey data.

to have the same proportionate impact on the poverty gap. This is borne out by calculations of the elasticities of the poverty gap index to growth in the mean, holding inequality constant (so that all levels of income grow at the same rate). The higher the mean income of the poor, the higher is the absolute elasticity of the poverty gap index to the overall mean. (It is readily verified that when all levels of income grow at the same rate, the elasticity of the poverty gap index to the overall mean is $-MP/[1 - MP]$.) Thus although this elasticity for the $1 a day poverty line in 2001 is –1.3 for Sub-Saharan Africa, it is –1.8 for Latin America and the Caribbean, –3.3 for East Asia (–3.2 for China), –3.7 for Eastern Europe and Central Asia, –3.9 in South Asia, and –4.3 for the Middle East and North Africa (though this is deceptive, because proportionately fewer people live below the $1 a day line; elasticity falls to –2.8 for the $2 a day line). The elasticity is –2.5 for the developing world overall. The elasticity has fallen (in absolute value) over time in Africa, though only slightly (from –1.4 in 1981), while rising in the developing world as a whole (from –1.9 in 1981).

Relative Poverty

The absolute poverty measures examined so far aim to treat the same consumption level the same way no matter what country a person lives in. To see how the results might be affected by making an allowance for relative deprivation, poverty is estimated based on the relative poverty lines described above (table 8 and figure 4).

As expected, the incidence of relative poverty is noticeably higher for Eastern Europe and Central Asia, Latin America, and the Middle East and North Africa. By this measure Latin America overtakes South Asia in the early 1990s, making it the second poorest region. And Eastern Europe and Central Asia overtakes East Asia by

Table 8. Relative Poverty Measures by Region, 1981–2001

Region	1981	1984	1987	1990	1993	1996	1999	2001
Headcount index (%)								
East Asia	63.15	44.45	33.92	35.31	30.17	21.48	20.86	19.69
China	63.76	41.01	28.45	33.01	28.36	17.38	17.77	16.64
Eastern Europe and Central Asia	8.11	7.53	6.41	7.77	22.65	23.17	27.17	21.49
Latin America and Caribbean	40.55	45.37	42.34	43.28	44.97	39.39	38.98	39.77
Middle East and North Africa	37.36	33.40	21.80	19.29	17.58	17.16	18.26	16.91
South Asia	58.17	50.65	47.72	41.45	40.33	36.87	32.09	31.41
India	62.55	54.50	49.43	42.07	42.31	42.25	35.33	34.70
Sub-Saharan Africa	45.93	50.48	51.27	47.61	47.56	48.71	49.66	50.18
Total	50.1	42.0	36.6	35.3	34.9	30.6	29.8	28.8
Number of poor (millions)								
East Asia	871.3	642.9	515.2	563.7	502.6	371.4	373.1	358.8
China	633.7	425.2	308.4	374.8	334.2	211.6	222.8	211.6
Eastern Europe and Central Asia	34.9	33.3	29.2	36.2	106.8	109.6	128.9	102.0
Latin America and Caribbean	149.1	177.6	175.6	189.8	207.8	191.3	198.1	208.3
Middle East and North Africa	67.1	66.1	47.3	45.8	45.0	46.8	52.8	50.8
South Asia	536.2	498.6	501.4	464.5	479.4	464.1	426.9	432.8
India	439.6	408.6	394.8	357.4	380.0	399.5	352.4	358.6
Sub-Saharan Africa	180.5	216.4	239.3	242.2	261.6	290.0	319.5	338.2
Total	1839.2	1634.9	1508.0	1542.1	1603.2	1473.2	1499.4	1490.8

Note: The relative poverty line is $1.08 or one-third of mean consumption, whichever is larger.

Source: Authors' calculations based on national household survey data.

Figure 4. Number of Poor People by Region for a Relative Poverty Line, 1981–2001

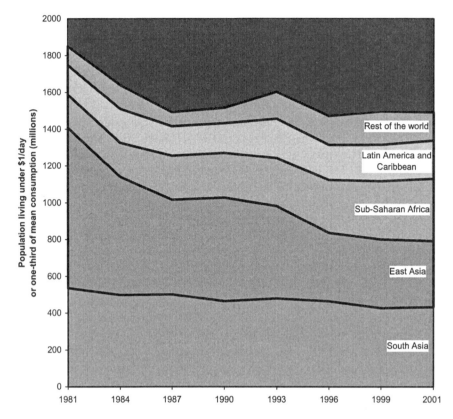

Note: The relative poverty line is $1.08 a day or one-third of mean consumption, whichever is larger.
Source: Authors' calculations based on national household survey data.

the mid-1990s. Although there are marked changes in regional rankings, the aggregate trends over time are quite similar. (This is at least in part a consequence of the fact that the relative poverty lines are absolute over time.) The incidence of relative poverty in the developing world as a whole is 29 percent in 2001, down from 50 percent in 1981. By this measure the total number of poor people is 1.5 billion in 2001. The total number of poor people by the relative poverty measure has shown no trend decline since the mid-1980s. Excluding China, the number of relatively poor people has remained at around 1.2 billion, though showing a slight upward trend in the 1990s.

Conclusions

In providing new estimates of the extent of poverty in the developing world over 1981–2001, we have followed previous practice in focusing primarily on an international poverty line that accords with poverty lines typical of the poorest countries. We used a poverty line of about $1 a day, though we also considered a line set at twice this value, as well as a relative poverty line that rises with average consumption when it exceeds about $3 a day. The estimates drew on newly available household surveys, and all past estimates have been revised in the light of the new data. Our estimates appear to be more internally consistent and comparable over time than past estimates, including those of World Bank (2002), which argued that there were 200 million fewer poor at the end of twentieth century than 20 years earlier.

We find that the 200 million figure is an underestimate and that the reduction in the number of poor people in the world was almost twice that size, entailing a near halving of the 1981 poverty rate of 40 percent by 2001.

The precise time period covered is crucial, however. Progress against extreme poverty has been uneven over time. The most dramatic reduction in poverty was in the early 1980s; about half of the 390 million drop in the $1 a day poverty count between 1981 and 2001 occurred in the first three years of that period. This coincided with the sharp drop in extreme poverty in China in the aftermath of the reforms that abandoned the socialist mode of agricultural production in favor of household-based farming. In contrast, during 1987–93 the number of people living on less than $1 a day stayed roughly constant, at around 1.2 billion. There was more progress in the 1990s, once growth had been restored in the most populous countries, China and India. There were 100 million fewer poor people by the $1 a day standard at the end of the 1990s than at the beginning. For assessing overall trends, we argue that the focus should be on the period 1984–2001.

Although the overall picture is good news, it is no cause for complacency. The 390 million fewer poor people by the $1 a day poverty line over 1981–2001 are still poor by the standards of middle-income developing economies and certainly very poor by the standards of what poverty means in rich countries. Our estimates indicate that the number of people living on less than $2 a day has risen. Clearly, a great many people remain poor and vulnerable to aggregate economic slowdowns.

Nor has this aggregate progress for the poorest over the 1980s and 1990s been shared by all regions. The dramatic progress against poverty in the early 1980s owes much to China. If one focuses on the developing world outside China, the number of poor people by the $1 a day standard has changed little—indeed, it has risen slightly.

The composition of world poverty has changed dramatically. The number of poor people has fallen in Asia but risen elsewhere. The share of the world's poor people living in Africa has risen appreciably. Not only has Africa emerged in the 1990s as the region with the highest incidence of poverty, but the depth of poverty is also markedly higher than in other regions—suggesting that future economic growth will have a harder time reducing poverty in Africa than elsewhere unless inequality falls.

If the trend rate of decline in the incidence of poverty by the $1 a day standard over 1984–2001 is maintained over 2001–15, it will be sufficient to halve the 1990 aggregate headcount index by 2015, consistent with the Millennium Development Goal. However, only one part of the world—East and South Asia—will have reached the goal.

Appendix: Survey Data Sets by Country, Date, and Welfare Indicator

Table A.1. Survey Data Set

Region	Share of 2001 population represented (%)	Country	Survey dates	Welfare indicator
East Asia	96.11	Cambodia	1997	Expenditure
		China	1980, 1981, 1984, 1985, 1987, 1990	Income
			1990, 1992, 1993, 1996, 1999, 2001	Expenditure
		Indonesia	1981, 1984, 1987, 1990, 1993, 1996, 1999, 2002	Expenditure
		Lao PDR	1992, 1997	Expenditure
		Malaysia	1984, 1987, 1989, 1992, 1995, 1997	Income
		Mongolia	1995,1998	Expenditure
		Philippines	1985, 1988, 1991, 1994, 1997, 2000	Expenditure
		Thailand	1981, 1988	Income
			1988, 1992, 1996, 1998, 1999, 2000, 2002	Expenditure
		Vietnam	1992/93, 1998	Expenditure
Eastern Europe and Central Asia	97.32	Albania	1997, 2002	Expenditure
		Armenia	1988, 1996	Income
			1996, 1998	Expenditure
		Azerbaijan	1988	Income
			1995, 2001	Expenditure
		Belarus	1988, 1993, 1995, 1998, 1999	Income
			1996–2000	Expenditure

(Continued)

Table A.1. (Continued)

Region	Share of 2001 population represented (%)	Country	Survey dates	Welfare indicator
		Bulgaria	1989, 1992, 1994, 1995, 1997, 2001	Expenditure
			1993, 1996	Income
		Croatia	1998, 1999, 2000, 2001	Expenditure
			1988, 1998	Income
		Czech Republic	1988, 1993, 1996	Income
		Estonia	1988, 1993, 1995, 1998	Income
		Georgia	1989, 1996, 1997	Income
			1996, 1998–2001	Expenditure
		Hungary	1989, 1993–1996, 1998	Income
		Kazakhstan	1988, 1993	Income
			1993, 1996, 2000	Expenditure
		Kyrgyz Republic	1988, 1993, 1996, 1998	Income
			1993, 1997–2001	Expenditure
		Latvia	1988, 1993, 1995, 1998	Income
		Lithuania	1988, 1993, 1994, 1996, 2000	Income
			1996, 1998, 2000	Expenditure
		Macedonia	1988	Income
			1998	Expenditure
		Moldova	1988, 1992, 1997	Income
			1997–2001	Expenditure
		Poland	1985, 1987, 1989, 1993, 1998	Income
			1990, 1992, 1993–96	Expenditure
		Romania	1989, 1992, 1994	Income
			1998, 2000	Expenditure
		Russian Federation	1988, 1993	Income
			1993, 1996, 1998, 2000	Expenditure
		Slovak Republic	1988, 1992, 1996	Income
		Slovenia	1987, 1993, 1996, 1998	Income
		Tajikistan	1998	Expenditure
		Turkey	1987, 1994, 2000	Expenditure
		Turkmenistan	1988, 1993, 1998	Income
		Ukraine	1988, 1992, 1997	Income
			1995, 1996, 1999	Expenditure
		Uzbekistan	1988, 1993	Income
			1998, 2000	Expenditure
Latin America and the Caribbean	95.31	Argentina	1980, 1982, 1989, 1992, 1996, 1998, 2001	Income
		Bolivia	1986, 1990, 1997, 1999	Income

Table A.1. (Continued)

Region	Share of 2001 population represented (%)	Country	Survey dates	Welfare indicator
		Brazil	1981, 1984, 1985, 1987, 1988–89, 1990, 1993, 1995–98, 2001	Income
		Chile	1987, 1990, 1992, 1994, 1996, 1998, 2001	Income
		Colombia	1980, 1988, 1989, 1991, 1995–96, 1998–1999	Income
		Costa Rica	1981, 1986, 1989, 1990, 1993, 1996–1998, 2001	Income
		Dominican Republic	1986, 1989, 1992,1996, 1998	Income
		Ecuador	1988, 1994–95, 1998	Income
			1994–95	Expenditure
		El Salvador	1989, 1995–98, 2000	Income
		Guatemala	1986, 1989, 1998, 2000	Income
		Guyana	1993, 1998	Expenditure
		Honduras	1986, 1989–90, 1992, 1994, 1996–1999	Income
		Jamaica	1988–94, 1996–2000	Expenditure
		Mexico	1984, 1992, 2000	Expenditure
			1989, 1995, 1996, 1998	Income
		Nicaragua	1993, 1998	Expenditure
		Panama	1979, 1989, 1991, 1995–98, 2000	Income
		Paraguay	1990, 1995, 1997–1999	Income
		Peru	1985, 1994, 1996	Expenditure
			1994, 1996, 2000	Income
		St. Lucia	1995	Income
		Trinidad and Tobago	1988, 1992	Income
		Uruguay	1981, 1989, 1996–1998, 2000	Income
		Venezuela	1981, 1987, 1989, 1991, 1993, 1995–98	Income
Middle East and North Africa	74.05	Algeria	1988, 1995	Expenditure
		Egypt, Arab Rep.	1991, 1995, 2000	Expenditure
		Iran	1986, 1990, 1994, 1998	Expenditure
		Jordan	1987, 1992, 1997	Expenditure
		Morocco	1985, 1990, 1998/99	Expenditure
		Tunisia	1985, 1990, 1995, 2000	Expenditure
		Yemen	1992, 1998	Expenditure

(Continued)

Table A.1. (Continued)

Region	Share of 2001 population represented (%)	Country	Survey dates	Welfare indicator
South Asia	98.09	Bangladesh	1983/84, 1984–85, 1988, 1992, 1996, 2000	Expenditure
		India	1977/78, 1983, 1986–91, 1993/94, 1995/96, 1999/2000	Expenditure
		Nepal	1985, 1995	Expenditure
		Pakistan	1986/87, 1990/91, 1992/93, 1996/97, 1998	Expenditure
		Sri Lanka	1980, 1985, 1990, 1995	Expenditure
Sub-Saharan Africa	77.86	Botswana	1985/86, 1993	Expenditure
		Burkina Faso	1994, 1998	Expenditure
		Burundi	1992, 1998	Expenditure
		Cameroon	1996	Expenditure
		Central African Republic	1993	Expenditure
		Côte d'Ivoire	1985–88, 1993, 1995, 1998	Expenditure
		Ethiopia	1981, 1995, 2000	Expenditure
		Gambia, The	1992, 1998	Expenditure
		Ghana	1987, 1989, 1998	Expenditure
		Kenya	1992, 1994, 1997	Expenditure
		Lesotho	1986, 1993, 1995	Expenditure
		Madagascar	1980, 1993, 1999	Expenditure
		Mali	1989, 1994	Expenditure
		Malawi	1997	Expenditure
		Mauritania	1988, 1993, 1995, 2000	Expenditure
		Mozambique	1996/97	Expenditure
		Namibia	1993	Expenditure
		Niger	1992, 1995	Expenditure
		Nigeria	1985, 1992, 1997	Expenditure
		Rwanda	1983/85	Expenditure
		Senegal	1991, 1994	Expenditure
		Sierra Leone	1989	Expenditure
		South Africa	1993, 1995, 2000	Expenditure
		Swaziland	1994	Expenditure
		Tanzania	1991	Expenditure
		Uganda	1988, 1992, 1996, 1999	Expenditure
		Zambia	1991, 1993, 1996, 1998	Expenditure
		Zimbabwe	1990/91, 1995	Expenditure

Source: National household surveys.

Notes

Shaohua Chen is senior information officer in the Development Research Group at the World Bank; her e-mail address is schen@worldbank.org. Martin Ravallion is research manager in the Development Research Group at the World Bank; his e-mail address is mravallion@worldbank.org. The authors are grateful to numerous colleagues at the World Bank who helped them obtain the necessary data and answered their many questions, and the staff of numerous governmental statistics offices who collected the primary survey data. The able assistance of Prem Sangraula is gratefully acknowledged. Angus Deaton, Johan Mistiaen, Dominique van de Walle, and the journal's editorial board made useful comments on the first draft.

1. Wade (2004) also questions the 200 million figure. However, he misdiagnoses the problem by confusing changes in the methods used to count the world's poor people with the methodological issues related to the way World Bank (2002) used different data sources. In fact, the Chen and Ravallion estimates used in World Bank (2002) would be judged internally consistent by Wade's criteria. The Deaton critique is more persuasive because it is grounded on a well-researched understanding of the methods involved.

2. For a critical overview of our estimation methods, see Deaton (2002a), which covers the main issues raised in the literature. Ravallion (2002a) replies to Deaton's comments; also see Ravallion (2003a) for further discussion.

3. The latest individual country estimates can be found online at www.worldbank.org/research/povmonitor. The latest year's estimates at the country level are also published in the World Bank's *World Development Indicators* (see, for example, World Bank 2004).

4. Because we are using the same PPP rates as Chen and Ravallion (2001), we use Penn World Tables 5.6, which was the latest available at that time. Version 6.1 has since become available.

5. Thus we do not accept the claims made by Reddy and Pogge (2002) and Wade (2004) that we have lowered the real value of the poverty line. They ignore the fact that there has been (in effect) a PPP devaluation of poor countries relative to the United States since the switch from the 1985- to 1993-based PPPs, reflecting both the new ICP price data and differences in methods of measuring the PPP rate. For further discussion of the Reddy and Pogge criticisms of our methods see Ravallion (2002b).

6. Note that the same poverty line is generally used for urban and rural areas. There are two exceptions. For China and India we estimate poverty measures separately for urban and rural areas and use sector-specific CPIs. For India we also use a corrected version of the rural CPI (the consumer price index for agricultural laborers), as discussed in Datt and Ravallion (1998).

7. For Nigeria we used the GDP per capita growth rate. Substantial changes in Nigeria's method of calculating private consumption made it impossible to construct a consistent series for consumption.

8. Thus $H93 = [(1995-1993)/(1995-1989)] \cdot H93(89) + [(1993-1989)/(1995-1989)] \cdot H93(95)$. In a small number of cases this method did not give sensible results in that either $M93(89)$ or $M93(95)$ was outside the interval $[M(89), M(95)]$ even though the national accounts growth rates were positive for both 1989–93 and 1993–95. In these cases we ignored the national accounts data and fell back on simply estimating $M(93)$, using the growth rate in survey means between 1989 and 1995.

9. This assumes that the trend is linear rather than exponential (linear in logs). The exponential trends are 2.9 percent a year using all eight years and 2.5 percent a year ignoring the first year.

References

Ahmad, Sultan. 2003. "Purchasing Power Parity for International Comparison of Poverty: Sources and Methods." World Bank, Development Data Group, Washington, D.C. Available online at www.worldbank.org/data/icp.

Atkinson, Anthony B., and François Bourguignon. 1999. "Poverty and Inclusion from a World Perspective." Paper presented for the Annual World Bank Conference on Development Economics, European Conference, Paris.

Bourguignon, Francois, and Christian Morisson. 2002. "The Size Distribution of Income among World Citizens, 1820–1990." *American Economic Review* 92(4):727–44.

Chen, Shaohua, and Martin Ravallion. 1996. "Data in Transition: Assessing Rural Living Standards in Southern China." *China Economic Review* 7:23–56.

———. 2000. "How Did the World's Poorest Fare in the 1990s?" Policy Research Working Paper 2409. World Bank, Washington, D.C. Available online at http://econ.worldbank.org/resource.php?type=5.

———. 2001. "How Did the World's Poor Fare in the 1990s?" *Review of Income and Wealth* 47(3): 283–300.

Chen, Shaohua, Gaurav Datt, and Martin Ravallion. 1994. "Is Poverty Increasing or Decreasing in the Developing World?" *Review of Income and Wealth* 40:359–76.

Datt, Gaurav, and Martin Ravallion. 1992. "Growth and Redistribution Components of Changes in Poverty Measures: A Decomposition with Applications to Brazil and India in the 1980s." *Journal of Development Economics* 38:275–95.

———. 1998. "Farm Productivity and Rural Poverty in India." *Journal of Development Studies* 34: 62–85.

———. 2002. "Has India's Post-Reform Economic Growth Left the Poor Behind?" *Journal of Economic Perspectives* 16(3):89–108.

Deaton, Angus. 2002a. "Counting the World's Poor: Problems and Possible Solutions." *World Bank Research Observer* 16(2):125–47.

———. 2002b. "Is World Poverty Falling?" *Finance and Development* 39(2):4–7.

———. 2003. "Adjusted Indian Poverty Estimates for 1999–00." *Economic and Political Weekly* 38(4): 322–26.

Foster, James, J. Greer, and E. Thorbecke. 1984. "A Class of Decomposable Poverty Measures." *Econometrica* 52:761–65.

Gibson, John, Jikun Huang, and Scott Rozelle. 2001. "Why Is Income Inequality So Low in China Compared to Other Countries? The Effect of Household Survey Methods." *Economics Letters* 71: 329–33.

Ravallion, Martin. 2002a. "Comment on 'Counting the World's Poor' by Angus Deaton." *World Bank Research Observer* 16(2):149–56.

———. 2002b. "How *Not* to Count the Poor: A Reply to Reddy and Pogge." World Bank, Development Research Group, Washington, D.C.

———. 2003a. "The Debate on Globalization, Poverty and Inequality: Why Measurement Matters." *International Affairs* 79(4):739–54.

———. 2003b. "Measuring Aggregate Economic Welfare in Developing Countries: How Well Do National Accounts and Surveys Agree?" *Review of Economics and Statistics* 85:645–52.

Ravallion, Martin, and Shaohua Chen. 2004. "China's (Uneven) Progress against Poverty." World Bank, Development Research Group, Washington, D.C.

Ravallion, Martin, Gaurav Datt, and Dominique van de Walle. 1991. "Quantifying Absolute Poverty in the Developing World." *Review of Income and Wealth* 37:345–61.

Reddy, Sanjay G., and Thomas W. Pogge. 2002. "How *Not* to Count the Poor." Working paper, Barnard College, New York.

Sen, Abhijit, and Himanshu. 2003. "Poverty and Inequality in India: Getting Closer to the Truth." Working paper, Jawaharlal Nehru University, New Delhi.

Sundaram, K., and Suresh D. Tendulkar. 2003. "Poverty in India in the 1990s. Revised Results for All-India and 15 Major States for 1993–94." *Economic and Political Weekly* 38(46):4865–72.

Wade, Robert Hunter. 2004. "Is Globalization Reducing Poverty and Inequality?" *World Development* 32(4):567–89.

World Bank. 1990. *World Development Report: Poverty*. New York: Oxford University Press.

———. 1997. *China 2020: Sharing Rising Income*. Washington, D.C.

———. 2000. *World Development Report 2000/2001: Attacking Poverty*. New York: Oxford University Press.

———. 2002. *Globalization, Growth and Poverty*. Washington, D.C.

———. 2004. *World Development Indicators*. Washington, D.C.

B
International Convergence or Divergence?

## 8

Journal of Economic Perspectives—Volume 11, Number 3—Summer 1997—Pages 3–17

Divergence, Big Time

Lant Pritchett

D
ivergence in relative productivity levels and living standards is the dominant feature of modern economic history. In the last century, incomes in
the "less developed" (or euphemistically, the "developing") countries
have fallen far behind those in the "developed" countries, both proportionately
and absolutely. I estimate that from 1870 to 1990 the ratio of per capita incomes
between the richest and the poorest countries increased by roughly a factor of five
and that the difference in income between the richest country and all others has
increased by an order of magnitude.[1] This divergence is the result of the very different patterns in the long-run economic performance of two sets of countries.

One set of countries—call them the "developed" or the "advanced capitalist" (Maddison, 1995) or the "high income OECD" (World Bank, 1995)—is
easily, if awkwardly, identified as European countries and their offshoots plus
Japan. Since 1870, the long-run growth rates of these countries have been rapid
(by previous historical standards), their growth rates have been remarkably similar, and the poorer members of the group grew sufficiently faster to produce
considerable convergence in absolute income levels. The other set of countries,
called the "developing" or "less developed" or "nonindustrialized," can be
easily, if still awkwardly, defined only as "the other set of countries," as they
have nothing else in common. The growth rates of this set of countries have
been, on average, slower than the richer countries, producing divergence in

---

[1] To put it another way, the standard deviation of (natural log) GDP per capita across all countries has
increased between 60 percent and 100 percent since 1870, in spite of the convergence amongst the
richest.

■ *Lant Pritchett is Senior Economist, World Bank, Washington, D.C.*

relative incomes. But amongst this set of countries there have been strikingly different patterns of growth: both across countries, with some converging rapidly on the leaders while others stagnate; and over time, with a mixed record of takeoffs, stalls and nose dives.

The next section of this paper documents the pattern of income growth and convergence within the set of developed economies. This discussion is greatly aided by the existence of data, whose lack makes the discussion in the next section of the growth rates for the developing countries tricky, but as I argue, not impossible. Finally, I offer some implications for historical growth rates in developing countries and some thoughts on the process of convergence.

Convergence in Growth Rates of Developed Countries

Some aspects of modern historical growth apply principally, if not exclusively, to the "advanced capitalist" countries. By "modern," I mean the period since 1870. To be honest, the date is chosen primarily because there are nearly complete national income accounts data for all of the now-developed economies since 1870. Maddison (1983, 1991, 1995) has assembled estimates from various national and academic sources and has pieced them together into time series that are comparable across countries. An argument can be made that 1870 marks a plausible date for a modern economic period in any case, as it is near an important transition in several countries: for example, the end of the U.S. Civil War in 1865; the Franco-Prussian War in 1870–71, immediately followed by the unification of Germany; and Japan's Meiji Restoration in 1868. Perhaps not coincidentally, Rostow (1990) dates the beginning of the "drive to technological maturity" of the United States, France and Germany to around that date, although he argues that this stage began earlier in Great Britain.[2]

Table 1 displays the historical data for 17 presently high-income industrialized countries, which Maddison (1995) defines as the "advanced capitalist" countries. The first column of Table 1 shows the per capita level of income for each country in 1870, expressed in 1985 dollars. The last three columns of Table 1 show the average per annum growth rate of real per capita income in these countries over three time periods: 1870–1960, 1960–1980 and 1980–1994. These dates are not meant to date any explicit shifts in growth rates, but they do capture the fact that there was a golden period of growth that began some time after World War II and ended sometime before the 1980s.

Three facts jump out from Table 1. First, there is strong convergence in per capita incomes within this set of countries. For example, the poorest six countries in 1870 had five of the six fastest national growth rates for the time period 1870–

_____

[2] For an alternative view, Maddison (1991) argues the period 1820–1870 was similar economically to the 1870–1913 period.

Table 1

Average Per Annum Growth Rates of GDP Per Capita in the Presently High-Income Industrialized Countries, 1870–1989

		Per annum growth rates		
Country	Level in 1870 (1985 P$)	1870–1960	1960–80	1980–94
Average	1757	1.54	3.19	1.51
Std dev. of growth rates		.33	1.1	.51
Australia	3192	.90	2.43	1.22
Great Britain	2740	1.08	2.02	1.31
New Zealand	2615	1.24	1.39	1.28
Belgium	2216	1.05	3.70	1.52
Netherlands	2216	1.25	2.90	1.29
USA	2063	1.70	2.48	1.52
Switzerland	1823	1.94	2.07	.84
Denmark	1618	1.66	2.77	1.99
Germany	1606	1.66	3.03	1.56
Austria	1574	1.40	3.81	1.58
France	1560	1.56	3.53	1.31
Sweden	1397	1.85	2.74	.81
Canada	1360	1.85	3.32	.86
Italy	1231	1.54	4.16	1.62
Norway	1094	1.81	3.78	2.08
Finland	929	1.91	3.77	1.09
Japan	622	1.86	6.28	2.87

Source: Maddison, 1995.
Notes: Data is adjusted from 1990 to 1985 P$ by the U.S. GDP deflator, by a method described later in this article. Per annum growth rates are calculated using endpoints.

1960; conversely, the richest five countries in 1870 recorded the five slowest growth rates from 1870 to 1960.[3] As is well known, this convergence has not happened at a uniform rate. There is as much convergence in the 34 years between 1960 and 1994 as in the 90 years from 1870 to 1960. Even within this earlier period, there are periods of stronger convergence pre-1914 and weaker convergence from 1914 to 1950.

Second, even though the poorer countries grew faster than the richer countries did, the narrow range of the growth rates over the 1870-1960 period is striking. The United States, the richest country in 1960, had grown at 1.7 percent per annum since 1870, while the overall average was 1.54. Only one country, Australia, grew either a half a percentage point higher or lower than the average, and the standard deviation of the growth rates was only .33. Evans (1994) formally tests the hypothesis

---

[3] The typical measure of income dispersion, the standard deviation of (natural log) incomes, fell from .41 in 1870 to .27 in 1960 to only .11 in 1994.

that growth rates among 13 European and offshoot countries (not Japan) were
equal, and he is unable to reject it at standard levels of statistical significance.

Third, while the long run hides substantial variations, at least since 1870 there
has been no obvious acceleration of overall growth rates over time. As Charles Jones
(1995) has pointed out, there is remarkable stability in the growth rates in the
United States. For instance, if I predict per capita income in the United States in
1994 based only on a simple time trend regression of (natural log) GDP per capita
estimated with data from 1870 to 1929, this prediction made for 65 years ahead is
off by only 10 percent.[4] Although this predictive accuracy is not true for every
country, it is true that the average growth rate of these 17 countries in the most
recent period between 1980 and 1994 is almost exactly the same as that of the 1870–
1960 period. However, this long-run stability does mask modest swings in the growth
rates over time, as growth was considerably more rapid in the period between 1950
to 1980, especially outside the United States, than either in earlier periods or since
1980.

These three facts are true of the sample of countries that Maddison defines as
the "advanced capitalist" countries. However, the discussion of convergence and
long-run growth has always been plagued by the fact that the sample of countries
for which historical economic data exists (and has been assembled into convenient
and comparable format) is severely nonrepresentative. Among a sample of now
"advanced capitalist" countries something like convergence (or at least nondiver-
gence) is almost tautological, a point made early on by De Long (1988). Defining
the set of countries as those that are the richest *now* almost guarantees the finding
of historical convergence, as either countries are rich now and were rich historically,
in which case they all have had roughly the same growth rate (like nearly all of
Europe) or countries are rich now and were poor historically (like Japan) and hence
grew faster and show convergence. However, examples of divergence, like countries
that grew much more slowly and went from relative riches to poverty (like Argentina) or countries that were poor and grew so slowly as to become relatively poorer
(like India), are not included in the samples of "now developed" countries that
tend to find convergence.

Calculating a Lower Bound For Per Capita GDP

This selectivity problem raises a difficult issue in trying to estimate the possible
magnitude of convergence or divergence of the incomes since 1870. There is no

---

[4] Jones (1995) uses this basic fact of the constancy of growth to good effect in creating a compelling
argument that the steadiness of U.S. growth implies that endogenous growth models that make growth
a function of nonstationary variables, such as the level of R&D spending or the level of education of the
labor force, are likely incorrect as they imply an accelerating growth rate (unless several variables working
in opposite directions just happen to offset each other). These issues are also discussed in his paper in
this issue.

historical data for many of the less developed economies, and what data does exist has enormous problems with comparability and reliability. One alternative to searching for historical data is simply to place a reasonable lower bound on what GDP per capita could have been in 1870 in any country. Using this lower bound and estimates of recent incomes, one can draw reliable conclusions about the historical growth rates and divergence in cross-national distribution of income levels.

There is little doubt life was nasty, brutish and short in many countries in 1870. But even deprivation has its limit, and some per capita incomes must imply standards of living that are unsustainably and implausibly low. After making conservative use of a wide variety of different methods and approaches, I conclude that $250 (expressed in 1985 purchasing power equivalents) is the lowest GDP per capita could have been in 1870. This figure can be defended on three grounds: first, no one has ever observed consistently lower living standards at any time or place in history; second, this level is well below extreme poverty lines actually set in impoverished countries and is inconsistent with plausible levels of nutritional intake; and third, at a lower standard of living the population would be too unhealthy to expand.

Before delving into these comparisons and calculations, it is important to stress that using the purchasing power adjustments for exchange rates has an especially important effect in poor countries. While tradable goods will have generally the same prices across countries because of arbitrage, nontradable goods are typically much cheaper in poorer countries because of their lower income levels. If one applies market exchange rates to convert incomes in these economies to U.S. dollars, one is typically far understating the "true" income level, because nontradable goods can be bought much more cheaply than market exchange rates will imply. There have been several large projects, especially the UN International Comparisons Project and the Penn World Tables, that through the collection of data on the prices of comparable baskets of goods in all countries attempt to express different countries' GDP in terms of a currency that represents an equivalent purchasing power over a basket of goods. Since this adjustment is so large and of such quantitative significance, I will denote figures that have been adjusted in this way by $P\$$. By my own rough estimates, a country with a per capita GDP level of $70 in U.S. dollars, measured in market exchange rates, will have a per capita GDP of $P\$250$.

The first criteria for a reasonable lower bound on GDP per capita is that it be a lower bound on measured GDP per capita, either of the poorest countries in the recent past or of any country in the distant past. The lowest five-year average level of per capita GDP reported for any country in the Penn World Tables (Mark 5) is $P\$275$ for Ethiopia in 1961–65; the next lowest is $P\$278$ for Uganda in 1978–1982. The countries with the lowest level of GDP per capita ever observed, even for a single year, are $P\$260$ for Tanzania in 1961, $P\$299$ for Burundi in 1965 and $P\$220$ Uganda in 1981 (in the middle of a civil war). Maddison (1991) gives estimates of GDP per capita of some less developed countries as early as 1820: $P\$531$ for India, $P\$523$ for China and $P\$614$ for Indonesia. His earliest estimates for Africa begin in 1913: $P\$508$ for Egypt and $P\$648$ for Ghana. Maddison also offers increasingly speculative estimates for western European countries going back much further in time; for example, he estimates that per capita GDPs in the Netherlands and the United Kingdom in 1700 were P$1515 and P$992, respectively, and ventures to guess that the average per capita GNP in western Europe was P$400 in 1400. Kuznets's (1971) guess of the trough of the average per capita GDP of European countries in 900 is around P$400.[5] On this score, P$250 is a pretty safe bet.

A complementary set of calculations to justify a lower bound are based on "subsistence" income. While "subsistence" as a concept is out of favor, and rightfully so for many purposes, it is sufficiently robust for the task at hand. There are three related calculations: poverty lines, average caloric intakes and the cost of subsistence. Ravallion, Datt and van de Walle (1991) argue that the lowest defensible poverty line based on achieving minimally adequate consumption expenditures is P$252 per person per year. If we assume that personal consumption expenditures are 75 percent of GDP (the average for countries with GDP per capita less than P$400) and that mean income is 1.3 times the median, then even to achieve median income at the lowest possible poverty line requires a per capita income of $437.[6]

As an alternative way of considering subsistence GDP per capita, begin with the finding that estimated average intake per person per day consistent with working productively is between 2,000 to 2,400 calories.[7] Now, consider two calculations. The first is that, based on a cross-sectional regression using data on incomes from the Penn World Tables and average caloric intake data from the FAO, the predicted caloric consumption at P$250 is around 1,600.[8] The five lowest levels of

---

[5] More specifically, Kuznets estimated that the level was about $160, if measured in 1985 U.S. dollars. However, remember from the earlier discussion that a conversion at market exchange rates—which is what Kuznets was using—is far less than an estimate based on purchasing power parity exchange rates. If we use a multiple of 2.5, which is a conservative estimate of the difference between the two, Kuznets's estimate in purchasing power equivalent terms would be equal to a per capita GDP of $400 in 1985 U.S. dollars, converted at the purchasing power equivalent rate.

[6] High poverty rates, meaning that many people live below these poverty lines, are not inconsistent with thinking of these poverty lines as not far above our lower bound, because many individuals can be in poverty, but not very far below the line. For instance, in South Asia in 1990, where 33 percent of the population was living in "extreme absolute poverty," only about 10 percent of the population would be living at less than $172 (my estimates from extrapolations of cumulative distributions reported in Chen, Datt and Ravallion, 1993).

[7] The two figures are based on different assumptions about the weight of adult men and women, the mean temperature and the demographic structure. The low figure is about as low as one can go because it is based on a very young population, 39 percent under 15 (the young need fewer calories), a physically small population (men's average weight of only 110 pounds and women of 88), and a temperature of 25° C (FAO, 1957). The baseline figure, although based on demographic structure, usually works out to be closer to 2,400 (FAO, 1974).

[8] The regression is a simple log-log of caloric intake and income in 1960 (the log-log is for simplicity even though this might not be the best predictor of the level). The regression is

$$\ln(\text{average caloric intake}) = 6.37 \quad + .183*\ln(\text{GDP per capita}),$$
$$(59.3) \ (12.56).$$

with *t*-statistics in parentheses, $N = 113$, and R-squared = .554.

caloric availability ever recorded in the FAO data for various countries—1,610 calories/person during a famine in Somalia in 1975; 1,550 calories/person during a famine in Ethiopia in 1985; 1,443 calories/person in Chad in 1984; 1,586 calories/person in China in 1961 during the famines and disruption associated with the Cultural Revolution; and 1,584 calories/person in Mozambique in 1987—reveal that nearly all of the episodes of average daily caloric consumption below 1,600 are associated with nasty episodes of natural and/or man-made catastrophe. A second use of caloric requirements is to calculate the subsistence income as the cost of meeting caloric requirements. Bairoch (1993) reports the results of the physiological minimum food intake at $291 (at market exchange rates) in 1985 prices. These calculations based on subsistence intake of food again suggest P$250 is a safe lower bound.

That life expectancy is lower and infant mortality higher in poorer countries is well documented, and this relation can also help establish a lower bound on income (Pritchett and Summers, 1996). According to demographers, an under-five infant mortality rate of less than 600 per 1000 is necessary for a stable population (Hill, 1995). Using a regression based on Maddison's (1991) historical per capita income estimates and infant mortality data from historical sources for 22 countries, I predict that infant mortality in 1870 for a country with income of P$250 would have been 765 per 1000.[9] Although the rate of natural increase of population back in 1870 is subject to great uncertainty, it is typically estimated to be between .25 and 1 percent annually in that period, which is again inconsistent with income levels as low as P$250.[10]

Divergence, Big Time

If you accept: a) the current estimates of relative incomes across nations; b) the estimates of the historical growth rates of the now-rich nations; and c) that even in the poorest economies incomes were not below P$250 at any point—then you cannot escape the conclusion that the last 150 years have seen divergence, big time. The logic is straightforward and is well illustrated by Figure 1. If there had been no divergence, then we could extrapolate backward from present income of the poorer countries to past income assuming they grew at least as fast as the United

---

[9] The regression is estimated with country fixed effects:

$$\ln(\text{IMR}) = -.59 \ln(\text{GDP per capita}) \underset{(23.7)}{} - .013 * \text{Trend} \underset{(32.4)}{} - .002 * \text{Trend} * (1 \text{ if } > 1960)$$
$$\phantom{\ln(\text{IMR}) =} (23.7) (32.4) (14.23)$$

$N = 1994$ and *t*-statistics are in parenthesis. The prediction used the average country constant of 9.91.

[10] Livi-Basci (1992) reports estimates of population growth in Africa between 1850 and 1900 to be .87 percent, and .93 percent between 1900 and 1950, while growth for Asia is estimated to be .27 1850 to 1900, and .61 1900 to 1950. Clark (1977) estimates the population growth rates between 1850 and 1900 to be .43 percent in Africa and India and lower, .33 percent, in China.

Figure 1
Simulation of Divergence of Per Capita GDP, 1870–1985
(showing only selected countries)

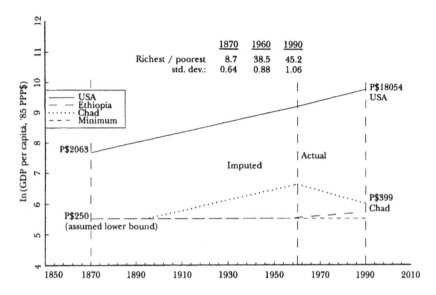

States. However, this would imply that many poor countries must have had incomes below P$100 in 1870. Since this cannot be true, there must have been divergence. Or equivalently, per capita income in the United States, the world's richest industrial country, grew about four-fold from 1870 to 1960. Thus, any country whose income was not fourfold higher in 1960 than it was in 1870 grew more slowly than the United States. Since 42 of the 125 countries in the Penn World Tables with data for 1960 have levels of per capita incomes below $1,000 (that is, less than four times $250), there must have been substantial divergence between the top and bottom. The figure of P$250 is not meant to be precise or literal and the conclusion of massive divergence is robust to any plausible assumption about a lower bound.

Consider some illustrative calculations of the divergence in per capita incomes in Table 2. I scale incomes back from 1960 such that the poorest country in 1960 just reaches the lower bound by 1870, the leader in 1960 (the United States) reaches its actual 1870 value, and all relative rankings between the poorest country and the United States are preserved.[11] The first row shows the actual path of the U.S. econ-

---

[11] The growth rate of the poorest country was imposed to reach P$250 at exactly 1870, and the rate of the United States was used for the growth at the top. Then each country's growth rate was assumed to be a weighted average of those two rates, where the weights depended on the scaled distance from the bottom country in the beginning period of the imputation, 1960. This technique "smushes" the distri-

Table 2

Estimates of the Divergence of Per Capita Incomes Since 1870

	1870	1960	1990
USA ($P\$$)	2063	9895	18054
Poorest ($P\$$)	250	257	399
	(assumption)	(Ethiopia)	(Chad)
Ratio of GDP per capita of richest to poorest country	8.7	38.5	45.2
Average of seventeen "advanced capitalist" countries from Maddison (1995)	1757	6689	14845
Average LDCs from PWT5.6 for 1960, 1990 (imputed for 1870)	740	1579	3296
Average "advanced capitalist" to average of all other countries	2.4	4.2	4.5
Standard deviation of natural log of per capita incomes	.51	.88	1.06
Standard deviation of per capita incomes	$P\$459$	$P\$2,112$	$P\$3,988$
Average absolute income deficit from the leader	$P\$1286$	$P\$7650$	$P\$12,662$

Notes: The estimates in the columns for 1870 are based on backcasting GDP per capita for each country using the methods described in the text assuming a minimum of $P\$250$. If instead of that method, incomes in 1870 are backcast with truncation at $P\$250$, the 1870 standard deviation is .64 (as reported in Figure 1).

omy. The second row gives the level of the poorest economy in 1870, which is $P\$250$ by assumption, and then the poorest economies in 1960 and 1990 taken from the Penn World Tables. By division, the third row then shows that the ratio of the top to the bottom income countries has increased from 8.7 in 1870 to 38 by 1960 and to 45 by 1990. If instead one takes the 17 richest countries (those shown in Table 1) and applies the same procedure, their average per capita income is shown in the fourth row. The average for all less developed economies appearing in the Penn World Tables for 1960 and 1990 is given in the fifth row; the figure for 1870 is calculated by the "backcasting" imputation process for historical incomes described above. By division, the sixth row shows that the ratio of income of the richest to all other countries has almost doubled from 2.4 in 1870 to 4.6 by 1990.

---

bution back into the smaller range between the top and bottom while maintaining all cross country rankings. The formula for estimating the log of GDP per capita (GDPPC) in the ith country in 1870 was

$$GDPPC_i^{1870} = GDPPC_i^{1960} * (1/w_i)$$

where the scaling weight w_i was

$$w_i = (1 - \alpha_i) * \min(GDPPC^{1960}) / P\$250 + \alpha_i * GDPPC_{USA}^{1960} / GDPPC_{USA}^{1870},$$

and where α_i is defined by

$$\alpha_i = (GDPPC_i^{1960} - \min(GDPPC^{1960})) / (GDPPC_{USA}^{1960} - \min(GDPPC^{1960})).$$

The magnitude of the change in the absolute gaps in per capita incomes between rich and poor is staggering. From 1870 to 1990, the average absolute gap in incomes of all countries from the leader had grown by an order of magnitude, from $1,286 to $12,662, as shown in the last row of Table 2.[12]

While the growth experience of all countries is equally interesting, some are more equally interesting than others. China and India account for more than a third of the world's population. For the conclusion of divergence presented here, however, a focus on India and China does not change the historical story. One can estimate their growth rates either by assuming that they were at $250 in 1870 and then calculating their growth rate in per capita GDP to reach the levels given by the Penn World Tables in 1960 (India, $766; China, $567), or by using Maddison's historical estimates, which are shown in Table 3, India's growth rate is a fifth and China's a third of the average for developed economies. Either way, India's and China's incomes diverged significantly relative to the leaders between 1870 and 1960.

The idea that there is some lower bound to GDP per capita and that the lower bound has implications for long-run growth rates (and hence divergence) will not come as news either to economic historians or to recent thinkers in the area of economic growth (Lucas, 1996). Kuznets (1966, 1971) pointed out that since the now-industrialized countries have risen from very low levels of output to their presently high levels, and that their previously very low levels of output were only consistent with a very slow rate of growth historically, growth rates obviously accelerated at some point. Moreover, one suspects that many of the estimates of income into the far distant past cited above rely on exactly this kind of counterfactual logic.

Considering Alternate Sources of Historical Data

Although there is not a great deal of historical evidence on GDP estimates in the very long-run for the less developed countries, what there is confirms the finding of massive divergence. Maddison (1995) reports time series data on GDP per capita incomes for 56 countries. These include his 17 "advanced capitalist" countries (presented in Table 1), five "southern" European countries, seven eastern European countries and 28 countries typically classified as "less developed" from Asia (11), Africa (10) and Latin America (7). This data is clearly nonrepresentative of the poorest countries (although it does include India and China), and the data for Africa is very sparse until 1960. Even so, the figures in Table 3 show substantially lower growth for the less developed countries than for the developed countries. If

---

[12] In terms of standard deviations, the method described in the text implies that the standard deviation of the national log of per capita GDP has more than doubled from 1870 to 1990, rising from .51 in 1870 to .88 in 1960 to 1.06 by 1990. In dollar terms, the standard deviation of per capita incomes rose from $459 in 1870 to $2,112 in 1960 to $3,988 in 1990 (again, all figures expressed in 1985 dollars, converted at purchasing power equivalent exchange rates).

Table 3
Mean Per Annum Growth Rates of GDP Per Capita

	1870–1960	1960–1979	1980–1994
Advanced capitalist countries (17)	1.5	3.2	1.5
	(.33)	(1.1)	(.51)
Less developed countries (28)	1.2	2.5	.34
	(.88)	(1.7)	(3.0)
Individual countries:			
India	.31	1.22	3.07
China	.58	2.58	6.45
Korea (1900)	.71	5.9	7.7
Brazil	1.28	4.13	−.54
Argentina (1900)	1.17	1.99	.11
Egypt (1900)	.56	3.73	2.21

Source: Calculations based on data from Maddison (1995).

one assumes that the ratio of incomes between the "advanced capitalist" countries and less developed countries was 2.4 in 1870, then the .35 percentage point differential would have produced a rich-poor gap of 3.7 in 1994, similar to the projected increase in the gap to 4.5 in Table 2.

Others have argued that incomes of the developing relative to the developed world were even higher in the past. Hanson (1988, 1991) argues that adjustments of comparisons from official exchange rates to purchasing power equivalents imply that developing countries were considerably richer historically than previously believed. Bairoch (1993) argues that there was almost no gap between the now-developed countries and the developing countries as late as 1800. As a result, his estimate of the growth rate of the "developed" world is 1.5 percent between 1870 and 1960 as opposed to .5 percent for the "developing" world, which implies even larger divergence in per capita incomes than the lower bound assumptions reported above.

Poverty Traps, Takeoffs and Convergence

The data on growth in less developed countries show a variety of experiences, but divergence is not a thing of the past. Some countries are "catching up" with very explosive but sustained bursts of growth, some countries continue to experience slower growth than the richest countries, and others have recently taken nosedives.

Let's set the standard for explosive growth in per capita GDP at a sustained rate of 4.2 percent; this is the fastest a country could have possibly grown from 1870 to 1960, as at this rate a country would have gone from the lower bound in 1870 to the U.S. level in 1960. Of the 108 developing countries for which there are available data in the Penn World Tables, 11 grew faster than 4.2 per annum over the 1960–1990 period. Prominent among these are east Asian economies like Korea (6.9 percent annual growth rate in per capita GDP from 1960–1992), Taiwan (6.3 percent annual growth) and Indonesia (4.4 percent). These countries are growing at an historically unprecedented pace. However, many countries that were poor in 1960 continued to stagnate. Sixteen developing countries had *negative* growth over the 1960–1990 period, including Mozambique (−2.2 percent per annum) and Guyana (−.7 percent per annum). Another 28 nations, more than a quarter of the total number of countries for which the Penn World Tables offers data, had growth rates of per capita GDP less than .5 percent per annum from 1960 to 1990 (for example, Peru with .1 percent); and 40 developing nations, more than a third of the sample, had growth rates less than 1 percent per annum.[13]

Moreover, as Ben-David and Papell (1995) emphasize, many developing countries have seen their economies go into not just a slowdown, but a "meltdown." If we calculate the growth rates in the Penn World Tables and allow the data to dictate one break in the growth rate over the whole 1960–1990 period, then of the 103 developing countries, 81 have seen a deceleration of growth over the period, and the average deceleration is over 3 percentage points. From 1980–1994, growth in per capita GDP averaged 1.5 percent in the advanced countries and .34 percent in the less developed countries. There has been no acceleration of growth in most poor countries, either absolutely or relatively, and there is no obvious reversal in divergence.

These facts about growth in less developed countries highlight its enormous variability and volatility. The range of annual growth rates in per capita GDP across less developed economies from 1960 to 1990 is from −2.7 percent to positive 6.9 percent.

Taken together, these findings imply that almost nothing that is true about the growth rates of advanced countries is true of the developing countries, either individually or on average. The growth rates for developed economies show convergence, but the growth rates between developed and developing economies show considerable divergence. The growth rates of developed countries are bunched in a narrow group, while the growth rates of less developed countries are all over with some in explosive growth and others in implosive decline.

Conclusion

For modern economists, Gerschenkron (1962) popularized the idea of an "advantage to backwardness," which allows countries behind the technological frontier to

---

[13] The division into developed and developing is made here by treating all 22 high-income members of the OECD as "developed" and all others as "developing."

experience episodes of rapid growth driven by rapid productivity catch-up.[14] Such rapid gains in productivity are certainly a possibility, and there have been episodes of individual countries with very rapid growth. Moreover, there are examples of convergence in incomes amongst regions. However, the prevalence of absolute divergence implies that while there may be a potential advantage to backwardness, the cases in which backward countries, and especially the most backward of countries, actually gain significantly on the leader are historically rare. In poor countries there are clearly forces that create the potential for explosive growth, such as those witnessed in some countries in east Asia. But there are also strong forces for stagnation: a quarter of the 60 countries with initial per capita GDP of less than $1000 in 1960 have had growth rates less than zero, and a third have had growth rates less than .05 percent. There are also forces for "implosive" decline, such as that witnessed in some countries in which the fabric of civic society appears to have disintegrated altogether, a point often ignored or acknowledged offhand as these countries fail to gather plausible economic statistics and thus drop out of our samples altogether. Backwardness seems to carry severe disadvantages. For economists and social scientists, a coherent model of how to overcome these disadvantages is a pressing challenge.

But this challenge is almost certainly not the same as deriving a single "growth theory." Any theory that seeks to unify the world's experience with economic growth and development must address at least four distinct questions: What accounts for continued per capita growth and technological progress of those leading countries at the frontier? What accounts for the few countries that are able to initiate and sustain periods of rapid growth in which they gain significantly on the leaders? What accounts for why some countries fade and lose the momentum of rapid growth? What accounts for why some countries remain in low growth for very long periods?

Theorizing about economic growth and its relation to policy needs to tackle these four important and distinct questions. While it is conceivable that there is an all-purpose universal theory and set of policies that would be good for promoting economic growth, it seems much more plausible that the appropriate growth policy will differ according to the situation. Are we asking about more rapid growth in a mature and stable economic leader like the United States or Germany or Japan? About a booming rapidly industrializing economy trying to prevent stalling on a plateau, like Korea, Indonesia, or Chile? About a once rapidly growing and at least semi-industrialized country trying to initiate another episode of rapid growth, like Brazil or Mexico or the Philippines? About a country still trying to escape a poverty trap into sustained growth, like Tanzania or Myanmar or Haiti? Discussion of the theory and policy of economic growth seems at times remarkably insensitive to these distinctions.

■ *I would like to thank William Easterly, Deon Filmer, Jonathan Isham, Estelle James, Ross Levine, Mead Over, Martin Rama and Martin Ravallion for helpful discussions and comments.*

---

[14] I say "for modern economists," since according to Rostow (1993), David Hume more than 200 years ago argued that the accumulated technological advances in the leading countries would give the followers an advantage.

16   Journal of Economic Perspectives

References

Bairoch, Paul, *Economics and World History: Myths and Paradoxes.* Chicago: University of Chicago Press, 1993.

Barro, Robert, "Economic Growth in a Cross Section of Countries," *Quarterly Journal of Economics,* May 1991, *106,* 407–43.

Barro, Robert, and Xavier Sala-i-Martin, "Convergence," *Journal of Political Economy,* April 1992, *100,* 223–51.

Barro, Robert, and Xavier Sala-i-Martin, *Economic Growth.* New York: McGraw Hill, 1995.

Baumol, William, "Productivity Growth, Convergence and Welfare: What the Long-Run Data Show," *American Economic Review,* December 1986, *76,* 1072–85.

Ben-David, Dan, "Equalizing Exchange: Trade Liberalization and Convergence," *Quarterly Journal of Economics,* 1993, *108:3,* 653–79.

Ben-David, Dan, and David Papell, "Slowdowns and Meltdowns: Post-War Growth Evidence from 74 countries." Centre for Economic Policy Research Discussion Paper Series No. 1111, February 1995.

Canova, Fabio, and Albert Marcet, "The Poor Stay Poor: Non-Convergence Across Countries and Regions." Centre for Economic Policy Research Discussion Paper No. 1265, November 1995.

Caselli, Franseco, Gerardo Esquivel, and Fernando Lefort, "Reopening the Convergence Debate: A New Look at Cross-Country Growth Empirics," mimeo, Harvard University, 1995.

Chen, Shaohua, Gaurav Datt, and Martin Ravallion, "Is Poverty Increasing in the Developing World?" World Bank Policy Research Working Paper No. 1146, June 1993.

Clark, Colin, *Population Growth and Land Use.* London: Macmillan, 1977.

De Long, Bradford, "Productivity Growth, Convergence, and Welfare: Comment," *American Economic Review,* December 1988, *78,* 1138–54.

Dollar, David, and Edward Wolff, *Competitiveness, Convergence, and International Specialization.* Cambridge, Mass.: Massachusetts Institute of Technology Press, 1993.

Easterly, William, Michael Kremer, Lant Pritchett, and Lawrence Summers, "Good Policy or Good Luck? Country Growth Performance and Temporary Shocks," *Journal of Monetary Economics,* December 1993, *32:3,* 459–83.

Evans, Paul, "Evaluating Growth Theories Using Panel Data," mimeo, Ohio State University, 1994.

de la Fuente, Angel, "The Empirics of Growth and Convergence: A Selective Review." Centre for Economic Policy Research No. 1275, November 1995.

FAO, *Calorie Requirements: Report of the Second Committee on Calorie Requirements.* Rome: FAO, 1957.

FAO, *Handbook on Human Nutritional Requirements.* Rome: Food and Agriculture Organization and World Health Organization, 1974.

Gerschenkron, Alexander, *Economic Backwardness in Historical Perspective, a Book of Essays.* Cambridge: Belknap Press, 1962.

Hanson, John R., "Third World Incomes before World War I: Some Comparisons," *Explorations in Economic History,* 1988, *25,* 323–36.

Hanson, John R., "Third World Incomes before World War I: Further Evidence," *Explorations in Economic History,* 1991, *28,* 367–79.

Hill, Kenneth, "The Decline of Childhood Mortality." In Simon, Julian, ed., *The State of Humanity.* Oxford: Blackwell, 1995, pp. 37–50.

International Rice Research Institute, *World Rice Statistics.* Los Banos: International Rice Research Institute, 1987.

Jones, Charles, "R&D Based Models of Economic Growth," *Journal of Political Economy,* August 1995, *103:4,* 759–84.

Kuznets, Simon, *Modern Economic Growth: Rate, Structure and Spread.* New Haven: Yale University Press, 1966.

Kuznets, Simon, *Economic Growth of Nations: Total Output and Production Structure.* Cambridge, Mass.: Belknap Press, 1971.

Livi-Basci, Massimo, *A Concise History of World Population.* Cambridge, Mass: Blackwell, 1992.

Loayza, Norman, "A Test of the International Convergence Hypothesis Using Panel Data." World Bank Policy Research Paper No. 1333, August 1994.

Lucas, Robert, "Ricardian Equilibrium: A Neoclassical Exposition," mimeo, Technion Israel Institute of Technology Economics Workshop Series, June 1996.

Maddison, Angus, "A Comparison of Levels of GDP Per Capita in Developed and Developing Countries, 1700–1980," *Journal of Economic History,* March 1983, *43,* 27–41.

Maddison, Angus, *Dynamic Forces in Capitalistic Development: A Long-Run Comparative View.* New York: Oxford University Press, 1991.

Maddison, Angus, "Explaining the Economic Performance of Nations, 1820–1989." In Baumol, William J., Richard R. Nelson, and Edward N. Wolff, eds., *Convergence of Productivity: Cross-*

National Studies and Historical Evidence. New York: Oxford University Press, 1994, pp. 20–61.

Maddison, Angus, *Monitoring the World Economy, 1820–1992.* Paris: Development Centre of the Organisation for Economic Co-operation Development, 1995.

Mankiw, N. Gregory, David Romer, and David Weil, "A Contribution to the Empirics of Economic Growth," *Quarterly Journal of Economics,* May 1992, *107*:2, 407–36.

Nuxoll, Daniel, "Differences in Relative Prices and International Differences in Growth Rates," *American Economic Review,* Decmeber 1994, *84,* 1423–36.

Pritchett, Lant, "Where Has All the Education Gone?," mimeo, June 1995a.

Pritchett, Lant, "Population, Factor Accumulation and Productivity." World Bank Policy Research Paper No. 1567, October 1995b.

Pritchett, Lant, and Lawence H. Summers, "Wealthier is Healthier," *Journal of Human Resources,* 1996, *31*:4, 841–68.

Quah, Danny, "Empirics for Economic Growth and Convergence." Centre for Economic Policy Research Discussion Paper No. 1140, March 1995.

Ravallion, Martin, Gaurav Datt, and Dominique van de Walle, "Quantifying Absolute Poverty in the Developing World," *Review of Income and Wealth,* 1991, *37*:4, 345–61.

Rebelo, Sergio, "Long-Run Policy Analysis and Long-Run Growth," *Journal of Political Economy,* June 1991, *99,* 500–21.

Rostow, W. W., *Theorist of Economic Growth from David Hume to the Present: With a Perspective on the Next Century.* New York: Oxford University Press, 1990.

Sachs, Jeffrey, and Andrew Warner, "Economic Convergence and Economic Policies." NBER Working Paper No. 5039, February 1995.

Sala-i-Martin, Xavier, "Regional Cohesion: Evidence and Theories of Regional Growth and Convergence." Centre for Economic Policy Research Discussion Paper No. 1074, November 1994.

Summers, Robert, and Alan Heston, "The Penn World Tables (Mark 5): An Expanded Set of International Comparisons, 1950–88," *Quarterly Journal of Economics,* 1991, *106*:2, 327–68.

World Bank, *World Development Report: Workers in an Integrating Economy.* Washington, D.C.: Oxford University Press for the World Bank, 1995.

## 9

The Economic Journal, 112 (*January*), 51–92. © Royal Economic Society 2002. Published by Blackwell Publishers, 108 Cowley Road, Oxford OX4 1JF, UK and 350 Main Street, Malden, MA 02148, USA.

TRUE WORLD INCOME DISTRIBUTION, 1988 AND 1993: FIRST CALCULATION BASED ON HOUSEHOLD SURVEYS ALONE*

Branko Milanovic

The paper derives world income or expenditure distribution of individuals for 1988 and 1993. It is the first paper to calculate world distribution for individuals based entirely on household surveys from 91 countries, and adjusted for differences in purchasing power parity between countries. Measured by the Gini index, inequality increased from 63 in 1988 to 66 in 1993. The increase was driven more by differences in mean incomes between countries than by inequalities within countries. The most important contributors were rising urban-rural differences in China, and slow growth of rural incomes in South Asia compared to several large developed economies.

1. The Objective

The issues of income inequality have gained increased prominence in the last decade. There are several reasons for this. Some are empirical: increasing inequality in Western countries in 1980s, then an 'explosion' of inequality in transition economies in the 1990's. Others are 'theoretical': economic theory is able to incorporate the issues of inequality better today than a few decades ago. There is greater interest in the growth-equality relationship (Lundberg and Squire, 1999); inequality plays a central role in the endogenous growth models; there are several new approaches to what determines inequality (Li *et al.*, 1998; Benabou, 2000); inequality and political economy are linked through the median voter hypothesis. Finally, not the least important reason, is a vastly increased availability of income distribution data. Without exaggeration, one could say that the increase in the coverage of the world by

* I am very grateful to Costas Krouskas for his truly excellent work in collection and processing the data. Prem Sangraula helped with some calculations at a later stage. I am very grateful too to a number of people who have helped me with identification of household surveys, and sometimes with the data processing and survey interpretation. They are individually acknowledged in Annex 1 where a short description of the surveys used is provided. A more detailed list of surveys, with their exact dates, number of data points available, and welfare metric used (income or expenditures) is given in Annex 2 available from the author on request. The actual data used can be downloaded from http://www.worldbank.org/research/transition/

I am also indebted to Shlomo Yitzhaki for discussion of the Gini decomposition procedure, and to Richard Adams, Francois Bourguignon, Ian Castles, Yuri Dikhanov, Hamid Davoodi, Francisco Ferreira, Richard Freeman, Timothy Heleniak, Aart Kraay, Stefano Paternostro, Thomas Pogge, Kalanidhi Subbarao, Michael Ward, three anonymous referees and Costas Meghir for helpful suggestions. I am grateful for comments and questions to the participants of the World Bank Macroeconomics seminar, Washington, June 1999, and International Economic Association meetings in Buenos Aires in July 1999 where the first version of the paper was presented. The research was financed by a World Bank Research Grant RPO 683-68, and a special grant by the World Bank Inequality Thematic Group. The paper represents only author's own views and the opinions expressed should not be attributed to the World Bank, member governments, or its affiliated institutions.

income or expenditure surveys plays the same role in heightening the importance of income inequality today, that the work on national income aggregates played in the early 1930's in paving the way for a more thorough study of macroeconomics.[1]

Recently, the fact of rising inequality within many countries was linked with the issues of globalisation. Several writers (Richardson, 1995; Wood, 1995) have asked if rising inequality may be related to globalisation, and others (Williamson, 1999) have pointed to similar spurs in inequality at the turn of the last century – which also was a period of globalisation. But globalisation also implies that national borders are becoming less important, and that every individual may, in theory, be regarded simply as a denizen of the world. Then, the question may be asked: is *world* inequality increasing? For, even if within-country inequalities are rising, world income inequality need not increase, or may even decline, if the poor (and populous) countries grow faster than the rich (and less populous) countries. In other words, even if globalisation can be shown to lead to an increase in within-country inequalities, globalisation may lessen income differences between *individuals* in the world.

The objective of the paper is to answer this question empirically – or more exactly, since we lack the data for any prolonged (in time) study of world income inequality, at least to establish the benchmark for world inequality in two years, 1988 and 1993. We shall derive the first personal world income distribution based *directly and solely* on household survey data, and adjusted for differences in purchasing powers of individuals in different countries. The two years, 1988 and 1993, are chosen because these are the years for which the direct international price comparison data are available. Of course, such a study is made possible only thanks to a massively expanded data base on income distribution. Over the last decade, many countries in Africa conducted their first national representative household income or expenditure surveys. The economic changes in China in the late 1970s, and the end of the Cold War in the late 1980s, opened up to the researchers the hitherto unavailable sources in China and the former Soviet Union. Thus, for the first time in human history, researchers have reasonably accurate data on distribution of income or welfare (= expenditures or consumption) amongst more than 90% of world population.

Now, other than for the reasons of intellectual curiosity, why should one be concerned with world inequality? There are, I think, several reasons that could be adduced. The awareness of a problem often begins, or is at least enhanced, by its conceptualisation and quantification. We need to measure world inequality in order to be able to say whether it is, in our view, large or not; whether current policies are contributing to it, or not; and finally, whether we need to do something about it – if we deem it too large. It may be, not unreasonably, conjectured that with globalisation and greater awareness of other peoples' cultures and their level of living, the concern

---

[1] See the recent discussion on the same topic by Kanbur and Lustig (1999).

with poverty and inequality at the world level might begin to resemble the concern with the same issues at the national level. That is not a fanciful prognostication: one needs to remember that the empirical interest in inequality and poverty at the level of the nation-state is also relatively recent. Although the states were in existence for a very long time, the first calculations of inequality were made at the turn of the 19th century; since then inequality within nations has become a much more researched, and hotly debated topic. In addition, knowing where individuals from different countries stand in the world income distribution helps us address such current issues as the probability that the Tobin or some similar tax levied at the citizens of the rich countries would end up in the pockets of wealthy individuals from the poor countries. Is this statistically likely? If proceeds from the tax were distributed randomly across citizens of poor countries, or even in proportion to their income, we can readily calculate the probability that the tax would result in a regressive transfer at the world level.

Section 2 will review the previous studies and explain how this one differs from them. In Section 3, I explain in detail the procedure of calculation, and look at the coverage. Sections 4 and 5 present the findings, dealing respectively with regional income inequalities, and world income inequality. Section 6 looks at factors that lie behind the calculated level of world inequality, and the 1988–93 change. Section 7 compares our results with those from other studies. Section 8 concludes the paper.

2. Previous Work

Most previous studies were studies of *international* inequality in the sense that they calculated what would be inequality in the world if the world were populated by representative individuals from all countries, that is by people having mean income of their countries. The most notable examples are several studies by Theil (Theil, 1979; Theil and Seale, 1994; Theil 1996; but see also Podder, 1993) who decomposed international inequality into regional components in order to show, among other things, decomposability properties of the Theil index of inequality. For income, these studies used GDP per capita, not survey data.

The second group of studies is better in the sense that they acknowledge the fact that the world is not populated by representative individuals from each country, and try somehow to take into account income distributions within countries. However, since they do not have access to the survey data, which alone provide information on distribution, such studies use countries' Gini coefficients or other indicators of inequality in order to estimate the entire distribution from a single statistic. A good example of this type of work is a recent paper by Schultz (1998). His analysis is based on a between-country component which reflects differences in Purchasing power parity ($PPP) GDPs per capita, and a within-country component where an inequality measure (log variance) for each individual country was obtained from a regression analysis using the Deininger and Squire (1996) data base. A very similar approach was adopted by Chotikapanich *et al.* (1997). They use the

GDP per capita (in PPP terms) and the Gini coefficient for each country (also obtained from the Deininger and Squire data base), and assume that income distributions of all countries follow a log-normal pattern. They thus obtain estimates of within-country income distributions needed to derive world inequality. The approach followed by these studies is unsatisfactory for two reasons. First, distributions cannot be well predicted from a single inequality statistic, nor is it acceptable to assume that all distributions follow the same pattern. Indeed, this is a *pis-aller*, explicitly acknowledged by Chotikapanich *et al.* when they observe that 'information on the income distributions, or, at least, the population and income shares for a number of income classes [by countries]...is not available' (1997, p. 535). Second, GDP is an imperfect indicator of household disposable income or expenditures, both because it often fails to account for home consumption, which is particularly important in poor countries, and includes (eg) undistributed profits or increase in stocks, which do not directly affect current welfare of the population. Moreover, as we shall see below, there is a systematic relationship between the ratio of income or expenditures obtained from household surveys (HS) to GDP, and level of GDP per capita.

More accurate studies use survey data. For example, Berry *et al.* (1983) and Grosh and Nafziger (1986) combine survey-derived income or expenditure shares with countries' per capita GDPs (in PPP-adjusted terms). Both papers derive world (not *international*) income distribution using income shares from household budget surveys for 'developed countries and about forty less developed countries' (Berry *et al.*, p. 219) and 71 countries (Grosh and Nafziger, 1986, p. 349). Income shares are multiplied by countries' GDPs per capita in order to get mean income for each quantile.[2] In other words, household surveys are used to get income shares, but the actual incomes for different income classes are *not* obtained directly from the surveys. The difference may be important because, as mentioned before, the ratio of mean per capita survey income or expenditure to per capita GDP is not constant across countries. In addition, for countries for which they did not have income distribution data, Berry *et al.* (1983) estimate income shares 'on the basis of observed relationships between the shares of seven quantiles in countries for which comparable...data do exist and a set of explanatory variables' (p. 219). For these countries they use a regression analysis to determine income/expenditure shares.[3] Recently, Korzeniewick and Moran (1997), use the same approach although they multiply income shares (quintiles for 46 countries) by dollar per capita GDPs (*not* per capita GDPs in PPP terms). Not surprisingly, they find that between-country differences –

[2] There is an inconsistency in Grosh and Nafziger (1986) which is due to the nature of the data they use. The income (decile) shares with which they multiply countries' GDP *per capita*, are derived from distributions of *household* income across *households*. Berry *et al.* (1983) use – correctly – distribution of per capita household income across individuals.

[3] Grosh and Nafziger (1986) similarly 'allocate' some 40 countries into several groups (low income, middle income, industrialised, capital-surplus oil exporters) and apply to them income distribution of 'their' group computed from the countries whose income distributions are available. For several centrally-planned countries they use wage distributions.

which are magnified when simple dollar per capita GDPs are used – explain most of world inequality. Thus they feel justified in expanding their sample from 46 countries for which they have income-share data, to 112 countries using simple GDPs per capita and ignoring within-country distributions. In effect, they revert to a study of inter-national inequality. Firebaugh (1999), in response to Korzeniewick and Moran (1997), also presents a study of international inequality but he uses per capita GDPs in PPP terms.

Since Berry *et al.* published their article, some 15 years ago, there has been a huge increase in the availability of surveys in the countries of the former Soviet Union, and Africa in particular. There are many more surveys from other countries as well, and data standardisation (insuring that variables are defined the same way as much as possible) has progressed tremendously, thanks mostly to the efforts of Luxembourg Income Study (LIS), and the World Bank (Living Standard Measurement Survey (LSMS), Africa Poverty Monitoring, Household Expenditure and Income Data for Transition Economies, HEIDE).

More recently, Bourguignon and Morrisson (1999), have returned to the topic of world inequality in a historical perspective. They study the evolution of world inequality between 1820 and 1990. Similarly to Berry *et al.* (1983), they use quantile shares multiplied by GDPs per capita (in PPP terms) to derive world income distribution. Since, obviously, the data for such a long period of 170 years are sparsely available, they divide the world in 33 country groups whose income distributions are approximated by one or more countries belonging to the group. For example, distribution of 37 Latin American countries is assumed to be the same as that of Brazil; distribution of Indonesia the same as that of India until, of course, the data for Indonesia become available in the late 1960s etc.

Finally, we come to the papers that are methodologically almost identical to this one. These are papers by Ravallion *et al.* (1991), Chen *et al.* (1994), and Ravallion and Chen (1997). The last study, for example, is based entirely on household survey data from 67 countries with 42 countries being represented with at least two surveys. These studies have produced the widely quoted World Bank estimates of the people living in absolute poverty (at less than $PPP1 per capita per day), and their results were repeatedly used in World Bank's *World Development Reports* and *World Development Indicators*. The major difference between their and this work is in the coverage (they do not include advanced market economies)[4] and focus (they are interested in changes in world poverty; not in world inequality).

This is therefore the first study which is based solely on household survey data and where world income distribution is derived the same way as we would derive a country's income distribution from regional distributions.

---

[4] Two out of three papers (1991 and 1994) include only developing countries (as mentioned in the titles of the papers). The third (1997) adds transition economies.

3. Methodology, Sources, and Coverage

3.1. *Methodology: Quality of Data and how Are the Calculations Done*

For each country for which nationally representative survey data are available, we take local currency (LC) mean income or expenditure per decile (if we have access to unit record data), or for any other population shares (eg 12 or 15 population groups).[5] The objective is that the number of such data points be at least ten in order to have a sufficiently precise description of a distribution. In total, for both years, there are 216 country surveys with an average of 10.8 data points in 1988 and 11.4 data points in 1993. Most countries' data are deciles; some countries however have 16, 18, 20 or more data points. There are only 12 surveys where we have only quintiles (5 data points). Each data point is weighted by the population it represents. For example, one decile in the US survey represents 1/10th of the US population, one decile in the Nigerian survey represents 1/10th of Nigeria's population etc.

The quality of the surveys is uneven. It could hardly have been otherwise because the surveys have all been conducted independently by countries' statistical offices, even if their objectives (to assess the average standard of living or income of the population and its distribution) and national representativeness are the same. In principle, we can distinguish two types of problems.

First, the issue of survey quality. Although the claim of national representativeness is shared by all surveys, they may not all achieve it. Moreover, even the definition of what 'national representativeness' means may vary. It varies even among the developed countries where the survey techniques are generally thought to be better. For example, Israeli surveys do not include the self-employed and rural population. Urban areas are defined as those with more than 2,000 inhabitants for Jewish localities, and more than 10,000 for non-Jewish localities (Achdut, 1997, p. 152). Japan's *Family Income and Expenditure Survey* seriously underrepresents farmers and one-person households (Tachibanaki and Yagi, 1997, p. 112). These problems are magnified when we use surveys from more than 100 countries, where such sources of bias often go unreported. However, no adjustments to the surveys were made first, because information on sources of the bias survey-by-survey is unavailable, and second, even if we had information regarding omission of certain population categories, it is simply beyond the scope of knowledge of any single researcher to make meaningful corrections for such a great and varied number of surveys.

The second source of potential problems has to deal with differences in the surveys' definition of income and expenditures – the two welfare categories we use to rank people. Here, fortunately, we can take a less agnostic attitude. For example, the source of our data for most OECD countries is the Luxembourg Income Study which, using the member country surveys,

---

[5] A more detailed list of the surveys used, their sources, and acknowledgements to people and organisations that kindly provided them is given in Annex 1.

© Royal Economic Society 2002

attempts to standardise the variable definitions (eg making sure that disposable income is defined the same way across all countries). For several transition economies and Latin American countries, I have used respectively the HEIDE database and a database created by the Inter-American Development Bank (described in Szekely and Hilgert (1999)) where variable definitions are also standardised. For the countries – about ¾ of their total number – where the quantiles were calculated from the individual level data, I have tried to define the variables in a consistent fashion: for example to have income include not only monetary income but home-consumption as well. In the remaining cases – even if unfortunately this group includes the single most important country for world income distribution, namely China – where I had access only to the pre-defined or grouped (not individual level) data I had to go by whatever the definition of income or expenditures was.

The unit of analysis is throughout the individual, which means that each decile includes 10% of *individuals* in a given country. Individuals are ranked by their household per capita income or expenditures (see Table 1).[6] When only published data were available, and if, for example, the distribution was that of households, so that each decile contained 10% of households, such data were not used. The tabulated distributions were used only if they gave percentage of individuals ranked by their household per capita income.

3.2. Coverage

Table 2 divides all the countries and territories[7] in the world into four groups: those included in our data base for both years (called 'common sample'), those included in 1988, but not in 1993; those included in 1993 but not in 1988; and those not included in either year. The common sample consists of 91 countries, inclusive of the data for large countries (China,

Table 1

Summary of World Income Distribution Characteristics

Unit of observation	Individual
Welfare concept	Disposable per capita income or expenditures per capita
Ranking criterion	Welfare concept per capita
Currency units	$PPP or $

[6] There are three reasons why I am not using 'equivalent adult' instead of per capita measurement. First, equivalence scales vary as a function of relative price of public versus private goods which is not the same across countries. Thus the 'correct' equivalence scale is country-specific and the more so since we deal with countries that are vastly different in terms of real income and household composition. Second, the use of equivalence scales would make difficult a direct comparison between income (and expenditure) measures used here and GDPs per capita. The third and sufficient reason is that the use of equivalent scales is impossible without access to individual-level data for all countries. Unfortunately for about a quarter of the countries in the sample I had to rely on pre-calculated per capita tabulations.

[7] For simplicity, in the rest of the paper, both will be called 'countries'. This includes not only territories such as Puerto Rico, but also 'units' whose legal positions changed between 1988 and 1993: the republics of the former USSR, Yugoslavia, and Czechoslovakia that have become independent countries, or Hong Kong that has rejoined China.

Table 2
CountriesIncluded in the Study

Countries in *both* 1988 and 1993	Countries included *only* in 1993

Western Europe, North America and Oceania (22)
Australia, Austria, Belgium, Canada, Cyprus,
  Denmark, Finland, France, Germany, Greece,
  Ireland, Israel, Italy, Luxembourg, Netherlands,
  Norway, New Zealand, Portugal, Sweden,
  Switzerland, United Kingdom, United States
Latin America and Caribbean (17)
Argentina(urban), Bolivia, Brazil, Chile, Colombia,
  Costa Rica, Dominican Republic, El Salvador
  (urban), Honduras, Jamaica, Mexico, Panama,
  Paraguay, Venezuela, Ecuador*, Uruguay†,
  Peru‡
Eastern Europe and FSU (22)
Armenia, Bulgaria, Czech Republic, East Germany,
  Georgia, Slovak Republic, Hungary, Poland,
  Romania, Belarus, Estonia, Kazakhstan, Kyrgyz
  Rep., Latvia, Lithuania, Moldova, Russia,
  Turkmenistan, Ukraine, Uzbekistan,
  FR Yugoslavia, Slovenia
Asia (17)
Bangladesh(rural), Bangladesh(urban), China(rural),
  China(urban), Hong Kong, India(rural),
  India(urban), Indonesia(rural), Indonesia(urban),
  Japan, Jordan, Korea South, Malaysia, Pakistan
  Philippines, Taiwan, Thailand
Africa (13)
Algeria, Egypt(urban), Egypt(rural), Ghana, Ivory
  Coast, Lesotho, Madagascar, Morocco,
  Nigeria, Senegal, Tunisia, Uganda, Zambia
Total: 91
	Western Europe, North America and Oceania (1)
	  Turkey
	Latin America and Caribbean (2)
	  Guyana, Nicaragua
	Eastern Europe and FSU (1)
	  Albania
	Asia (8)
	  Laos, Mongolia(urban), Mongolia(rural),
	  Nepal, Papua New Guinea, Singapore,
	  Vietnam, Yemen Rep.
	Africa (16)
	  Guinea Bissau, Burkina Faso, Djibouti, Ethiopia,
	  Gambia, Guinea, Kenya, Mali, Mauritania, Namibia,
	  Niger(rural), Niger(urban), RCA, South
	  Africa, Swaziland, Tanzania
	Total: 28

Countries included *only* in 1988	Countries *not* included in either year

Western Europe, North America and Oceania (1)
  Spain
Latin America and Caribbean (2)
  Guatemala, Trinidad & Tobago
Eastern Europe and FSU (5)
  Azerbaijan, Bosnia, Croatia, Macedonia, Tajikistan
Asia (1)
  Sri Lanka
Africa (1)
  Rwanda
Total: 10
	Western Europe, North America,
	and Oceania (1)
	  Iceland
	Latin America and Caribbean (21)
	  Antigua and Barbuda, Argentina(rural),
	  Aruba, Bahamas, Barbados, Belize, Bermuda,
	  Cuba, Dominica, El Salvador(rural),
	  French Guyana, Grenada, Guadeloupe,
	  Haiti, Netherlands Antilles, Puerto Rico,
	  St. Kitts and Nevis, St. Lucia,
	  St. Vincent and Gr., Suriname,
	  Virgin Islands
	Asia (18)
	  Afghanistan, Bahrain, Bhutan, Brunei,
	  Cambodia, Iran, Iraq, Korea North, Kuwait,
	  Lebanon, Macao, Maldives, Myanmar, Oman,
	  Qatar, Saudi Arabia, Syria, United Arab
	  Emirates
	Africa (21)
	  Angola, Benin, Botswana, Burundi, Cameroon,
	  Cape Verde Is, Chad, Comoros, Congo,
	  Gabon, Liberia, Malawi, Mauritius,
	  Mozambique, Seychelles, Sierra Leone,
	  Somalia, Sudan, Togo, Zaire, Zimbabwe
	Total: 61

* In 1988 only urban; in 1993 the whole country. † In 1988 the whole country; in 1993 only urban.
‡ In 1988 only Lima; in 1993 the whole country.

India, Bangladesh, and Indonesia) that have been divided into rural and urban parts. For 1988, other than the common sample, I had the data for 10 additional countries, and for 1993, for 28 additional countries. Thus the full 1993 sample was 119 countries.

The largest difference between 1988 and 1993 is a much better coverage of African countries. While in 1988, I had data for only 14 African countries, their number increased to 29 in 1993. This is mostly thanks to a number of surveys in Africa conducted or organised by the World Bank, or whose results were compiled and made more easily accessible to researchers by the Africa Region of the World Bank. Note the significant increase in the full-sample coverage of Africa shown in Table 4: the share of African population included went up from slightly under ½ to almost ¾. The share of GDP covered reached almost 90%.

Sixty-one countries are not included in either year. However, our coverage, both in terms of income or population is much greater than this number suggests, because most of the non-included countries are very small, measured either by their GDPs or population. For example, the total population of 22 non-included Latin American and Caribbean countries (see Table 2) is 42 million, and their combined GDP in 1993 was $80 billion. This is about equal to the population and GDP of Poland.

The countries are divided into five geographical regions: Africa, Asia, Eastern Europe and the former Soviet Union, Latin America and the Caribbean (LAC), and Western Europe, North America and Oceania (WENAO). The last region is the 'old OECD' region short of Japan, that is it includes the 'old' OECD countries before the recent expansion of the organisation in Eastern Europe, Mexico, and South Korea. The distribution of countries by region is shown in Table 2.

The countries included in 1988 and 1993 represent respectively about 4.4 and 5 billion people, or respectively 86 and 91% of world population. The common-sample countries cover about 84% of world population (Tables 3 and 4). The total current dollar GDP of the countries covered is about 95% of world GDP in both years. The common-sample countries account for about 93% of world GDP (Table 4).

Turning to the regions, WENAO and Eastern Europe/FSU are covered in the full sample almost in full (92 to 99% of population; not less than 95% of GDP). Asia and LAC are covered about 90%, both in terms of population and GDP. Finally, Africa's coverage, as already mentioned, has substantially increased between 1988 and 1993: from around ½ in both population and GDP to almost 90% in terms of GDP and ¾ in terms of population. The common-sample coverage is still low in Africa. It is the reflection of unavailability of household surveys until the very recent period. On the other hand, a significant jump in African coverage (for the full-sample) between 1988 and 1993 shows that in terms of household survey availability Africa is approaching the other continents.

A special consideration is due to China and India. These two countries have respectively 1.2 and 0.9 billion people, that is almost 40% of world

Table 3

World Population (in millions)

	World population		Population included in the study (full sample)		Population included in the study (common sample)	
	1988	1993	1988	1993	1988	1993
Africa	607	672	293	503	286	306
Asia	2,959	3,206	2,682	2,984	2,665	2,868
E. Europe/ FSU	425	411	422	391	399	388
LAC	427	462	373	423	363	418
WENAO	707	755	653	716	614	656
World	5,125	5,506	4,423	5,017	4,328	4,635

Table 4

How Much of the World do our Data Cover? (in %)

	Population		Current dollar GDP	
	1988	1993	1988	1993
Full sample				
Africa	48.3	74.8	52.0	89.2
Asia	90.6	93.1	91.0	91.3
E. Europe/FSU	99.3	95.2	99.4	96.3
LAC	87.4	91.6	90.2	92.5
WENAO	92.4	94.8	99.3	96.4
World	86.3	91.1	95.8	94.7
Common sample				
Africa	47.2	45.5	51.4	49.9
Asia	90.1	89.5	90.8	89.8
E. Europe/FSU	93.8	94.2	95.0	96.1
LAC	85.1	90.5	88.8	92.3
WENAO	86.8	86.9	96.5	95.6
World	84.4	84.2	93.7	93.1

population. In order to improve the analysis, their populations are shown separately for rural and urban areas (the same way that the data are generated in their Surveys). Thus, the largest single 'country' in the world is rural China with 860 million people in 1993. The same breakdown into rural and urban populations was done for three other large countries (Bangladesh, Indonesia and Pakistan)[8] for which such survey data were available.

3.3. *Problems*

Other than the issue of differential reliability (quality) of individual country surveys, the main problem is the mixing of income and expenditures. Ideally, there could be two different distributions, one based on incomes, another on expenditures. However, the number of countries which would have been

---

[8] Pakistan though was divided into rural and urban in 1988 only.

included in each would have been substantially lower than when both income and expenditures are combined. Moreover since countries tend to conduct either income or expenditures surveys, there would have been two unrelated distributions, none of which would represent the 'world'. One distribution would have been for that part of the world where most of the surveys are expenditure-based (Africa and Asia; see Table 5); another for the part of the world where almost all surveys are income-based (WENAO, Eastern Europe/ FSU, and Latin America).[9] Since expenditure surveys are more frequent in the poorer part of the world (Africa and Asia), and since they tend to yield lower inequality and higher mean than income-based surveys,[10] the mixing of income and expenditure data probably biases Gini downward.

Another problem is the use of a single PPP exchange rate for the whole country even if we know that regional price differences may be large. This is particularly a problem in the case of the four countries for which the survey data are broken down into rural and urban parts, because presumably different PPP rates should apply to each part. For all of them but China, I use the same PPP rates however. For China, in 1993, I use the rate reported in the International comparison project (ICP) for urban areas only (since the rate itself was obtained from surveys conducted in two cities: Guandong and Shanghai), and reduce the price level in rural areas by an estimated 20% (see Yao and Zhu, 1998, p. 138).

There are also possible inconsistencies and mistakes between the PPP rates calculated for 1988 and 1993. Small errors in the estimates of large countries'

Table 5

Welfare Indicators Used in Surveys: Income or Expenditures (number of countries)

	1988		1993	
	Income	Expenditure	Income	Expenditure
Africa	3	11	2	27
Asia	9	9	8	16
Eastern Europe	27	0	19	3
LAC	18	1	16	3
WENAO	23	0	23	0
World	80	21	68	49

Note. The difference between 117 surveys for 1993 here, and 119 countries in 1993 as listed in Table 2 stems from the fact that East Germany, existing in 1988, was incorporated into the West Germany, and in 1988 Pakistan was divided into rural and urban areas while that was not the case in 1993. In 1993, we thus have 117 surveys, but 119 'countries'.

[9] There are seven countries (Armenia, Ecuador, Georgia, Jamaica, Madagascar, Thailand, and Zambia) that are 'cross-overs', that is they have income-based surveys in the 1988 data set, and expenditure-based HS in the 1993 data set. Peru is the 'cross-over' in the other direction: from expenditures to income. But, the total importance of these countries is small. Their total population in 1993 is 126 million (or 2.7% of world population), and they account for a mere 0.6% of world $PPP income.

[10] For example, Li *et al.* (1998) report that, everything else being the same, income-based Ginis are on average greater than expenditure-based Ginis by some 6.6 Gini points. Consequently, in their regressions, they increase expenditure-based Ginis by 6.6 points, and that practice has recently been adopted by other researchers (see Banerjee and Duffo, 2000).

PPPs may produce large effects on the calculated world inequality. Table 6 shows the ratio between the domestic and world price levels in 1988 and 1993 for China, India, Bangladesh, and Indonesia. The four countries' price levels ranged from 27 to 34% of the world level in 1988; in 1993, they ranged from 23 to 30%. In three countries out of four, the relative price level went down, which – bearing in mind that these are poor countries – should reduce world inequality. We note, however, the opposite trends in India's and Indonesia's relative price levels. While in 1988, the price level in India was the highest of the four countries, and some 20% higher than in Indonesia, in 1993, India's price level is the lowest of the four, and almost ¼ *less* than Indonesia's. This is a fairly large swing.

Finally, the fact that we assume that that all people within each quantile (data point) have the same income/expenditures biases the overall inequality downward. We calculate the 'minimum' or lower-bound Gini (see Kakwani, 1980, pp. 97–100). Although with only six or seven optimally selected data points, the 'minimum' Gini approximates the 'true' Gini within a few percentage points, this result is obtained within the context of income distribution for a single country (Davies and Shorrocks, 1989, pp. 100–3). The problem is more complex in our case because the span of world incomes, from the poorest income class to the richest, is much wider than in any single country, some of the data points are very large, and they are not optimally selected (that is, data points are not necessarily created at 'best' places along income distribution). Thus the minimum Gini might underestimate the true Gini by more than we would normally expect. Yet the use of minimum Gini was made necessary because in many important cases (eg China's and India's data points), we do not have information on income bounds of each income class. For example, the sixth income class of rural population in China has the mean annual income of $PPP 615 and it contains 180 million people (the largest data point in the study). Since the mean income of the income classes just below and above this one is respectively $PPP 486 and $PPP 789, we know that all the 180 million people

Table 6

RatioBetween Domestic and International Price Level in China, India, Indonesia and Bangladesh, 1988 and 1993

	Purchasing power exchange rate (LC per $)		Nominal exchange rate (annual average)		Ratio of domestic to world price level	
	1988	1993	1988	1993	1988	1993
India	4.756*	6.997*	13.917	30.493	0.342	0.229
China (urban)	1.038*	1.414*	3.72	5.762	0.279	0.245
Indonesia	453.453†	626.130*	1685.7	2087.1	0.269	0.300
Bangladesh	8.822†	9.496*	31.733	39.567	0.278	0.240

Sources: * Data from ICP tables provided by Yonas Biru (World Bank). † Data from Heston and Summers (1991).

in our group must have incomes between these two values, most likely between $PPP 500 and $PPP 700. Yet this is only one estimate of the bounds; it could as well be that the true bounds are $PPP 550 and $PPP 720, or a variety of other values. I therefore thought it more prudent to stay with a conservative estimate of the minimum Gini – that is, of inequality where it is assumed that all individuals within each data point have same income.

4. Regional Income Inequalities

4.1. *Average Regional Incomes*

Table 7 shows mean regional GDP and income per capita. In 1993, the ratio between the richest (WENAO) and the poorest (Africa) region was 30 to 1 using GDP per capita in current dollars, 11 to 1 using GDP per capita in international dollars (PPP), and 8 to 1 using the data from household surveys adjusted for the differences in purchasing power.

We know since Kravis *et al.*'s (1982) work and UN International Comparison Project that adjusting for the differences in countries' price levels reduces the gap between poor and rich countries, because price level systematically increases with GDP per capita. This reduces differences between rich and poor countries compared to what they would have been if we used market exchange rates to convert GDPs. In addition, we find here that there is – similar in its effect on the poor-to-rich nation gap – a systematic relationship between (i) the ratio of per capita income or expenditures from household surveys to GDP per capita (*RATIO*), and (ii) level of per capita GDP: as GDP per capita increases, the *RATIO* variable decreases (see Fig. 1). In other words, differences between rich and poor countries are less when measured by incomes or expenditures per capita calculated from household surveys than when measured by GDP per capita (some reasons why this may be so are given below).

If we regress for 1988 and 1993, *RATIO* against (i) GDP per capita (in $PPP terms), (ii) a dummy variable taking a value of 1 if HS data are

Table 7

GDPand Income Per Capita

	GDP per capita ($)		GDP per capita ($PPP)		Household survey income or expenditure per capita ($PPP)	
	1988	1993	1988	1993	1988	1993
Africa	619	673	1,320	1,757	1,036	1,233
Asia	1,422	2,007	1,927	2,972	1,175	1,752
E. Europe	1,889	1,194	6,355	4,522	3,634	2,646
LAC	1,967	3,027	4,829	5,923	2,702	3,483
WENAO	16,255	20,485	14,713	19,952	7,581	9,998
World	3,649	4,531	4,442	5,642	2,475	3,092

Note. All amounts are annual. Full-sample countries.

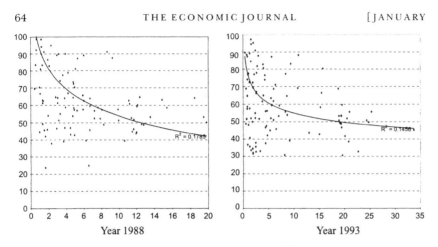

Year 1988   Year 1993

Fig. 1. *RATIO as function of $PPP GDP per capita*
Note. Vertical axis: ratio (in %) between average household survey income (or expenditure) and GDP. Horizontal axis: GDP per capita in thousand international dollars. The fitted curve is based on a simple regression between $PPP GDP per capita and RATIO

expenditures-based and 0 if income-based, and (iii) the interaction term between GDP per capita and the expenditure dummy, all the variables (but one in 1993) are significant at the 5% level (see Table 8). Every $PPP 1,000 increase in GDP per capita lowers *RATIO* by about 1 percentage point in 1993 and 2 percentage points in 1988. The expenditure dummy is also significant implying that expenditure-based surveys (more common in poor countries) yield *RATIO* values that are 30 to 40 percentage points higher than income-based surveys. However, since the interaction term is negative and

Table 8
Explaining RATIO Variable

	1988	1993
Intercept	80.84	70.84
	(p = 0.000)	(p = 0.000)
GDP per capita (in $PPP)	−0.002	−0.001
	(p = 0.015)	(p = 0.067)
Expenditure dummy	41.1	29.9
	(p = 0.015)	(p = 0.008)
Interaction (GDP per capita and expenditure dummy)	−0.023	−0.009
	(p = 0.008)	(p = 0.029)
R^2	0.17	0.16
F	6.4	7.1

Note. The dependent variable is *RATIO* (income or expenditure per capita from household surveys divided by GDP per capita expressed in percent). Significance levels between brackets.

significant, the *RATIO* variable declines faster as income goes up when household surveys are expenditure-based. The difference between expenditure- and income-based surveys in their *RATIO* values vanishes for GDP levels of about $PPP 1,800 per capita in 1988 and $PPP 3,300 in 1993.

What explains the decrease in *RATIO* as GDP per capita goes up? The cause seems to lie in the systematic accounting divergence between GDP and household surveys. Four components, imperfectly or not at all included in household survey data, tend to rise with GDP per capita. They are (i) undisbursed corporate profits, (ii) income from property, (iii) personal taxes, and (iv) government transfers in kind. Undisbursed corporate profits (and build-up of inventories) are a component of GDP, but not of household income. Their share in GDP is, of course, higher in richer countries, where the enterprise sector is larger and 'formalised'. Income from capital (property) is also greater in relative terms in richer countries, simply because income-rich countries are also capital-rich. Capital income is also the most underreported type of income in household surveys, with underreporting estimated at up to 40% in some European OECD countries.[11] Finally, disposable income as covered by surveys is defined as factor income (wages, property income, self-employment income etc.) *plus* government cash transfers *minus* personal income taxes. In richer countries, taxes withdrawn at source (and thus not included in household surveys) as well as personal income taxes are a larger share of GDP than in poorer countries. While one part of transfers financed by taxes (cash transfers) is included in HS's, the other part – often very sizeable – government education and health expenditures is not. Moreover, if there is a current surplus in the financing of cash transfers (so that contributions and fees exceed the outlays), disposable income in a country where such contributions are deducted at source will be underestimated compared to a country where there is only private insurance. In the latter case, all contributions and fees will be part of disposable income (see Lindbeck, 1990, pp. 6–7). Most poor countries belong to this category; most developed countries belong to the former (social security contributions deducted at source).

These are the reasons why the difference between the rich and poor countries will be less if we use their HS disposable income or expenditures than if we use their GDPs. It is reflected in the fact that while in Africa household surveys account for over 70% of GDP, in WENAO countries, the ratio is 50–51%. Asia, Eastern Europe/FSU, and Latin America and the Caribbean are in between with the ratio of around 60% (Table 9). Therefore, one important source of smaller world income inequality than that calculated using GDP per capita will lie in the systematic difference – varying with income level – between the survey-collected incomes or expenditures, and GDP.

---

[11] For example, Concialdi (1997, p. 261) writes that the best available French household surveys conducted by the *Institut National de Statistique et Etudes Economiques* underestimates capital incomes by about 40%.

Table 9

RatioBetween Household Income/Expenditure from Surveys and GDP

	1988	1993
Africa	78.5	70.2
Asia	61.0	58.9
E. Europe/FSU	57.2	58.5
LAC	55.9	58.8
W. Europe	51.5	50.1
World	54.5	53.4

Note. Weighted average.

4.2. *Regional Ginis*

Table 10 shows regional Gini coefficients for the common-sample countries. A regional Gini shows inequality in a given region (say, Asia) where each individual is treated equally – simply as an inhabitant of a given region. In other words, the aggregation of country distributions at the regional level proceeds in the same way as the aggregation of country distributions to generate world income distribution. (This is important to underline to show that the regional inequality is *not* simply *inter-national* inequality within the region.)

Note, first, that the most unequal regions are Asia and LAC with Ginis between 55 and almost 62 (Table 10). They are followed by Africa where Gini has increased sharply from 43 in 1988 to 49 in 1993. Eastern Europe/FSU, and WENAO have traded places. In 1988, the former socialist bloc was the most equal region with a Gini of 26. However, the transition which has led to massive increases of inequality within individual countries (Milanovic, 1998) has also led to an 'explosion' of inequality in the region as a whole. Its Gini in 1993 was more than 20 points higher than before the transition. It has surpassed the West European and North American region whose inequality has remained at the Gini level of 37, about the same as the Gini coefficient for the United States.

As Table 10 makes clear, between 1988 and 1993, inequality increased in three regions, went down slightly in WENAO, and decreased by 1½ Gini

Table 10

RegionalGini Coefficients in 1988 and 1993
(Common-sample Countries; Distribution of Persons by $PPP Income/
Expenditures Per Capita)

	1988	1993
Africa	42.7	48.7
Asia	55.9	61.8
Latin America and Caribbean	57.1	55.6
Eastern Europe, FSU	25.6	46.4
Western Europe, North America, Oceania	37.1	36.6

Note. For the list of countries included in each region, see Table 2.

points in Latin America and the Caribbean. The most important increase occurred in Eastern Europe/FSU, while inequality in both Asia and Africa went up by 6 Gini points.

Comparison between Asia and Africa is instructive. While their mean and median incomes are quite similar (eg in 1993, mean income in Asia was about $PPP 1,600, and in Africa about $1,200; the medians were respectively $PPP680 and PPP750), the shape of the income distribution curve is very different (Fig. 2). This is a reflection of much greater heterogeneity in Asia (presence of rich countries) than in Africa. Consequently, the frequency of the very poor people is much greater in Africa. Note that up to $PPP 300, the density function for Africa lies significantly above the one for Asia. Africa's modal income is extremely low ($PPP200), one-half of Asia's modal income ($PPP400). Asian distribution extends much further to the right. Five percent of Asian population have per capita incomes in excess of $PPP7,600 per year while only ½% of Africans have such high incomes. This is, of course, mostly because of people living in rich Asian countries: 83% of the Japanese have incomes higher than $PPP7,600 per year, as do 60% of the South Koreans, 50% of the Taiwanese and 50% of citizens of Hong Kong. By contrast, there are almost no such people (in statistically significant numbers) in Africa.

Tables 11–15 show for each region the Pyatt (1976)-type decomposition where the overall Gini is broken into three components: (a) within-country

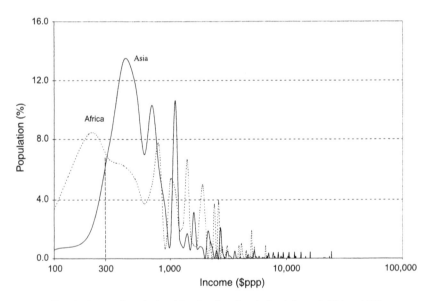

Fig. 2. *Income Distribution* (density functions) *for Asia and Africa, 1993*
Note. *x*-axis in logs. The distribution function is smoothed using kernel function with a bandwidth 0.005

Table 11

Africa: Gini Decomposition, 1988 and 1993

	1988	1993	Change
Within countries	6.2	6.2	0
Between countries	20.9	30.1	+9.2
Overlapping	15.6	12.4	−3.2
Total Gini	42.7	48.7	+6.0
Number of countries	13	13	
Mean country Gini	41.8	41.4	−0.4
Coefficient of variation of Gini	25.2	19.6	−5.6
Average income/expenditures per capita ($PPP)	1,078	1,217	+12.9
Standard deviation income/expenditure per capita ($PPP)	695	806	
Coefficient of variation (%)	64	66	+2

Table 12

Asia: Gini Decomposition, 1988 and 1993

	1988	1993	Change
Within countries	3.2	3.0	−0.2
Between countries	46.3	53.6	+7.3
Overlapping	6.4	5.3	−1.1
Total Gini	55.9	61.8	+5.9
Number of countries	17	17	
Mean country Gini	32.8	34.3	+1.5
Coefficient of variation of Gini	21.4	22.2	+0.8
Average income/expenditures per capita ($PPP)	1,129	1,613	+42.9
Standard deviation income/expenditures per capita ($PPP)	2,178	3,587	
Coefficient of variation (%)	193	222	+29

Table 13

Latin America and the Caribbean: Gini Decomposition, 1988 and 1993

	1988	1993	Change
Within countries	15.0	11.7	−3.3
Between countries	13.9	13.6	−0.3
Overlapping	28.2	30.3	+2.1
Total Gini	57.1	55.6	−1.5
Number of countries	17	17	
Mean country Gini	48.1	49.1	+1.0
Coefficient of variation of Gini	13.4	12.9	−0.5
Average income/expenditures per capita ($PPP)	2,814	3,634	+29.1
Standard deviation income/expenditures per capita ($PPP)	1,221	1,899	
Coefficient of variation (%)	43	52	+9

Table 14

Eastern Europe and FSU: Gini Decomposition, 1988 and 1993

	1988	1993	Change
Within countries	3.9	9.5	+5.6
Between countries	12.5	26.4	+13.9
Overlapping	9.1	10.4	+1.3
Total Gini	25.6	46.4	+20.8
Number of countries	22	22	
Mean country Gini	21.7	32.6	+10.2
Coefficient of variation of Gini	14.6	23.9	+7.2
Average income/expenditures per capita ($PPP)	3,681	2,795	−24.0
Standard deviation income/expenditures per capita ($PPP)	2,000	1,472	
Coefficient of variation (%)	54	53	−1

Table 15

Western Europe, North America, Oceania: Gini Decomposition, 1988 and 1993

	1988	1993	Change
Within countries	8.5	8.3	−0.2
Between countries	14.4	8.9	−5.5
Overlapping	14.1	19.4	+5.3
Total Gini	37.1	36.6	−0.5
Number of countries	22	22	
Mean country Gini	30.4	31.8	+1.4
Coefficient of variation of Gini	15.9	22.0	+6.1
Average income/expenditures per capita ($PPP)	7,817	10,684	+36.7
Standard deviation income/expenditures per capita ($PPP)	3,751	5,284	
Coefficient of variation (%)	48	49	+1

Note. Ginis in Tables 11–15 calculated for individuals within each region ranked according to their household per capita $PPP income or expenditures. Common-sample countries. Regional mean Ginis and their standard deviations are unweighted (it is the simple average Gini, and standard deviation of the Gini for all the countries of the region). Regional mean incomes and their standard deviations are population-weighted. Change in average income per capita is in current $PPP.

inequality, (b) between-country inequality, and (c) an overlapping component.[12] The first component shows that part of inequality which is due to the differences in income between the recipients in individual countries. The second component accounts for inequality due to people living in countries with different mean incomes. In other words, even if within-country inequalities were zero, there would still be differences between individual incomes due to the fact that mean incomes in each country are different. Finally, the third ('overlapping') component appears because the Gini coefficient is not exactly decomposable by recipients. The overlapping component accounts for

---

[12] The same decomposition formula is derived also by Mookherjee and Shorrocks (1982) and Shorrocks (1984). For different Gini decomposition rules see Silber (1989), Sastry and Kelkar (1994), Yitzhaki and Lerman (1991), Yitzhaki (1994).

the fact that somebody who lives in a richer country may still have an income lower than somebody from a poorer country. One interpretation of the 'overlapping' component is 'homogeneity' of population (Yitzhaki and Lerman, 1991; Yitzhaki, 1994, Lambert and Aronson, 1993). The more important the 'overlapping' component compared to the other two, the more homogeneous the population – or differently put, the less one's income depends on where she lives. Thus, the third, residual component may be viewed as providing some additional information compared to the measures, like Theil index, which are exactly decomposable. The decomposition formula of the Gini is:

$$
\begin{aligned}
GINI &= \sum_{i=1}^{n} G_i p_i \pi_i + \sum_{i}^{n} \sum_{j>i}^{n} \left(\frac{y_j - y_i}{y_i} \right) \pi_i p_j + L \\
&= \sum_{i=1}^{n} G_i p_i \pi_i + \frac{1}{\mu} \sum_{i}^{n} \sum_{j>i}^{n} (y_j - y_i) p_i p_j + L
\end{aligned}
\tag{1}
$$

where y_i = mean income of country i, G_i = Gini coefficient of country i; π_i = income share of country i in total income of the region (where countries are ranked by their mean incomes so that $y_j > y_i$); p_i = country's population share, and μ = mean income of the region.

A glance at Tables 11–15 reveals that in Africa, Asia, and Eastern Europe/FSU, the between-country component is the largest. In 1993, it was about 54 Gini points in Asia (87% of total inequality in Asia), 30 Gini points in Africa (almost two-thirds of total inequality), and 26.4 Gini points in Eastern Europe/FSU (57% of total inequality).[13] In LAC and WENAO, inequality in countries' mean incomes is indeed important – it 'explains' about ¼ of total inequality – but overlapping is even more important. These two are consequently the most homogeneous regions: note also that they have the lowest coefficient of variation of population weighted income/expenditure per capita. Asia, on the other hand, is by far the most heterogeneous region.

As for the importance of within-country inequality, it is largest in Latin America and the Caribbean (11.7 Gini points), followed by Eastern Europe/FSU, and Western Europe and North America (respectively 9.5 and 8.3 Gini points). In both Africa and Asia, 'within country' inequality is of little importance. This is because the size of the within component depends on the product of the population and income weights (see (1)). Countries with large population weights in Asia (rural India and rural China) have relatively low income weights. The issue is discussed in greater detail in Section 6 below.[14]

[13] When we use the entire sample of countries for Africa (29) rather than the common sample, the 1993 Gini becomes 52.9, the between-country component 32.9, within-country 3.6, and the overlap component 16.4.

[14] In addition, the most populous countries in Asia have relatively low inequality: rural China (30% of Asia's population) has the Gini of 32.9 in 1993; urban China (12% of population) has the Gini of 27; rural India (23% of population) has the Gini of 29; urban India (8% of the population) has the Gini of 35. Therefore, countries accounting for 73% of Asia's population, have Ginis between 27 and 35. In Africa, a similar role is played by three countries: Egypt – 11% of Africa's population with the Gini of 38, Algeria (5% of population) with the Gini of 35, and Morocco (5% of population) with the Gini of 36.

However, the relevance of regional inequality is limited – both because regional 'borders' are often arbitrary, and because study of regional inequality is not fundamentally different from a study of country-level inequality. Our primary interest is world inequality. We turn to this next.

5. World Income Inequality

Fig. 3 shows the density function of world income distribution in 1988 and 1993. It illustrates the rising number of people with extremely low incomes: note that the 1993 curve lies above the 1988 curve for incomes up to $PPP200 per year. The two modes of the distribution are around $PPP400 and a little over $PPP1,100. The mean world income in 1993 was $PPP3,160, some 29% higher than in 1988 (when it was $PPP2,450). These are amounts in current international dollars. In order to be comparable we need to deflate the 1993 value by 22% which is equal to the increase in the US price level (PPP numeraire). We thus find that between 1988 and 1993, mean per capita world income increased by 5.7% in real terms (or by 1.1% p.a. on average). The median income in 1993 was $PPP1,041, some 18% higher than in 1988, or 3% less in real terms.[15] The fact that the mean real income would increase while the median would go down suggests that inequality (skewness) of the distribution increased.

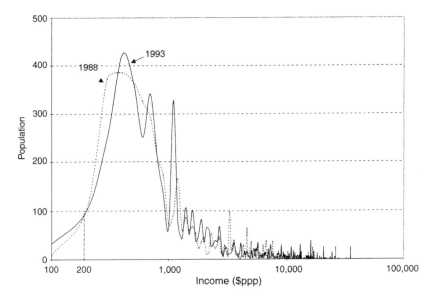

Fig. 3. *World Income Distribution in 1988 and 1993 (in millions of persons)*
Note: x-axis in logs. Distribution functions are smoothed using kernel function with the bandwidth of 0.005

[15] The median world per capita income in 1988 was $PPP 885.

5.1. *How Great is World Inequality?*

In 1993, the Gini coefficient for world per capita $PPP income/expenditure distribution was 66.0. The value is almost the same whether we use the common-sample countries or the full sample. Compared to 1988, inequality has increased by 3.2 Gini points (for the common-sample countries) or 3.4 Gini points (for the full sample).[16] The implied increase of about 0.6 Gini points per year is very high. During the 1980s, inequality in the United States and the United Kingdom increased by about ½ a Gini point per year (Atkinson *et al.*, 1995, p. 25). Similarly, Li *et al.* (1998, p. 32) in the panel analysis of 49 countries find that only two countries (China and Chile) had increases averaging more than ½ Gini point per year. Using the Theil index, world inequality is estimated at about 87, an increase of about 11 Theil points compared to 1988. The increase is more important if measured by the Theil index (13%) than if measured by the Gini index (6%). What is remarkable about the increase is that (i) it occurs at an already very high level of inequality, and (ii) is present in all measures reported here – that is, whether we use common-country sample or the full sample, PPP dollars or current dollars, Gini or Theil index (Table 16). Of course, the current dollar inequality is even higher. It reaches a Gini of 80 in 1993.

5.2. *Lorenz Dominance*

A comparison between the Lorenz curves for 1988 and 1993 shows that income distribution for 1988 is Lorenz-dominant (Fig. 4). For any cumulative percent of world population, the 1988 curve lies above the 1993 curve. This is illustrated also by the data in Table 17. Note that the share of the bottom quintile of the population has decreased from 2.3% of total world $PPP income to 2.0%; that of the bottom half from 9.6% to 8.5% etc. Thus, not

Table 16

WorldInternational Dollar Inequality in 1988 and 1993

(Distribution of Persons by $PPP and $ Income Per Capita)

	Full sample		Common sample	
	1988	1993	1988	1993
International dollars				
Gini index	62.5 (3.1)	65.9 (2.6)	62.8 (3.1)	66.0 (2.7)
Theil index	75.8	86.4	76.5	87.3
Dollars				
Gini index	77.8 (2.3)	80.7 (2.0)	78.2 (2.3)	80.5 (2.2)

Note. Gini standard errors given in parentheses.

[16] The standard errors for the calculated Gini were 3.1 Gini points in 1988, and 2.7 Gini points in 1993. This means that the one-standard error range within which the 'true' Gini might have lain in 1988 was 59.7–65.9, and in 1993 63.3–68.7. The standard errors were calculated using the 'jackknife' technique developed by Sandstrom *et al.* (1988).

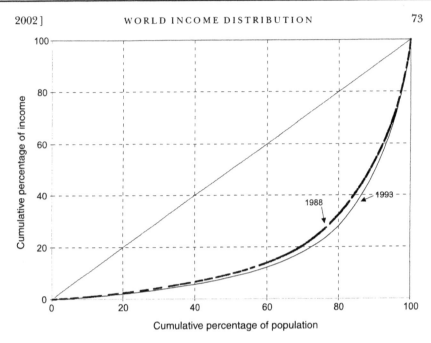

Cumulative percentage of income

Cumulative percentage of population

Fig. 4. *World Lorenz curves for 1988 and 1993*

Table 17

Cumulative Percentage of Persons and Income/expenditures

Cumulative percentage of world population	Cumulative percentage of world income/expenditures	
	1988	1993
Bottom 10	0.9	0.8
Bottom 20	2.3	2.0
Bottom 50	9.6	8.5
Bottom 75	25.9	22.3
Bottom 85	41.0	37.1
Top 10	46.9	50.8
Top 5	31.2	33.7
Top 1	9.3	9.5

only is the Gini higher in 1993, but any quasi-convex social welfare function would rank the 1988 distribution above the 1993 distribution – provided, of course, mean incomes are the same. This condition, however, is not satisfied because the 1993 real income was higher than the 1988 real income. We thus move to the investigation of stochastic dominance.

5.3. *Stochastic Dominance*

Lorenz dominance simply shows that inequality in 1993 was unambiguously greater than in 1988. But, as we have seen, world real per capita income increased between 1993 and 1988 by 5.7%. It is therefore possible that at each percentile of income distribution real income in 1993 was higher than in 1988 (first order stochastic dominance). Table 18 shows the data needed to test first order stochastic dominance. It is rejected.[17] We see that income of the bottom 75% of people was less in real terms in 1993 than in 1988. The largest difference was for the bottom five percent and the 70–75th percentile who have lost 14–16% in real terms. Between the 10th and the 30th percentile, the loss amounts to about 10%; it then becomes smaller and nil for the 50th percentile before rising again around the 70th percentile.[18] The 1993 distribution dominates the 1988 distribution for the top quintile only. The people in the top quintile have gained between 3 and 18% in real terms. Thus, in a nutshell, a description of inequality changes that have occurred in the world between 1988 and 1993 is: the poorest 5% have lost almost 1/4 of their real income,[19] the top quintile has gained 12%. Fig. 5a displays the charts of first order stochastic dominance for each region. As already mentioned, a distribution *A* is first-order dominant over distribution *B*, if at any given percentile of income distribution, a person in distribution *A* has a higher income than a person in distribution *B*. If we accept that these are the same people (which they obviously are not when we compare two distributions in two different points in time), we can say that distribution *A* is Pareto-superior to *B*.[20] Only WENAO displays the first order stochastic dominance: 1993 dominates 1988. In Eastern Europe and FSU, in contrast, the 1988 distribution would be first-order dominant were it not for the slightly higher incomes at the very top of income distribution in 1993. For other regions, and the world, the two distributions intersect. However, the situation varies between the regions. In Africa, real income of the population up to the 55th percentile was higher in 1988 than in 1993. In LAC, the bottom decile has lost between 1988 and 1993, while for the rest the two distributions criss-cross, although on balance incomes are higher in 1993. Finally, in Asia, the two curves almost coincide up to the 60th percentile, and those above are better off in 1993 than in 1988. These results highlight the well-known decline in real incomes practically across the board in Eastern

---

[17] The tests of stochastic dominance are done using software DAD developed by Jean-Yves Duclos, Abdelkarim Araar and Carl Fortin (downloadable from http://www.ecn.ulaval.ca/~jyves/#dad).

[18] This last loss is largely caused by income declines in Eastern Europe and the FSU: a large chunk of East European population had incomes around the 70th world percentile in 1988, they slipped downwards, and those who replaced them have lower incomes.

[19] The data in Table 18 are calculated at the exact percentage points. Thus, the real income of a person at the 5th percentile went down by 14% between 1988 and 1993. But the total real income of the bottom 5% of people is 23% less in 1993 than in 1998. The same concern applies to the top quintile.

[20] Note, however, that while *A* may be first-order dominant, distribution *B* can still be Lorenz-dominant. For example, income distribution in (say) Mali can Lorenz-dominate that in the United States, although absolute income level for every percentile may be higher in the United States than in Mali.

Table 18

FirstOrder Stochastic Dominance: Real Per Capita Income by Percentile of Income Distribution in 1988 and 1993 (World)

Percentile of income distribution	(1) Income in 1988	(2) Income in 1993	Ratio (2): (1) (in %)
5	277.4	238.1	86
10	348.3	318.1	91
15	417.5	372.9	89
20	486.1	432.1	89
25	558.3	495.8	89
30	633.2	586.0	93
35	714.5	657.7	92
40	802.7	741.9	92
45	908.3	883.2	97
50	1,047.5	1,044.1	100
55	1,314.4	1,164.9	89
60	1,522.7	1,505.0	99
65	1,898.9	1,856.8	98
70	2,698.5	2,326.8	86
75	3,597.0	3,005.6	84
80	4,370.0	4,508.1	103
85	5,998.9	6,563.3	109
90	8,044.0	9,109.8	113
95	11,518.4	13,240.7	115
99	20,773.2	24,447.1	118

Note. All values expressed in 1993 international dollars. The values show income exactly at a given percentile of income distribution.

Europe/FSU, but also the worsening position of the bottom half of the population in Africa (an issue which should be of greatest concern), and of the bottom decile in Latin America and the Caribbean.

In Fig. 5*b* we look at the second-order stochastic dominance.[21] In this case, the requirement for distribution *A* to dominate distribution *B* is that at each percentile of income distribution mean cumulative income of those in *A* be greater than mean cumulative income of those in distribution *B*. In other words, we require that (say) the bottom 20% of the population have a higher cumulative income – not necessarily that each individual percentile (18th, 19th, 20th) have a higher income as in the case of first-order dominance. Here only Eastern Europe/FSU and Africa pass the test. In both cases, the 1988 distribution dominates the 1993 distribution. For the world, the bottom four quintiles received cumulatively less in real terms in 1993 than in 1988. Income gains were concentrated in the top quintile. For Asia, the 1988 distribution dominates the 1993 distribution up to the 60th percentile, although the difference is small; for LAC countries, the 1988 distribution is better only for the lowest decile.

---

[21] The first-order dominance implies the second-order dominance. The second-order stochastic dominance means the same thing as generalised Lorenz curve dominance (as in Shorrocks (1983)).

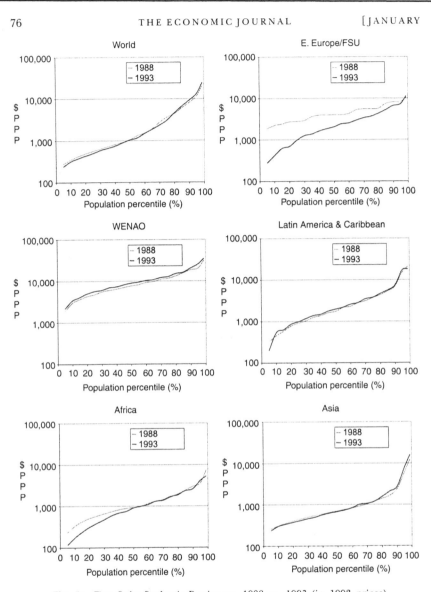

Fig. 5a. *First Order Stochastic Dominance, 1988 vs. 1993* (in 1993 prices)

6. How to Explain the Level, and Change in World Inequality?

6.1. *Decomposition of Total Inequality*

Using the same decomposition formula as before, the between-country component for the world turns out to be 57.8 Gini points in 1993, and

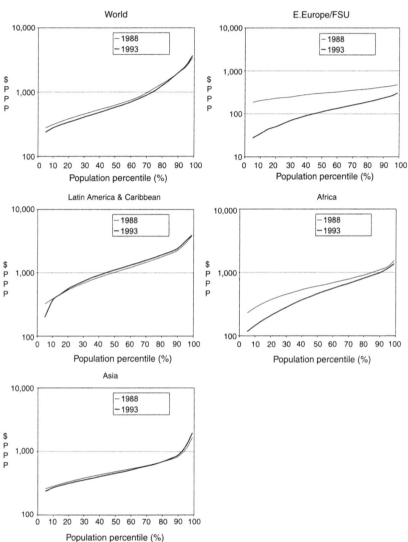

Fig. 5b. *Second Order Stochastic Dominance: 1988 vs. 1993* (in 1993 prices)
Note: First-order stochastic dominance implies that, at each percentile, income of distribution A is greater than income of distribution B. Second-order stochastic dominance implies that, at each percentile, cumulative income of distribution A is greater than cumulative income of distribution B

55.1 Gini points in 1988 (Table 19). This means that 88% of world inequality is due to differences in countries' mean incomes. The within-country inequality accounts for only 1.3 Gini points or 2% of total world inequality. The remainder (10% of world inequality) is due to the 'overlap' component.

According to the Theil index which is exactly decomposable, between-country differences explain ¾ of world inequality, and within-country inequality the remaining ¼ in both 1988 and 1993. According to both Theil and Gini indices, the individual components of inequality increased in step – keeping the composition of inequality the same in both years.

The decomposition results raise three questions that we shall address in turn. They are: (i) what lies behind the very high between-country component of inequality; (ii) why is the 'pure' within-country inequality component in the Gini coefficient so small, and (iii) what drove the increase of 2.7 Gini points in the between-country component which was the main factor behind the increase in the overall world inequality? The first two questions are 'static': they refer to the decomposition of the 1993 measures of inequality. The third question is 'dynamic': it asks why inequality increased between 1988 and 1993.

In the rest of the analysis, I shall consider only inequality adjusted for purchasing power ($PPP) and, in order to avoid spurious changes due to the difference in the composition of the sample, I shall consider only common-sample countries.

What are the main contributors to the between-country inequality? As we know from (1), the between-country component is equal to

$$\sum_{i}^{n}\sum_{j>i}^{n}\left(\frac{y_j - y_i}{y_i}\right)\pi_i p_j = \frac{1}{\mu}\sum_{i}^{n}\sum_{j>i}^{n}(y_j - y_i)p_i p_j \tag{2}$$

Table 19

WorldIncome Inequality in 1988 and 1993
(Common-sample Countries; Distribution of Persons by $PPP Income/ Expenditure Per Capita)

	Gini 1988	Gini 1993	Theil 1988	Theil 1993
Within-country inequality	1.3 (2%)	1.3 (2%)	19.4 (25%)	22.4 (26%)
Between-country inequality	55.1 (88%)	57.8 (88%)	57.1 (75%)	64.9 (74%)
Overlap	6.4 (10%)	6.8 (10%)	–	–
Total world inequality	62.8	66.0	76.5	87.3
Number of countries	91	91	91	91
Mean country Gini/Theil	33.7	36.9	23.7	26.7
Standard deviation of Gini/Theil	11.2	9.9	19.6	17.1
Average income/expenditures per capita ($PPP)	2,450	3,160		
Standard deviation of per capita income/expenditures	2,552	3,591		
Coefficient of variation	1.04	1.14		

Note. Percentage contribution to total inequality between brackets. Mean country Gini and Theil and their standard deviations are unweighted. Average world income and its standard deviation are population-weighted.

For each pair of countries (i,j), its value depends on (i) the difference in mean incomes between these two countries, and (ii) the two countries' shares in total population. The view of the world implicit in Pyatt's decomposition is one populated by representative individuals having mean income of their countries. The greater the number of countries, the greater – under *ceteris paribus* conditions – the between-country component of total inequality.[22] The largest inter-country terms (ICT) will be those interacting poor and rich populous countries. Not surprisingly, therefore, the single largest contributors to total inequality belong, on the one hand, to China-rural and China-urban, and India-rural and India-urban, and, on the other, to the United States, Japan, Germany, France and the United Kingdom. India and China (both rural and urban) account for 45.2% of world population in 1993,[23] and the five rich countries for 12.6%. The difference in mean incomes between these nine countries accounts for 18.9 Gini points or almost 30% of total world inequality (see Table 20).[24]

The greatest contributors to the world Gini are therefore large countries that are at the two poles of the income distribution spectrum, the so-called 'twin peaks' (Quah, 1997). One pole is represented by more than 2.4 billion people who live in countries whose mean income is less than $PPP1,000 per year (Fig. 6).[25] They include both rural and urban India, rural and urban Indonesia, and rural China. The next pole occurs for the income level of over $PPP 11,500. There are more than ½ billion people who live in such rich countries. They include United States,

Table 20

TheLargest Between-country Contributors to Inequality in 1993 (in Gini Points)

	Poor					
Rich	China (rural)	India (rural)	China (urban)	India (urban)	Total Gini points	Population share (%)
United States	3.8	3.0	1.3	1.0	9.1	5.6
Japan	1.7	1.4	0.6	0.5	4.2	2.7
Germany	1.0	0.8	0.3	0.3	2.4	1.8
France	0.7	0.6	0.2	0.2	1.7	1.2
United Kingdom	0.6	0.5	0.2	0.2	1.5	1.3
Total	7.8	6.2	2.7	2.2	18.9	12.6
Population share (%)	18.5	14.3	7.3	5.1		57.8

[22] The approximation to the Lorenz curve implied in Pyatt's decomposition is that of a number of straight lines (one for each country) whose length is proportional to country's population share. The greater the number of such lines, the closer the resulting polygon comes to the true Lorenz curve based on individual incomes. A different view of the world and a different Gini decomposition formula is proposed by Yitzhaki (1994). The latter is not a standard decomposition formula though, and a comparison between it and Pyatt's decomposition is addressed in Yitzhaki and Milanovic (forthcoming).

[23] More exactly, of the common-sample population.

[24] The difference in mean incomes between China (rural and urban), India (rural and urban), and the United States alone explains 9.1 Gini points, or more than 15% of world inequality.

[25] Note that the difference between Fig. 3 and Fig. 6 illustrates the difference between world and international income distribution.

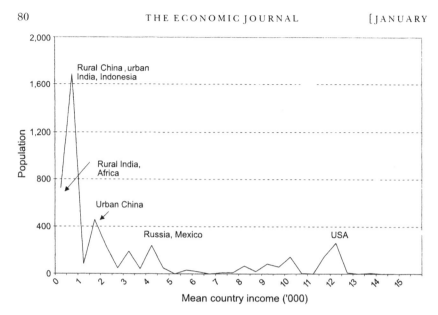

Fig. 6. *Distribution of Population* (in millions) *According to Average per capita Income of Country where They Live* (in '000 $PPP per year)

Japan, Germany, France and the United Kingdom. The poor pole accounts for 45% of world (more exactly, common-sample) population and about 9% of world PPP income; the rich pole accounts for almost 13% of world population and 45% of world PPP income. Populous countries that have 'middling' per capita incomes (eg Brazil, Mexico, Russia) do contribute to inequality but much less so than the two polar sets. Fast economic growth of China and India would therefore have a huge impact on reducing world inequality since the difference between their mean incomes and those of OECD countries would go down. In 1993, the difference in mean per capita income between the United States and rural China was $PPP 11,506, or 3.6 times greater than the average world $PPP income. Suppose that due to faster growth in rural China the difference is reduced to 3 times world average. With unchanged world population shares of rural China and the United States, the ICT will be 3.2 Gini points instead of 3.6 Gini points now. The overall world inequality would be reduced by much more – by almost 4 Gini points due to the decreasing difference between the mean income in rural China and mean income in other richer countries.

However, every synthetic index of inequality, and the Gini is no exception to that, is a very complex statistic. We have just seen that faster per capita growth of China reduces the ITCs between China, and the rich populous OECD countries. It is also absolutely crucial for the reduction of world inequality. As Table 21 shows, if China's and India's income were to increase

Table 21

WorldGini and its Components as China's and India's Per Capita Incomes Increase
(Simulations)

	Percent income increase						
	0	10	20	50	70	85	100
Gini points							
Within countries	1.3	1.4	1.4	1.5	1.5	1.6	1.6
Between countries	57.8	56.9	56.0	53.6	52.2	51.2	50.3
Overlapping	6.9	7.0	7.0	7.4	7.5	7.8	7.9
Total Gini	66.0	65.2	64.4	62.5	61.2	60.6	59.8

by between 10 and 100%, while incomes of all other countries are assumed unchanged, world inequality would be reduced by between 0.8 and 6.2 Gini points.[26] All of the decrease occurs through a lower between-country component, while the 'overlap' component – as we would expect since more rich Chinese/Indians would have greater incomes than poor citizens of richer countries – goes up. However, if we suppose that China and India continue to grow faster than other populous countries, there may be a point where the gain in world equality achieved through them getting closer to the rich OECD countries may be offset by the growing difference between China and India, on the one hand, and Indonesia, Nigeria, and Bangladesh on the other, which we assume – for the sake of the argument – not to grow at all. This point occurs only for an extremely high increase in China's and India's per capita income: more than 7 times the current level so that urban China's income would be equal to that of Hong Kong, and rural India's income would equal that of Bulgaria. However, this illustrates the fact that the Gini coefficient is U-shaped even in income growth of the two largest, and among the poorest, countries. A situation might then ensue where instead of a bi-polar world, depicted in Fig. 6, we might have a tri-polar world, with one or several large countries with incomes around the median. Yet this might imply the same or even higher Gini inequality.

6.2. *Why is the Within-country Inequality so Small?*

There are two reasons for this. First, it is because the countries with large total incomes (most OECD countries) have relatively small populations, and the reverse for countries like China and India. (Recall that the *within* component of the Gini coefficient is equal to $\Sigma G_i \pi_i p_i$.) The largest population in the common sample is that of rural China with 18.5% of world population but with only 5% of world $PPP income. Largest income weight is that of the United States with 29% of world income but with only 5.6% of world population. Since the weight attached to the individual country Gini in the Pyatt decomposition is the product of country's income and population shares, this means that the largest weight is

---

[26] Populations are assumed unchanged throughout.

0.0145 (ie 0.29 times 0.05). For most countries, the weights attached to their Ginis are thus very small and the sum of weights is far smaller than 1 (in 1993, the sum was 0.038). Obviously, if a very large country, like China and India, were also a very rich country its weight in both population and total income would be great, and it would strongly influence the within component. However, in reality, even if the Ginis of a number of countries were to increase significantly, the within-country component would not go up by much. For example, if both China's – rural and urban – Ginis increased to 50 (from the current values of respectively 33 and 27), and the US Gini increased to 60 (from the current value of 37), the within-country component would increase by only ½ Gini point.

This is but a mechanical explanation for the low within-country inequality component. A substantive explanation is as follows. Mean country incomes are very close to each other particularly among poor countries (see Fig. 7). 62 countries have mean HS incomes that are less than $PPP 4,000 per capita p.a. In other words, the countries' mean incomes are 'crowded'.

If mean incomes are very close, then the only way for the overlap component to be small, and for the within-country component to be relatively large, is if countries' own income density functions are very narrow with Ginis close to 0 (see Fig. 8*b*).[27] But since individual country Ginis are, of course, not zero, poor people from a slightly richer country will overlap with the rich

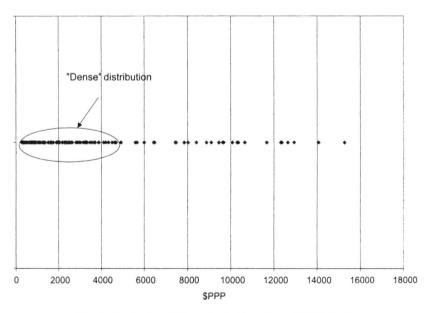

Fig. 7. *Distribution of Countries by Mean Annual $PPP Income Calculated from Household Surveys (1993)*

[27] Imagine the situation where all mean country income differ by only Δx. Then, the overlap component will be 0 *only* if individual country Ginis are 0.

(a)

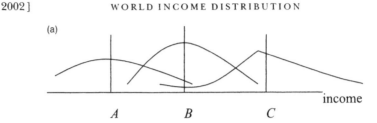

Fig. 8a. *Large Overlap Component in Gini Decomposition*

(b)

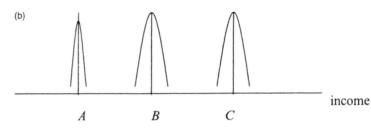

Fig. 8b. *Small Overlap Component in Gini Decomposition*
Note: vertical lines represent countries mean incomes

people from a slightly poorer country (see Fig. 8*a*). To see this, superimpose density functions from Fig. 8*a* onto the mean incomes (dots) in Fig. 7. There would be a lot of overlapping particularly among the poorer countries, whose incomes are not only more 'crowded' but where inequality is also greater so that the density functions have longer tails.[28] Thus any inequality above 0 will 'feed' the overlap component and detract from 'within' component. Or, in other words, the overlap component will be small only if (i) mean incomes are very far (different) from each other, or (ii) individual country distributions are very equal.[29] Neither is the case here.

Another question raised by the finding that most of world inequality is due to the differences between countries mean incomes is, how sensitive world Gini is to distributional changes within countries (which leave mean incomes unchanged). The answer is that it is sensitive although most of the change may occur through the overlap component. For example, if we let US, UK and German distributions experience regressive transfers such that each of the bottom nine deciles loses 10% of its income in favour of the top decile, world Gini in 1993 increases by 0.4 Gini points, 0.3 of which is due to the greater overlap.[30] What happens is that the poor, middle-class etc. end of distribution of these rich countries now shifts to the left (see Fig. 8*a*), and more of those people overlap with people from poorer countries.

[28] The simple correlation coefficient between Gini and level of per capita income (in $PPP) is −0.31 in 1988, and −0.25 in 1993.
[29] This point is also made by Lambert and Aranson (1993, p. 1226) in their reinterpretation of the Gini decomposition.
[30] The assumed distributional changes are significant: they increase Ginis of the three countries by between 5 and 5.5 Gini points.

Finally note that a relatively small importance of within-country inequality and the overlap component in Pyatt-type Gini decomposition does not mean that one can ignore them and, in the absence of large distributional changes within the countries, use the between component as a fully satisfactory proxy for world inequality (as is sometimes argued; see Melchior *et al.* (2000, p. 18)). This is not the case though: when incomes of poor countries like India and China grow relative to those of the rich countries, it does not only reduce the distance between the countries' mean incomes and lowers the value of (2), but also affects – even in the absence of distributional change – the two other Gini components. First, greater weight of China's and India's GDP in the world might increase the within-country component depending on whether India's and China's Ginis are greater than the mean Gini in the world. Second, and more importantly, there is an increase in the overlap term as more people from these poor countries 'mingle' with people from rich countries. This is reflected in the rising overlap component in our simulations in Table 21: while the between term went down by $7\frac{1}{2}$ Gini points, the overlap term increased by 1 Gini point. Using the changes in the between component alone will give a biased view of changes in world inequality.

6.3. *What Factors Were Behind the 2.7 Gini Points Increase in between-country Inequality Between 1988 and 1993?*

We have already seen that the most significant contributor to the overall Gini is the between-country component, and within it, the income differences between the poor populous countries of Asia (India and China), and the rich, but less populous, five OECD countries (United States, Japan, France, Germany and the United Kingdom). But while these ICTs are large they may not be the ones that have *increased* the most between 1988 and 1993, and may not therefore be the ones driving the increase in inequality between the two years. Indeed, as seen in Table 22, some of them have decreased in importance, that is they have contributed to *reducing* inequality. Shrinking difference between, on the one hand, China's mean rural and urban income and, on the other, the mean US income has shaved off almost $\frac{1}{2}$ Gini points from world inequality. Similarly, decreasing income differences between (i) China and rural India, and (ii) three large countries (Brazil, Russia and Ukraine) whose per capita real incomes have gone down, have reduced the world Gini by 1.3 points (Table 22).[31]

But in addition the ICT between rural China and the United States decreased also on account of the shrinking percentage of world population living in rural China. In 1988, 19.5% of world population lived in rural

---

[31] However, income declines in Eastern Europe/FSU region did not have an overall equalising effect on world income inequality. If we conduct a simulation exercise for 1993 keeping real incomes and inequality in the Eastern Europe/FSU region at their 1988 level, world income Gini becomes 64.7 instead of the actual 66.0. Thus, changes *outside* the transition countries are responsible for an increase of almost 2 Gini points in world inequality (64.7 minus 62.8), while the changes in transition economies added another 1.3 Gini points (66.0 minus 64.7).

Table 22

LargestNegative (Inequality-reducing) Changes in Inter-country Terms Between 1988 and 1993 (in Gini Points)

	China (rural)	China (urban)	India (rural)	Japan
United States	−0.40	−0.05		−0.14
Russia	−0.30	−0.12	−0.17	
Ukraine	−0.21		−0.14	
Brazil	−0.19	−0.09	−0.09	

China; in 1993, that percentage was 18.5. Thus, both the fact that China's income rose compared to the US income, and that its population moved out of the poorer rural areas, contributed to reducing world inequality.

This calculation allows us to illustrate the following problem. Consider growth of rural incomes in India vs. United States. Rural incomes in India increased by only 5%, the mean income in the United States increased by 24%. Since United States started as a richer country, this should, at first glance, imply that the inter-country Gini component should increase, and not decrease. However, note that the formula for each ICT is

$$\frac{y_j - y_i}{\mu} p_i p_j$$

so that – given unchanged p_i and p_j – it will go up only if the difference between the incomes increases faster than the mean world income. (One might remember that Gini is a mean-standardised measure of inequality.) In the case of rural India–United States, the difference between these two countries' mean incomes increased from $PPP 9,495 to $11,870. However, this increase (25%) was less than the increase in the mean world income (29%). Thus the difference between mean income in rural India and income in the United States *decreased* from being 3.87 times world mean income to being 3.75 times world mean income. This example illustrates that for a single ICT to go up, and thus to add to world inequality, it is not sufficient that a rich country grow faster than a poor country. The absolute difference between the two countries' incomes must increase faster than world mean income.[32]

What were then the main factors underlying the increase in inequality between 1988 and 1993? They were two. First, slower growth of rural areas in large South Asian countries (India and Bangladesh) and in rural China compared to several OECD countries (France, Japan, Germany)[33] is responsible for 2 Gini points increase of world inequality (see Table 23). Mean per

[32] This can be shown by the total differentiation of the ICT term (denoted by Δ): $d\Delta = 1/\mu[dy_j - dy_i - 1/\mu(y_j - y_i)d\mu]p_ip_j = 1/\mu[r_jy_j - r_jy_i - r_\mu(y_j - y_i)]p_ip_j$ where r_i = growth rate of country i and p_ip_j assumed constant. After some further rearrangements, the condition for $d\Delta > 0$ becomes: $r_j > y_i/y_j(r_i - r_\mu) + r_\mu$. The latter expression is greater than r_i whenever $r_\mu > r_i$. This means that whenever world mean income grows faster than the income of the poorer country, for the ICP to increase it is not sufficient that the rich country simply grow faster than the poor.

[33] And to some extent, with respect to the United States; see the Bangladesh–United States cell in Table 23.

Table 23

LargestPositive (Inequality-increasing) Changes in Inter-country Terms Between 1988 and 1993 (in Gini Points)

	Bangladesh	India(rural)	China(rural)
Japan	0.20	0.28	0.23
Germany	0.12	0.25	0.25
France		0.14	0.14
United States	0.42		
Subtotal	0.74	0.67	0.61
China(urban)		0.22	0.23
Total	0.74	1.11	1.08

capita rural income in India increased by 5% in current $PPP between 1988 and 1993; in Bangladesh the increase was 14%, and in rural China 21%. Meanwhile, mean current $PPP incomes in the United States increased by 24%, in Japan by 60%, and in Germany by 43%.[34] The absolute income differences between a few large OECD countries and populous rural areas in Asia thus increased faster than did world income overall; this in turn increased the ICTs, and added to world inequality.

Second, the widening differences within China between urban and rural areas, and between urban China and rural India, pushed world inequality up by about 0.45 Gini points.[35]

In conclusion, what happens to world inequality is to a large extent determined by what happens to inequality between the countries, and what happens to the inequality between the countries depends, to a large extent, on what is the relationship between mean incomes in China, India, and several large OECD countries. This explains the ambiguous effects produced by the relatively fast growth of mean income in urban China. On the one hand, Chinese urban growth reduced its distance from the middle-income and rich countries and thus the world Gini; on the other hand, though, the widening gap between urban and rural China, and between urban China and rural India, increased world inequality.

7. Comparison with Other Studies

Table 24 shows the estimates of world inequality collected from several other studies mentioned in Section 2. In terms of methodology, Bourguignon and Morrisson (1999) and Berry et al. (1983) are the closest to our study because they use income shares derived from household surveys. However, in both cases, income shares for a number of countries are approximated using income shares of 'similar' countries – whether it is done by using econometric

---

[34] This translates into 2% per capita real growth in the United States, 17% in Germany and about 30% in Japan (all over the 1988–93 period). Compare this with real GDP growth over the same period of 9% in the United States, 15% in Germany, and 16% in Japan.

[35] While current $PPP incomes in rural China increased by 21%, the growth in urban areas was over 70%.

Table 24

World and International Inequality as Estimated by Different Authors

	Gini	Theil	Note
World inequality			
Berry, Bourguignon and Morrisson (1982)	64.9 (1970)		Uses GDP per capita and income shares; approximates distributions for a number of countries
Grosh and Nafziger (1986)	63.6 (1970s)		Uses GDP per capita and income shares; approximates distributions for some 40 countries
Chotikapanich, Valenzuela and Rao (1997)	64.8 (1990)		Uses GDP per capita data; approximates distributions.
Bourguignon and Morrisson (1999)	66.3 (1992)	86.4 (1992)	Uses GDP per capita and income shares; approximates distributions for a number of countries
Milanovic (this paper)	62.8 (1988) 66.0 (1993)	76.5 (1988) 87.3 (1993)	Uses actual HS data
Inter-national inequality			
Theil and Seale (1994)		64.5 (1986)	Only between-country component; uses GDP per capita
Podder (1993)	53.1 (1987)		Only between-country inequality; uses GDP per capita
T. Paul Schultz (1998)	55.2 (1989)		Only between-country component; uses GDP per capita
Firebaugh (1999)	54.3 (1989)	52.6 (1989)	Only between-country inequality; uses GDP per capita
Milanovic (this paper)	55.1 (1988) 57.8 (1993)	57.1 (1988) 64.9 (1993)	Uses actual HS data

Note: Year of estimation between brackets. All GDP per capita are in $PPP terms.

techniques (as in the 1982 paper), or by simply 'assigning' what are deemed to be similar countries. Yet the results for the world inequality are very similar to the ones obtained here. The world Gini coefficient for 1992 is estimated by Bourguignon and Morrisson as 66.3; we find that, in 1993, it is equal to 66.0. Everything else being the same, we would expect to find a lower Gini value than Bourguignon and Morrisson because they use GDPs per capita and we use actual mean incomes from surveys. As mentioned above. the differences between the rich and poor countries are less when we use HS incomes or expenditures than when we use GDP per capita. On the other hand, the fact that for all countries we use actual survey data with at least 10 data points (while they mostly use quintiles) means that our estimation of within-country inequality and the overlap term is more precise and the two terms thus greater. The two effects apparently offset each other. In effect, all four studies of world inequality by other authors as well and ours, show world Gini to lie within a narrow range of 63 to 66. Studies of inter-national inequality, on the other hand, show that the between-country Gini ranges between 53 and 55. Therefore using the standard Gini decomposition, about (or more than) 4/5 of world inequality is due to differences in mean PPP incomes between the countries.

8. Summary and Conclusions

Our main conclusions from the first calculation of world income and expenditure inequality based solely on household surveys – which cover about 84% of world population and 93% of world GDP – can be summarised in several points:

1. World income inequality is very high: the Gini coefficient is 66 if one uses incomes adjusted for differences in countries' purchasing power, and almost 80 if one uses current dollar incomes.

2. World inequality has increased (using the same sample of countries) from a Gini of 62.8 in 1988 to 66.0 in 1993. This represents an increase of 0.6 Gini points per year. This is a very fast increase, faster than the increase experienced by the United States and the United Kingdom in the decade of the 1980s. (The Gini coefficient is scale-invariant: thus larger and smaller units can legitimately be compared.)

3. Differences between countries' mean incomes is the most important factor behind world inequality. It explains between 75 and 88% of overall inequality (depending on whether we use Gini or Theil coefficient to measure inequality).

4. The increase of inequality between 1988 and 1993 occurred as both between-country and within-country inequality increased. However, since their relative proportions remained the same, it was the between-country inequality which, being much larger, drove overall inequality up. More specifically, slow growth of rural per capita incomes in populous Asian countries (China, India and Bangladesh) compared to income growth of several large and rich OECD countries, plus fast growth of urban China compared to rural China and rural India, were the main reasons why world Gini increased.

5. World income distribution in 1988 Lorenz-dominates the distribution in 1993. Neither year is stochastically dominant (either first- or second-order). However, if one considers different regions, in the Western Europe, North America and Oceania (WENAO) region, 1993 stochastically dominates 1988. Other regions display no such regularity. In Africa, and Eastern Europe/FSU, though, 1988 displays a second-order stochastic dominance over 1993.

6. What happens to world inequality depends to a large extent on what happens to the relative position of China and India (on the one end of the spectrum), and United States, Japan, France, Germany and the United Kingdom, on the other end.

7. The bottom 5% of the world grew poorer, as their real incomes decreased between 1988 and 1993 by ¼, while the richest quintile grew richer. It gained 12% in real terms, that is its income grew more than twice as much as mean world income (5.7%).

8. A number of other statistics can be generated from world income distribution. These are some examples:

• The richest 1% of people in the world receive as much as the bottom 57%, or in other words, less than 50 million income-richest people receive as much as 2.7 billion poor.

• An American having the average income of the bottom US decile is better-off than 2/3 of world population.

• The top 10% of the US population has an aggregate income equal to income of the poorest 43% of people in the world, or differently put, total income of the richest 25 million Americans is equal to total income of almost 2 billion poor people.

• The ratio between average income of the world top 5% and world bottom 5% increased from 78 to 1 in 1988, to 114 to 1 in 1993.

• 75% of world population receive 25 of world $PPP income; and the reverse.

• 84% of world population receive 16% of world (unadjusted) dollar income; and the reverse.

The World Bank
Date of receipt of the first submission: April 2000
Date of receipt of the final transcript: April 2001

Annex 1. Data sources

All data come from nationally representative household surveys. Most of the data for Western Europe, Northern America and Oceania come from the Luxembourg Income Study (LIS). For some European countries not fully included in the LIS (Greece, Portugal, France), the data were provided by individual researchers, or by countries' statistical offices (Ireland, Switzerland).

Most of the data for Eastern Europe and former Soviet Union are taken from Milanovic (1998) and different World Bank sources (eg poverty assessments for Georgia, Armenia).

For Latin American countries, most of the 1988 data are from Psacharopoulos *et al.* (1997). The 1993 data come from various World Bank sponsored surveys, in particular Living Standard Measurement Surveys, LSMSs (eg Ecuador, Jamaica, Guyana, Nicaragua etc.) and countries' own surveys available in the Bank (kindly provided by Kihoone Lee and Julie Van Domelen). Some of the surveys were obtained from an extensive data base created and maintained by the Inter-American Development Bank (Dominican Republic, Costa Rica, Mexico, Peru, El Salvador, and Venezuela). They were kindly provided by Miguel Szekely, Mariane Hilgert, and Ricardo Fuentes. Finally, several surveys were obtained directly from countries' statistical offices (Brazil, Honduras).

For Africa, most of the data come from World Bank organised surveys which have been assembled and standardised in the Africa ISP-Poverty monitoring group. They have been kindly supplied by Olivier Dupriez and Hyppolite Fofack. In addition, some of the surveys were provided by the countries' statistical offices directly (South Africa, Mauritius).

For most Asian countries, the data were kindly supplied by Shaohua Chen and Benu Bidani. Some of these data were used in the book on East Asia by Ahuja *et al.* (1997), and in Ravallion and Chen (1997) work on world poverty. Again, LSMS data and Diane Steele's help were invaluable. Data for some countries (Singapore, Hong Kong, South Korea) were supplied by the countries' statistical offices. For some of the countries (Nepal), household surveys were obtained from a very good and expanding World Bank's Poverty Monitoring Database maintained by Giovanna Prennuschi. The Database either provides the surveys themselves or identifies the institutions or people who might be contacted.

Many other people in the World Bank (Luisa Ferreira, Paul Glewwe, Jacqueline Baptist, Richard Adams, Bahjat Achikbakche, Peter Lanjouw, Ruslan Yemtsov, Francisco Ferreira, Kihoone Lee, Boniface Essama Nssah, Roy Canagaraja, Jeanine Braithwaite) and outside (Peter Krause for the East German data; Carlos Farinha Rodriguez for the Portuguese data; Carol Ernst tor the Swiss data; Panos Tsakloglou for the Greek data; Yap Yee Liong for the Singapore data) also helped with the information. Yonas Biru and Yuri Dikhonov helped me generously with the International Comparison (ICP) data. I am extremely grateful to all of them: clearly the project would have been impossible without their help. Costas Krouskas and (in the very early stages of the project, Nadia Soboleva) have done a splendid job in interlinking the country and regional files and providing research assistance.

About ¾ of the country data used in the study are calculated from individual (unit record) data. Most of them come from four sources: HEIDE data base for East European and FSU countries, LSMS Surveys, Africa ISP-Poverty monitoring group, and Luxembourg Income study.[36] This, of course, means that variables and recipient units could be defined to reflect precisely what I needed.

References

Achdut, L. (1997). 'Income inequality and poverty under transition from rapid inflation to stabilization: Israel, 1979–1990', in Gottschalk et al. (1977) pp. 132–53.

Ahuja, V., Bidani, B., Ferreira, F. and Walton, M. (1997). *Everyone's Miracle? Revisiting Poverty and Inequality in East Asia,* Washington: World Bank.

Atkinson, A. B., Rainwater, L. and Smeeding, T. (1995). 'Income distribution in advanced economies: evidence from the Luxembourg Income Study', Luxembourg Income Study (LIS) Working paper no. 12.

Banerjee, A. and Duffo, E. (2000). 'Inequality and growth: what do the data say?', manuscript.

Bauer, J. and Mason, A. (1992). 'The distribution of income and wealth in Japan', *Review of Income and Wealth,* vol. 38, no. 4, (December), pp. 403–28.

Bénabou, R. (2000). 'Unequal societies: income distribution and the social contract', *American Economic Review,* vol. 90, no. 1, (March), pp. 96–129.

Berry, A., Bourguignon, F. and Morrisson, Ch. (1983). 'Changes in the world distribution of income between 1950 and 1977', ECONOMIC JOURNAL, vol. 93 (June), pp. 331–50.

Bourguignon, F. and Morrisson, Ch. (1999). 'The size distribution of income among world citizens, 1820–1990', manuscript (June).

Chen, S., Datt, G. and Ravallion, M. (1994). 'Is poverty increasing in the developing world', *Review of Income and Wealth,* vol. 40, no. 4, (December), pp. 359–76.

Chotikapanich, D., Valenzuela, R. and Rao, D. S. P. (1997). 'Global and regional inequality in the distribution of income: estimation with limited and incomplete data', *Empirical Economics,* vol. 22, pp. 533–46.

Concialdi, P. (1997). 'Income distribution in France: the mid 1980s turning point', in Gottschalk et al. (1997) pp. 239–64.

Davies, J. B. and Shorrocks. A. F. (1989). 'Optimal grouping of income and wealth data', *Journal of Econometrics,* vol. 42, pp. 97–108.

Deininger, K. and Squire L. (1996). 'A new data set measuring income inequality', *World Bank Economic Review.* vol. 10, (September), pp. 565–91.

Firebaugh, G. (1999). 'Empirics of world income inequality', *American Journal of Sociology,* vol. 104, pp. 1597–630.

Freeman, R. B. (1995). 'Are your wages set in Beijing?', *Journal of Economic Perspectives,* vol. 9, no. 3, (Summer), pp. 15–32.

Gottschalk, P. Gustafson, B. and Palmer E. (1997). *Changing Patterns in the Distribution of Economic Welfare: An International Perspective.* Cambridge: Cambridge University Press.

Grosh, M. E. and Nafziger, E. W. (1986). 'The computation of world income distribution', *Economic Development and Cultural Change,* vol. 35, pp. 347–59.

[36] The web sites are: for HEIDE data base: http://www.worldbank.org/research/transition/index.htm; for LSMS surveys: http://www.worldbank.org/html/prdph/lsms/lsmshome.html; for Luxembourg Income Study: http://lissy.ceps.lu/index.htm

Heston and Summers (1991). Author to complete, see Table 6.

Kakwani, N. (1980). *Income Inequality and Poverty*. Washington, D.C.: World Bank and Oxford University Press.

Kanbur, R. and Lustig, N. (1999). 'Why is inequality back on the agenda?', manuscript (April 21).

Kravis, I. B., Heston, A. and Summers, R. (1982). *World Product and Income: International Comparisons of Real Gross Product* . New York and Washington, D.C.: United Nations and the World Bank.

Korzeniewick, R. P. and Moran, T. (1997). 'World-economic trends in the distribution of income, 1965–1992', *American Journal of Sociology*, vol. 102, pp. 1000–39.

Lambert, P. and Aranson, J. R. (1993). 'Inequality decomposition analysis and the Gini coefficient revisited', ECONOMIC JOURNAL, vol. 103, (September), pp. 1221–7.

Lerman, R. and Yitzhaki, Sh. (1984). 'A note on the calculation and interpretation of the Gini index', *Economic Letters*, vol. 15, pp. 363–8.

Li, H., Squire, L. and Zou, H. (1998). 'Explaining international and intertemporal variations in income inequality', ECONOMIC JOURNAL, vol. 108 (January), pp. 26–43.

Lindbeck, A. (1990). 'The Swedish experience', A Paper prepared for OECD – World Bank conference 'The transition to a market economy in Central and Eastern Europe', Paris, 28–30 November.

Lundberg, M. and Squire, L. (1999). 'Growth and inequality: extracting the lessons for policy-makers', manuscript (February).

Melchior, A., Telle, K. and Wiig, H. (2000). 'Globalisation and inequality: world income distribution and living standards, 1960–1998', Royal Norwegian Ministry of Foreign Affairs, Studies on Foreign Policy Issues, Report 6B: 2000, October.

Milanovic, Branko, (1998). *Income, Inequality, and Poverty during the Transition from Planned to Market Economy*. Washington, D.C.: World Bank.

Mookherjee, D. and Shorrocks, A. F. (1982). 'A decomposition analysis of the trend in the UK income inequality', ECONOMIC JOURNAL, vol. 92 (December), pp. 886–902.

Psacharopoulos. G., Morley, S., Fiszbein, A., Lee, H. and Wood, B. (1997). *Poverty and Income Distribution in Latin America: The Story of the 1980s*. Washington, D.C.: The World Bank.

Podder, N. (1993). 'A profile of international inequality', *Journal of Income Distribution*, vol. 3, (Fall), no. 2.

Pyatt, G. (1976). 'On the interpretation and disaggregation of the Gini coefficient', ECONOMIC JOURNAL, vol. 86, (June), pp. 243–54.

Quah. D. (1997). 'Empirics for growth and distribution: stratification, polarization and convergence clubs', London School of Economics and Political Science, Center for Economic Performance Discussion Paper no. 324.

Ravallion, M. and Chen, S. (1997). 'What can new survey data tell us about recent changes in distribution and poverty?', *World Bank Economic Review*, vol. 11, no. 2, pp. 357–82.

Ravallion, M., Datt, G. and van der Walle, D. (1991). 'Quantifying absolute poverty in the developing world', *Review of Income and Wealth*, vol. 37, no. 4, (December), pp. 345–61.

Richardson, D. J., (1995). 'Income inequality and trade: how to think, what to conclude', *Journal of Economic Perspectives*, vol. 9, no. 3, (Summer), pp. 33–56.

Sandstrom, A., Wretman, J. H. and Walden, B. (1988). 'Variance estimators of the Gini coefficient – probability sampling', *Journal of Business and Economic Statistics*, vol. 6, no. 1, (January), pp. 113–9.

Sastry, D. V. and Kelkar, U. R. (1994). 'Note on the decomposition of Gini inequality', *Review of Economics and Statistics*, vol.76, no. 3, pp. 584–6.

Schultz, T. P. (1998). 'Inequality in the distribution of personal income in the world: how it is changing and why', *Journal of Population Economics*, vol. 11, no. 3, pp. 307–44.

Shorrocks, A. F. (1983). 'Ranking income distributions', *Economica*, vol. 50 (February), pp. 3–17.

Shorrocks. A. F. (1984). 'Inequality decomposition by population subgroups', *Econometrica*, vol. 52, (November), pp. 1369–86.

Silber, J. (1989). 'Factor components, population subgroups and the computation of the Gini index of inequality', *Review of Economics and Statistics*, vol. 71, (February), pp. 107–15.

Summers, R. and Heston, A. (1991). 'Penn world table (Mark 5): an expanded set of international comparisons, 1950–1988', *Quarterly Journal of Economics*, vol. 106, (May), pp. 327–68.

Summers, R. and Kravis, I. B. (1984). 'Changes in the world income distribution', *Journal of Policy Modeling*. vol. 6, (May), pp. 237–69.

Szekely, M. and Hilgert, M. (1999). 'What's behind the inequality we measure?: an investigation using Latin American data', OCE Working Paper Series no. 409, Research Department, Inter-American Development Bank, Washington, D.C.

Tachibanaki, T. and Yagi, T. (1997). 'Distribution of economic well-being in Japan: towards a more unequal society', in Gottschalk *et al.* (1997), pp. 108–31.

Theil, H. (1979). 'World income inequality', *Economics Letters*, vol. 2, pp. 99–102.

Theil, H. (1996). *Studies in Global Econometrics*. Amsterdam: Kluwer Academic Publishers.
Theil, H. and Seale, J. L. (1994). 'The geographic distribution of world income, 1950–90', *De Economist*, no. 4, pp. 387–419.
Williamson, J. G. (1999). 'Globalization and inequality then and now: the late 19th and late 20th centuries compared', National Bureau of Economic Research Working Paper no. 5491, Cambridge, Mass.
Wood, A. (1995). 'How trade hurt unskilled workers', *Journal of Economic Perspectives*, vol. 9, no. 3, (Summer), pp. 57–80.
Yao, S. and Zhu, L. (1998). 'Understanding income inequality in China: a multi-angle perspective', *Economics of Planning*, vol. 31, no. 2–3, pp. 133–50.
Yitzhaki, Sh. (1994). 'Economic distance and overlapping of distributions', *Journal of Econometrics*, vol. 61, pp. 147–59.
Yitzhaki, Sh. and Lerman, R. I. (1991). 'Income stratification and income inequality', *Review of Income and Wealth*, vol. 37, no. 3, pp. 313–29.
Yitzhaki, Sh. and Milanovic, B. (forthcoming). 'Decomposing world income distribution by continents and regions: does the world have a middle class', manuscript.

C
Regional Convergence or Divergence?

[10]

EQUALIZING EXCHANGE: TRADE LIBERALIZATION AND INCOME CONVERGENCE*

DAN BEN-DAVID

How does movement toward freer trade affect income disparity among countries? This paper attempts to shed some light on the issue by examining episodes of major postwar trade liberalization within specified groups of countries. The findings suggest a strong link between the timing of trade reform and income convergence among countries.

I. INTRODUCTION

In 1969 Arghiri Emmanuel wrote about the "unequal exchange" that he believed was brought about by the "imperialism of trade."[1] This paper provides evidence that movement toward free trade may actually have just the opposite effect, leading to a *reduction* in income disparity among countries.

Income divergence, or at best, nonconvergence, appears to characterize the behavior of most cross-country income differentials (see, for example, Romer [1986, 1989] and Baumol [1986]). On the other hand, there has been some evidence [Baumol, 1986; Abramowitz, 1986; Baumol, Blackman, and Wolff, 1989; and Dowrick and Nguyen, 1989] of convergence within the OECD. Most of this convergence took place during the postwar period, which has also been a period of increasing trade liberalization. The question is, are these two episodes related?

The factor price equalization (FPE) theorem [Samuelson, 1948, 1949, 1953; Helpman and Krugman, 1985] provides a framework for relating trade's impact on income convergence. Alternatively, the traditional growth literature [Solow, 1956, 1957; Cass, 1965; Koopmans, 1965] postulates that, even in the absence of internationally mobile goods and factors, convergence to a steady state path should occur between countries provided that

*I would like to thank Robert E. Lucas, Jr., Paul M. Romer, Sherwin Rosen, Andrei Shleifer, Robert H. Topel, and two anonymous referees for their insightful comments and suggestions. I have also benefited from discussions with John J. Antel, Richard Baldwin, Shaul Ben-David, David M. Gould, Dan Levin, Michael Loewy, Pin Ng, Roy J. Ruffin, and James Smith as well as from comments by seminar participants at the University of Chicago, Stanford University, the Econometric Society Winter Meetings, University of New Mexico, the Federal Reserve Bank of Dallas, the University of Houston, and the NBER Summer Institute workshop in International Trade and Investment.

1. Samuelson [1975] referred to Emmanuel's proposition as "reformulated Marxist theory."

The Quarterly Journal of Economics, August 1993

they have identical production technologies, population growth, savings rates, etc.

Abramowitz [1986] uses the catch-up hypothesis to explain his findings of convergence in labor productivity among the OECD countries. The premise of this hypothesis is that the potential for growth is greatest for those countries that are the farthest behind. A variant of this idea is provided by Jovanovic and Lach [1990] who posit that income inequality among countries is due to differences in the rate that countries implement new technologies. They state that varying speeds of technology diffusion can account for large amounts of variation in levels of GNP. The question, in this context is, what determines the rate of diffusion? Dollar, Wolff, and Baumol suggest that there exists "strong circumstantial evidence that technology diffusion through trade in goods and international investment . . . [has] played an important role in the convergence of productivity levels" [1988, p. 44].

The experience of the European Economic Community (EEC) provides a very useful arena for examining the link between freer trade and incomes. The attractiveness of the Community, particularly during its evolutionary period, is due to the fact that the EEC exhibited significantly increased trade, while exhibiting negligible improvements in factor flows [El-Agraa, 1985; Jensen and Walter, 1965; Balassa, 1975; Collins, 1975; Mayes, 1985]. An examination of the EEC also alleviates the question of sample selection that, as De Long [1988] pointed out, may affect the determination of convergence/divergence outcomes. The EEC represents a fixed grouping of countries[2] created with the goal of eliminating trade restrictions among its members. To isolate trade's impact on cross-country income disparity, the behavior of the Community's income differentials *during* the period of liberalization will be compared with their pre-liberalization years, as well as with other benchmark groups that vary in the degree and timing of their openness.

A formal agreement creating the European Economic Community was signed over 30 years ago, in 1957, between six countries[3] in Europe. The bulk of the economic integration by the original members of the Community took place during a ten-year span, called the *transition period* which lasted from 1959 until 1968.

To get an idea of the relationship between the income differen-

2. The size of the EEC remained constant for a decade and a half.
3. France, West Germany, Belgium, the Netherlands, Luxembourg, and Italy.

tials within the European Economic Community, and the *timing* of its trade liberalization, it is useful to examine the behavior of the annual cross-country standard deviations of log per capita incomes.[4] The annual dispersion of real per capita income is plotted in Figure I, along with the important dates in the integration of the EEC. The behavior of income differentials appears to indicate a strong relationship between the removal of trade barriers and reductions in the degree of income disparity across EEC countries.[5] This contrasts with the nonconvergence, and even divergence that appears to be the rule in the other studies cited above.[6] Are these results due to a historical accident, or are they related to the movement toward economic integration by the EEC countries?[7] The remainder of this paper attempts to examine this issue.

Methodology

It is important to establish, from the outset, the boundaries of this paper. Its primary purpose is to provide a descriptive account of the relationship between trade and income disparity, within the context of a specific setting. No attempt is made to broaden the theoretical motivations (mentioned above) of why such a relationship should exist. The contribution of this paper is solely within the realm of empirically ascertaining the existence of such a linkage.

The timing of trade liberalization, as well as the extensiveness of its implementation, will be the key evidence for examining the impact of liberalization on income differentials. While the primary focus will be on the EEC (its liberalization was by far the most comprehensive, while trade between its members comprised most of their overall trade), other major instances of postwar trade liberalization are also examined. In these cases, the timing of trade reform differed from that of the EEC. These results are compared

4. Unless specified otherwise, the data source is Summers and Heston [1988].
5. It should be pointed out that while "official" barriers were phased out, nontariff barriers would sometimes be substituted instead. Trade in agricultural products was also exempted from some of the measures that governed the rest of the internal EEC trade. The bottom line, however, is that these aberrations were not strong enough to completely cancel out the general liberalization effects on the income differentials.
6. Using cointegration techniques, Bernard and Durlauf [1990] conclude that, while they can find little evidence of convergence among fifteen industrialized countries, there does appear to be significant convergence among a European subset of six of these countries (of which four were original members of the EEC, and one joined later).
7. One obvious question is whether this is nothing but a continuation of a long-term convergence trend. Another possibility is that this reduction in income disparity is simply due to German recovery from the Second World War.

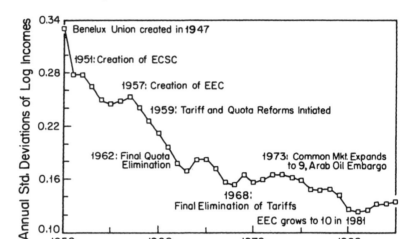

FIGURE I
Per Capita Income Dispersion: Between Six Original EEC Countries, 1950–1985

with benchmarks at opposite ends of the spectrum. At one end is the relationship among U. S. states, where there is relatively uninhibited movement of goods *and* factors, while at the other end are cases where liberalization was nonexistent, or minimal in comparison.

Section II details the main features of the EEC trade liberalization, including evidence of its impact on trade. Section III examines the changes in income differentials within the EEC that have occurred as a result of the freer trade and compares these with other benchmarks. Other episodes of trade liberalization are examined in the fourth section. Section VI summarizes.

II. LIBERALIZATION AND TRADE

Internal Tariffs

The Treaties of Rome, signed in 1957, provided a relatively strict timetable for the elimination of internal tariffs. This *transition period* was implemented on January 1, 1959, and comprised three stages. Internal tariffs were reduced in a series of 10 percent drops at specified dates, with minimum targets set for the end of each stage (Figure II). The customs union was completed on July 1, 1968, when all remaining internal tariffs were abolished and national customs duties in trade with the rest of the world were

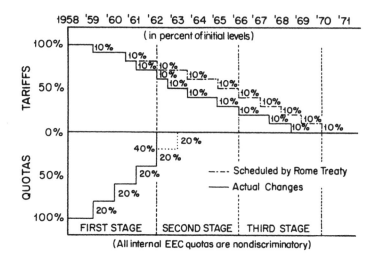

FIGURE II

Reduction of Internal EEC Trade Barriers
This graph was first used by Jensen and Walter [1965]. It was slightly altered here to include information from Bourdot [1988]. The first tariff reduction was 10 percent on *all* goods. The remaining reductions were 10 percent *on average*, and as little as 5 percent on any *one* good. Quotas were increased in steps of 20 percent *on average*, with a minimum of 10 percent on any *one* good.

replaced by the *Common Customs Tariff*. The main difference between the EEC tariff reductions and those imposed by GATT was in their scope. While GATT negotiations produced tariff cuts on a commodity-by-commodity basis, the EEC lowered them on all goods at once, in a step-by-step progression specified in advance at the time of the signing of the Treaties of Rome. This across-the-board form of tariff reductions did in fact have some exceptions, particularly regarding some agricultural products that were exempted from the overall timetable and were instead governed by special regulations. Internal agricultural quotas, as well as minimum prices, came to be replaced by variable levies.

It should also be noted that only the initial tariff reduction of 10 percent in 1959, and the final removal of all customs duties in 1968, were to be applied uniformly across all goods. Countries were given discretion in the degree of reduction they imposed on each commodity, as long as they averaged the 10 percent drops agreed upon in the original timetable. They were further required to reduce the internal duties on each product by at least 25 percent and 50 percent, at the end of the first and second stages of the transition period, respectively.

Internal Quotas

The Rome Treaties decreed that all nonagricultural quotas between member countries become nondiscriminatory as of 1959. Furthermore, intra-EEC quotas were simultaneously increased by 20 percent on average, and by a minimum of 10 percent for any given product (Figure II). Quota restrictions on industrial commodities were completely lifted by the end of 1961, with a few exceptions.

In the following year, limits were imposed on the minimum levels of agricultural quotas, and all quotas between members became nondiscriminatory. Several were replaced altogether by a system of variable levies whose purpose was to compensate for price differences between the importing and exporting EEC countries.

The Impact on Trade

The effect of this liberalization process on the Community's trade can be seen in Figures III and IV. Total imports from the non-EEC world divided by total EEC GDP are compared in Figure

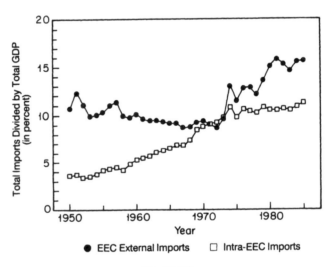

FIGURE III
Ratio of EEC Imports to GDP

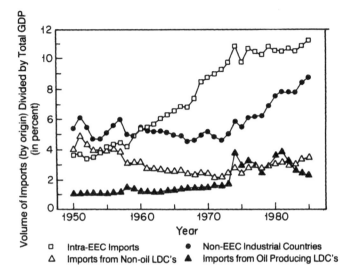

FIGURE IV
Origin of Imports, as a Percent of GDP

III with the ratio of total intra-EEC imports to GDP.[8] In the pretransition period, the volume of imports from the rest of the world was stable, at approximately 11 percent of GDP. During these years there was a slight, though significant, rise in the intra-EEC imports to GDP ratio. This coincided with the partial liberalization that had already begun between the countries which would later form the European Economic Community.

During the transition period that followed, imports from the rest of the world declined a little, relative to GDP, while the ratio of intra-EEC trade doubled. In the twelve years following 1973, when nearly all the barriers on trade between the members of the European Economic Community had been removed, the fraction of intra-EEC trade, out of GDP, stabilized and remained between 10 and 11 percent. This compares with a rise in the ratio of non-EEC imports to GDP, which was due in large part to the liberalization of trade with other industrialized countries (which included the Community's new members). This is illustrated in Figure IV. The less pronounced, but significant, increase in imports from the

8. Data source: IMF, *International Financial Statistics* and *Direction of Trade Statistics*.

nonoil-producing developing nations coincided with a concentrated effort on the part of the Community to aid these countries through partial and full waivers of many external EEC barriers. Imports from the oil-producing countries experienced *a level* change in 1974. In the years that followed, the import ratio from these countries remained at the higher level, albeit with much greater fluctuations than before.

The rise in the importance of trade within the EEC contrasts with the declining share of trade among the top 25 non-EEC countries in the world as well as among the 14 non-EEC countries with incomes that ranged (in 1960) between the wealthiest and poorest EEC countries (see Figures V and VI, respectively).[9]

III. LIBERALIZATION AND INCOME CONVERGENCE

For convergence to occur, there must exist a negative relationship between a country's initial level of per capita product and its per capita growth rates. In a sample of 98 countries, Barro [1991] calculated a correlation coefficient of 0.09 for the years 1960 through 1985, indicating that average annual rates of growth (ROGs) are uncorrelated with initial levels of income. In the case of the EEC, however, this relationship was found to be significant (at the 1 percent level), with a correlation coefficient of -0.95 for the years 1950 to 1985.

The objective of the next two parts of this section will be to relate the convergence more decisively to the actual removal of trade barriers. This is done by (1) contrasting the postwar period to the years preceding World War II, and (2) examining the income differentials of the three countries that joined the Community in 1973.

Comparison of the Postwar Period with Earlier Trends

Could the postwar convergence among the EEC countries be due to shocks induced by the Second World War? In other words, was the postwar fall in the disparity of incomes due primarily to the rebuilding of war-shattered economies, or alternatively, was it a continuation of a long-term convergence trend? Verification of

9. Saudi Arabia was excluded from both graphs due to poor and incomplete direction of trade and GDP data. The United States was omitted from the top graph because it was an outlier that exhibited a rising share of imports to GDP, while its extremely large size (as a producer and trader) reversed the otherwise declining trade share for the remainder of the group. The U. S. trading behavior is further discussed in Section IV. The countries included in these two groups are listed in the Appendix.

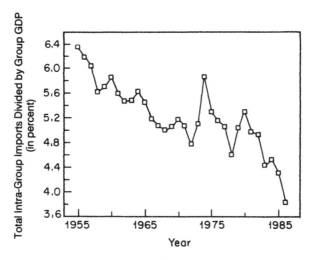

FIGURE V
Ratio of Imports to GDP: Top 25 Countries

either of these scenarios would weaken the case for a link between trade liberalization and income convergence.

Using Maddison's [1982] data, it was possible to analyze these alternative propositions by calculating the standard deviations

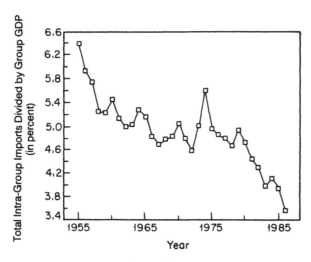

FIGURE VI
Ratio of Imports to GDP: Middle 14 Countries

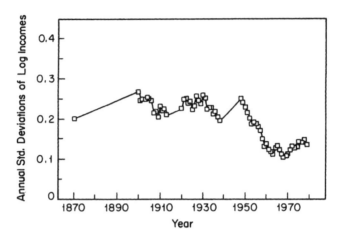

FIGURE VII
Per Capita Income Dispersion: Between Belgium, France, the Netherlands, and
Italy, 1870–1979

(σ's) for the founding members of the EEC all the way back to
1870.[10] The standard deviations displayed in Figure VII measure
the income dispersion without Germany. The country is omitted to
show that the postwar convergence which took place was not
simply an outcome of German rebuilding following the war.[11]

The behavior of the σ's clearly indicates that, during the
prewar years, *neither* of the above two scenarios appears to hold.
The dispersion of real per capita incomes was fairly stable from
1870 until the mid-1950s, with the σ's fluctuating between 0.194
and 0.268. Only after the onset of trade liberalization did the
standard deviations exhibit a level change (the minimum level of
0.104 was attained in 1968, the final year of the transition period).

Income Behavior of the Three New EEC Member-Countries

Shifting the focus to the next three countries to join the EEC
(Ireland, Denmark, and the United Kingdom) examines the ques-

10. Maddison's data include all of the original EEC countries, with the
exception of the smallest, Luxembourg. From Summers and Heston's data,
however, it can be shown that exclusion of Luxembourg does not appreciably alter
the main conclusions enumerated above. Therefore, its omission here should not be
considered too serious a problem.

11. Germany was always among the poorest, in per capita terms, of the six
countries. Today, it is one of the wealthiest countries in Europe. As a result of its
heightened prosperity, it might be claimed that all of the convergence that has been
witnessed within the EEC is due to the behavior of Germany. Thus, its exclusion
should bias the results away from convergence.

tion of whether their income differentials behaved in a manner similar to those of the original Six during the entire postwar period, despite the differences in the timing of their trade reforms. Furthermore, if these countries exhibited convergence upon elimination of their trade barriers, was this behavior any different than their preliberalization behavior?

Figure VIII displays the annual disparity among the Three. In contrast with the convergence that occurred among the Six, the σ's of the Three actually increased until the mid-sixties. At that time the countries began to relax the trade restrictions that existed among themselves and later in the decade they began to liberalize trade with the Six. This coincided with a stabilization in the σ's, followed by a reduction in the degree of income disparity. The rise in the income differentials of the Three during the eighties coincides with an increase in the σ's of the Six. This could be due to expansion of the EEC to include Greece (and later Spain and Portugal), as well as heightened benefits to LDCs.

Comparison of the EEC to Opposing Benchmarks

While the EEC countries have exhibited a significant reduction in the degree of income disparity among themselves, this has not been a prevalent feature of the international data. The remainder of this section focuses on a comparison of the EEC with opposing benchmark cases.

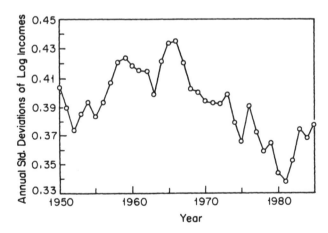

FIGURE VIII
Per Capita Income Dispersion: Between the United Kingdom, Denmark, and Ireland, 1950–1985

United States evidence will be used as a best-case scenario for what may be accomplished within a completely integrated world economy, where there is relatively unrestricted movement of goods *and* factors.[12] Empirical evidence [Ben-David, 1990; Barro and Sala-i-Martin, 1992] suggests that income differentials between U. S. states have exhibited a significant decline over much of the recent century. At the other end of the spectrum is the cross-country, or *world* case, where there exist curbs on the mobility of goods and factors between countries. The EEC provides the intermediate case that depicts a steady liberalization of trade that places it between the restrictive world case and the free trade, free factor flow, United States case.

In 1950 the average income dispersion in the European Economic Community was 30 percent higher than in the United States. However, as can be seen in Figures IX and X, the σ's for the United States and the EEC became very similar. This is in contrast to the degree of income inequality across the 107 market economies (marked "world" in the figure). Partitioning the world also yields divergence for most income groups [Ben-David, 1990], though the high-income groups exhibit fairly stable standard deviations. This is highlighted in Figure IX by the income differentials between the top 25 countries (in terms of 1960 per capita income). This lack of a significant increase, or decrease, in disparity, is very similar to the relatively stable income differentials displayed by the EEC members in the years *before* they began to remove their internal barriers on trade (see Figure VII). However, once these barriers were eliminated, the EEC countries achieved the rates, and even levels, of convergence found within the United States—despite the fact that interstate factor flows were considerably more widespread and uninhibited than they were within the European Community.

The following model may be used to describe the convergence/divergence behavior of each group. Let

$$(1) \qquad\qquad y_{i,t+1} - \bar{y}_{t+1} = \phi(y_{i,t} - \bar{y}_t),$$

where

$\qquad$ $y_{i,t}$ = country i's log per capita income in year t

$\qquad$ $\bar{y}_t$ = unweighted average of the log per capita

$\qquad\qquad$ incomes for the group in year t.

12. Data source: U. S. Department of Commerce, Bureau of Economic Analysis.

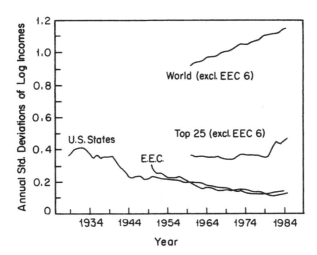

FIGURE IX
Comparison of Income Dispersions, 1929–1985

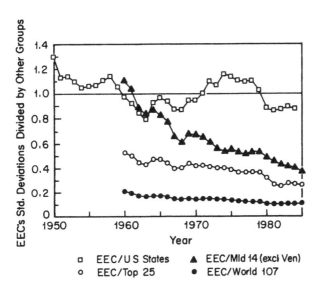

FIGURE X
Ratio of Disparity in EEC to Disparity in Other Groups
(relative standard deviations)

Letting $z_{i,t} = y_{i,t} - \bar{y}_t$, the above equation may be rewritten as

$$(2) \qquad\qquad \Delta z_{i,t+1} = -\kappa z_{i,t}$$

where $\Delta z_{i,t+1} = z_{i,t+1} - z_{i,t}$. The convergence coefficient κ, which equals $1 - \phi$, represents the rate of convergence of country i's per capita income to the group's average income level.[13] The larger the κ, the faster the convergence. This model is used to test how the convergence behavior within the EEC compares with the benchmark cases.

To estimate the equation, the countries of each group were pooled together. In such instances, there arises a question regarding the robustness of the results with respect to outlier countries (if they should exist) as well as the possibility of the sample beginning, or ending, in years that exhibited particularly large, or small, income discrepancies and thereby influencing the final outcomes. The convergence results in Table I were tested with this in mind, and the reduction in income differentials, when these are reported, was found to be robust among the group members.[14] Two-tailed t-tests were calculated in each case to determine whether the estimated κ's differ significantly from zero (the standard deviations for the κ's appear in parentheses). The number of years required for the average disparity to be cut in half (when $\kappa > 0$), or doubled (when $\kappa < 0$) are indicated in the two columns on the right.[15]

The convergence coefficient for the EEC countries is not significantly different from zero during the prewar years, implying that the disparity between the countries remained relatively constant. During the postwar years, however, there occurred a very significant convergence, with the strongest decline in the income disparity taking place during the transition period. It is interesting

13. Squaring both sides of equation (1) and then summing over the countries gives the relationship between σ_t and σ_{t+1}, where ϕ represents the rate of decline (if $\phi < 1$) in the group's average level of dispersion (when the group averages are geometric means).

14. For example, exclusion of the two EEC members that lost WWII, Germany and Italy (which also happened to be the two poorest EEC countries in 1950), does not alter the significant convergence among the remaining countries. Alternatively, removal of the wealthiest country alone, as well as the two wealthiest countries together, still leaves significant convergence among the other EEC countries. Ben-David and Bohara [1992] use the Seemingly Unrelated Regression approach to account for the existence of contemporaneous shocks and find that the postwar convergence within the EEC is still significant while prewar incomes did not converge.

15. The half-life (x) may be calculated as follows. If $z_{t+1} = \phi z_t$, then $z_{t+x} = \phi^x z_t$. Since $z_{t+x} = 0.5 z_t$ by definition, then $0.5 z_t = \phi^x z_t$, or $0.5 = \phi^x$. Taking logs of both sides and dividing by $\log \phi$ gives x.

EQUALIZING EXCHANGE 667

TABLE I
CONVERGENCE COEFFICIENTS, BY GROUP[a]

	$\hat{\kappa}$	N	R^2	t-stat. $H_0: \kappa = 0$	Half-life	Double life
EEC						
Prewar,[b] 1900–1933	0.0091 (0.0094)	135	0.988	0.98	75.5	
Postwar, 1951–1985	0.0291 (0.0066)	204	0.991	4.39**	23.5	
Transition period, 1959–1968	0.0506 (0.0103)	60	0.993	4.90**	13.3	
United States, 1931–1984	0.0442 (0.0038)	2554	0.961	11.64**	15.3	
World (excl. EEC 6), 1960–1985						
All 107 countries	−0.0074 (0.0012)	2675	0.996	−6.42**		93.9
Top 25 countries	−0.0027 (0.0056)	625	0.981	−0.47		260.9
14 Countries[c] (excluding Venezuela)	−0.0132 (0.0093)	325	0.973	−1.42		52.7

a. Standard deviations are in parentheses.
b. Does not include Luxembourg due to lack of data and excludes the WWI years, 1914–1919.
c. These are the fourteen countries within the same per capita income range as the EEC six countries in 1960.
**Significant at the 1 percent level.

to note that the half-life during the transition period was very similar to the half-life of the United States convergence over the past half century.

The *world* was examined as one large group, as well as in smaller breakdowns of the wealthier countries. The group of 107 countries displayed a propensity toward doubling their average income gap within 94 years. The top 25 industrialized countries exhibited no significant tendency in either direction, which is quite similar to the prewar "stability" of the EEC countries. All fourteen countries with per capita incomes below Luxembourg (the wealthiest nation in the EEC in 1960) and above Italy (the poorest) were lumped together as a comparison group that had achieved approximately the same level of development and the same degree of income disparity in 1960 as that which existed within the European Economic Community. This group showed no inclination whatever toward convergence over the next quarter century.

IV. LIBERALIZATION AND INCOME DISPARITY ELSEWHERE

While convergence has not appeared to be the dominant trend for most countries, there is evidence that income differentials among OECD countries have been declining during the postwar period. Although the EEC comprises a sizable proportion of these countries, not all the OECD convergence is due to EEC convergence. Furthermore, the *timing* of the EEC convergence was not identical to the timing among the other countries.

The impact of trade on convergence within the OECD becomes somewhat more plausible when one considers the origins of the OECD. Its predecessor, the OEEC (Organization for European Economic Cooperation), was established in 1948 to promote free trade within Europe and to provide suggestions regarding the distribution of American aid, which was contingent on relaxation of obstacles to trade. Most of the OEEC's success, as far as trade liberalization was concerned, came with the removal of up to 80 percent of the quantitative restrictions [Bourdot, 1988; Graduate Institute of International Studies, 1968] between its member countries, though it met with less success in eliminating tariff barriers.

In the 1960s the OEEC was supplanted by the OECD (Organization for Economic Cooperation and Development) with the addition of non-European countries. Some of the trade liberalization within the OECD resulted from multilateral agreements under the auspices of the GATT, while a considerable amount of

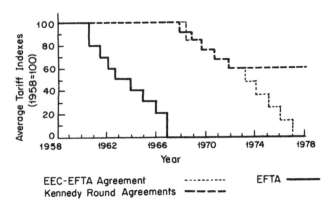

FIGURE XI
Tariff Elimination Schedules: 1958–1978

the elimination of trade barriers was carried out within subgroupings of countries (the most prominent of these being the EEC).

Figure XI and Table II provide a comparison of the major postwar tariff reforms. While there were five earlier postwar multilateral conferences, the Kennedy Round was by far the most important [Preeg, 1970]. It was also the first time that the GATT adopted across-the-board tariff reductions (which replaced the earlier item-by-item approach) of the type first implemented by the EEC. Beginning in 1968, and continuing over the next five years in equal installments, tariff reductions on industrial products, averaging approximately 35 to 40 percent (with two-thirds of the cuts exceeding 50 percent), were carried out by the signatories of the Kennedy Round.

Two of the non-European countries belonging to the OECD, the United States and Canada, provide an interesting illustration of the behavior of income differentials and the possible effects of trade liberalization. Until the late sixties, the United States and

TABLE II
DATES OF TARIFF ELIMINATIONS

Avg. tariff index (in percent)	EEC	EFTA	EFTA-EEC agreement*	Kennedy Round
100	1/58	1/58	1/58	1/58
92				1/68
90	1/59			
84			7/68	1/69
80	7/60	7/60		
76			1/70	1/70
70	1/61	7/61		
68			1/71	1/71
60	1/62	3/62	1/72	1/72
50	7/62	10/62		
48			4/73	
40	7/63	12/63		
36			1/74	
30	1/65	1/65		
24			1/75	
20	1/66	1/66		
12			1/76	
10	7/67			
0	7/68	1/67	1/77	

*The first phases of this agreement were part of the Kennedy Round.
Sources. Jensen and Walter [1965], Bourdot [1988], and Curzon [(1974].

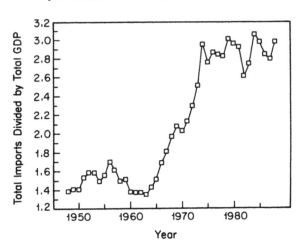

FIGURE XII
Ratio of United States-Canada Bilateral Trade to GDP

Canada—which were also the primary trading partners of each other (Figure XII)—exhibited an income gap that tended to fluctuate between 0.15 and 0.22 (Figure XIII). With the implementation of the Kennedy Round Agreement, the fall in tariffs coincided with a noticeable drop in the income gap between the United States and Canada.

Among the European countries, creation of the European Economic Community in the late fifties by the members of the European Coal and Steel Community followed the breakdown of talks on a pan-European free trade area. Subsequently, an additional European trade group was formed by some of the countries that had been unable to come to terms with the EEC. This group, called EFTA (the European Free Trade Association), comprised eight countries,[16] though Finland was officially just an associate member due to the sensitivities of its Soviet neighbor, and Portugal received exemptions from clauses requiring the abolishment of trade barriers (in fact, it was allowed to implement additional tariffs in some instances [Graduate Institute of International Studies, 1968], and for this reason, Portugal will not be included in the subsequent analysis). EFTA began abolishing tariffs on trade in manufactured goods in 1961 and completed the process by 1967.

16. Austria, Denmark, Finland, Norway, Portugal, Sweden, Switzerland, and the United Kingdom.

EQUALIZING EXCHANGE 671

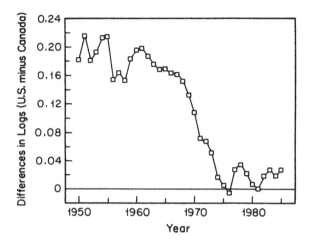

FIGURE XIII
Gap in Per Capita Incomes: Between the United States and Canada, 1950–1985

Three times during this period, the United Kingdom Denmark, and Norway applied for EEC membership, finally signing the Treaty of Accession in January 1972. While Norway eventually opted to stay out of the EEC, the United Kingdom and Denmark, together with Ireland decided to join, becoming members of the EEC in January 1973. The remaining EFTA countries each tried to come to terms with the EEC during the sixties, but without success.

Austria, which ranked second in terms of per capita income among the five remaining countries before World War I, had fallen to last place by the end of World War II. After the Second World War, it rebounded dramatically, and this led to a steady decline in income differentials among the five throughout the postwar period. Austria, however, appears to be an outlier, as income differentials among the remaining countries (Switzerland, Sweden, Finland, and Norway) stayed fairly steady until the early sixties, beginning a slight decline during EFTA's liberalization period from 1961 through 1967. But the biggest decline in σ came *after* EFTA had abolished its internal trade barriers (Figure XIV).[17] One possible explanation may be that, with the exception of the United Kingdom, the size of the EFTA countries is very small (compared with the EEC) and the ratio of their internal trade to their external

17. Income disparity among all six EFTA countries (that is, with the inclusion of the United Kingdom and Denmark) was very similar to that of the four.

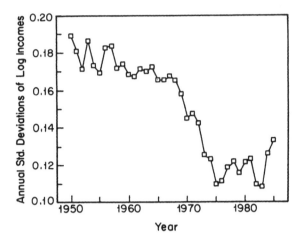

FIGURE XIV
Per Capita Income Dispersion Among EFTA 6: Switzerland, Sweden, Denmark,
Norway, Finland, and the United Kingdom

trade is fairly small.[18] A much larger proportion of EFTA's trade
was with the EEC, so trade liberalization with the EEC may have
had more of an impact on disparity within EFTA than its own,
internal, liberalization.

Tariffs between EFTA and the EEC were reduced starting in
mid-1968, in accordance with the Kennedy Round Agreements.
Further agreements between the EEC and the EFTA countries
provided for the continuation of this process, until the eventual
elimination of nearly all tariffs on industrial goods by 1977 (the
impact of this agreement on EFTA imports from the EEC may be
seen in Figure XV).[19] In fact, not only did disparity within EFTA
decline from 1968 through the mid-seventies, so also did the
income gap between the EFTA and EEC mean incomes.

Table III gives an indication of how the timing of the convergence differed between the EEC and the other groups. The postwar
period is divided into four periods. In the first period, which ran
from 1951 to 1958 (the years prior to the formation of the EEC and

18. The ratio of EFTA 6's internal trade (measured by its imports) to its total
imports rose from 17 percent (8 percent for the EFTA 4) prior to liberalization, to 22
percent (12 percent for the EFTA 4) by the end of the transition period in 1967. By
comparison, total intra-EEC imports comprised 46 percent of total EEC imports by
the end of their transition period, up from 30 percent at its inception.
19. Trade reform with the EFTA countries that became EEC members in the
early seventies proceeded at the same pace as the overall liberalization between the
EEC and the countries that remained in EFTA.

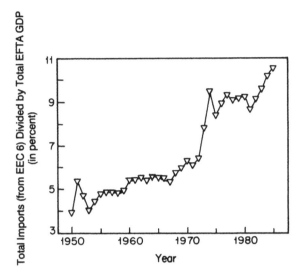

FIGURE XV
Ratio of EFTA 6 Imports to EFTA 6 GDP: Switzerland, Sweden, Denmark,
Norway, Finland, and the United Kingdom

EFTA), none of the groups exhibited significant changes in their levels of disparity. However, the differences between the EFTA countries and the EEC were reduced during this period. This may be related to the impact of the OEEC in abolishing 80 percent of the quantitative restrictions in Europe during the fifties.[20] The EEC's transition years of trade liberalization comprise the second period, which extends from 1959 until 1967 (this period also includes EFTA's liberalization years). The results corroborate the visual evidence of significant convergence only among the EEC countries.

The third period begins with the implementation of the Kennedy Round agreements and ends when all tariffs between the EEC and EFTA were abolished.[21] In the case of the United States and Canada, only the five years of the Kennedy Round tariff cuts plus one additional year were used. During this period, the EEC displayed no convergence tendencies, compared with the significant convergence in EFTA and between the United States and

20. It is possible that these restrictions were more extensive (prior to their elimination) between the two groups of countries than within them. This might explain why the reductions among the EEC countries and among the EFTA countries were not significant.
21. The EEC's transition period actually ended in July 1968. However, since the Kennedy Round agreements also became effective in 1968, the year was used as the beginning of the third period.

674   QUARTERLY JOURNAL OF ECONOMICS

TABLE III
Convergence Coefficients in Postwar, by Group[a]

Period	Group	$\hat{\kappa}$	Std. dev.	N	R^2	t-stat. $H_0: \kappa = 0$	Half-life	Double life
1951–1985	EEC6	0.0291	0.0066	204	0.991	4.39**	23.5	
	EFTA6	0.0191	0.0097	204	0.981	1.98	35.9	
	US-Can[a]	0.0466	0.0240	34	0.980	1.95	14.5	
	EF6-EC6[b]	0.0324	0.0091	204	0.976	3.58**	21.0	
1951–1958	EEC6	0.0248	0.0144	42	0.991	1.73	27.6	
	EFTA6	0.0142	0.0180	42	0.987	0.79	48.5	
	US-Can[a]	0.0565	0.0559	7	0.979	1.01	11.9	
	EF6-EC6[b]	0.0456	0.0151	42	0.980	3.02*	14.8	
1959–1967	EEC6	0.0504	0.0118	48	0.993	4.28**	13.4	
	EFTA6	0.0097	0.0144	48	0.990	0.68	71.0	
	US-Can[a]	0.0155	0.0154	8	0.998	1.01	44.3	
	EF6-EC6[b]	0.0166	0.0125	48	0.988	1.33	41.3	
1968–1977	EEC6	0.0107	0.0154	54	0.987	0.70	64.1	
	EFTA6	0.0540	0.0230	54	0.970	2.35*	12.5	
	US-Can[a,c]	0.1855	0.0416	5	0.990	4.46**	3.4	
	EF6-EC6[b]	0.0746	0.0247	54	0.958	3.02*	8.9	
1978–1985	EEC6	0.0216	0.0159	42	0.989	1.35	31.8	
	EFTA6	0.0028	0.0293	42	0.966	0.10	242.9	
	US-Can[a,d]	0.2343	0.2298	11	0.526	1.02	2.6	
	EF6-EC6[a,d]	−0.0242	0.0313	42	0.959	−0.77		29.0

EEC 6 includes Belgium, France, Netherlands, Germany, Italy, and Luxembourg.
EFTA 6 includes Sweden, Switzerland, Finland, Norway, the United Kingdom, and Denmark.
a. The annual US-CAN data are gaps, rather than differences from a group mean as in the case of the other groups.
b. The annual EF6-EC6 data are differences between each of the EFTA 6 incomes and the EEC 6 average income rather than from the EFTA average as in the EFTA 6 rows.
c. Period: 1968–1973.
d. Period: 1974–1985.
**Significant at the 1 percent level.
*Significant at the 5 percent level.

Canada as well as between EFTA and the EEC. The post-liberalization years comprise the final period and none of the groups gives any indication of significant convergence or divergence.[22]

    22. It is interesting to note that the EEC and EFTA convergence episodes were not a reflection of European-wide convergence. In fact, income differentials among the remaining European countries which were neither members of EFTA nor among the first nine members of the EEC, exhibited no tendency toward income convergence (or divergence for that matter) during the entire postwar period. This lack of convergence closely resembles the fairly stable income differentials in the prewar EEC as well as among the other postwar industrialized countries that did not significantly liberalize their trade.

Ben-David [1993] uses a different method to gauge the relationship between the timing of trade reform and the reduction in income disparity. By creating indexes of trade barriers (TBI's) within each group, the study finds that annual changes in disparity are significantly related to the annual changes in the TBI's, and are not related to a simple straight-line trend during the postwar years.

Other than the EEC, EFTA, and the GATT-sponsored agreements, there have been several other attempts at liberalizing trade on a regional basis (e.g., in South America, Africa, and Southeast Asia). Since these met with far less success in eliminating trade barriers than their European counterparts, there was very little, if any, impact on income disparity among these countries that might be attributed to trade reform.

V. SUMMARY AND CONCLUSIONS

This paper examined the proposition that liberalization of trade may contribute to income convergence. The primary focus of this analysis was on the six original members of the European Economic Community.

During the postwar period of trade reform, the convergence of incomes within the EEC was found to be quite substantial. The link between trade liberalization and income convergence was demonstrated in a couple of settings related to the Community. Examination of pre-WWII data indicates that the income convergence witnessed after 1950 was not due to some enormous earlier divergence caused by World War II (i.e., postwar σ's were not returning to some earlier level) nor was it a continuation of some long-term trend as was the case within the United States. In a related example, the σ's of the next group of countries to join the EEC (in 1973) were examined. Not only did the incomes among the three new members fail to replicate the behavior of the original Six and converge during the postwar years, the degree of disparity actually increased. Their income differentials began to fall only after these countries began to remove the trade barriers among themselves and with the six original members of the Community.

The focus of the analysis then shifted to a comparison of the EEC with other benchmark cases. The United States, which is characterized by (1) a relative absence of barriers on commodity flows and factor movements and (2) a central government, provides an illustration of the type of income convergence that an integrated world economy might exhibit. The behavior of income differentials at the opposite end of the mobility spectrum, where there are restrictions on the movements of both goods and factors, was also examined. The 107 market economies in the sample exhibited significant income divergence. A noticeable lack of convergence was also evident among the world's 25 wealthiest countries, as well among the 14 countries with incomes in the range of the EEC spectrum. This was very similar to the prewar behavior of income differentials between the countries that would later make up the Community, which were also fairly constant and high. However, as trade became more liberalized, the EEC incomes began to converge, at rates of income convergence that closely resembled the rates observed in the United States among states.

The postwar convergence among OECD countries may also be related to their liberalization of trade. The timing of income convergence among the non-EEC countries differed from the EEC convergence, and it coincided with the Kennedy Round agreements and (in the case of the EFTA countries) the EFTA-EEC agreement for trade liberalization.

To summarize, convergence among specific industrialized countries does not appear to be due simply to their being developed since the convergence phenomenon was not apparent among other industrialized country groupings nor among these same countries prior to their liberalization of trade. Furthermore, the convergence within the EEC and EFTA does not appear to be due to any European-wide movement toward reductions in income disparity, as evidenced by the lack of convergence among the non-EEC and non-EFTA European countries. When evidence of convergence was found, it appeared to coincide closely with the timing of trade reform among major trading partners. Different periods of liberalization were related to different periods of convergence.

The results in this paper provide prima facie evidence that trade liberalization may have an impact on incomes, even to the extent of bringing about the sort of convergence results attained in the integrated economy case, as exemplified by the United States. In the absence of free trade, however, there is no reason to assume convergence in income levels, as is evidenced by the analysis of the world case.

DATA APPENDIX

The per capita GDP data used in this paper come from Summers and Heston [1988] and Maddison [1982]. Per capita personal income data from the Bureau of Economic Analysis [1984] was used for the U. S. states.

The intragroup trade statistics were calculated by summing the imports by each country from the remaining group members and dividing by the group's total aggregate GDPs. The external trade statistics (in the case of the EEC) use the same denominator as in the intra-EEC measure, while the numerator sums up total imports (from external sources) into the EEC countries. Trade data came from various IMF *Direction of Trade Statistics* yearbooks, while the aggregate GDP data came from various IMF *International Financial Statistics* yearbooks.

Groups examined include the following countries. EEC 6: Belgium, France, Germany, Italy, Luxembourg, and the Netherlands. EEC 3: Denmark, Ireland, and the United Kingdom. EFTA: Austria, Denmark, Finland, Norway, Portugal, Sweden, Switzerland, and the United Kingdom. Mid-14: Australia, Austria, Canada, Denmark, Finland, Iceland, New Zealand, Norway, Saudi Arabia, Sweden, Trinidad and Tobago, United Kingdom, Uruguay, and Venezuela. Top 25 include the mid-14 plus Argentina, Chile, Iraq, Ireland, Israel, Japan, Mexico, South Africa, Spain, Switzerland, and the United States. All 48 states within the continental United States comprised the intra-U. S. group.

UNIVERSITY OF HOUSTON

REFERENCES

Abramovitz, Moses, "Catching Up, Forging Ahead, and Falling Behind," *Journal of Economic History*, XLVI (1986), 385–406.
Balassa, Bela, "Structural Policies in the European Common Market," in Bela Balassa, ed., *European Economic Integration* (Amsterdam: North-Holland, 1975), pp. 225–74.
Barro, Robert J., "Economic Growth in a Cross Section of Countries," *Quarterly Journal of Economics*, CVI (1991), 407–43.
Barro, Robert J., and Xavier Sala-i-Martin, "Convergence," *Journal of Political Economy*, C (1992), 223–51.
Baumol, William J., "Productivity Growth, Convergence, and Welfare: What the Long-Run Data Show," *American Economic Review*, LXXVI (1986), 1072–85.
Baumol, William J., Sue Ann B. Blackman, and Edward N. Wolff, *Productivity and American Leadership: The Long View* (Cambridge, MA: MIT Press, 1989).
Ben-David, Dan, "From Liberalization to Equalization: Some Evidence on the Impact of Freer Trade on Income Differentials," University of Chicago, Ph.D., thesis, 1990.
——, "Income Disparity Among Countries and the Effects of Freer Trade," in *Economic Growth and the Structure of Long Run Development*, Luigi L. Pasinetti and Robert M. Solow, eds. International Economic Association (London: Macmillan, 1993), forthcoming.

Ben-David, Dan, and Alok Bohara, "Income Disparity Among Countries in Western Europe: Before and After the Second World War," 1992.

Bernard, Andrew B., and Steven N. Durlauf, "Convergence of International Output Movements," 1990.

Bourdot, Yves, *International Integration, Market Structure and Prices* (New York: Routledge, 1988).

Bureau of Economic Analysis, *State Personal Income: Estimates for 1929–82 and a Statement of Sources and Methods* (Washington, DC: U. S. Department of Commerce, 1984).

Cass, David, "Optimum Growth in an Aggregative Model of Capital Accumulation," *Review of Economic Studies*, XXXII (1965), 233–40.

Collins, Doreen, *The European Communities: The Social Policy of the First Phase* (London: Martin Robertson & Co. Ltd., 1975), Chs. 2 and 3.

Curzon, Victoria, *The Essentials of Economic Integration: Lessons of the EFTA Experience* (New York: St. Martins Press, 1974).

De Long, J. Bradford, "Productivity Growth, Convergence, and Welfare: Comment," *American Economic Review*, LXXVIII (1988), 1138–54.

Dollar, David, Edward N. Wolff, and William J. Baumol, "The Factor-Price Equalization Model and Industry Labor Productivity: An Empirical Test across Countries," in Robert C. Feenstra, ed., *Empirical Methods for International Trade* (Cambridge: MIT Press, 1988), pp. 23–47.

Dowrick, Steve, and Duc-Tho Nguyen, "OECD Comparative Economic Growth 1950–85: Catch-Up and Convergence," *American Economic Review*, LXXIX (1989), 1010–30.

El-Agraa, A. M., "Measuring the Impact of Economic Integration," in A. M. El-Agraa, ed., *The Economics of the European Community*, 2nd ed. (Oxford: Philip Allan Publishers Ltd., 1985), pp. 112–23.

Emmanuel, Arghiri, *Unequal Exchange: A Study of the Imperialism of Trade* (Monthly Review Press, 1972); originally, *L'échange inégal* (Paris: Librairie Francois Maspero, 1969).

Graduate Institute of International Studies, Geneva, *The European Free Trade Association and the Crisis of European Integration: An Aspect of the Atlantic Crisis?* (London: Michael Joseph, 1968).

Helpman, Elhanan, and Paul R. Krugman, *Market Structure and Foreign Trade* (Cambridge: MIT Press, 1985).

International Monetary Fund, *International Financial Statistics Yearbook* (Washington, DC), various editions.

____, *Direction of Trade Statistics Yearbook* (Washington, DC), various editions.

Jensen, Finn B., and Ingo Walter, *The Common Market: Economic Integration in Europe* (Philadelphia: J. B. Lippincott Co., 1965), Ch. 3.

Jovanovic, Boyan, and Saul Lach, "The Diffusion of Technology and Inequality Among Nations," Paper presented at the NBER Workshop on Economic Growth, 1990.

Koopmans, Tjalling C., "On the Concept of Optimal Economic Growth," *The Econometric Approach to Development Planning*, Pontificia Academia Scientiarum (Amsterdam: North-Holland Publishing Co., 1965).

Maddison, Angus, *Phases of Capitalist Development* (Oxford: Oxford University Press, 1982).

Mayes, D. G., "Factor Mobility," in A. M. El-Agraa, ed., *The Economics of the European Community*, 2nd ed. (Oxford: Philip Allan Publishers Ltd., 1985), Ch. 7.

Preeg, Ernest H., *Traders and Diplomats: An Analysis of the Kennedy Round of Negotiations under the General Agreement on Tariffs and Trade* (Washington, DC: Brookings Institution, 1970).

Romer, Paul M., "Increasing Returns and Long-Run Growth," *Journal of Political Economy*, XCIV (1986), 1002–38.

____, "Capital Accumulation in the Theory of Long-Run Growth," in Robert Barro, ed., *Modern Business Cycle Theory* (Cambridge: Harvard University Press, 1989).

EQUALIZING EXCHANGE   **679**

Samuelson, Paul A., "International Trade and the Equalisation of Factor Prices," *Economic Journal*, LVIII (1948), 163–84.

____, "International Factor-Price Equalisation Once Again," *Economic Journal*, LIX (1949), 181–97.

____, "Prices of Factors and Goods in General Equilibrium," *Review of Economic Studies*, XXI (1953), 1–20.

____, "Trade Pattern Reversals in Time-Phased Ricardian Systems and Intertemporal Efficiency," *Journal of International Economics*, V (1975), 309–63.

Solow, Robert M., "A Contribution to the Theory of Economic Growth," *Quarterly Journal of Economics*, LXX (1956), 65–94.

____, "Technical Change and the Aggregate Production Function," *Review of Economics and Statistics*, XXXIX (1957), 312–20.

Summers, Robert, and Alan Heston, "A New Set of International Comparisons of Real Product and Price Levels Estimates for 130 Countries, 1950–1985," *Review of Income and Wealth*, Series 34, No. 1 (March 1988), 1–25.

[11]

The Economic Journal, 113 (*October*), 747–761. © Royal Economic Society 2003. Published by Blackwell Publishing, 9600 Garsington Road, Oxford OX4 2DQ, UK and 350 Main Street, Malden, MA 02148, USA.

WINNERS AND LOSERS FROM REGIONAL INTEGRATION AGREEMENTS*

Anthony J. Venables

How are the benefits and costs of a customs union divided between member countries? Outcomes depend on the comparative advantage of members, relative to each other and relative to the rest of the world. Countries with a comparative advantage between that of their partners and the rest of the world do better than countries with an 'extreme' comparative advantage. Consequently, integration between low income countries tends to lead to divergence of member country incomes, while agreements between high income countries cause convergence. Results suggest that developing countries are likely to be better served by 'north-south' than by 'south-south' agreements.

How are the gains and losses associated with membership of a customs union divided between member countries? Do unions promote convergence of *per capita* income levels amongst member states, or divergence? The theory of economic integration (from Viner (1950) onwards) tells us that the effects of membership are ambiguous but gives little guidance on these questions.[1]

The empirical literature is slightly more suggestive. For customs unions containing relatively high income countries there is evidence of convergence. For example, the work of Ben-David (1993, 1996) charts convergence within the European Union. From the late 1940s to early 1980s he finds that *per capita* income differences narrowed, falling by about two thirds over the period, due mainly to more rapid growth of the lower income countries.[2] More recently there has been the strong performance of Ireland, Spain and Portugal, which have made substantial progress in closing the gap with richer members of the EU. Whereas in the mid 1980s these countries' *per capita* incomes were, respectively, 64%, 67% and 57% of the income of the large EU countries,[3] by the end of the 1990s the numbers had risen to 113%, 80% and 71%. Clearly, the prospect of convergence is motivating the queue of entrants to the EU.

For low income countries there is some evidence that the opposite process is at work, with regional integration promoting divergence. Perhaps the best documented example of this is the concentration of manufacturing in the old East African Common Market. In the 1960s Kenya steadily enhanced its position as the industrial centre of the Common Market, producing more than

* This paper was produced as part of the Globalisation Programme of the UK Economic and Social Research Council funded Centre for Economic Performance, London School of Economics. Thanks to referees and to participants in seminars at Columbia University, the LSE, the University of Sao Paolo, and the University of Sussex for helpful comments.

[1] Two recent surveys are Baldwin and Venables (1995) and Panagariya (2000).

[2] Differences measured by the standard deviation across countries of log *per capita* incomes.

[3] The average of France, Germany, Italy and the UK. All numbers in this and the next paragraph for *per capita* income PPP, from World Bank, World Development Indicators.

70% of the manufactures, exporting a growing percentage of them to its two relatively less developed partners, and achieving faster GDP growth (Eken, 1979). The Common Market collapsed in 1977, partly because of the internal tensions that this divergent performance created. More recent examples include the concentration of industry and services in and around Guatemala City and San Salvador in the Central American Common Market, and Abidjan and Dakar in the Economic Community of West Africa. El Salvador and Guatemala now account for over 80% of manufacturing value added in the Central American Common Market, up from 68% in 1980; over the same time period their *per capita* incomes have gone from 117% and 112% of the average for CACM to 138% and 116% respectively. In the Economic Community of West Africa the combined share of Cote d'Ivoire and Senegal in manufacturing value added has risen from 55% in 1972 to 71% in 1997, although Cote d'Ivoire's income lead has narrowed.[4] Understanding the effects of regional integration on the distribution of income in 'South-South' agreements is particularly important given the recent rapid growth in the number of such agreements (World Bank, 2000).

Many factors may be driving these changes but this paper concentrates just on comparative advantage and its implications for trade creation and trade diversion. We show how careful consideration of a country's comparative advantage – relative to the world as a whole *and* relative to its partners in the customs union (CU) – yields predictions about the winners and losers from CU formation. It turns out that countries with 'extreme' comparative advantage in a CU will generally be more vulnerable to trade diversion than are those with an 'intermediate' comparative advantage. If comparative advantage is associated with *per capita* income (via physical or human capital endowments) then CU membership will lead to convergence of income levels within a union composed of high income countries, and divergence in a union composed of low income members.

The argument is based on the comparative advantages of member countries, relative to each other and to the rest of the world. Suppose that countries differ in their endowments of skilled and unskilled labour, and that these differences form the basis of their comparative advantage. Let us take two countries that are unskilled labour abundant relative to the rest of the world (say 'Uganda' and 'Kenya'), and suppose that one of them, Uganda, is also unskilled abundant relative to the other, Kenya. Uganda therefore has an 'extreme' comparative advantage, and Kenya an 'intermediate' one. What happens if these two countries form CU? The comparative advantage of Kenya relative to Uganda will cause Kenya to export the skilled labour intensive good (say manufactures) to Uganda, which will export the unskilled labour intensive good (agriculture) in return. The first of these flows is trade diverting: Uganda is getting its imports of manufactures from Kenya not from the rest of the world, in line with intra-union

---

[4] Another good example is the divergence in economic performance between East and West Pakistan which was one of the factors leading to the break up of the country. See World Bank (2000) for fuller discussion of these cases.

not global comparative advantage. The second is trade creating: by increasing imports of agriculture from Uganda, Kenya is trading with the global, not just intra-union, lowest cost supplier.

The general argument here is that the country with an 'intermediate' comparative advantage will do better from the union than the one with the 'extreme' comparative advantage. Intuitively, interposing an intermediate country between the extreme one and the rest of the world is exactly the circumstance likely to divert the extreme country's trade. For two poor countries this unequal division of costs and benefits causes income divergence; the extreme country is the one with the least skilled labour, and hence initially poorest. However, for two rich economies (both with above world average skilled labour abundance) the extreme country is the one with the highest skilled–unskilled labour ratio. Thus, exactly the same force that drives income divergence in a CU between Kenya and Uganda, leads to income convergence in a CU between, say, France and Spain.

The remainder of the paper is devoted to developing these ideas more fully. First (Section 1), we present a two-good diagrammatic analysis of the relationship between comparative advantage and trade creation/ diversion. Then we develop the argument in a multi-good Ricardian trade model (Section 2). Finally (Section 3), we present a simulation based exploration of a two-factor and two-sector model which combines a Heckscher-Ohlin structure with product differentiation by location of production (Armington). The model shows how, given the endowment of the rest of the world, the gains and costs of CU membership depend on each country's own endowment and that of its partner. We also use this model to look at the question of South-South versus North-South CUs, arguing, as do Spilimbergo and Stein (1998), that the latter are likely to be preferable for Southern countries.

How does the present paper, with its focus on comparative advantage, relate to existing literature? Much recent work analyses regional integration in models with product differentiation and intra-industry trade, generally abstracting from comparative advantage. This is partly because of the intrinsic importance of some product market issues (eg, competition effects) and partly because these models provide a tractable framework in which to analyse dynamic effects and political economy considerations (Krugman, 1993; Krishna, 1998; Baldwin, 1995). In the competitive equilibrium tradition, the Kemp-Wan-Ohyama (Kemp and Wan, 1976) analysis establishes sufficient conditions for gain, but does not investigate the distribution of costs and benefits when these conditions do not hold. Much of the rest of the competitive equilibrium literature is devoted to models in which a very specific structure of trade is assumed; for example, the three-country and three-good models (following Meade (1955) and reviewed in Lloyd (1982)), in which integrating countries are simply assumed to export different goods. These models have the drawbacks that a very large number of trade configurations are possible (Lloyd 1982), and that the failure to connect with underlying determinants of comparative advantage makes it impossible to ask questions such as, is a South-South agreement better than a North-South agreement? The objective of this paper is precisely to show how analysis of countries' comparative advantage can produce insights on the extent to which they experience trade creation or trade diversion.[5]

The fundamental difficulty in the development of the literature perhaps arises from the fact that, in the obvious benchmark trade model, CU formation has no effect whatsoever. If the integrating countries are small and their pattern of trade with a large 'rest of the world' is the same before and after formation of the CU, then prices of all goods so traded are set in the rest of the world and unchanged by formation of the union; formation of the CU then has no effect. An interesting model must therefore have one of the following characteristics. Either goods must switch source of supply, or terms of trade effects must be introduced, so that price changes can occur. In this paper, we develop a family of models in order to pursue both approaches. In the diagrammatic analyses (Sections 1 and 2) CU formation has the effect of causing changes in the sourcing of imports. In the Heckscher-Ohlin-Armington model (Section 3) product differentiation means that fixed prices of rest of the world goods are consistent with variation of the prices of goods produced and exported by the integrating economies. We have no completely general theorem but show how consideration of countries' comparative advantage, relative to their partner and relative to the rest of the world, yields some important insights about the costs and benefits of CU membership, insights that are robust across the family of models studied. The focus is on the relationships between comparative advantage, trade creation, and trade diversion, and in the last Section of the paper we link this back to income levels and the convergence–divergence issue.

1. Internal and External Comparative Advantage: A Diagrammatic Example

The basic argument can be made most simply – yet rigorously – through a diagrammatic example. Figure 1 describes a world with two goods, A and M, and three countries, a large rest of the world (country 0), and two small countries, 1 and 2. The Figure has on the axes quantities of goods A and M, consumption of which takes place in fixed proportions, along the consumption line illustrated. The world price of good M in terms of A is p_0.[6]

Production possibilities for countries 1 and 2 are illustrated by the solid lines A_1M_1 and A_2M_2. They are constructed such that both 1 and 2 have comparative advantage in good A relative to the rest of the world, and 2 also has a comparative advantage in A relative to 1. Thus, with free trade and prices p_0 countries 1 and 2

---

[5] A recent paper that does address this issue and makes explicit the endowments of the countries is Spilimbergo and Stein (1998). They undertake numerical analysis of a model in which there are two identical low income (capital-scarce) countries and two identical high-income (capital-rich) countries, investigating the effects of alternative trading arrangements. Our analysis provides for a larger set of configurations of comparative advantage, permitting analysis of gains and losses within South-South and North-North agreements. Levy (1997) uses a factor endowment based model to analyse the political economy of CU formation but allows only for situations of completely free trade or autarky: thus, countries in a CU are assumed to have no trade with the rest of the world.

[6] p_0 is the relative price on international markets. There are no trade or transport costs, and internal prices differ from p_0 only because of tariffs.

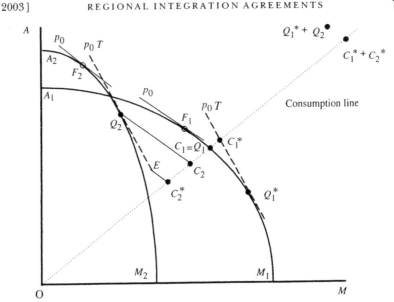

Fig. 1. *Preferential liberalisation*

would produce at points F_1 and F_2. They would both export good A, country 2 more than country 1, since it has the more extreme comparative advantage (like Uganda in our earlier example).

The initial situation is not free trade but a position in which all imports by countries 1 and 2 are subject to tariffs at rate $T > 1$.[7] We set this rate sufficiently high that country 1 is self sufficient at point $C_1 = Q_1$, with the domestic price of good M in terms of good A given by the gradient of the production possibility frontier at this point. This price ratio lies between the domestic price ratio that would rule if good M were to be imported ($p_0 T$), and that which would rule if good A were to be imported (p_0 / T), so confirming that trade is not profitable. Country 2 has the same tariffs, but its more extreme comparative advantage means that it has some trade in the initial situation, producing at Q_2 and consuming at C_2. It imports good M, meaning that the domestic price ratio is $p_0 T$, at which Q_2 is profit maximising. The budget constraint holds at world prices, p_0, so country 2's trade vector is $Q_2 C_2$.

What happens if these two countries form a customs union? In the Figure, the new equilibrium has the CU as a whole continuing to import M from the rest of the world, so the internal price ratio is $p_0 T$. Production then occurs at points Q_1^* and Q_2. (Adding these production vectors to point $Q_1^* + Q_2$ confirms that the CU imports good M, since the CU's production is less M intensive than consumption.) The trade of each of the countries is as follows. Country 1 has a comparative

---

[7] We use *ad valorem* tariff factors throughout, so $T = 1$ is free trade.

advantage in M relative to country 2, so trades vector $Q_1^* C_1^*$ with country 2, at price ratio $p_0 T$. Correspondingly, country 2 has internal trade vector $Q_2 E = Q_1^* C_1^*$. It also has external trade vector EC_2^*, this being conducted at world price p_0, and equalling the external trade of the CU as a whole, vector $EC_2^* = (Q_1^* + Q_2) - (C_1^* + C_2^*)$.

The welfare effects of the CU are given by comparison of consumption points. Country 1 gains from the union as C_1^* is above C_1; it now has some gains from trade, where previously it had none. Notice that this arises despite the fact that country 1's production structure has moved in the opposite direction from the way it would go under free trade. In contrast, country 2 loses, going from C_2 to C_2^*. The reason is trade diversion: it was getting all its imports of M from the rest of the world and is now getting some of them from its higher cost partner. As we argued in the introduction, the imports of the extreme country (2) are diverted to a partner country with comparative advantage between it and the rest of the world. However, for the intermediate country (1), trade with the partner and with the rest of the world are less close substitutes, and therefore less vulnerable to trade diversion.

This diagrammatic analysis provides a rigorous argument but perhaps seems rather contrived – one of the countries is in autarky in the initial situation and trades only with its partner once the CU is in place. This reflects the problem noted at the end of the introduction, and is why we now turn to more general models.

2. A Generalised Ricardian Model

If there are many goods with technical coefficients varying across countries, then CU formation will generally bring both trade creation and trade diversion as goods change source of supply. How is the distribution of these effects related to countries' comparative advantage? Once again, a diagrammatic approach provides the main insights.

The vertical axis of Figure 2 measures the cost of producing a good in country 2, and the horizontal the cost in country 1. The points labelled with Greek letters represent goods, and their coordinates the costs of producing them in each country. These costs are composed of the wage in each country, w_i, times the unit labour coefficients, b_i, which vary across goods and countries reflecting Ricardian efficiency differences. All goods have rest of the world price 1 (by choice of units) and initially face country 1 and 2 import tariffs at rate T.

Looking first at efficiency levels in country 1, we see that good α has the lowest country 1 unit labour requirement.[8] This good will therefore be exported by country 1 and, since the world price of the good is unity, this sets the country 1 wage at $w_1 b_1(\alpha) = 1$. In the initial situation where all imports bear tariff T, country 1 is self sufficient in goods β, γ, and ε since domestic costs ($w_1 b_1$) are less than the private unit costs of import ($= T$) and greater than unit export receipts ($= 1$). Goods δ and ζ are imported from the rest of the world, since for each of them

[8] Is furthest to the left on the horizontal axis.

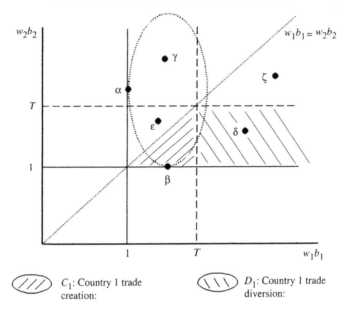

Fig. 2. *Sourcing of Manufactures*

$w_1 b_1 > T$. The analogous configuration for country 2 can be read off the vertical axis. Good β has the lowest unit labour requirement, so the country 2 wage is set by $w_2 b_2(\beta) = 1$. Country 2 is self sufficient in goods δ and $\varepsilon(1 < w_2 b_2 < T)$ and imports α, γ, and $\zeta(w_2 b_2 > T)$.

Formation of a CU will change the pattern of trade in some goods and not others. Wages in both economies remain constant, because they continue to supply their respective export goods to the rest of the world. However, country 1 will now buy from country 2 any good for which $w_2 b_2 < w_1 b_1$ (below the 45° line) and $w_2 b_2 < T$ (so it is cheaper to import duty free from the partner than import from rest of the world). As illustrated, this includes two goods. Good δ goes from being imported from the rest of the world to being imported from the partner country; this is trade diversion with additional cost per unit of $w_2 b_2(\delta) - 1$. Good β goes from country 1 self sufficiency to being imported from 2; this is trade creation, with cost saving per unit of $w_1 b_1(\beta) - w_2 b_2(\beta)$.

Analogously, country 2 now imports from 1 any good for which $w_1 b_1 < w_2 b_2$ and $w_1 b_1 < T$. Good γ therefore experiences trade diversion, now being supplied by country 1 instead of the rest of the world (since $T > w_1 b_1(\gamma) > 1$). Good ε goes from being locally produced in 2 to imported from 1, and this is trade creation, since $w_1 b_1(\varepsilon) < w_2 b_2(\varepsilon)$, bringing unit cost saving equal to this cost difference.

These effects are summarised in Table 1 (in which 0 denotes rest of the world), and the regions of product space within which country 1 experiences trade creation and diversion are illustrated by the shaded areas on Figure 2; (analogous country 2 zones are not marked).

Table 1

The Direction of Trade

	Initial		CU		Welfare Change	
	Country 1	Country 2	Country 1	Country 2	Country 1	Country 2
α	Exp. to 0	Imp. from 0	Exp. to 0	Imp. from 0		
β	No trade	Exp. to 0	Imp. from 2	Exp. to 0 & 1	↑, TC	
γ	No trade	Imp. from 0	Exp. to 2	Imp. from 1		↓, TD
δ	Imp. from 0	No trade	Imp. from 2	Exp. to 1	↓, TD	
ε	No trade	No trade	Exp. to 2	Imp. from 1		↑, TC
ζ	Imp. from 0	Imp. from 0	Imp. from 0	Imp. from 0		

This approach can be generalised to arbitrarily many commodities. To calculate the overall welfare effect we then need to know the distribution of commodities over the space and the consumption levels of each, before and after CU formation. If products are indexed χ and consumed in fixed quantity $c(\chi)$ then the change in country 1 welfare is simply

$$\Delta w_1 = \sum_{\chi \in D_1} [1 - w_2 b_2(\chi)] c(\chi) + \sum_{\chi \in C_1} [w_1 b_1(\chi) - w_2 b_2(\chi)] c(\chi)$$

where D_1 and C_1 are the sets in which there is trade diversion and trade creation.

Can we now link this to our discussion of countries' comparative advantage relative to each other and relative to the rest of the world? Suppose that the set of products that exist are uniformly distributed within the ellipse shape area on Figure 2. Then, intuitively, country 1 is 'more like' the rest of the world than is country 2. Country 1's production costs relative to the rest of the world (with unit cost = 1) vary at most by an amount equal to the width of the ellipse, and on average by half of this; in contrast, country 2's production costs vary according to the height of the ellipse. More precisely, country 1 has comparative disadvantage relative to the world but comparative advantage relative to country 2 ($1 < w_1 b_1 < w_2 b_2$), in all products in the ellipse and above the 45° line. Thus, for this majority of commodities, it lies 'between' country 2 and the rest of the world.

Comparing the shape of the ellipse with the regions of trade creation and diversion completes the argument. As illustrated, a low proportion of country 1's goods change source of supply (the intersection of the ellipse and the shaded areas) and for most of those that do, this is trade creation. For country 2, a much higher proportion of goods change source of supply, and most of these changes are trade diversion. Thus, this multi-commodity framework confirms our earlier finding. The 'extreme' country does worse than the 'intermediate' one.

A formal model of this case can be easily developed if the set of products is restricted to lie on a line in $b_1 b_2$ space, as is usual in such a model, e.g. Dornbusch *et al.* (1977). Results confirm the conclusions drawn from Figure 2.[9]

---

[9] Such a model is developed in Venables (2000).

3. Income Divergence and Convergence: A Heckscher-Ohlin-Armington Model

We now turn to a variant of the standard trade model in which comparative advantage arises from differences in factor endowments. We add to the standard Heckscher-Ohlin model an assumption of product differentiation at the national level, in order to maintain non-specialisation of production and to allow output prices to change rather than being set by supply of homogeneous products from the rest of the world. Analysis of this model requires numerical simulation, although most of the intuition comes from Heckscher-Ohlin.

The model structure is as follows. There are two factors of production, skilled and unskilled labour (S and U), and two sectors, differing in factor intensity. There are three countries, one of which, the rest of the world, is large and is endowed with equal quantities of the two factors. The other countries, 1 and 2, have factor endowment ratios different from each other and from the rest of the world, and these differences are the basis of their comparative advantage. All countries have the same technology and preferences, although we assume some national ('Armington') product differentiation. Thus, products in each sector are differentiated by location of production, although the amount of differentiation is set at minimal levels – the elasticity of substitution between different countries' products in each sector is 50 in the examples that follow. For ease of interpretation we impose a symmetric structure on production and consumption, assuming that consumer expenditure is equally divided between sectors, and that the factor intensity in one industry is the reciprocal of that in the other industry (using Cobb-Douglas technologies, see Appendix for details).

Because of the symmetry that is built into the model the equilibrium price ratio of output produced in the rest of the world is unity; this world price ratio is held constant in all experiments that follow. In the initial equilibrium all imports face the same tariff rate (set at 30%). The internal price ratios and trade patterns of countries 1 and 2 reflect these tariffs and each country's factor abundance. The experiment we study is the removal of the tariff between countries 1 and 2, and we show how outcomes depend on their endowments, relative to each other and to the rest of the world.

Results are illustrated on Figures 3–5, which give contours of welfare change as a function of the factor endowments of countries 1 and 2. Axes measure the factor abundance ratios of each country, and in Figures 3 and 4 are constructed with $S_i + U_i = 1$, $i = 1,2$. Each country's factor abundance relative to the rest of the world depends on whether S_i/U_i is greater or less than unity, while intra-union comparative advantage is measured relative to the 45° line, above which country 1 is S abundant relative to country 2.

We look first at relative utility changes, by mapping on Figure 3 the contours of the proportionate change in utility in country 2 minus that in country 1. The bold straight lines marked 00 are the zero contours, and the surface is saddle shaped, with regions in which country 2 does better than country 1 marked +. Consider the case in which both countries' endowment ratios are on the same side of those of the rest of the world. In the bottom left quadrant both countries are unskilled

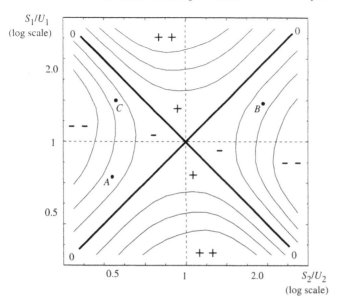

Fig. 3. *Relative Changes in Welfare* (country 2 minus country 1)

labour abundant relative to the world as a whole. Then country 2 loses relative to country 1 if and only if it is the more unskilled labour abundant of the two economies, i.e. at a point such as A, above the diagonal, with $S_1/U_1 > S_2/U_2$. Conversely, in the upper right quadrant both countries are skilled labour abundant (relative to the world) and the more skilled labour abundant country suffers the relative loss – at point B this is country 2. Both these cases illustrate that, as with the previous models, the 'extreme' country fares relatively badly, the reason being that its imports are diverted to the 'intermediate' country in line with intra-CU comparative advantage but not global comparative advantage.

In the upper left and lower right quadrants countries 1 and 2 lie on opposite sides of the rest of the world endowment ratio. Along the downward sloping line 00 countries 1 and 2 are symmetric, so experience the same welfare change.[10] Off this line the country that has endowment closer to the world average is the relative gainer. Thus, at point C country 2 is the relative loser, since S_2/U_2 is further from unity (horizontal distance) than is S_1/U_1 (vertical distance). The intuitive reason is that although country 2's union partner is S abundant relative to the world, the CU as a whole is S scarce. Trade diversion is experienced by country 2 as it switches its sourcing of the S intensive good from the rest of the world to the CU.

How general are these results? Providing country differences arise only from endowments of two factors, then the surface is quite generally a saddle with a zero-contour on the 45% line from the origin, along which the two economies are

---

[10] Country 1's endowment ratio is the reciprocal of country 2's.

identical. However, the second zero-contour line need not be straight, nor necessarily downwards sloping everywhere; its linearity in Figure 3 is a consequence of the symmetry built into the model.

The symmetry of Figure 3 derives from the fact that it gives utility change in country 2 minus that in country 1. Figure 4 focuses just on country 2 welfare change, expressed as a proportion of 2's initial welfare. This, like the relative change of the previous Figure, forms a saddle on endowment space. The lines marked 00 are zero contours, and the plus and minus signs indicate regions of country 2 gain and loss. There are very small gains along the 45° line, arising from the product differentiation in the model. However, the main message of the Figure is that the relative losses we saw in Figure 3 can also be associated with absolute losses. These regions of absolute loss are subsets of regions in which country 2 suffers relative loss (Figure 3), and the intuition is as before. Thus, at the left and right hand sides of the Figure country 2 has 'extreme' endowments, and trade diversion causes it to lose from CU membership.

In Figures 3 and 4 the factors S and U enter the model symmetrically, so to refer to them as skilled and unskilled labour is a misnomer – the wage of S is on average no higher than that of U and countries with much S are on average no richer than those with much U. To capture the idea that S abundant economies are relatively high income we now modify the analysis in the following way. In Figure 3 and 4, if an economy gained a unit of S it lost a unit of U (since $S_i + U_i = 1$). Now, in Figure 5, we hold U constant ($= \bar{U}$), and simply vary the amount of S. Perhaps the best way to think of this is that countries 1 and 2 both have $\bar{U}$ workers, a fraction $S_i/\bar{s}$ of whom

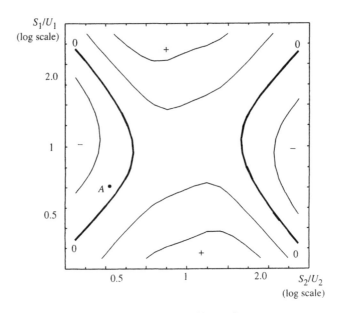

Fig. 4. *Country 2 Welfare Change Contours*

are endowed with one unit of unskilled labour and $\bar{s}$ units of skilled labour, while the fraction $1 - S_i/\bar{s}$ have no skill. Thus, at a high value of S_i/U_i a higher proportion of the population are endowed with skilled labour. S and U enter production as before but S abundant economies will now tend to be richer. For example, moving from $S_i/U_i = 0.5$ to $S_i/U_i = 2$ in the example of Figure 5 raises the proportion of the population with skills and approximately doubles country i *per capita* income.

Contours in Figure 5 illustrate, like Figure 4, the country 2 welfare change due to CU formation. Two main messages come from the Figure. The first is the original argument, that CU formation between two poor countries tends to lead to income divergence and between rich countries leads to convergence. Consider point A. At this point country 2 is poorer than country 1 (it is S scarce relative to its partner), and suffers a welfare reduction, while country 1 experiences a welfare gain, causing divergence. (The country 1 gain is not illustrated directly, but can be seen by reversing country labels and looking at point A', the reflection of A around the 45° line). Conversely, at point B both countries are S abundant, but country 2 relatively more so, and therefore relatively rich. It is now country 2 that loses and country 1 that gains, causing convergence of their real incomes.

The second point concerns the attractiveness of 'North-South' agreements for low income countries. Let us take a fixed and low value of S_2/U_2, and ask: what type of partner is country 2 best off forming a CU with? The answer is a skilled labour abundant economy (high S_1/U_1). There are two forces driving this. One is that trade creation is maximised and trade diversion minimised with such a partner (as in

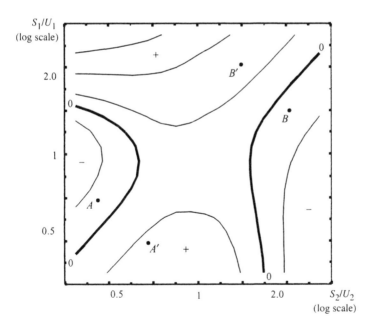

Fig. 5. *Country 2 Welfare Change Contours* (U_i = constant)

previous cases). The other is a terms of trade gain. If the skill abundant country has relatively high total income, then the low income country experiences relatively large growth in export demand which improves its terms of trade, giving it a larger share of the aggregate gains from CU formation. The argument is similar to that of Spilimbergo and Stein (1998), derived by computing outcomes in a model with two identical low income countries and two identical high income countries.

4. Concluding Comments

Systematic analyses of the comparative advantage of customs union members – relative to each other and relative to the rest of the world – establish how the real income effects of regional integration are distributed amongst member countries. In general, countries with 'extreme' comparative advantage do worse than those with comparative advantage intermediate between the partner and the rest of the world. If comparative advantage is systematically related to income *per capita*, then this is a way of resolving the paradox that formation of a CU containing high income members may be a force for convergence of *per capita* incomes, while developing country CUs have sometimes been associated with divergence. In the former case the extreme countries are those with the highest *per capita* incomes, while in the latter they are those with the lowest. The analysis warns of the dangers from 'South-South' integration schemes, showing how they may draw manufacturing production into richer countries at the expense of poorer members of the union. It also suggests that low income countries are better served by integration with high income countries.

The mechanism underlying the analysis is comparative advantage. To focus on comparative advantage we have abstracted from all differences between economies except in endowments or technologies. It would be interesting to explore how other differences – such as in initial tariff rates – affect results. We have also abstracted from other mechanisms that are undoubtedly important in determining the outcome of regional integration agreements. These include policy stance, technology flows, foreign direct investment and agglomeration forces.[11] Agglomeration forces can lead to clustering of manufacturing in selected locations in a CU and might be particularly powerful in developing countries, possibly reinforcing the divergence argument made in this paper. If manufacturing starts from a small base and if activities complementary to manufacturing (for example, provision of business services, telecommunications and transport infrastructure) are thinly distributed, then the likelihood of manufacturing development agglomerating in a few locations is relatively high. This suggests that, particularly for developing countries, the forces analysed in this paper might understate the extent of divergence that could be caused by regional trade agreements.

London School of Economics and CEPR

Date of receipt of first submission: February 2001
Date of receipt of final typescript: February 2003

---

[11] See Puga and Venables (1997, 1998) for analysis of the way in which integration might trigger agglomeration in a subset of *ex ante* identical countries.

Appendix

There are two goods, x and y, (indicated by superscripts), two countries 1 and 2 (indicated by subscripts) and the rest of the world (indicated by subscript 0). Factor endowments are S_i and U_i with respective prices v_i and w_i. Technologies are described by cost functions,

$$c_i^x = w_i^\lambda v_i^{1-\lambda}, \quad c_i^y = w_i^{1-\lambda} v_i^\lambda, \quad \lambda = 0.25. \tag{A1}$$

Factor market clearing takes the form

$$S_i = \frac{\partial c^x}{\partial v_i} q_i^x + \frac{\partial c^y}{\partial v_i} q_i^y, \quad U_i = \frac{\partial c^x}{\partial w_i} q_i^x + \frac{\partial c^y}{\partial w_i} q_i^y, \quad i = 1, 2, \tag{A2}$$

where q_i^k denotes the quantity of good k produced in country i.

Preferences are described by

$$m_i = u_i (G_i^x G_i^y)^{1/2}, \tag{A3}$$

where m_i is income, u_i is utility, and G_i^k is the price index of good k in country i, defined by

$$G_i^k = \left[(p_i^k)^{1-\sigma} + (t p_j^k)^{1-\sigma} + T^{1-\sigma} \right]^{1/(1-\sigma)}, \quad i, j = 1, 2, \ i \neq j. \tag{A4}$$

where p_i^k denotes the price of good k produced in country i, equal to unit cost, t denotes the internal tariff and T the external tariff. σ is set at 50, and t and T both take initial value 1.3, t dropping to 1 when the customs union is formed. Demands are derived from utility maximisation, and income is given by

$$m_i = w_i U_i + v_i S_i + p_j^x q_{ji}^x (t - 1) + p_j^y q_{ji}^y (t - 1) + q_{0i}^x (T - 1) + q_{0i}^y (T - 1), \quad i, j = 1, 2, \tag{A5}$$

where q_{ij}^k denotes the quantity of good k produced in j and sold in i. In addition, country 0 has demands q_{i0}^k which have price elasticity σ and are scaled such that in the initial equilibrium an average of 10% of the output of countries 1 and 2 are exported to country 0.

In Figures 3 and 4 endowments vary in the interval $S_i = [0.25, 0.75]$ with $U_i = 1 - S_i$.

In Figure 5 endowments vary in the interval $S_i = [0.1667, 1.5]$ with $U_i = 0.5$.

References

Baldwin, R. (1995). 'A domino theory of regionalism', in (R. Baldwin, P. Haaparanta and J. Kiander, eds.), *Expanding Membership of the European Union*, Cambridge: Cambridge University Press.

Baldwin, R. and Venables, A. J. (1995). 'Regional economic integration', in (G. Grossman and K. Rogoff, eds.), *Handbook of International Economics*, vol. 3, Amsterdam: North Holland.

Ben-David, D. (1993). 'Equalizing exchange; trade liberalization and income convergence', *Quarterly Journal of Economics*, vol. 108, pp. 653–79.

Ben-David, D. (1996). 'Trade and convergence among nations', *Journal of International Economics*, vol. 40, pp. 279–98.

Dornbusch, R., Fischer, S. and Samuelson, P. A. (1977). 'Comparative advantage, trade and payments in a Ricardian model with a continuum of products', *American Economic Review*, vol. 67, pp. 823–39.

Eken, S. (1979). 'Breakup of the East African Community', *Finance and Development*, vol. 16, pp. 36–40.

Kemp, M. and Wan, H. (1976). 'An elementary proposition concerning the formation of customs unions', *Journal of International Economics*, vol. 6, pp. 95–7.

Krishna, P. (1998). 'Regionalism and multilateral; a political economy approach', *Quarterly Journal of Economics*, vol. 113, pp. 227–51.

Krugman, P. R. (1993). 'Regionalism versus multilateralism; analytical notes', in (J. de Melo and A. Panagariya, eds.), *New Dimensions in Regional Integration*, Cambridge: Cambridge University Press.

Levy, P.I. (1997). 'A political economic analysis of free-trade agreements', *American Economic Review*, vol. 87, pp. 506–19.

Lloyd, P. J. (1982). '3 × 3 theory of customs unions', *Journal of International Economics*, vol. 12, pp. 41–63.

Meade, J. E. (1955). *The Theory of Customs Unions*, Amsterdam: North-Holland.

Panagariya, A. (2000). 'Preferential trade liberalization; the traditional theory and new developments', *Journal of Economic Literature*, vol. 2, pp. 287–331.

Puga, D. and Venables, A. J. (1997). 'Preferential trading arrangements and industrial location', *Journal of International Economics*, vol. 43, pp. 347–68.

Puga, D. and Venables, A. J. (1998). 'Trading arrangements and industrial development', *World Bank Economic Review*, vol. 12, pp. 221–49.

Spilimbergo, A. and Stein, E. (1998). 'The welfare implications of trading blocs among countries with different endowments', in (J. Frankel, ed.) *The Regionalization of the World Economy*, Chicago: NBER and Chicago University Press.

Venables, A. J. (2000). 'Winners and losers from regional integration agreements', CEPR Discussion Paper no 2528.

Viner, J. (1950). *The Customs Union Issue*, New York: Carnegie Endownment for International Press.

World Bank (2000). *Trade Blocs*. Policy Research Report, Washington DC.

D
Domestic Inequality and Poverty

[12]

Journal of Economic Growth, 7, 195–225, 2002

Growth is Good for the Poor

DAVID DOLLAR

Development Research Group, The World Bank

AART KRAAY

Development Research Group, The World Bank

Average incomes of the poorest quintile rise proportionately with average incomes in a sample of 92 countries spanning the last four decades. This is because the share of income of the poorest quintile does not vary systematically with average income. It also does not vary with many of the policies and institutions that explain growth rates of average incomes, nor does it vary with measures of policies intended to benefit the poorest in society. This evidence emphasizes the importance of economic growth for poverty reduction.

Keywords: income inequality, poverty, growth

JEL classification: D3, I3, O1

> *Globalization has dramatically increased inequality between and within nations . . .*
> Jay Mazur
> ''Labor's New Internationalism,'' Foreign Affairs (Jan/Feb 2000)

> *We have to reaffirm unambiguously that open markets are the best engine we know of to lift living standards and build shared prosperity.*
> Bill Clinton
> Speech at World Economic Forum (2000)

1. Introduction

The world economy grew well during the 1990s, despite the financial crisis in East Asia. However, there is intense debate over the extent to which the poor benefit from this growth. The two quotes above exemplify the extremes in this debate. At one end of the spectrum are those who argue that the potential benefits of economic growth for the poor are undermined or even offset entirely by sharp increases in inequality that accompany growth. At the other end of the spectrum is the argument that liberal economic policies such as monetary and fiscal stability and open markets raise incomes of the poor and everyone else in society proportionately.

In light of the heated popular debate over this issue, as well as its obvious policy relevance, it is surprising how little systematic cross-country empirical evidence is available on the extent to which the poorest in society benefit from economic growth. In this paper, we define the poor as those in the bottom fifth of the income distribution of a country, and empirically examine the relationship between growth in average incomes of the poor and growth in overall incomes, using a large sample of developed and developing countries spanning the last four decades. Since average incomes of the poor are proportional to the share of income accruing to the poorest quintile times average income, this approach is equivalent to studying how a particular measure of income inequality— the first quintile share—varies with average incomes.

In a large sample of countries spanning the past four decades, we cannot reject the null hypothesis that the income share of the first quintile does not vary systematically with average incomes. In other words, we cannot reject the null hypothesis that incomes of the poor rise equiproportionately with average incomes. Figure 1 illustrates this basic point. In the top panel, we plot the logarithm of per capita incomes of the poor (on the vertical axis) against the logarithm of average per capita incomes (on the horizontal axis), pooling 418 country-year observations on these two variables. The sample consists of 137 countries with at least one observation on the share of income accruing to the bottom quintile, and the median number of observations per country is 3. There is a strong, positive, linear relationship between the two variables, with a slope of 1.07 which does not differ significantly from one. Since both variables are measured in logarithms, this indicates that on average incomes of the poor rise equiproportionately with average incomes. In the bottom panel we plot average annual growth in incomes of the poor (on the vertical axis) against average annual growth in average incomes (on the horizontal axis), pooling 285 country-year observations where we have at least two observations per country on incomes of the poor separated by at least five years. The sample consists of 92 countries and the median number of growth episodes per country is 3. Again, there is a strong, positive, linear relationship between these two variables with a slope of 1.19. In the majority of the formal statistical tests that follow, we cannot reject the null hypothesis that the slope of this relationship is equal to one. These regressions indicate that within countries, incomes of the poor on average rise equiproportionately with average incomes. This is equivalent to the observation that there is no systematic relationship between average incomes and the share of income accruing to the poorest fifth of the income distribution. Below we examine this basic finding in more detail and find that it holds across regions, time periods, growth rates and income levels, and is robust to controlling for possible reverse causation from incomes of the poor to average incomes.

Given the strong relationship between incomes of the poor and average incomes, we next ask whether policies and institutions that raise average incomes have systematic effects on the share of income accruing to the poorest quintile which might magnify or offset their effects on incomes of the poor. We focus attention on a set of policies and institutions whose importance for average incomes has been identified in the large cross-country empirical literature on economic growth. These include openness to international trade, macroeconomic stability, moderate size of government, financial development, and strong property rights and rule of law. We find little evidence that these policies and institutions have systematic effects on the share of income accruing to the poorest quintile. The only exceptions are that there is some weak evidence that smaller government size and stabilization from high inflation disproportionately benefit the poor by raising the share of

Levels

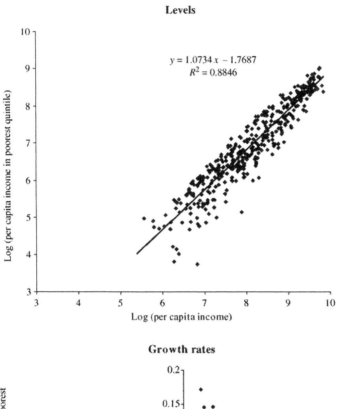

Growth rates

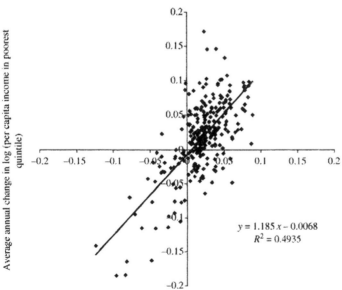

Figure 1. Incomes of the poor and average incomes.

income accruing to the bottom quintile. These findings indicate that growth-enhancing policies and institutions tend to benefit the poor—and everyone else in society—equiproportionately. We also show that the distributional effects of such variables tend to be small relative to their effects on overall economic growth.

We next examine in more detail the popular idea that greater economic integration across countries is associated with increases in inequality within countries. We first consider a range of measures of international openness, including trade volumes, tariffs, membership in the World Trade Organization, and the presence of capital controls, and ask whether any of these has systematic effects on the share of income accruing to the poorest in society. We find little evidence that they do so, and we find that this result holds even when we allow the effects of measures of openness to depend on the level of development and differences in factor endowments as predicted by the factor proportions theory of international trade. We therefore also cannot reject the null hypothesis that on average, greater economic integration benefits the poorest in society as much as everyone else.

In recent years there has been a great deal of emphasis in the development community on making growth even more "pro-poor." Given our evidence that neither growth nor growth-enhancing policies tend to be systematically associated with changes in the share of income accruing to the poorest fifth of societies, we interpret this emphasis on "pro-poor" growth as a call for some other policy interventions that raise the share of income captured by the poorest in society. We empirically examine the importance of four such potential factors in determining the income share of the poorest: primary educational attainment, public spending on health and education, labor productivity in agriculture relative to the rest of the economy, and formal democratic institutions. While it is likely that these factors are important in bettering the lot of poor people in some countries and under some circumstances, we are unable to uncover any evidence that they systematically raise the share of income of the poorest in our large cross-country sample.

In short, we find little evidence that either average incomes, or a wide variety of policy and other variables, are significantly associated with the income share of the poorest quintile. We therefore cannot reject the null hypothesis that incomes of the poor on average rise equiproportionately with average incomes. This of course does not mean that growth is all that is required to improve the lot of the poorest in society, and that the distributional effects of policies should be ignored. As we discuss in greater detail below, existing cross-country data on income distribution that we use contains substantial measurement error. We therefore cannot rule out the possibility that our failure to uncover systematic effects of average incomes and policy on the income share of the poorest quintile is simply a consequence of this measurement error. We also cannot rule out the possibility that there are complex interactions between inequality and growth, not captured by our simple empirical models, that net out to small changes in the former that are uncorrelated with the latter.[1] What we can conclude however is that policies that raise average incomes are likely to be central to successful poverty reduction strategies, and that existing cross-country evidence—including our own—provides disappointingly little guidance as to what mix of growth-oriented policies might especially benefit the poorest in society.

Our work builds on and contributes to two strands of the literature on inequality and growth. Our basic finding that (changes in) income and (changes in) inequality are unrelated is consistent with the findings of several previous authors including Deininger and Squire (1996), Chen and Ravallion (1997), and Easterly (1999) who document this same regularity in smaller samples of countries. We build on this literature by considering a significantly larger sample of countries and by employing more elaborate econometric techniques that take into account the possibility that income levels are endogenous to inequality as suggested by the large theoretical and empirical literature on the effects of inequality on growth. Our results are also related to the small but growing literature on the determinants of the cross-country and intertemporal variation in measures of income inequality, including Li et al. (1998), Gallup et al. (1998), Spilimbergo et al. (1999), Leamer et al. (1999), Barro (2000), Lundberg and Squire (2000), and Foster and Székely (2001). Our work expands on this literature by considering a wider range of potential determinants of inequality using a consistent methodology in a large sample of countries, and can be viewed as a test of the robustness of these earlier results obtained in smaller and possibly less representative samples of countries. We discuss how our findings relate to these other papers throughout the discussion below. The rest of this paper proceeds as follows. Section 2 describes the data and empirical specification. Section 3 presents our main findings. Section 4 concludes.

2. Empirical Strategy

2.1. *Measuring Income and Income of the Poor*

We measure mean income as real per capita GDP at purchasing power parity in 1985 international dollars, based on an extended version of the Summers–Heston Penn World Tables Version 5.6.[2] In general, this need not be equal to the mean level of household income, due to a variety of reasons ranging from simple measurement error to retained corporate earnings. We nevertheless rely on per capita GDP for two pragmatic reasons. First, for many of the country-year observations for which we have information on income distribution, we do not have corresponding information on mean income from the same source. Second, using per capita GDP helps us to compare our results with the large literature on income distribution and growth that typically follows the same practice. In the absence of evidence of a systematic correlation between the discrepancies between per capita GDP and household income on the one hand, and per capita GDP on the other, we treat these differences as classical measurement error, as discussed further below.[3]

We use two approaches to measuring the income of the poor, where we define the poor as the poorest 20 percent of the population.[4] We are able to obtain information on the share of income accruing to the poorest quintile constructed from nationally representative household surveys for 796 country-year observations covering 137 countries. For these observations, we measure mean income in the poorest quintile directly, as the share of income earned by the poorest quintile times mean income, divided by 0.2. For a further 158 country-year observations we have information on the Gini coefficient but not the first quintile share. For these observations, we assume that the distribution of income is lognormal, and we obtain the share of income accruing to the poorest quintile as the 20th percentile of this distribution.[5]

Our data on income distribution are drawn from four different sources. Our primary source is the UN-WIDER World Income Inequality Database, which is a substantial extension of the income distribution dataset constructed by Deininger and Squire (1996). A total of 706 of our country-year observations are obtained from this source. In addition, we obtain 97 observations originally included in the sample designated as "high-quality" by Deininger and Squire (1996) that do not appear in the UN-WIDER dataset. Our third data source is Chen and Ravallion (2000) who construct measures of income distribution and poverty from 265 household surveys in 83 developing countries. Since the Deininger–Squire and UN-WIDER compilations directly report many of the observations from this and earlier Chen–Ravallion compilations, we obtain only an additional 118 recent observations from this source. Finally, we augment our dataset with 32 observations primarily from developed countries not appearing in the above three sources, that are reported in Lundberg and Squire (2000). This results in an overall sample of 953 observations covering 137 countries over the period 1950–1999. To our knowledge this is the largest dataset used to study the relationship between inequality, incomes, and growth. Details of the geographical composition of the dataset are shown in the first column of Table 1. Definitions and sources for all of the variables used in the paper are provided in a short data appendix.

This dataset forms a highly unbalanced and irregularly spaced panel of observations.

Table 1. Sources for income distribution data.

	Number of Observations		
	Total	Spaced Sample	Changes
By Source			
UN-WIDER World Income Inequality Database	706	289	199
Deininger and Squire High Quality Sample	97	45	28
World Bank Poverty Monitoring Website	118	68	45
Lundberg and Squire (2000)	32	16	13
By Region			
East Asia and Pacific	178	77	22
E. Europe and Central Asia	172	52	66
Latin America and Caribbean	160	88	95
Middle East/North Africa	41	31	24
South Asia	73	28	18
Sub-Saharan Africa	90	59	29
Other	239	83	31
Total	953	418	285

Notes: This table shows the four sources of data on income distribution on which we rely to construct estimates of mean incomes of the poor. Total refers to the total number of annual observations. Spaced sample refers to observations separated by at least five years from each other within countries. Changes refers to the source of the final year for each pair of observations for which it is possible to construct a five-year change within countries in incomes of the poor.

While for a few countries continuous time series of annual observations on income distribution are available for long periods, for most countries only one or a handful of observations are available, with a median number of observations per country of 4. Since our interest is in growth over the medium to long run, and since we do not want the sample to be dominated by those countries where income distribution data happen to be more abundant, we filter the data as follows. For each country we begin with the first available observation, and then move forward in time until we encounter the next observation subject to the constraint that at least five years separate observations, until we have exhausted the available data for that country.[6] This results in an unbalanced and irregularly spaced panel of 418 country-year observations on mean income of the poor separated by at least five years within countries, and spanning 137 countries. The median number of observations per country in this reduced sample is 3. In our econometric estimation (discussed in the following subsection) we restrict the sample further to the set of 285 observations covering 92 countries for which at least two spaced observations on mean income of the poor are available, so that we can consider within-country growth in mean incomes of the poor over periods of at least five years. The median length of these intervals is six years. When we consider the effects of additional control variables, the sample is slightly smaller and varies across specifications depending on data availability. The data sources and geographical composition of these different samples are shown in the second and third columns of Table 1.

As is well known there are substantial difficulties in comparing income distribution data across countries.[7] Countries differ in the coverage of the survey (national versus subnational), in the welfare measure (income versus consumption), the measure of income (gross versus net), and the unit of observation (individuals versus households). We are only able to very imperfectly adjust for these differences. We have restricted our sample to income distribution measures based on nationally representative surveys. For all surveys we have information on whether the welfare measure is income or consumption, and for the majority of these we also know whether the income measure is gross or net of taxes and transfers. While we do have information on whether the recipient unit is the individual or the household, for most of our observations we do not have information on whether the Lorenz curve refers to the fraction of individuals or the fraction of households.[8] As a result, this last piece of information is of little help in adjusting for methodological differences in measures of income distribution across countries. We therefore implement the following very crude adjustment for observable differences in survey type. We pool our sample of 418 observations separated by at least five years, and regress both the Gini coefficient and the first quintile share on a constant, a set of regional dummies, and dummy variables indicating whether the welfare measure is gross income or whether it is consumption. We then subtract the estimated mean difference between these two alternatives and the omitted category to arrive at a set of distribution measures that notionally correspond to the distribution of income net of taxes and transfers.[9] The results of these adjustment regressions are reported in Table 2. As noted in the introduction however, it is clear that very substantial measurement error remains in this income distribution data, and so we cannot rule out the possiblity that our failure to find significant determinants of the income share of the poorest quintile is due to this measurement error.

Table 2. Adjustments to Gini coefficients and income shares.

	Gini Coefficient		Income Share of Bottom Quintile	
	Coefficient	Std. Err.	Coefficient	Std. Err.
Constant	31.160	0.664***	0.072	0.002***
Gross Income Dummy	4.046	1.011***	− 0.011	0.003***
Expenditure Dummy	− 1.397	1.412	0.002	0.003
East Asia and Pacific	4.673	1.088***	− 0.001	0.003
E. Europe and Central Asia	− 2.656	1.502*	0.022	0.004***
Middle East/North Africa	9.095	1.625***	− 0.007	0.004
Latin America and Caribbean	15.550	1.015***	− 0.023	0.003***
South Asia	3.519	1.502**	0.009	0.004**
Sub-Saharan Africa	16.186	1.772***	− 0.018	0.005***

Notes: This table reports the results of a pooled OLS regression of the indicated inequality measures on the indicated variables. Standard errors are White-corrected for heteroskedasticity. * (*) (***) denote significance at the 10 (5) (1) percent levels.

2.2. *Estimation*

In order to examine how incomes of the poor vary with overall incomes, we estimate variants of the following regression of the logarithm of per capita income of the poor (y^P) on the logarithm of average per capita income (y) and a set of additional control variables (X):

$$y_{ct}^P = \alpha_0 + \alpha_1 \cdot y_{ct} + \alpha_2' X_{ct} + \mu_c + \varepsilon_{ct}, \tag{1}$$

where c and t index countries and years, respectively, and $\mu_c + \varepsilon_{ct}$ is a composite error term including unobserved country effects. We have already seen the pooled version of equation (1) with no control variables X_{ct} in the top panel of Figure 1 above. Since incomes of the poor are equal to the the first quintile share times average income divided by 0.2, it is clear that equation (1) is identical to a regression of the log of the first quintile share on average income and a set of control variables:

$$\ln\left(\frac{Q1_{ct}}{0.2}\right) = \alpha_0 + (\alpha_1 - 1) \cdot y_{ct} + \alpha_2' X_{ct} + \mu_c + \varepsilon_{ct}. \tag{2}$$

Moreover, since empirically the log of the first quintile share is almost exactly a linear function of the Gini coefficient, equation (1) is almost equivalent to a regression of a negative constant times the Gini coefficient on average income and a set of control variables.[10]

We are interested in two key parameters from equation (1). The first is α_1, which measures the elasticity of income of the poor with respect to mean income. A value of $\alpha_1 = 1$ indicates that growth in mean income is translated one-for-one into growth in income of the poor. From equation (2), this is equivalent to the observation that the share of income accruing to the poorest quintile does not vary systematically with average incomes ($\alpha_1 - 1 = 0$). Estimates of α_1 greater or less than one indicate that growth more than or less than proportionately benefits those in the poorest quintile. The second parameter of interest is α_2 which measures the impact of other determinants of income of the poor over and above their impact on mean income. Equivalently from equation (2), α_2 measures the impact of these other variables on the share of income accruing to the poorest quintile, holding constant average incomes.

Simple ordinary least squares (OLS) estimation of equation (1) using pooled country-year observations is likely to result in inconsistent parameter estimates for several reasons.[11] Measurement error in average incomes or the other control variables in equation (1) will lead to biases that are difficult to sign except under very restrictive assumptions.[12] Since we consider only a fairly parsimonious set of right-hand side variables in X, omitted determinants of the log quintile share that are correlated with either X or average incomes can also bias our results. Finally, there may be reverse causation from average incomes of the poor to average incomes, or equivalently from the log quintile share to average incomes, as suggested by the large empirical literature which has examined the effects of income distribution on subsequent growth. This literature typically estimates growth regressions with a measure of initial income inequality as an explanatory variable, such as:

$$y_{ct} = \beta_0 + \rho \cdot y_{c,t-k} + \beta_1 \cdot \ln\left(\frac{Q1_{c,t-k}}{0.2}\right) + \beta_2' Z_{c,t-k} + \eta_c + v_{ct}. \tag{3}$$

This literature has found mixed results using different sample and different econometric techniques. On the one hand, Alesina and Rodrik (1994), Persson and Tabellini (1994), Perotti (1996), Barro (2000), and Easterly (2001) find evidence of a negative effect of various measures of inequality on growth (i.e., $\beta_1 > 0$). On the other hand, Forbes (2000) and Li and Zou (1998) both find positive effects of income inequality on growth (i.e., $\beta_1 < 0$).[13] Whatever the true underlying relationship, it is clear that as long as β_1 is not equal to zero, OLS estimation of equations (1) or (2) will yield inconsistent estimates of the parameters of interest. For example, high realizations of μ_c which result in higher incomes of the poor relative to mean income in equation (1) will also raise (lower) mean incomes in equation (3), depending on whether β_1 is greater than (less than) zero. This could induce an upwards (downwards) bias into estimates of the elasticity of incomes of the poor with respect to mean incomes in equation (1).

A final issue in estimating equation (1) is whether we want to identify the parameters of interest using the cross-country or the time-series variation in the data on incomes of the poor, mean incomes, and other variables. An immediate reaction to the presence of unobserved country-specific effects μ_c in equation (1) is to estimate it in first differences.[14] The difficulty with this option is that it forces us to identify our effects of interest using the more limited time-series variation in incomes and income distribution.[15] This raises the possibility that the signal-to-noise ratio in the within-country variation in the data is too unfavorable to allow us to estimate our parameters of interest with any precision. In contrast, the advantage of estimating equation (1) in levels is that we can exploit the large cross-country variation in incomes, income distribution, and policies to identify our effects of interest. The disadvantage of this approach is that the problem of omitted variables is more severe in the cross-section, since in the differenced estimation we have at least managed to dispose of any time-invariant country-specific sources of heterogeneity.

Our solution to this dilemma is to implement a system estimator that combines information in both the levels and changes of the data.[16] In particular, we first difference equation (1) to obtain growth in income of the poor in country c over the period from $t - k(c, t)$ to t as a function of growth in mean income over the same period, and changes in the X variables:

$$
y_{ct}^P - y_{c,t-k(c,t)}^P = \alpha_1 \cdot (y_{ct} - y_{c,t-k(c,t)}) + \alpha_2'(X_{ct} - X_{c,t-k(c,t)}) + (\varepsilon_{ct} - \varepsilon_{c,t-k(c,t)}),
\tag{4}
$$

where $k(c, t)$ denotes the country- and year-specific length of the interval over which the growth rate is calculated. We then estimate equations (1) and (4) as a system, imposing the restriction that the coefficients in the levels and differenced equation are equal. We address the three problems of measurement error, omitted variables, and endogeneity by using appropriate lags of right-hand-side variables as instruments. In particular, in equation (1) we instrument for mean income using growth in mean income over the five years prior to time t. This preceding growth in mean income is by construction correlated with contemporaneous mean income, provided that ρ is not equal to zero in equation (3). Given the vast body of evidence on conditional convergence, this assumption seems reasonable a priori, and we can test the strength of this correlation by examining the corresponding first-stage regressions. Differencing equation (3), it is straightforward to see that past growth is also uncorrelated with the error term in equation (1), provided that ε_{ct} is not correlated over time. In equation (4), we instrument for growth in mean income using the level of mean income at the beginning of the period, and growth in the five years preceding $t - k(c, t)$. Both of these are by construction correlated with growth in mean income over the period from $t - k(c, t)$ to t. Moreover it is straightforward to verify that they are uncorrelated with the error term in equation (4) using the same arguments as before.

In the version of equation (1) without control variables, these instruments provide us with three moment conditions with which to identify two parameters, α_0 and α_1. We combine these moment conditions in a standard generalized method of moments (GMM) estimation procedure to obtain estimates of these parameters. In addition, we adjust the standard errors to allow for heteroskedasticity in the error terms as well as the first-order autocorrelation introduced into the error terms in equation (4) by differencing. Since the model is overidentified we can test the validity of our assumptions that the instruments are uncorrelated with the error terms using tests of overidentifying restrictions.

When we introduce additional X variables into equation (1) we also need to take a stand on whether or not to instrument for these as well. Difficulties with measurement error and omitted variables provide as compelling a reason to instrument for these variables as for income. It is also possible that at least some of the policy variables may respond endogenously to inequality.[17] Nevertheless, in what follows we choose not to instrument for the X variables, for two reasons. First and pragmatically, using appropriate lags of these variables as instruments greatly reduces our sample size. Second, we take some comfort from the fact that tests of overidentifying restrictions pass in the specifications where we instrument for income only, providing indirect evidence that the X variables are not correlated with the error terms. In any case, we find qualitatively quite similar results in the smaller samples where we instrument, and so we only report selected instrumented results for brevity.

3. Results

3.1. Growth is Good for the Poor

We start with our basic specification in which we regress the log of per capita income of the poor on the log of average per capita income, without other controls (equation (1) with $\alpha_2 = 0$). The results of this basic specification are presented in detail in Table 3. The five columns in the top panel provide alternative estimates of equation (1), in turn using information in the levels of the data, the differences of the data, and finally our preferred system estimator which combines the two. The first two columns show the results from estimating equation (1) in levels pooling all of the country-year observations, using OLS and single-equation two-stage least squares (2SLS), respectively. OLS gives a point estimate of the elasticity of income of the poor with respect to mean income of 1.07, which is (just) significantly greater than 1. As discussed in the previous section there are reasons to doubt the simple OLS results. When we instrument for mean income using growth in mean income over the five preceding years as an instrument, the estimated elasticity increases to 1.19. However, this elasticity is much less precisely estimated, and so we do not reject the null hypothesis that $\alpha_1 = 1$. In the first-stage regression for the levels equation, lagged growth is a highly significant predictor of the current level of income, which gives us some confidence in its validity as an instrument.

The third and fourth columns in the top panel of Table 3 show the results of OLS and 2SLS estimation of the differenced equation (4). We obtain a point estimate of the elasticity of income of the poor with respect to mean income of 0.98 using OLS, and a slightly smaller elasticity of 0.91 when we instrument using lagged levels and growth rates of mean income. In both the OLS and 2SLS results we cannot reject the null hypothesis that the elasticity is equal to one. In the first-stage regression for the differenced equation (reported in the second column of the bottom panel), both lagged income and twice-lagged growth are highly significant predictors of growth. Moreover, the differenced equation is overidentified. When we test the validity of the overidentifying restrictions we do not reject the null of a well-specified model for the differenced equation alone at conventional significance levels.

In the last column of Table 3, we combine the information in the levels and differences in the system GMM estimator, using the same instruments as in the single-equation estimates reported earlier. The system estimator delivers a point estimate of the elasticity of 1.008, which is not significantly different from 1. Since the system estimator is based on minimizing a precision-weighted sum of the moment conditions from the levels and differenced data, the estimate of the slope is roughly an average of the slope of the levels and differenced equation, with somewhat more weight on the more-precisely estimated differenced estimate. Since our system estimator is overidentified, we can test and do not reject the null that the instruments are valid, in the sense of being uncorrelated with the corresponding error terms in equations (1) and (4). Finally, the bottom panel of Table 3

Table 3. Basic specification.

	Estimates of Growth Elasticity				
	(1) Levels No Inst	(2) Inst	(3) Differences No Inst	(4) Inst	(5) System
Intercept	−1.762 (0.210)***	−2.720 (1.257)**			−1.215 (0.629)*
Slope	1.072 (0.025)***	1.187 (0.150)***	0.983 (0.076)***	0.913 (0.106)***	1.008 (0.076)***
P-Ho: $\alpha_1 = 1$	0.004	0.213	0.823	0.412	0.916
P-OID				0.174	0.163
T-NOSC					−0.919
# Observations	269	269	269	269	269

	First-Stage Regressions for System	
	Dependent Variable:	
	ln (Income)	Growth
Intercept	8.238 (0.064)***	
Lagged Growth	0.956 (0.293)***	
Lagged Income		0.011 (0.002)***
Twice Lagged Growth		0.284 (0.094)***
P-Zero Slopes	0.007	0.001

Notes: The top panel reports the results of estimating equation (1) (columns 1 and 2), equation (4) (columns 3 and 4), and the system estimator combining the two (column 5). OLS and IV refer to ordinary least squares and instrumental variables estimation of equations (1) and (4). The bottom panel reports the corresponding first-stage regressions for IV estimation of equations (1) and (4). The row labeled P-Ho: $\alpha_1 = 1$ reports the p-value associated with the test of the null hypothesis that $\alpha_1 = 1$. The row labeled P-OID reports the p-value associated with the test of overidentifying restrictions. The row labeled T-NOSC reports the t-statistic for the test of no second-order serial correlation in the differenced residuals. Standard errors are corrected for heteroskedasticity and for the first-order autocorrelation induced by first differencing using a standard Newey–West procedure. * (*) (***) denote significance at the 10 (5) (1) percent levels.

reports the first-stage regressions underlying our estimator, and shows that our instruments have strong explanatory power for the potentially endogenous income and growth regressors.

We next consider a number of variants on this basic specification. First, we add regional dummies to the levels equation, and find that dummies for the East Asia and Pacific, Latin America, Sub-Saharan Africa, and the Middle East and North Africa regions are negative and significant at the 10 percent level or better (first column of Table 4). Since the omitted category consists of the rich countries of Western Europe plus Canada and the United States, these dummies reflect higher average levels of inequality in these regions relative

Table 4. Variants on the basic specification.

	Regional Dummies		Regional Dummies Common Trend		Regional Dummies Slopes Differ by Decade		Regional Dummies Slopes Differ by Region		Regional Dummies Slopes Differ with Income		Regional Dummies Slopes Differ +/- Growth	
	Coefficient	Std. Err.	Coefficient	Std. Err.	Coefficient	Std. Err.	Coefficient	Std. Err.	Coefficient	Std. Err.	Coefficient	Std. Err.
Constant	−0.114	0.876	−0.050	4.824	−0.465	0.698	−4.308	1.421***	−0.762	0.815	−1.254	0.647*
ln (per capita GDP)	0.905	0.094***	1.003	0.139***	0.941	0.079***	1.355	0.153***	0.988	0.196***	1.027	0.070***
EAP	−0.168	0.102*	−0.079	0.143	−0.127	0.088	3.733	1.568**	−0.103	0.064	−0.050	0.081
ECA	−0.023	0.147	0.085	0.202	0.003	0.131	2.965	3.944	0.050	0.115	0.132	0.109
LAC	−0.618	0.121***	−0.512	0.166***	−0.572	0.101***	8.244	3.083***	−0.542	0.095***	−0.490	0.095***
MENA	−0.275	0.140**	−0.152	0.199	−0.246	0.118**	2.213	2.380	−0.189	0.100*	−0.127	0.109
SA	−0.079	0.208	0.128	0.311	0.000	0.166	2.615	1.616	0.055	0.135	0.185	0.154
SSA	−0.685	0.288**	−0.369	0.355	−0.550	0.243**	2.111	2.008	−0.422	0.170**	−0.384	0.210*
Time			0.000	0.003								
$y \times 1970s$					−0.001	0.008						
$y \times 1980s$					0.003	0.010						
$y \times 1990s$					0.005	0.010						
$y \times EAP$							−0.413	0.173**				
$y \times ECA$							−0.290	0.474				
$y \times LAC$							−1.019	0.368***				
$y \times MENA$							−0.243	0.285				
$y \times SA$							−0.239	0.188				
$y \times SSA$							−0.230	0.256				
$y \times y90$									−0.001	0.013		
$y \times$ (Dummy Negative Growth)											0.009	0.008
P-Ho: $\alpha_1 = 1$	0.313		0.983		0.455		0.020		0.949		0.694	
P-OID	0.390		0.240		0.126		0.133		0.209		0.174	
T-NOSC	−0.948		−0.921		−0.938		−1.571		−0.932		−0.907	
# Observations	269		269		269		269		269		269	

Notes: The row labeled P-Ho: $\alpha_1 = 1$ reports the p-value associated with the test of the null hypothesis that $\alpha_1 = 1$. The row labeled P-OID reports the p-value associated with the test of overidentifying restrictions. The row labeled T-NOSC reports the t-statistic for the test of no second-order serial correlation in the differenced residuals. Standard errors are corrected for heteroskedasticity and for the first-order autocorrelation induced by first differencing using a standard Newey–West procedure. * (*) (***) denote significance at the 10 (5) (1) percent levels.

to the rich countries. Including these regional dummies reduces the estimate of the elasticity of average incomes of the poor with respect to average incomes slightly to 0.91, but we still cannot reject the null hypothesis that the slope of this relationship is equal to one (the p-value for the test of this hypothesis is 0.313, and is shown in the fourth-last row of Table 4). We keep the regional dummies in all subsequent regressions.

Next we add a time trend to the regression, in order to capture the possibility that there has been a secular increase or decrease over time in the share of income accruing to the poorest quintile (second column of Table 4). The coefficient on the time trend is statistically insignificant, indicating the absence of systematic evidence of a trend in the share of income of the bottom quintile. Moreover, in this specification we find a point estimate of $\alpha_1 = 1.00$, indicating that average incomes in the bottom quintile rise exactly proportionately with average incomes.

A closely related question is whether the elasticity of incomes of the poor with respect to average incomes has changed over time. In order to allow for the possibility that growth has become either more or less pro-poor in recent years, we augment the basic regression with interactions of income with dummies for the 1970s, 1980s and 1990s. The omitted category is the 1960s and so the estimated coefficients on the interaction terms capture differences in the relationship between average incomes and the share of the poorest quintile relative to this base period. We find that none of these interactions are significant, consistent with the view that the inequality-growth relationship has not changed significantly over time. We again cannot reject the null hypothesis that $\alpha_1 = 1$ ($p = 0.455$).

In the next two columns of Table 4 we examine whether the slope of the relationship between average incomes and incomes of the poorest quintile differs significantly by region or by income level. We first add interactions of each of the regional dummies with average income, in order to allow for the possibility that the effects of growth on the share of income accruing to the poorest quintile differ by region. We find that the coefficients on these interactions with average income all enter negatively, indicating that the elasticity of incomes of the poor with respect to average incomes is highest in the omitted category of the rich countries. In two regions (East Asia/Pacific and Latin America/Caribbean) we find significantly lower slopes than the omitted category of the rich countries. However, we cannot reject at the 5 percent significance level the null hypotheses that all of the region-specific slopes are individually or jointly equal to one.[18]

Another hypothesis regarding the deviations from our general relationship is the Kuznets hypothesis which suggests that inequality rises at low levels of development and only declines as countries pass a certain threshold level of income. In order to allow the relationship between income and the share of the bottom quintile to vary with the level of development, we interact average incomes in equation (1) with real GDP per capita in 1990 for each country. When we do this, we find no evidence that the relationship is significantly different in rich and poor countries, contrary to the Kuznets (1955) hypothesis that inequality increases with income at low levels of development.

In the last column of Table 4 we ask whether the relationship between growth in average incomes and incomes of the poor is different during periods of negative and positive growth. This allows for the possibility that the costs of economic crises are borne disproportionately by poor people. We add an interaction term of average incomes with a dummy variable which takes the value one when growth in average incomes is negative.

These episodes certainly qualify as economic crises since they correspond to negative average annual growth over a period of at least five years. However, the interaction term is tiny and statistically indistinguishable from zero, indicating that there is no evidence that the share of income that goes to the poorest quintile systematically rises or falls during periods of negative growth. Of course, it could still be the case that the same proportional decline in income has a greater impact on the poor if social safety nets are weak, and so crises may well be harder on the poor. But this is not because their incomes tend to fall more than those of other segments of society. A good illustration of this general observation is the recent financial crisis in East Asia in 1997. In Indonesia, the income share of the poorest quintile actually increased slightly between 1996 and 1999, from 8.0 to 9.0 percent, and in Thailand from 6.1 to 6.4 percent between 1996 and 1998, while in Korea it remained essentially unchanged after the crisis relative to before.

3.2. Growth Determinants and Incomes of the Poor

The previous section has documented that average incomes in the bottom quintile tend to rise equiproportionately with average incomes. This finding suggests that a range of policies and institutions that are associated with higher growth will also benefit the poor proportionately. However, it is possible that growth from different sources has differential impact on the poor. In this section we take a number of the measures of policies and institutions that have been identified as pro-growth in the empirical growth literature, and examine whether there is any evidence that any of these variables has disproportionate effects on the poorest quintile. The five indicators that we focus on are inflation, which Fischer (1993) finds to be bad for growth; government consumption, which Easterly and Rebelo (1993) find to be bad for growth; exports and imports relative to GDP, which Frankel and Romer (1999) find to be good for growth; a measure of financial development, which Levine et al. (2000) have shown to have important causal effects on growth; and a measure of the strength of property rights or rule of law. The particular measure is from Kaufmann et al. (1999).[19] The importance of property rights for growth has been established by, among others, Knack and Keefer (1995).

First, we take the basic regression from the first column of Table 4 and add these variables one at a time (shown in the first five columns of Table 5). Since mean income is included in each of these regressions, the effect of these variables that works through overall growth is already captured there. The coefficient on the growth determinant itself therefore captures any differential impact that this variable has on the income of the poor, or equivalently, on the share of income accruing to the poor. In the case of trade volumes, we find a small, negative, and statistically insignificant effect on the income share of the bottom quintile. The same is true for government consumption as a share of GDP, and inflation, where higher values of both are associated with lower income shares of the poorest quintile, although again insignificantly so. The point estimates of the coefficients on the measure of financial development and on rule of law indicate that both of these variables are associated with higher income shares in the poorest quintile, but again, each of these effects is statistically indistinguishable from zero. When we include all five measures together, the coefficients on each are similar to those in the simpler regressions.

Table 5. Growth determinants and incomes of the poor.

	Trade Volumes		Government Consumption/GDP		log(1 + Inflation Rate)		Financial Development		Rule of Law Index		All Growth Variables		All Growth Variables, Instrument	
	Coefficient	Std. Err.	Coefficient	Std. Err.	Coefficient	Std. Err.	Coefficient	Std. Err.	Coefficient	Std. Err.	Coefficient	Std. Err.	Coefficient	Std. Err.
ln (per capita GDP)	**1.094**	**0.108*****	**1.050**	**0.085*****	**1.020**	**0.089*****	**0.995**	**0.119*****	**0.914**	**0.105*****	**1.140**	**0.100*****	**1.020**	**0.128*****
(Export + imports)/GDP	−0.039	0.088									0.023	0.056	−0.067	0.208
Government consumption/GDP			−0.571	0.419							−0.746	0.386*	0.401	1.013
ln(1 + inflation)					−0.136	0.103					−0.163	0.107	−0.216	0.077***
Commercial bank assets/total bank assets							0.032	0.257			−0.209	0.172	0.264	0.282
Rule of law									0.084	0.069	−0.032	0.060	−0.011	0.071
P-Ho: $\alpha_1 = 1$	**0.386**		**0.555**		**0.825**		**0.968**		**0.412**		**0.164**		**0.876**	
P-OID	0.257		0.168		0.159		0.350		0.279		0.393		0.716	
T-NOSC	−0.751		−0.506		−0.261		−0.698		−0.945		−0.762		−0.563	
# Observations	223		237		253		232		268		189		137	

Notes: All regressions include regional dummies. The row labeled P-Ho: $\alpha_1 = 1$ reports the p-value associated with the test of the null hypothesis that $\alpha_1 = 1$. The row labeled p-OID reports the P-value associated with the test of overidentifying restrictions. The row labeled T-NOSC reports the t-statistic for the test of no second-order serial correlation in the differened residuals. Standard errors are corrected for heteroskedasticity and for the first-order autocorrelation induced by first differencing using a standard Newey–West procedure. * (*) (***) denote significance at the 10 (5) (1) percent levels.

However, government consumption as a share of GDP now has an estimated effect on the income share of the poorest that is negative and significant at the 10 percent level. In addition, inflation continues to have a negative effect, which just falls short of significance at the 10 percent level.[20]

Finally, in the last column of Table 5, we report results which treat these measures of policy as endogenous to the income share of the poorest quintile, and use appropriate lags of these policy variables as instruments. As discussed above, this substantially reduces our sample size. However, we find results that are qualitatively not too different in this smaller sample. The main differences are that the negative effect of inflation becomes larger and more significant, while the effect of government consumption changes sign and becomes insignificant. Since we find throughout the rest of this paper that instrumented and uninstrumented results are generally quite similar, for reasons of space we report only the uninstrumented results below.

Our empirical specification only allows us to identify any differential effect of these macroeconomic and institutional variables on incomes of the poor relative to average incomes. What about the overall effect of these variables, which combines their effects on growth with their effects on income distribution? In order to answer this question we also require estimates of the effects of these variables on growth based on a regression like equation (3). Since equation (3) includes a measure of income inequality as one of the determinants of growth, we estimate it using the same panel of irregularly spaced data on average incomes and other variables that we have been using thus far.[21] Clearly this limited dataset is not ideal for estimating growth regressions, since our sample is very restricted by the relative scarcity of income distribution data. Nevertheless, it is useful to estimate this equation in our data set for consistency with the previous results, and also to verify that the main findings of the cross-country literature on economic growth are present in our sample.

We include in the vector of additional explanatory variables a measure of the stock of human capital (years of secondary schooling per worker) as well as the five growth determinants from Table 5. We also include the human capital measure in order to make our growth regression comparable to that of Forbes (2000) who applies similar econometric techniques in a similar panel data set in order to study the effect of inequality on growth. In order to reduce concerns about endogeneity of these variables with respect to growth, we enter each of them as an average over the five years prior to year $t - k$. We estimate the growth regression in equation (3) using the same system estimator that combines information in the levels and differences of the data, although our choice of lags as instruments is slightly different from before.[22] In the levels equation, we instrument for lagged income with growth in the preceding five years, and we do not need to instrument for the remaining growth determinants under the assumption that they are predetermined with respect to the error term v_{ct}. In the differenced equation we instrument for lagged growth with the twice-lagged log-level of income, and for the remaining variables with their twice-lagged levels.

The results of this growth regression are reported in the first column of Table 6. Most of the variables enter significantly and with the expected signs. Secondary education, financial development, and better rule of law are all positively and significantly associated with growth. Higher levels of government consumption and inflation are both negatively

Table 6. Growth and distribution effects.

	Growth Regression		Income of Poor Regression		Standard Deviation	Growth Effect	Distribution Effect
	Coefficient	Std. Err.	Coefficient	Std. Err.			
Income			1.140	0.101***			
Lagged income	0.668	0.169***					
Lagged inequality	− 0.089	0.062					
Secondary education	0.097	0.057*					
Trade volumes	0.045	0.074	0.024	0.056	0.280	0.035	0.012
Inflation	− 0.145	0.131	− 0.162	0.107	0.275	− 0.104	− 0.059
Government consumption	− 0.973	0.415**	− 0.744	0.387*	0.054	− 0.143	− 0.060
Financial development	0.374	0.167**	− 0.208	0.172	0.153	0.175	− 0.007
Rule of law	0.180	0.082**	− 0.032	0.060	0.250	0.133	0.011

Notes: The first column reports the results of estimating the growth regression in Equation All regressions include regional dummies. The row labeled P-Ho: $\alpha_1 = 1$ reports the *p*-value associated with the test of the null hypothesis that $\alpha_1 = 1$. The row labeled P-OID reports the *p*-value associated with the test of overidentifying restrictions. The row labeled T-NOSC reports the *t*-statistic for the test of no second-order serial correlation in the differenced residuals. Standard errors are corrected for heteroskedasticity and for the first-order autocorrelation induced by first differencing using a standard Newey–West procedure. * (*) (***) denote significance at the 10 (5) (1) percent levels.

associated with growth, although only the former is statistically significant. Trade volumes are positively associated with growth, although not significantly so, possibly reflecting the relatively small sample on which the estimates are based (the sample of observations is considerably smaller than in Table 5 given the requirement of additional lags of right-hand side variables to use as instruments). Interestingly, the log of the first quintile share enters negatively (although not significantly), consistent with the finding of Forbes (2000) that greater inequality is associated with higher growth.

We next combine these estimates with the estimates of equation (1) to arrive at the cumulative effect of these growth determinants on incomes of the poor. From equation (1) we can express the effect of a permanent increase in each of the growth determinants on the level of average incomes of the poor as:

$$\frac{\partial y_{ct}^P}{\partial X_{ct}} = \frac{\partial y_{ct}}{\partial X_{ct}} + \left((\alpha_1 - 1) \cdot \frac{\partial y_{ct}}{\partial X_{ct}} + \alpha_2 \right), \qquad (5)$$

where $\partial y_{ct}/\partial X_{ct}$ denotes the impact on average incomes of this permanent change in X. The first term captures the effect on incomes of the poor of a change in one of the determinants of growth, holding constant the distribution of income. We refer to this as the "growth effect" of this variable. The second term captures the effects of a change in one of the determinants of growth on incomes of the poor through changes in the distribution of income. This consists of two pieces: (i) the difference between the estimated income elasticity and one times the growth effect, i.e., the extent to which growth in average incomes raises or lowers the share of income accruing to the poorest quintile; and (ii) the direct effects of policies on incomes of the poor in equation (1).

In order to evaluate equation (5) we need an expression for the growth effect term. We obtain this by solving equations (1) and (3) for the dynamics of average income, and obtain:

$$y_{ct} = \beta_0 + \beta_1 \cdot \alpha_0 + (\rho + \beta_1 \cdot \alpha_1) \cdot y_{c,t-k} + (\beta_1 \cdot \alpha_2 + \beta_2)' X_{c,t-k} + \eta_c$$
$$+ \beta_1 \cdot \mu_c + v_{ct} + \beta_1 \cdot \varepsilon_{ct}. \tag{6}$$

Iterating equation (6) forward, we find that the estimated long-run effect on the level of income of a permanent change in one of the elements in X is:

$$\frac{\partial y_{ct}}{\partial X_{ct}} = \frac{\beta_1 \cdot \alpha_2 + \beta_2}{1 - (\rho + \beta_1 \cdot \alpha_2)}. \tag{7}$$

The remaining columns of Table 6 put all these pieces together. The second column repeats the results reported in the penultimate column of Table 5. The next column reports the standard deviations of each of the variables of interest, so that we can calculate the impact on incomes of the poor of a one-standard deviation permanent increase in each variable.[23] The remaining columns report the growth and distribution effects of these changes, which are also summarized graphically in Figure 2. The main story here is that the growth effects are large and the distribution effects are small. Improvements in rule of law and greater financial development of the magnitudes considered here, as well as reductions in government consumption and lower inflation all raise incomes in the long run by 15–20 percent. The point estimate for more trade openness is at the low end of existing results in the literature: about a 5 percent increase in income from a one standard deviation increase in openness. This should therefore be viewed as a rather conservative estimate of the benefit of openness on incomes of the poor. In contrast, the effects of these policies that operate through their effects on changes in the distribution of income are much smaller in magnitude, and with the exception of financial development work in the same direction as the growth effects.

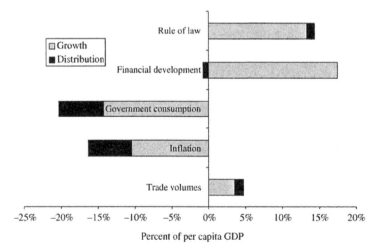

Figure 2. Growth and distribution effects of policies.

3.3. Globalization and the Poor

One possibly surprising result in Table 5 is the lack of any evidence of a significant negative impact of openness to international trade on incomes of the poor. While this is consistent with the finding of Edwards (1997) who also finds no evidence of a relationship between various measures of trade openness and inequality in a sample of 44 countries, a number of other recent papers have found evidence that openness is associated with higher inequality. Barro (2000) finds that trade volumes are significantly positively associated with the Gini coefficient in a sample of 64 countries, and that the disequalizing effect of openness is greater in poor countries. In a panel data set of 320 irregularly spaced annual observations covering 34 countries, Spilimbergo et al. (1999) find that several measures of trade openness are associated with higher inequality, and that this effect is lower in countries where land and capital are abundant and higher where skills are abundant. Lundberg and Squire (2000) consider a panel of 119 quinquennial observations covering 38 countries and find that an increase from zero to one in the Sachs–Warner openness index is associated with a 9.5 point increase in the Gini index, which is significant at the 10 percent level.

Several factors may contribute to the difference between these findings and ours, including (i) differences in the measure of inequality (all the previous studies consider the Gini index while we focus on the income share of the poorest quintile, although given the high correlation between the two this factor is least likely to be important); (ii) differences in the sample of countries (with the exception of the paper by Barro, all of the papers cited above restrict attention to considerably smaller and possibly non-representative samples of countries than the 76 countries which appear in our basic openness regression, and in addition the paper by Spilimbergo et al. uses all available annual observations on inequality with the result that countries with regular household surveys tend to be heavily overrepresented in the sample of pooled observations); (iii) differences in the measure of openness (Lundberg and Squire, 2000, for example focus on the Sachs–Warner index of openness which has been criticized for proxying the overall policy environment rather than openness *per se*[24]); (iv) differences in econometric specification and technique.

A complete accounting of which of these factors contribute to the differences in results is beyond the scope of this short section. However, several obvious extensions of our basic model can be deployed to make our specification more comparable to these other studies. First, we consider several different measures of openness, some of which correspond more closely with those used in the other studies mentioned above. We first (like Barro, 2000, and Spilimbergo et al., 1999) purge our measure of trade volumes of the geographical determinants of trade, by regressing it on a trade-weighted measure of distance from trading partners, and a measure of country size and taking the residuals as an adjusted measure of trade volumes.[25] Since these geographical factors are time invariant, this will only influence our results to the extent that they are driven by the cross-country variation in the data and to the extent that these geographical determinants of trade volumes are also correlated with the share of income of the poorest quintile. Second, we use the Sachs–Warner index in order to compare our results more closely with those of Lundberg and Squire (2000). Finally, we also consider three other measures of openness not considered by the above authors: collected import taxes as a share of imports, a dummy variable taking the value one if the country is a member of the World Trade Organization (or its predecessor the GATT), and a dummy variable taking the value one if the country has restrictions on international capital movements as reported in the International Monetary Fund's Report on Exchange Arrangements and Exchange Controls.

We also consider two variants on our basic specification. First, in order to capture the possibility that greater openness has differential effects at different levels of development, we introduce an interaction of the openness measures with the log-level of real GDP per capita in 1990 for each country. Given the high correlation in levels between per capita income and capital per worker, this interaction may be thought of as capturing in a very crude way the possibility that the effects of trade on inequality depend on countries' relative factor abundance. The second elaboration we consider is to add an interaction of openness with the logarithm of arable land per capita, as well as adding this variable directly. This allows a more general formulation of the hypothesis that the effects of openness depend on countries' factor endowments.

The results of these extensions are presented in Table 7. Each of the columns of Table 7 corresponds to a different measure of openness, and the three horizontal panels correspond to the three variants discussed above. Two main results emerge from this table. First, in all of the specifications considered below, we continue to find that average incomes of the poor rise proportionately with average incomes: in each regression, we do not reject the null hypothesis that the coefficient on average incomes is equal to one. This indicates that our previous results on the lack of any significant association between average incomes and the log first quintile share are robust to the inclusion of these additional control variables. Second, we find no evidence whatsoever of a significant negative relationship between any of these measures of openness and average incomes of the poor. In all but one case, we cannot reject the null hypothesis that the relevant openness measure is not significantly associated with the income share of the bottom quintile, holding constant average incomes. The only exception to this overall pattern is the measure of capital controls, where the presence of capital controls is significantly (at the 10 percent level) associated with a lower income share of the poorest quintile. Overall, however, we conclude from this table that there is very little evidence of a significant relationship between the income share of the poorest quintile and a wide range of measures of exposure to the international economy. The only other finding of interest in this table is unrelated to the question of openness and incomes of the poor. In the bottom panel where we include arable land per capita and its interaction with openness measures, we find some evidence that countries with greater arable land per worker have a lower income share of the poorest quintile. This is consistent with Leamer et al. (1999) who find that cropland per capita is significantly associated with higher inequality in a cross-section of 49 countries.

3.4. Other Determinants of Incomes of the Poor

Finally we consider a number of other factors that may have direct effects on incomes of the poor through their effect on income distribution. We consider four such variables: primary educational attainment, social spending, agricultural productivity, and formal democratic institutions. Of these four variables, only the primary education variable tends

Table 7. Openess and incomes of the poor.

	Trade Volumes		Adjusted Trade Volumes		Sachs–Warner Trade Policy Index		Import Taxes As Share of Imports		Dummy for WTO Membership		Dummy for Capital Controls	
	Coefficient	Std. Err.	Coefficient	Std. Err.	Coefficient	Std. Err.	Coefficient	Std. Err.	Coefficient	Std. Err.	Coefficient	Std. Err.
Basic												
ln (per capita GDP)	**1.094**	**0.108*****	**1.047**	**0.133*****	**1.077**	**0.092*****	**0.936**	**0.136*****	**0.917**	**0.104*****	**0.869**	**0.116*****
Openess measure	−0.039	0.088	−0.038	0.167	−0.071	0.065	−0.161	0.358	0.021	0.043	−0.090	0.051*
P-Ho: $\alpha_1 = 1$	**0.386**		**0.724**		**0.407**		**0.638**		**0.428**		**0.259**	
P-OID	0.257		0.135		0.431		0.074		0.425		0.183	
T-NOSC	−0.751		−0.767		−0.677		1.263		−0.998		−1.084	
# Observations	223		213		234		137		269		208	
Interaction with per capita GDP												
ln (per capita GDP)	**1.102**	**0.092*****	**0.991**	**0.126*****	**1.066**	**0.076*****	**1.013**	**0.082*****	**1.012**	**0.078*****	**0.969**	**0.084*****
Openess measure	−0.323	1.363	1.188	1.601	0.237	0.573	0.604	3.133	−0.026	0.558	−0.515	0.587
Openess measure × ln (per capita GDP)	0.030	0.146	−0.123	0.169	−0.036	0.072	−0.085	0.396	0.002	0.070	0.052	0.064
P-Ho: $\alpha_1 = 1$	**0.267**		**0.942**		**0.386**		**0.873**		**0.876**		**0.708**	
P-OID	0.218		0.144		0.567		0.126		0.226		0.121	
T-NOSC	−0.742		−0.816		−0.696		1.253		−0.905		−1.005	
# Observations	223		213		234		137		269		208	
Interaction with per capita GDP and land												
ln (per capita GDP)	**1.120**	**0.105*****	**0.901**	**0.099*****	**1.046**	**0.084*****	**1.063**	**0.083*****	**1.101**	**0.072*****	**1.009**	**0.081*****
Openess measure	0.304	1.780	1.161	1.485	0.109	0.605	2.552	2.858	0.513	0.569	−0.574	0.607
ln(arable land/worker)	−0.090	0.031***	−0.086	0.023***	−0.018	0.032	−0.037	0.029	−0.054	0.039	−0.038	0.025
Openess measure × ln (per capita GDP)	−0.036	0.198	−0.074	0.170	−0.024	0.075	−0.378	0.385	−0.066	0.072	0.050	0.066
Openess measure × ln (arable land per worker)	0.061	0.070	0.245	0.111**	−0.041	0.035	−0.366	0.262	0.016	0.039	−0.023	0.031
P-Ho: $\alpha_1 = 1$	**0.253**		**0.322**		**0.582**		**0.443**		**0.163**		**0.915**	
P-OID	0.030		0.062		0.267		0.082		0.208		0.095	
T-NOSC	−0.755		−0.896		−1.134		0.421		−1.019		−1.492	
# Observations	207		207		219		131		243		193	

Notes: All regressions include regional dummies. The row labeled P-Ho: $\alpha_1 = 1$ reports the *p*-value associated with the test of the null hypothesis that $\alpha_1 = 1$. The row labeled P-OID reports the *p*-value associated with the test of overidentifying restrictions. The row labeled T-NOSC reports the *t*-statistic for the test of no second-order serial correlation in the differenced residuals. Standard errors are corrected for heteroskedasticity and for the first-order autocorrelation induced by first differencing using a standard Newey–West procedure. * (*) (***) denote significance at the 10 (5) (1) percent levels.

Table 8. Other determinants of incomes of the poor.

	Year Primary Education		Social Spending		Agricultural Productivity		Voice		Voice with Macro Controls	
	Coefficient	Std. Err.	Coefficient	Std. Err.	Coefficient	Std. Err.	Coefficient	Std. Err.	Coefficient	Std. Err.
ln(per capita GDP)	**1.067**	**0.088***	**1.025**	**0.101***	**0.985**	**0.104***	**0.933**	**0.095***	**1.117**	**0.098***
Years primary education	0.014	0.031								
Government consumption/GDP			−1.553	0.547***						
Social spending/Total public spending			−0.664	0.429						
Agricultural relative productivity					0.060	0.081				
Voice							0.095	0.053*	0.029	0.058
P-Ho: $\alpha_1 = 1$	**0.448**		**0.803**		**0.886**		**0.480**		**0.233**	
P-OID	0.213		0.028		0.166		0.302		0.419	
T-NOSC	−0.384		0.594		−0.837		−0.970		−0.767	
# Observations	222		111		197		265		207	

Notes: All regressions include regional dummies. The row labeled P-Ho: $\alpha_1 = 1$ reports the *p*-value associated with the test of the null hypothesis that $\alpha_1 = 1$. The row labeled P-OID reports the *p*-value associated with the test of overidentifying restrictions. The row labeled T-NOSC reports the *t*-statistic for the test of no second-order serial correlation in the differenced residuals. Standard errors are corrected for heteroskedasticity and for the first-order autocorrelation induced by first differencing using a standard Newey–West procedure. * (*) (***) denote significance at the 10 (5) (1) percent levels.

to be significantly correlated with economic growth, and even here recent evidence suggests that much of this correlation reflects reverse causation from growth to greater schooling (Bils and Klenow, 2000).

However, these policies may be especially important for the poor. Consider for example primary enrollment rates. Most of the countries in the sample are developing countries in which deviations from complete primary school enrollments are most likely to reflect the low enrollment among the poorest in society. This in turn may be an important factor influencing the extent to which the poor participate in growth. Similarly, depending on the extent to which public spending on health and education is effective and well-targeted towards poor people, a greater share of social spending in public spending can be associated with better outcomes for poor people. Greater labor productivity in agriculture relative to the rest of the economy may benefit poor people disproportionately to the extent that the poor are more likely to live in rural areas and derive their livelihood from agriculture. And finally, formal democratic institutions may matter to the extent that they give voice to poor people in the policymaking process.

Table 8 reports the results we obtain adding these variables to the basic specification of Table 4. We find that while years of primary education and relative productivity in agriculture both enter positively, neither is significant at conventional levels. In the regression with social spending, we also include overall government consumption in order to capture both the level and compositional effects of public spending. Overall government spending remains negatively associated with incomes of the poor, and the share of this spending devoted to health and education does not enter significantly. This may not be very surprising, since in many developing countries, these social expenditures often benefit the middle class and the rich primarily, and the simple share of public spending on the social sectors is not a good measure of whether government policy and spending is particularly pro-poor.[26] Finally, the measure of formal democratic institutions enters positively and significantly (although only at the 10 percent level). However, this result is not very robust. In our large sample of developed and developing countries, measures of formal democratic institutions tend to be significantly correlated with other aspects of institutional quality, especially the rule of law index considered earlier. When we include the other growth determinants in the regression, the coefficient on the index of democratic institutions is no longer significant.

4. Conclusions

Average incomes of the poorest fifth of a country on average rise or fall at the same rate as average incomes. This is a consequence of the strong empirical regularity that the share of income of the poorest fifth does not vary systematically with average incomes, in a large sample of countries spanning the past four decades. This relationship holds across regions and income levels, and in normal times as well as during crises. We also find that a variety of pro-growth macroeconomic policies, such as low inflation, moderate size of government, sound financial development, respect for the rule of law, and openness to international trade, raise average incomes with little systematic effect on the distribution of income. This supports the view that a basic policy package of private property rights, fiscal discipline, macroeconomic stability, and openness to trade on average increases the income of the poor to the same extent that it increases the income of the other households in society. It is worth emphasizing that our evidence does not suggest a "trickle-down" process or sequencing in which the rich get richer first and eventually benefits trickle down to the poor. The evidence, to the contrary, is that private property rights, stability, and openness contemporaneously create a good environment for poor households—and everyone else—to increase their production and income. On the other hand, we find little evidence that formal democratic institutions or a large degree of government spending on social services systematically affect incomes of the poor.

Our findings do not imply that growth is all that is needed to improve the lives of the poor. Rather, we simply emphasize that growth on average does benefit the poor as much as anyone else in society, and so standard growth-enhancing policies should be at the center of any effective poverty reduction strategy. This also does not mean that the potential distributional effects of growth, or the policies that support growth, can or should be ignored. Our results do not imply that the income share of the poorest quintile is immutable—rather, we simply are unable to relate the changes across countries and over time in this income share to average incomes, or to a variety of proxies for policies and institutions that matter for growth and poverty reduction. This may simply be because any effects of these policies on the income share of the poorest quintile are small relative to the substantial measurement error in the very imperfect available income distribution data we are forced to rely upon. It may also be due to the inability of our simple empirical models to capture the complex interactions between inequality and growth suggested by some theoretical models. In short, existing cross-country evidence—including our own—provides disappointingly little guidance as to what mix of growth-oriented policies might especially benefit the poorest in society. But our evidence does strongly suggest that economic growth and the policies and institutions that support it on average benefit the poorest in society as much as anyone else.

Appendix: Variable Definitions and Data Sources

Variable	Source	Comments
Real GDP Per Capita	Summers and Heston Penn World Tables, World Bank Data	Constant 1985 US dollars. Extended to 1998 using constant price local currency growth rates. Extended cross-sectionally as described in Kraay, Loayza, Serven and Ventura (2000).
First Quintile Share	UN-WIDER (2000), Deininger and Squire (1996), Ravallion and Chen (2000), Lundberg and Squire (2000)	Combination of data from different sources described in text.

Variable	Source	Comments
Gini Coefficient	UN-WIDER (2000), Deininger and Squire (1996), Ravallion and Chen (2000), Lundberg and Squire (2000)	Combination of data from different sources described in text.
(Exports + Imports)/GDP	World Bank Data, Summers and Heston Penn World Tables	Exports and imports are in constant 1985 US dollars at market exchange rates. Denominator is in constant 1985 dollars at PPP.
Government Consumption/GDP	World Bank Data	Numerator and denominator are in current local currency units.
ln(1+inflation)	World Bank Data	Inflation is CPI-based where available, otherwise use growth of GDP deflator.
Commercial Bank Assets/Total Bank Assets	Beck, Demirguc-Kunt, and Levine (1999)	
Rule of Law	Kaufmann, Kraay and Zoido-Lobaton (1999).	Index, greater values indicate better rule of law.
Secondary Education	Barro and Lee (2000)	Stock of years of secondary education.
Frankel-Romer Distance Measure	Frankel and Romer (1999)	Trade-weighted average of distance from trading partners.
Population	World Bank Data	
Sachs-Warner Index	Sachs and Warner (1995)	
Import Taxes/Total Imports	World Bank Data	Data on import taxes in numerator originally from IMF Government Finance Statistics. Numerator and denominator in current local currency units.
WTO Membership Dummy	www.wto.org	
Capital Controls Dummy	International Monetary Fund Report on Exchange Arrangements and Exchange Controls, various issues.	
Years Primary Education	Barro and Lee (2000)	Stock of years of primary education
Social Spending/Total Public Spending	Government Finance Statistics	
Arable Land Per Worker	World Bank Data	Total arable land in hectares divided by population aged 15–64.
Agricultural Relative Labor Productivity	World Bank Data	Current price share of agriculture in GDP divided by share of workforce in agriculture.

Note: The dataset used in this paper is available at www.worldbank.org/research/growth.

Acknowledgments

We are grateful to Dennis Tao for excellent research assistance, and to two anonymous referees and the editor of this journal for helpful comments. This paper and the accompanying dataset are available at www.worldbank.org/research/growth. The opinions expressed here are the authors' and do not necessarily reflect those of the World Bank, its Executive Directors, or the countries they represent.

Notes

1. For example, economic growth might raise earnings inequality, but if earnings of the poor rise fast enough, credit constraints that limit educational opportunities for the poor become less binding, thus offsetting the initial effects on inequality. See Galor and Zeira (1993) for an early reference on the links between credit constraints, inequality, and growth.

2. We begin with the Summers and Heston Penn World Tables Version 5.6, which reports data on real per capita GDP adjusted for differences in purchasing power parity through 1992 for most of the 156 countries included in that dataset. We use the growth rates of constant price local currency per capita GDP from the World Bank to extend these forward through 1997. For a further set of 29 mostly transition economies not included in the Penn World Tables we have data on constant price GDP in local currency units. For these countries we obtain an estimate of PPP exchange rate from the fitted values of a regression of PPP exchange rates on the logarithm of GDP per capita at PPP. We use these to obtain a benchmark PPP GDP figure for 1990, and then use growth rates of constant price local currency GDP to extend forward and backward from this benchmark. While these extrapolations are necessarily crude, they do not matter much for our results. As discussed below, the statistical identification in the paper is based primarily on within-country changes in incomes and incomes of the poor, which are unaffected by adjustments to the levels of the data.

3. Ravallion (2001a) provides an extensive discussion of sources of discrepancies between national accounts and household survey measures of living standards and finds that, with the exception of the transition economies of Eastern Europe and the Former Soviet Union, growth rates of national accounts measures track growth rates of household survey measures fairly closely on average.

4. At least three other measures of welfare of the poor have been used in this literature. First, one could define "the poor" as those below a fixed poverty line such as the dollar-a-day poverty line used by the World Bank, and measure average incomes of those below the poverty line, as is done by Ali and Elbadawi (2001). The relationship between growth in average incomes and growth in this measure of average incomes of the poor is much more difficult to interpret. For example, if the distribution of income is very steep near the poverty line, distribution-neutral growth in average incomes will lift a large fraction of the population from just below to just above the poverty line with the result that average incomes of those below the poverty line fall. Not surprisingly in light of their different definition, these authors find an elasticity of incomes of the poor with respect to average incomes that is less than one. Second, Foster and Székely (2001) measure incomes of the poor using a "generalized mean" which assigns greater weight to the poorest in society and is closely related to the Atkinson class of inequality measures. They find that the greater is the weight assigned to the incomes of the poor in the generalized mean, the lower is the elasticity of incomes of the poor to average incomes. However, Kraay and Ravallion (2001) show that this result is likely to be an artifact of the greater sensitivity to measurement error of the Atkinson class of inequality measures as the degree of inequality-aversion increases. Finally, a number of papers have examined how the fraction of the population below some pre-specified poverty line varies with average income. See, for example, Ravallion (1997, 2001b) and Ravallion and Chen (1997). These papers generally find a strong negative relationship between growth and the change in the headcount.

5. If the distribution of income is lognormal, i.e., log per capita income $\sim N(\mu,\sigma)$, and the Gini coefficient on a scale from 0 to 100 is G, the standard deviation of this lognormal distribution is given by

$$\sigma = \sqrt{2} \cdot \Phi^{-1}\left(\frac{1 + G/100}{2}\right)$$

where $\Phi(\cdot)$ denotes the cumulative normal distribution function. (Aitchinson and Brown, 1966). Using the properties of the mean of the truncated lognormal distribution (e.g., Johnston, Kotz and Balakrishnan, 1994) the 20th percentile of this distribution is given by $\Phi(\Phi^{-1}(0.2) - \sigma)$.

6. We prefer this method of filtering the data over the alternative of simply taking quinquennial or decadal averages since our method avoids the unnecessary introduction of noise into the timing of the distribution data and the other variables we consider. Since one of the most interesting of these, income growth, is very volatile, this mismatch in timing is potentially problematic.

7. See Atkinson and Brandolini (1999) for a detailed discussion of these issues.

8. This information is only available for the Chen–Ravallion dataset which exclusively refers to individuals and for which the Lorenz curve is consistently constructed using the fraction of individuals on the horizontal axis.

9. Our main results do not change substantially if we use three other possibilities: (1) ignoring differences in survey type, (2) including dummy variables for survey type as strictly exogenous right-hand side variables in our regressions, or (3) adding country fixed effects to the adjustment regression so that the mean differences in survey type are estimated from the very limited within-country variation in survey type.

10. In our sample of spaced observations, a regression of the log first quintile share on the Gini coefficient delivers a slope of -23.3 with an R^2 of 0.80.

11. It should also be clear that OLS standard errors will be inconsistent given the cross-observation correlations induced by the unobserved country-specific effect.

12. While at first glance it may appear that measurement error in per capita income (which is also used to construct our measure of incomes of the poor) will bias the coefficient on per capita income towards one in equation (1), this is not the case. From equation (2) (which of course yields identical estimates of the parameters of interest as does equation (1)) it is clear that we only have a problem to the extent that measurement error in the first quintile share is correlated with average income. Since our data on income distribution and average income are drawn from different sources, there is no a priori reason to expect such a correlation. When average income is taken from the same household survey, under plausible assumptions even measurement error in both variables will not lead to inconsistent coefficient estimates (Chen and Ravallion, 1997).

13. While we follow most of the empirical literature in specifying a linear relation between inequality and growth in equation (3), it is worth noting that this need not be the case. Bannerjee and Duflo (1999) present some simple models and empirical evidence that changes in inequality in either direction lower growth. Galor and Moav (2001) develop a theoretical model in which inequality raises growth at low levels of development (where returns to physical capital are high, and so a reallocation of wealth to richer households with higher saving propensities raises growth), but lowers growth at higher levels of development (where returns to human capital are high, and so a reallocation of wealth to richer households makes it more difficult for poor households to invest in education).

14. Alternatively one could enter fixed effects, but this requires the much stronger assumption that the error terms are uncorrelated with the right-hand side variables at all leads and lags.

15. Li et al. (1998) document the much greater variability of income distribution across countries compared to within countries. In our sample of irregularly spaced observations, the standard deviation of the Gini coefficient pooling all observations in levels is 9.4. In contrast the standard deviation of changes in the Gini coefficient is 4.7 (an average annual change of 0.67 times an average number of years over which the change is calculated of 7).

16. This type of estimator has been proposed in a dynamic panel context by Arellano and Bover (1995) and evaluated by Blundell and Bond (1998).

17. For example Easterly (2001) finds an effect of inequality on inflation and financial development, but not openness to international trade.

18. The estimated coefficients imply an elasticity of incomes of the poor with respect to average incomes in Latin America of 0.33 which is very low. This somewhat surprising result appears not to be very robust and may be attributable to the unusually poor performance of our instruments in this particular subsample of countries.

Uninstrumented results for this region alone produce a slope of 0.98 with a standard error of 0.06, which is more consistent with our priors. Moreover, Foster and Székely (2001) find an elasticity of average incomes of the bottom quintile with respect to average incomes statistically indistinguishable from one in a sample consisting primarily of Latin American countries.

19. This particular measure of institutional quality refers to the period 1997–98 and does not vary over time. We therefore can only identify the effects of this variable using the cross-country variation in our data using the levels equation.

20. This particular result is primarily driven by a small number of very high inflation episodes in our sample. However, it is consistent with several existing findings: Agenor (1998) finds an adverse effect of inflation on the poverty rate, using a cross-section of 38 countries; Easterly and Fischer (2000) show that the poor are more likely to rate inflation as a top national concern, using survey data on 31,869 households in 38 countries; and Datt and Ravallion (1999) find evidence that inflation is a significant determinant of poverty using data for Indian states.

21. Since our panel is irregularly spaced, the coefficient on lagged income in the growth regression should in principle be a function of the length of the interval over which growth is calculated. There are two ways to address this issue. In what follows below, we simply restrict attention to the vast majority of our observations which correspond to growth spells between 5 and 7 years long, and then ignore the dependence of this coefficient on the length of the growth interval. The alternative approach is to introduce this dependence explicitly by assuming that the coefficient on lagged income is $\rho^{k(c,t)}$. Doing so yields very similar results to those reported here.

22. See, for example, Levine et al. (2000) for a similar application of this econometric technique to cross-country growth regressions.

23. The only exception is the rule of law index which by construction has a standard deviation of one. Since perceptions of the rule of law tend to change only very slowly over time, we consider a smaller change of 0.25, which still delivers very large estimated growth effects.

24. See, for example, the criticism of Rodriguez and Rodrik (2000), who note that most of the explanatory power of the Sachs–Warner index derives from the components that measure the black market premium on foreign exchange and whether the state holds a monopoly on exports.

25. Specifically, we use the instrument proposed by Frankel and Romer (1999) and the logarithm of population in 1990 as right-hand side variables in a pooled OLS regression.

26. Existing evidence on the effects of social spending is mixed. Bidani and Ravallion (1997) do find a statistically significant impact of health expenditures on the poor (defined in absolute terms as the share of the population with income below one dollar per day) in a cross-section of 35 developing countries, using a different methodology. Gouyette and Pestiau (1999) find a simple bivariate association between income inequality and social spending in a set of 13 OECD economies. In contrast, Filmer and Pritchett (1997) find little relationship between public health spending and health outcomes such as infant mortality, raising questions about whether such spending benefits the poor.

References

Ali, A. G. A., and I. Elbadawi. (2001). "Growth Could Be Good for the Poor," Manuscript, Arab Planning Institute and the World Bank.

Aitchinson, J., and J. A. C. Brown. (1966). *The Lognormal Distribution*. Cambridge: Cambridge University Press.

Agenor, P.-R. (1998). "Stabilization Policies, Poverty, and the Labour Market," Manuscript, International Monetary Fund and the World Bank.

Alesina, A., and D. Rodrik. (1994). "Distributive Politics and Economic Growth," *Quarterly Journal of Economics* 109(2), 465–490.

Arellano, M., and O. Bover. (1995). "Another Look at the Instrumental-Variable Estimation of Error-Components Models," *Journal of Econometrics* 68, 29–52.

Atkinson, A. B., and A. Brandolini. (1999). "Promise and Pitfalls in the Use of 'Secondary' Data-Sets: Income Inequality in OECD Countries," Manuscript. Nuffield College, Oxford and Banca d'Italia: Research Department.

Beck, T., A. Demirguc-Kunt, and Ross Levine. (1999). "A New Database on Financial Development and Structure," World Bank Policy Research Department Working Paper No. 2146.

Banerjee, A. V., and E. Duflo. (1999). "Inequality and Growth: What Can the Data Say?" Manuscript, MIT.

Barro, R. J. (2000). "Inequality and Growth in a Panel of Countries," *Journal of Economic Growth* 5, 5–32.

Barro, R. J., and J. -W. Lee. (2000). "International Data on Educational Attainment: Updates and Implications," Harvard University Center for International Development Working Paper No. 42.

Bidani, B., and M. Ravallion. (1997). "Decomposing Social Indicators Using Distributional Data," *Journal of Econometrics* 77, 125–139.

Bils, M., and P. Klenow. (2000). "Does Schooling Cause Growth?" *American Economic Review* 90(5), 1160–1183.

Blundell, R., and S. Bond. (1998). "Initial Conditions and Moment Restrictions in Dynamic Panel Data Models," *Journal of Econometrics* 87, 115–143.

Chen, S., and M. Ravallion. (1997). "What Can New Survey Data Tell Us about Recent Changes in Distribution and Poverty?" *The World Bank Economic Review* 11(2), 357–382.

Chen, S., and M. Ravallion. (2000). "How Did the World's Poorest Fare in the 1990s?" Manuscript, the World Bank. Data and paper available at http, //www.worldbank.org/research/povmonitor/.

Datt, G., and M. Ravallion. (1999). "When is Growth Pro-Poor?" Manuscript, The World Bank.

Deininger, K., and L. Squire. (1996). "A New Data Set Measuring Income Inequality," *The World Bank Economic Review* 10(3), 565–591.

Easterly, W. (1999). "Life During Growth," *Journal of Economic Growth* 4, 239–276.

Easterly, W. (2001). "The Middle-Class Consensus and Economic Development," *Journal of Economic Growth* 6, 317–335.

Easterly, W., and S. Fischer. (2000). "Inflation and the Poor," World Bank Policy Research Department Working Paper No. 2335.

Easterly, W., and S. T. Rebelo. (1993). "Fiscal Policy and Economic Growth: An Empirical Investigation," *Journal of Monetary Economics* 32(3), 417–458.

Edwards, S. (1997). "Trade Policy, Growth, and Income Distribution," *American Economic Review* 87(2), 205–210.

Filmer, D., and L. Pritchett. (1997). "Child Mortality and Public Spending on Health: How Much Does Money Matter?" Policy Research Working Paper No. 1864, The World Bank.

Fischer, S. (1993). "The Role of Macroeconomic Factors in Growth," *Journal of Monetary Economics* 32(3), 485–512.

Forbes, K. J. (2000). "A Reassessment of the Relationship between Inequality and Growth," *American Economic Review* 90(4), 869–897.

Foster, J., and M. Székely. (2001). "Is Economic Growth Good for the Poor? Tracking Low Incomes Using General Means," Interamerican Development Bank Research Department Working Paper No. 453.

Frankel, J. A., and D. Romer. (1999). "Does Trade Cause Growth?" *The American Economic Review* (June), 379–399.

Gallup, J. L., S. Radelet, and A. Warner. (1998). "Economic Growth and the Income of the Poor," Manuscript, Harvard Institute for International Development.

Galor, O., and J. Zeira. (1993). "Income Distribution and Macroeconomics," *Review of Economic Studies* 60(1), 35–52.

Galor, O., and O. Moav. (2001). "From Physical to Human Capital Accumulation: Inequality and the Process of Development," Brown University Working Paper 99–27.

Gouyette, C., and P. Pestieau. (1999). "Efficiency of the Welfare State," *Kyklos* 52, 537–553.

Johnston, N, S. Kotz, and N. Balakrishnan. (1994). *Continuous Univariate Distributions* 2 edn, Vol. 2, New York: Wiley.

Kaufmann, D., A. Kraay, and P. Zoido-Lobatón. (1999). "Governance Matters," World Bank Policy Research Department Working Paper No. 2196.

Knack, S., and P. Keefer. (1995). "Institutions and Economic Performance: Cross-Country Tests Using Alternative Institutional Measures," *Economics and Politics* 7(3), 207–227.

Kraay, A., and M. Ravallion. (2001). "Measurement Error, Aggregate Growth, and the Distribution-Corrected Mean: A Comment on Foster-Székely," Manuscript, The World Bank.

Kuznets, S. (1955). "Economic Growth and Income Inequality," *The American Economic Review* 45(1), 1–28.

Leamer, E., H. Maul, S. Rodriguez, and P. Schott. (1999). "Does Natural Resource Abundance Increase Latin American Income Inequality?" *Journal of Development Economics* 59, 3–42.

Levine, R., N. Loayza, and T. Beck. (2000). "Financial Intermediation and Growth: Causality and Causes," *Journal of Monetary Economics* 46, 31–77.

Li, H., and H. Zou. (1998). "Income Inequality is not Harmful for Growth: Theory and Evidence," *Review of Development Economics* 2(3), 318–334.

Li, H., L. Squire, and H. Zou. (1998). "Explaining International and Intertemporal Variations in Income Inequality," *The Economic Journal* 108, 26–43.

Lundberg, M., and L. Squire. (2000). "The Simultaneous Evolution of Growth and Inequality," Manuscript, The World Bank.

Perotti, R. (1996). "Growth, Income Distribution and Democracy: What the Data Say," *Journal of Economic Growth* 1, 149–187.

Persson, T., and G. Tabellini. (1994). "Is Inequality Harmful for Growth?" *American Economic Review* 84(3), 600–621.

Ravallion, M. (1997). "Can High-Inequality Countries Escape Absolute Poverty?" *Economics Letters* 56(1), 51–57.

Ravallion, M. (2001a). "Measuring Aggregate Welfare in Developing Countries: How Well do National Accounts and Surveys Agree?" World Bank Policy Research Department Working Paper No. 2665.

Ravallion, M. (2001b). "Growth, Inequality, and Poverty: Looking Beyond Averages," *World Development* 29(11), 1803–1815.

Rodriguez, F., and D. Rodrik. (2000). "Trade Policy and Economic Growth: A Skeptic's Guide to the Cross-National Evidence," In B. Bernanke, and K. Rogoff (eds), *Macroeconomics Annual 2000*, MIT Press for NBER.

Sachs, J. D., and A. Warner. (1995). "Economic Reform and the Process of Global Integration," *Brookings Papers on Economic Activity* (1), 1–118.

Spilimbergo, A., J. L. Londono, and M. Szekely. (1999). "Income Distribution, Factor Endowments, and Trade Openness," *Journal of Development Economics* 59, 77–101.

Summers, R., and A. Heston. (1991). "The Penn World Table (Mark 5): An Expanded Set of International Comparisons, 1950–88," *Quarterly Journal of Economics* 106(2), 327–368.

United Nations University—World Institute for Development Economics Research (2000). World Income Inequality Database. Available online at http://www.wider.unu.edu/wiid/wiid.htm.

[13]

Pergamon

www.elsevier.com/locate/worlddev

World Development Vol. 29, No. 11, pp. 1803–1815, 2001
© 2001 Elsevier Science Ltd. All rights reserved
Printed in Great Britain
0305-750X/01/$ - see front matter

PII: S0305-750X(01)00072-9

Growth, Inequality and Poverty:
Looking Beyond Averages

MARTIN RAVALLION *
World Bank, Washington, DC, USA

Summary. — The available evidence suggests that the poor in developing countries typically do share in the gains from rising aggregate affluence, and in the losses from aggregate contraction. But there are large differences between countries in how much poor people share in growth, and there are diverse impacts among the poor in a given country. Crosscountry correlations are clouded in data problems, and undoubtedly hide welfare impacts; they can be deceptive for development policy. There is a need for deeper micro empirical work on growth and distributional change. Only then will we have a firm basis for identifying the specific policies and programs that are needed to complement growth-oriented policies. © 2001 Elsevier Science Ltd. All rights reserved.

Key words — economic growth, inequality, poverty

1. INTRODUCTION

The recent backlash against globalization has given new impetus to an old debate on whether the poor benefit from economic growth. The following quotes from *The Economist* represent well the two main opposing views on the matter:

> Growth really does help the poor: in fact it raises their incomes by about as much as it raises the incomes of everybody else...In short, globalization raises incomes, and the poor participate fully (*The Economist*, May 27, 2000, p. 94).

> There is plenty of evidence that current patterns of growth and globalization are widening income disparities and hence acting as a brake on poverty reduction (Justin Forsyth, Oxfam Policy Director, Letter to *The Economist*, June 20, 2000, p. 6).

Here we seem to have irreconcilable positions about how much the world's poorest benefit from the economic growth that is fueled by greater openness to foreign trade and investment. *The Economist*'s own article is adamant that such growth is poverty reducing, drawing on a recent study by Dollar and Kraay (2000) which found that average incomes of the poorest quintile moved almost one-for-one with average incomes overall. In commenting on *The Economist*'s article, Oxfam's Policy Director seems equally confident that rising inequality is choking off the potential benefits to the poor, in seeming contradiction to the

Dollar and Kraay results and earlier results in the literature pointing in the same direction. [1]

As this paper will argue, however, there is some truth in both the quotes above. Indeed, it is not difficult to reconcile these two views, with important implications for development policy. In critically reviewing the arguments in this debate, I will draw heavily on evidence from a new compilation of household-level data for developing countries. The following section discusses these data. Section 3 looks at what they show about how much the poor have benefited from rising average living standards in developing countries, and how much they have lost from contractions. Section 4 looks at how distribution has been changing, to see if there is evidence to support the second quote above. The section first looks at how aggregate distribution in the developing world has been changing in the 1990s, and then it looks at what has been happening at country level. The paper then considers in more detail the ways in which

_____

* Helpful comments on this paper were received from Nancy Birdsall, Bill Easterly, Gary Fields, Paul Isenman, Ravi Kanbur, Aart Kraay, Branko Milanovic, Giovanna Prennushi, Dominique van de Walle, Nicolas van de Walle, Michael Walton and participants at presentations at the World Bank and the World Institute of Development Economics Research. These are the views of the author, and need not reflect those of the World Bank or any affiliated organization. Final revision accepted: 15 June 2001.

distribution matters to the outcomes for the poor—both as an impediment to growth (Section 5) and as an impediment to poverty-reducing growth (Section 6). Section 7 then points to some potential pitfalls in drawing policy implications from the evidence of a weak correlation between growth and distributional changes across countries. Section 8 concludes with some observations about directions for future research.

2. NEW EVIDENCE ON AN OLD DEBATE

Data on poverty and inequality are obtained from household surveys, in which random samples of households are interviewed using a structured questionnaire. The main data I draw on here relate to "spells" defined by the periods of time spanning two successive household surveys for a given country. From the latest update of the data base on which the World Bank's tabulations of income distribution are based (Chen & Ravallion, 2001), one can assemble two or more household surveys over time for about 50 developing countries, to create 120 such spells, mostly in the 1990s.[2] The estimates of poverty and inequality measures were done from the primary data (rather than using secondary sources), so that it was possible to eliminate obvious inconsistencies in existing compilations from secondary sources. Comparisons over time between any two surveys use the same indicator of economic welfare, which was either income or expenditure per person; half the time it is expenditure, which is taken to be the preferred indicator. Imputed values are included for income or consumption-in-kind from own-farm output. All measures are population weighted (taking account of household size and sample expansion factors). The underlying household surveys are nationally representative.

The data are not without problems.[3] Among the concerns about the data used here, there are clearly underlying differences (between countries and over time) in the original household surveys that were the source of the data on household incomes and expenditures. There are also concerns about how best to deflate nominal values for changes in the cost-of-living; the available consumer price indices do not always reflect well the spending behavior of the poor. On top of these problems, there is likely to be underestimation of incomes and spending in household surveys, particularly (but probably not only) by the rich, who often do not want to participate, or are hard to reach, or deliberately understate their incomes or spending. Nothing much can be done to fix these problems. One can still take partial account of the data problems by using methods of analysis that are not likely to be too sensitive to the errors in the data.

In examining the effect of growth on poverty there is also a question: "growth of what?" We want to know whether the poor are sharing in the growth in average living standards. There are, however, two quite distinct, and largely independent, sources of data on a country's average welfare, as measured by households' command over commodities. The level of private consumption expenditure (PCE) per capita from the national accounts (NAS) is widely used for this purpose. On the other hand, measures of average household living standards are available from the same household surveys used to measure poverty.

These two measures do not agree in general, either in the levels or in their growth rates. This is not surprising, given the differences in coverage, definitions and methods. There are the aforementioned problems in survey data. But national accounts have their own data problems. For example, PCE is typically determined residually in the NAS, after accounting for other uses of domestic output and imports at the commodity level. In developing countries, there are concerns about how well both output and consumption by unincorporated ("informal sector") businesses is measured, though it is not clear how this would affect NAS consumption. A further problem is that it is not generally possible to separate the spending by nonprofit institutions (such as nongovernmental organizations, religious groups, and political parties) from that of households. In many developing countries, the nonhousehold sectors that are implicitly lumped together with households appear to be sizable and possibly growing, so PCE may well overstate the growth rate in household welfare. There are also consistency problems between the two sources, such as arising from imperfect matching between survey dates (which also vary between types of commodities, according to assumed recall periods) and the accounting periods used in the NAS.

There are differences in the extent of these data concerns both between regions and between types of surveys. India stands out as an unusual case in the 1990s. The growth rates in consumption that we have seen in the national accounts for India in the 1990s have not been reflected in the main national household survey of expenditures on consumption (the National Sample Survey). This divergence is naturally putting a brake on how much poverty reduction we are seeing in the survey data during this period of economic growth (Datt, 1999). At the same time, there are signs that measured inequality is increasing, which is also slowing the rate of poverty reduction given the rate of growth (Ravallion, 2000).

How one interprets the data for India depends critically on why we are seeing this rising divergence between the two data sources on consumption. One interpretation assumes that all consumptions are being underestimated by the surveys, and so concludes that poverty is falling faster than the survey data suggest (Bhalla, 2000). While agreeing that the surveys are probably missing a share of the aggregate consumption gains, an alternative interpretation is that the problem is more likely to be due to underestimation of consumption by the nonpoor. The latter interpretation would appear to accord better with our limited knowledge of the problems of underreporting and noncompliance in consumption and income surveys (see, for example, Groves & Couper, 1998). The fact that the divergence is correlated with growth (over time and across states) of India is also consistent with an income effect on survey underestimation, which one expects to hold also between households (Ravallion, 2000). If the problem is entirely due to underreporting of consumption by the nonpoor, who are nonetheless correctly weighted in the survey design, then one will still get the poverty measures right. But, there could well be problems of sample weighting and underestimation of consumption by the poor, leading to an underestimation of the rate of poverty reduction.

If one is willing to discount income (rather than expenditure) surveys for measuring average levels of economic welfare, and if one puts aside the (highly problematic) data from the transition economies of Central and Eastern Europe for growth rates, then the tests for bias reported in Ravallion (2001) do not point to a systematic overall discrepancy between national accounts and survey-based estimates of aggregate consumption. (This holds in the aggregate across countries; large discrepancies can still be found for specific countries, in both directions.) Nonetheless, it is notable that in the aggregate, and for most regions, the elasticity

of the survey mean to NAS consumption growth is less than one (even though the difference is often not statistically significant). This could well be an attenuation bias due to measurement error. By implication, elasticities of measured poverty to NAS growth will be less than those implied by the measured elasticities of poverty to growth in the survey mean.

The fact that the mean from the surveys is consistent with the data used to calculate poverty measures makes it an appealing candidate for measuring the growth rate. This creates a further problem, however, namely that survey measurement errors can create a spuriously high correlation between poverty measures and the means of the distributions on which those measures are based. The fact that there is measurement error in the surveys (probably creating a spurious negative correlation between measured poverty and the measured mean) speaks to the use of econometric methods that are robust to this type of problem. Examples will be given later.

3. POVERTY REDUCTION AND GROWTH IN AVERAGE LIVING STANDARDS

There is little or no correlation in these data between growth in average household income per person and the change in measured inequality. The correlation coefficient between the annualized change in the log of the Gini index and the annualized change in the log of the survey mean is -0.09 ($n = 115$). The correlation is even lower if one uses growth rates in consumption from the national accounts (a correlation coefficient of 0.01). This finding is consistent with previous research. Earlier versions of this data set also indicated that growth in average household income per person and the change in measured inequality are virtually orthogonal (Ravallion, 1995; Ravallion & Chen, 1997). Similarly, Dollar and Kraay (2000) find that, across countries, log mean income of the poorest quintile (inferred from distributional shares and GDP per capita) changes one-to-one with the overall log GDP per capita. This is equivalent to saying that the share of the poorest quintile is uncorrelated with log GDP per capita.

It does not follow, however, that growth raises incomes of the poor "...by about as much as it raises the incomes of everybody else" (in the quote from *The Economist* at the beginning of this paper). Finding that the share of income going to the poor does not change on average with growth does not mean that growth raises the incomes of the poor as much as for the rich. Given existing inequality, the income gains to the rich from distribution-neutral growth will of course be greater than the gains to the poor. For example, the income gain to the richest decile in India will be about four times higher than the gain to the poorest quintile; it will be 19 times higher in Brazil.[4] The fact that, on average, the rich will tend to capture a much larger share of the increment to national income from growth than the poor is directly implied by the empirical results in the literature, including Dollar and Kraay (2000).

Of course, if distributional shares do not change on average then the poor will gain in absolute terms: growth is poverty reducing, and contraction is poverty increasing. Figure 1 plots the proportionate changes in the poverty rate against the growth rate in average income. The poverty measure is the proportion of people living below $1/day (using 1993 Purchasing Power Parity exchange rates), though other poverty lines show a similar pattern.[5]

The figure also gives the regression line that fits the data best. The line virtually passes through the origin, implying that the average rate of poverty reduction at zero growth is zero—consistent with the pattern of zero change in inequality on average. The line has a slope of -2.50 with a (heteroskedasticity corrected) standard error of 0.30 ($R^2 = 0.44$). This can be thought of as an overall "growth elasticity" of poverty, since the two variables are proportionate changes. Thus for every 1% increase in the mean, the proportion of the population living below $1/day (at 1993 Purchasing Power Parity) falls by an average of 2.5%. For example, in a large enough sample of countries for which exactly half of the population lives below $1/day, a 3% increase in the mean will bring that proportion down to about 0.46. A 3% drop in mean income will push the poverty rate up to about 0.54 on average.

There is no indication in the data that the elasticity is any different when the mean is increasing versus decreasing; one cannot reject the null hypothesis that the elasticity is the same in both directions (the t-statistic is 0.11). So there is no sign that distributional changes help protect the poor during contractions in average living standards.

The relationship looks similar if one uses PCE per capita from the national accounts instead of the mean from the survey, although then the correlation is not as strong, and the elasticity is -1.96 with a considerably higher standard error of 0.89 (though still statistically

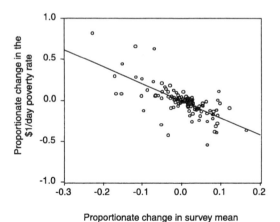

Proportionate change in survey mean

Figure 1. *Poverty tends to fall with growth in mean household income or expenditure. (Note: Based on data for 47 developing countries in the 1980s and 1990s (multiple spells for most countries). The horizontal axis is the annualized change in the log of the real value of the survey mean; the vertical axis is the annualized change in the log of the percentage of the population living below $1/day at 1993 Purchasing Power Parity. The figure has been trimmed of extreme values, but this does not alter the line of best fit indicated.)*

significant at the 3% level). This is partly because of measurement problems, such as the fact that survey periods do not match exactly the periods used in National Accounts. It is also partly because changes in PCE can arise solely from the nonhousehold sector of the economy (notably spending by nonprofit organizations). Nor is there any sign that the elasticity to growth from the national accounts is any different in expansions versus contractions.

A possible concern about this estimate of the average growth elasticity of poverty reduction is that there may be negatively correlated measurement errors in the rate of poverty reduction and the rate of growth in the survey mean. If the second survey overestimated the mean for some reason (relative to the first survey) it will probably overestimate the rate at which poverty is falling. To check for a bias due to this problem, I used the growth rate in private consumption per capita from the national accounts as the instrumental variable for estimating the regression line in Figure 1, i.e., as the predictor of the growth rate in the survey mean. This assumes that the errors in the national accounts growth rate are uncorrelated with the errors in the growth rates based on the survey means. This instrument is not valid, however, for the countries of Eastern Europe and Central Asia for which there is no correlation between the growth rates from the surveys and those from the national accounts (Ravallion, 2001). So I dropped the data for that region. This estimation method gave a growth elasticity of −2.07 with a standard error of 0.72 (significant at the 1% level).

Therein lies the truth in the first quote at the start of this paper. The incidence of absolute poverty in developing countries tends to fall with growth. This is not a new point; indeed, the empirical relationship has been well known for some time (Bruno *et al.*, 1998, provide a survey). But it is worth emphasizing in the context of the recent debate.

Looking behind the averages, however, the experience is diverse. Even ignoring extreme values, the 95% confidence interval of the last estimate above of the growth elasticity implies that a 1% rate of growth in average household income or consumption will bring anything from a modest drop in the poverty rate of 0.6% to a more dramatic 3.5% annual decline. We will now try to better understand this variance in growth elasticities of poverty.

4. IS RISING INEQUALITY IMPEDING POVERTY REDUCTION?

Let us look first at distribution in the developing world as a whole in the 1990s. In the same way that rising inequality in one country can clearly put a brake on prospects for poverty-reducing growth, rising inequality in the developing world as a whole can inhibit overall poverty reduction. Has that been happening?

The proportion of the population of the developing world living in households with consumption per capita less than about $1/day in 1998 (at 1993 Purchasing Power Parity) is estimated to be 23% which was only five percentage points lower than in 1987 (Chen & Ravallion, 2001). The total number of poor by this standard was about the same in 1998 as in 1987, with roughly 1.2 billion people living below $1/day. Chen and Ravallion (2001) try to assess what role worsening distribution played in aggregate poverty reduction during the 1990s. They simulate what would have happened if there had been no change in the overall interpersonal distribution for developing and transitional countries during 1987–98. In other words, all household consumptions and incomes grow at the same rate, given by the growth rate in the (population-weighted) survey mean over their entire data set. The 1987 Lorenz curve of interpersonal consumption for the developing world as a whole would thus remain fixed over the period. If it were true that distribution is worsening over time in the developing world as a whole then this distribution-neutral simulation would give lower poverty in 1998 than actually observed. Chen and Ravallion find, however, that the poverty rate in 1998 would have been 24.4% in the distribution neutral case, instead of 23.4% as calculated from the data.

It can be inferred from this that there was no worsening in the overall interpersonal distribution from the point of view of the poor. Indeed, the actual distributional changes were slightly pro-poor, since the measured poverty rate in 1998 is slightly lower than the simulated rate without any change in distribution. On investigating this finding more closely, one finds that the difference is almost entirely attributable to growth in China. If one takes China out of the calculation then the actual poverty rate in 1998 of 25.2% is almost exactly the same as the simulated rate (25.9%). So income distribution has not been deteriorating overall in the 1990s, from the point of view of the poor.[6]

This aggregate picture hides more than it reveals. The previous section pointed to the heterogeneity in the gains to the poor from a given rate of growth. Underlying this heterogeneity lies the fact that during spells of growth or contraction one sees changes in inequality over time within most developing economies— changes in both directions.

Table 1 divides the data points of Figure 1 (each spell representing two surveys for a given country) into four groups, according to whether the mean is increasing or not, interacted with whether inequality is increasing or not. Even in the countries in which inequality is rising with growth in average living standards, poverty is falling on average. But it typically falls at a much slower rate than in countries experiencing more equitable growth. The median rate of decline in the proportion of the population living below $1/day among countries with both rising average income and rising inequality was 1.3% per year (Table 1). By contrast, the median rate of poverty reduction was seven times higher, at about 10% per year, among the countries that combined growth in average living standards and falling inequality. Among contracting economies it also mattered greatly what was happening to inequality; when inequality was rising while average living standards fell, the poverty rate was rising by a dramatic 14% per year on average, while with falling inequality the poverty rate rose by less than 2%.

There have been plenty of cases of rising inequality during spells of growth. Indeed, inequality increases about half the time (Table 1; also see Ravallion & Chen, 1997). Therein lies the truth in the second quote at the beginning of this paper. The first quote implicitly averages over this diversity; the second looks not at the averages, but the cases in which the poor share little in the gains from growth.

The fact that we are seeing plenty of cases of rising inequality during spells of growth does not, however, imply that the rising inequality is putting a brake on the rate of poverty reduction. It cannot be concluded from the information in Table 1 that the growing economies with rising inequality could have achieved something like a 9.6% rate of poverty reduction—instead of 1.3% on average—if only inequality had been falling. For that to hold one requires the assumption that the growth rate would have been no lower with falling inequality. Possibly there is an aggregate tradeoff between growth and inequality reduction. That depends critically on exactly how the reduction in inequality is achieved. The next section considers this point further.

5. INEQUALITY AS AN IMPEDIMENT TO GROWTH

One way inequality can matter to the rate of poverty reduction is through the rate of growth in average income. There are a number of arguments that have been made as to why greater equality can actually be good for growth, belying the presumption of an aggregate tradeoff. A seemingly plausible argument points to the existence of credit market failures such that people are unable to exploit growth-promoting opportunities for investment in (physical and human) capital (see, for example, Aghion, Caroli, & Garcia-Penalosa, 1999; Benabou, 1996). With declining marginal products of capital, the output loss from the market failure will be greater for the poor. So the higher the proportion of poor people there are in the economy the lower the rate of growth.[7] Crosscountry comparisons of growth rates provide some support for the claim that countries with higher initial inequality in incomes

Table 1. *Diverse impacts on poverty underlie the fact that changes in inequality are uncorrelated with economic growth*[a]

		What is happening to average household income between the surveys?	
		Falling	Rising
What is happening to inequality between the surveys?	Rising	16% *of spells* Poverty is rising at a median rate of 14.3% per year	30% *of spells* Poverty is falling at a median rate of 1.3% per year
	Falling	26% *of spells* Poverty is rising at a median rate of 1.7% per year	27% *of spells* Poverty is falling at a median rate of 9.6% per year

[a] Based on 117 spells between two household surveys covering 47 developing countries in the 1980s and 1990s. Poverty is measured by the % of the population living below $1/day at 1993 Purchasing Power Parity. Inequality is measured by the Gini index.

experienced lower rates of growth controlling for other factors such as initial average income, openness to trade and the rate of inflation. [8] The robustness of this finding has been called into question in some studies. There are difficult problems in identifying this relationship empirically, and the results in the literature have not been robust to alternative specifications, such as allowing for country fixed effects (Barro, 2000; Forbes, 1997; Li & Zou, 1998).

Again, there are a number of concerns about the data and methods used. There are measurement errors in both the levels and changes in measured income inequality, including comparability problems between countries and over time arising from survey error (sampling and non-sampling) and heterogeneity in survey design and processing (see, for example, Atkinson & Brandolini, 1999). One expects that this will matter more to tests which allow for country fixed effects than to standard growth regressions, since the signal-to-noise ratio could well be quite low for changes in measured inequality in existing data sets. Greater attenuation bias should be expected in the fixed-effects regressions of growth on inequality. Using a pooled regression of growth on inequality, Knowles (2001) finds that trimming the data set to reduce the comparability problems changes the results obtained in important ways. Knowles finds, however, that using more recent and more comparable measures of inequality in consumption expenditures does indicate significant negative effects of inequality on growth.

Another concern is that spurious inequality effects in an aggregate growth regression can arise from the assumptions made in aggregating across micro relationships, given credit market failures (Ravallion, 1998). The direction of this bias could go either way, though results for China indicate that regional aggregation hides the adverse effect of inequality on growth. The validity of the common assumption that initial inequality has a linear effect on aggregate growth is also questionable; Banerjee and Duflo (1999) find evidence that changes in income inequality are bad for growth, which ever way the changes go. The choice of control variables in identifying the relationship is also open to question; for example, past tests of the effect of inequality on growth have controlled for the human capital stock, yet reducing investment in human capital is presumably one of the ways that inequality matters to growth.

On balance, the existing evidence using crosscountry growth regressions appears to offer more support for the view that inequality is harmful to growth than the opposite view, which was the prevailing view in development economics for decades. That does not imply, however, that any reduction in inequality will enhance growth; indeed, it can have the opposite effect if it comes at the expense of other factors that are also known to matter to growth. Reducing inequality by adding further distortions to external trade or domestic economy will have ambiguous effects on growth and poverty reduction.

Given the concerns about past tests based on crosscountry aggregates, it is of interest to ask if there might be some other way of testing for an effect of initial distribution on growth. Returning to the various theories about why initial distribution might matter, one finds that many of the proposed models share some strong and testable implications for micro data. An example is the common feature of a number of the theoretical models based on credit-market failures that individual income or wealth at one date is an increasing concave function of its own past value. This implication of the class of models of distribution-dependent growth based on credit market failures is testable on micro panel data; Lokshin and Ravallion (2001) provide supportive evidence in panel data for Hungary and Russia. [9]

As with macro tests of whether inequality is bad for growth, finding the appropriate non-linearity in household-level income dynamics would not constitute a case for public redistribution as a means of stimulating aggregate growth. But, with the right data, dynamic micro models of income or consumption can be augmented to allow for (possibly endogenously placed) public programs. [10] Micro structural modeling of growth in the presence of specific redistributive interventions may offer hope of a deeper understanding of the policy implications.

6. INEQUALITY AS AN IMPEDIMENT TO PRO-POOR GROWTH

Even when inequality is not rising, a high initial level of inequality can stifle prospects for pro-poor growth. In an economy where inequality is persistently low, one can expect that the poor will tend to obtain a higher share of the gains from growth than in an economy in which inequality is high. To put this another way, an important determinant of the rate of poverty reduction is the *distribution-corrected rate of growth* in average income, given by a measure of initial equality (100 minus the measure of inequality) times the rate of growth. Indeed, the distribution-corrected growth rate knocks out the ordinary growth rate when both are used in a regression for the rate of poverty reduction (Ravallion, 1997). It is not the rate of growth that matters, but the distribution-corrected rate of growth.

One can represent this in the form of a very simple model in which the proportionate rate of change in the incidence of poverty (P) between surveys is directly proportional to the distribution-corrected rate of growth; on adding an error term, this can be written as:

$$\Delta \ln P_{it} = \gamma (1 - G_{i,t-\tau}) \Delta \ln Y_{it} + \varepsilon_{it}, \qquad (1)$$

where the difference is taken between surveys that are τ years apart (which varies between countries and over time), $G_{i,t-\tau}$ is the Gini index (between zero and one) for country i at the beginning of the spell, Y_{it} is real value of the survey mean at date t, and γ is a parameter to be estimated. Using the same data as in Figure 1, I obtained an estimate of -3.74 for γ, with standard error of 0.68 (this is very close to the estimate in Ravallion, 1997, on an earlier and smaller data set). A possible concern about this estimate is that there may be (negatively) correlated measurement errors in the changes in P and Y. Using the growth rate in PCE per capita from the national accounts as the instrumental variable for the growth rate in the survey means and dropping the observations for Eastern Europe and Central Asia (where the instrument fails) I found a lower estimate of γ, namely -2.94, with standard error of 1.18.

The elasticity of poverty to growth declines appreciably as the extent of initial inequality rises. Consider a per capita growth rate of (say) 2% per annum (roughly the mean for low-income countries in the 1990s). With $\gamma = -3$ a country with high inequality (a Gini index of 60% say) can expect to see a rate of poverty reduction of 2.4% per year. By contrast, a relatively low-inequality country, with a Gini of 30%, can expect a rate of poverty reduction of 4.2% per year.

The above results are unrevealing about what specific aspects of inequality matter. The theoretical arguments based on credit-market failures point to the importance of asset inequality, not income inequality *per se*. There is evidence of adverse effects of asset inequality in growth (Birdsall & Londono, 1997; Deininger & Ol-

into, 2000, both using crosscountry data; Ravallion, 1998, using regional data for China).

Some clues have been found by comparing rates of poverty reduction across states of India, for which we can compile a long series of reasonably comparable survey data back to about 1960. The analyzes of these data confirm that economic growth has tended to reduce poverty in India. Higher average farm yields, higher public spending on development, higher (urban and rural) nonfarm output and lower inflation were all poverty reducing (Ravallion & Datt, 2001). But, the response of poverty to nonfarm output growth in India has varied significantly between states. The differences reflected systematic differences in initial conditions. Low farm productivity, low rural living standards relative to urban areas and poor basic education all inhibited the prospects of the poor participating in growth of the nonfarm sector. Rural and human resource development appear to be strongly synergistic with poverty reduction though an expanding nonfarm economy.

7. "NO CORRELATION" DOES NOT MEAN "NO IMPACT"

We have seen that the data suggest little or no correlation between growth and changes in inequality across countries. The same holds for indicators of growth promoting policies for which significant correlations have rarely been found, one way or the other. This is confirmed by Dollar and Kraay (2000), who find negligible correlation between changes in inequality and indicators of policy reform, including greater openness.[11] If there is no effect on inequality then the outcomes for the poor depend solely on the growth effects.

There are three main reasons to be cautious in drawing implications for policy from this lack of correlation between growth and changes in inequality. First, this apparent distribution-neutrality of reform (on average) could simply reflect the fact that changes in inequality are not well measured as a rule. For example, it should be emphasized again that although the main data set used above has been constructed to try to eliminate as many of the problems as possible, there are still changes in survey design that can add considerable noise to the measured changes in inequality.

Second, the data relate to averages within countries. Aggregate inequality or poverty may change relatively little over time, and yet there are both gainers and losers at all levels of living. Indeed, in cases in which the survey data have tracked the same families over time ("panel data"), it is quite common to find considerable churning under the surface; Baulch and Hoddinott (2000) provide evidence of this for a number of countries. Some of this reflects measurement error, but probably not all, since the changes seen in the data are partially explicable in terms of observable characteristics and measurable shocks (see, for example, Jalan & Ravallion, 2000, using data for rural China).

One can find that many people have escaped poverty while others have fallen into poverty, even though the overall poverty rate may move rather little. For example, comparing household incomes immediately after the 1998 financial crisis in Russia with incomes of the same households two years earlier, one finds a seemingly small 2% point increase in the poverty rate. But, this was associated with a large proportion of the population (18%) falling into poverty, while a slightly smaller proportion (16%) escaped poverty over the same period (Lokshin & Ravallion, 2000).

People are often hurting behind the averages. Panel data and observations from the ground can reveal this, but the aggregate statistics cannot. It is important to know the aggregate balance of gains and losses, but it will be of little consolation to those suffering to be told that poverty is falling on average.

A third reason why the low correlations found between policy reform and changes in overall inequality can be deceptive is that starting conditions vary a lot between reforming countries. Averaging across this diversity in initial conditions can readily hide systematic effects. This argument warrants further elaboration since it holds lessons for policy.

One obvious way that countries differ is in their initial level of economic development. It has been argued that greater openness to external trade will have very different effects on inequality depending on the level of economic development—increasing inequality in rich countries and decreasing it in poor ones (Wood, 1994, makes a qualified argument along these lines). The opposite outcome is possible, however, when economic reforms, including greater openness to external trade, increase demand for relatively skilled labor, which tends to be more inequitably distributed in poor countries than rich ones.[12] Geographic disparities in access to infrastructure also impede prospects for participating in the growth generated by reform, and these disparities tend to be correlated with incomes.

A simple test for the effect of openness on inequality is suggestive. Using the same data set as Li, Squire, and Zou (1998), I found no significant effect of exports as a share of GDP on the Gini index across 50 countries (100 observations). The regression included controls for schooling, financial sector development, urbanization and the black-market premium (the same explanatory variables used by Li *et al.*, 1998). But, I found a strong *negative* interaction effect with initial GDP per capita (with openness entering positively on its own in the same regression). This suggests that openness is associated with *higher* inequality in poor countries. Barro (2000) also reports a significant negative interaction effect between GDP per capita and openness in a regression for inequality, using different controls.

Heterogeneity might also be expected at given levels of economic development. Suppose that reforming developing countries fall into two categories: those in which pre-reform controls on the economy were used to benefit the rich, keeping inequality artificially high, and those in which the controls had the opposite effect, keeping inequality low. The reforms may well entail sizable redistribution between the poor and the rich, but in opposite directions in the two groups of countries. Then one should not be surprised to find that there is zero correlation between growth and changes in inequality or that the average impact of policy reform on inequality is not significantly different from zero. Yet there could well be nonrandom distributional change going on under the surface of this average impact calculation. This can arise when policy reforms shift the distribution of income in different directions in different countries. Moreover, it is not implausible that they would do so, given the diversity in initial conditions across developing countries at the time reforms begin.

There is evidence to support this interpretation. As noted already, using the same data set underlying Figure 1, one finds virtually zero correlation between changes in the Gini index of inequality and growth in mean income or consumption. But, suppose that the true relationship is one in which initial inequality interacts with growth, such that the growth attenuates high inequality, but it increases inequality when it is initially low. Using the same set of developing countries as used for Figure 1, one finds evidence for such an interaction effect by regressing the change in the log of the Gini index on the growth rate in PCE and the product of that growth rate with initial inequality. More precisely, the test regression takes the form:

$$\Delta \ln G_{it}/\tau = (\beta_0 + \beta_1 \ln G_{it-\tau})\Delta \ln Y_{it}/\tau + \mu_{it}, \quad (2)$$

where G_{it} is the Gini index in country i at date t, and Y_{it} is the private consumption per capita of country i at date t and τ is the time between surveys. The estimate of β_0 is significantly positive (6.03, with a standard error of 2.14), while β_1 is significantly negative (a regression coefficient of -1.60 with a standard error of 0.57). (Again, the standard errors are heteroskedasticity-consistent.) Thus one finds a significant *negative* interaction effect between growth and initial inequality.[13] At a value of the log Gini index of $-\beta_0/\beta_1$, growth has no effect; this occurs at a Gini index of 0.433, which is very close to the median Gini index in the sample of 0.425.

A possible concern about this test is that the interaction effect with initial inequality might be due to measurement error in the latter variable. If the Gini index is over- (under-) estimated this year, then the growth rate in the Gini index will tend to be under- (over-) estimated, which will be reflected in a negative interaction effect with growth in the above test (a version of a problem known as "Galton's Fallacy"). But, the negative interaction effect remained significant (at the 2% level) when I used a higher lag of the inequality measure as the instrument for "initial" inequality.[14] This will eliminate any bias due to measurement error as long as the errors are serially independent. The turning point was almost the same (a Gini index of 0.432). So for roughly the lower half of countries in terms of inequality, growth tends to come with higher inequality, while for the upper half, growth tends to attenuate inequality.

None of this denies that growth-oriented reforms have an important role in fighting poverty or that policies can intervene to alter the distributional outcomes. But these observations do point to the need for a deeper understanding of the evident diversity in the impacts on poverty, and what role other policies have played. This requires further research on the role of initial conditions (including distribution) and how they interact with policy change.

Economic reforms in developing countries can create opportunities for poor people. But only if the conditions are in place for them to take advantage of those opportunities will absolute poverty fall rapidly. Given initial inequalities in income and nonincome dimensions of welfare, economic reforms can readily bypass the poor. The conditions for pro-poor growth are this closely tied to reducing the disparities in access to human and physical capital, and sometimes also to differences in returns to assets, that create income inequality and probably also inhibit overall growth prospects.

Policy discussions have often emphasized the need to combine policies conducive to growth with investments in the human and physical assets of poor people.[15] But, many questions remain unanswered. What specific interventions should have priority in specific circumstances? Should reform be redesigned or delayed when initial conditions are not favorable, and take time to change?

8. CONCLUSIONS

The seemingly opposing positions taken in this ongoing debate are not as hard to reconcile as it might seem at first sight. The poor typically do share in the benefits of rising aggregate affluence, and they typically do suffer from economic contraction. But, there is a sizable variance around the "typical" outcomes for the poor. One source of variance is that "economic growth," as measured in the national accounts, is not always reflected in average household living standards as measured in surveys, at least in the short run.

The sources of the heterogeneity in outcomes for the poor go deeper than that, however. Finding zero average impact on inequality of growth-oriented policy reforms does not mean that reforms are generally distribution neutral. An average is just that, and it is deceptive when one averages over large differences across countries in their starting points. There are important differences in initial inequalities, with implications for how much the poor share in aggregate growth and contraction. The churning that is found under the surface of the aggregate outcomes also means that there are often losers during spells of growth, even when poverty falls on average. While various papers in the literature have found that growth-promoting policies have little or no average impact on inequality, that finding is perfectly consistent with sizable distributional impacts in specific countries, albeit in different directions. Average neutrality is consistent with strong distributional effects at the country level. There is truth in both the quotes at the beginning of this paper, though each is potentially deceptive on its own.

These observations point to the importance of more micro, country-specific, research on the factors determining why some poor people are able to take up the opportunities afforded by an expanding economy—and so add to its expansion—while others are not. Individual endowments of physical and human capital have rightly been emphasized in past work, and suggest important links to policy. Other factors that may well be equally important have received less attention, such as location, social exclusion and exposure to uninsured risk.

While good policy-making for fighting poverty must obviously be concerned with the aggregate impacts on the poor, it cannot ignore the diversity of impacts underlying the averages, and it is here that good micro empirical work can help. That diversity also holds potentially important clues as to what else needs to be done by governments to promote poverty reduction, on top of promoting economic growth.

NOTES

1. Earlier contributions include Fields (1989), World Bank (1990, Chapter 3), Squire (1993), Ravallion (1995), Ravallion and Chen (1997) and Bruno, Ravallion, and Squire (1998).

2. The latest version of the data set can be found a http://www.worldbank.org/research/povmonitor/. This web site is updated regularly; the results in this paper are based on the data set at mid-2000, as used in Chen and Ravallion (2001).

3. For a critical review of the methods underlying the data set used here, see Deaton (2001).

4. These are based on income shares for Brazil in 1996 and consumption shares for India in 1997; in both cases the ranking variable is per capita (World Bank, 2000a).

5. One possible concern is that the poverty line is fixed (in PPP terms) across countries. While this is valid for making comparisons of absolute poverty in terms of command over commodities, actual poverty lines tend to rise with mean consumption or income in a country (Chen & Ravallion, 2001). But, comparisons of national poverty lines with mean consumption (both at PPP) indicate that the "income" elasticity of the poverty line is very low among poor countries, only rising at middle to upper income levels (Chen & Ravallion, 2001). Thus the growth elasticity of poverty in low- and middle-income countries is unlikely to be affected much by using relative poverty lines consistent with the way national poverty lines vary.

6. Here I am only referring to distribution in the developing world as it affects poverty. There is evidence of rising overall interpersonal inequality in the world (developing and developed); see Milanovic (2001) for 1987–93.

7. Banerjee and Duflo (1999) sketch a simple but elegant model of the intergenerational accumulation of wealth in which individuals start with an endowment from the previous generation but face a borrowing constraint. In this model, individual wealth at one date is a concave function of the individual's endowment, given declining marginal products of capital. Thus mean wealth in the economy at one date is a quasi-concave function of the vector of endowments left over from the previous period. It follows from well-known properties of concave functions that higher initial inequality will entail lower future mean wealth for any given initial mean wealth.

8. Examples include Persson and Tabellini (1994), Alesina and Rodrik (1994), Birdsall, Ross, and Sabot (1995), Clarke (1995), Perotti (1996), Deininger and Squire (1998) and Deininger and Olinto (2000).

9. Distribution-dependent growth is possible without nonlinear income or wealth dynamics at the micro level. Such models that have been driven instead by their assumptions about political economy, notably the way initial distribution influences the balance of power over public spending (Alesina & Rodrik, 1994; Persson & Tabellini, 1994).

10. For example, research on government anti-poverty programs in China suggests that there have been dynamic consumption gains from the program at farm-household level (Jalan & Ravallion, 1998).

11. Dollar and Kraay (2000) do find that stabilizing against inflation is associated with lower inequality. This is consistent with other evidence that inflation hurts the poor (including Easterly & Fischer, 2001, using cross-country data, and Datt & Ravallion, 1998, using data for India).

12. Disparities in returns to schooling need not favor the poor either. For evidence on this point see, van de Walle's (2000) results for Vietnam.

13. This test has used the data for developing market economies. The negative interaction effect vanishes if one includes the transition economies of Eastern Europe and Central Asia. This is not too surprising given that these economies are going through a transition process to a market economy in which the

economies are tending to contract, and inequality is rising, which may well be confounding the true relationship.

14. Naturally the number of observations drops considerably, to $n = 69$.

15. Arguments along these lines can be found in World Bank (1990, 2000b), Bruno et al. (1998) and Kanbur and Squire (1999) among others.

REFERENCES

Aghion, P., Caroli, E., & Garcia-Penalosa, C. (1999). Inequality and economic growth: the perspectives of the new growth theories. *Journal of Economic Literature, 37*(4), 1615–1660.

Alesina, A., & Rodrik, D. (1994). Distributive politics and economic growth. *Quarterly Journal of Economics, 108*, 465–490.

Atkinson, A. B., & Brandolini, A. (1999). *Promise and pitfalls in the use of secondary data sets: income inequality in OECD countries*. Mimeo, Nuffield College Oxford.

Banerjee, A., & Duflo, E. (1999). *Inequality and growth: what can the data say?* Mimeo, Department of Economics, MIT.

Barro, R. (2000). Inequality and growth in a panel of countries. *Journal of Economic Growth, 5*, 5–32.

Baulch, B., & Hoddinott, J. (2000). Economic mobility and poverty dynamics in developing countries. *Journal of Development Studies., 36*(6), 1–24.

Benabou, R. (1996). Inequality and growth. In B. Bernanke, & J. Rotemberg (Eds.), *National bureau of economic research macroeconomics annual* (pp. 11–74). Cambridge, MA: MIT Press.

Bhalla, S. (2000). Growth and poverty in India—myth and reality, available from http://www.oxusresearch.com/economic.asp.

Birdsall, N., & Londono, J. L. (1997). Asset inequality matters: an assessment of the World Bank's approach to poverty reduction. *American Economic Review Papers and Proceedings, 87*(2), 32–37.

Birdsall, N., Ross, D., & Sabot, R. (1995). Inequality and growth reconsidered: lessons from East Asia. *World Bank Economic Review, 9*(3), 477–508.

Bruno, M., Ravallion, M., & Squire, L. (1998). Equity and growth in developing countries: old and new perspectives on the policy issues. In V. Tanzi, & K. Chu (Eds.), *Income distribution and high-quality growth*. Cambridge, MA: MIT Press.

Chen, S., & Ravallion, M. (2001). How did the world's poorest fare in the 1990s? *Review of Income and Wealth* (in press).

Clarke, G. R. G. (1995). More evidence on income distribution and growth. *Journal of Development Economics, 47*, 403–428.

Datt, G. (1999). Has poverty in India declined since the economic reforms. *Economic and Political Weekly, 34*(December), 11–17.

Datt, G., & Ravallion, M. (1998). Farm productivity and rural poverty in India. *Journal of Development Studies, 34*, 62–85.

Deaton, A. (2001). Counting the world's poor: problems and possible solutions. *World Bank Research Observer*.

Deininger, K., & Olinto, P. (2000). *Asset distribution inequality and growth*. Policy Research Working Paper 2375 Washington, DC: World Bank.

Deininger, K., & Squire, L. (1998). New ways of looking at old issues: inequality and growth. *Journal of Development Economics, 57*(2), 259–287.

Dollar, D., & Kraay, A. (2000). *Growth is good for the poor*. Washington, DC: World Bank.

Easterly, W., & Fischer, S. (2001). Inflation and the poor. *Journal of Money Credit and Banking, 33*(2), 160–179.

Fields, G. (1989). Changes in poverty and inequality in developing countries. *World Bank Research Observer, 4*, 167–186.

Forbes, K. J. (1997). *A reassessment of the relationship between inequality and growth*. Mimeo. Department of Economics, MIT.

Groves, R. M., & Couper, M. P. (1998). *Nonresponse in household surveys*. New York: Wiley.

Jalan, J., & Ravallion, M. (1998). Are there dynamic gains from a poor-area development program? *Journal of Public Economics, 67*(1), 65–86.

Jalan, J., & Ravallion, M. (2000). Is transient poverty different? Evidence for rural China. *Journal of Development Studies, 36*, 82–99.

Kanbur, R., & Squire, L. (1999). *The evolution of thinking about poverty: exploring the interactions*. Department of Agricultural Resource and Managerial Economics Paper, 99-24. Cornell University.

Knowles, S., (2001). *Inequality and economic growth: the empirical relationship reconsidered in the light of comparable data*. Paper prepared for the WIDER Conference on Growth and Poverty. WIDER, Helsinki.

Li, H., & Zou, H. (1998). Income inequality is not harmful to growth: theory and evidence. *Review of Development Economics, 2*(3), 318–334.

Li, H., Squire, L., & Zou, H. (1998). Explaining international and intertemporal variations in income inequality. *Economic Journal, 108*, 26–43.

Lokshin, M., & Ravallion, M. (2000). Welfare impacts of Russia's 1998 financial crisis. *Economics of Transition, 8*(2), 269–295.

Lokshin, M., & Ravallion. M. (2001). *Nonlinear household income dynamics in two transition economies.* Mimeo, Development Research Group, World Bank.

Milanovic, B. (2001). True world income distribution: 1988 and 1993: First calculations based on household surveys alone. *Economic Journal.*

Perotti, R. (1996). Growth income distribution and democracy: what the data say. *Journal of Economic Growth, 1*(2), 149–187.

Persson, T., & Tabellini, G. (1994). Is inequality harmful for growth? *American Economic Review, 84*, 600–621.

Ravallion, M. (1995). Growth and poverty: evidence for developing countries in the 1980s. *Economics Letters, 48*, 411–417.

Ravallion, M. (1997). Can high inequality developing countries escape absolute poverty? *Economics Letters, 56*, 51–57.

Ravallion, M. (1998). Does aggregation hide the harmful effects of inequality on growth? *Economics Letters, 61*(1), 73–77.

Ravallion, M. (2000). Should poverty measures be anchored to the national accounts? *Economic and Political Weekly.* September.

Ravallion, M. (2001). Measuring aggregate welfare in developing countries: How well do national accounts and surveys agree? Policy Research Working Paper, World Bank.

Ravallion, M., & Chen, S. (1997). What can new survey data tell us about recent changes in distribution and poverty? *World Bank Economic Review, 11*(2), 357–382.

Ravallion, M., & Datt, G. (2001). Why has economic growth been more pro-poor in some states of India than in others? *Journal of Development Economics* (in press).

Squire, L. (1993). Fighting poverty. *American Economic Review Papers and Proceedings, 83*(2), 377–382.

van de Walle, D. (2000). *Are returns to investment lower for the poor? Human and physical capital interactions in rural Vietnam.* Policy Research Working Paper, WPS 2425. Washington, DC: World Bank.

Wood, A. (1994). *North–South trade employment and inequality. Changing fortunes in a skill driven world.* Oxford: Clarendon Press.

World Bank. (1990). *World development report: Poverty.* New York: Oxford University Press.

World Bank. (2000a). *World development indicators.* Washington, DC: The World Bank.

World Bank. (2000b). *World development report: Attacking poverty.* New York: Oxford University Press.

[14]

Dollar and Kraay on 'Trade, Growth, and Poverty': A Critique[1]

Howard L.M. Nye[2] and Sanjay G. Reddy[3]

In their paper, 'Trade, Growth, and Poverty',[4] Dollar and Kraay claim to present evidence that trade liberalisation leads to faster growth in average incomes, and that this growth in average incomes in turn increases the incomes of the poor 'proportionately', thus leading to decreased absolute poverty. The paper suggests that one of the surest ways for less developed countries to alleviate poverty is to pursue policies of trade liberalisation. We argue, however, that the arguments and evidence presented by Dollar and Kraay are unconvincing. The record of the effects of trade on growth and poverty appears to be considerably more mixed than claimed by Dollar and Kraay.

Dollar and Kraay attempt to show on the basis of empirical evidence that: (1) Post-1980 'globalisers' – or developing countries that undertook greater shifts in favor of a more open trade regime than others did in the period from the early 1980s to the late 1990s – have experienced greater increases in growth of per capita incomes; (2) growth of the share of trade in gross domestic product (henceforth, trade volume) is positively associated with increases in the growth rate of average income; and (3) there is no *systematic* tendency for the share of national income captured by the bottom quintile of the income distribution to change as per capita national income grows. The first two claims are each intended to support the view that 'trade liberalisation leads to higher growth of average incomes' while the third claim is intended to support the view that 'growth of average incomes increases the incomes of the poor proportionately'. We critically examine below the claims of Dollar and Kraay.

1. The Identification and Relative Growth Performance of 'Globalisers'

The authors' first exercise is a descriptive comparison of the growth comparison of 'globalisers' and 'non-globalisers'. Although the authors do not intend this to substitute for an econometric analysis that controls for confounding factors, they consider it informative enough to present. A problem that arises immediately concerns how to identify a group of 'globalisers'. As Dollar and Kraay themselves note, trade liberalisation often occurs at the same time as many other reforms (see also Rodriguez and Rodrik (2000)). Thus, identification problems plague inferences that differences in growth rates are due to differences in trade policy. Differences in growth rates between countries identified according to their trade policies may be due to other policy changes that also differentiate these groups of countries.

How should globalizing countries, or 'countries that have significantly opened up to foreign trade' be distinguished from non-globalizing ones, or 'countries that have remained more closed'?[5] An obvious possibility is to differentiate countries by measures that indicate the extent of the obstacles to trade that they erect, such as tariff and non-tariff barriers, since the concepts of being closed or open are ultimately related to the presence or absence of such barriers. However, Dollar and Kraay assert that such direct measures of trade policies (e.g. the average level of tariff rates) capture poorly the extent of actual openness.[6] Instead, they use changes in trade volumes as a percentage of GDP as a 'proxy' for the extent of trade liberalisation.

Is this a reasonable strategy for distinguishing globalisers and non-globalisers? Clearly, many factors *other* than policies affect the volume of trade (such as geography, country size, technological and organizational capabilities, domestic institutions, and the attitudes of potential trading partners). Dollar and Kraay recognize that this dependence of trade volumes on multiple factors makes it difficult to draw inferences that differences in the level of trade volumes are due to trade policies alone. We argue below that the dependence of trade volumes on multiple factors *also* makes it difficult to make credible inferences that changes in trade volumes are due to changes in trade policies, as Dollar and Kraay wish to do.

A related issue is that there are many reasons that *causal* inferences about the relation between trade volumes and growth may be formed incorrectly when applying the authors' framework. First, it is possible that higher growth rates cause a country to have higher volumes of trade relative to GDP. This is both because growth in incomes typically leads to growth in import demand, and because income growth may lead to faster export growth. There are many reasons that more rapid export growth may be triggered by income growth. For a variety of reasons, firms may achieve more competitive costs on international markets as national income increases. Higher incomes may strengthen public finances or otherwise bring about investment in public infrastructure which reduces the costs of producing goods and bringing them to market, or may make possible the overcoming of the asset, liquidity and credit constraints that had previously limited firms from investing adequately in their export capacity.[7]

Second, factors unrelated to trade policy that cause countries to have higher growth rates may *also* cause countries to have higher trade volumes relative to GDP, creating a correlation between these two factors despite the absence of any direct causal connection. For instance, investment in domestic infrastructure (e.g. in transportation and marketing) may facilitate domestic market development (and therefore growth) while simultaneously reducing the costs of bringing domestically produced goods to international markets and international goods to domestic markets, thereby increasing the share of exports and imports in GDP. Higher growth may be the cause of higher trade volumes (rather than the other way), and there may exist unidentified third factors that are causes of both increased growth and trade volumes.[8]

Recognizing some of the possible shortcomings of using trade volumes as the primary selection criterion for globalisers, Dollar and Kraay identify 'globalisers' according to two other criteria: countries that had the greatest reductions in average tariffs and countries that were *both* among those that saw the greatest increases in trade volumes and among those that saw the greatest reductions in average tariffs. Dollar and Kraay claim that for all three groups of 'globalisers' (i.e. those which had the largest increase in trade volumes, those which had the largest reductions in average tariffs, and those which were on both of these lists), globalisers saw greater increases in growth rates than non-globalisers. These claims are superficially plausible, but as we discuss below, do not withstand scrutiny.

Conflicting results

Because very little tariff data was available before 1985, Dollar and Kraay use data on tariff reductions between 1985–89 and 1995–97. The data on changes in trade volumes that they use is based on the interval from 1975–79 to 1995–97. Because the construction of the group of globalisers using reductions in average tariffs is based only on reductions in average tariffs from the 1985–89 period to the 1995–97 period, the comparison of the performance of this group of 'globalisers' with that of 'non-globalisers' has no straightforward interpretation when undertaken for the period before 1985–89.[9] It is true that each group of 'globalisers' saw greater increases in growth from the 1970s period to the 1990s than did 'non-globalisers'. However, it is *not* the case that all three groups of 'globalisers' saw greater increases in growth than non-globalisers during a reasonably *meaningful* period for such comparisons, which in the case of globalisers selected on the basis of reductions in tariffs must at least roughly correspond to the period from 1985–89 to 1995–97. Dollar and Kraay's own Table 3 (reproduced in part in our Table 1) shows that for the group of globalisers and non-globalisers constructed on the basis of reductions in average tariffs from 1985–89 to 1995–97, non-globalisers saw increases in growth rates of 1.7% for the weighted average (going from –0.6% in the 1980s to 1.1% in the 1990s) and 1.3% for the unweighted average (going from –0.4% in the 1980s to 0.9% in the 1990s) as against increases in growth rates for the globalisers of 1.3% for the weighted average (going from 3.6% in the 1980s to 4.9% in the 1990s) and 1.1% for the unweighted average (going from 1.0% in the 1980s to 2.1% in the 1990s). Thus, for a period in which it is reasonably *meaningful* to compare the performance of globalisers and non-globalisers selected on the basis of reductions in average tariffs (i.e. the 1980s to the 1990s), 'non-globalisers' actually *outperformed* 'globalisers' in terms of increases in the growth rate of GDP!

Dollar and Kraay state that 'Given the problems of measuring trade liberalisation that we have discussed, there cannot be a definitive list of recent liberalisers: any one of our three groups of countries constitutes a reasonable candidate set of "globalisers".'[10] If it is believed, as Dollar and Kraay appear to, that increases in trade volumes relative to GDP, reductions in tariffs (and the combination of both) are all plausible selection criteria for 'globalisers' (or countries that have pursued rapid trade liberalisation) then applying these criteria over meaningful comparison periods must lead to the conclusion that the relative growth performance of globalisers and non-globalisers presents a *mixed* record. Globalisers identified on the basis of changes in trade volumes relative to GDP from 1975–79 to 1995–97 saw greater increases in growth over this period than non-globalisers, while globalisers identified on the basis of reductions in average tariffs from 1985–89 to 1995–97 actually saw smaller increases in growth over this period than non-globalisers.[11]

Table 14.1 Performance of 'Globalisers' vs. 'Non-Globalisers' According to the Various Selection Criteria Employed by Dollar and Kraay

Criterion 1: Top One-Third of Developing Countries With Greatest Increases in the Ratio of Trade Volumes Relative to GDP Between the 1975–79 Period and the 1995–97 Period

Average Trade Volumes

	1970s	1980s	1990s	Change, 1970s–1990s	Change, 1980s–1990s
Globalisers Simple Average	37.9%	47.7%	72.4%	34.5%	24.7%
Globalisers Weighted Average	16.0%	24.7%	32.6%	16.6%	7.9%
Non-Globalisers Simple Average	71.7%	68.2%	63.9%	-7.8%	-4.3%
Non-Globalisers Weighted Average	59.9%	51.8%	49.1%	-10.8%	-2.7%

Average Growth in GDP per Capita

	1970s	1980s	1990s	Change, 1970s–1990s	Change, 1980s–1990s
Globalisers Simple Average	3.1%	0.5%	2.0%	-1.1%	1.5%
Globalisers Weighted Average	2.9%	3.5%	5.0%	2.1%	1.5%
Non-Globalisers Simple Average	2.4%	0.1%	0.6%	-1.8%	0.5%
Non-Globalisers Weighted Average	3.3%	0.8%	1.4%	-1.9%	0.6%

DID THE 'GLOBALISERS' GROW FASTER? YES

Criterion 2: Top Third of Developing Countries With the Greatest Declines in Average Tariffs Between the 1985–89 Period and the 1995–97 Period

Average Tariffs

	1970s	1980s	1990s	Change, 1970s–1990s	Change, 1980s–1990s
Globalisers Simple Average	NA	44.3%	23.4%	NA	-20.9%
Globalisers Weighted Average	NA	57.6%	34.7%	NA	-22.9%
Non-Globalisers Simple Average	NA	21.0%	16.5%	NA	-4.5%
Non-Globalisers Weighted Average	NA	21.0%	17.3%	NA	-3.7%

Average Growth in GDP per Capita

	1970s	1980s	1990s	Change, 1970s–1990s	Change, 1980s–1990s
Globalisers Simple Average	1.8%	1.0%	2.1%	0.3%	1.1%
Globalisers Weighted Average	2.8%	3.6%	4.9%	2.1%	1.3%
Non-Globalisers Simple Average	3.1%	-0.4%	0.9%	-2.2%	1.3%
Non-Globalisers Weighted Average	4.2%	-0.6%	1.1%	-3.1%	1.7%

DID THE 'GLOBALISERS' GROW FASTER? CANNOT COMPARE — NO

Criterion 3: Top Third of Developing Countries With both the Greatest Increases in the Ratio of Trade Volumes Relative to GDP Between the 1975–79 Period and the 1995–97 Period and the Greatest Declines in Average Tariffs Between the 1985–89 Period and the 1995–97 Period

Average Trade Volumes

	1970s	1980s	1990s	Change, 1970s–1990s	Change, 1980s–1990s
Globalisers Simple Average	25.6%	31.0%	45.8%	20.2%	14.8%
Globalisers Weighted Average	14.2%	22.5%	27.8%	13.6%	5.3%
Non-Globalisers Simple Average	63.8%	60.8%	71.0%	7.2%	10.2%
Non-Globalisers Weighted Average	56.6%	52.8%	58.5%	1.9%	5.7%

Average Tariffs

	1970s	1980s	1990s	Change, 1970s–1990s	Change, 1980s–1990s
Globalisers Simple Average	NA	51.4%	24.4%	NA	-27.0%
Globalisers Weighted Average	NA	61.3%	36.6%	NA	-24.7%
Non-Globalisers Simple Average	NA	27.3%	19.6%	NA	-7.7%
Non-Globalisers Weighted Average	NA	32.6%	22.6%	NA	-10.0%

Average Growth in GDP per Capita

	1970s	1980s	1990s	Change, 1970s–1990s	Change, 1980s–1990s
Globalisers Simple Average	2.3%	1.4%	3.8%	1.5%	2.4%
Globalisers Weighted Average	2.8%	3.8%	5.4%	2.6%	1.6%
Non-Globalisers Simple Average	2.8%	-0.1%	0.8%	-2.0%	0.9%
Non-Globalisers Weighted Average	3.9%	0.8%	1.8%	-2.1%	1.0%

DID THE 'GLOBALISERS' GROW FASTER? CANNOT COMPARE — YES

Source: Drawn from Dollar and Kraay (2001), Table 3

Tariffs vs. trade volumes

As we have seen, the use of changes in tariffs as the criterion for the selection of globalisers leads to the inference that liberalisation is linked to *lower* growth over a meaningful period of comparison. Rodrik (2000) argues that while average tariffs may not accurately capture the degree of protection of relatively more important commodities or the extent of non-tariff barriers, they are nevertheless an important means of capturing the degree of overall openness or restrictiveness of trade policy regimes. This is because tariffs tend to be highly correlated across a wide range of commodities and because countries tend to employ similar levels of tariff and non-tariff barriers to trade. Rodrik presents a table of countries with the highest and lowest average tariffs, and argues that none of the countries in these groups would be badly misclassified as possessing more restrictive or open trade regimes, respectively. Tariff data is an important source of information on trade policy openness. However, the selection of globalisers on the basis of tariff data and the use of a meaningful time period for comparison between globalisers and non-globalisers leads to results contrary to those claimed by Dollar and Kraay.

Openness – levels vs. changes

Dollar and Kraay refer to the countries with the largest reductions in tariffs or increases in trade volumes in the period that they study as globalisers. Strikingly, however, the countries with the largest reductions in tariffs are those that retain the highest tariffs, and the countries with the largest increase in trade volumes are those with the lowest trade volumes.[12] In what sense are Dollar and Kraay's 'globalisers' really globalisers then? As we mentioned above, 'globalisers' selected on the basis of reductions in average tariffs from 1985–89 to 1995–97 had *lower* increases in growth rates over this period than did non-globalisers. It is true that 'globalisers' selected on this basis had higher *levels* of growth than 'non-globalisers' in both the 1980s and the 1990s. However, 'globalisers' selected on the basis of *reductions* in average tariffs from the 1985–89 period to the 1995–97 period actually had *higher levels* of average tariffs than 'non-globalisers' in both the 1980s and 1990s. The countries with higher levels of average tariffs in the 1980s undertook greater cuts in tariffs from 1985–89 to 1995–97, but still had higher levels of average tariffs after the cuts (in the 1990s). The *greater cuts* in average tariffs were associated with *lower increases* in growth, while the *higher levels* of average tariffs in both the 1980s and 1990s were associated with *higher levels* of growth in both decades. Dollar and Kraay's own data thus seems to suggest, if anything, that when it comes to tariffs, countries with the least open trade regimes perform the best in terms of the growth rate of average income, and that countries that open their trade regimes the least perform the best in terms of increases in the growth rate of average income!

As evident in Table 1, the only group of 'globalisers' selected by the authors that outperform 'non-globalisers' over a meaningful period of comparison are those selected on the basis of having the greatest changes in trade volumes. However, the countries with the greatest change in trade volumes happen to be those with the lowest initial and final trade volumes. It is rather surprising in this context to refer to these countries as 'globalisers'. It is possible that countries with higher initial levels of trade volumes had initially rather open trade regimes and did not further liberalise their trade policies over the period in question, while countries with lower initial trade volumes were initially more closed and began to liberalise their trade policies during this period. If this is the case, while it might be true that the latter group had 'significantly opened up to foreign trade' over the period, it would be misleading to characterize the former group as those 'that have remained more closed', as Dollar and Kraay do. If the purpose of the selection and evaluation of the growth performance of 'globalisers' and 'non-globalisers' is to gain insight into the efficacy of trade liberalisation, it would be important to look not only at how much a country liberalised its trade policy over a given period, but at how liberalised that country's trade policy was at the beginning and the end of the period. Dollar and Kraay's results suggest that countries that had the greater increases in trade volumes saw the greater increases in growth, but that countries with greater levels of trade volumes saw lower levels of growth. This would seem to suggest that the effects of trade liberalisation on growth are mixed.[13] In Dollar and Kraay's sample, 'globalisers' selected on the basis of changes in trade volumes relative to GDP are found to have higher increases in growth. However, it is also true that the countries with more open economies (in level terms) had lower increases in growth![14]

2. Cross-Country Relationships between Changes in Trade Volumes and Average Incomes

The authors' second exercise is a cross-country regression analysis of the effects of trade liberalisation on growth, using changes in trade volumes as a proxy for changes in trade policy. The authors begin by reviewing many of the problems with the existing literature on this subject. They revisit the difficulties involved in measuring trade policy either directly through tariffs or indirectly through trade volumes. They also note the issue (raised prominently in Rodriguez and Rodrik (2000) and Rodrik (1997)) that causal inferences based on statistical associations found in such regressions are plagued by the possible presence of omitted variables. The 'true' causes of higher growth may be empirically correlated with changes in trade policy (or more specifically with changes in trade volumes) for entirely contingent reasons. For example, macroeconomic stabilization or institutional changes (such as clearer definition of property rights) often take place alongside trade liberalisation. If they are omitted from the analysis, then their effect may be misattributed to trade policy.

The authors assert that they have taken measures to avoid this problem. In particular, they claim that their focus on the relationship between *changes* in trade volumes and *changes* in growth rates allows them to control for the effect of unchanging factors, among which they identify geography and institutions, on the level of trade volumes. Unfortunately, the approach of Dollar and Kraay is still prone to the problem. One (already mentioned) reason for this is that the effect of omitted country-specific factors that *do* change over time and that influence growth and trade (such as institutions and infrastructure) will be misattributed to trade by this procedure. The authors claim that their focus on *changes* in trade volumes controls for the effect of omitted variables that lead to both growth and trade policy (or trade volumes) and that do not change over time. By their own admission, therefore, the effect of such variables that *do* change over time may not be adequately controlled for and may be misattributed to trade. Dollar and Kraay suggest that institutions probably do not change much over time, but since their sample spans decades, there is no reason to assume this.[15] Similarly (as we mentioned above in our discussion of Dollar and Kraay's use of changes in trade volumes as a selection criterion for 'globalisers'), there are numerous reasons to believe that higher growth may cause higher trade volumes (rather than the other way around), or that there may exist overlooked third factors unrelated to trade policy (such as improvements to domestic infrastructure and to the productivity of firms) that are simultaneously the causes both of increased growth and of increased trade volumes. A second reason why Dollar and Kraay may misattribute to trade the effect of other factors is that unchanging non-trade-policy factors (such as geography or institutions) may have *different* effects on trade volumes at *different* points in time, either because of structural changes in the national or world economy or because of omitted 'interaction effects' in which the effect of unchanging factors depends on the effects of changing ones. Changes in the global economic system may have made certain unchanging features of countries (such as their geography) more or less relevant over time to explaining the impact of *other* causal factors (including trade policy) on growth, for example, lower communications and transportation costs might make geography a decreasingly significant determinant of trade volumes. These effects will not be adequately accounted for simply by including time as an explanatory variable in the regression analysis, as the authors do. There exist additional reasons to question the authors' econometric methodology and results, concerning, for instance, the validity of their other attempts to control for the presence of omitted variables[16] and for reversed causation, and concerning the robustness of their results to alternative specifications and choices of data.[17]

3. The Relationship between Growth in Average Overall Incomes and the Average Income of the Bottom Quintile

To support their third claim, Dollar and Kraay make reference to their previous paper, Dollar and Kraay (2000), which presents an econometric argument that there is no *systematic* tendency for the share of income possessed by the bottom quintile of the income distribution in countries to change as countries grow. However, this is very different from the claim that in any *given* country an increase in growth rates ... leads to *proportionate* increases in the incomes of the poor. Even if across countries the average factor of proportionality between the growth of average overall income and the growth of average income of those in the bottom quintile of the income distribution is one, this does not imply (indeed it is not the case!) that in most countries the factor of proportionality actually *is* one. Indeed, for many countries in the Dollar and Kraay sample, the factor of proportionality relating the incomes of the bottom quintile and average incomes was either significantly less than or significantly more than one; few saw incomes of the bottom quintile rise exactly (or even nearly) 'one for one' with income. The result arrived at by Dollar and Kraay is the consequence of the co-presence of cases in which the income of the bottom quintile rises more than proportionately with average income and cases in which it rises less than proportionately with average income.[18]

It would therefore be incorrect, when, in considering the possible consequences of growth in aggregate income in a specific country, to claim that based on other countries' experiences, there is no reason to expect any large change in household income inequality. Because the majority of countries in the Dollar and Kraay sample *did* see deviations from 'one-for-one' movements between aggregate income and the income of the bottom quintile, if anything it can be expected that a given country would experience a change in household income inequality that could be quite substantial.[19] The direction and magnitude of this change would obviously depend upon the structural specificities of the country's economy. It would be necessary to enquire into these specificities to determine exactly what effects might reasonably be anticipated. There is little evidence that the income of the bottom quintile will increase 'one-for-one' with average incomes in any *given* country (or even in most), as suggested by Dollar and Kraay.

A way to think about the efficacy of growth in terms of poverty reduction under a scenario in which the incomes of the poor rise 'one-for-one' with average incomes is to consider how effective aggregate growth is from the point of view of targeting. If the objective of a policy-maker is to increase the income of the bottom quintile by a certain amount, a completely targeted policy would identify members of this group and increase their incomes by that amount. A completely untargeted alternative would increase the incomes of everyone reached by the same amount, incidentally increasing those of persons in the bottom quintile in the process. If targeting is costless or inexpensive, then the first policy is a more efficient means of attaining the objective than the second. However, from this standpoint aggregate growth would under the 'one-for-one' assumption be *even less* efficient at reducing poverty than a completely untargeted policy: in an unequal society, it would increase the incomes of the non-poor by *more* than those of the poor! Even if the authors were right that trade liberalisation reduces poverty, they would not have given us much guidance concerning how relatively effective it is as a poverty reducing policy.

Further, what does any of this concern about the bottom quintile of the *income* distribution have to do with poverty? If what is meant by poverty is the possession of inadequate resources with which to attain a relevant set of valued ends (e.g. elementary capabilities), then the income of the bottom quintile is not a very reliable measure of it. As Foster and Szekely (2001) point out, using the bottom quintile of income distribution as the measure of poverty will overstate absolute poverty (understood as income inadequate to achieve elementary capabilities) in wealthy countries (since many in the bottom quintile will have sufficient access to the material preconditions of basic capabilities) and understate it in poorer countries (since many people with income above that of those in the bottom quintile still will not possess elementary capabilities). Although Dollar and Kraay's focus on the poorest quintile may perhaps be justified as a simplifying device, it must not be thought to be what it is not!

It is also widely recognized that it is necessary to account not only for the extent of deprivation (just how many poor people there are) but also for the depth of deprivation (just how poor the poor are). To address this concern, Foster and Szekely adopt a family of measures they call 'general means'. These measures aggregate the wealth of each person in a society, but give a person progressively less 'weight' in the aggregate the more wealth the person has. Such measures are 'absolutist' in that they focus on the absolute level of real incomes, but do not employ an arbitrary poverty line, and incorporate concern for the depth of poverty by giving more weight to a person the poorer the person is. Using a set of 144 household surveys from 20 countries over 25 years, Foster and Szekely examine the relationship between average incomes and poverty as measured by the class of 'general means'. They find that the more sensitive to the lowest incomes a 'general mean' measure of poverty is, the less it increases with increases in average income (i.e. the lower the proportion by which the general mean measure will increase for a given increase in average income). Thus, if a measure of poverty that is sensitive to the bottom of the income distribution is used, it *does* appear that there is a systematic discrepancy between the rate of growth of average incomes and the rate of poverty reduction, and moreover that growth is *less* effective at reducing poverty (understood in this way) the *more* weight one gives to the very poorest people, because their incomes are weakly tied to overall incomes. It is perhaps not entirely surprising that this should be so, as the poorest are often the most excluded from opportunities to participate in markets and otherwise to benefit from aggregate economic growth.

Dollar and Kraay do not present convincing evidence that increased trade liberalisation leads to growth in average incomes or that growth in average incomes reduces poverty 'one-for-one' in a sense that is ultimately relevant to policy selection. The authors' strategy of identifying a group of 'globalisers' that supposedly experienced both more trade liberalisation and more growth is dogged by problems. The criteria adopted to select 'globalisers' are deeply flawed. 'Globalisers' selected by the authors on the basis of having had the highest reductions in average tariffs from the period 1985–89 to the period 1995–97 actually performed slightly *worse* in terms of increases in growth than non-globalisers over this period; it is only by selecting globalisers on the basis of changes in trade volumes (a suspect criterion because of its imperfect relationship to trade policy – the ultimate focus of the concept of trade liberalisation) or by undertaking an inappropriate comparison over mismatched time periods, that Dollar and Kraay come to their conclusions. Countries with large increases in trade volumes often have low levels of trade, casting doubt on whether they can really be characterized as 'globalisers'.

Dollar and Kraay's cross-country regression analysis of the relationship between changes in growth and changes in trade volumes fails adequately to isolate the effect of trade liberalisation on growth. Many factors other than trade policy affect the size of trade volumes. The use of changes rather than levels of trade volumes does not avoid this problem, as it neither controls fully for the influence of time-invariant factors that influence trade volumes in a varying way over time, nor for important omitted variables that do change over time. Among determinants of growth that may have these features are important ones such as infrastructure and institutions.

The authors claim that trade-induced growth will reduce poverty because, on average across countries, the income of the bottom quintile of the population rises in the same proportion as does average income. The jump from this proposition to the conclusion that poverty reduction strategies should focus heavily on producing growth in aggregate incomes is unjustified. Even if proportionate changes in the income of the bottom quintile were on average the same as proportionate changes in average income, this fact would have *no* policy implications for any *specific* country. Further, even if this were true in a particular country, it would not imply that the bottom quintile benefits to the same *extent* as does the rest of the nation from an increase in national income. In any event, there is evidence that the incomes of the poor (as distinguished from those of the bottom quintile of the income distribution) do grow at a slower rate than do average incomes. In particular, there is some evidence that the factor of proportionality between growth in average incomes and growth in the incomes of the poor becomes progressively smaller as poorer people are considered,

The relations between trade, growth, and poverty are real, but our understanding of the links is not advanced by the presupposition that they are simple.

Notes

1. We would like to thank Rodrigo Dias, Camelia Minoiu, Michael Polak and Francisco Rodriguez for helpful comments. Aart Kraay was kind enough to respond to an earlier version of this comment. We would also like to thank Kevin Watkins, who was a coauthor of an earlier version.
2. University of Michigan, hlmnye@umich.edu.
3. Dept. of Economics, Barnard College, Columbia University, sr793@columbia.edu.
4. See http://www/wider.unu.edu/conference/conference-2001-1/dollar%20and%20kraay.pdf. We comment on the version dated March 2001. Dollar and Kraay's paper was subsequently published in the *Economic Journal* in 2004. We provide additional page references for the published version (Dollar and Kraay (2004)) where possible.
5. See Dollar and Kraay (2001), p. 7 and Dollar and Kraay (2004), pp. F30–F31, for these descriptions of what it means for countries to be 'globalisers' or 'non-globalisers'.
6. In support of this view, Dollar and Kraay cite reasons such as that there may be unobserved 'non-tariff barriers to trade, that average tariff rates may not accurately capture the obstructions created by tariffs, that the level of enforcement of tariffs may vary across countries, and that trade-weighted measures of tariffs give little or no weight to commodities for which trade is low or non-existent precisely because tariffs are high.
7. This is only one example. Domestic markets for many products may also expand, allowing firms to become more productive due to the presence of economies of scale. Development may also increase the competitiveness of domestic market environments, forcing firms to reduce 'X-inefficiency' and to approach the 'frontier' of potential productivity, or bring about advances in firm-level technology.
8. While Dollar and Kraay do recognize the problems with the use of trade volumes as a proxy for trade policies and *attempt* (as we discuss below) to deal with some of these problems in the context of their cross country growth regressions, they make no attempt to correct for these problems in the current context (the comparison of the growth performance of groups of countries classified as 'globalisers' and 'non-globalisers'). It is interesting to note that the use of changes in trade volumes as a proxy for changes in trade policy leads to a number of the problems we identify. These problems could in many instances have been avoided if changes in tariffs had been used instead, although if this had been done the authors' conclusions would also have been rather different.
9. In order meaningfully to compare the performance of globalisers versus non-globalisers from 1975–79 and 1995–97, one would need to select globalisers on the basis of those that had reduced tariffs the most from 1975–79 and 1995–97, but as Dollar and Kraay point out it is impossible to construct such a group, as they only have tariff data from the 1985–89 period to the 1995–97 period.
10. Dollar and Kraay (2001), p. 8, and Dollar and Kraay (2004), p. F31.
11. There is some evidence that even the result that globalisers identified on the basis of trade volumes had greater increases in growth rates is somewhat dependent upon the period examined. As Rodrik (2000) has noted, using changes in trade volumes from the 1985–89 period to the 1995–97 period to select globalisers (as opposed to the 1975–79 to 1995–97 comparison employed by Dollar and Kraay) leads to the selection of a very different group of 'globalisers', and one whose growth rates are significantly lower than that obtained by Dollar and Kraay. Moreover, the group obtained by Rodrik using the same data and using the same initial years (of 1985–89) for both tariffs and trade volume shows higher growth rates *before* the 1980s and 1990s than after, which would suggest, if anything, that globalisation had been detrimental in the later period.
12. See Figures 1 and 2 and Table 3 (reproduced in part in our Table 1) in Dollar and Kraay (2001, 2004).
13. If anything this pattern might suggest an 'inverse-U-shaped' relation between openness and growth. In this case there might be an 'optimal' level of openness. In particular, a country possessing a trade regime more closed than this 'optimal' level would increase growth by liberalising, but a country possessing a trade regime more open than this 'optimal' level would see lower levels of growth.
14. It is entirely possible (as indeed Dollar and Kraay argue) that levels of trade volumes may be more influenced by variables not related to trade policy (such as geography and institutional factors)

than changes in trade policy. We concede that the inference that the level of a country's trade volume is due to its trade policy is *more* problematic than the inference that the *change* in the country's trade volumes is due to change in its trade policy. However, it is nevertheless the case that trade policies *are* among the determinants of the level of trade volumes and (as we argue elsewhere) that there are non-trade policy determinants of changes in trade volumes. For both of these reasons, Dollar and Kraay's inferences are misplaced. In particular, we wish only to point out the anomaly that countries with greater increases in trade volumes had lower initial and final levels of trade volumes, while countries with smaller increases in trade volumes had higher initial and final levels of trade volumes, and to raise the *possibility* that this could be due to the fact that the countries in the former group began and ended the period with more closed trade policies while the countries in the latter group began and ended the period with more open trade policies. In this case, it would not be correct to infer that more open trade policy increases growth, as it may be that the more open trade policy of countries with already high trade volumes is the *cause* of their lower growth.

15. In particular, Rodrik (2000) lists Chile, Korea, and China as counter examples.
16. We are not, for instance, convinced that 'contract-intensive money' is a suitable proxy for institutional quality.
17. For instance, it is reasonable to ask whether the same results would be identified if there had been a focus on developing countries alone.
18. Ravallion (2001) presents evidence from a sample of 47 developing countries that in 46 percent of cases inequality rose with changes in income, while in 53 percent of cases inequality fell with changes in income.
19. As one can see from a look at Dollar and Kraay's figure 4, the deviations from 'one-for-one' movement between aggregate income and the income of the bottom quintile in the Dollar and Kraay data are in many cases quite substantial. Figure 4 shows that there is a sizable number of cases in which aggregate income increased but the income of the bottom quintile actually decreased.

References

Foster, James E., and Miguel Szekely (2001), 'Is Economic Growth Good for the Poor? Tracking Low Incomes Using General Means', presented at the WIDER conference on Growth and Poverty, Helsinki, May 25–26. Interamerican Development Bank, Research Department Working Paper No. 453, available at: http://www.iadb.org/res/publications/pubfiles/pubWP-453.pdf.

Ravallion, Martin (2001), 'Growth, Inequality, and Poverty: Looking Beyond the Averages', presented at the WIDER conference on Growth and Poverty, Helsinki, May 25–26, World Bank Policy Research Working Paper No. 2558.

Rodriguez, Francisco and Dani Rodrik (2000), 'Trade Policy and Economic Growth: A Skeptic's Guide to the Cross-National Evidence', in Ben Bernanke and Kenneth Rogoff (eds), *Macroeconomics Annual*, MIT Press for NBER.

Rodrik, Dani (1997), 'Trade Policy and Economic Performance in Sub-Saharan Africa', manuscript, prepared for the Swedish Ministry for Foreign Affairs, November. National Bureau of Economic Research Working Paper No. 6562.

Rodrik, Dani (2000), 'Comments on "Trade, Growth, and Poverty", by D. Dollar and A. Kraay', manuscript, October.

[15]

ELSEVIER

www.elsevier.com/locate/worlddev

World Development Vol. 33, No. 7, pp. 1045–1063, 2005
© 2005 Elsevier Ltd. All rights reserved
Printed in Great Britain
0305-750X/$ - see front matter
doi:10.1016/j.worlddev.2005.04.003

Openness and Inequality in Developing Countries: A Review of Theory and Recent Evidence

EDWARD ANDERSON [*]
Overseas Development Institute, London, UK

Summary. — Increased openness affects income inequalities within developing countries by affecting factor price ratios, asset inequalities, spatial inequalities, gender inequalities, and the amount of income redistribution. Most time-series studies find that greater openness has increased the relative demand for skilled labor, but most cross-country studies find that greater openness has had little impact on overall income inequality. One possible explanation is that countries selected for time-series analysis are not representative of all developing countries. Another is that the effects of openness on income inequality *via* the relative demand for skilled labor have been offset by its effects *via* other channels.
© 2005 Elsevier Ltd. All rights reserved.

Key words — trade, technology transfer, FDI, income distribution

1. INTRODUCTION

This paper reviews existing theory and recent empirical evidence regarding the links between openness and inequality in developing countries. It defines openness by the ease and cost with which goods and services, factors of production (e.g., capital, labor, skills), and technology can flow into and out of a country. As is well known, many developing countries have become more open in recent decades according to this definition. The many potential consequences of this trend have been debated extensively in both academic and policy circles. This paper focuses on its consequences for inequalities in income levels between individuals within countries.

An understanding of the links between openness and inequality is important for three reasons. First, when combined with evidence on links between openness and economic growth, it can tell us about the effect of openness on absolute poverty. For example, if we know that openness raises economic growth, but has no effect on the distribution of income, we can be reasonably confident that openness reduces absolute poverty. Second, it can tell us about the likelihood that openness-increasing policies will in fact be implemented. Trade liberalization is less likely to be implemented if the costs associated with it are concentrated on specific groups

in society, while the benefits are widely spread—especially if those groups are vocal or influential politically. Third, it tells us more about how openness affects individuals' and households' well-being. This is because of widespread evidence that people are concerned not only by their absolute levels of income and consumption, but also by their levels relative to others.

Other surveys of the literature on openness and inequality in developing countries do exist. Wood (1997), O'Conner and Lunati (1999), Arbache (2001), Cooper (2002), and Rama (2003) all review recent theory and empirical evidence relating to the effects of openness on wage inequalities between skilled and less-skilled workers. The contribution lies in updating some of these earlier reviews, and extending the discussion of theory and evidence to include the effects of openness on other sorts of inequalities.

The paper proceeds as follows. Section 2 outlines the various channels through which greater openness can affect inequality in theory, and discusses the mechanisms involved in each case. Section 3 then describes recent evidence

_____

[*] I am grateful for many helpful comments and suggestions from Simon Maxwell, Andrew McKay, Oliver Morrissey, Tony Killick, Dirk Willem te Velde, Adrian Wood, and three anonymous referees. Final revision accepted: January 31, 2005.

regarding the direction and magnitude of these effects in practice, while Section 4 summarizes. Two points of clarification are required at the outset. First, the paper focuses purely on the effects of increased openness on inequality within countries, and ignores any effects on inequality between countries. Second, it focuses purely on the effects of increased openness on inequalities between individuals' incomes, averaged over time. The extent to which increased openness has affected other inequalities—for example, in levels of income between countries, or in broader measures of well-being within or between countries—are clearly also important issues, but ones which cannot also be addressed adequately in a single paper.

2. THEORY

(a) Basic framework

This section outlines a basic framework for identifying the various channels through which greater openness can affect income inequality. The first step is to link inequalities in income among individuals to inequalities in the ownership of assets or factors of production (e.g., land, capital, labor, skill). We begin by expressing the income of any one individual i as the sum of their ownership of each factor multiplied by its return. In algebraic terms, this is shown by

$$y_i \equiv w_{1i}E_1\omega_{1i} + \cdots + w_{ji}E_j\omega_{ji}, \qquad (1)$$

where y_i is the income of individual i, w_{ji} is the return to factor j for individual i, E_j is the total amount of factor j available in the country, and ω_{ji} is the share of the total amount of factor j owned by individual i. We then derive an expression for overall inequality, under the assumption that the returns to each asset do not vary across individuals ($w_{ji} = w_j$ for all i). For instance, dividing each side by total income and summing over the poorest quintile of individuals (by income) yields

$$\varphi_P \equiv \lambda_1\omega_{P1} + \cdots + \lambda_j\omega_{Pj}, \qquad (2)$$

where φ_P is the share of national income received by the poorest 20% (one common measure of overall inequality), λ_j is the share of national income received by factor j, and ω_{Pj} is the share of the jth factor owned by the poorest 20% (White & Anderson, 2001). [1] Eqn. (2) highlights the fact that, although the underlying sources of income inequality are inequalities in

the ownership of assets, the distribution of national income among factors also affects inequality. In particular, if the ownership of some factor j is distributed more equally than some factor k, an increase in the share of factor j in national income relative to factor k will reduce income inequality, and *vice versa*.

The next step is to link the relative shares of any two factors in national income to their relative return and relative quantity available. In a purely accounting sense, the share of each factor in total income depends on the total amount of it available and its return. In algebraic terms, this is shown by

$$\lambda_j \equiv \frac{w_j E_j}{Y}, \qquad (3)$$

where Y is national income. This implies that the ratio of any two factor shares in national income is

$$\frac{\lambda_j}{\lambda_k} \equiv \frac{w_j}{w_k} \cdot \frac{E_j}{E_k}, \qquad (4)$$

where E_j/E_k is the relative quantity of the factors j and k, and w_j/w_k is their relative return.

The last step is to link changes in relative returns and quantities to shifts in relative demand and relative supply. Assuming a constant elasticity of substitution (CES) production function, we can express the relative demand schedule as

$$\frac{E_j}{E_k} = a\left(\frac{w_j}{w_k}\right)^{-\sigma}, \qquad (5)$$

where a is a term representing the exogenous level of relative demand (for factor j relative to factor k), and σ is the elasticity of substitution between factor j and factor k. It is then convenient to express the relative supply schedule as

$$\frac{E_j}{E_k} = b\left(\frac{w_j}{w_k}\right)^{\varepsilon}, \qquad (6)$$

where b is a term representing the exogenous level of relative supply (of factor j relative to factor k), and ε is the elasticity of relative supply. Under these assumptions, an increase in the demand for some factor j relative to another factor k raises their relative return (w_j/w_k) and their relative shares in national income (λ_j/λ_k). An increase in the supply of some factor j relative to another factor k reduces their relative return, but its effect on their relative shares in national income depends on whether the elasticity of substitution between them is greater or less than unity. [2]

A final consideration is that people may differ in the amount by which they adjust their ownership of an asset in response to a change in its return. In this case, changes in relative factor returns will also affect the distribution of factors among individuals, as well as their relative shares in national income, with additional implications for inequality. If, for instance, the elasticity of supply of some factor j relative to another factor k (e.g., human capital relative to unskilled labor) is greater among people who own a large amount of factor j, a rise in its return (relative to factor k) will increase inequality in its ownership, as well as raise its share of national income (and its aggregate relative quantity).

This simple framework suggests therefore that there are two main channels through which an increase in openness could affect overall income inequality. First, it may affect the relative shares of the factors of production in national income, by affecting the relative demand for, or the relative supply of, those factors. Second, it may affect the amount of inequality in the ownership of the factors of production, either by affecting the underlying sources of asset inequality, or by affecting relative factor returns. There are two other channels which may be significant in practice but which cannot be written down simply in the above framework. Greater openness may also affect income inequality by altering gaps between individuals in the returns to a given factor of production, for example between men and women, or between regions, or between rural and urban areas. It may also affect income inequality by altering the ability or willingness of governments to redistribute income *via* taxes and transfers. We now discuss each of these four channels in more detail.

(b) *Openness and relative factor shares*

The standard model used by economists to analyze the effect of trade on the relative returns to different factors of production is the Heckscher–Ohlin (HO) model. In its standard and simplest form, its predictions in developing countries are well known: greater openness boosts the demand for unskilled relative to skilled labor, which raises their wage and share of national income relative to skilled la-

bor. Given that unskilled labor is a more equally distributed asset than skill, this reduces overall income inequality.

This hypothesis needs to be qualified in two main ways. On the one hand, there are additional considerations arising from models which, although retaining the central assumptions of HO theory, include more countries or more factors or production. For instance, in HO models which include natural resources as a factor of production (e.g., Leamer, 1987), greater openness may well raise overall inequality in those developing countries which have abundant supplies of those resources (relative to other factors). The reason is that greater openness will raise the relative returns to natural resources in such countries, and that natural resources are typically, although not necessarily, less equally distributed than other assets. [3] Alternatively, in HO models which assume many countries, greater openness will raise the relative demand for skilled labor in any middle-income developing countries whose supply of skilled relative to unskilled labor is higher than the effective world average.

On the other hand, there are additional considerations arising from models which depart from the central assumptions of HO theory. In particular, once we relax the HO assumption that all countries have equal access to the best available production technology, greater openness to that technology may well increase the relative demand for skilled labor, even in low-income developing countries. This might be for three reasons. First, learning and adapting to a new technology is a difficult task which requires the use of skilled labor (Pissarides, 1997). Second, recent technological progress in developed countries—e.g., personal computers, automated assembly lines—has reduced firms' demand for unskilled labor, and is likely to have the same effect when transferred to developing countries (Berman & Machin, 2000). Third, cheaper access to foreign technology allows developing countries to compete internationally in more skill-intensive goods, which raises their average skill intensity of production, and thus the relative demand for skilled labor (Feenstra & Hanson, 1997). [4]

A synthesis of some of these arguments with those associated with traditional HO theory is provided by Wood (2002). He distinguishes between two different forms of increased openness in developing countries: falling barriers to trade, mainly through lower freight, tariffs, finance, and insurance charges, and falling barriers to movements of know-how, mainly through lower travel and communication (T&C) costs. He assumes two types of labor in developing countries: medium-skilled (E) and unskilled (U), and two types of goods: low-quality non-tradable (B), and high-quality tradable (A). All A-goods require the input of foreign know-how, which comes at a cost, equal to the additional time spent by highly skilled (K) workers based in developed countries traveling to and from, and working in, developing countries.

Under these assumptions, a reduction in T&C costs causes a shift in A-sector production from developed to developing countries, and encourages a reallocation of labor out of the B-sector in developing countries. This either increases or reduces the demand for E-workers relative to U-workers in developing countries, depending on whether new A-sector production requires a higher or a lower ratio of E-workers to U-workers than is available in the B-sector. Lower trade costs, by contrast, cause a reallocation of production within the A-sector, toward goods which require a lower ratio of E-workers to U-workers, which always reduces the demand for E-workers relative to U-workers (in accordance with HO principles). The overall impact of openness therefore depends on the balance between reductions in trade costs and reductions in T&C costs, and on the existing relative supply of E-workers in the B-sector.

Two other implications of the Wood (2002) model are worth noting. First, there are interactions between the effects of reductions in trade costs and reductions in T&C costs. In particular, the effect of a decline in trade costs on relative demand is smaller when the level of T&C costs is high. The reason is that, when T&C costs are high, the A-sector accounts for a small proportion of total employment, and a reallocation of labor within it has little impact on the economywide demand for E-workers relative to U-workers. Second, the shift in A-sector production from developed to developing countries also tends (at least initially) to increase the demand for E-workers relative to U-workers in developed countries, as it is the goods which require the lowest ratio of E-workers to U-workers which shift first. It is therefore conceivable that greater openness raises the relative demand for E-workers in both developed and developing countries.

(c) *Openness and asset inequality*

Greater openness may affect asset inequality *via* two main channels. The first is *via* income effects. If greater openness raises the real incomes of poorer groups, this will tend to relax the constraints they face in obtaining credit, increase their investment in asset accumulation, and lower asset inequality. If greater openness reduces the real incomes of poorer groups, the effect works in the opposite direction, tending to raise asset inequality.

The second is *via* differences between individuals in the amount by which they adjust their holdings of assets in response to changes in the return to those assets. To take the case of human capital, one expectation is that the more human capital people already have, the less responsive they will be to a rise in its return. This might be because they have less time before retiring to benefit from additional human capital, or because they pay a higher opportunity cost for additional time spent out of work acquiring human capital. If this is this case, a rise in the return to human capital will lead to a decline in the amount of inequality in its ownership, and the effect of the rise in the return to human capital on overall inequality will be dampened. However, an alternative scenario is that the more human capital people already have, the more responsive they will be to a rise in its return. This might be because they also possess higher amounts of other assets, and can finance additional spending on education and training by running down other assets (e.g., financial savings) at a constant opportunity cost, without resorting to reductions in other components of household expenditure. If this is the case, a rise in the return to human capital will lead to an increase in the amount of inequality in its ownership, and the effect of the rise in the return to human capital on overall inequality will be reinforced. [5]

As a result, it is not generally possible to predict in advance the effect of a change in the relative returns to some asset, such as human capital, on the amount of inequality in its ownership. However, the former outcome, where a rise in the return to an asset leads to reduction in the amount of inequality in its ownership, is more likely, the easier it is for poorer groups to obtain access to credit. In this case, the relative advantage of wealthier groups in financing additional investments in human capital (or other assets) will be lower.

(d) *Openness and spatial inequality*

Understanding of disparities in income and factor prices between regions has expanded rapidly in recent years thanks to developments in the field of economic geography. One hypothesis is that income disparities between regions within a country are smaller if the country is well integrated into international trade (Fujita, Krugman, & Venables, 1999). The reasoning is as follows: Under a policy of import substitution, domestic firms will prefer to locate close to national centers of final demand and intermediate inputs, in order to lower transport costs. As they do so, they encourage other firms to do the same, setting in motion a process of cumulative causation, leading to a concentration of population and economic activity in one region, and an increase in gaps between regions in the real earnings of immobile factors of production (e.g., land). Following trade liberalization, however, firms can make use of foreign sources of demand and intermediate inputs. Assuming that access to foreign markets is similar across regions within a country, this reduces firms' incentives to locate in the core region and reduces the concentration of economic activity there. Gaps between regions in the real earnings of immobile factors decline as a result.

Although not directly concerned with spatial inequality, the effects of trade on the sectoral structure of production predicted by the HO theory may have indirect effects on inequality between urban and rural areas. In countries with a comparative advantage in manufactures, greater openness raises the returns to human resources relative to natural resources. This will tend to increase average income gaps between urban and rural areas, because the ratio of human to natural resources is typically higher in urban areas than in rural areas (on account of the fact that manufacturing typically concentrates in urban areas, while primary production is typically tied to rural areas). The opposite— that is, a narrowing of average income gaps between urban and rural areas—will occur in countries with a comparative advantage in primary products.

(e) *Openness and gender inequality*

Where men and women have different average skill levels, increased openness will affect the size of wage gaps between men and women through its effect on the size of wage gaps between skilled and unskilled labor. However, it may also affect the "residual" gender wage gap, namely that proportion of the gender wage gap which remains after controlling for measured gaps in skill levels between men and women. It has been argued, for example, that the expansion of manufactured exports has increased the demand for female relative to male labor in developing countries. This is either because female workers are perceived by exporting firms as less likely to make demands for improved wages and/or working conditions, or because women possess a comparative advantage relative to men in performing the light industrial tasks associated with developing country exports such as clothing, footwear, and basic electronics. In either case, the consequence of increased openness will be an increase in women's labor market participation and wages relative to men. It is also argued that, by increasing competition in product markets, increased openness to trade will reduce wage gaps between men and women based on discrimination (Becker, 1971).

However, there may be offsetting effects. First, increases in the relative earnings and employment opportunities of women may be offset by a decline in their leisure time, in absolute terms and relative to men (Fontana & Wood, 2000). Second, where agriculture predominates in export activity, women may not benefit directly from increased openness, either because their property rights in land are limited, or because they have limited access to credit, inputs, and marketing channels (Fontana, Joekes, & Masika, 1998). For these reasons, impacts of openness on gender inequality are in practice more likely to be mixed, depending in particular on the type of goods a country exports and on institutions governing women's access to land and other productive assets.

(f) *Openness and redistribution*

Most economists believe that governments in open economies should engage in some form of income redistribution, for purely instrumental reasons. The reason is that unless the people who are made worse off by trade, in absolute terms, are compensated in some way by those who gain, they will prevent a policy of free trade from being implemented, and the aggregate gains from free trade from being realized. Of course, many people also believe that governments should redistribute income from richer to poorer citizens as an independent goal in itself.

It has been argued that greater openness reduces the ability of national governments to redistribute income (e.g., Rodrik, 1997; Rodrik & van Ypersele, 1999). The main argument is that as some factors of production (e.g., capital, highly skilled labor) become internationally mobile, they become more sensitive to differences between countries in the amount of tax they have to pay. Any attempt to raise taxes on their earnings will simply cause them to relocate to countries where taxes are lower. The result is that the tax burden is shifted onto immobile factors of production (e.g., land), and redistribution from mobile to immobile factors becomes impossible.

Again however, the argument needs qualifying. First, it is not that national governments in open economies cannot redistribute (from mobile to immobile factors of production), it is that they cannot do so by more than other open economies. If all countries have similar ideas about the amount of redistribution they would like to achieve, and set taxes accordingly, there is no conflict between redistribution and openness. Second, in the presence of agglomeration forces, even perfectly mobile capital becomes "tied" to specific locations and integration need not lead to falling tax rates (Baldwin & Krugman, 2000). [6]

3. EVIDENCE

This section describes the empirical research which has been undertaken in recent years toward testing the various hypotheses about the effects of greater openness on inequality within developing countries described in the previous section.

(a) *Openness and aggregate inequality*

Several studies have tested hypotheses outlined in the previous section using aggregate measures of overall inequality, such as the Gini coefficient or the share of the poorest 20% in national income. Details of some of these are shown in Table 1. Attention is restricted to published studies using the Deininger and Squire (D&S) (1996) dataset, or recent extensions of it, and which have regressed the level of openness on the level of inequality, the change in openness on the change in inequality, or some combination of the two. [7] A distinc-

tion is drawn between tests of the three different hypotheses. The first is that greater openness raises overall inequality in all countries. Section 2(b) showed that this hypothesis can be derived from recent theoretical models including Feenstra and Hanson (1997) and Wood (2002). Tests of this hypothesis involve regressions of the form:

$$INQ_{it} = \alpha_0 + \alpha_1 OPEN_{it} + \alpha_2 Z_{it} + e_{it}, \qquad (7)$$

where INQ is an aggregate measure of inequality, $OPEN$ is a measure of a country's openness to international trade or capital flows, and Z is a set of control variables also thought to affect inequality. Support for the hypothesis requires that $\alpha_1 > 0$.

The second hypothesis is that greater openness reduces overall inequality in developing countries, but increases overall inequality in developed countries. This hypothesis is typically derived from the basic HO model of trade outlined in Section 2(b), in which developed countries have an abundant supply of skilled relative to unskilled labor, and developing countries have an abundant supply of unskilled relative to skilled labor. Tests of this hypothesis involve regressions of the form:

$$INQ_{it} = \beta_0 + \beta_1 OPEN_{it} + \beta_2 OPEN_{it} \cdot Y_{it}$$
$$+ \beta_3 Z_{it} + \varepsilon_{it}, \qquad (8)$$

where Y is a qualitative or quantitative measure of development, such as OECD/non-OECD (qualitative) or GDP per capita (quantitative). The coefficient β_2 measures the direction and amount by which the effect of openness on inequality varies by level of development. The coefficient β_1 measures the effect of openness on inequality when y is zero (equal to its effect at all other values if $\beta_2 = 0$). Support for the hypothesis requires that $\beta_1 < 0$ and $\beta_2 > 0$.

The third hypothesis is that the effects of greater openness on overall inequality vary, depending on the factor endowments of the country opening up. This hypothesis is derived from HO models with many countries (see, for example, Wood, 1997). In such models, the higher is the endowment of any one factor j relative to labor, the greater (more positive or less negative) will be the effect of an increase in openness on the return to factor j, and the share of factor j in national income, relative to labor. Because labor is the most equally distributed asset, this in turn implies that the higher is the endowment of any one factor j relative to labor, the greater (more positive or less negative) will be the effect of an increase in openness on overall inequality. Tests of this third hypothesis therefore involve regressions of the form:

$$INQ_{it} = \chi_0 + \chi_1 OPEN_{it} + \chi_{2j} OPEN_{it} \cdot E_{ijt}$$
$$+ \beta_3 Z_{it} + \varepsilon_{it}, \qquad (9)$$

where E is a set of variables measuring the factor endowments of country i, all relative to labor. Each coefficient χ_{2j} measures the direction and amount by which the effect of openness on inequality varies according to a country's endowment of factor j (relative to labor). Support for the hypothesis requires that each χ_{2j} is positive.

Even when distinguishing between these different types of studies, there remains considerable variety among them, in the measure of openness used, the countries and periods included in the sample, and the econometric strategy, making the results difficult to compare. However, it is possible to draw three broad conclusions. First, there is almost no support for the first hypothesis, that greater openness raises aggregate inequality in all countries. Its null cannot be rejected in the studies by White and Anderson (2001), Ravallion (2001), Dollar and Kraay (2002), Edwards (1997), and Calderon and Chong (2001). The two exceptions where its null can be rejected are Barro (2000) and Lundberg and Squire (2003). Second, there is conflicting evidence regarding the second hypothesis. Calderon and Chong (2001) find that greater openness does reduce inequality in developing countries. However, Barro (2000) and Ravallion (2001) both find that the effect of openness on inequality *declines* as per capita GDP increases. Moreover, Dollar and Kraay (2002), Edwards (1997), and Higgins and Williamson (1999) all find no significant effect of openness on inequality at any level of development. Finally, there is qualified support for the third hypothesis. In particular, both Spilimbergo, Londono, and Szekely (1999) and Fischer (2001) find that the effect of openness on inequality increases as countries' endowments of human capital increase. However, they also both find that the effect of openness declines as countries' endowments of capital increase, and that the effect of openness is unaffected by countries' endowments of arable land per capita (as do Dollar & Kraay, 2002).

Further empirical work along these lines would be useful. There is scope for extending tests of the third hypothesis, for example, by testing the interaction of openness measures with a wider range of factor endowment measures. There is also scope for testing the predictions of the Wood (2002) model, which would involve including measures of both openness to trade and openness to foreign technology and know-how. However, studies of the effects of openness on aggregate inequality do suffer certain inherent drawbacks. First, there are concerns regarding the quality of the underlying data. Although most studies using the Deininger and Squire (1996) dataset restrict the analysis to "high-quality" observations, there remain differences in survey design between countries and over time (income- *vs.* expenditure-based; personal *vs.* household income; gross *vs.* net income) which reduce levels of statistical significance. Second, there is the possibility that any observed impact of openness on inequality is spurious, because observable indicators of openness are correlated with unobserved variables which may also affect inequality. [8] Perhaps most importantly, they tell us little about the channels through which openness affects inequality—through relative factor returns, spatial or gender inequality, government redistribution, asset inequality, and so on—information which is important to policy makers.

(b) *Openness and relative factor returns*

There has been a large amount of research into the effect of openness on one particular factor price ratio, the wage of skilled relative to unskilled labor. Details of some of these studies are shown in Table 2. Attention here is restricted to publicly accessible, time-series studies which span a period of at least five years, which use either education attainment, occupation, or the wage itself as a proxy for skill level, and which make some attempt to measure the effect of increased openness on any change in the relative wage.

Among these, a distinction can again be drawn between tests of three different hypotheses. The first is that reductions in barriers to trade reduce the relative demand for skilled labor, by shifting the structure of production toward more labor-intensive sectors, as predicted by standard HO theory. The second is that reductions in barriers to foreign investment increase the relative demand for skilled labor, by shifting the structure of production toward more skill-intensive sectors, as

Table 1. *Cross-country econometric studies of the effect of openness on inequality*

Study	Hypothesis	Measure of inequality	Measure of openness	Sample	Controlling variables	Results
White and Anderson (2001)	(1)	Q1, Q1 + Q2	Trade–GDP ratio	SYs, 1960–90	ETHNIC, GDPpc, initial Gini, INFL, LE, POL, URBAN	$\alpha_1 = 0$
Lundberg and Squire (2003)	(1)	Gini	S&W (1995); trade–GDP ratio	5-Year PAs, 1960–94, $N = 38$	EDUC, FINANCE, GDPpc, GOV, INFL, LGINI, POL, TOT	$\alpha_1 > 0$, S&W (1995) $\alpha_1 = 0$, trade–GDP ratio
Edwards (1997)	(1), (2)	Gini; Q1	Five measures of policy barriers to trade	DAs, 1970s and 1980s, $N = 44$	EDUC, GDPpc, INFL	$\beta_1, \beta_2 = 0$
Higgins and Williamson (1999)	(1), (2)	Gini; Q5/Q1	S&W (1995); capital controls; tariffs/ quotas on imports; trade–GDP ratio; adjusted trade–GDP ratio	DAs, 1960s, 1970s, 1980s and 1990s, $N = 85$	AGE, EDUC, FINANCE, GDPpw, GDPpw2, LAND, POL; AFR, LA, OBTYPE	$\alpha_1 = 0$, $\beta_2 = 0$
Barro (2000)	(1), (2)	Gini	Adjusted trade–GDP ratio	SYs; 1960–90, $N = 84$	EDUC, GDPpc, GDPpc2; AFR, LA, OBTYPE	$\alpha_1 > 0$, $\beta_1 > 0$, $\beta_2 < 0$
Ravallion (2001)	(1), (2)	Gini	Exports-to-GDP ratio	5-Year PAs, 1947–94, $N = 50$	BLPREM, EDUC, FINANCE, POL, URBAN	$\alpha_1 = 0$, $\beta_1 > 0$, $\beta_2 < 0$
Calderon and Chong (2001)	(2)	Gini	Trade-to-GDP ratio	5-Year PAs, 1960–95, $N = 102$	BLPREM, EDUC, FINANCE, GDPpc, lagged Gini, RER, TOT	$\beta_1 < 0$, $\beta_2 = 0$,

Study	Models	Measure of inequality	Measure of openness	Sample	Controlling variables	Results
Dollar and Kraay (2002)	(1), (2), (3)	Average income of Q1	Trade–GDP ratio; adjusted trade–GDP ratio; S&W (1995); import taxes-import value ratio; membership of WTO; capital controls	SYs, 1950–99, N = 92	FINANCE, GDPpc, GOV, INFL, LAW; REGION	$\alpha_1 = 0$, β_1, $\beta_2 = 0$, $x_1, x_{2j} = 0$
Spilimbergo et al. (1999)	(3)	Gini; Q1–Q5	Adjusted trade–GDP ratio	SYs, 1965–92, N = 34	CAPITAL, EDUC, GDPpc, GDPpc2, LAND	$x_{2j} > 0$ (EDUC), $x_{2j} < 0$ (CAPITAL), $x_{2j} = 0$ (LAND)
Fischer (2001)	(3)	Gini	S&W (1995)	5-Year PAs, 1965–90, N = 66	CAPITAL, EDUC, LAND	$x_{2j} > 0$ (EDUC), $x_{2j} < 0$ (CAPITAL), $x_{2j} = 0$ (LAND)

Measure of inequality: Gini = Gini coefficient; Q1 = share of 1st (poorest) quintile in national income, Q2 = share of 2nd quintile in national income, ..., Q5 = share of 5th (richest) quintile.

Measures of openness: S&W (1995) = Sachs and Warner (1995). The trade–GDP ratio is the sum of the value of imports and exports, divided by GDP. The adjusted trade–GDP ratio is the residual value of this variable obtained from a regression of the actual trade–GDP ratio on geographical characteristics.

Sample: All studies use data from both developed and developing countries. DAs = decade averages, PAs = period averages, SYs = single years, N = number of countries in sample.

Controlling variables: Quantitative: AGE = age structure of population, BLPREM = black market premium on exchange rate, CAPITAL = capital per worker, EDUC = education per worker, ETHNIC = ethno-linguistic fragmentation, FINANCE = financial sector development, GDPpc = GDP per capita, GDPpc2 = GDP per capita squared; GDPpw = GDP per worker, GDPpw2 = GDP per worker squared, GOV = government size (% of GDP), INFL = inflation, LAW = rule of law, LAND = arable land per capita, LE = life expectancy, LGINI = Gini coefficient of land holdings, POL = political and civil liberties, RER = real exchange rate, TOT = terms of trade, URBAN = urban population (% of total). Qualitative: LA = Latin America, AFR = Africa, REGION = all regions, OBYTPE = type of inequality observation (gross/net income, personal/household, income/consumption).

Results: >0 indicates a coefficient is statistically significant and positive; <0 indicates a coefficient is statistically significant and negative; =0 indicates a coefficient is not statistically significant.

Table 2. *Time-series empirical studies of the effect of openness on the relative wage of skilled labor*

Study	Countries	Period	Data source	Measure of skill	Methodology
Robbins (1996)	Argentina, Chile, Colombia, Costa Rica, Malaysia, Mexico, Philippines, Taiwan, Uruguay	Mid-1970s to early 1990s*	Household surveys	Education	Supply and demand
Beyer *et al.* (1999)	Chile	1960–96	Household survey	Education	Supply and demand
Robbins and Gindling (1999)	Costa Rica	1976–93	Household survey	Education	Supply and demand
te Velde and Morrissey (forthcoming)	Hong Kong, Philippines, Singapore, South Korea, Thailand	1983–98*	ILO wage data, from Freeman and Oostendorp (2000)	Occupation	Supply and demand
te Velde (2003)	(a) Chile, Bolivia, Costa Rica, Colombia	(a) 1978–2001*	(a) Household surveys	Education, occupation**	Supply and demand
	(b) Argentina, Bolivia, Chile, Colombia, Costa Rica, Ecuador, El Salvador, Guatemala, Honduras, Mexico, Nicaragua, Panama, Paraguay, Uruguay, Venezuela	(b) 1990–99*	(b) ECLAC (2002) wage data		
Feenstra and Hanson (1997)	Mexico	1975–88	Industrial Census	Occupation	Cost function
Berman and Machin (2000)	Bangladesh, Chile, Colombia, Egypt, Ethiopia, Guatemala, India, Malaysia, Pakistan, Peru, Philippines (1970s only), South Korea, Tanzania, Uruguay, Venezuela	1970–80 and 1980–90*	UN General Industrial Statistics Database	Occupation	Cost function

Gorg and Strobl (2002)	Ghana	1991–97	Firm survey (longitudinal)	Occupation	Cost function
Mazumdar and Quispe-Agnoli (2002)	Peru	1991–97	Employment survey	Occupation	Cost function
Wood (1994)	Taiwan, South Korea, Hong Kong, Singapore	1960s to late 1980s*	Varied	Education, occupation, wage**	Discursive
Hanson and Harrison (1999)	Mexico	(a) 1965–88 (b) 1984–90	(a) Industrial Census (b) Firm survey	Occupation	Mainly discursive
Robertson (2000)	Mexico	1987–95	Employment survey	Education, wage	Mandated wage regressions
Gindling and Robbins (2001)	Chile, Costa Rica	1974–90 (Chile), 1987–95 (Costa Rica)	Household surveys	Wage	Discursive
Green et al. (2001)	Brazil	1981–99	Household survey	Education, wage	Discursive

Notes: * Exact years vary by country. ** Exact measure of skill varies by country.

predicted by Feenstra and Hanson (1997) and, in some cases, Wood (2002). The third is that reductions in barriers to trade and investment increase the relative demand for skilled labor, by increasing the use of foreign, skill-biased, technologies by individual firms and enterprises, as predicted by Pissarides (1997) and Berman and Machin (2000).

Two main empirical approaches have been used to test these hypotheses. The first is the "supply-and-demand" approach. This begins by assuming that the quantity of skilled relative to unskilled labor is unaffected by their relative wage. In this case, Eqn. (5) in Section 2(a) can be re-expressed as

$$\ln \left(\frac{w_s}{w_u}\right) = \ln(a/\sigma) - \frac{1}{\sigma} \ln \left(\frac{E_S}{E_U}\right), \qquad (10)$$

where E_S/E_U is the supply of skilled relative to unskilled labor (assumed exogenous), a is the demand for skilled relative to unskilled labor, w_s/w_u is the relative wage, and σ is the elasticity of substitution between skilled and unskilled labor. One can then test econometrically whether a proxy measure of openness to trade (e.g., trade–GDP ratio, FDI–GDP ratio) or the use of foreign technology (e.g., imports of capital equipment) has a significant effect on the relative wage, controlling for relative supply. If so, it can be inferred that openness to trade, or the use of foreign technology, affects relative demand. [9] Examples of this approach include Beyer, Rojas, and Vergara (1999), Robbins (1996), Gindling and Robbins (2001), te Velde and Morrissey (forthcoming), and te Velde (2003).

The second is the "cost function" approach. This begins by assuming that firms minimize their costs of production, by varying the use of skilled and unskilled labor, in response to changes in production technology and in the economywide relative wage of skilled labor. Assuming a translog production function, the share of skilled wages in firm i's total wage bill (s_{it}) can then be expressed as

$$s_i = a + b \ln \left(\frac{w_s}{w_u}\right) + c \ln K_i + d \ln Y_i + e \ln T_i, \qquad (11)$$

where w_s/w_u is the economywide wage of skilled relative to unskilled labor, K_i is capital used by firm i, Y_i is firm value added, and T_i is a set of variables reflecting the type of technology used by firm i. One can then test econometrically

whether a proxy measure of the use of foreign technology (e.g., imports of capital equipment) raises the share of skilled labor in the total wage bill, controlling for the relative wage. If so, it can be inferred that the use of foreign technology raises the relative demand for skilled labor. [10] Examples of this approach include Gorg and Strobl (2002), Mazumdar and Quispe-Agnoli (2002), Feenstra and Hanson (1997), and Berman and Machin (2000). The "supply and demand" and "cost-function" approaches are not the only ways of linking increased openness to changes in relative wages; others include the "mandated wage approach" (e.g., Robertson, 2000), and the more discursive approaches of Wood (1994), Hanson and Harrison (1999), Green, Dickerson, and Saba Arbache (2001), and Gindling and Robbins (2001).

What do the results of these studies show? Wood (1994) shows that the relative wage of skilled workers narrowed in Taiwan, South Korea and Singapore after they shifted to export-oriented strategies during the 1960s and 1970s, although they did not in Hong Kong, mainly because the relative supply of unskilled labor was boosted by immigration from China. Robbins (1996), however, shows that the relative demand for skilled workers rose during episodes of trade liberalization in Argentina, Costa Rica, Colombia, Chile, Mexico, and Uruguay during the 1980s and the early 1990s. This was confirmed by subsequent studies on Chile and Costa Rica (Beyer et al., 1999; Gindling & Robbins, 2001; Robbins & Gindling, 1999). Green et al. (2001) show that the relative demand for college-educated workers also rose significantly in Brazil during the first half of the 1990s, a period of substantial trade liberalization. On this basis therefore, there is little support for the hypothesis that reductions in barriers to trade reduce the relative demand for skilled labor.

It is possible, however, that by the 1980s and the early 1990s, the supply of skilled relative to unskilled labor in most Latin American countries was higher than the effective world average. In this case, HO theory predicts that reductions in barriers to trade will increase the relative demand for skilled labor. Evidence consistent with this hypothesis is found by Hanson and Harrison (1999) and Robertson (2000), who show that in Mexico prior to liberalization, tariffs were highest in labor-intensive sectors, suggesting that Mexico did not have a comparative advantage in labor-intensive products. Robertson (2000) finds that the reduction in the relative price of labor-intensive products caused by liberalization can account for 50% of the rise in the relative wage of skilled labor. In other words, the lack of empirical support for the first hypothesis does not in itself amount to a rejection of HO theory.

Nevertheless, there is more direct evidence to support the second and third hypotheses, that reductions in barriers to trade and foreign investment increase the relative demand for skilled labor, either by shifting the structure of production toward more skill-intensive sectors, or by increasing the use of foreign, skill-biased, technologies by individual firms and enterprises. With regard to the former, Feenstra and Hanson (1997) themselves show that the relative demand for skilled workers in Mexico is positively affected by the number of foreign manufacturing establishments, and by te Velde and Morrissey (forthcoming) and te Velde (2003), who show that the stock of foreign direct investment (FDI) has a positive and significant effect on the relative demand for skilled workers in Chile, Bolivia, and Thailand (although it also has a negative and significant effect in Hong Kong, the Philippines, and Colombia, and no significant effect in South Korea, Singapore, or Costa Rica). With regard to the latter, Mazumdar and Quispe-Agnoli (2002) and Gorg and Strobl (2002) show that industries or firms in Peru and Ghana, respectively, which use more imported foreign equipment employ a higher ratio of skilled relative to unskilled workers. It is also supported by Robbins (1996), who shows that the size of the imported capital stock has a positive and statistically significant effect on the relative demand for university graduates, in a pooled sample including Argentina, Chile, Colombia, Costa Rica, Malaysia, and the Philippines, and by Robbins and Gindling (1999), who obtain a similar result using time-series data for Costa Rica. Berman and Machin (2000) show that the share of skilled wages in the total manufacturing wage bill increased during the 1980s in 10 out of 14 low- and middle-income countries for which they were able to collect data. The exceptions were Malaysia and India (where it declined), and Chile and South Korea (where there was no significant change).

Further research along these lines would be useful. There is a particular need for more research on low-income countries. There is evidence that the relative wage of skilled labor has risen in some low-income countries in re-

cent years, including Ghana (Gorg & Strobl, 2002; Teal, 2000), Nicaragua (te Velde, 2003) and, depending on the measure of the relative wage used, Vietnam (Gallup, 2002), trends which clearly cannot be explained by HO theory. However, other than the study by Gorg and Strobl, there have been no attempts to assess the effect of increased openness on these trends. More research is required to assess whether relative wages have risen in other low-income countries, and if so why. That there have been significant increases in employment in formal exporting sectors in several low-income countries following liberalization is now well documented (e.g., Jenkins & Sen, 2003). We still know little about whether, and if so how, greater openness has affected other factor–price ratios, such as the return to land (and other natural resources) relative to labor, skilled or unskilled, in low- or middle-income countries. Movements in this latter ratio may in fact have a much larger impact on overall inequality in Africa and Latin America, with their relatively abundant supplies of land and other natural resources.

(c) *Openness and asset inequality*

There have been few empirical attempts to link openness and asset inequality. One exception is Wood and Ridao-Cano (1999). They find that openness had a negative effect on enrollment rates in secondary and tertiary education during 1960–90 in countries with low levels of educational attainment. This is the direction of change one would expect if increased openness reduces the relative return to secondary and tertiary education in countries with low levels of education, as HO theory predicts, and if the supply of education is at least partly responsive to its return. They also find that openness has had little significant effect on enrollment rates in primary education, which implies that inequalities in levels of educational attainment in low-education countries have been reduced by increased openness (although at the expense of lowering the average level).

Further research along these lines would also be useful. Wood and Ridao-Cano (1999) do not provide a direct test of the hypothesis that a fall in the labor market returns to secondary and tertiary education caused the decline in the secondary and tertiary enrollment rates, although their evidence is consistent with the fact. There also remains little direct evidence about the extent to which the responsiveness of the supply of education to changes in its return varies, either among countries or among individuals within countries according, for instance, to the availability of credit for education expenditures or government expenditure on basic education.

(d) *Openness and spatial inequality*

It is now well known that inequalities in income between regions and between rural and urban areas within developing countries are often very large. Unfortunately, we know much less about whether these disparities have been changing in recent years, and even less about whether any changes are linked to greater openness. However, IFAD (2001) show that ratios of rural to urban poverty have risen in many South and East Asian countries since 1985, especially in China, while in Africa, rural–urban poverty ratios have fallen. The same broad pattern is also found by Eastwood and Lipton (2000). This pattern is consistent with the indirect effects one would expect increased openness to have on the basis of HO theory, operating through changes in the relative demand for the different factors of production. Broadly speaking, the comparative advantages of most South and East Asian countries lie in manufactures (Mayer & Wood, 2001), while the comparative advantages of the majority of African countries lie in primary products (Wood & Mayer, 2001). Establishing the precise magnitude of these effects would, however, require more research.

Evidence regarding the links between openness and spatial inequality predicted by new economic geography models remains limited. Ades and Glaeser (1995) show that, in a sample of 85 countries, the population of the largest city is negatively related to the share of imports in GDP, and positively related to the extent of tariff barriers. They do not, however, examine the link between the extent of urban concentration and income inequality. Hanson (1997) shows that the concentration of manufacturing industry in Mexico around Mexico City—in 1980, the capital accounted for more than 40% of the country's manufacturing employment—declined following trade liberalization and integration into NAFTA. At the same time, the amount by which the wages paid by manufacturing firms in the capital exceeded other regions declined. However, this evidence relates to nominal rather than real wage differentials. There is a potential for further work, on different countries and real as well as nominal income differentials.

(e) *Openness and gender inequality*

There are relatively few estimates of the effect of openness on gender wage differentials. In a recent cross-country study based on occupational wage data from the ILO october Inquiry, Oostendorp (2004) finds that higher trade and FDI net inflows caused gender wage gaps in relatively low-paid occupations in low and lower-middle income developing countries to narrow. Rama (2001) finds that the gender gap in earnings (controlling for educational attainment and work experience) declined from 39% to 26% in Vietnam during the 1990s (a period of trade liberalization), while Artecona and Cunningham (2001) report a similar change associated with trade liberalization in Mexico. Tzannatos (1999) shows that male–female wage gaps fell at an average rate of 1% per year in a sample of 12 developing countries between the late 1970s and the early 1990s. These studies support the hypotheses outlined in Section 2(e) as to why increased openness may narrow gender wage gaps.

At the same time, however, Seguino (1997, 2000) finds that the gender wage gap narrowed only marginally in South Korea between 1975 and 1990, despite an average increase in exports of 15% per year, while Berik, Rodgers, and Zveglich (2002) find that rising import shares in Taiwan during 1981–99 caused the wage gap between men and women (controlling for observed productivity differences) to widen. The hypothesis that greater openness reduces the gender wage gap is therefore not always supported by the evidence.

(f) *Openness and redistribution*

Evidence of links between openness and fiscal redistribution is difficult to come by, not least because it is difficult to measure the extent to which governments do in fact redistribute income. The reason is that the people who are legally responsible for paying a tax are often not the same people who ultimately bear the tax. Calculating the real burden of taxation instead requires detailed knowledge of elasticities of supply and demand, and the structure of markets more generally, which is often lacking in developing countries (Shah & Whalley, 1991).

If greater openness has reduced the ability of governments in developing countries to redistribute income, we would, at the very least, expect to see a combination of lower taxes on capital owners, highly skilled workers, and corporations, and higher taxes on land and less-skilled labor; multinational corporations adjusting their location decisions in response to differences in taxes and wage rates; and taxes on capital income in one country influencing rates set in another. As yet, we do not have any convincing evidence one way or the other. Evidence for OECD countries suggests that tax rates on labor income are higher in more open economies, and tax rates on capital income lower (Rodrik, 1997), that reductions in corporation tax in one country increase the likelihood of reductions in another (Devereux, Lockwood, & Redoano, 2002), and that the responsiveness of the demand for labor to changes in wages has increased in recent decades (Slaughter, 2001). These results are all consistent with the hypothesis that greater openness has reduced the ability of governments to redistribute income. However, Wheeler and Mody (1992) find that rates of corporate taxation had only limited impact on the locational choices of US multinationals during the 1980s, compared to other variables including the quality of infrastructure, market size, and the number of other foreign investors. This finding suggests the governments in fact have more flexibility in setting tax rates than is typically thought. [11]

4. CONCLUSION

There are several channels through which an increase in the openness of a country, to international flows of goods and services, factors of production, and technology, can affect inequalities in income between individuals within it. Most of the theoretical work linking greater openness to domestic inequality focuses on its effect on the relative demand for domestic factors of production, and in particular, the demand for skilled relative to unskilled labor. There is less theoretical work linking increases in openness to domestic inequality *via* other channels. Those links may nevertheless be significant. Greater openness can affect asset inequality by affecting the real incomes of credit-constrained groups, or by affecting relative factor returns. Greater openness can also affect gaps between regions in the real incomes

of immobile factors of production, by affecting the spatial concentration of economic activity. Greater openness can also reduce "residual" wage gaps between men and women, at least in theory, by increasing the relative demand for female labor or by reducing discrimination. Finally, greater openness may affect inequality by reducing the ability of the government to redistribute income *via* taxes and transfers.

Recent years have witnessed many empirical studies on the effects of openness on inequality in developing countries. This body of work has suggested something of a puzzle. On the one hand, several detailed time-series studies of individual (or small groups of) developing countries have shown that increased openness has raised the relative demand for skilled labor. On the other hand, cross-country econometric evidence suggests that increased openness has had little impact on overall inequality in developing countries, when controlling for other observable influences on inequality. This is a puzzle, because we would expect a rise in the relative demand for skilled labor to increase overall inequality, all else being equal.

There are, broadly speaking, two plausible explanations for this puzzle. One is differences in samples. Most cross-country studies focus on the period since the 1960s, and include low- and middle-income countries, while the time-series studies have focused mostly on the 1980s and 1990s, and cover mostly middle-income countries. HO theory predicts that increased openness will increase the relative demand for skilled labor in many middle-income developing countries, especially in those which became more open during the 1980s and 1990s (following the entry of more low-income countries into world markets, e.g., China, Indonesia, and Bangladesh). It is possible therefore that in the cross-country econometric analysis, the positive effect of openness on inequality in middle-income countries during the 1980s and 1990s is offset by a negative impact in middle-income countries during the 1960s and 1970s, and in low-income countries during the 1980s and 1990s. [12]

The other plausible explanation is offsetting effects. Greater openness may affect inequality through several channels, of which changes in the relative wage of skilled labor is only one, and not necessarily the most important, in terms of accounting for changes in overall inequality. Given the evidence discussed in Sections 3(c)–3(e), increases in the relative demand for skilled labor could plausibly have been offset by reductions in the average wages of men relative to women, in average incomes in core relative to peripheral regions, and in the level of inequality in the ownership of human capital.

These explanations remain hypotheses, and their testing will require further research. There are, in particular, two main priorities: first, whether greater openness has also raised the relative demand for skilled labor in low-income countries in recent decades, and second, whether greater openness has affected domestic inequality through other channels, in either low- or middle-income countries. A greater understanding as to which groups have been made relatively worse off and which have been made relatively better off through increased openness, and in which countries, will assist policy makers in designing compensatory mechanisms aimed at ensuring a fair distribution of the aggregate net benefits of increased openness.

NOTES

1. One can express another common measure of inequality, the Gini coefficient, in a similar way (Fei, Ranis, & Kuo, 1978).

2. For other production functions (e.g., the translog), or under alternative assumptions regarding the precise form of Eqn. (6), these relationships will typically be more complicated. Nevertheless, the broader point remains, that changes in the relative shares of the different factors of production in national income are driven by exogenous shifts in the relative demand for, and relative supply of, those factors.

3. HO models which include physical capital as a factor of production generally predict that greater openness reduces overall inequality in developing countries. This is because most developing countries are capital scarce by world standards (so that greater openness reduces the returns to capital relative to labor), and because capital is, almost always, a less equally distributed asset than labor (so that a fall in the share of capital relative to that of labor in national income reduces overall inequality). Many HO models do not include physical capital as a factor of production, however, on the grounds that it is much more internationally mobile than other factors of production (see Wood, 1994, pp. 32–40, for further discussion).

4. One might also relax the assumption of fully competitive product and labor markets. In models which include wage bargaining, the wages of less-skilled workers are affected by the extent of their bargaining power over firms. Greater openness may reduce that bargaining power, by increasing firms' ability to relocate or outsource production overseas, and therefore lower the returns to less-skilled labor relative to other, more mobile, factors of production (Mezzetti & Dinopoulos, 1991; Rodrik, 1997).

5. Similar arguments can be applied to other assets, such as land. One would expect, for example, that land-owning households will increase their investments in the quality of land when the returns to land increase, but that the size of this response will differ across households, causing the (quality-adjusted) distribution of land ownership to change.

6. The literature on fiscal decentralization has argued that, because of the internal mobility of economic units, central rather than state or local government should be responsible for income redistribution (e.g., Musgrave, 1959). However, there are theoretical arguments for income redistribution at the state or local level, and in practice many state and local governments do engage in a significant amount of redistribution (see Oates, 1999, pp. 1121–1122, for more details).

7. Most studies use only "high-quality" observations, defined as those which are based on household surveys, cover all sources of income, and are representative of the population at the national level. Estimates of Gini coefficients and income shares still vary, however, according to whether household surveys are income based or expenditure based, refer to net or gross income, or are based on individual-level or household-level data. Most, although not all, studies control for this source of variation.

8. The limitations of the many different measures of openness, including policy measures (e.g., tariff averages) and outcome measures (e.g., trade/GDP ratios) are discussed by Rodriguez and Rodrik (2000) and Rodrik (2000), in the context of studies testing for links between openness and aggregate economic performance. Such limitations apply equally to the studies reviewed in Table 1.

9. The analysis is usually carried out using national-level data on relative wages and relative supply, which makes the assumption of exogenous relative factor supplies more reasonable. Sometimes a value of the elasticity of substitution between skilled and unskilled workers is assumed *a priori*, based on the results of

previous studies. This is then used to impute changes in relative demand over time, on which proxy measures of openness are then regressed.

10. This analysis is usually done using time-series data on individual firms, or narrowly defined industries, which makes the assumption of exogenous relative wages more reasonable.

11. Rodrik (1998) shows that openness has a positive effect on the size of the government, as measured by government consumption, investment or employment, or by the tax–GDP ratio. He argues that this is because openness increases external risk, and because citizens demand that governments grow in size as a way of insuring against such risk. The provision of such insurance by governments need not, however, imply a redistribution of income.

12. The entry of large low-income countries into the world market is the explanation favored by Wood (1997) for a related conflict in the evidence, described in Section 3(b), namely that time-series studies of the East Asian experience in the 1960s and 1970s suggest that greater openness narrowed wage differentials between skilled and unskilled labor, while similar studies of the Latin American experience in the 1980s and the early 1990s suggest that greater openness widened those differentials.

REFERENCES

Ades, A., & Glaeser, E. (1995). Trade and circuses: Explaining urban giants. *Quarterly Journal of Economics, 110*(1), 195–227.

Arbache, J. S. (2001). Trade liberalisation and labour markets in developing countries: Theory and evidence. Mimeo, University of Brasilia and University of Kent.

Artecona, R., & Cunningham, W. (2001). Effects of trade liberalisation on the gender wage gap in Mexico. Mimeo, World Bank.

Baldwin, R., & Krugman, P. (2000). Agglomeration, integration and tax harmonisation. Discussion Paper No. 2630, Centre for Economic Policy Research.

Barro, R. (2000). Inequality and growth in a panel of countries. *Journal of Economic Growth, 5*(1), 5–32.

Becker, G. (1971). *The economics of discrimination.* Chicago: University of Chicago Press.

Berik, G., Rodgers, Y., & Zveglich, J. (2002). Does trade promote gender wage equity? Evidence from East Asia. Working Paper 2002-14, Centre for Economic Policy Analysis, New York University.

Berman, E., & Machin, S. (2000). Skill-biased technology transfer around the world. *Oxford Review of Economic Policy, 16*(3), 12–22.

Beyer, H., Rojas, P., & Vergara, R. (1999). Trade liberalization and wage inequality. *Journal of Development Economics, 59*(1), 103–123.

Calderon, C., & Chong, A. (2001). External sector and income inequality in interdependent economies using a dynamic panel data approach. *Economics Letters, 71*(2), 225–231.

Cooper, R. (2002). Growth and inequality: The role of foreign trade and investment. Annual World Bank Conference on Development Economics 2001/2002, World Bank.

Deininger, K., & Squire, L. (1996). A new dataset measuring income inequality. *World Bank Economic Review, 10*(3), 565–591.

Devereux, M., Lockwood, B., & Redoano, M. (2002). Do countries compete over corporate taxes? CSGR Working Paper 97/02, University of Warwick.

Dollar, D., & Kraay, A. (2002). Growth is good for the poor. *Journal of Economic Growth, 7*(3), 195–225.

Eastwood, R., & Lipton, M. (2000). Rural-urban dimensions of inequality change. Working Paper 200, World Institute for Development Economics Research.

Edwards, S. (1997). Trade policy, growth and income distribution. *American Economic Review, 87*(2), 205–210.

Feenstra, R. C., & Hanson, G. H. (1997). Foreign direct investment and relative wages: Evidence from Mexico's maquiladoras. *Journal of International Economics, 42*(3–4), 371–393.

Fei, J., Ranis, G., & Kuo, S. (1978). Growth and the family distribution of income by factor components. *Quarterly Journal of Economics, 92*(1), 17–53.

Fischer, R. (2001). The evolution of inequality after trade liberalisation. *Journal of Development Economics, 66*(2), 555–579.

Fontana, M., Joekes, S., & Masika, R. (1998). Global trade expansion and liberalisation: Gender issues and impacts. BRIDGE Report 42, Institute of Development Studies, University of Sussex.

Fontana, M., & Wood, A. (2000). Modeling the effects of trade on women, at work and at home. *World Development, 28*(7), 1173–1190.

Fujita, M., Krugman, P., & Venables, A. (1999). *The spatial economy: Cities, regions and international trade.* Cambridge, MA: MIT Press.

Gallup, J. (2002). The wage labour market and inequality in Vietnam in the 1990s. Policy Research Working Paper 2896, World Bank.

Gindling, T. H., & Robbins, D. (2001). Patterns and sources of changing wage inequality in Chile and Costa Rica during structural adjustment. *World Development, 29*(4), 725–745.

Gorg, H., & Strobl, E. (2002). Relative wages, openness and skill-biased technological change. Discussion Paper 596, Institute for the Study of Labour (IZA), Bonn.

Green, F., Dickerson, A., & Saba Arbache, J. (2001). A picture of wage inequality and the allocation of labour through a period of trade liberalization: The case of Brazil. *World Development, 29*(11), 1923–1939.

Hanson, G. H. (1997). Increasing returns, trade and the regional structure of wages. *Economic Journal, 107*(440), 113–133.

Hanson, G. H., & Harrison, A. E. (1999). Trade liberalization and wage inequality in Mexico. *Industrial Labor Relations Review, 52*(2), 271–288.

Higgins, M., & Williamson, J. G., (1999). Explaining inequality the world round: Cohort size, Kuznets curves, and openness. Working Paper 7224, National Bureau of Economic Research.

IFAD (International Fund for Agricultural Development) (2001). *Rural poverty report 2001: The challenge of ending rural poverty.* Oxford: Oxford University Press.

Jenkins, R., & Sen, K. (2003). Globalisation and manufacturing employment. *Insights, 47*, 2–3.

Leamer, E. (1987). Paths of development in the three-factor, *n*-good general equilibrium model. *Journal of Political Economy, 95*(5), 961–999.

Lundberg, M., & Squire, L. (2003). The simultaneous evolution of growth and inequality. *Economic Journal, 113*(487), 326–344.

Mayer, J., & Wood, A. (2001). South Asia's export structure in a comparative perspective. *Oxford Development Studies, 29*(1), 5–29.

Mazumdar, J., & Quispe-Agnoli, M. (2002). Trade and the skill premium in developing countries: The role of intermediate goods and some evidence from Peru. Working Paper No. 2002-11, Federal Reserve Bank of Atlanta.

Mezzetti, C., & Dinopoulos, E. (1991). Domestic unionisation and import competition. *Journal of International Economics, 31*(1/2), 79–100.

Musgrave, R. (1959). *The theory of public finance.* New York: McGraw-Hill.

Oates, W. (1999). An essay on fiscal federalism. *Journal of Economic Literature, 37*(3), 1120–1149.

O'Conner, D., & Lunati, M. (1999). Economic opening and the demand for skills in developing countries: A review of theory and evidence. Technical Paper No. 99/6, OECD Development Centre.

Oostendorp, R. (2004). Globalisation and the gender wage gap. Policy Research Working Paper 3256, World Bank.

Pissarides, C. (1997). Learning by trading and the returns to human capital in developing countries. *World Bank Economic Review, 11*(1), 17–32.

Rama, M. (2001). The gender implications of public sector downsizing: The reform program of Vietnam. Policy Research Working Paper 2573, World Bank.

Rama, M. (2003). Globalisation and workers in developing countries. Policy Research Working Paper 2958, World Bank.

Ravallion, M. (2001). Growth, inequality and poverty: Looking beyond averages. *World Development, 29*(11), 1803–1815.

Robbins, D. J. (1996). Evidence on trade and wages in the developing world. Technical Paper 119, OECD Development Centre.

Robbins, D. J., & Gindling, T. H. (1999). Trade liberalisation and the relative wages of more-skilled workers in Costa Rica. *Review of Development Economics, 3*(2), 140–154.

Robertson, R. (2000). Trade liberalisation and wage inequality: Lessons from the Mexican experience. *The World Economy, 23*(6), 827–849.

Rodriguez, F., & Rodrik, D. (2000). Trade policy and economic growth: A skeptic's guide to the cross-national evidence. In B. Bernanke & K. Rogoff (Eds.), *NBER macroeconomics annual 2000.* Cambridge, MA: MIT Press.

Rodrik, D. (1997). *Has globalisation gone too far?* Washington, DC: Institute for International Economics.

Rodrik, D. (1998). Why do more open economies have bigger governments? *Journal of Political Economy, 106*(5), 997–1032.

Rodrik, D. (2000). Comments on "Trade, Growth and Poverty", by D. Dollar and A. Kraay. Mimeo, Harvard University.

Rodrik, D., & van Ypersele, T. (1999). Capital mobility, distributive conflict and international tax coordination. *Journal of International Economics, 54*(1), 57–73.

Seguino, S. (1997). Gender wage inequality and export-led growth in South Korea. *Journal of Development Studies, 34*(2), 102–132.

Seguino, S. (2000). The effects of structural change and economic liberalisation on gender wage differentials in South Korea and Taiwan. *Cambridge Journal of Economics, 24*(4), 437–459.

Shah, A., & Whalley, J. (1991). Tax incidence analysis of developing countries: An alternative view. *World Bank Economic Review, 5*(3), 535–552.

Slaughter, M. (2001). International trade and labour-demand elasticities. *Journal of International Economics, 54*(1), 27–56.

Spilimbergo, A., Londono, J. L., & Szekely, M. (1999). Income distribution, factor endowments, and trade openness. *Journal of Development Economics, 59*(1), 77–101.

Teal, F. (2000). Real wages and the demand for skilled and unskilled male labour in Ghana's manufacturing sector: 1991–1995. *Journal of Development Economics, 61*(2), 447–461.

te Velde, D. W. (2003). *Foreign direct investment and income inequality in Latin America: Experiences and Policy Implications.* London: Overseas Development Institute.

te Velde, D. W., & Morrissey, O. (forthcoming). Foreign direct investment, skills and wage inequality in East Asia. *Journal of the Asia Pacific Economy.*

Tzannatos, Z. (1999). Women and labour market changes in the global economy: Growth helps, inequalities hurt and public policy matters. *World Development, 27*(3), 551–570.

Wheeler, D., & Mody, A. (1992). International investment location decisions: The case of US firms'. *Journal of International Economics, 33*(1/2), 57–76.

White, H., & Anderson, E. (2001). Growth versus distribution: Does the pattern of growth matter? *Development Policy Review, 16*(3), 267–289.

Wood, A. (1994). *North–south trade, employment and inequality*. Oxford: Clarendon Press.

Wood, A. (1997). Openness and wage inequality in developing countries: The Latin American challenge to East Asian conventional wisdom. *World Bank Economic Review, 11*(1), 33–58.

Wood, A. (2002). Globalisation and wage inequalities: A synthesis of three theories. *Weltwirtschaftliches Archiv, 138*(1), 54–82.

Wood, A., & Mayer, J. (2001). Africa's export structure in a comparative perspective. *Cambridge Journal of Economics, 25*(3), 369–394.

Wood, A., & Ridao-Cano, C. (1999). Skill, trade and international inequality. *Oxford Economic Papers, 51*(1), 81–119.

Available online at www.sciencedirect.com

SCIENCE @ DIRECT®

E
Country Perspectives

[16]

Review of Development Economics, 9(1), 87–106, 2005

Fifty Years of Regional Inequality in China: a Journey Through Central Planning, Reform, and Openness

*Ravi Kanbur and Xiaobo Zhang**

Abstract

The paper constructs and analyzes a long-run time series for regional inequality in China from the Communist Revolution to the present. There have been three peaks of inequality in the last fifty years, coinciding with the Great Famine of the late 1950s, the Cultural Revolution of the late 1960s and 1970s, and finally the period of openness and global integration in the late 1990s. Econometric analysis establishes that regional inequality is explained in the different phases by three key policy variables—the ratio of heavy industry to gross output value, the degree of decentralization, and the degree of openness.

1. Introduction

The second half of the twentieth century saw a tumultuous history unfold in China—the early years of communist rule in the 1950s culminating in the Great Famine, the Cultural Revolution and its aftermath in the late 1960s and the 70s, the reform of agriculture in the late 1970s and the 80s, and an explosion of trade and foreign direct investment in the late 1980s and the 90s. All these events have affected the course of economic growth and income distribution. However, while a large literature has studied growth through these different phases of Chinese history (e.g. McMillan et al., 1989; Lin, 1992; Fan et al., 2003), few studies have matched the evolution of inequality over the long run with these different periods in Communist Chinese history over its entire course.

This paper presents and analyzes the evolution of Chinese regional inequality since the Communist Revolution right up to the present. Most studies on China's inequality (e.g. Hussain et al., 1994; Khan and Riskin, 2001; Chen and Ravallion, 1996; Aaberge and Li, 1997; Tsui, 1998) have focused on relatively short periods, mostly during the post-reform years, making use of the new household surveys that became available during this period. Of the studies which come closest to the spirit of our interest in Chinese inequality over the long run, Tsui (1991) stopped in 1985 and Lyons (1991) stopped in 1987, just as the increase in trade and foreign direct investment was beginning; Yang and Fang (2000) went up to 1996, but focused only on the rural–urban gap at the national level; and Kanbur and Zhang (1999) disaggregated down to the rural–urban level within provinces to calculate a regional inequality index, and present a decomposition of regional inequality by its rural–urban and inland–coastal components, but their study is only for the post-reform years of 1983–1995.

Using a dataset of provincial and national data covering the second half of the twentieth century, we are able to construct a comprehensive time series of regional

* Kanbur: Cornell University. Zhang: International Food Policy Research Institute, 2033 K Street NW, Washington, DC 20006, USA. Tel: (202) 862-8149; Fax: (202) 467-4439; E-mail: x.zhang@cgiar.org. The authors would like to thank participants at seminars held in George Washington University, IFPRI, Kansas State University, and at the WIDER conference on Spatial Inequality in Asia.

88　*Ravi Kanbur and Xiaobo Zhang*

inequality in China, including its decompositions into rural–urban and inland–coastal components, from 1952 to 2000. We find that changes in regional inequality match the phases of Chinese history remarkably well, as do its rural–urban and inland–coastal components. The peaks of inequality in China have been associated with the Great Famine, the Cultural Revolution, and the current phase of openness and decentralization. We further use econometric analysis to establish that regional inequality is explained to different degrees in different phases by three key policy variables: the share of heavy industry in gross output value, the degree of decentralization, and the degree of openness.

2. Constructing a Long-run Time Series for Regional Inequality in China

Ideally, for an analysis of the evolution of inequality over Communist Chinese history we would have available representative national household surveys over the entire period. Unfortunately, while such surveys have been conducted throughout the last 50 years, they are available to researchers only for the post-reform period, and in any case sporadically, for restricted years with varying but limited coverage. Thus, for example, Chen and Ravallion (1996) had access to official household survey data but only for four provinces between 1986 and 1990. Aaberge and Li (1997) analyzed urban household surveys for Liaoning and Sichuan provinces for the same period, while Tsui (1998) analyzed rural surveys for 1985, 1988, and 1990, but only for Guangdong and Sichuan. Yang (1999) analyzed both rural and urban parts of the household survey for four years between 1986 and 1994, and for Guangdong and Sichuan. This different coverage across studies reflects the differential access to official data. Researchers have also conducted and analyzed independent surveys—for example, Hussain et al. (1994) did one for 1986, Rozelle (1994) for township and village enterprises between 1984 to 1989 in Jiangsu province, and Khan et al. (1993) conducted a household survey for 1988.

The inequality analysis that has been done on household surveys for the late 1980s and 90s has been extremely valuable in illuminating specific aspects of the distributional dimensions of Chinese development. In general these analyses decompose inequality by income sources but few have aligned the patterns of inequality with national development policies. The bottom line is that researchers simply do not have access to comprehensive household surveys which are national and which cover the entire, or even a substantial part of, the half-century sweep of Chinese history that is of interest to us in this paper.

In the face of this data restriction, we are forced to look for data availability at higher levels of aggregation than at the household level. As it turns out, certain types of data are indeed available at the province level, disaggregated by rural and urban areas, stretching back to 1952. This paper constructs a time series of inequality by building up information on real per capita consumption in the rural and urban areas of 28 of China's 30 provinces (unfortunately, data availability is not complete for Tibet and Hainan provinces).[1]

With these sub-provincial rural and urban per capita consumption figures, and population weights for these areas, a national distribution of real per capita consumption can be constructed, and its inequality calculated, for each year between 1952 and 2000, thus covering the vast bulk of the period from 1949 to the present. Of course what this means is that overall household-level inequality is being understated, since inequality within the rural and urban areas of each province is being suppressed. Moreover, we cannot say anything about the evolution of household-level inequality *within* these areas. Our measures do provide a lower bound on inequality over this entire period.

But the fact remains that our study of inequality is essentially a study of regional inequality.

A detailed discussion of our basic data is provided in the Appendix. A number of studies have used province-level data to study regional inequality in the past. Many of them used Soviet-type statistics, largely because long-term data series existed for these (Lyons, 1991; Tsui, 1991), and they did not in general disaggregate by rural and urban areas within provinces. With the availability of rural–urban disaggregations on consumption per capita stretching back to the 1950s, these studies can be substantially improved and extended in terms of time and space coverage. In the recent literature, Yang and Fang (2000) used the same data sources as we have used, but focused solely on the average rural–urban gap at the national level, and did not go into inequalities across provinces.

Using the information available, we calculate the Gini coefficient of inequality using the standard formula. But the bulk of our analysis is done with a second inequality index, a member of the decomposable generalized entropy (GE) class of inequality measures as developed by Shorrocks (1980, 1984):

$$I(y) = \begin{cases} \sum_{i=1}^{n} f(y_i) \left\{ \left(\dfrac{y_i}{\mu} \right)^c - 1 \right\} & \text{for } c \neq 0, 1, \\[2ex] \sum_{i=1}^{n} f(y_i) \left(\dfrac{y_i}{\mu} \right) \log\left(\dfrac{y_i}{\mu} \right) & \text{for } c = 1, \\[2ex] \sum_{i=1}^{n} f(y_i) \log\left(\dfrac{\mu}{y_i} \right) & \text{for } c = 0. \end{cases} \tag{1}$$

In the above equation, y_i is the ith income measured as Chinese yuan, μ is the total sample mean, $f(y_i)$ is the population share of y_i in the total population, and n is total population. For c less than 2, the measure is transfer-sensitive, in the sense that it is more sensitive to transfers at the bottom end of the distribution than those at the top. The key feature of the GE measure is that it is additively decomposable. For K exogenously given, mutually exclusive and exhaustive groups indexed by g:

$$I(y) = \sum_{g}^{K} w_g I_g + I(\mu_1 e_1, \ldots, \mu_K e_K), \tag{2}$$

where

$$w_g = \begin{cases} f_g \left(\dfrac{\mu_g}{\mu} \right)^c & \text{for } c \neq 0, 1, \\[2ex] f_g \left(\dfrac{\mu_g}{\mu} \right) & \text{for } c = 1, \\[2ex] f_g & \text{for } c = 0. \end{cases}$$

In equation (2), I_g is inequality in the gth group, μ_g is the mean of the gth group, and e_g is a vector of 1s of length n_g, where n_g is the population of the gth group. If n is the total population of all groups, then $f_g = n_g/n$ represents the share of the gth group's population in the total population. The first term on the right-hand side of (2) represents the within-group inequality. The second term is the between-group, or intergroup, component of total inequality. For simplicity, we present results in this paper only for

$c = 0.$[2] The within-group inequality part in (2) represents the spread of the distributions in the subgroups; the between-group inequality indicates the distance between the group means. With our time series of inequality in China over the long term, we are now in a position to investigate dimensions of inequality in the different phases of Chinese development over the past half century.

3. Inequality Change through the Phases of Chinese History: a Narrative

Following standard discussions, Communist Chinese history can be divided into several phases: 1949–56 (revolution and land reform), 1957–61 (the Great Leap Forward and the Great Famine), 1962–65 (post-famine recovery), 1966–78 (Cultural Revolution and transition to reform), 1979–84 (rural reform), and 1985–present (post-rural reform, decentralization, and opening up to trade and foreign direct investment).

Table 1 presents economic indicators for China from 1952 to 2000. It includes three key indicators of economic policy—the share of heavy industry in gross value of total output (a measure of the bias against agriculture and China's comparative advantage), the ratio of trade volume to total GDP (a measure of the degree of openness), and the ratio of local government expenditure to total government expenditure (a measure of decentralization).[3] Figure 1 shows the evolution of real per capita GDP through the different phases identified above. Table 2 presents long-run inequality series, and Figure 2 graphs the evolution of Chinese regional inequality, as measured by the Gini and the GE indices, through the six phases of development identified above. The two indices move in close relation to each other, and match the different phases of Chinese development remarkably well.

Inequality was relatively low and steady in the early first years of communist rule when land reform was introduced. However, it rose precipitously during the Great Leap Forward and the Great Famine, reaching a peak in 1960. It fell during the recovery from the Great Famine, reaching a trough in 1967. But the effects of the Cultural Revolution, which began in late 1966, started an increase in inequality which peaked in 1976. The transition from the Cultural Revolution to the period of rural reform saw a decline in inequality which gathered pace in the early 1980s and reached its trough in 1984. In the post-rural reform period after 1984, when China decentralized, opened up, and experienced an explosion of trade and foreign direct investment, inequality rose steadily and sharply right through to the end of our data series, in 2000.

Thus over the past 50 years inequality has peaked three times—during the Great Famine, at the end of the Cultural Revolution, and in the current period of global integration. In fact, the Gini coefficient of regional inequality in China in 2000 exceeds the peaks of inequality reached at the end of the Cultural Revolution in 1976, and at the Great Famine in 1960. Using the Gini coefficient, inequality in 2000 is about 16% higher than that in 1960.

Similarly, there are three major troughs in the overall evolution of inequality—in 1952, right at the beginning of the data series; in 1967, at the end of the recovery from the Great Famine and before the effects of the Cultural Revolution set in; and in 1984, at the end of the rural reform period and the start of the expansion based on global integration. Overall, inequality seems to have been low when policy was encouraging to agriculture and the rural sector generally, and high when this sector was relatively neglected. These effects can be further investigated by decomposing overall inequality into subcomponents and examining the evolution of these.

As discussed in the previous section, the GE index is subgrouped additively decomposable, allowing us to look deeper into the make-up of inequality. The 56 data points

Table 1. Economic Indicators, 1952–2000

Year	GDP (billion)	Imports (billion)	Total expenditure (billion)	GOV (billion)	Tariff rate (%)	Trade ratio (%)	Decentralization (%)	Industrialization (%)
1952	67.9	3.8	17.2	81.0	12.8	9.5	25.9	15.3
1953	82.4	4.6	21.9	96.0	11.0	9.8	26.1	17.5
1954	85.9	4.5	24.4	105.0	9.2	9.9	24.7	18.9
1955	91.0	6.1	26.3	110.9	7.6	12.1	23.5	19.7
1956	102.8	5.3	29.9	125.2	10.2	10.6	29.6	21.7
1957	106.8	5.0	29.6	124.1	9.6	9.8	29.0	25.5
1958	130.7	6.2	40.0	164.9	10.4	9.8	55.7	35.2
1959	143.9	7.1	54.3	198.0	9.9	10.4	54.1	43.8
1960	145.7	6.5	64.4	209.4	9.2	8.8	56.7	52.1
1961	122.0	4.3	35.6	162.1	14.5	7.4	55.0	37.7
1962	114.9	3.4	29.5	150.4	14.3	7.0	38.4	32.3
1963	123.3	3.6	33.2	163.5	11.6	6.9	42.1	33.5
1964	145.4	4.2	39.4	188.4	10.4	6.7	42.9	34.4
1965	171.6	5.5	46.0	223.5	10.3	6.9	38.2	30.4
1966	186.8	6.1	53.8	253.4	10.6	6.8	36.9	32.7
1967	177.4	5.3	44.0	230.6	7.3	6.3	38.7	28.1
1968	172.3	5.1	35.8	221.3	12.4	6.3	38.7	26.9
1969	193.8	4.7	52.6	261.3	13.5	5.5	39.3	31.7
1970	225.3	5.6	64.9	313.8	12.5	5.0	41.1	36.4
1971	242.6	5.2	73.2	348.2	9.5	5.0	40.5	39.5
1972	251.8	6.4	76.6	364.0	7.8	5.8	43.7	40.2
1973	272.1	10.4	80.9	396.7	8.7	8.1	44.4	39.9
1974	279.0	15.3	79.0	400.7	9.2	10.5	49.7	38.7
1975	299.7	14.7	82.1	446.7	10.2	9.7	50.1	40.2
1976	274.4	12.9	80.6	453.6	11.6	9.6	53.2	40.3
1977	320.2	13.3	84.4	497.8	19.8	8.5	53.3	41.9
1978	362.4	18.7	112.2	563.4	15.3	9.8	52.6	42.8
1979	403.8	24.3	128.2	637.9	10.7	11.3	48.9	41.3
1980	451.8	29.9	122.9	707.7	11.2	12.6	45.7	38.5
1981	486.0	36.8	113.8	758.1	14.7	15.1	45.0	34.5
1982	530.2	35.8	123.0	829.4	13.3	14.5	47.0	34.9
1983	595.7	42.2	141.0	921.1	12.8	14.4	46.1	36.1
1984	720.7	62.1	170.1	1083.1	16.6	16.7	47.5	37.0
1985	898.9	125.8	200.4	1333.5	16.3	23.0	60.3	38.6
1986	1020.1	149.8	220.5	1520.7	10.1	25.3	62.1	38.6
1987	1195.5	161.4	226.2	1848.9	8.8	25.8	62.6	38.7
1988	1492.2	205.5	249.1	2408.9	7.5	25.6	66.1	38.4
1989	1691.8	220.0	282.4	2855.2	8.3	24.6	68.5	39.4
1990	1859.8	257.4	308.4	3158.6	6.2	29.9	67.4	38.3
1991	2166.3	339.9	338.7	3478.2	5.5	33.4	67.8	41.5
1992	2665.2	444.3	374.2	4368.4	4.8	34.2	68.7	44.8
1993	3456.1	598.6	464.2	5939.8	4.3	32.6	71.7	49.7
1994	4667.0	996.0	579.3	8592.7	2.7	43.7	69.7	35.5
1995	5749.5	1104.8	682.4	11223.5	2.6	40.9	70.8	33.1
1996	6685.1	1155.7	793.8	12195.3	2.6	36.1	72.9	30.0
1997	7314.3	1180.7	923.4	13749.7	2.7	36.9	72.6	29.2
1998	7801.8	1162.2	1079.8	14320.5	2.7	34.4	71.1	27.0
1999	8206.8	1373.7	1318.8	15063.0	4.1	36.4	68.5	23.6
2000	8940.4	1863.9	1588.7	n.a	4.0	43.9	65.3	n.a.

in each year from which the overall distribution is constructed, a rural and an urban observation for each of 28 provinces, can be divided into rural and urban observations across the provinces and, using equation (2), the GE can be decomposed into "within rural–urban" and "between rural–urban" components (we will call it rural–urban inequality hereafter). The overall GE and the between rural–urban component are

92   *Ravi Kanbur and Xiaobo Zhang*

Figure 1. Per Capita GDP (in logs) in Constant 1980 Prices

shown in Table 2. The within rural–urban component is the difference of the above two.

A key dimension of inequality in China, especially in the post-reform period, is that between inland and coastal provinces (Tsui, 1993; Chen and Fleisher, 1996; Yao 1997; Zhang and Kanbur, 2001). We follow the practice of classifying the provinces of Beijing, Liaoning, Tianjin, Hebei, Shandong, Jiangsu, Shanghai, Zhejang, Fujian, Guangdong, and Guangxi as coastal and the other provinces as inland. We therefore divide our 56 observations into 22 coastal and 34 inland observations and decompose the GE measure accordingly. The "between inland–coastal" component (we will call it inland–coastal inequality hereafter) is reported in Table 2.

Figures 3–5 go a long way in translating the above narrative into impacts on overall inequality and the rural–urban and inland–coastal inequalities, and provide some initial hypotheses for econometric testing in the next section. Under the central planning system, the central government had large powers to allocate and utilize financial revenues to achieve the goal of equity, albeit at the expense of efficiency. With economic reforms, the central government has granted local governments more autonomy in allocating their resources and bearing more responsibilities (Ma, 1997; Lin et al., 1997; Qian and Roland, 1998). Figure 3 shows that in general the share of local government expenditure increased in the reform period, although there were some blips as the government reassessed its priorities periodically. With the new fiscal structure, local governments have more incentive to promote economic growth. However, because of differences in historical development level and geographical locations, the rate of growth may differ across regions. Under fiscal decentralization, regions with agriculture as the major means of production must rely more on the extraction of levies and compulsory apportionment, which hinder local economic growth. Regions with more diverse economic structure and larger revenue base have a larger degree of freedom to finance their economic development (Zhang et al., 2004). Not surprisingly, as shown in Figure 3, inequality moved closely in tandem with decentralization.

FIFTY YEARS OF REGIONAL INEQUALITY IN CHINA 93

Table 2. Inequalities and Decompositions, 1952–2000

Year	Gini (%)	GE (%)	Rural–Urban	Inland–Coastal
1952	22.4	9.0	6.9	0.6
1953	24.7	10.7	8.6	0.7
1954	23.2	9.4	7.9	0.6
1955	22.0	8.6	7.3	0.3
1956	22.9	9.4	8.2	0.2
1957	23.8	9.8	8.5	0.1
1958	24.4	10.2	8.8	0.2
1959	29.7	14.3	11.6	0.2
1960	32.2	16.6	13.5	0.3
1961	30.3	14.5	11.2	0.2
1962	28.5	13.1	10.7	0.2
1963	27.6	12.4	9.6	0.2
1964	28.2	12.8	9.5	0.2
1965	26.7	11.8	8.7	0.2
1966	26.6	11.7	9.1	0.2
1967	25.5	10.8	8.5	0.2
1968	26.3	11.3	8.7	0.3
1969	27.1	12.2	9.9	0.3
1970	27.0	12.1	9.8	0.3
1971	26.9	12.1	9.8	0.3
1972	28.1	12.8	9.8	0.3
1973	27.9	12.7	9.9	0.3
1974	28.8	13.5	10.3	0.3
1975	29.5	14.2	11.2	0.5
1976	30.9	15.5	12.1	0.5
1977	30.8	15.4	12.1	0.5
1978	29.3	14.0	11.0	0.4
1979	28.6	13.3	10.1	0.4
1980	28.2	13.1	9.9	0.5
1981	27.0	12.0	9.1	0.6
1982	25.6	10.6	7.2	0.5
1983	25.9	11.1	6.8	0.4
1984	25.6	10.9	6.3	0.4
1985	25.8	11.1	6.6	0.5
1986	26.8	11.9	6.9	0.5
1987	27.0	12.0	6.8	0.6
1988	28.2	13.1	7.7	0.8
1989	29.7	14.4	9.3	1.0
1990	30.1	14.9	9.5	1.0
1991	30.3	14.9	9.9	1.2
1992	31.4	16.0	10.2	1.5
1993	32.2	16.8	10.9	1.7
1994	32.6	17.2	10.8	2.0
1995	33.0	17.7	11.5	2.3
1996	33.4	18.2	11.7	2.6
1997	33.9	18.9	11.7	2.7
1998	34.4	19.6	12.2	2.9
1999	36.3	23.4	12.8	3.2
2000	37.2	24.8	13.9	3.8

Notes: Calculated by the authors. GE refers to the generalized entropy index with $c = 0$.

GE with $c = 1$ was also calculated but the results are similar and not reported here.

94   *Ravi Kanbur and Xiaobo Zhang*

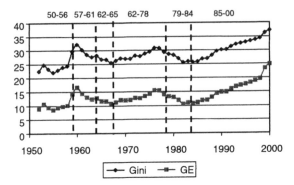

Figure 2. Trends of Regional Inequality (from Table 2)

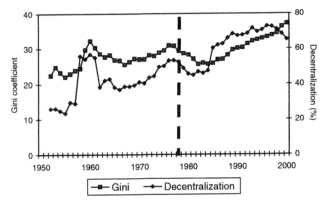

Figure 3. Decentralization and Overall Inequality (Gini coefficient)

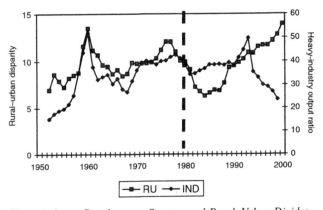

Figure 4. Heavy-industry Development Strategy and Rural–Urban Divides

FIFTY YEARS OF REGIONAL INEQUALITY IN CHINA 95

While Lin et al. (1997) and Zhang and Zou (1998) have in particular analyzed the relationship between fiscal decentralization and economic growth for China, few studies except Tsui (1991) have investigated the effect of decentralization on regional inequality. Tsui (1991) detected a positive relationship between decentralization and worsening regional inequality using a graph analysis based on data series up to 1985. Based on lessons drawn from other countries, Prud'homme (1995) has cautioned on the possible detrimental effects of decentralization on inequality. This leads to the following hypothesis.

HYPOTHESIS 1. *Decentralization affects regional inequality during the economic transition from a planned economy to a market economy.*

In order to accelerate the pace of industrialization after the initial period of land reform, the state extracted massive resources from agriculture, mainly through the suppression of agricultural prices and restrictions on labor mobility (Lin et al., 1996). Almost all the scarce investment funds were allocated to heavy industry in preference to light industry and agriculture. As shown in Figure 4, the share of heavy industry in gross output value rose from 0.22 in 1956 to 0.52 in 1960. Because this policy greatly violated China's comparative advantage, it could not be implemented unless administrative distortions were imposed. The main enforcement mechanisms were a trinity of institutions, including the household registration system, the unified procurement and sale of agricultural commodities, and the people's communes.

In particular, the government established the *Hukou* system of household registration in this period, confining people to the village or city of their birth, in order to ensure there was enough agricultural labor to produce sufficient grain for urban workers (Solinger, 1993). Although, to some extent, the urban wage was also suppressed, employment was guaranteed and the urban residents enjoyed many exclusive subsidies, such as free housing and numerous in-kind transfers from the government. Consequently, the large rural–urban divide became a major feature of China's inequality (Yang, 1999; Yang and Fang, 2000), and the policies eventually led to the Great Famine. During the famine, however, most urban residents were protected from starvation at the expense of about 30 million deaths in the rural areas (Lin and Yang, 2000). These developments are reflected in the sharp increases, up to 1960, in the rural–urban inequality in Table 2 and in Figure 4.

In reaction to the Great Famine, agriculture was once again given priority. The slogan "Yi Liang Wei Gang, Gang Ju Mu Zhang" [Grain must be taken to be the core; once it is grasped, everything falls into place] reflects the spirit of this policy. In the years between 1961 and 1964, 20 million state workers and 17 million urban high school students were sent to the countryside for "re-education" by participating in agricultural production (Selden, 1992). Meanwhile, central planning was loosened a little, boosting agricultural productivity (Fan and Zhang, 2002). Not surprisingly, the share of heavy industry fell and the rural–urban divide narrowed. This is reflected in the declining rural–urban disparity during this period, which pulled down overall inequality to its next trough, just before the start of the Cultural Revolution.

With the start of the Cultural Revolution in 1966, pro-Mao leftists came into the ascendancy. The combination of a lack of incentives in the agricultural sector and investment in military and heavy industry during the Cold War atmosphere of the time, as reflected in the rise in the share of heavy industry in Figure 4, led to the rural–urban divide increasing to its peak at the end of the Cultural Revolution, on the eve of the 1979 reforms.

96   *Ravi Kanbur and Xiaobo Zhang*

With the end of the Cultural Revolution, the Chinese economy was on the verge of collapse. In response to the agricultural crisis, the government started to give greater incentives to household producers. The "household responsibility" system spread from its origins in Anhui province to cover 98% of all villages in China by 1983 (Lin, 1992). These and other market-oriented strategies led to a remarkable growth in agricultural output, and the share of heavy industry dropped. The first five years of the post-1979 reforms saw a sharp decline in the rural–urban divide. Overall inequality fell as well, as shown in Figure 3.

In general, the heavy-industry development strategy in the pre-reform period violated China's comparative advantage at the time that capital was scarce and labor was abundant. To ensure low food cost for urban workers and to extract funds from the agricultural sector, agricultural product prices had to be suppressed as well, and the mobility of rural residents was severely restricted. This leads to our second hypothesis.

HYPOTHESIS 2. *The heavy-industry development strategy, particularly in the pre-reform period, was a major contributing factor to the large rural–urban divide and to overall inequality.*

The latest phase in Chinese history began in the mid-1980s. As is well known, this has been a period of accelerating integration into the global economy through greater openness in trade and especially in foreign direct investment. As seen in Figure 5, the trade ratio, after showing no trend for 35 years, began a steady increase from the mid-1980s both because of reductions in nominal tariffs and because of increases in import volumes. Between 1984 and 2000, the value of exports grew 11% per year. Changes in FDI flows are even more astonishing. We do not of course have long-run time series for these; but from an almost isolated economy in the late 1970s, China has become the largest recipient of FDI among developing countries. In order to speed up integration with world markets, China has implemented a coastal-biased policy, such as establishing special economic zones in coastal cities and providing favorable tax breaks to coastal provinces. Obviously, the policy is biased against inland regions and may

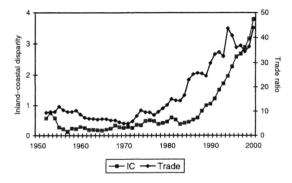

Figure 5. Openness and Inland–Coastal Disparity

have enlarged inland–coastal disparity. In other words, the opening process has been intertwined with the regional-biased development policy.

As is well appreciated, and as shown in Figure 1, there has been spectacular growth largely due to the reforms and open-door policy. But the gains have not been evenly distributed across regions. Coastal provinces have attracted far more foreign direct investment and generated more trade volume than inland provinces during the liberalization process. In 2000, the three coastal provinces, Guangdong, Jiangsu, and Shanghai, were the top three, while the three inland provinces, Guizhou, Inner Mongolia, and Jilin, were the bottom three in terms of attracting FDI. The above three coastal provinces alone contributed more than 60% of total foreign trade in 2000. The difference in the growth rates between the coastal and inland regions has been as high as three percentage points during the past two decades (Zhang and Zhang, 2003).

We can use Guangdong and Sichuan provinces to illustrate how internal geography affects the response to openness. In 1978, the coastal Guangdong province ranked 14th in labor productivity, which was almost the same as the 15th rank of inland Sichuan province. In a closed economy, Guangdong did not enjoy any obviously better resource endowments than inland provinces. However, since China opened its door to the world, Guangdong has become one of the most favored places for foreign direct investment and international trade, in large part due to its proximity to Hong Kong. Meanwhile, the ranking of labor productivity in Sichuan has declined from 15th in 1978 to 23rd in 2000. Clearly, the relative comparative advantages between the two provinces have changed significantly and are associated with the opening up to the outside and the decentralization which facilitated this response.

The above story of Guangdong and Sichuan is reflected nationwide in the behavior of the inland–coastal component of inequality. The major change in the behavior of these components over the entire 50-year period comes in the mid-1980s. After relative stability up to this point, inland–coastal inequality began to increase sharply. Although still quite small as a contributor to overall inequality, its contributions to *changes* in inequality increased dramatically. As shown in Figure 5, inland–coastal disparity has closely followed the path of the trade ratio.

When an economy opens up to world markets, theory suggests that there could well be affects on regional inequality, as argued recently by Fujita et al. (1999). External trade liberalization can change internal comparative advantage and hence location patterns. Coupled with decentralization, opening up to world markets provides local governments with an opportunity to better exploit a comparative advantage. Trade liberalization could also lead to specialization and industry clustering. Empirical evidence for the impact of globalization on income distribution in developing countries has been limited, and the findings of existing studies are at best mixed. The existing work for developing countries has been limited to the effects of trade liberalization on wage inequality (e.g. Wood, 1997; Hanson and Harrison, 1999), shedding little light on the effect on regional inequality. Jian et al. (1996) have argued that China's regional inequality is associated with internal geography. China's rapid change from a closed economy to open economy provides a good testing ground for our third hypothesis.

HYPOTHESIS 3. *Greater openness is associated with greater regional inequality in a spatially large country such as China.*

Our narrative of the phases of Chinese development, and of the evolution of inequality and its components, is suggestive of the forces behind the changes in inequality over this half century. We now turn to an econometric analysis of the correlates of inequality, to see whether these hypotheses can be confirmed statistically.

4. Correlates of Regional Inequality: an Econometric Analysis

Our task is to test the association between inequality and its components on the one hand, and heavy industrialization, decentralization, and openness, on the other. Following several analyses on Chinese data (e.g. Lin, 1992), we use one-period lagged values of the independent variables as regressors to reduce potential endogeneity problems.[4] In the regressions, all the variables are in logarithms. We have compared regressions in levels and log levels and the latter gives a better fit based on R^2 and RESET misspecification test. In addition, the heteroskedasticity problem is greatly reduced after taking logarithms.

A central issue in this long-run time series is that of structural breaks. It is common in the econometric literature on China (e.g. Lin 1992; Li, 2000) to locate the break at the start of the reforms in the late 1970s. As shown in regression R1 in Tables 3 and 4 on overall inequality and rural–urban inequality, the Chow tests indicate a significant break in 1979. The Chow-test p-value is 0.105 in the regression on inland–coastal inequality (R1 in Table 5), indicating a marginally significant structural break.

Table 3. Regression Results: Total Inequality

	R1	R2	
Variables	Whole period (1952–2000)	Before reform (1952–1978)	Reform (1979–2000)
Decentralization	0.279**	0.011	0.267**
	(0.072)	(0.068)	(0.056)
Trade ratio	0.295**	0.151**	0.455**
	(0.060)	(0.071)	(0.056)
Heavy-industry ratio	0.003	0.488**	−0.161
	(0.111)	(0.113)	(0.128)
Chow-test p-value	0.000	0.997	
F-test for coefficients (p-value)		0.001	
Phillips–Ouliaris test	−3.350	−5.012	
KPSS statistic	0.116	0.054	
Adjusted R^2	0.675	0.817	

Notes: All the variables are in logarithmic form and independent variables have one-year lag. Figures in parentheses are robust standard errors. * and ** indicate statistical significance at 10% and 5%, respectively. The null hypothesis of the Chow test is that there is no structural break in 1979. The F-test is for testing whether the coefficients are the same across the two periods. The Phillips–Ouliaris Z_t test is for testing the null hypothesis of no cointegration. Phillips and Ouliaris (1990) report the critical values for regressions with independent variables only up to 5. The critical values to reject this null hypothesis with three and five independent variables at the 10% significant level are −3.833 and −4.431, respectively. The KPSS statistic is for testing the null hypothesis of cointegration. If the statistic is larger than 0.347, the null will be rejected at the 10% significance level.

FIFTY YEARS OF REGIONAL INEQUALITY IN CHINA 99

Table 4. Regression Results: Rural–Urban Inequality

Variables	R1	R2	
	Whole period (1952–2000)	Before reform (1952–1978)	Reform (1979–2000)
Decentralization	0.256**	−0.018	0.369**
	(0.078)	(0.060)	(0.079)
Trade ratio	0.128**	0.208**	0.406**
	(0.036)	(0.087)	(0.067)
Heavy-industry ratio	−0.080	0.458**	0.121
	(0.108)	(0.102)	(0.159)
Chow-test *p*-value	0.000	0.993	
F-test for coefficients		0.001	
Phillips–Ouliaris test	−2.596	−4.529	
KPSS statistic	0.153	0.036	
Adjusted *R*²	0.302	0.669	

Notes: All the variables are in logarithmic form and independent variables have one-year lag. Figures in parentheses are robust standard errors. * and ** indicate statistical significance at 10% and 5%, respectively. The null hypothesis of the Chow test is that there is no structural break in 1979. The *F*-test is for testing whether the coefficients are the same across the two periods. The Phillips–Ouliaris Z_t test is for testing the null hypothesis of no cointegration. Phillips and Ouliaris (1990) report the critical values for regressions with independent variables only up to 5. The critical values to reject this null hypothesis with three and five independent variables at the 10% significant level are −3.833 and −4.431, respectively. The KPSS statistic is for testing the null hypothesis of cointegration. If the statistic is larger than 0.347, the null will be rejected at the 10% significance level.

There are two ways to handle a structural break. One way is to estimate the equations separately for the pre-reform period (1952–78) and the post-reform period (1979–99). However, in so doing, some degrees of freedom will be lost. Here, we adopt the second way by estimating the equations for the whole period but allowing coefficients to vary across the two periods. Regression R2 in Tables 3–5 provide the estimation results under the varying-coefficient specifications. The Chow-test *p*-values indicate that a structural break has been correctly captured in the new specification.

Because the three inequality series are not stationary, it is important to check whether regressing one on other policy variables produces stationary residuals, which means cointegration among variables. If the residuals are not stationary, the regressions with nonstationary data may give spurious results. Here we adopt two cointegration tests. The first one is the Phillips–Ouliaris test (1990, PO for short). The PO test is designed to detect the presence of a unit root in the residuals of regressions among the levels of time series. The null hypothesis is that the residuals have unit roots (no cointegration). The critical values for the PO test can be found in the appendix of Phillips and Ouliaris (1990). In addition to the Phillips–Ouliaris test, we also perform the KPSS test (Kwiatkowski et al., 1992) to check the cointegrated relationship. In contrast to the PO test, the KPSS tests the null hypothesis that the regression residuals are stationary (the variables are cointegrated).

Consider Table 3 first and start with the results for overall inequality. Regression R2 has better specification than R1 as it does not have structural breaks and passes both

100   *Ravi Kanbur and Xiaobo Zhang*

cointegration tests. The *F*-test indicates that the coefficients in the two periods are statistically different. In the pre-reform period, the heavy-industry coefficient is significant and has the highest value (0.488), suggesting that the heavy-industry development strategy implemented in the central planning era was a dominant force behind the overall inequality. Turning to the post-reform period, the coefficients for decentralization and trade ratio are significantly positive. In particular, trade ratio has the largest impact on overall inequality in this period. The coefficient for decentralization has changed from insignificant to significant, confirming the observation in Figure 3 that decentralization has a closer relationship with the overall inequality in the reform period. Despite the importance of the heavy-industry ratio in the pre-reform period, it faded into insignificance in the reform period as China changed its development strategies.

As in Table 3, regression R2 with varying coefficients in Table 4 has a better specification than regression R1 with constant coefficients. The *F*-test shows a systematic difference in coefficients across the two periods. The results are similar to Table 3. In the pre-reform period, a greater favoring of heavy industry increases rural–urban spread. The impact of openness on the rural–urban divide almost doubled as China transformed from a closed economy to a more open economy. In the reform period, greater decentralization widened the rural–urban disparity.

In Table 5 the two specifications on inland–coastal inequality produce similar results. The PO test and KPSS test indicate that the first regression R1 is cointegrated in levels.

Table 5. Regression Results: Inland–Coastal Inequality

Variables	R1 Whole period (1952–2000)	R2 Before reform (1952–1978)	Reform (1979–2000)
Decentralization	0.564**	0.341*	0.440**
	(0.119)	(0.203)	(0.163)
Trade ratio	1.409**	1.070**	1.412**
	(0.072)	(0.280)	(0.133)
Heavy-industry ratio	−0.611**	−0.260	−1.100**
	(0.293)	(0.421)	(0.363)
Chow-test *p*-value	0.105	0.242	
F-test for coefficients		0.566	
Phillips–Ouliaris test	−3.908	−3.895	
KPSS statistic	0.152	0.137	
*R*²	0.828	0.825	

Notes: All the variables are in logarithmic form and independent variables have one-year lag. Figures in parentheses are robust standard errors. * and ** indicate statistical significance at 10% and 5%, respectively. The null hypothesis of the Chow test is that there is no structural break in 1979. The *F*-test is for testing whether the coefficients are the same across the two periods. The Phillips–Ouliaris Z_t test is for testing the null hypothesis of no cointegration. Phillips and Ouliaris (1990) report the critical values for regressions with independent variables only up to 5. The critical values to reject this null hypothesis with three and five independent variables at the 10% significant level are −3.833 and −4.431, respectively. The KPSS statistic is for testing the null hypothesis of cointegration. If the statistic is larger than 0.347, the null will be rejected at the 10% significance level.

FIFTY YEARS OF REGIONAL INEQUALITY IN CHINA 101

The coefficients for all the three policy variables are significant with signs consistent with our hypotheses. In particular, the trade ratio has the largest impact on inland–coastal inequality, reflecting the dramatic changes in regional comparative advantage as a result of coastal-biased policy as well as the opening up to the world market. The negative coefficient for the heavy-industry ratio tells the same story. In the planned era, most heavy industries were established in the interior regions, thereby reducing the inland–coastal disparity. When China opened up, the coastal region found itself with a pronounced comparative advantage in labor-intensive exporting sectors (usually light industries) in world markets. The faster growth in the coastal region widened the inland–coastal gap. In the second regression R2, the coefficient for decentralization has increased by nearly 30% from the pre-reform period to the reform period, indicating that greater decentralization played a larger detrimental effect on inland–coastal inequality.

Overall, these results represent broad support for the hypotheses advanced earlier on heavy industry, decentralization, and openness. Heavy industry increased inequality, especially its rural–urban component, and particularly in the pre-1979 period. Decentralization, when it is significant, increased overall inequality, rural–urban inequality, and inland–coastal inequality. The trade ratio was associated with greater overall inequality and, in particular, inland–coastal disparity in the reform period.

5. Conclusions

The tremendous growth in per capita GDP since the reform period, and its impact on poverty in China, has been much discussed and celebrated (Piazza and Liang, 1998; Fan et al., 2002). But this has not stopped a concern with growing inequality, for at least two reasons. First, as is well known, the poverty-reducing effects of a given growth rate on poverty are lower at higher levels of inequality (e.g. Ravallion, 2001). Second, rising inequality may itself lead to tensions within a country and impede the prospects for future growth through a variety of social, political, and economic mechanisms (Kanbur, 2000; Kanbur and Lustig, 2000). In the case of China, such concerns have been expressed widely (Wang et al., 2002).

This study tries to comprehend the driving forces behind the changes in China's regional inequality over half a century. We find that the evolution of inequality matches different political–economic periods in Chinese history. In particular, we find that the heavy-industry development strategy played a key role in forming the enormous rural–urban gap in the pre-reform period, while openness and decentralization contributed to the rapid increase in inland–coastal disparity in the reform period of the 1980s and 90s.

The empirical finding also has relevance to the ongoing debate on how globalization affects regional inequality in developing countries. Convergence or divergence of a nation's economy is dependent not only on its domestic polices but also on its openness. With China joining the WTO, the economy will become more liberalized, and open, likely resulting in more dramatic shifts in regional comparative advantages. If the government continues to favor the coastal region in its investment strategy, then regional disparity may widen even more. Further liberalizing and investing in the economy in the inland region is thus an important development strategy for the government to both promote economic growth and reduce regional inequality.

102   *Ravi Kanbur and Xiaobo Zhang*

Data Appendix

GDP

The nominal gross domestic product is from *China Statistical Yearbook* (2001, p. 49). The constant GDP (1980 prices) used in Figure 1 is calculated based on the nominal GDP value in 1980 as well as the annual real growth rate of GDP in *China Statistical Yearbook* (2001, p. 49).

Per Capita Consumption

Following Kanbur and Zhang (1999) and Yang and Zhou (1999), this study uses rural and urban per capita consumption data at the provincial level, but covering a longer period, 1952 to 2000. Prior to 1990, the data are from *Regional Historical Statistical Materials Compilation (1949–1989)*. Alongside the nominal per capita consumption, the accumulative growth rates of real per capita consumption for rural and urban residents at a provincial level with 1952 as a basis are also published. By assuming the prices were the same across provinces in 1952, we can derive real per capita consumption by province with a rural–urban divide since 1952. For the period 1990–2000, the annual real growth rates are available from various issues of *China Statistical Yearbook*. Using the calculated per capita consumption in 1989 and the annual real growth rates since 1989, we can obtain the real capita consumption for this period. However, the published real growth rates are identical to nominal growth rates for the years of 1999 and 2000.[5] So for these two years, we further adjust the real growth rates with rural and urban consumer price indexes by province.

There do exist differences between this dataset and another dataset (per capita living expenditure) in the section of People's Livelihood in *China Statistical Yearbook*. Yang and Zhou (1999) provide discussions on the differences between the two sets of measures. The consumption dataset may be more consistently compiled over time for three reasons. First, the data includes information on real growth rates while the other dataset lacks this information. Second, per capita expenditure data were estimated based on survey data, which carry different imputation at different times. Third, the consumption data include consumption in-kind, such as the value of housing, food subsidies from the government to urban households, according the explanatory notes in the yearbook. As a result, the consumption estimate is significantly higher than the living expenditure estimate.

We should be aware that there exists some incomparability between rural and urban resident consumptions. For instance, urban residents enjoy some housing and medical care subsidies while rural residents do not. In addition, the calculation of price index may have not reflected the improvement in quality of consumer goods, which is more evident in cities. The relatively higher increase in urban price may be partly due to quality improvement. In addition, price support in cities has been gradually phased out over the past decades while the procurement price for major grains in rural areas has long been very low, which may also lead to differences in price levels between rural areas and cities. In spite of these shortcomings of the consumption measure, it is the only summary measure at a provincial level that is readily available, consistently compiled, and covering both rural and urban populations in all the provinces for nearly half a century.

Population

When calculating inequality measures, we also need to use population by province as weights. There are two sets of population data. One is agricultural and nonagricultural population and the other is rural and urban population. In general, these two sets of population are rather close except for several provinces, such as Heilongjiang and Xinjiang, where state farming is a large sector. In this paper, we use rural and urban population with per capital consumption data that have a rural and urban divide as well.

The population data prior to 1978 are from *Regional Historical Statistical Materials Compilation (1949–1989)*. For several provinces without the rural and urban population, we use the agricultural and nonagricultural population data instead. The total population data from 1978 to 2000 are from *Comprehensive Statistical Data and Materials on 50 Years of New China,* while the rural population for the same period are available from *Comprehensive Agricultural Statistical Data and Materials on 50 Years of New China.* The total population and rural population in 1999 and 2000 are from *China Statistical Yearbook* (2001 and 2001) and *China Rural Statistical Yearbook* (2000 and 2001). The difference between the total and rural population is urban population.

Urban and rural residencies refer to the status registered in the household register system. Principally speaking, rural and urban residents are supposed to specialize in farm work and nonfarm work in their registration areas, respectively. The strict household registry system used to prevent population from moving freely to a large extent. However, with the success of rural reform, many workers are freed up from agriculture activities and move to urban areas, especially to big cities, to seek opportunities without any entitlement to subsidies like urban residents. These floating migrants are not covered in the SSB sample that includes only the registered resident households. Hence, possible biases result from using the official registered numbers of rural and urban population. However, more than 80% of these floating migrants are laborers who work outside during the off-harvest season (*China Development Report 1998*). These migrants usually send money back home (Tsui, 1998), to some extent reducing the bias resulting from migration that is not captured by the official population statistics.

Decentralization

We use the share of local governments' expenditure in total government expenditure as a proxy for fiscal decentralization. Although, in the literature, some other measures are also used as a proxy for decentralization, they are not long enough for our time-series analysis. For example, Lin et al. (1997) create a fiscal decentralization index based on the revenue-sharing formula, but their index dates back to only 1985. The total, central, and local governments' expenditure data from 1953 to 2000 are available from *China Statistical Yearbook* (2001, p. 258). The data for 1952 are obtained from *Comprehensive Statistical Data and Materials on 50 Years of New China* (p. 19).

Openness

There are two ways to measure openness. One is the effective tariff rate, which is defined as the ratio of tariff revenue to total imports. The other commonly used measure is the trade ratio—the share of trade (imports plus exports) in total GDP. The

104   *Ravi Kanbur and Xiaobo Zhang*

data on imports and exports prior to 1999 are from *Comprehensive Statistical Data and Materials on 50 Years of New China* (p. 60). Information on the two last years is from *China Statistical Yearbook* (2001, p. 586). The tariff data are from *China Statistical Yearbook* (2001, p. 248).

Heavy-Industry Ratio

This is defined as the ratio of the gross heavy-industrial output value relative to the gross agricultural and industrial output value. From 1949 to 1998, the gross agricultural output value, the gross industrial output value, and the gross heavy-industrial output value are available from *Comprehensive Statistical Data and Materials on 50 Years of New China* (p. 30 and 38). For 1999, the gross agricultural output value and the gross industrial output value are from *China Statistical Yearbook* (2000, p. 374 and 409). The gross output value of heavy industry is from the same source (p. 412). For the year 2000, the *China Statistical Yearbook* publishes gross output values of enterprises with only revenue of over five million Chinese yuan. Therefore the data are incompatible with previous years. Because we take a one-year lag for this variable and other policy variables in regressions, the omission of data in 2000 does not affect the results.

References

Aaberge, Rolf and Xuezeng Li, "The Trend in Urban Income Inequality in Two Chinese Provinces, 1986–90," *Review of Income and Wealth* 43 (1997):335–55.

Chen, Jian and Belton M. Fleisher, "Regional Income Inequality and Economic Growth in China," *Journal of Comparative Economics* 22 (1996):141–64.

Chen, Shaohua and Martin Ravallion, "Data in Transition: Assessing Rural Living Standards in Southern China," *China Economic Review* 7 (1996):23–56.

Fan, Shenggen and Xiaobo Zhang, "Production and Productivity Growth in Chinese Agriculture: New National and Regional Measures," *Economic Development and Cultural Change* 50 (2002):819–38.

Fan, Shenggen, Xiaobo Zhang, and Sherman Robinson, "Structural Change and Economic Growth in China," *Review of Development Economics* 7 (2003):360–77.

Fan, Shenggen, Linxiu Zhang, and Xiaobo Zhang, *Growth and Poverty in Rural China: the Role of Public Investment*, International Food Policy Research Institute Policy Report 125 (2002).

Fujita, Masahisa, Paul Krugman, and Anthony J. Venables, *The Spatial Economy*, Cambridge, MA: MIT Press (1999).

Hanson, G. and A. Harrison, "Trade Liberalization and Wage Inequality in Mexico," *Industrial and Labor Relations Review* 52 (1999):271–88.

Hussain, Athar, Peter Lanjouw, and Nicholas Stern, "Income Inequalities in China: Evidence from Household Survey Data," *World Development* 22 (1994):1947–57.

Jian, T., Jeffrey Sachs, and Andrew Warner, "Trends in Regional Inequality in China," NBER working paper 5412 (1996).

Kanbur, Ravi, "Income Distribution and Development," in A. B. Atkinson and F. Bourguigon (eds), *Handbook of Income Distribution*, Vol. 1. Amsterdam: North-Holland (2000).

Kanbur, Ravi and N. Lustig, "Why is Inequality Back on the Agenda?" in *Proceedings of the Annual World Bank Conference in Development Economics*, World Bank (2000).

Kanbur, Ravi and Xiaobo Zhang, "Which Regional Inequality: Rural–Urban or Coast–Inland? An Application to China," *Journal of Comparative Economics* 27 (1999):686–701.

Khan, Azizur Rahman and Car Riskin, *Inequality and Poverty in China in the Age of Globalization*, Oxford: Oxford University Press (2001).

FIFTY YEARS OF REGIONAL INEQUALITY IN CHINA   105

Khan, Azizur R., Keith Griffin, Carl Riskin, and Renwei Zhao, "Sources of Income Inequality in Post-reform China," *China Economics Review* 4 (1993):19–35.

Kwiatkowski, D., P. C. B. Phillips, P. Schmidt, and Y. Shin, "Testing the Null Hypothesis of Stationarity Against the Alternative of a Unit Root: How Sure Are We That Economic Time Series Have a Unit Root?" *Journal of Econometrics* 54 (1992):159–78.

Li, Xiao-Ming, "The Great Leap Forward, Economic Reforms, and the Unit Root Hypothesis: Testing for Breaking Trend Functions in China's GDP Data," *Journal of Comparative Economics* 27 (2000):814–27.

Lin, Justin Yifu, "Collectivization and China's Agricultural Crisis in 1959–1961," *Journal of Political Economy* 98 (1992):1228–52.

———, "Rural Reforms and Agricultural Growth in China," *American Economic Review* 82 (1992):34–51.

Lin, Justin Yifu and Dennis T. Yang, "Food Availability, Entitlement and the Chinese Famine of 1959–61," *Economic Journal* 110 (2000):136–58.

Lin, Justin Yifu, Cai Fang, and Zhou Li, *The China Miracle: Development Strategy and Economic Reform*, Hong Kong: Chinese University Press (1996).

Lin, Justin Yifu, Zhiqiang Liu, and Funing Zhong, "Fiscal Decentralization and Rural Development in China," China Center for Economic Research working paper E1997012 (1997).

Lyons, Thomas P., "Interprovincial Disparities in China: Output and Consumption, 1952–1987," *Economic Development and Cultural Change* 39 (1991):471–506.

Ma, Jun, *Intergovernmental Relations and Economic Management in China*, New York: St Martin's Press (1997).

McMillan, John, John Whalley, and Lijing Zhu, "The Impact of China's Economic Reforms on Agricultural Productivity Growth," *Journal of Political Economy* 97 (1989):781–807.

Piazza, A. and E. Liang, "Reducing Absolute Poverty in China: Current Status and Issues," *Journal of International Affairs* 52 (1998):253–73.

Phillips, P. C. B. and S. Ouliaris, "Asymptotic Properties of Residual Based Tests for Cointegration," *Econometrica* 58 (1990):165–93.

Prud'homme, Remy, "The Danger of Decentralization," *World Bank Research Observer* 10 (1995):201–20.

Qian, Yingyi and Gérard Roland, "Federalism and the Soft Budget Constraint," *American Economic Review* 88 (1998):1143–62.

Rodrik, Dani, "Comments on 'Trade, Growth, and Poverty,' by Dollar and Kraay." Available at http://ksghome.harvard.edu/~.drodrik.academic.ksg/Rodrik%20on%20Dollar-Kraay.PDF (2000).

Rozelle, Scott, "Rural Industrialization and Increasing Inequality: Emerging Patterns in China's Reforming Economy," *Journal of Comparative Economics* 19 (1994):362–91.

Selden, M., *The Political Economy of Chinese Development*, New York: M. E. Sharpe (1992).

Shorrocks, Anthony F., "The Class of Additively Decomposable Inequality Measures," *Econometrica* 48 (1980):613–25.

———, "Inequality Decomposition by Population Subgroups," *Econometrica* 52 (1984):1369–85.

Solinger, Dorothy, "China's Transients and the State: a Form of Civil Society?" *Politics & Society* 21 (1993):98–103.

State Statistical Bureau (SSB), *Historical Statistical Materials for Provinces, Autonomous Regions and Municipalities 1949–1989 (Quanguo Gesheng Zizhiqu Zhixiashi Lishi Tongji Ziliao Huibian)*. Beijing: China Statistical Publishing House (1990).

———, *China Development Report (Zhongguo Fazhan Baogao)*. Beijing: China Statistical Publishing House (1998).

———, *Comprehensive Statistical Data and Materials on 50 Years of New China (Xin Zhongguo wushinian Tonji Ziliao Huibian)*. Beijing: China Statistical Publishing House (1999).

———, *Comprehensive Agricultural Statistical Data and Materials on 50 Years of New China (Xin Zhongguo Wushinian Nongye Tonji Ziliao Huibian)*. Beijing: China Statistical Publishing House (2000).

106   *Ravi Kanbur and Xiaobo Zhang*

———, *China Statistical Yearbook (Zhongguo Tongji Nianjian)*. Beijing: China Statistical Publishing House, various years.

Tang, Xianguo, *The Reform of China's Pricing System*, Geneva: Institut universitaire de hautes études internationals (1987).

Tsui, Kai-yuen, "China's Regional Inequality, 1952–1985," *Journal of Comparative Economics* 15 (1991):1–21.

———, "Decomposition of China's Regional Inequalities," *Journal of Comparative Economics* 17(1993):600–27.

———, "Factor Decomposition of Chinese Rural Income Inequality: New Methodology, Empirical Findings, and Policy Implications," *Journal of Comparative Economics* 26 (1998):502–28.

Wang, Shaoguang, Angang Hu, and Yuanzhu Ding, "Inequality 'Threatens Social Explosion'" by reporter Josephine Ma. *South China Morning Post*, 10 August (2002).

Wood, A., "Openness and Wage Inequality in Developing Countries: the Latin American Challenge to East Asian Conventional Wisdom," *World Bank Economic Review* 11 (1997):33–57.

Yang, Danis Tao, "Urban-based Policies and Rising Income Inequality in China," *American Economic Review* 89 (1999):306–10.

Yang, Danis Tao and Cai Fang, "The Political Economy of China's Rural–Urban Divide," Center for Research on Economic Development and Policy Reform working paper 62, Stanford University (2000).

Yang Dennis and Hao Zhou, "Rural–Urban Disparity and Sectoral Labour Allocation in China," *Journal of Development Studies* 35 (1999):105–33.

Yao, Shujie, "Industrialization and Spatial Income Inequality in Rural China, 1986–92," *Economics of Transition* 5 (1997):97–112.

Zhang, Tao and Heng-fu Zou, "Fiscal Decentralization, Public Spending, and Economic Growth in China," *Journal of Public Economics* 67 (1998):221–40.

Zhang, Xiaobo and Ravi Kanbur, "What Difference Do Polarisation Measures Make? An Application to China," *Journal of Development Studies* 37 (2001):85–98.

Zhang, Xiaobo and Kevin H. Zhang. "How Does Globalisation Affect Regional Inequality within a Developing Country? Evidence from China," *Journal of Development Studies* 39 (2003):47–67.

Zhang, Xiaobo, Shenggen Fan, Linxiu Zhang, and Jikun Huang, "Local Governance and Public Goods Provision, in Rual China," *Journal of Public Economics* 88(2004):2857–71.

Notes

1. Data for Hainan province since 1988 are incorporated into Guangdong province, while data for Chongqing province since 1997 are included in Sichuan province.

2. Results for $c = 1$ are similar and not reported here.

3. We note here criticisms of Rodrik (2000) on various standard measures of "openness." Since our measure is based partly on trade volume it does not fully isolate the pure effects of a policy of openness.

4. Given data restrictions it is impossible to find suitable alternative instruments covering the entire 50-year period under consideration.

5. We thank Professor D. Gale Johnson for pointing this out. In fact, the inflation (deflation) rates in the two years were rather low.

[17]

ARVIND PANAGARIYA

Columbia University

India's Trade Reform

Among developing countries, India's growth experience during the past five decades has been unique. Unlike many of its East and Southeast Asian neighbors, India did not grow at "miracle" rates that exceeded 6 percent and reached as high as 10 percent. Nor, unlike Africa and Latin America, did it suffer periods of prolonged stagnation or decline. For three of the five decades (1950–80), India's economy grew steadily at the so-called Hindu rate of $3\frac{1}{2}$ percent a year in real terms, and during the next two decades it grew at annual rates between 5 and 6 percent.

Although the credit for this steady growth without prolonged stagnation or decline goes to the macroeconomic stability and policy credibility that the government provided, the blame for the relatively low rate of growth, especially during 1950–80, must be assigned to the myriad microeconomic distortions and heavy state intervention that straitjacketed India's entrepreneurs.[1] The government effectively stamped out domestic competition through strict investment licensing and eliminated foreign competition through strict import licensing. It was only during the second half of the 1980s that the government began to loosen its grip on investment and import licensing; this was followed by a more systematic and comprehensive opening up in the 1990s and after.

This paper discusses India's external sector policies, focusing especially on the past two decades; the impact of these policies on trade flows, efficiency, and growth; and the future direction trade policies must take. It begins with a discussion of the major policy developments in trade in both goods and services. This is followed by a discussion of the evolution of trade flows—their growth, composition, and direction. The next section describes the impact of trade liberalization on efficiency and growth.

The author thanks Pranab Bardhan, Suman Bery, Govinda Rao, Jagadeesh Sivadasan, and participants in the India Policy Forum 2004 in New Delhi for excellent comments on an earlier draft.

1. Policy changes, whether good or bad, have been largely predictable in India. Consultations with the relevant parties, extensive discussions, and special committee reports have usually preceded all major policy actions.

The penultimate section considers policy options available to India and the most appropriate course for the country. The final section concludes.

The Reforms to Date

The history of India's external sector policies since independence can be divided into three phases: 1950–75, when the trend was toward tighter controls, culminating in virtual autarky by the end of the period; 1976–91, when some liberalization took place, especially during the last five to seven years; and from 1992 onward, when deeper and more systematic liberalization was undertaken.

Toward Virtual Autarky, 1950–75

Although the history of tariff protection in India goes further back in time, quantitative import controls were introduced in May 1940 to conserve foreign exchange and shipping during World War II.[2] Starting in 1947, however, regulation of the balance of payments became the central concern, and the government introduced explicit restrictions on the rate at which foreign exchange could be run down. From then until the launch of the First Five Year Plan in 1951, India alternated between liberalization and tighter controls. But the period covered by the first plan was one of progressive liberalization. In particular, the India Tariff (Second Amendment) Act of 1954 stepped up tariff rates for thirty-two items and paved the way for the liberalization of import quotas through additional licenses over and above normal entitlements.

A balance-of-payments crisis in 1956–57 led to a major reversal of this liberalization, as India resorted to comprehensive import controls.[3] The crisis left a sufficiently deep impression on the political leadership that it made the allocation of foreign exchange across various activities the central objective of trade and foreign exchange policy. The interaction of this objective with an ambitious, powerful, and self-interested bureaucracy produced a regime that was highly protectionist and without a clear sense of

2. This section draws heavily on part 7, especially chapters 15 and 22, of the most remarkable contribution by Jagdish Bhagwati and Padma Desai (1970), which foresaw the pitfalls of the license raj early on and offered a thorough analytical case for an open, pro-market policy regime, paying due attention to the political economy and institutional context of the time.

3. India's financial year starts on April 1 and ends on March 31. Therefore, 1956–57 covers the period from April 1, 1956, to March 31, 1957; it is also called fiscal year 1957.

economic priorities. The number of criteria to be taken into account was large—private versus public sector, small versus large enterprises, and capital versus intermediate versus consumer goods—and the number of industries across which foreign exchange had to be allocated even larger: within the machinery sector alone they included paper machinery, chemical machinery, mining machinery, tea machinery, and metallurgical machinery, to name just a few. Unsurprisingly, the process quickly degenerated into a system of ad hoc rules. As Bhagwati and Desai describe graphically, "The problem was Orwellian: all industries had priority and how was each sponsoring authority to argue that some industries had more priority than others?"[4] They conclude, "It is not surprising, therefore, that the agencies involved in determining industry-wise allocation fell back on vague notions of 'fairness,' implying *pro rata* allocations with reference to capacity installed or employment, or shares defined by past import allocations and similar other rules of thumb without any clear rationale."[5]

Under the regime that evolved, producers needed to make only minimal effort to get absolute protection against imports. The authorities applied the principle of indigenous availability, according to which the government denied the allocation of foreign exchange for importing a product if domestic import substitutes were available in sufficient quantity. Therefore all a producer needed to do to block the entry of imports of a product was to let the relevant agency know that the producer made a substitute for it in the requisite quantity. The quality of the substitute, the price at which it was supplied, and any delay in delivery were of secondary importance to the authorities.

An important switch in policy came in June 1966, when India undertook a major devaluation from 4.7 rupees to 7.5 rupees to the dollar and, alongside, took steps toward liberalization of import licensing, tariffs, and export subsidies.[6] The liberalization measures gave fifty-nine industries, covering 80 percent of output in the formal ("organized") sector, freedom to import

4. Bhagwati and Desai (1970, p. 288).

5. Bhagwati and Desai (1970, p. 290). The authors quote an unpublished doctoral thesis by Arun Shourie (1966), which offers systematic evidence supporting the hypothesis that, rather than devise a set of priorities based on proper economic criteria, the government agencies essentially fell back on simple rules of thumb. For example, the cuts imposed on various industries immediately following the Sino-Indian war in late 1962 and early 1963 were overwhelmingly uniform.

6. Some industrial de-licensing and limited decontrol of steel distribution on the recommendation of the Swaminathan Committee on Industries Development Procedures had taken place just before and after these steps on the external front. But the de-licensing was mainly aimed at reducing delays in the issuance of licenses. For details see Bhagwati and Desai (1970, p. 477).

4 INDIA POLICY FORUM, 2004

their raw materials and components.[7] Paradoxically, however, the need to obtain a license remained. Because the licensing procedures continued to apply the principle of "indigenous availability," the actual liberalization turned out to be very limited ex post.[8]

The impetus for the devaluation and other measures had come from the World Bank, which promised a package of $900 million annually for several years to help finance the expansion of imports that would result from the liberalizing measures.[9] Unfortunately, this policy measure coincided with a second consecutive crop failure, which led to an industrial recession.[10] As a result, a large proportion of the World Bank aid remained unutilized in 1966–67. More important, the timing of the recession gave credence to the widely held and popular view that the measures forced by the World Bank were the wrong prescription in the first place. Intense domestic criticism, a political leadership that was keen to distribute export subsidies, and an industry that had learned to profit from protection came together to reverse the policy in less than two years.[11] Bhagwati and Desai describe the political economy of the reversal:

> In a very real sense, therefore, the timing of import liberalization was not ideal, in retrospect: a burgeoning economy would have increased the chances of making an effective dent in the practice of granting automatic protection to every activity. On the other hand, it was clear that it was quite naïve to expect industrialists . . . to agree to switch over to an efficient system involving competition . . . . In this, the pressure groups were often in the company of disinterested politicians (such as the Finance Minister Morarji Desai) whose thinking had also been conditioned by the planning philosophy of the earlier period: that anything which could be produced and supplied from domestic capacity must automatically be protected from imports.[12]

---

7. The "organized" sector in India is defined as consisting of central, state, and local administrations and public and private firms with ten or more workers if using electrical power and twenty or more workers if not using power. Firms in the organized sector are required to register with an appropriate governmental agency.

8. Bhagwati and Desai (1970, p. 483).

9. The World Bank had acted on the recommendation of the Bell mission, which also advised a shift away from industry and toward agriculture. Starting in 1960–61, the performance of Indian agriculture had deteriorated rapidly, and the aid consortium had become concerned about an impending "quiet crisis." The Bell mission was a response to that concern. For details see Joshi and Little (1994, chapter 4).

10. Industrial growth fell from 5.6 percent in 1965–66 to 2.6 percent in 1966–67 and 1.4 percent in the first three quarters of 1967–68.

11. Around this time, under pressure from the United States, the World Bank also went back on its promise of $900 million in annual aid; this further strengthened the hands of the protectionist forces, which had more or less full control of the process in any case. See Joshi and Little (1994, chapter 4).

12. Bhagwati and Desai (1970, pp. 486–87).

The late 1960s and early 1970s saw a reversal of the 1966 liberalization measures and a further tightening of the import controls. The U.S. policy of isolating Prime Minister Indira Gandhi immediately before and after the Bangladesh war in 1971 drove her further toward economic isolationism. By the mid-1970s India's trade regime had become so repressive that the share of nonoil, noncereals imports in GDP fell from an already low 7 percent in 1957–58 to 3 percent in 1975–76.

Two factors paved the way for a return to liberalization in the late 1970s, however. First, industrialists came to feel the adverse effect of the tight import restrictions on their profitability and began to lobby for liberalization of imports of the raw materials and machinery for which domestically produced substitutes did not exist. Second, improved export performance and remittances from overseas workers in the Middle East led to the accumulation of a healthy foreign exchange reserve, raising the comfort level of policymakers with respect to the effect of liberalization on the balance of payments.

Ad Hoc Liberalization: 1976–91

The new phase of liberalization began in 1976 with the reintroduction of the Open General Licensing (OGL) list, which had been a part of the original wartime regime but had become defunct as controls were tightened in the wake of the 1966 devaluation. The system operated on a positive-list basis: unless an item was on the OGL list, its importation required a license from the Ministry of Commerce. Inclusion on the OGL list did not necessarily mean that the good could be imported freely, however, since the importer usually had to be the actual user and, in the case of machinery imports, could be subject to clearance from the industrial licensing authority if the sector in which the machinery was to be employed was subject to industrial licensing.

Upon its introduction in 1976, the OGL list contained only 79 capital goods items. But by April 1988 it had expanded to cover 1,170 capital goods items and 949 intermediate inputs. By April 1990 OGL imports had come to account for approximately 30 percent of total imports.[13] Although tariff rates were raised substantially during this period, items on the OGL list were given large concessions on those rates through "exemptions," so that the tariffs did not significantly add to the restrictive effect of licensing. Mainly, they allowed the government to capture the quota rents, thus helping relieve the pressure on the budget. The government also introduced

13. See Pursell (1992).

several export incentives, especially after 1985, which partly neutralized the antitrade bias of import controls. Above all, during 1985–90 the rupee was devalued in nominal effective terms by a hefty 45 percent, leading to a real depreciation of 30 percent.

In addition, by 1990 thirty-one sectors had been freed from industrial licensing. This measure had a trade-liberalizing dimension as well, since it freed machinery imports in these sectors from industrial licensing clearance. Import flows were also helped by improved agricultural performance and by the discovery of oil, which made room for nonoil, nonfood imports, mainly machinery and intermediate inputs. As Garry Pursell, a long-time follower of India's trade regime, notes, "The available data on imports and import licensing are incomplete, out of date, and often inconsistent. Nevertheless, whichever way they are manipulated, they confirm very substantial and steady import liberalization that occurred after 1977–78 and during 1980s."[14] During 1985–90, nonoil imports grew at an annual rate of 12.3 percent.

The liberalization, complemented by expansionary fiscal policy, raised India's growth rate from the Hindu rate of approximately 3.5 percent during 1950–80 to 5.6 percent during 1981–91. The jump in the average annual growth rate was particularly significant during 1988–91, when it reached 7.6 percent. Nevertheless, the external and internal borrowing that supported the fiscal expansion was unsustainable and culminated in a balance-of-payments crisis in June 1991. This time, however, the government turned the crisis into an opportunity: instead of reversing the course of liberalization, it launched a truly comprehensive, systematic, and systemic reform program that continues to be implemented today.

Deeper and Systematic Liberalization: 1992 to Date

The collapse of the Soviet Union, the phenomenal economic rise of China following its adoption of outward-oriented policies, and India's own experience, first with protectionist policies for three decades and then with liberalization in the 1980s, finally persuaded policymakers of the merits of the policy approach that pro-market and pro–free trade economists, most notably Jagdish Bhagwati, had advocated for nearly two decades. Starting with the July 1991 budget, there was a clear switch in favor of a move toward an outward-oriented, market-based economy. The trade liberalization program initiated in the 1991 budget was comprehensive, although the pace remained gradual and there were occasional hiccups.

14. Pursell (1992, p. 441).

MERCHANDISE TRADE LIBERALIZATION. The July 1991 reforms did away with import licensing on all but a handful of intermediate inputs and capital goods. Consumer goods, accounting for approximately 30 percent of tariff lines, remained under licensing. Only a decade later, after a successful challenge by India's trading partners at the World Trade Organization (WTO), were these goods freed of licensing. Today, except for a handful of goods that are disallowed on environmental or health and safety grounds, and a few (including fertilizer, cereals, edible oils, and petroleum products) that are "canalized" (meaning they can be imported by government only), all goods may be imported without a license or other restrictions. As called for under the Uruguay Round Agreement on Agriculture, all border measures on agricultural goods have been replaced by tariffs.

As noted earlier, tariff rates in India had been raised substantially during the 1980s, so as to turn quota rents for industry into tariff revenue for the government. Accordingly, tariff revenue as a proportion of imports rose from 20 percent in 1980–81 to 44 percent in 1989–90. In 1990–91 the highest tariff rate stood at 355 percent, the simple average of all tariff rates at 113 percent, and the import-weighted average of tariff rates at 87 percent.[15] With the removal of licensing, these tariff rates became effective restrictions on imports. Therefore a major task of the reforms in the 1990s and since has been to lower tariffs.

Tariff reductions have been confined to nonagricultural, industrial goods, however. Therefore the liberalization described below applies strictly to these goods. The reduction in tariffs has been accomplished through a gradual compression of the top tariff rates, with a simultaneous rationalization of the tariff structure through a reduction in the number of tariff bands. The top rate fell to 85 percent in 1993–94 and to 50 percent in 1995–96. Despite some reversals along the way in the form of special duties and through unification of two successive bands at the higher rate, the general direction has been toward liberalization. Before the most recent elections in May 2004, the then finance minister announced that the top tariff rate would be lowered from 25 percent to 20 percent and that the Special Additional Duty (SAD), which could be as high as 4 percent, would be eliminated. The incoming government has approved this change, so that the top tariff rate on industrial goods now stands at 20 percent, with no other additional custom duties, such as the SAD, on top of this rate.

There remain exceptions to this rule, however, as evidenced by table 1, which is taken from the latest Trade Policy Review of India by the WTO.[16]

15. WTO (1998) and Panagariya (1999a).
16. WTO (2002)

TABLE 1. Tariff Structure and Average Tariff Rates by Product Type, India

Product type	No. of lines	MFN tariff rates, 1997–98			MFN tariff rates, 2001–02		
		Average (percent)	Range (percent)	Coefficient of variation	Average (percent)	Range (percent)	Coefficient of variation
All products							
By WTO definition							
Agricultural products	676	35.1	0–260	0.9	40.7	0–210	0.7
Live animals and products	81	25.4	15–45	0.6	39.8	35–100	0.4
Dairy products	20	31.5	0–35	0.3	38.0	35–60	0.2
Coffee and tea, cocoa, sugar, etc.	128	37.6	15–192	0.4	39.6	35–170	0.4
Cut flowers and plants	34	25.1	10–45	0.6	29.9	10–35	0.3
Fruit and vegetables	150	32.7	0–127	0.5	36.6	25–115	0.3
Grains	16	0.0	0–0	...	49.4	0–100	0.8
Oils, seeds, fats, and oil products	71	38.9	15–45	0.2	56.2	15–100	0.5
Beverages and spirits	31	114.8	15–260	0.8	96.9	35–210	0.8
Tobacco	9	45.0	45–45	...	35.0	35–35	...
Other agricultural products, n.e.s.[a]	136	27.8	0–45	0.5	28.1	0–50	0.4
Nonagricultural products (excl. petroleum)	4,435	35.4	0–192	0.3	31.1	0–170	0.3
Fish and fishery products	108	20.3	0–65	0.6	35.0	35–35	...
Mineral products, precious stones, etc.	335	37.5	0–45	0.3	30.6	0–55	0.3
Metals	588	32.5	10–45	0.2	32.0	5–35	0.2
Chemicals and photographic supplies	840	34.6	0–192	0.2	33.8	0–170	0.2
Leather, rubber, footwear, travel goods	146	39.8	0–45	0.3	32.1	0–35	0.2
Wood, pulp, paper, and furniture	248	30.1	0–45	0.4	29.3	0–35	0.4
Textiles and clothing	830	43.7	25–55	0.1	31.3	15–35	0.2
Transport equipment	122	41.7	3–45	0.2	40.5	3–105	0.6

Nonelectric machinery	525	27.1	10–45	0.2	25.9	0–35	0.2
Electric machinery	257	34.7	15–45	0.3	26.8	0–35	0.4
Nonagricultural products, n.e.s.	436	37.1	0–55	0.2	30.0	0–35	0.2
Petroleum	2	31.0	37–35	0.2	25.0	15–35	0.6
By sector[b]							
Agriculture and fisheries	289	26.5	0–45	0.6	33.1	0–100	0.4
Mining	105	26.2	0–45	0.5	21.9	5–55	0.5
Manufacturing	4,718	36.1	0–260	0.4	32.5	0–210	0.4
By stage of processing							
First stage	628	25.7	0–127	0.6	29.4	0–115	0.5
Semi-processed products	1,673	35.7	0–192	0.2	32.3	0–170	0.2
Fully processed products	2,812	37.3	0–260	0.4	33.0	0–210	0.5

Source: World Trade Organization (2002).

a. n.e.s., not elsewhere specified.

b. International Standard Industrial Classification, Revision 2; excludes electricity, gas, and water (one tariff line).

10 INDIA POLICY FORUM, 2004

The table compares in detail the structure of tariffs in 2001–02 with that in 1997–98, when the top tariff rate was still 35 percent. According to the table, chemicals and photographic supplies were subject to tariff rates as high as 170 percent, and transport equipment to rates reaching 105 percent, both well beyond the official "top" tariff rate applicable to industrial goods. Within transport equipment, automobiles constitute a major potential import and are currently subject to a 60 percent duty. In addition, numerous exemptions remain, based on end-user or other criteria.[17]

In agriculture, India took essentially the same approach as the member countries of the Organization for Economic Cooperation and Development, choosing excessively high tariff bindings, ranging from 100 to 300 percent, to replace border measures agreed to be discontinued under the Uruguay Round Agreement on Agriculture. On some agricultural products such as skimmed milk powder, rice, corn, wheat, and millet, India traditionally had zero or very low bound rates. These were renegotiated under Article XXXVIII of the General Agreement on Tariffs and Trade in December 1999 in return for concessions on other products.[18] According to the WTO, India's average bound rate in agriculture is 115.2 percent.[19] For comparison, the applied most-favored-nation tariff rate was 35.1 percent in 1997–98 and 41.7 percent in 2001–02.

Traditionally, India has also restricted exports of several commodities. As part of its liberalization policy, the government began to reduce the number of products subject to export controls in 1989–90. But until the July 1991 reforms, exports of 439 items were still subject to controls, including (in declining order of severity) prohibition (185 items), licensing (55 items), quantitative ceilings (38 items), canalization (49 items), and prespecified terms and conditions (112 items). The March 1992 Export-Import Policy reduced the number of items subject to controls to 296, with prohibited items reduced to 16. The process continued thereafter, so that today export prohibitions apply to only a small number of items on health, environmental, or moral grounds, and export restrictions

17. According to the WTO (2002), there are more than 100 kinds of exemptions, each running into several pages. The general notification for exemptions has 378 entries. The WTO (2002, p. 35) notes, "The use of such exemptions not only increases the complexity of the tariff, it also reduces transparency and hampers efficiency-increasing tools such as computerization of customs."

18. For example, in its negotiations with the United States, India gave market access in apples. It has been suggested that removing or reducing the exemptions and introducing a lower and uniform most-favored-nation duty structure would be more simple and transparent, with clear implications for governance.

19. WTO (2002, table III.1).

are maintained mainly on cattle, camels, fertilizers, cereals, groundnut oil, and pulses.

The lifting of exchange controls and the elimination of overvaluation of the rupee, both of which had served as additional barriers in the traded goods sector, also accompanied the 1990s reforms. As part of the 1991 reform, the government devalued the rupee by 22 percent, from 21.2 rupees to 25.8 rupees to the dollar. In February 1992, a dual exchange rate system was introduced, which allowed exporters to sell 60 percent of their foreign exchange receipts in the free market; the rest had to be sold to the government at the lower official price. Importers were authorized to purchase foreign exchange in the open market at the higher market price, effectively ending the exchange control regime. Within a year of establishing this market exchange rate, the official exchange rate was unified with it. Starting in February 1994, many current account transactions, including all current business transactions, education, medical expenses, and foreign travel, were also permitted at the market exchange rate. These steps culminated in India accepting the International Monetary Fund's Article VIII obligations, which made the rupee officially convertible on the current account. In recent years, bolstered by the accumulation of approximately $120 billion worth of foreign exchange reserves, India has freed up many capital account transactions. Two provisions are of special significance: first, residents can remit up to $25,000 abroad every year, and second, firms can borrow freely abroad as long as the maturity of the loan is five years or more.

LIBERALIZATION OF TRADE IN SERVICES. Since 1991, India has also substantially liberalized trade in services. Traditionally, the services sector has been subject to heavy government intervention. The public sector presence has been conspicuous in the key sectors of insurance, banking, and telecommunications. Nevertheless, considerable progress has been made toward opening the door wider to participation by the private sector, including foreign investors.

Until recently insurance was a state monopoly. On December 7, 1999, the Indian parliament passed a law establishing an Insurance Regulatory and Development Authority and opening the door to private entry, including entry by foreign investors. Up to 26 percent foreign ownership of a domestic firm was permitted, provided a license was obtained from the IRDA. In the 2004–05 budget this limit was raised to 49 percent.

Although public sector banks dominate the banking sector, private sector banks are permitted to operate. Foreign direct investment (FDI) in private sector banks, up to 74 percent of ownership, is permitted under the automatic route. In addition, foreign banks are allowed to open a specified number of new branches every year. More than 25 foreign banks with full banking licenses and approximately 150 foreign bank branches are in operation today. Under the 1997 WTO Financial Services Agreement, India committed itself to permitting twelve foreign bank branches to be established each year.

The telecommunications sector has experienced much greater opening to the private sector, including foreign investors. Until the early 1990s the sector was a state monopoly. The 1994 National Telecommunications Policy provided for opening cellular as well as basic and value-added telephone services to the private sector, with foreign investors granted entry. Rapid changes in technology led to the adoption of the New Telecom Policy in 1999, which sets the current policy framework. Accordingly, in basic, cellular mobile, paging, and value-added services, and in global mobile personnel communications by satellite, FDI of up to 49 percent of ownership, subject to licensing by the Department of Telecommunications, was permitted until recently. The 2004–05 budget raised this limit to 74 percent. FDI of up to 100 percent ownership is allowed, with some conditions for Internet service providers not providing gateways (for both satellite and submarine cables), infrastructure providers providing dark fiber, electronic mail, and voice mail. Additionally, subject to licensing and security requirements and the restriction that proposals with FDI beyond 49 percent must be approved by the government, up to 74 percent foreign investment is permitted for Internet service providers with gateways, radio paging, and end-to-end bandwidth.

FDI of up to 100 percent of ownership is permitted in e-commerce. Automatic approval is available for foreign equity in software and almost all areas of electronics. Full foreign ownership is permitted in information technology units set up exclusively for exports. These units can be set up under several schemes including export-oriented units, export processing zones, special economic zones, software technology parks, and electronics hardware technology parks.

The infrastructure sector has also been opened to foreign investment. Full foreign ownership under the automatic route is permitted in projects for construction and maintenance of roads, highways, vehicular bridges, toll roads, vehicular tunnels, ports, and harbors. In projects for construction and maintenance of ports and harbors, automatic approval for foreign equity up to 100 percent is available. In projects providing support services to water transport, such as the operation and maintenance of piers and loading and the discharging of vehicles, no approval is required for foreign equity up to 51 percent. FDI up to 100 percent ownership is permitted in airports, although FDI above 74 percent requires prior approval. Foreign equity up to 40 percent and investment by nonresident Indians up to 100 percent is permitted in domestic air transport services. Only railways remain off limits to private entry.

Since 1991, several attempts have been made to bring private sector investment, including FDI, into the power sector, but without perceptible success. The most recent attempt is the Electricity Act of 2003, which replaces the three existing laws on electric power dated 1910, 1948, and 1998. The act offers a comprehensive framework for restructuring of the power sector and builds on the experience in the telecommunications sector. It attempts to introduce competition through private sector entry side by side with public sector entities in generation, transmission, and distribution. The act completely eliminates licensing requirements in generation and freely permits captive generation. Only hydroelectric projects would henceforth require clearance from the Central Electricity Authority. Distribution licensees would be free to undertake generation, and generating companies would be free to enter the distribution business. Trading has been recognized as a distinct activity, with the regulatory commissions authorized to fix ceilings on trading margins, if necessary. FDI is permitted in all three activities.

Impact on Trade Flows

The policy changes discussed above have brought with them important changes in trade flows. These can be discussed under three headings: growth in trade, the composition of trade, and its direction.

Growth in Trade

India's share in world exports of goods and services, which had declined from 2 percent at independence to 0.5 percent by the mid-1980s, bounced back to 0.8 percent by 2002.[20] Thus, since the mid-1980s, India's exports of goods and services have grown faster than world exports. Table 2 offers an overview of the evolution of India's external sector during the 1980s and 1990s compared with that of China. The numbers leave little doubt that the liberalizations of the 1990s have had a more significant impact on India's trade than those of the 1980s. Although trade has performed less

20. Trade in services refers to nonfactor services and does not include remittances.

14 INDIA POLICY FORUM, 2004

TABLE 2. Exports and Imports of India and China, 1980–2000

	Billions of current dollars			Average growth (percent per year)	
Category[a]	1980	1990	2000	1980–90	1990–2000
India					
Exports of goods and services	11.2	23.0	63.8	7.4	10.7
Merchandise, f.o.b.	8.5	18.5	44.9	8.1	9.3
Manufactures	5.1	13.0	34.5	9.8	10.3
Imports of goods and services	17.8	31.5	75.7	5.9	9.2
Merchandise, c.i.f.	15.9	27.9	59.3	5.8	7.8
Capital goods	2.4	5.8	8.8	9.2	4.2
Fuel and energy	6.7	6.0	15.7	–1.0	10.0
China					
Exports of goods and services	20.2	68.0	279.6	12.9	15.2
Merchandise, f.o.b.	18.3	62.1	249.2	13.0	14.9
Manufactures	9.0	46.2	223.8	17.8	17.1
Imports of goods and services	20.9	55.5	250.7	10.3	16.3
Merchandise, c.i.f.	20.0	53.4	225.1	10.3	15.5
Capital goods	5.1	16.9	91.9	12.6	18.5
Fuel and energy	0.2	1.3	26.0	20.1	35.2

Source: World Bank (2002).
a. f.o.b., free on board; c.i.f., cost including insurance and freight.

spectacularly in India than in China, the claim by some that the 1990s did not see a perceptible shift in the growth of exports and imports is simply wrong.

As table 2 shows, exports of goods and services grew 7.4 percent a year on average in the 1980s but 10.7 percent a year during the 1990s. The pace also picked up on the imports side, with growth rising from 5.9 percent a year in the 1980s to 9.2 percent a year in the 1990s. Thus the growth rates of both exports and imports rose by 3.3 percentage points. Nevertheless, these growth rates are substantially lower than those experienced by China since its opening to the world economy. China's exports of goods and services grew at a 12.9 percent average annual rate during the 1980s and at 15.2 percent a year during the 1990s, and its imports grew at an average annual rate of 10.3 percent during the 1980s and 16.3 percent during the 1990s. These higher growth rates are reflected in the higher degree of openness achieved by China in terms of its trade-to-GDP ratio.

According to table 3, the ratio of total exports of goods and services to GDP in India nearly doubled between 1990 and 2000, rising from 7.3 percent to 14 percent. The rise was less dramatic on the import side but still significant: from 9.9 percent in 1990 to 16.6 percent in 2000. Over these ten

TABLE 3. Indicators of Trade Openness for India and China, 1980, 1990, and 2000
Percent of GDP

Indicator	1980	1990	2000
India			
Merchandise exports	4.6	5.8	9.8
Merchandise imports	8.7	8.8	13.0
Goods and services exports	6.2	7.3	14.0
Goods and services imports	9.7	9.9	16.6
Total trade in goods and services[a]	15.9	17.2	30.6
China			
Merchandise exports	8.5	17.1	23.1
Merchandise imports	4.2	12.7	20.8
Goods and services exports	9.3	18.7	26.0
Goods and services imports	9.6	15.3	23.3
Total trade in goods and services	18.9	34.0	49.3

Source: World Bank (2002).
a. Exports plus imports.

years the ratio of total goods and services trade to GDP rose from 17.2 percent to 30.6 percent. Although this is substantially lower than the corresponding ratio of 49.3 percent for China over the same period, it is comparable to the ratio that China had achieved twelve years after its opening: 34.0 percent in 1990.

Composition of Trade

Tables 4 and 5 summarize the broad composition of merchandise exports and imports, respectively, in three periods—1987–88, 1992–93, and 2001–02—and table 6 provides details on the composition of services and transfers ("invisibles" in the official Indian terminology) for 1980–81, 1990–91, and 2001–02.[21] Table 7 provides additional details on invisibles receipts for 2001–02 and 2002–03 that are not available for other years. One can draw five important conclusions from these tables together with table 2.

First, services exports have grown more rapidly than merchandise exports. As table 2 shows, the share of services in total exports of goods and services rose from 19.6 percent in 1990 to 29.6 percent in 2000. More

---

21. Changes in the classification system do not allow one to go farther back than 1987–88 on a comparable basis; 1992–93 has been chosen to represent the baseline at the beginning of the reform, instead of 1991–92, because the latter was off trend as a result of the June 1991 crisis.

TABLE 4. Composition of Merchandise Exports, India, 1987–88, 1992–93, and 2001–02

Percent of total exports except as indicated

	1987–88	*1992–93*	*2001–02*
Primary products	26.1	20.9	16.1
Agriculture and allied products	21.2	16.9	13.4
Tea	3.8	1.8	0.8
Coffee	1.7	0.7	0.5
Rice	2.2	1.8	1.5
Cotton raw including waste	0.7	0.3	0.0
Tobacco	0.9	0.9	0.4
Cashews including cashew nut shell liquid	2.0	1.4	0.9
Spices	2.1	0.7	0.7
Oil Meals	1.4	2.9	1.1
Fruits and vegetables	0.8	0.6	0.5
Processed fruits, juices, misc. processed items	1.1	0.4	0.7
Marine products	3.4	3.2	2.8
Sugar and molasses	0.1	0.7	0.9
Meat and meat preparations	0.6	0.5	0.6
Other			
	0.5	1.0	2.1
Ores and minerals	5.0	4.0	2.8
Iron ore	3.5	2.1	0.9
Mica	0.1	0.0	0.0
Other	1.3	1.9	1.8
Manufactured goods	67.8	75.7	75.6
Leather and manufactures	8.0	6.9	4.3
Chemicals and allied products	4.7	6.6	9.2
Drugs, pharmaceuticals, and fine chemicals	2.1	2.9	4.7
Other	2.6	3.8	4.6
Plastic and linoleum products	0.4	0.8	2.2
Rubber, glass, paints, enamels and products	1.4	2.1	2.2
Engineering goods	9.5	13.4	15.7
Readymade garments	11.6	12.9	11.4
Textile yarn, fabrics, made-ups, etc.	9.0	10.3	10.1
Cotton yarn, fabrics, made-ups, etc.	7.3	7.3	6.9
Natural silk yarn, fabrics, made-ups, etc.	0.9	0.7	0.6
Other	0.8	2.2	2.5
Jute manufactures	1.5	0.7	0.3
Coir and manufactures	0.2	0.2	0.1
Handicrafts	20.2	20.4	18.8
Gems and jewelry	16.7	16.6	16.7
Carpets (handmade exclusive silk)	2.1	2.3	0.8
Works of art (exclusive floor coverings)	1.4	1.5	1.3
Sports goods	0.4	0.2	0.2
Others	0.9	1.3	1.1
Petroleum products	4.1	2.6	4.8
Other	1.9	0.8	3.5
Total exports (billions of dollars)	12.1	18.5	43.8

Source: Author's calculations using data from Reserve Bank of India (2002, table 124).

TABLE 5. Composition of Merchandise Imports, India,
1987–88, 1992–93, and 2001–02

Percent of total imports except as indicated

	1987–88	1992–93	2001–02
Bulk imports	40.9	44.9	39.4
Petroleum, crude and products	18.2	27.9	27.2
Bulk consumption goods	6.6	2.3	4.0
Cereals and cereal preparations	0.3	1.5	0.0
Edible oils	4.4	0.3	2.6
Pulses	1.1	0.5	1.3
Sugar	0.9	0.0	0.0
Other bulk items	16.1	14.7	8.2
Fertilizers	2.3	4.5	1.3
Crude	0.6	0.7	0.3
Sulphur and unroasted iron pyrites	0.8	0.6	0.1
Manufactured	0.8	3.2	0.9
Nonferrous metals	2.9	1.8	1.3
Paper, paperboards, manufactures, including newsprint	1.2	0.8	0.9
Crude rubber, including synthetic and reclaimed	0.5	0.4	0.3
Pulp and waste paper	1.1	0.6	0.6
Metalliferous ores, metal scrap, etc.	2.2	3.0	2.2
Iron and steel	5.9	3.6	1.6
Non-bulk imports	59.1	55.1	60.6
Capital goods	29.5	20.7	18.1
Manufactures of metals	0.7	0.7	0.8
Machine tools	1.0	0.8	0.4
Machinery, except electrical and electronic	11.8	7.6	5.8
Electrical machinery, except electronic	4.9	3.8	1.2
Electronic goods			7.3
Computer goods			0.4
Transport equipment	3.4	2.1	1.2
Project goods	7.8	5.8	1.1
Mainly export related items	15.1	19.0	16.0
Pearls, precious and semi-precious stones	9.1	11.2	9.0
Organic and inorganic chemicals	4.9	6.5	5.4
Textile yarn, fabrics, made-ups, etc.	0.8	0.7	1.4
Cashew nuts	0.3	0.6	0.2
Other	14.5	15.4	26.5
Artificial resins and plastic materials, etc.	2.5	1.9	1.3
Professional, scientific, and controlling instruments[a]	2.2	2.3	2.0
Coal, coke, and briquettes, etc.	1.0	2.2	2.2
Medicinal and pharmaceutical products	0.8	1.3	0.8
Chemical materials and products	0.9	0.8	0.9
Nonmetallic mineral manufactures	0.5	0.4	0.8
Others	6.6	6.5	18.4
Total imports (billions of dollars)	17.2	21.9	51.4

Source: Author's calculations using data from Reserve Bank of India (2002, table 124).
a. Including photographic and optical goods.

18   INDIA POLICY FORUM, 2004

T A B L E   6 .   Composition of Invisibles Receipts and Payments, India,
1980–81, 1990–91, and 2001–02
Percent of total except as indicated

Item	Receipts			Payments		
	1980–81	*1990–91*	*2001–02*	*1980–81*	*1990–91*	*2001–02*
Nonfactor services	39.0	61.0	57.0	71.2	46.3	74.6
Travel	17.0	19.5	8.2	5.4	5.1	10.6
Transportation	6.4	13.2	5.5	21.2	14.2	11.0
Insurance	0.9	1.5	0.7	2.0	1.1	1.2
Government, not						
included elsewhere	1.5	0.2	1.3	2.8	2.2	1.3
Miscellaneous	13.2	26.6	41.2	39.7	23.7	50.5
Investment income	12.8	4.9	7.7	28.0	53.5	25.1
Transfers						
Private	37.7	27.9	34.2	0.7	0.2	0.3
Official	10.5	6.2	1.1	0.2	0.0	0.0
Total (billions of dollars)	7.2	7.5	35.6	2.1	7.7	21.6

Source: Author's calculations using data from Reserve Bank of India (2002, table 137).

T A B L E   7 .   Composition of Invisibles Receipts, India, 2001–02 and 2002–03
Percent of total except as indicated

Item	*2001–02*	*2002–03*
Transfers	34.3	35.4
Software services	20.6	22.3
Miscellaneous services other than software	20.4	21.2
Travel	7.9	7.0
Transportation	5.4	5.9
Income	9.4	6.6
Insurance and GNIE[a]	2.0	1.6
Total receipts (billions of dollars)	36.7	43

Source: Reserve Bank of India (2003, table 6.4).
a. GNIE: Government, not included elsewhere

recent data from the World Bank show that this ratio rose further, to
33.1 percent, in 2001.[22] H. A. C. Prasad places India's share of world
services exports in 2002 at 1.3 percent.[23]

Second, at the relatively broad level of aggregation shown in table 4, the
commodity composition of India's trade has changed only modestly.[24]

22. World Bank (2003).
23. H. A. C. Prasad, *Business Line*, August 27, 2003.
24. The next section will show that in the more finely disaggregated data, changes in the
composition of both exports and imports are quite dramatic. Products with no or very low
trade initially have grown very rapidly.

During 1992–2002 the share of manufactures in total commodity exports remained unchanged at approximately 75 percent. Within manufactures the sectors that have grown more rapidly than the average for all merchandise exports are the capital- and skilled labor–intensive sectors, including chemicals and allied products and engineering goods. Within the former category, drugs, other pharmaceuticals, and fine chemicals have done especially well; within engineering goods, automobiles and auto parts have lately shown impressive growth. The key unskilled labor–intensive sectors have grown at best at the average pace of all merchandise exports. For example, leather manufactures have grown at rates well below the average, whereas ready-made garments and textiles, yarn, fabrics, and made-up goods have grown at approximately the average rate of all merchandise exports.

Third, on the import side, perhaps the most remarkable observation is that the share of capital goods imports declined drastically during the 1990s (table 5). From 29.5 percent in 1987–88, this share fell to 18.1 percent in 2001–02. In part this decline reflects a bias in liberalization in the 1980s in favor of capital goods over intermediate inputs, whereas in the 1990s both capital and intermediate goods (but not consumer goods) were freed from licensing. But the decline also reflects the general slowdown in private investment activity during the 1990s relative to the late 1980s.

Fourth, on the invisibles account, two key items that have shown very rapid growth are remittances from Indians residing overseas and software exports. The former are reported under "private transfers" in tables 6 and 7. The latter are subsumed within the category "miscellaneous" in table 6 but are reported separately for the last two years in table 7. Software exports (including business process outsourcing) accounts for the greater part of the growth in the miscellaneous category during the 1990s. According to table 7, software exports have risen from $7.6 billion in 2001–02 to $9.6 billion in 2002–03. Interestingly, a substantial part of the growth in remittances has also come from the software industry, since these remittances include the repatriation of earnings by temporary Indian workers in the United States (mainly H1B visa holders). This component rose from $2.1 billion in 1990–91 to $12.2 billion in 2001–02.

Finally, it comes as no surprise that India is far from achieving its potential in tourism. After reaching $3.2 billion in 2000–01, tourism receipts fell to $2.9 billion in 2001–02 in the wake of the September 11 tragedy and recovered only slightly to $3.0 billion in 2002–03. Given

India's attractiveness as a tourist destination and its low costs, this level of tourism is well below what the country could achieve.

Direction of Trade

Table 8 summarizes the direction of India's merchandise trade for 1987–88, 1992–93, and 2001–02. On the export side the major shift has been away from Russia and Japan toward developing Asia. The share of India's exports going to Japan declined from 10.3 percent in 1987–88 to 3.4 percent in 2001–02. The share taken by Russia declined from 12.5 percent to a paltry 1.8 percent over the same period. The share of developing countries as a whole grew from 14.2 percent to 30.9 percent, with each major region—Asia, Africa, and Latin America—absorbing a larger share of India's total exports than before. The share taken by developing Asia rose from 11.9 percent to 23.6 percent. The United States meanwhile has remained a steady trading partner, accounting for approximately one-fifth of India's merchandise exports throughout the period.

On the import side, the major shift has been away from the industrial countries and Russia to the OPEC nations and other developing countries. India's imports from the European Union declined from 33.3 percent of the total in 1987–88 to 22.1 percent in 1999–2000.[25] The decline in the U.S. share over the same years was from 9.0 percent to 7.2 percent, and that in the Japanese share from 9.6 percent to 5.1 percent. Russia also lost share, with imports from that country declining from 7.5 percent to 1.3 percent of India's total imports. OPEC and the other developing countries meanwhile gained share. The share of imports coming from OPEC rose from 13.3 percent to 25.9 percent, and that from developing countries from 17.3 percent to 29.2 percent.

An interesting ongoing development is the rapid expansion of India's trade with China. From just $18 million in 1990–91, India's exports to China rose to approximately $2 billion in 2002–03. India's imports from China similarly expanded from $35 million to $2.8 billion over the same period. India's exports to China have consisted of medium- to high-technology products. In 2002–03 three product groups—engineering goods, iron ore, and chemicals—accounted for more than 70 percent of India's exports to China. On the import side, electronic goods, chemicals, and textiles, yarn, fabric, and made-up articles together accounted for approximately half of the total value of India's imports from China.

25. The available direction-of-trade data on imports for years 2000–01 and after are not consistent with those for the earlier years.

TABLE 8. Direction of Trade, India, Selected Years

Percent of total exports or imports except as indicated

Country or group	1987–88 Exports	1987–88 Imports	1992–93 Exports	1992–93 Imports	2001–02 Exports	1999–2000 Imports[a]
OECD countries	58.9	59.8	60.5	56.1	49.3	43.0
European Union	25.1	33.3	28.3	30.2	22.5	22.1
Germany	6.8	9.7	7.7	7.6	4.1	3.7
United Kingdom	6.5	8.2	6.5	6.5	4.9	5.4
North America	19.7	10.3	20.0	11.7	20.8	7.9
Canada	1.1	1.3	1.0	1.9	1.3	0.8
United States	18.6	9.0	19.0	9.8	19.4	7.2
Asia and Oceania	11.6	12.0	9.1	10.6	4.5	7.5
Australia	1.1	2.3	1.2	3.8	1.0	2.2
Japan	10.3	9.6	7.7	6.5	3.4	5.1
Other OECD countries	2.5	4.2	3.0	3.6	1.6	5.5
Switzerland	1.3	1.1	1.1	1.7	0.9	5.2
OPEC	6.1	13.3	9.6	21.8	11.9	25.9
United Arab Emirates	2.0	3.4	4.4	5.1	5.7	4.7
Eastern Europe	16.5	9.6	4.4	2.5	2.9	2.0
Russia	12.5	7.2	3.3	1.2	1.8	1.3
Developing countries	14.2	17.3	22.9	19.6	30.9	29.2
Asia	11.9	12.1	18.8	14.6	23.6	20.0
SAARC members[b]	2.6	0.4	4.0	0.8	4.6	0.8
Other	9.3	11.7	14.8	13.8	19.0	19.2
Hong Kong	2.8	0.5	4.1	0.8	5.4	1.6
South Korea	0.9	1.5	0.9	1.6	1.1	2.6
Malaysia	0.6	3.8	1.0	1.9	1.8	4.1
Singapore	1.7	1.9	3.2	2.9	2.2	3.1
Thailand	0.5	0.3	1.4	0.3	1.4	0.7
Africa	2.0	2.9	3.1	3.5	5.2	7.3
Latin America	0.3	2.3	1.0	1.5	2.1	1.9
Other	0.0	0.0	0.1	0.0	0.2	0.0
Total trade (billions of dollars)	12.1	17.2	18.5	21.9	43.8	49.7

Source: Author's calculations from Reserve Bank of India (2002, table 130).

a. Available direction of trade data on imports for 2000–01 and beyond are not consistent with those for earlier years.

b. In addition to India, members of the South Asian Association for Regional Cooperation include Bangladesh, Bhutan, Maldives, Nepal, Pakistan, and Sri Lanka.

Impact on Efficiency and Growth

The benefits of liberalization may be measured in terms of static efficiency gains and economic growth.[26] This section will discuss each of these approaches briefly.

Static Efficiency

Measurements of efficiency gains inevitably rely on simulations using partial- or general-equilibrium models.[27] The dominant approach today is to construct a general-equilibrium model and parameterize it such that it reproduces the equilibrium in the base year with the existing policy distortion in place. The model is then subjected to a comparative statics exercise by removing specific distortions and solved for the changes in various endogenous variables, including consumption, output, net imports of various goods, and real income. The results of these exercises critically depend on the choice of the model, functional forms, and parameter values.[28] Moreover, the effects on sectoral consumption, output, and trade predicted by these models do a very poor job of tracking the actual outcomes.[29] For these reasons estimates based on these studies must be taken with a grain of salt.

With this caveat, the only comprehensive study that quantitatively measures the impact of India's liberalization on welfare is that by Rajesh Chadha and others.[30] Using the Michigan Computable General Equilibrium model, this study concludes that trade liberalization corresponding approximately to what has been accomplished to date had the potential to raise GDP permanently by approximately 2 percent. If the same liberalization were done after a competitive regime replaced the existing regime, however, the gain from trade liberalization would rise to as much as 5 percent of GDP.

The traditional analyses of the static gains from trade liberalization fail to emphasize some key sources of such gains: specialization in production that eliminates certain sectors entirely and gives rise to new ones; reduced costs due to the availability of higher-quality inputs; and the

---

26. An examination of the effects on poverty reduction is beyond the scope of this paper.

27. See Panagariya (2002a).

28. Panagariya and Duttagupta (2001) demonstrate this fact in the context of computable general-equilibrium models of preferential trading.

29. See Kehoe (2003).

30. Chadha and others (1998).

availability of new and higher-quality products to consumers.[31] Because these sources are particularly relevant for India, given its regime of across-the-board protection, it is useful here to consider briefly each of these sources of gains.

When a country's production structure is excessively diversified as a result of a policy of wholesale, indiscriminate import substitution, as was the case in India, opening to trade is likely to lead to the disappearance of certain activities and sectors altogether. Conversely, the availability of new inputs and higher-quality substitutes for low-quality inputs produced domestically will likely give rise to new products and sectors capable of competing in world markets. Benefits from these changes can potentially give rise to gains much larger than the traditional triangular efficiency gains from the expansion or contraction of existing activities that are relatively small.

Even in the case of products that continue to be produced domestically, the availability of newer and higher-quality inputs is likely to yield large savings. For years India prohibited imports of machinery and intermediate inputs whenever domestic substitutes were available, even if the latter were of dubious quality. This resulted in low efficiency as well as poor quality of the final product. Vijay Kelkar makes this point forcefully:

> In the manufacturing sector we opted for an across-the-board import substitution strategy where we sought to produce everything in a production chain whether the product was a commercial vehicle or a steel mill. And by this, the weakest link decided the fate of the strength of the whole production chain. We entered into production of a number of activities in which we just did not possess the competitive edge. It resulted in a loss of efficiency for the entire industry. For instance, forcing the Indian fertilizer industry to use only Indian designed catalyst, the entire fertilizer industry's productivity suffered. Same was the case for electronics sector where our software industry took time to take off because of the insistence on the use of domestic computer hardware.[32]

Pursell expresses a similar sentiment when describing India's trade regime until the mid-1970s:

> During this period, import-substitution policies were followed with little or no regard to costs. They resulted in an extremely diverse industrial structure and high degree of self-sufficiency, but many industries had high production costs. In addition, there was a general problem of poor quality and technological backwardness, which beset even low-cost sectors with comparative advantage such

31. Chadha and others (1998) do allow for economies of scale and are thus able to capture some of the pro-competitive effects of reduced protection on production costs. But they apparently hold the numbers of domestic and foreign products fixed.

32. Kelkar (2001, p. 5).

as the textiles, garment, leather goods, many light industries, and primary industries such as cotton.[33]

A final source of static welfare gains is the availability of new and perhaps higher-quality variants of existing products. As Paul Romer has emphasized using an elegant analytical model, when new products become available, the benefits are not limited to the traditional welfare triangles but the entire area under the demand curve.[34] For many years India either prohibited imports of consumer goods or allowed them only under very stringent conditions. As a result, products that were readily available elsewhere commanded a very large premium in India. In addition, the quality of domestically produced counterparts of foreign goods was often extremely poor.[35] This situation changed drastically after the liberalization of consumer goods imports, first through the easing of baggage rules and the issuance of tradable special import licenses for specified consumer goods, and subsequently, in April 2001, through an end to all licensing.[36] The availability of high-quality products has contributed to consumer welfare not only directly but also indirectly, by making consumers more discriminating and therefore forcing domestic manufacturers to upgrade the quality of their products.

Two sectors in which the impact of opening up on the quality and availability of new products is highly visible are automobiles and telecommunications. Indian consumers had long suffered the 1950s models sold by Ambassador and Fiat, and even then they had to wait in queues that were several years long. Today virtually all of the world's major car manufacturers are represented in the Indian market, and consumers have immediate access to a wide variety of models. Continued high tariffs on automobile imports notwithstanding, consumers have reaped large benefits because automobile manufacturers have been able to enter the market through tariff-jumping investments.

33. Pursell (1992, pp. 433–34).

34. Romer (1994).

35. Bhagwati tells an anecdote that aptly captures the deleterious impact that protectionist policies had on the quality of the Indian products. Upon his return from study abroad in the early 1960s, Bhagwati initially shared the intellectual attitudes that helped India turn inward, although he quickly changed his mind in light of the realities on the ground. In a letter to Harry Johnson written during his tenure at the Indian Statistical Institute in the early 1960s, Bhagwati happened to complain about the craze he observed in India for everything foreign. Harry Johnson promptly responded that if the quality of the paper on which Bhagwati had written his letter was any indication of the quality of homemade products, the craze for the foreign seemed perfectly rational to him.

36. "Baggage rules" are those applicable to imports entering India as a part of passengers' baggage.

In the same vein, not too long ago, telephone service was considered a luxury even among upper-middle-class Indians in urban areas, and they had to wait in long queues to obtain it. The few "lucky" ones who did manage to get a telephone usually found that half the time they could not get a dial tone, and the other half of the time they got a wrong number.[37] In contrast, telephone service today, whether it be fixed line or cellular, is available on demand in most regions, and absence of a dial tone and inability to connect to the number dialed are no longer at issue. India has made full use of the rapid advances in technology in this sector, with benefits to consumers that many now take for granted. Had it not freed imports of information technology products (and undertaken other reforms in the telecommunications sector), India could not have taken advantage of these advances.

The benefits of new imported inputs and final products are not limited to these obvious, highly visible examples. In her doctoral thesis, Purba Mukerji analyzes the changes in trade flows during the 1990s at a highly disaggregated level.[38] She finds that, at the five-digit SITC classification, the total number of products imported jumped from 2,120 in 1991 to 2,611 in 1999, or 23 percent, and that of exports from 2,273 to 2,549, or 12 percent, over the same period.

More important, following Timothy Kehoe and Kim Ruhl, Mukerji studies the change in the share of new goods in total merchandise imports and exports using the five-digit SITC data.[39] Contrary to the impression of relatively minor changes in the composition of imports and exports conveyed by the aggregate data, she finds movements in the composition of imports and exports that could not be more dramatic. The available data span the years 1988 to 1999. Mukerji first sorts products in ascending order of the value of their imports. She then divides them into ten categories, with each category accounting for 10 percent of the total imports in 1988. By construction, the first category consists of products that individually

---

37. Prompted by his unhappy experience with the Indian telephone system, Bhagwati once quipped that one way to distinguish between a developed and a developing country is that in the former one gets tired of *receiving* phone calls, whereas in the latter one is exasperated *making* them. Tharoor (1997, p. 167) offers a more direct indictment of the telecommunications sector in India in the early 1980s and the government's attitude toward it: "The government's indifferent attitude to the needs to improve India's communications infrastructure was epitomized by Prime Minister Indira Gandhi's communications minister, C. M. Stephens, who declared in Parliament, in response to questions decrying the rampant telephone breakdowns in the country, that telephones were a luxury, not a right, and that any Indian who was not satisfied with his telephone service could return his phone—since there was an eight-year waiting list of people seeking this supposedly inadequate product."

38. Mukerji (2004).

39. Kehoe and Ruhl (2002).

contributed little or nothing to the volume of imports in 1988 and therefore contains the largest number of products. By the same token, the last category contains products that individually contributed the largest volume of imports in 1988 and hence contains the fewest products.[40] Mukerji then fixes the categories and computes the change in the share of each category in the following years. She does a similar exercise for exports.

Mukerji's results for imports are reproduced in the top panel of table 9. Because so many products were allowed to be imported only in tiny quantities, or not at all, in 1988, as many as 2,312 out of 2,742 importable items accounted for 10 percent of imports in the first category. That is to say, the remaining 429 products, or just 15.6 percent of all importable items, accounted for 90 percent of India's merchandise imports. In the following years, especially after the major liberalization in July 1991, the proportions shifted dramatically. By 1999, products in the first category had increased their share in total imports from 10 percent to 35 percent, with products in most other categories experiencing a declining trend.

A similar if slightly less dramatic story emerges on the export side. According to the bottom panel of table 9, in 1988 only 8.4 percent of all products accounted for 90 percent of India's exports, with the remaining 91.6 percent of products accounting for the remaining 10 percent. By 1999 the share of the products in the latter category had climbed to 27 percent. Again, the pattern is one in which products with zero or minuscule shares initially are the ones that grew fastest. Only the first two categories in table 9, which contain those products with the smallest initial shares, show gains, with the rest experiencing either a decline or no change in 1999.

Growth and Productivity

The bulk of the benefits from liberalization has evidently come from faster growth. Although India has seen a clear shift in its growth rate during the last two decades, its connection to liberalization has been questioned. Bradford DeLong argues that since the shift in the growth rate took place during the 1980s whereas the reforms began only in 1991, reforms cannot be credited with the shift.[41] Dani Rodrik endorses DeLong's view, asserting that "the change in official attitudes in the 1980s, towards encouraging rather than discouraging entrepreneurial activities and integration into the world economy, and a belief that the rules of the economic game had

40. The last category contains 20 percent of the imports initially, to overcome a problem posed by a switch in classification in 1992.
41. DeLong (2003).

TABLE 9. Composition of Trade According to New versus Old Products

Percent of total imports or exports

Category[a]	No. of products	1988	1989	1990	1991	1992	1993	1994	1995	1996	1997	1998	1999
Imports													
9	2,312	10	13	15	15	17	20	28	26	28	32	38	35
8	211	10	10	11	9	9	11	11	11	11	11	9	10
7	97	10	10	11	10	11	13	13	14	12	11	10	8
6	49	10	9	9	8	8	7	7	7	6	5	5	4
5	29	10	8	9	9	8	8	9	9	8	7	6	6
4	19	10	9	9	8	7	6	5	5	4	5	3	2
3	13	10	8	7	6	5	5	7	8	8	7	8	8
2	8	10	12	11	10	9	6	6	6	5	5	3	6
1	3	20	21	18	25	26	24	14	14	18	17	18	21
Exports													
9	2,533	10	13	14	18	20	22	23	24	26	27	25	27
8	132	10	10	11	10	10	11	11	12	12	12	12	11
7	52	10	11	10	11	11	8	9	7	8	8	7	8
6	23	10	10	11	10	8	7	7	7	7	7	7	7
5	11	10	10	10	11	10	11	11	11	12	12	11	10
4	7	10	11	11	10	11	10	9	8	9	8	8	7
3	5	11	9	10	11	10	10	11	12	10	10	11	8
2	1	3	3	3	2	2	1	1	1	1	1	1	1
1	1	26	23	20	17	18	20	18	18	15	15	18	21

Source: Mukerji (2004).

a. Products are ranked according to quantities imported or exported and then divided into categories according to import or export quantity in 1988, with the first category including the products accounting for the most imports or exports, and the ninth category the least (the latter including products in which there was no trade in 1988). Thus an increase in the share of trade accounted for by products in a given category indicates an expansion of trade in products in that category or (in the ninth category) the introduction of trade in formerly nontraded products. Category 1 contains 20 percent of imports in 1988 to overcome a problem posed by a switch in classification in 1992.

28 INDIA POLICY FORUM, 2004

changed for good may have had a bigger impact on growth than any specific policy reforms."[42]

Elsewhere I have subjected this view to a systematic critique, offering four counterarguments.[43] First, growth during the 1980s was fragile, exhibiting significantly higher variance than in the 1990s. It was the super-high growth rate of 7.6 percent a year during the last three years of 1980s that makes overall growth in the 1980s look comparable to that in the 1990s. Second, growth in the 1980s, especially the extremely rapid growth of the last three years of the decade, took place in the presence of significant liberalization of both investment and import licensing, notably during the second half of the decade. Third, growth during the 1980s was also fueled by fiscal expansion. As such, it was unsustainable, with the result that the economy crash-landed in 1991. Finally, even if DeLong were right that changes in attitudes rather than in policies led to the shift in the growth rate in the 1980s, without further liberalization that growth would not have been sustained. It is on the strength of continued liberalization that India sustained a 6 percent annual growth rate from 1992–93 onward. It is also because of the 1990s liberalization that India has been able to build a foreign exchange reserve of $120 billion, putting it beyond the immediate reach of another macroeconomic crisis despite fiscal deficits that are currently as large as those in the late 1980s.[44]

In assessing the contribution of liberalization to growth more directly, one may ask whether liberalization was accompanied by increased growth in total factor productivity (TFP). Before reviewing the evidence from India in this area, however, it is important to recall that the literature on productivity has been, in general, controversial and inconclusive on the role of policy in stimulating growth. In the context of East Asia, Alwyn Young set off a major debate with his conclusion that the super-high growth rates of the Asian miracle economies were almost entirely due to capital accumulation, and that policies—whether outward-oriented and pro-market, or inward-oriented and interventionist—played no role.[45] Later findings by Jong-Il Kim and Lawrence Lau, Susan Collins and Barry Bosworth, and Ishaq Nadiri and Wanpyo Son have reinforced Young's conclusions, leading Paul Krugman to colorfully describe the East Asian

42. Rodrik (2003).
43. Panagariya (2004).
44. Nevertheless, the deficits are not sustainable in the long run and impose a short-term cost by crowding out private investment.
45. See Young (1992, 1995).

growth experience as one of Soviet-style perspiration rather than policy-induced inspiration.[46]

Bhagwati argues forcefully, however, that the traditional measures of TFP fail to capture the effect that policies have on capital accumulation itself.[47] Good policies can raise the rate of saving and therefore of investment. Approaching the issue from the productivity perspective, Charles Hulten has long argued that increased productivity due to innovation raises the return to capital and induces greater capital accumulation.[48] The conventional productivity measures do not take this innovation-induced accumulation into account. For example, Hulten and Mieko Nishimizu study the direct and indirect effects of innovation on growth in nine industrialized countries for the period 1960–73 and find that the conventional TFP measure accounts for 45 percent of output growth, but that when innovation-induced capital accumulation is taken into account, the contribution of innovation jumps to 84 percent.[49]

Empirical studies aimed at measuring TFP in India focus virtually exclusively on manufacturing and may be divided into two categories, those relying on industry-level data and those relying on firm-level data. Their findings are not unambiguous, because of differences in methodology, the unit of analysis, and the quality of the data, but the weight of the evidence is in favor of trade liberalization leading to productivity gains.

Among studies based on industry-level data, the key source of the differences in results is the manner in which gross output and intermediate inputs are deflated. Isher Ahluwalia initially looked for effects of the early reforms on productivity using industry data from 1959–60 to 1985–86.[50] She concluded that although there was no net TFP growth during the entire period, a mildly accelerating pattern of productivity growth did emerge after liberalization began in the late 1970s.

P. Balakrishnan and K. Pushpangandan and J. Mohan Rao rejected this finding, however, on the ground that Ahluwalia had used a "single-deflation" procedure that assumes that prices of output and intermediate inputs grow at the same rate.[51] Instead they used a "double-deflation"

---

46. See Kim and Lau (1994), Collins and Bosworth (1996), Nadiri and Son (1998), and Krugman (1994).
47. Bhagwati (1999).
48. Hulten (1975).
49. Hulten and Nishimizu (1980).
50. See Ahluwalia (1991). For a discussion of the earlier literature on productivity growth in India, see Bhagwati and Srinivasan (1975).
51. See Balakrishnan and Pushpangandan (1994) and Rao (1996).

method, with separate estimates of prices for final output and for intermediate goods, and found the opposite pattern of TFP growth, with TFP growth collapsing during 1985–92.

More recently, Hulten and Syleja Srinivasan have taken a fresh look at the data for 1973–92.[52] They begin by noting that the finding by Balakrishnan and Pushpangandan and by Rao, that TFP increased rapidly until 1982–83 and then plummeted 35 percent by the end of the period, is rather implausible, and they share the skepticism expressed subsequently by Ahluwalia and by B. H. Dholakia and R. H. Dholakia about the Balakrishnan-Pushpangandan-Rao double-deflation method.[53] They then proceed to recalculate productivity growth applying different and, in their view, superior methods of measurement of output and intermediate input prices. Their price indexes lead to the same results as in the Balakrishnan-Pushpangandan-Rao papers for the entire sample period (1973–92) but yield major differences for the subperiods 1973–82 and 1983–92. In particular, whereas the output price index used by Rao accelerates from the first half of the sample period to the second, the output price index used by Hulten and Srinivasan decelerates. In the same vein, the Hulten and Srinivasan input price index shows a less rapid deceleration between the two subperiods than the Rao index.

These differences in price indexes lead to different productivity outcomes in the two subperiods. They smooth out the TFP path, and the sudden collapse found in the Balakrishnan-Pushpangandan-Rao papers disappears. At the same time, no pickup in TFP growth in the second period is found: the growth rates are 2.2 percent and 2.1 percent in the two subperiods, respectively.

Hulten and Srinivasan argue, however, that the lack of pickup in TFP growth still leaves open the possibility that the surge in investment in the second subperiod reflected an improved investment climate due to reform. Therefore they proceed to make the process of capital accumulation itself endogenous and calculate the total growth in productivity (direct productivity growth plus that through productivity-induced capital accumulation). This leads to estimates of 5.0 percent and 5.7 percent growth in productivity in the two subperiods, respectively, indicating at least a small pickup in productivity growth.

In a more recent study, Satish Chand and Kunal Sen break up the time period more finely and use a different methodology, one that incorporates

52. Hulten and Srinivasan (1999).
53. Ahluwalia (1994) and Dholakia and Dholakia (1994).

TABLE 10. **Change in Protection and Growth in Total Factor Productivity, India, 1974–88**

Percent

	Industry classification		
	Consumer goods	Intermediate goods	Capital goods
Change in protection			
1974–78	4.5	0.4	−1.8
1979–83	−1.1	1.4	1.7
1984–88	−0.4	−5.4	−4.3
Growth in TFP			
1974–78	−0.5	−1.2	−1.6
1979–83	−1.2	−3.1	−1.5
1984–88	5.1	4.8	3.7

Source: Chand and Sen (2002).

the productivity effects of new inputs made available by trade liberalization.[54] They use three-digit industry data covering thirty industries that account for 53 percent of gross value added and 45 percent of employment in manufacturing over the period under study, 1973–88. The industries are divided approximately equally among consumer, intermediate, and capital goods. Chand and Sen measure protection by the proportionate wedge between the Indian and the U.S. price and estimate TFP growth in the three industry groups averaged over three nonoverlapping periods: 1974–78, 1979–83, and 1984–88. They then relate this productivity growth to liberalization.

Table 10 presents Chand and Sen's findings.[55] By their measure, protection declines over the sample period in the intermediate and capital goods sectors but not in the consumer goods sector. Moreover, all three sectors see a significant improvement in TFP growth in 1984–88 compared with the two earlier periods. Thus the jump in TFP growth coincides with the liberalization of capital and intermediate goods.

Chand and Sen perform further tests by pooling their sample and employing fixed-effects estimators to allow for intrinsic differences across industries with respect to the rate of technological progress. Their estimates show that, on average, a 1 percentage point reduction in the price wedge leads to a 0.1 percent rise in TFP. For the intermediate goods sector, the effect is twice as large. The impact of liberalization of the intermediate

54. Chand and Sen (2002).
55. See Chand and Sen (2002, table 3).

goods sector on productivity turns out to be statistically significant in all of their regressions.[56]

Several studies focus principally on the impact of the 1990s reforms on productivity growth using firm- or plant-level data; these include the contributions by Pravin Krishna and Devashish Mitra; Balakrishna, Pushpangandan, and M. Babu; Petia Topalova; and Jagadeesh Sivadasan.[57] The first three of these studies employ the PROWESS firm-level database maintained by the Center for Monitoring the Indian Economy (CMIE), whereas the last one uses, for the first time, the plant-level data underlying the industry-level data used by earlier researchers, which come from the Annual Survey of the Industries (ASI). The three papers using the PROWESS/CMIE data reach conflicting conclusions, perhaps because they employ different subsets of the dataset or different techniques, but possibly also because of the same differences in price deflators that have been at the heart of the conflict between industry-level studies.

The PROWESS database includes information on a number of variables on an annual basis for all of the roughly 4,000 industrial firms listed on the Bombay Stock Exchange. Krishna and Mitra choose firms in four sectors: electronics (90 firms), electrical machinery (90 firms), nonelectrical machinery (72 firms), and transport equipment (111 firms). They allow for scale economies and imperfect competition and find strong evidence of a pro-competitive effect, as reflected in a decline in the price-cost margin, as well as some evidence of an increase in productivity growth following the 1991 reform. Balakrishna, Pushpangandan, and Babu employ essentially the same methodology as Krishna and Mitra but apply it to a much larger sample of 2,300 firms spanning the period 1988–89 to 1997–98. They fail to find any acceleration in productivity growth following the 1991 reform, however.

Topalova carries out a more comprehensive analysis, with a sample that covers 1989–2001 and includes the largest number of firms (which varies across years) of the three studies using the CMIE/PROWESS database. She

---

56. Two recent studies by Das (2003) and Unel (2003) extend the industry-level analysis to the 1990s. The results of these two studies contradict each other, however. Whereas Unel finds substantial growth in productivity in the 1980s and 1990s (with the growth rate higher in the latter decade), Das finds the opposite: TFP growth accounts for only 7 percent of the manufacturing growth during the 1980s and almost none of that in the 1990s. Once again, the differences arise from the deflators used. Whereas Unel effectively uses a common deflator for output and intermediate inputs, Das uses separate deflators for each of them.

57. Krishna and Mitra (1998); Balakrishnan, Pushpangadan, and Babu (2000); Topalova (2003); Sivadasan (2003).

finds very strong evidence that tariff reductions have a positive effect on both the level of productivity and its growth rate. The results are highly statistically significant and robust to different specifications.

A criticism applicable to all three of these firm-level studies is that the CMIE/PROWESS data are of poor quality. Often the totals and mean values of several variables do not match those available from other, more reliable sources. There is also the possibility that since firms file the information to the stock exchange as a part of their profit-loss statements, they may misrepresent it in order to influence investors. Most important, however, the CMIE data do not report the number of a firm's employees. This makes it difficult to measure labor input. The usual way around this (as, for example, in Krishna and Mitra, 1998) is to use the deflated wage bill as the labor input, but this suffers from the problem that if TFP growth is shared by workers through higher wages, the change in TFP would be underestimated. These deficiencies of the data make the recent, carefully executed study by Sivadasan using the ASI data particularly important.

Sivadasan estimates the effects of tariff liberalization, FDI, and the removal of investment licensing at the plant level on aggregate productivity, using annual data on 40,000 plants from 1986–87 to 1994–95. A key appeal of his analysis, among many, is that he applies the double-deflation method advocated by Hulten and Srinivasan and experiments with several aggregations for the deflation of inputs, finding the results to be robust across the different deflators.

Sivadasan finds a 30 to 35 percent increase in mean intraplant productivity in those industries subject to tariff liberalization. He also finds a 25 percent increase in aggregate output growth and a 20 percent increase in aggregate productivity growth following tariff liberalization. The change in intraplant productivity growth turns out to be the biggest component of the change in aggregate productivity and output growth. He finds similar results for de-licensing and for liberalization of FDI.

To sum up, the four studies do not uniformly demonstrate an acceleration in productivity growth following the reforms, but the more careful of them, using reliable data, clearly point in that direction. At the industry level, the careful study by Chand and Sen offers clear evidence of the acceleration in productivity that coincided with the reforms in the second half of the 1980s. At the plant level, the careful study by Sivadasan, who is able to exploit the variation within plants over time as well as across plants during a given year, is particularly persuasive. His findings are robust and uniform in the expected direction for the level as well as the growth rate of

34 INDIA POLICY FORUM, 2004

productivity, and not just for tariff liberalization but also for investment de-licensing and FDI.

Three additional points are worth noting. First, for reasons discussed briefly in the next section, Indian industry was not a stellar performer during either the 1980s or the 1990s, despite the reforms. Average annual growth in this sector was only 6.8 percent during 1981–91 and 6.4 percent during 1991–2001. Therefore, regardless of what view one takes on the productivity story, the bigger puzzle to solve is why industry has grown relatively slowly.

Second, to a considerable degree, the rapid growth during the 1990s was driven by services, which today account for approximately half of India's GDP. In the aggregate, services grew at a 6.9 percent annual rate during 1981–91 and 8.1 percent during 1991–2001. Because of a lack of data, there are no studies on productivity growth in this important sector. But the record of some of the services sectors clearly looks sparkling. According to Jim Gordon and Poonam Gupta, the faster growth in services during the 1990s than during the 1980s was driven mainly by fast growth in communications services, financial services, business services (which include the information technology sector), and community services.[58] Trade liberalization has played a direct role in the growth of at least some of these sectors, namely, telecommunications and business services.

Finally, insofar as output is measured at prereform domestic relative prices, it is likely to be undervalued in a liberalizing environment. The point is readily made with the help of figure 1, which shows the production possibilities frontier between two goods, with good 1 imported. Lines *AA′* and *TT′* give the world price. Initially, a tariff keeps the domestic price at *AB,* with production and consumption taking place at *A* and *C,* respectively. Elimination of the tariff changes the domestic price to *TT′* and moves the output and consumption points to *T* and *C′.* If output is measured at prereform domestic prices, however, income is given by line *RR′,* suggesting a *decline* in income. Insofar as a movement toward exportables and away from importables accompanies the growth process, this undervaluation of output will be observed with a changing level of the capital stock as well. Thus the growth rate is likely to be understated in an environment in which domestic prices are being progressively realigned with world prices. In view of the much smaller realignment of the prices during the 1980s than during the 1990s, this fact suggests that the growth rate in the latter period relative to that in the former is understated.

58. Gordon and Gupta (2003).

FIGURE 1.   GDP at Domestic and World Prices

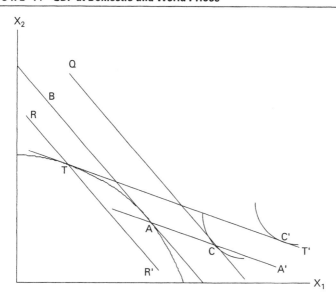

Future Policy

Although this paper focuses only on trade policy, the discussion cannot be totally divorced from some key domestic policy issues that necessarily impinge on trade flows and patterns of specialization. This section is therefore divided into five parts. The first part discusses some key domestic policy reforms necessary to allow the Indian economy to specialize in sectors where India has comparative advantage. The second takes up the issue of autonomous trade policy reform—also called unilateral trade reform—arguing in favor of adopting a uniform tariff regime and lowering the single tariff rate to below 10 percent in the next three years. The third part discusses the reforms necessary in the area of contingent protection—antidumping and safeguards. The fourth part takes up the issue of bilateral trade arrangements, and, the fifth the state of play in the ongoing Doha Round of multilateral trade negotiations under the auspices of the WTO.

Domestic Policy Reforms

Two important related facts emerge from our review of trade flows and growth from the viewpoint of domestic policy reform: the overall response of trade to India's opening up has been weaker than in countries such as China, and the economy has failed to move rapidly into the manufacturing of labor-intensive products. Both facts point to the need for some key domestic policy reforms.

The response of trade to liberalization has been an order of magnitude weaker in India than in China. In China, exports of goods and services grew at annual rates of 12.9 and 15.2 percent during the 1980s and the 1990s, respectively. Imports performed similarly. Consequently, China's ratio of total trade to GDP rose from 18.9 percent in 1980 to 34 percent in 1990 and to 49.3 percent in 2000.

Although foreign investment is not the subject of this paper, it may be noted that the differences between India and China on this front are even starker. FDI into China rose from $60 million in 1980 to $3.5 billion in 1990 and then to a whopping $42.1 billion in 2000. China was slower to open its market to portfolio investment, but once it did, inflows quickly surpassed those into India, reaching $7.8 billion in 2000. Even if one allows for an upward bias in these figures, as some China specialists suggest, and a downward bias in the figures for India, there is little doubt that foreign investment flows into China are several times those into India.

Part of the difference in performance between India and China can be attributed to the presence of Chinese entrepreneurs in Hong Kong and Taiwan, who have been eager to escape rising wages in their home economies by moving to China. However, a more central explanation lies in differences in the composition of GDP in the two countries and the asymmetric responses of their industries to opening up. Among developing countries, India is unique in having a very large share of its GDP in the mostly informal part of the services sector. Whereas in other countries a decline in the share of agriculture in GDP has been accompanied by a substantial expansion of industry in the early stages of development, in India this has not happened. For example, in 1980 the proportion of GDP originating in industry was already 48.5 percent in China, whereas in India it was only 24.2 percent. Services, on the other hand, contributed only 21.4 percent to GDP in China, but as much as 37.2 percent in India.

In the following twenty years, despite considerable growth, the share of industry did not rise in India. Instead the entire decline in the share of agriculture was absorbed by services. In China, in contrast, the share of industry started out very high in 1980, fell to 41.6 percent in 1990, but went back up to 50.9 percent in 2000. Correspondingly, services rose from its low

1980 level of 21.4 percent to 31.3 percent in 1990 and just 33.2 percent in 2000. The key point is that industry already accounted for a large share of GDP in China in 1980, and what it lost during the 1980s it more than recovered in the 1990s.[59]

Why does this matter? Because under liberal trade policies, developing countries are much more likely to be able to expand exports and imports if a large proportion of their output originates in industry. Not only is the scope for expanding labor-intensive manufactures greater in a labor-abundant country, but a larger industrial sector also requires more imported inputs, thereby offering greater scope for the expansion of imports. In India, not only have exports failed to grow rapidly, but the response of imports has been just as muted. Consequently, in recent years the Reserve Bank of India has had to purchase large volumes of foreign exchange to keep the rupee from appreciating. Even then it was unsuccessful and had to let the currency appreciate by 5 to 7 percent against the dollar during 2003. Given the poor performance of industry, imports have simply failed to absorb the foreign exchange generated by remittances and relatively modest foreign investment flows.

This same factor is also at work in explaining the relatively modest response of FDI to more liberal policies. Investment in industry, whether domestic or foreign, has been sluggish. Foreign investors have been hesitant to invest in industry for much the same reasons as domestic investors. At the same time, the capacity of the formal services sector to absorb foreign investment is limited.

Therefore the solution to both trade and FDI expansion in India lies in stimulating growth in industry. Here again this paper's review of the composition of trade flows gives some clear clues. On the export side, as noted above, unskilled labor–intensive sectors such as apparel and footwear have grown at no more than the average rate for total exports, whereas the capital- and skilled labor–intensive sectors have shown above-average growth. This pattern clearly points to bottlenecks facing the labor-intensive sectors. On the import side, machinery imports have seen their share of the total decline during the 1990s relative to the 1980s. Given the removal of trade barriers on both capital goods and intermediate inputs, this fact is also explained by relatively sluggish growth in industry.

If industrial growth is to pick up, three key domestic reforms are essential. First, the fiscal deficit must be brought down, to release funds for investment in the private sector. A major surge in industrial growth

---

59. These data are taken from World Bank (2002).

38   INDIA POLICY FORUM, 2004

will have to come from increased investment, and that will require the availability of savings to the private sector. Because the productivity of private investment depends crucially on public investment in infrastructure, the fiscal deficit cannot be contained at the expense of public investment. Therefore containing the revenue deficit is the only choice. This means cutting and streamlining current expenditure and raising more revenue.

Second, a large majority of labor-intensive manufacturing products still remain on the small-scale industries reservation list. Without an end to this reservation, there is little hope that industry will begin to grow rapidly. The large multinationals that, in China, have driven the growth of labor-intensive industry in sectors ranging from toys to apparel can hardly be expected to enter manufacturing in India on a small scale. Nor can India count on sustained rapid growth of industry on the back of the capital- and skilled labor–intensive sectors, because the scarcity of skilled labor places an automatic limit on the potential growth of these sectors. If India is to transform itself from a primarily agricultural to a primarily industrial economy, rapid growth of labor-intensive industry is essential.

Finally, the end to the small-scale industries reservation is also insufficient by itself to ensure rapid industrial growth. Current labor laws that virtually prohibit even the reassignment of workers, let alone their dismissal, must be reformed as well. The virtual ban on the exit of firms with 100 or more workers is a major disincentive to firms interested in entering the market on a large scale. Reliance on contract labor, the use of capital-intensive techniques, and the concentration of production activity in skilled labor–intensive industries—practices that get around the hiring and firing regulations relating to unskilled workers—have been deployed by many manufacturers. But this solution exacts a heavy toll in terms of drastically reduced employment opportunities or (in the case of contract labor) low worker morale, resulting in low productivity and poor product quality.

The effect of these twin regulations—the small-scale industries reservation and stringent labor laws—is best illustrated by a comparison of the apparel industry in India with that in China. According to a 2001 McKinsey Global Institute report,[60] India's share in apparel imports of the top ten importing countries not constrained by Multifibre Arrangement (MFA) quotas, at 1.6 percent, is less than its share of 3.2 percent among the MFA quota-constrained countries. The reverse holds true for the more competitive China: its share in apparel imports of the top ten non-quota-constrained

60. McKinsey Global Institute (2001).

countries is 38.1 percent, and that among the top quota-constrained countries is 11.3 percent. This difference in performance derives to a large degree from the vastly different organization of apparel factories in the two countries. Whereas the average clothing plant in India employs 50 machines, the average Chinese plant employs 500. Without reform of the small-scale industries reservation and of labor law, this organizational difference and the accompanying differences in the cost and quality of production cannot be eliminated.

Some leading economists in India question the importance of reforming the Industrial Disputes Act and related labor laws to give firms the power to retrench workers, subject to appropriate compensation, on the ground that these laws impact less than 10 percent of the labor force that is employed in firms with 100 workers or more. This is a nonsensical argument. The reason the number of firms with 100 or more workers in India is so small is precisely that labor laws remain a major barrier to the entry of firms with 100 or more workers. If India wishes to create a large number of jobs that pay decent wages, it must make the business environment friendly to labor-intensive industries. Labor law reform is a necessary condition for the creation of that environment.

Autonomous Trade Reform

Turning back to trade policy, India's autonomous trade reform program must continue until all tariffs have fallen well below 10 percent. In addition, India must address the issue of its tariff structure, which, despite substantial compression and rationalization, remains complex.

For example, the peak tariff on nonagricultural goods is ostensibly 20 percent. But nearly 10 percent of nonagricultural tariff rates are still not subject to this peak. With respect to complexity, the situation is even grimmer: approximately twenty tariff bands currently exist. As was shown in table 1, tariff rates on chemicals and photographic supplies ranged from 0 to 170 percent in 2001–02, and those on transport equipment from 3 to 105 percent.[61] The situation is not much different today, with the multi-billion-dollar automobile industry receiving nominal protection at the ad valorem rate of 60 percent. With lower input tariff rates, the effective rate of protection is even higher.

This tariff structure has little economic rationale but is rather the result of two sets of forces. First, some politically powerful sectors such as chemicals and automobiles have managed to evade the tariff compression

61. WTO (2002).

40   INDIA POLICY FORUM, 2004

applied to other sectors during the past decade. Second, the misconception remains among policymakers that somehow final goods must be protected at tariff rates higher than those applied to raw materials and intermediate inputs. As a result, tariffs on final goods have been compressed less than those on inputs. The process has been slowed recently, however: tariff reductions have been largely limited to products subject to the "peak" tariff rate, which happen to be final goods, and some of the lower tariff rates applying to intermediate inputs have been raised as a part of the rationalization process.

As part of further reform, it will be best for India to move to a single uniform tariff of 15 percent for nonagricultural goods starting in financial year 2005–06. This will involve ending the plethora of exemptions and raising tariffs on approximately 5 percent of tariff lines currently subject to tariffs below 15 percent. The uniform tariff should then be lowered to 10 percent and by a further 2 to 3 percentage points in each of the subsequent two years, to achieve a 5 percent uniform tariff rate by the beginning of 2008–09.

The adoption of a uniform tariff has the major advantage that it will take politics out of trade policy. When the government is willing to offer protection at different rates, industrial lobbies have a field day. Politically more powerful sectors such as the automobile and chemical sectors can lobby for sweetheart deals at the expense of the consumer. But once the rule is that all will receive equal protection, the incentive for any single industry to lobby diminishes dramatically. Simultaneously, the government has a logical defense against the demands of specific industries for higher protection: because it must raise the tariff for all if it does so for one, its hands are tied.[62]

The single tariff rate also has the advantage of transparency and administrative simplicity. It eliminates the prospect of industries getting a higher tariff by classifying their product as a finished rather than an intermediate good. It also does away with all kinds of exemptions. As noted earlier, according to the WTO, India's current tariff code has more than 100 kinds of exemptions, each of which runs to several pages. In addition to creating distortions, these exemptions hamper the deployment of efficiency-increasing tools such as computerization of customs.

---

62. Panagariya and Rodrik (1993) present a number of formal models that yield the uniform tariff rule as the optimal outcome. In these models tariffs are determined by lobbying. The adoption of a uniform tariff rule then creates a free rider problem in the lobbying activity, since the protection granted to one industry is automatically granted to all industries. This feature of the uniform tariff rule has a strong dampening effect on incentives to lobby.

A single uniform tariff of 15 percent would also be superior to the two-part structure proposed by the Indian government in a previous budget, with rates of 10 percent on inputs and 20 percent on final goods. A tariff structure that levies a 10 percent tariff on inputs and a 20 percent tariff on final goods grants excessively high effective protection to the latter. For example, suppose the world price of a cell phone is $100 and that its components cost $80. The proposed two-part tariff would raise the prices of the cell phone and its components to $120 and $88, respectively. This would allow domestic value added in cell phone assembly to rise from $20 to $32, thus providing effective protection of 60 percent.

Critics of the uniform tariff may argue that it would fail to minimize the distortion cost of raising revenue. In a strict sense, this is correct. The theory of optimal taxation states that, under certain technical assumptions, goods with inelastic import demand should be subject to higher tariffs than those with elastic demand. The problem, however, is that India's actual tariff structure bears little relationship to this theoretical ideal. The relevant counterfactual is not some optimal tariff structure based on various elasticities about which information is lacking, but rather the one actually in place. Compared with that structure, the uniform tariff is a vastly superior alternative.

A key issue concerning the progressive reduction in tariffs is its connection to government revenue and therefore to domestic tax reform. Even if tariff reductions initially increased tariff revenue as imports rose or compliance improved, eventually tariff revenue must fall. In the extreme case, a zero tariff rate raises no tariff revenue at all.

In India, tariff revenue has been declining for some time, as a proportion both of imports and of GDP. Tariff revenue fell as a proportion of imports from 40 percent to 17.5 percent between 1991 and 2001, and as a proportion of GDP from 3.3 percent to 1.6 percent. On the one hand, this loss of revenue may share some of the blame for the increased fiscal deficit, but, on the other, it may be credited with having forced the government's hand on reforming the domestic tax system, a process that is ongoing. Optimal efficiency dictates that revenue be raised through domestic taxes. This implies that tariff liberalization and domestic tax reform must go hand in hand. Here China provides an interesting contrast to India: tariff revenue in China is currently less than 3 percent of total imports.

India can also achieve—and benefit from—considerable compression of agricultural tariffs through autonomous liberalization. India has export potential in agriculture, but that potential will not be fully exploited without the liberalization of India's own agricultural trade regime. The World

Bank and several influential nongovernmental organizations such as Oxfam have repeatedly asserted in recent years that agricultural protection is a problem of the rich countries, and that it is wrong to ask poor countries to liberalize when rich countries maintain high protection. Their position, however, effectively ties the hands of Indian politicians in this area, who now routinely express the view that, without an end to agricultural subsidies and considerable liberalization by the rich countries, India cannot risk liberalizing its agriculture, which employs 65 percent of its work force. Given this state of political play, liberalization in agriculture will have to be left to multilateral negotiations.[63]

Fortunately, politics is less of a constraint on the autonomous liberalization of services trade. India has the potential to become a major exporter not just of information technology–related services but of health and education services and tourism as well. India's costs in these sectors are relatively low, but in the education sector, considerable internal liberalization will be required. Currently, India does not permit private universities, but without them India cannot hope to become an education hub of Asia. In the health care and tourism sectors, it will be essential to improve the country's infrastructure, including its aviation infrastructure.

On the import side, India will benefit further through liberalization of its FDI rules. Sectoral caps on FDI remain in such areas as insurance, effectively denying foreign investors control of firms. These caps should be simply abolished, to allow foreign investors 100 percent ownership. There also seems little justification in many cases for the requirement that the Foreign Investment Promotion Board approve foreign investments. Indeed, the board should also be disbanded.

Contingent Protection

The WTO permits temporary protection of domestic industry through two main measures: antidumping and safeguard duties. In WTO terminology, dumping is said to occur when one or more foreign firms sell a product for less than fair value, where "fair value" is measured, for example, by the price the exporting firm charges in its home market. If such dumping causes injury to the domestic industry, the country can subject the dumping firms to antidumping duties equal to the dumping margin, measured as the difference between the "fair value" and the price actually charged. Safeguard

---

63. For reasons to be explained below in the section on a possible India-U.S. Free Trade Agreement, bilateral trade agreements also do not offer an effective channel for the liberalization of agriculture.

duties are permitted if import competition resulting from trade liberalization causes serious injury to the domestic industry. Whereas antidumping
duties are applied only to the firms found to be dumping and other firms
from the same countries, safeguard duties are applied to all trading partners
on a nondiscriminatory basis.

Traditionally, Indian industry enjoyed sufficient permanent protection
through tariffs and licensing that it did not require protection through
antidumping measures and safeguards. But the end to licensing and the liberalization of tariffs led India to institute administrative mechanisms for
these measures. India's first three antidumping cases were initiated in
1992–93. Since then the number of cases has risen steadily, especially following the Asian financial crises in 1997–98 and the end to the Indian
licensing regime in 2001. According to the WTO, from July 2001 through
June 2002, India was the largest initiator of antidumping cases, with sev-
enty-six, followed by the United States with fifty-eight.[64] In terms of cumulative measures in force, the United States topped the list, followed by the
European Union and India, in that order. By far the country most frequently
targeted by India has been China. In contrast, India has made only limited
use of safeguard measures, having initiated only six cases as of March 1999.

Many of the antidumping measures have been imposed with a clear
protectionist intent, hurting buyers of the product subject to the duties.
Moreover, insofar as antidumping measures tend to target the most
competitive firms, the potential losses from higher domestic prices are
likely to be large. It is critical that the use of antidumping measures be
restrained considerably if India is to reap the benefits of its liberalization. It
makes little sense to replace one instrument of protection with another. An
effective remedy to limit the use of antidumping measures would be to
make the injury criteria more demanding.

India also needs to streamline its antidumping procedures. Currently, the
same agency carries out both the investigation to establish the dumping
margin and the investigation to determine injury to the domestic industry.
In other countries, such as the United States, the dumping investigation is
carried out by the Department of Commerce and the injury investigation by
the International Trade Commission. To ensure the independence of the
two investigations, it is important that they be carried out by different agencies. The natural agency to be entrusted with the injury investigation in
India is the Tariff Commission, which needs to be strengthened and made
more independent.

64. WTO (2003).

A final important reform in the area of contingent protection is to encourage the use of safeguard rather than antidumping duties. Because the former are applied on a nondiscriminatory basis to all trading partners, they are inherently more efficient. Moreover, since they cover all potential sources of imports, duty rates can be much lower than the duty rates in antidumping cases, which are often very high.

Replacing antidumping with safeguard duties will require a key change in India's safeguards legislation, however. Currently, unlike the antidumping mechanism, the safeguard mechanism can be invoked only if the domestic industry can provide persuasive evidence that it is capable of restructuring itself during the period when safeguard duties are in force. This requirement is an entirely Indian invention and is not required by the WTO rules. Therefore it would be best to drop it.

Regional Arrangements

Recently, India has embarked upon an ambitious program of regional trade arrangements.[65] It has signed free trade area (FTA) agreements with Sri Lanka and Thailand and is in the advanced stages of negotiating an agreement with Singapore. India has also signed a framework agreement for an FTA with the members of the Association of South East Asian Nations (ASEAN) and an agreement to create a South Asian Free Trade Area (SAFTA). Recently, it has also approached more distant trading partners such as South Africa and Brazil to negotiate FTA arrangements.

A number of mutually reinforcing factors have contributed to this upsurge in FTA activity on India's part. First, the proliferation of regional trade arrangements around the world has made India feel that it is being left behind in this area. In the wake of the failure to make progress in multilateral talks at Cancún in September 2003, the U.S. Trade Representative announced that the United States would now aggressively move to free up trade preferentially with those countries willing to liberalize. This announcement prompted Indian leaders to seek to respond in kind. The framework agreement with the ASEAN members, SAFTA, and the offers for FTA negotiations with Brazil and South Africa are all post-Cancún developments.

65. The usefulness of regional trade agreements is a vast and controversial topic, and the discussion here is highly selective. Bhagwati and Panagariya (1996) and Panagariya (1999b, 2000) discuss various analytical and policy issues surrounding these agreements in greater detail.

Second, having seen the Indian economy adjust relatively painlessly to very substantial trade liberalization over the last two decades, Indian leaders have acquired greater confidence in their country's ability to withstand the competition that would result from the complete elimination of trade barriers even against selected trading partners.

Third, India's rising economic strength has made other countries keen to gain preferential access to the potentially large Indian market. This was clearly a factor in the ASEAN members' decision to accept the framework agreement, which India had sought for some time.

Fourth, political factors have been clearly dominant in the decision by India and Pakistan—and perhaps other countries in the region—to sign the SAFTA agreement. Regardless of the economic implications, the leaders foresaw a major payoff to such an agreement in terms of easing tensions between the two rivals.

Finally, during the last year of the National Democratic Alliance government, India had an external affairs minister who had previously served as finance minister for several years and whose heart was more in economic diplomacy than in political diplomacy. In contrast to Jaswant Singh, his predecessor, Yashwant Sinha demonstrated much less interest in political diplomacy and much greater keenness in seeking trade agreements abroad.

The critical question is whether this aggressive pursuit of FTAs is a good idea from the Indian perspective and, if so, what kinds of agreements should be pursued and with which countries. This subsection will consider first the potential downside of these arrangements and then the potential benefits. It will then outline what may be the best and most pragmatic strategy for India.

THE DOWNSIDE. At least three important factors weigh against India proceeding along the route toward preferential trade agreements. First, given its own high external trade barriers, India faces the obvious risk of losses due to trade diversion that preferential liberalization brings with it. Although economists have long recognized and stressed this risk, it continues to be underestimated in policy discussions and is worth spelling out explicitly here.

To make the point most dramatically, consider the proposed India-Singapore FTA. Suppose for the sake of argument that India's tariff on steel imports is 20 percent. If the world price of steel is $500 a ton, the tariff-inclusive price in India would be $600 a ton. An FTA with Singapore would give that country's steel exporters tariff-free access to the Indian market, allowing them to displace some of the steel previously imported from third countries such as South Korea and Russia. A perhaps surprising

Globalization and Poverty I

point is that, despite this "liberalization," as long as some steel continues to be imported from those third countries, the internal price of steel would remain unchanged at $600. The third countries would continue to receive $500 per ton of steel, and the Indian customs authorities would collect $100 in duties on each ton. Since Singaporean steel would be exempt from the duty, however, their exporters would now receive an extra $100 a ton in revenue. What used to be tariff revenue collected by India would now become extra revenue for Singaporean firms.

One might ask why the price of steel in India would not drop to $500 a ton as a result of the FTA. This could happen, but only if Singapore produced enough steel to supply all of India's steel imports at $500 a ton. But as long as even a small quantity of steel continued to be imported from non-members, it would have to be sold at $600, and thus the price would not change.

One way around this outcome would be for Singaporean firms to buy steel from Korean and Russian suppliers for $500 a ton and then resell it in India at the higher internal Indian price. If enough Singaporean exporters did this, the price of steel in India would drop to $500. The outcome would be the same as if India removed the duty not just on Singapore but on all its trading partners. However, this type of transshipment is prohibited under most FTA arrangements through what are called rules of origin. For example, to claim duty-free status, Singaporean exporters would have to prove to the satisfaction of a commerce ministry bureaucrat that a minimum, prespecified percentage of value added in each ton of steel being brought into India originated in Singapore. This regulation would eliminate trans-shipments from third countries.

It is tempting to conjecture that although India might lose on the goods it imports from Singapore, the losses might be offset by tariff preferences received on exports to Singapore. The catch, however, is that Singapore is already a free-trading country. The FTA gives Indian exporters no tariff preference whatsoever in the Singaporean market. More generally, in an FTA, a high-tariff member is likely to lose, since it gives up more in preferences to its partner than it receives in return. The lesson is that it is best to have low external tariffs, as does Singapore, if a country wants to benefit from FTAs.

The second risk of FTAs is their likely adverse effect on autonomous, nondiscriminatory liberalization, as illustrated by the Latin American experience. Several countries in Latin America had already been liberalizing their external trade barriers aggressively before the North American Free Trade Agreement (NAFTA) went into effect in 1994. Following NAFTA, however, they all turned to FTAs with a vengeance, and the move toward nondiscriminatory liberalization came to a standstill. These countries felt they had a better chance of forming FTAs if they kept their external tariffs as a bargaining chip to be exchanged for preferential access to partner-country markets.

Finally, the move toward FTAs may also undermine the Doha WTO negotiations aimed at multilateral liberalization. Because FTAs give exporters of a member country preferential access to the partner country's market, exporters prefer them to multilateral liberalization. This constituency's incentive to push for multilateral liberalization declines even more once preferential agreements with major trading partners are in place. For example, Mexico, which has preferential access to the U.S. and EU markets, is unlikely to push hard for multilateral liberalization, because such liberalization would result in the loss of its preferential access. For India's part, it can scarcely afford to let the multilateral route close. Because of the numerous FTAs that already exist in the Americas and Europe, India faces considerable discrimination against its products in those markets. The only way to end this discrimination is to bring tariffs down to near zero on a multilateral basis in the Doha negotiations.

POTENTIAL BENEFITS. On the benefits side of the equation, two main factors may be noted. First, the strategic issue is of paramount importance: The proliferation of FTAs in the Americas and in Europe and its neighbors has led to increasing discrimination against Asian goods. The countries of Asia have two options: either they can either try to persuade these other countries to put an end to the preferences through a multilateral bargain in the near future, or they can form their own FTAs in an attempt to create discrimination against European and American goods and thereby raise their bargaining power in a future negotiation. The first option is clearly superior, but the second can serve as insurance against failure to end discrimination in the near future. It is also a good way of demonstrating to the Americas and Europe that discrimination is a two-way street.

Second, through its FTAs, the United States is systematically creating an FTA template that makes labor and environmental standards, WTO-plus intellectual property protection, and even restrictions on the use of capital controls a part of the agreements. The eventual objective of such a template is to apply it to a future multilateral agreement. For countries such as India that oppose the inclusion of these nontrade issues in trade agreements, FTAs provide an opportunity to create an alternative template. Confronted by U.S. assertions that nontrade issues already exist in the bilateral trade agreements, and that therefore their inclusion in multilateral agreements is justified, India and other developing countries can point to their own template that does not admit their inclusion.

Some analysts view FTAs as an additional instrument for promoting liberalization. The argument is that a country may find it politically difficult to eliminate tariffs against all trading partners as part of its autonomous liberalization program, but that it may be able to do so against a handful of trading partners on a reciprocal basis. Once this is accomplished, it may find that the pressure against liberalization for the remainder has become muted. This argument is unpersuasive. Logically, the incentive for autonomous liberalization will instead decline, because the existing FTA partners will see such liberalization as an assault on their preferences, and the potential future FTA partners will become reluctant to enter an agreement when they see that the potential preferences to be won are minimal. As noted above, the available evidence from Latin America points in the same direction.

THE PRAGMATIC COURSE. Given the incentives and the pressures they face today, governments find it difficult to restrain the move toward FTAs. If all the big players are chasing every FTA they see, how can smaller players resist the temptation? It is as though the alternative to opt out of such agreements no longer exists. Given this reality, the right question to ask is, How should India approach the FTAs it chooses to seek?

The first point to note is that if India stays the course on its autonomous liberalization program, the risks of preferential liberalization will be considerably ameliorated. After some hiccups during the second half of the 1990s, India has recently been remarkably steady in bringing its external tariffs down. If this process is continued, with the external tariff on industrial goods unified and brought down to between 5 and 10 percent by 2007–08, India will be well positioned to take advantage of the regional approach to liberalization, just as Singapore is today.

In addition, if India wishes to maximize the strategic advantage from FTAs, it must work toward the creation of an Asia-wide FTA. At present, India and China both have separate framework agreements with the ASEAN members to forge FTAs with them. But if India's strategic advantage vis-à-vis the Americas and Europe is to be maximized, India must eventually form an FTA with China, thereby creating pressure for Japan, Korea, and Taiwan to join to create an Asia-wide FTA.

To keep a clean FTA template, India should also be careful to keep nontrade issues, whatever they may be, out of its FTA agreements. For example, the recent SAFTA agreement incorporates many issues that are of mutual interest—infrastructure projects and rules for competition and the promotion of venture capital—but that are unrelated to trade.[66] This practice creates a bad precedent. It also risks making valuable projects of mutual benefit hostage to trade negotiations and trade disputes. The appropriate forum for pursuing these nontrade issues in South Asia is the South Asian Association for Regional Cooperation (SAARC), of which SAFTA should be a distinct part that focuses only on trade.

Because theoretical analysis does not give an unambiguous answer to the question of whether FTAs improve or worsen economic welfare, it is useful to subject any such agreements to quantitative empirical analysis. Unfortunately, much of this type of analysis relies on computable general-equilibrium (CGE) models, which, as mentioned above, have rather poor predictive power. As Kehoe demonstrates, not one of the numerous CGE models of NAFTA came even close to predicting the actual outcome.[67] A key reason, Kehoe notes, is that in reality the most pronounced trade effects of the agreement are in products that are initially traded in small quantities or not at all. The models, in contrast, focus on products that are already extensively traded.

Therefore my own inclination is to encourage future researchers to carry out sectoral studies that are much more deeply grounded in actual data than the CGE models. The benefits from an FTA are likely to arise in sectors where trade with third countries is minimal and the scope for increasing trade with the partner is large. Likewise, the losses are likely to be seen in sectors where trade with third countries is large and may be displaced by the partner. Such studies should focus on identifying these two types of sectors and assessing how the proposed FTA will alter the picture in them.

AN INDIA-U.S. FTA. Many observers, including the Confederation of Indian Industry, have proposed negotiations toward an India-U.S. FTA. Given that India now faces considerable actual or potential discrimination in the North American market vis-à-vis Mexico, Canada, Chile, Central America, Australia, and other countries, the affirmative case for such a move from the Indian perspective is straightforward. I will argue, however, that, so far as an FTA in goods is concerned, the overall case is weak and the political impediments are insurmountable.

First, at current levels of tariffs on industrial goods in India, there is considerable scope for trade diversion and the losses that accompany it. Tariffs in India are still very high compared with U.S. tariffs, so that India stands to experience the tariff revenue loss noted above in the context of

66. Panagariya (2003) discusses the economics of SAFTA.
67. Kehoe (2003).

Globalization and Poverty I

the India-Singapore FTA. Of course, if India carries out the liberalization outlined above, this objection will lose its force.

Second, in the area of agriculture, even though India stands to benefit from increased imports as well as increased exports, political pressures preclude the inclusion of this sector in a potential India-U.S. FTA. On the import side, benefits arise simply because Indian imports from third countries are currently limited, so that the scope for trade diversion is likewise limited. Moreover, because the United States is a globally efficient producer of agricultural products, opening to it will open India to competition against the world's most efficient producers in many sectors. The difficulty, however, is that with large domestic and export subsidies in place in the United States, which cannot be negotiated within the FTA but only in a multilateral context, any liberalization by India in agriculture is a pipedream. India's position on agriculture even in the multilateral context, with possibilities of substantial reductions in export subsidies and some reductions in domestic subsidies by the rich countries, has been squarely protectionist. The dominant view in the government is that, with 650 million people living on farm income, India cannot afford to open its agriculture to foreign competition.

Finally, the emerging U.S. FTA template, which requires the inclusion of labor and environmental standards and WTO-plus intellectual property rights in its agreements, is yet another insurmountable barrier. The U.S. Congress insists on the inclusion of these provisions in FTA agreements to which the United States is a party. India, on the other hand, is squarely opposed to them. Neither side is likely to compromise: the United States wants to establish as many precedents as possible, so as to make the linkage acceptable in the multilateral WTO agreements, whereas India has the diametrically opposite objective.

A limited case can be made, however, in favor of a mutually beneficial and politically acceptable FTA in *services* between the two countries, although even here the recent acrimonious debate on outsourcing in the United States points to potentially serious political barriers. The WTO General Agreement on Trade in Services (GATS) provides for such agreements, and there are already several precedents. Although a detailed analysis is beyond the scope of this paper, three preliminary points favoring the proposal can be made.

First, looking at the issue from the Indian perspective, to the extent the two countries' barriers in services take the form of anticompetitive regulations that cannot be eliminated on a discriminatory basis, preferential liberalization effectively becomes nondiscriminatory. Moreover, in sectors where no external liberalization has yet taken place, there is no possibility of trade diversion. In many services the United States may well be the most efficient supplier, in which case preferential liberalization will mimic multilateral liberalization.

Against these arguments one must consider that trade diversion of at least two forms cannot be ruled out. In cases where liberalization has already taken place under the GATS, trade from more efficient suppliers could be diverted. For example, India is committed to allowing twelve foreign bank branches to be opened annually as a part of its current GATS obligations. Should U.S. banks, as a result of an FTA, decide to open additional branches in India, India could count these toward fulfilling its GATS obligations. In the extreme case, if U.S. banks opened twelve or more branches a year, other countries would effectively be barred from entry into the Indian market, even if they were more efficient. Trade diversion may also happen in the potential sense in sectors that start from a position of autarky. If an FTA precedes multilateral liberalization, the U.S. firms would acquire an incumbency advantage. This would give rise to a different and inferior outcome than would have prevailed if the FTA had not preceded multilateral liberalization.[68]

Second, within these qualifications, there are several sectors in which the United States and India could benefit from an FTA in services. The U.S. comparative advantage in such sectors as telecommunications, banking, and insurance is well known. Indian firms in these sectors remain inefficient and would benefit from competition from the U.S. firms. An FTA might also spur further reforms, including privatization and the lifting of sectoral caps on FDI on a nondiscriminatory basis.

But there are other, less obvious sectors in which U.S. suppliers might benefit from market access in India. One of these is the "hospitality" sector of the tourism industry. On the one hand, India is beginning to emerge as a major attraction for foreign tourists, while, on the other, rapidly rising incomes are expanding the demand for tourism by the local population. This market could prove lucrative for U.S. suppliers of tourist services. For example, members of the Asian American Hotel Owners Association, most of whom are Americans of Indian origin, own 20,000 U.S. hotels with a total of 1 million rooms, accounting for 37 percent of all hotel properties in the United States, with a market value placed at $40 billion. These Indian American hoteliers could benefit greatly from setting up middle-tier motels

---

68. Mattoo and Fink (2002) offer a detailed and thoughtful discussion of potential benefits and costs of preferential trade liberalization in services and how they differ from preferential liberalization in goods.

along the national highways being constructed to link India's four major metropolises.[69]

In the same vein, the U.S. hospital and education sectors may benefit from market access in India. India can offer relatively cheap nursing and mid-level medical services, whereas Americans can bring excellent hospital management and top-tier medical skills. Similarly, there may be scope for cooperation in higher education if the FTA can serve to open the Indian market to the entry of private universities.

For its part, India would benefit not only from imports in the areas just described but also from increased exports. The provision of various services to U.S. firms under the broad rubric of "outsourcing" has emerged as a major export area for India. A services FTA could be a useful instrument for cementing market access in this important area. India may also benefit from an increased share of temporary worker visas in the United States. At present India is losing share because the United States is using the fixed number of H1B visas to first make good on its commitments to countries such as Mexico and Chile that already have services FTAs with it. In addition to the workers it provides in the information technology sector, India can offer many professional workers in such sectors as nursing and hospitality.

Finally, in a services FTA it may be possible to set aside the divisive issue of labor standards. In goods trade the United States faces the prospect of increased competition in unskilled labor–intensive sectors such as footwear and apparel. The "fair trade" argument for linking market access to labor standards has greater political salience in these sectors than in the skilled labor–intensive activities likely to be opened up to Indian services suppliers in the U.S. market.

Multilateral Negotiations

This paper would be incomplete without some discussion of the ongoing multilateral trade negotiations at Doha. Perhaps the single most important objective for India in the trade domain is to bring the Doha negotiations to a conclusion. It would be unrealistic to expect the round to close by the end of 2004 as originally planned, but a conclusion by the end of 2006 is both feasible and in India's interest.[70]

69. "Indian-American Hotel Owners See Prospects in Hospitality Industry," *News India-Times*, January 23, 2004, p. 16.

70. As discussed in detail in Panagariya (2002b), India has approached the Doha negotiations with great suspicion, which has not served its own best interests. The case for why and how India must support the liberalization agenda of the Doha negotiations is outlined in Bhagwati and Panagariya (2003).

After the failure to make progress in Cancún, the United States has revised its position in favor of a narrower round. India can readily make common cause with the United States around this position. Thus, in a letter dated January 11, 2004, and addressed to the trade ministers of the WTO member countries, U.S. Trade Representative Robert Zoellick expressed willingness to drop all Singapore issues from the agenda except for trade facilitation.[71] India has been willing to negotiate on trade facilitation, so that there is no more disagreement with the United States in this area. Moreover, Zoellick's proposal would considerably narrow the scope of the round, focusing it on trade liberalization just as India had sought originally. And India surely stands to benefit from liberalization in all areas: industry, agriculture, and services.

INDUSTRIAL TARIFFS. In his letter to the trade ministers, Zoellick renewed his proposal to achieve zero tariffs on industrial goods by 2015. Given its own autonomous trade liberalization program, this is a feasible goal for India. But if India wants more of a cushion, it can surely ask for a more relaxed deadline for developing countries, until 2020 or even 2025. The benefits to India from accepting this proposal as is or in modified form are quite unambiguous.

India has long sought to eliminate tariff peaks against labor-intensive products in developed countries. Top World Bank officials and many nongovernmental organizations have recently raised hopes that repeated public exhortations to the effect that developed country barriers cost developing countries more than what they give the latter in aid might shame them into dismantling these barriers unilaterally. But the experience of the last forty years leads to a different conclusion. The U.N. Conference on Trade and Development, the leaders of developing countries, trade and development experts, and even World Bank reports have condemned the barriers against developing country exports for decades. As early as 1965, developing countries successfully deployed moral suasion to add Part IV to the General Agreement on Tariffs and Trade, explicitly committing the developed countries to "accord high priority to the reduction and elimination of barriers to products currently or potentially of particular export interest to less developed contracting parties" and to "refrain from introducing, or increasing the incidence of customs duties or non-tariff barriers on products currently or potentially of particular export interest" to them.

71. The first WTO ministerial meeting in 1996, held in Singapore, introduced four new issues into the WTO study agenda: investment, competition policy, government procurement, and trade facilitation. New issues are initially taken up as study issues, and if there is enough support for them, they may be turned into negotiating issues.

54 INDIA POLICY FORUM, 2004

Yet because developing countries insisted on one-way concessions, little progress was actually made. On the contrary, textiles and apparel imports by developed countries came under severe restrictions through no fewer than 3,000 bilateral treaties under the MFA. Likewise, footwear and steel were frequently subject to the imposition of "orderly market arrangements" by the United States, and tariff peaks systematically discriminated against developing country exports. The only "concession" that the developing countries received was the Generalized System of Preferences, which now even Oxfam correctly cites as evidence against the United States' sincerity about opening its markets to developing countries.

The main substantive break that developing countries received in gaining improved market access for themselves in the last forty years was the agreement in the Uruguay Round to end the MFA. India would be deluding itself if it hung onto the notion that hard-core developed country barriers can be eliminated through moral suasion alone, without reciprocity.

India also gains a tactical advantage through the proposed initiative. In one stroke it would knock down its image as an "obstructionist" in the negotiations and announce its emergence as a truly confident player on the world economic stage, as it already has on the world political stage. Indeed, such a move would put the United States on the defensive, since, according to some, the U.S. government put forward the zero-tariff proposal, despite immense political pressure against it from domestic lobbies, precisely in the hope that developing countries would refuse to go along. India can call this bluff and turn the U.S. tactical advantage into its own.

There are two more reasons why India stands to benefit big from the proposed initiative. First, India's own liberalization, to which it would commit itself as a part of the deal, benefits India. India has now fully recognized this fact in its economic reforms program, with the Kelkar task force (the Task Force on Indirect Taxes) recommending that virtually all tariffs be lowered to 10 percent or less by 2006–07.[72] All that India will be doing under the proposed initiative is to bind this liberalization at the WTO and push it to its logical conclusion of zero tariffs by 2025. Second, as noted above, with NAFTA, the European Union, and numerous other preferential trade areas both between the European Union and its neighbors and within Latin America, Africa, and even East Asia already in existence, India's products today face discrimination in virtually every major market. Through the zero-tariff option, India would eliminate this discrimination in one stroke.

72. Government of India (2002).

AGRICULTURE. Effectively admitting his mistake in trying to make common cause with the European Union on agriculture at Cancún, Zoellick made the elimination of agricultural export subsidies a priority in his letter to the trade ministers. This is something India has sought as well. Nevertheless, India remains defensive in this area. India's main concern, as already noted, is that with 650 million or more Indians living on farm income, India cannot afford to open its agriculture.

Agriculture is indeed a politically charged issue in India, but the story is not altogether different in other parts of the world. Therefore, if India seeks agricultural liberalization, including substantial cuts in domestic subsidies by the rich countries, it has to be willing to place its own agricultural barriers on the table. This is not a particularly risky course for two reasons. First, like many rich countries, India has bound its agricultural tariffs at very high levels ranging from 100 to 300 percent. Bringing these bindings down to even 50 percent would lead to minimal effective opening up. All India would be doing is to eliminate the existing headroom in its tariffs. But if, in return, India could win additional market access in rich country markets, it could only contribute to boosting agricultural incomes in India. Second, according to available studies, if the developed country subsidies were substantially reduced, Indian agriculture would be competitive in a large majority of commodities. Thus any loss of market at home could be substantially made up by the market access achieved in the partner countries.

SERVICES. Services negotiations have been relatively less controversial. The discussion above of a possible services FTA between India and the United States illustrates the potential benefits to India from negotiating actively in this area. One priority for India ought to be to seek binding commitments from its trading partners, especially the United States, in those business services that fall under the heading of business process outsourcing. But India can also benefit from negotiations in areas in which it can offer low-cost services, such as health and accounting services. In return, India can offer binding commitments in areas such as banking, insurance, and telecommunications. Many of India's liberalizing measures in services are unbound and therefore can be used as bargaining chips.

Conclusions

This paper has discussed India's record on trade liberalization; its impact on trade flows, efficiency, and growth; and future choices for India's trade policy. It has demonstrated that liberalization has had a major impact on both the volume of trade and its composition. In particular, if one looks at India's trade at a highly disaggregated level, India's opening has led to the emergence of many new products on the imports and exports lists.

Trade liberalization has led to improved static efficiency in production as well as consumption. According to the calculations done by Chadha and others discussed above, total annual gains from these sources may have been as much as 5 percent of India's GDP. Liberalization was a key ingredient in sustaining India's growth rate of nearly 6 percent a year on average during the last two decades. The studies dealing with productivity have produced mixed evidence, but on balance they suggest that a considerable increase in both the level and the growth rate of productivity has accompanied liberalization. Specifically, the recent study by Sivadasan based on plant-level data offers robust evidence of tariff liberalization leading to increased productivity.[73]

To date, liberalization has failed to stimulate India's labor-intensive industries to any great degree. The industries that have shown the fastest export growth are typically capital- or skilled labor–intensive industries. This paper has identified the policy of small-scale industry reservation and stringent labor laws as the key reasons why labor-intensive exports have failed to grow rapidly. Reform in these areas is a necessary condition for the transformation of India from a primarily agricultural to a primarily industrial economy.

This paper has also argued that, by 2004–05, India should adopt a uniform 15 percent tariff rate on industrial goods and then gradually bring this rate down to 5 percent by the beginning of 2008–09. This reform would allow the country to end the plethora of exemptions that currently afflict the tariff regime and would help bring administrative costs down. In agriculture, although unilateral liberalization would still be beneficial, the current political climate seems against it. Therefore the best course is to take a more flexible approach in the Doha negotiations, which may help bring the level of subsidies and protection in the rich countries down quite substantially. Liberalization by India within the context of this rich country liberalization would provide considerable scope for the expansion of agricultural exports.

This paper has taken a generally cautious view on regional arrangements. If India must pursue these arrangements, it should work toward an Asia-wide FTA that includes China. Such an FTA would have strategic value in attracting attention to the diversion of Asian exports from the

73. Sivadasan (2003).

North American and European markets caused by NAFTA and the European Union, respectively. The desirability of smaller arrangements such as the SAFTA rests primarily on their political value. Economically, given the high tariffs in the region, trade diversion is likely to dominate. But the arrangement may prove to be a useful instrument for eventually establishing better political ties between India and Pakistan. All such FTA arrangements, however, should be limited to trade issues. Issues of cooperation in other areas, such as infrastructure projects of common interest, are better handled in the context of the SAARC rather than the SAFTA.

Finally, should India seek an FTA with the United States? A conventional India-U.S. FTA that focuses on goods trade is politically a nonstarter. Such an FTA would have to include agriculture but could not be expected to end agricultural subsidies in the United States (since these subsidies can only be eliminated in the multilateral context), and this would be unacceptable to India. This same issue has marred the current negotiations on the Free Trade Area of the Americas, with Brazil and the United States finding themselves at odds. The United States would also insist on the inclusion of labor and environmental standards and WTO-plus intellectual property protection in such an FTA, which would likewise be unacceptable to India. Therefore this paper has argued for studying the benefits and feasibility of an India-U.S. FTA limited to services trade. Evidence suggests that an FTA in this area could be mutually beneficial and politically feasible, but more work is required before a definitive conclusion can be reached.

Comments and Discussion

M. Govinda Rao: In this paper, Arvind Panagariya provides a comprehensive account of the evolution of India's trade policy in the context of the public sector–dominated, heavy industry–based, import-substituting industrialization strategy that the country followed in the initial phase of planned development and explores its impact on the productivity and growth of the Indian economy. The author shows how the strategy, pursued with vigor during the first twenty-five years of planning, evolved into an autarkic foreign trade and investment regime marked by tight export controls and culminated in economic isolationism. The next phase, which was characterized by ad hoc liberalization (1976–91), saw acceleration in economic growth, but expansionary fiscal policy created an unstable macroeconomic environment. The "progressive liberalization" phase, which began in 1991, has seen the increasing globalization of the Indian economy. The paper analyzes the broadening and deepening process of trade liberalization in terms of commodity composition and the direction of trade; it also reviews available evidence on the impact of liberalization on the efficiency and growth of the economy. The paper explores various policy options and charts an appropriate course for India to follow.

This is a well-researched paper. There can be hardly any disagreement on the various phases of trade policy analyzed, on the asserted impact of trade policy on the productivity and growth of India's economy, or on the policy options recommended. This comment attempts instead to supplement the analysis with some additional issues and argues for greater emphasis with respect to some of the issues discussed.

The author deals with the ill effects of India's autarkic trade policy as well as several microlevel distortions in considerable detail. The important issue, however, is that the country's protectionist trade policy and interventionist domestic policy combine to create adverse growth consequences that are much more than the sum of the impact of the two policies implemented separately. Combined, the two have created havoc with the economic system and the structure of incentives in the economy. Indeed, as the author notes, "the myriad microeconomic distortions and heavy state intervention straightjacketed the entrepreneurs." I would like to add that the ill effects

58

were even more far-reaching. The combination of these policies led to "structural stagnation" by creating powerful special interestgroups, a large rent-seeking society, in every sphere of economic activity.

The issue is important because India's autarkic international trade regime was closely followed by total central control of the banking and financial system in 1969, with the nationalization of fourteen major commercial banks. This, the single most important act of centralization of the financial system, has been, in combination with other dirigistic policies, a cause of several microeconomic distortions and inequities.

While the paper devotes considerable space to the discussion of the microlevel distortions created by various domestic policies, the analysis of total factor productivity (TFP) seems to attribute its growth entirely to trade liberalization. In particular, the evidence cited from the Chand and Sen paper covers only the phase in which trade policies were tinkered with. It may well be difficult to attribute the growth of TFP in 1984–88 to trade liberalization per se because it was a period of significant liberalization of both trade and internal regulation.

The importance of the Panagariya paper lies in highlighting the emerging policy issues. To be sure, tariffs have to be lowered within the next few years to the levels prevailing in the Southeast Asian economies, but it is important to phase out fiscal imbalances before significant external liberalization can be attempted. The task force chaired by Kelkar to achieve the targets set out in the Fiscal Responsibility and Budget Management Act 2003 has laid out a roadmap for augmenting revenues, primarily by levying a national goods and services tax.[1] However, the "grand bargain" required for such a levy is unlikely to materialize in the short, and even in the medium, terms. If containing the fiscal deficit is vigorously pursued, deficit reduction may be achieved at the cost of infrastructure investments. The paper, therefore, emphasizes the need to focus on reducing the revenue deficit in the near term.

Indeed, infrastructure development—particularly of ports, roads, railways, and most of all power facilities—is a critical determinant of the competitiveness of domestic producers. It is also important to provide adequate funds for maintaining physical infrastructure, which is considered as revenue expenditure. In the absence of infrastructure development, a tariff reduction could result in a flood of imports of finished consumer goods from neighboring countries such as China, Thailand, Malaysia, and Singapore. At the same time, it is important that the outlay on education and health care be increased, both to accelerate growth and to reduce poverty.

1. Government of India (2004).

Therefore the focus of fiscal restructuring should shift to the primary deficit rather than to either the revenue or the fiscal deficit.

The paper refers to the need to complement reductions in tariffs with domestic trade tax reforms. In particular, freeing internal trade from impediments to the movement of factors and products is critical in order to take advantage of the large common market. Equally, at the micro level there is too much protection (through exemption from various labor laws and freedom from the plethora of inspectors who implement them) of small-scale industry, which hinders its growth into medium- and large-scale enterprises. Small-scale industry also is exempt from domestic taxes, particularly the central excise duty. Panagariya rightly refers to the distortions and inefficiency created by the policy of reserving items for manufacture in small-scale industries. However, by merely de-reserving the items in the small-scale sector we may not be able to solve the problem, unless there is an incentive for small enterprises to grow into medium- and large-scale industries.

To conclude, the Panagariya paper makes a valuable contribution to the debate on trade policy. Its most important contribution lies in its recommendation for a future course of action, and one hopes that policymakers will heed its sound advice.

Pranab Bardhan: I found the Panagariya paper to be a lucid and fairly comprehensive survey of the main trends and issues of India's trade policy. I also agree with the main thrust of the paper in terms of policy recommendations. I would endorse the author's ideas on trade reform—in particular, on uniform and low tariffs—and I find his thoughts on the regional trade agreements sensible and pragmatic. A few suggestions that I had for the earlier version of the paper have been largely incorporated, so I have very little to say now, except for one minor and one quasi-major point.

It is not central to Panagariya's main empirical discussion on growth and productivity, but it seems to me that the brief discussion of the general literature on the role of total factor productivity growth (with particular reference to East Asia) vis-à-vis capital accumulation is somewhat incomplete. I have always found this literature to be unnecessarily controversial, particularly when much of the technological progress in developing countries (including that in East Asia) results from improved technologies that are embodied in imported capital goods, so that the distinction between TFP growth and investment is necessarily blurred. Also, before deriding

East Asian growth as "Soviet-style perspiration," American commentators should keep in mind that almost all countries, including the United States in large parts of the nineteenth century, have shown a similar pattern in the early stages of industrialization.[2]

I agree with Panagariya on the importance of two key domestic reforms if trade reform is to stimulate industrial growth: containing the public revenue deficit in order to release funds for public investment in infrastructure and dismantling the existing small-scale industries reservation program. But the practical importance of labor reform for industrial growth is a substantive point on which I and the author somewhat disagree. It is clear that the labor laws that are now on the books can hamper flexibility and ultimately harm the unemployed and workers who have to crowd the informal sector, but I would like to see more convincing evidence on how much of a hindrance to business investment they really are. Beyond repeated assertions by pro-reform economists and the "pink" (financial) press in India, there is very little hard evidence to go by.

Most of the anecdotes one hears about inefficient job secure workers in India are based on common encounters with lazy public sector, white-collar workers protected by their unions. However, there are counter-anecdotes that suggest that labor laws are commonly flouted by industrial employers in many states (particularly in west and south India) while the state government looks the other way. Jenkins (2000) has described this as "reform by stealth."

Nagaraj (2004) has raised the question of why, if labor laws made sacking workers and closing plants so difficult, Annual Survey of Industries data show that between 1995–96 and 2000–01 about 15 percent of workers in the organized manufacturing sector (about 1.1 million workers) lost their jobs. This loss of jobs was spread across industries and states in India.

Let me refer now to two careful microeconometric studies that I have seen that may also be relevant to the question of job security laws. One is by Dutta Roy (2004), who fits dynamic labor demand functions for sixteen industry groups (separately for production and nonproduction workers) for the period from 1960–61 to 1994–95. She shows that the impact of job security regulations in India is statistically insignificant, except in the cement industry. The rigidities in the adjustment of labor were about the same even before the introduction of stringent job security clauses in the

2. See Eichengreen (2002).

1976 and 1982 amendments to the Industrial Disputes Act. This suggests there are other reasons for any rigidities in the labor market.

The second study, by Daveri, Manasse, and Serra (2003), was part of a joint project with the World Bank on the impact of globalization on industrial labor market outcomes in India. Using a new dataset from a World Bank survey of 895 Indian firms in 1997–99, covering five manufacturing sectors, they find that employees of firms subject to foreign competition face much more uncertainty with regard to their earnings and employment prospects (there is, of course, a positive incentive effect—they are more likely to be involved in training and skill-upgrading programs).

All of this suggests that it is not socially responsible to talk about the beneficial effects of trade reform without at the same time making concrete suggestions for creating social adjustment programs for displaced workers. In a country where social safety nets for poor workers are either nonexistent or extremely inadequate and where authorities often renege on their compensation promises, academic demonstrations of the long-run benefits of trade reform are not going to be convincing. In this respect the attempt, though small scale, of the Department of International Development of the U.K. government in collaboration with a local NGO to financially assist and retrain displaced industrial workers in some bankrupt public sector firms in West Bengal is a step in the right direction. Social protection should be part of a comprehensive trade and labor reform package if reform is to be desirable as well as feasible.

General Discussion

Surjit Bhalla believed that the role of labor reform in explaining India's disappointing industrial performance was overstated. Instead, he felt that macroeconomic policies, particularly tight monetary policy, were more important. As evidence for this view he pointed out that the 1991 reforms had indeed led to a growth spurt in industry in the years immediately following, but that it had petered out in 1996, not to revive until 2002–03. He also felt that India's exchange rate policy had led to a loss of competitiveness, particularly with respect to China. Rajesh Chadha felt that policy uncertainty had been important in depressing industrial activity. He cited the sudden reduction in the customs duty on certain capital goods as an example of policy uncertainty that might dampen the investment intentions of other potential investors. John Williamson noted that there was a tendency to focus on the rupee-dollar rate, while even over 2003 the rupee had continued to depreciate in effective terms. He also queried the concept of the "capital intensity" of Indian exports, citing a recent McKinsey study that found that India's auto industry was much less capital intensive than China's, in part because of the greater skill level and flexibility of the Indian labor force.

Suman Bery asked whether there were any studies on the political economy of trade reforms that could explain both the liberalization episodes and the occasional backtracking. He also asked what the international experience was with a uniform tariff rate: If it is so pure, why is it not adopted more widely? Are the forces that determine more complex tariff structures revenue-driven or the result of lobbying for effective protection? Rajnish Mehra tended to agree with political explanations of industrial sluggishness, attributing it to the power of existing interests to prevent competition and extract rents. Noting Panagariya's caution on free trade agreements, Anil Sharma asked whether there was really any alternative, given the difficulties faced during the Doha Round of trade talks and the reduced appeal of unilateral action. Vijay Kelkar asked how realistic it is to impose a uniform tariff when the taxation of domestic inputs is not properly offset by drawback schemes. A uniform customs tariff would lead to negative rates of protection in a number of activities because the incidence of domestic indirect taxes is not uniform. Given the realities, he believed that a uniform low rate of custom duties in an environment of exchange rate appreciation would lead to a backlash from Indian industry and a possible reversal of the progress made. He agreed with Panagariya that the special and differential treatment provisions of GATT had outlived their utility for India and also that India's antidumping machinery needed review. Montek Ahluwalia and Vijay Joshi both pursued the issue, raised by Bardhan, of the link between India's intellectual property regime and the rise of India's pharmaceutical industry. Ahluwalia believed that the export orientation of the big Indian pharmaceutical firms in the past had as much to do with domestic price controls as with the intellectual property regime. Since these controls affected primarily the large players, these firms found foreign markets more lucrative than the domestic market.

Ahluwalia also concurred that the emphasis on labor reform might be overdone. He noted that import restrictions on labor-intensive sectors had been lifted only recently, as was the case with the liberalization of the small-scale industry regime. He believed that competition in product markets would be reflected in the behavior of the labor force, which would adjust to ensure company survival. Barry Bosworth noted, though, that labor legislation could have a major impact on foreign firms, which do not have the

64   INDIA POLICY FORUM, 2004

option of entering the informal sector. This could be one reason for the disappointing response of foreign direct investment to India's liberalization. Panagariya disagreed with the points made on labor reform and on uniform customs duties, indicating that both industry's stagnant share of GDP and the low share of organized sector employment in the labor force were indicators of serious obstacles to the expansion of modern industrial employment. He also rejected the view that the existing (and proposed) differential customs duty structure had anything to do with distortions in domestic taxation; in his view this structure reflects attempts by lobbies to secure effective protection and would lead only to further rent-seeking behavior and difficulties in implementation.

References

Ahluwalia, Isher J. 1991. *Productivity and Growth in Indian Manufacturing.* Delhi: Oxford University Press.

_____. 1994. "TFPG in Manufacturing Industry." *Economic and Political Weekly,* October 22, p. 2836.

Balakrishnan, P., and K. Pushpangandan. 1994. "Total Factor Productivity Growth in Manufacturing Industry: A Fresh Look." *Economic and Political Weekly,* July 30, pp. 2028–35.

Balakrishnan, P., K. Pushpangandan, and M. S. Babu. 2000. "Trade Liberalization and Productivity Growth in Manufacturing: Evidence from Firm-Level Panel Data." *Economic and Political Weekly,* October 7, pp. 3679–82.

Bhagwati, Jagdish. 1999. "The 'Miracle' That Did Happen: Understanding East Asia in Comparative Perspective." In *Taiwan's Development Experience: Lessons on Roles of Government and Market,* edited by Erik Thorbecke and Henry Wan. Boston: Kluwer Academic Publishers.

Bhagwati, Jagdish, and Padma Desai. 1970. *India: Planning for Industrialization.* London: Oxford University Press.

Bhagwati, Jagdish, and Arvind Panagariya. 1996. "Preferential Trading Areas and Multilateralism: Strangers, Friends or Foes?" In *The Economics of Preferential Trading,* edited by Jagdish Bhagwati and Arvind Panagariya. Washington: AEI Press. Reproduced as chapter 2 in *Trading Blocs: Alternative Approaches to Analyzing Preferential Trade Agreements,* edited by Jagdish Bhagwati, P. Krishna, and Arvind Panagariya. MIT Press, 1999.

_____. 2003. "Defensive Play Simply Won't Work." *Economic Times,* August 29, p. 15.

Bhagwati, Jagdish, and T. N. Srinivasan. 1975. *Foreign Trade Regimes and Economic Development: India.* New York: National Bureau of Economic Research.

Chadha, Rajesh, Alan Deardorff, Sanjib Pohit, and Robert Stern. 1998. *The Impact of Trade and Domestic Policy Reforms in India: A CGE Modeling Approach.* University of Michigan Press.

Chand, Satish, and Kunal Sen. 2002. "Trade Liberalization and Productivity Growth: Evidence from Indian Manufacturing." *Review of Development Economics* 6, no. 1: 120–32.

Collins, Susan M., and Barry P. Bosworth. 1996. "Economic Growth in East Asia: Accumulation versus Assimilation." *Brookings Papers on Economic Activity,* no. 2, pp. 135–91.

Das, Deb Kusum. 2003. "Manufacturing Productivity under Varying Trade Regimes: India in the 1980s and 1990s." Working Paper 107. New Delhi: Indian Council for Research on International Economic Relations.

Daveri, F., P. Manasse, and D. Serra. 2003. "The Twin Effects of Globalization." Turin, Italy: Luca d'Agliano Foundation.

DeLong, J. Bradford. 2003. "India Since Independence: An Analytic Growth Narrative." In *In Search of Prosperity: Analytic Narratives on Economic Growth,* edited by Dani Rodrik. Princeton University Press.

Dholakia, B. H., and R. H. Dholakia. 1994. "Total Factor Productivity Growth in Manufacturing Industry." *Economic and Political Weekly,* December 31, pp. 3342–44.

Dutta Roy, S. 2004. "Employment Dynamics in Indian Industry: Adjustment Lags and the Impact of Job Security Regulations." *Journal of Development Economics* 73, no. 1: 233–56.

Eichengreen, B. 2002. "Capitalizing on Globalization." *Asian Development Review* 19, no. 1: 17–69.

Gordon, Jim, and Poonam Gupta. 2003. "Understanding India's Services Revolution." Paper presented at the IMF-NCAER Conference, "A Tale of Two Giants: India's and China's Experience with Reform," New Delhi, November 14–16.

Government of India. 2002. "Reports of the Task Force on Indirect Taxes." Chairman, Vijay L. Kelkar. New Delhi: Ministry of Finance and Company Affairs.

————. 2004. "Report of the Task Force on Implementation of the Fiscal Responsibility and Budget Management Act, 2003." Chairman, Vijay L. Kelkar. New Delhi: Ministry of Finance.

Hulten, Charles R. 1975. "Technical Change and the Reproducibility of Capital." *American Economic Review* 65, no. 5: 956–65.

Hulten, Charles R., and Mieko Nishimizu. 1980. "The Importance of Productivity Change in the Economic Growth of Nine Industrialized Countries." In *Lagging Productivity Growth: Causes and Remedies,* edited by Shlomo Maital and Noah M. Meltz. Cambridge, Mass.: Ballinger.

Hulten, Charles, and Syleja Srinivasan. 1999. "Indian Manufacturing Industry: Elephant or Tiger? New Evidence on the Asian Miracle." Working Paper 7441. Cambridge, Mass.: National Bureau of Economic Research.

Jenkins, R. S. 2000. *Democratic Politics and Economic Reform in India.* Cambridge University Press.

Joshi, Vijay, and Ian M. D. Little. 1994. *India: Macroeconomics and Political Economy: 1961–91.* Washington: World Bank.

Kehoe, Timothy J. 2003. "An Evaluation of the Performance of Applied General Equilibrium Models of the Impact of NAFTA." Research Department Staff Report 320. Federal Reserve Bank of Minneapolis.

Kehoe, Timothy J., and Kim J. Ruhl. 2002. "How Important is the New Goods Margin in International Trade?" University of Minnesota.

Kelkar, Vijay. 2001. "India's Reform Agenda: Micro, Meso and Macro Economic Reforms." Fourth Annual Fellows Lecture, Center for the Advanced Study of India, University of Pennsylvania.

Kim, Jong-Il, and Lawrence J. Lau. 1994. "The Sources of Economic Growth of the East Asian Newly Industrialized Countries." *Journal of Japanese and International Economies* 8: 235–27.

Krishna, Pravin, and Devashish Mitra. 1998. "Trade Liberalization, Market Discipline and Productivity Growth: New Evidence from India." *Journal of Development Economics* 56: 447–62.

Krugman, Paul. 1994. "The Myth of Asia's Miracle." *Foreign Affairs* 73, no. 6: 62–77.

Mattoo, Aaditya, and Carsten Fink. 2002. "Regional Agreements and Trade in Services: Policy Issues." Policy Research Working Paper 2852. Washington: World Bank.

McKinsey Global Institute. 2001. *India: The Growth Imperative.* San Francisco.

Mukerji, Purba. 2004. "Essays in International Trade." Ph.D. dissertation, University of Maryland.

Nadiri, M. Ishaq, and Wanpyo Son. 1998. "Sources of Growth in East Asian Economies." New York University (July).

Nagaraj, R. 2004. "Fall in Organized Manufacturing Employment: A Brief Note." *Economic and Political Weekly* 39, no. 30.

Panagariya, Arvind. 1999a. "WTO Trade Policy Review of India, 1998." *World Economy* 22, no. 6: 799–824.

_____. 1999b. "The Regionalism Debate: An Overview." *World Economy* 22, no. 4: 477–511.

_____. 2000. "Preferential Trade Liberalization: The Traditional Theory and New Developments." *Journal of Economic Literature* 38: 287–331.

_____. 2002a. "Cost of Protection: Where Do We Stand?" *American Economic Review, Papers and Proceedings* 92, no. 2: 175–79.

_____. 2002b. "India at Doha: Retrospect and Prospect." *Economic and Political Weekly,* January 26, pp. 279–84.

_____. 2003. "South Asia: Does Preferential Trade Liberalization Make Sense?" *World Economy* 26, no. 9 (special issue on Global Trade Policy): 1279–91.

_____. 2004. "Growth and Reforms During 1980s and 1990s." *Economic and Political Weekly,* June 19, pp. 2581–94.

Panagariya, Arvind, and Rupa Duttagupta. 2001. "The 'Gains' from Preferential Trade Liberalization in the CGEs: Where Do They Come From?" In *Regionalism and Globalization: Theory and Practice,* edited by Sajal Lahiri. London: Routledge.

Panagariya, Arvind, and Dani Rodrik. 1993. "Political Economy Arguments for a Uniform Tariff." *International Economic Review,* August, pp. 685–703.

Pursell, Garry. 1992. "Trade Policy in India." In *National Trade Policies,* edited by Dominick Salvatore. New York: Greenwood Press.

Rao, J. Mohan. 1996. "Manufacturing Productivity Growth, Method and Measurement." *Economic and Political Weekly,* November 2, pp. 2927–36.

Reserve Bank of India. 2002. *Handbook of Statistics on Indian Economy.* Mumbai.

_____. 2003. *Annual Report 2002-2003.* Mumbai.

Rodrik, Dani. 2003. "Institutions, Integration, and Geography: In Search of the Deep Determinants of Economic Growth." In *In Search of Prosperity: Analytic*

Narratives on Economic Growth, edited by Dani Rodrik. Princeton University Press.

Romer, Paul. 1994. "New Goods, Old Theory, and the Welfare Costs of Trade Restrictions." *Journal of Development Economics* 43: 5–38.

Shourie, Arun. 1966. "Allocation of Foreign Exchange in India." Ph.D. dissertation, Syracuse University.

Sivadasan, Jagadeesh. 2003. "Barriers to Entry and Productivity: Micro-Evidence from Indian Manufacturing Sector Reforms." Graduate School of Business, University of Chicago.

Tharoor, Shashi. 1997. *From Midnight to the Millennium.* New York: Harper Perennial.

Topalova, Petia. 2003. "Trade Liberalization and Firm Productivity: the Case of India." Massachusetts Institute of Technology.

Unel, Bulent. 2003. "Productivity Trends in India's Manufacturing Sectors in the Last Two Decades." IMF Working Paper WP/03/22. Washington: International Monetary Fund.

World Bank. 2002. *World Development Indicators 2002.* Washington.

_____. 2003. *World Development Indicators 2003.* Washington.

World Trade Organization (WTO). 1998. "Trade Policy Review—India." Geneva.

_____. 2002. "Trade Policy Review—India." Geneva.

_____. 2003. *Annual Report.* Geneva.

Young, Alwyn. 1992. "A Tale of Two Cities: Factor Accumulation and Technical Change in Hong Kong and Singapore." In *NBER Macroeconomics Annual*, edited by Olivier J. Blanchard and Stanley Fischer. MIT Press.

_____. 1995. "The Tyranny of Numbers: Confronting the Statistical Realities of the East Asian Experience." *Quarterly Journal of Economics* 110, no. 3: 641–80.

[18]

The Experience of Economic Growth in Latin America and the Caribbean

Norman Loayza, World Bank; Pablo Fajnzylber, World Bank; César Calderón, World Bank

After repeated international crises, cases of interrupted reforms, and instances of macroeconomic mismanagement, several countries in Latin America and the Caribbean are experiencing severe economic downturns at the start of the new century. Just as in the aftermath of the Tequila crisis, the success of market-oriented reforms is called into question, and people from politicians to academics propose a change of economic policy away from the 'Washington Consensus'. In this context, it becomes necessary to reassess the growth performance of countries in the region, explain the underlying sources of their economic growth – or lack thereof –, and design a strategy for further reform. This study intends to contribute to this effort.

We cannot overstate the importance of income growth for economic, social, and even political development. Countries that grow strongly and for sustained periods of time are able to reduce significantly their poverty levels, strengthen their democratic and political stability, improve the quality of their natural environment, and even diminish the incidence of crime and violence. Economic growth is not a panacea; but even in the cases where it does not have a direct beneficial impact, it facilitates the implementation of public programs that deal with the people, places, and issues left behind.

No wonder, then, that enormous amount of talent and effort has been invested in understanding the process of economic growth. The recent surge in academic research on endogenous growth and the policy preoccupation with poverty-alleviating growth are only two of many demonstrations that economic growth is at the center of attention in research and policy circles. This study takes advantage of the received literature to analyze the growth performance in Latin America and the Caribbean, using in particular the methods and findings of macroeconomic and cross-national empirical studies.

The objectives of the study are the following. First, describe the basic characteristics (or stylized facts) of economic growth in Latin American and Caribbean countries. Second, explain the differences across countries and over time in economic growth based on regression analysis. And, third, forecast the changes in economic growth for the next decade based on both regression results and projections on the future behavior of growth determinants.

Our goal is to contribute with insights, arguments, and evidence to answer some of the central questions surrounding economic growth in Latin America and the Caribbean, among them,

- How similar are countries in Latin America and the Caribbean with each other regarding their patterns of economic growth? Can we speak of common regional trends? What are the major exceptions? And, is Latin America and the Caribbean unique in the world, or to what extent are its growth characteristics shared by other regions?
- Is physical capital investment crucial to start up growth? And, is investment responsible for the major shifts in economic growth, or is it factor productivity?
- What lies behind the economic downturn of the 'lost decade' of the 1980s? And, what explains the economic recovery of the 1990s? In particular, what is the role of structural and stabilization policy reform? To what extent can business-cycle movements and shifting external conditions explain the patterns of fall and recovery experienced in the last decades?
- What can be realistically expected for economic growth in Latin America and the Caribbean for the first decade of the new century? If Latin America and the Caribbean make significant progress in economic reforms, what is the region's growth potential? What are the areas of economic policy that are more likely to render an increase in economic growth?

As mentioned above, this study will take a cross-country perspective. That is, it will derive implications for Latin American and Caribbean countries from the international evidence on the patterns and determinants of economic growth. Thus, in its descriptive section, the study will examine the growth performance of individual countries in the context of regional and world trends; and, in its econometric section, the study will apply the estimates from cross-country regressions to analyze the economic and social factors that drive per capita GDP growth in each country in the region. This report can be seen as a complement to individual country-case studies. It can provide them with the basic international context in terms of both descriptive patterns and empirical explanations of output growth behavior.

The cross-country approach to the study of economic growth in Latin America has produced a rich literature. Table I.1 presents some of the most prominent papers in this area. They differ in the sample of countries and periods used, in their estimation techniques, and in the explanatory variables considered as growth determinants. Despite these differences, there are notable similarities in some basic results. First, there is clear evidence of conditional convergence among LAC countries, meaning that poorer countries tend to grow faster than richer ones, other things equal. Second, structural factors such as human capital (proxied by years of schooling, enrollment rates, or literacy indices), financial depth (measured as the ratio of broad money or private credit to GDP), public infrastructure (proxied by the availability of phones, roads, and electricity), and low government burden have a positive and robust relationship with growth. Third, growth is discouraged by high and volatile inflation rates as well as by real exchange rate misalignment, indicating a link between macroeconomic stability and long-run growth. And, fourth, external shocks (as captured, for instance, by terms of trade or capital flow shocks) impact significantly on economic growth.

Table 1.1   Literature Review on Economic Growth in Latin America and the Caribbean

(a) Sample and Estimation Technique		
Authors	Sample	Estimation Technique
De Gregorio (1992)	12 LAC Countries. 1950–85 (6-year period averages)	Panel Data. Generalized Least Squares (GLS) with Random Effects.
Corbo and Rojas (1993)	20 LAC Countries. 1960–88 (5-year averages)	Panel Data. Instrumental Variables (IV) with Random Effects.
Easterly, Loayza and Montiel (1997)	70 Countries (16 LAC). 1960–93 (5-year averages, except last one)	GMM-Difference Estimator (Arellano and Bond, 1991).
Campos and Nugent (1998)	19 LAC Countries. 1960–85 (10-year averages)	Panel Data. Fixed and Random Effects Estimators.
De Gregorio and Lee (1999)	81 Countries (21 LAC). 1965–95 (10-year averages)	Panel Data. Seemingly Unrelated Regressions (SUR) and 3SLS.
Fernández-Arias and Montiel (2001)	69 Countries (18 LAC). 1961–95 (5-year averages)	Panel Data. Instrumental Variables (IV) with Random Effects.
Calderon and Schmidt-Hebbel (2003)	56 Developing Countries (18 LAC). 1970–00 (5-year averages)	GMM-IV System Estimator (Arellano and Bover, 1995; Blundell and Bond, 1998).
Calderón and Servén (2003)	121 Countries (21 LAC). 1960–00 (5-year averages)	GMM-IV System Estimator (Arellano and Bover, 1995; Blundell and Bond, 1998).
De Gregorio and Lee (2003)	85 Countries (21 LAC). 1970–00 (5-year averages)	Three-Stage Least Squares (3SLS).
Blyde and Fernández-Arias (2004)	73 Countries (20 LAC). 1970–99 (5-year averages)	Panel Data. Instrumental Variables (IV) with Fixed Effects.

(b) Growth Determinants		
Category	Variable	Impact
Transitional Convergence	Initial GDP	[–]: 1,3,4,5,6,7,8,9,10
Structural Policies and Institutions		
Physical Capital	Investment to GDP ratio	[+]: 1,2,3,4,9 [0]: 5
Human Capital	Schooling (years, enrollment)	[+]: 2,3,4,5,7,8,10 [0]: 1,6,9
	Literacy	[+]: 1,5,9
	Fertility	[–]: 9
Financial Development	Credit to Private Sector (% GDP)	[+]: 7,8,10
	M2/GDP	[+]: 3,6
Trade Openness	Exports and Imports (% GDP)	[+]: 3,5,8,9,10 [0]: 1,7
Government Burden	Government Consumption (% GDP)	[–]: 1,2,3,5,6,7,8,9
Income Inequality	Income Shares	[0]: 1
Governance	Civil Liberties, Political Rights	[+]: 1,4,7,8,10
	Rule of Law	[+]: 5,9
Infrastructure	Telephones per capita	[+]: 8
	Energy per capita	[0/+]: 8
	Roads per area	[+]: 8
Stabilization Policies		
Inflation	CPI Inflation Rate	[–]1,2,3,5,6,7,8,10
	Inflation Volatility	[–]: 1
Real Exchange Rate (RER) Overvaluation	Degree of RER Overvaluation	[–]: 7,8,9
	Black Market Premium	[–]: 3,10 [0]: 2
Balance of Payments (BoP) Crisis	Frequency of BoP Crises Episodes	[0]: 9
External Conditions		
Terms of Trade Shocks	Changes in the terms of trade index	[+]: 2,3,5,6,7,8,9 [0]: 1,10
Capital Flows	Private Capital Flows (% GDP)	[+]: 1,7
	Foreign Direct Investment (% GDP)	[+]: 7

Notes:

[+] indicates a positive and significant relationship with economic growth, [–] indicates a negative and significant relationship with economic growth, and [0] indicates that the variable has no robust association with growth. The references to the results in the empirical growth literature are listed in chronological order: [1] De Gregorio (1992). [2] Corbo and Rojas (1993). [3] Easterly, Loayza and Montiel (1997). [4] Campos and Nugent (1998). [5] De Gregorio and Lee (1999). [6] Fernández-Arias and Montiel (2001). [7] Calderón and Schmidt-Hebbel (2003). [8] Calderón and Servén (2003). [9] De Gregorio and Lee (2003). [10] Blyde and Fernández-Arias (2004).

The plan of the report is the following. Section I describes the main stylized facts of growth in Latin America and the Caribbean from four different macro perspectives. We first review the growth performance of Latin American and Caribbean countries by decades (1960s to 1990s) in comparison to the typical countries in the region and in the world. Then, we conduct Solow-type growth accounting to assess the contribution of capital accumulation, expansion of the labor force, and improvement of total factor productivity.

In section II, we attempt to explain the economic growth performance in Latin American and Caribbean countries from a cross-country perspective. We follow the approach in Barro and Lee (1994) and Easterly, Loayza, and Montiel (1997), which consists of linking aggregate economic, political, and social variables to growth rates in GDP per capita for a large sample of countries. The estimated model is then used to project the growth rates in most Latin American and Caribbean countries and examine whether their performance has been close to expected values.

Section III presents some forecasts for the future growth performance of Latin American and Caribbean countries considering the cross-country empirical results and using a variety of assumptions. In this respect, we also start an evaluation of further sources for growth in these countries. Section IV concludes.

I. Stylized Facts

1. Growth in Latin America and the Caribbean and the World, 1960–2000

For the world as a whole, the rate of growth of output per capita has followed a declining path since the 1960s (see Figure I.1 and Table I.2). To some extent, this reflects the trend in industrialized countries and their influence on the developing world. There are, however, some notable differences across geographic regions. The economic growth rate in East Asia and the Pacific increased in the 1970s and 1980s and declined slightly in the 1990s. This region experienced the highest growth rates in the last four decades of the 20th century. Although at a lower level, the growth experience in South Asia in the last two decades has also been one of success, reaching rates of per capita output growth beyond 3% per year with remarkable stability.

Other regions, including Latin America and the Caribbean, have had rather unsatisfactory growth performances. The rates of economic growth of Eastern Europe and Central Asia exhibit the fastest decline from the 1960s onwards, arriving at negative rates in the 1990s that reveal the high costs of adjustment from planned to market economies. The regions of Latin America and the Caribbean, the Middle East and North Africa, and Sub-Saharan Africa share some interesting features – they had their best growth rates in the 1960s and 1970s, suffered a large decline in the 1980s, and then recovered somewhat in the 1990s. For the first two regions, the recovery of the 1990s meant an increase in output per capita, while for Sub-Saharan Africa this only implied a deceleration of its downward spiral. The negative growth rates from which Sub-Saharan Africa suffered in the last two decades are a major concern and appear to be the result of an unfortunate combination of poor policies, social conflict, and negative external shocks.

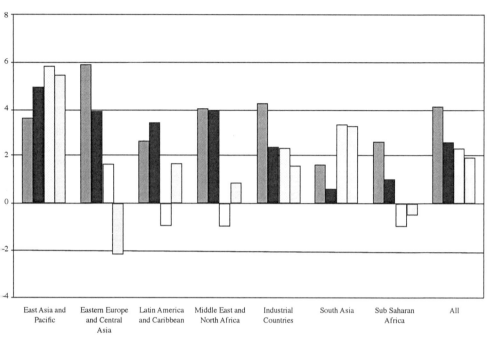

□ 1961–70 ■ 1971–80 □ 1981–90 □ 1991–00

Source: WDI and Authors' calculations.

Figure I.1   *Growth Rates of GDP per Capita, GDP-Weighted Average, by Regions:*
1961–2000 (constant sample)

Table 1.2   *Growth Rates of GDP per Capita, GDP-Weighted Average by Regions:*
1961–2000

	No obs.	1961–00	1961–70	1971–80	1981–90	1991–00
Constant Sample Over Time						
All Countries	108	2.76%	4.15%	2.68%	2.29%	1.90%
Industrial Countries	21	2.68%	4.28%	2.50%	2.42%	1.68%
Developing Countries:						
East Asia	14	4.96%	3.58%	4.90%	5.88%	5.53%
Eastern Europe	4	1.78%	5.92%	3.94%	1.73%	–2.11%
Latin America and the Caribbean	25	1.78%	2.63%	3.46%	–0.82%	1.75%
Middle East	9	2.20%	4.11%	4.00%	–0.86%	0.90%
South Asia	5	2.24%	1.72%	0.64%	3.40%	3.34%
Sub-Saharan Africa	30	0.66%	2.68%	1.08%	–1.00%	–0.42%

Source: WDI, and authors' calculations.

Coming back to Latin America and the Caribbean, there are some interesting disparities as well as common features across countries in the region regarding economic growth in the last four decades (see Table 1.3). Fifteen out of seventeen countries in continental Latin America experienced negative growth rates in the 1980s, a truly 'lost decade'. The exceptions were Chile and Colombia: during the 1980s, Chile had the merit of being an early reformer, and Colombia was the country with the best record of macroeconomic stability and external credit worthiness in the region. The 1990s was a decade of reform and recovery. Except for Ecuador, Paraguay, and, surprisingly, Colombia, all countries in continental Latin America underwent an increase in growth rates in the 1990s with respect to the previous decade. In several countries the improvement was quite notable; such is the case of Argentina, Chile, Uruguay, Bolivia, Peru, Costa Rica, El Salvador, Guatemala, Mexico, Nicaragua, and Panama. These countries have in common that they conducted strong market-oriented reforms and/or accomplished processes of economic and political stabilization. However, only in a few instances – Argentina, Chile, Costa Rica, El Salvador, and Peru –, the recovery in the 1990s resulted in economic growth rates that surpassed or at least matched those of the 1960s and 1970s.

The Caribbean countries showed less uniform patterns of economic growth. The Dominican Republic, Trinidad and Tobago, Guyana, and Suriname are similar to Latin American countries in that they experienced a sharp drop in economic growth in the 1980s and a substantial recovery in the 1990s. On the other hand, The Bahamas, Barbados, Belize, and the small island countries share in common a decreasing trend in growth rates since the 1960s and 1970s. Even more worrisome is the situation of Haiti and Jamaica. Marred by political instability and economic mismanagement, Haiti has suffered negative growth in three decades of the last 40 years; and Jamaica, afflicted from crime and violence and repeated banking crises, failed to sustain the increase in growth in the 1980s and came back to negative rates in the 1990s.

These growth trends raise several interesting questions. One of them is whether the ups and downs in economic growth observed in countries and regions can be traced to changes in domestic economic policies or to differing external conditions. For instance, is the growth decline in Latin America and the Caribbean in the 1980s and subsequent recovery in the 1990s a product of misguided policies in the former period and economic reform in the latter? Another, possibly more difficult question is whether the apparently good growth performance in some years is fueled by unsustainable policies that eventually lead to sharp economic contractions. This could have been the case in Latin America and the Caribbean and, to a larger extent, Eastern Europe and Central Asia in the 1960s and 1970s – strong growth promoted by distortionary policies that eventually resulted in the crises of the 1980s. In the second section of the report, we address directly the first question – on the sources of growth – and indirectly the second one – on the long-run merits of various policies for economic growth.

2. Growth Accounting

As documented in the first section of this report, the growth performance of most Latin American and Caribbean countries changed radically in the course of the past four decades. During the 1980s most countries had to deal with severe recessions and experienced rates of

Table 1.3   *Growth Rates of GDP per Capita, by Country: 1961–2000*

Region / Countries	1961–00	1961–70	1971–80	1981–90	1991–00
A. South Cone					
Argentina	0.95%	2.31%	1.32%	−2.99%	3.18%
Brazil	2.45%	3.18%	5.75%	−0.42%	1.27%
Chile	2.50%	1.82%	1.22%	2.08%	4.89%
Paraguay	1.62%	1.79%	5.69%	−0.30%	−0.69%
Uruguay	1.13%	0.36%	2.60%	−0.66%	2.24%
B. Andean Community					
Bolivia	0.37%	0.35%	1.67%	−1.95%	1.40%
Colombia	1.82%	2.21%	3.05%	1.26%	0.74%
Ecuador	1.52%	1.24%	5.65%	−0.47%	−0.35%
Peru	0.61%	2.31%	0.84%	−2.99%	2.28%
Venezuela, RB	−0.30%	1.46%	−0.76%	−1.75%	−0.15%
C. Central America					
Costa Rica	1.87%	1.93%	2.75%	−0.32%	3.13%
El Salvador	0.73%	2.15%	−0.18%	−1.47%	2.40%
Guatemala	1.29%	2.56%	2.87%	−1.62%	1.35%
Honduras	0.79%	1.52%	2.06%	−0.73%	0.31%
Mexico	2.11%	3.37%	3.58%	−0.29%	1.81%
Nicaragua	−0.77%	3.36%	−2.84%	−4.07%	0.46%
Panama	2.02%	4.70%	1.47%	−0.71%	2.62%
D. Caribbean – Continental					
Belize	2.72%	2.27%	5.07%	2.22%	1.32%
Guyana	0.59%	1.26%	0.66%	−3.90%	4.34%
Suriname	0.95%	–	1.81%	−1.68%	2.90%
E. Caribbean – Large Island					
Bahamas, The	1.36%	3.73%	0.70%	0.90%	0.10%
Barbados	2.55%	6.00%	2.37%	0.82%	1.03%
Dominican Republic	2.74%	2.47%	4.17%	0.31%	4.00%
Haiti	−0.99%	−1.48%	2.53%	−2.31%	−2.70%
Jamaica	0.47%	3.33%	−2.12%	1.24%	−0.56%
Trinidad and Tobago	2.52%	3.79%	5.13%	−1.20%	2.35%
F. Caribbean – Small Island*					
Antigua and Barbuda	4.09%	–	6.93%	5.43%	1.90%
Dominica	3.08%	–	0.60%	5.34%	1.56%
Grenada	3.69%	–	3.97%	5.00%	2.29%
St. Kitts and Nevis	5.26%	–	7.14%	5.56%	4.40%
St. Lucia	3.29%	–	–	5.34%	1.24%
St. Vincent and the Grenadines	3.68%	–	4.49%	4.95%	2.17%

* Countries in this group and Suriname are not included in the constant sample used in Tables I.1–I.2. Each country's starting and ending year for the full sample depends on data availability.

Source: WDI, and authors' calculations.

growth well below those of the 1960s and 1970s. The 1990s, on the contrary, were years of recovery in most of the region. Although cyclical recovery plays a role, trend changes are mostly behind the growth fluctuations from decade to decade. This suggests that the structural components of growth must be considered in any attempt to explain the growth performance of the region. On this basis, this section uses growth accounting methodologies to decompose the sources of output growth into the accumulation of factors of production and the growth rate of total factor productivity.

The analysis of the sources of economic growth dates back to the late 1950s, when Jan Tinbergen, Moses Abramovitz and, most notably, Robert Solow first decomposed output growth in a weighted average of the rate of growth of labor and capital, and a residual that became known as total factor productivity growth (TFP). Although the so-called 'Solow residual' was nothing more than the unexplained part of economic growth, economists increasingly became accustomed to viewing the residual as a measure of technological change. During the 1960s and 1970s new contributions by Edward Denison, Zvi Grilliches, Dale Jorgenson and John Kendrick, among others, led to the use of more general production functions and a more accurate measurement of inputs and outputs. Denison made the important contribution of taking into consideration the changes in both the quantity and quality of labor and capital inputs. In the case of labor, for instance, Denison accounted not only for changes in the size of the labor force but also for shifts related to age, gender, hours of work, and unemployment. These and other improvements in the basic growth accounting methodology led to TFP estimates for the US that were much lower than Solow's.

Despite the use of these adjustments, the contribution of TFP was still found to be large: a comparative study by Christensen, Cummings and Jorgenson (1980) found that over the 1947–73 period TFP accounted for 33% of GDP growth in the United States, 42% in Japan and more than 50% in several European countries. More recently, the lower rates of GDP growth of developed countries seem to have been accompanied by lower rates of productivity growth – the so-called 'productivity slowdown'.

For Latin America, the most detailed study to date of the sources of growth is Elias (1992), covering seven countries from 1940 to 1980. He found an average TFP contribution to GDP growth of 28%. There was, however, considerable variation across countries, with TFP contributions ranging from zero in Peru and 10% in Venezuela, to 37% in Mexico and 40% in Chile. Although less detailed than Elias's, the exercise performed by De Gregorio (1992) covered a larger number of Latin American countries (twelve), during the period 1950–1985. As in the case of developed countries, De Gregorio finds a positive correlation between GDP growth rates and TFP contributions to overall growth.

Additional comparisons between the sources of growth in Latin America and in other regions can be performed using the results of aggregate growth accounting exercises covering large cross-sections of countries. Collins and Bosworth (1996), for example, produce growth decompositions for 88 countries during the periods 1960–1973 and 1973–1994. In the former period, they find that TFP was responsible for 53% of the region's growth in output per worker, compared to 42% in the United States, 46% in other industrial countries, and 31% in East Asia. During the same period, the TFP contribution to the growth of output per worker was 49% in the Middle East, 16% in Africa and 6% in South Asia. After 1973, productivity growth slows down in almost all regions of the World – the only exception being South Asia where it accelerates – but the reductions are sharpest in Latin

America, the Middle East and Africa, where the TFP contribution to growth becomes negative.

Taken together, these studies point to two quite relevant results. The first is that the contribution of TFP to overall growth is larger when growth itself becomes larger. The second is that whatever the contribution of TFP to the *level* of the output growth, movements in TFP explain to a large extent the *changes* that output growth experiences. The latter result is confirmed by Easterly and Levine (2001), who in addition find that the cross-country variation in GDP growth rates is mostly driven by cross-country differences in total factor productivity.

Before presenting the new detailed evidence collected in this paper for Latin America, it is worth emphasizing some of the general limitations of the growth accounting methodology. First, the TFP component of growth is by definition a residual, being calculated as the difference between output growth and a weighted average of the growth in the quantity and quality of factors of production. As such, any measurement errors present in the variables used to measure labor and capital are mechanically imputed to TFP. If, for instance, we fail to account for improvements in the quality composition of capital stocks or the labor force, we will tend to over-estimate the TFP component. Similarly, if the quantities of labor and capital that are actually used in production are considerably lower than their available stocks (or installed capacity), the resulting TFP estimates will be under-estimated.

A second limitation is associated with the fact that growth accounting is a descriptive methodology and does not provide specific insights into the factors that underlie the TFP growth component. Thus, although most economists tend to think of TFP as a measure of technological change, one could also make the case that TFP reflects the role played by economies of scale and externalities in many of the 'new' growth models, or even the occurrence of changes in the sectoral composition of output.

Finally, although growth accounting exercises provide a useful first approximation to the sources of economic growth, the results depend to some extent on the assumption of independence between employment growth, capital accumulation and productivity growth. This assumption, however, can be criticized on several grounds. For instance, as argued by Klenow and Rodriguez-Clare (1997), TFP growth can help materialize previously unprofitable investment projects, so that the rate of capital accumulation would depend on productivity growth. Similarly, many technological innovations are embodied in capital goods and, thus, associated with investment, which makes TFP growth dependent on the rate and factors that determine capital accumulation, including the availability of a labor force with minimum levels of human capital.

All these limitations suggest that great caution should be used when employing growth accounting results for more than descriptive purposes. For instance, we believe that these problems are important enough to warrant skepticism regarding regressions analysis that employs the TFP residual as dependent variable. Although below we find that the TFP component of growth is largely responsible for the shifts in growth from decade to decade for most Latin American countries, we will not attempt to distinguish the determinants of capital accumulation from those of TFP growth via regression analysis. Rather, in the second part of the paper, we will focus on GDP growth as a whole as the dependent variable of interest for econometric analysis.

With these caveats in mind, we now turn to the growth accounting exercise. It covers twenty Latin American countries over the 1960–2000 period. The data sources are given in the full version of the paper (Loayza, Fajnzylber, Calderon, 2005), Appendix A; these include several international organizations, national agencies, as well as previous local and international studies. As others before, we apply a Solow-style procedure to decompose output growth into the contributions of capital, labor, and productivity growth. The contribution of total factor productivity is obtained as a residual once the growth contributions of capital and labor have been imputed. The decomposition adjusts for the 'quality' of labor, as measured by the average level of educational attainment and introduces adjustments for the actual utilization of the stocks of labor and capital.

To describe the approach, consider a neoclassical production function that depends on physical capital K, labor L, and the level of total factor productivity A. Assuming a Cobb-Douglas production function, we have,

$$Y = A K^{\alpha} L^{1-\alpha}$$

We assume that there are no adjustment costs in capital accumulation, and that there is perfect competition in the markets for production factors, so that the latter are paid their social marginal products. Taking logs and time derivatives, leads to the standard estimate for the growth rate of productivity,

$$TFP\ Growth1 = GdpGrowth - S_K * CapGrowth - (1 - S_K) * LaborGrowth$$

where S_K is the share of capital in income. This is the simplest Solow decomposition, in which capital growth consists simply of investment net of depreciation and labor growth comprises only the expansion of the working-age population.

A further refinement consists of adjusting for changes in the quality of labor associated with increases in educational attainment. We thus consider the following human-capital-augmented variation of the previous production function,

$$Y = A K^{\alpha} (HL)^{1-\alpha}$$

where H is an index of the quality of the labor force, based on its educational attainment. Following Collins and Bosworth (1996) and Bernanke and Gurkaynak (2001), for each country 'i' we construct H_i as a weighted average of the shares E_{ij} of the population with educational levels 'j',

$$H_i = \sum_j W_j E_{ij}$$

where the weights W_j are based on the social returns to schooling at each educational level. We use estimates of W_j based on Psacharopoulos (1994) for the primary, secondary and tertiary levels of education, and data on educational attainment from Barro and Lee (2000). Considering this adjustment, TFP growth would then be calculated as,

$$TFP\ Growth2 = GdpGrowth - S_K * CapGrowth - (1 - S_K) * (LaborGrowth + SchoolGrowth)$$

where *SchoolGrowth* is the log difference of the H index.

Finally, we control for the rate of utilization or employment of capital and labor. We adjust for the degree of utilization of the capital stock by using, as a proxy, the rate of labor employment. Regarding labor, we adjust for employment by, first, deducting from the working-age population the number of inactive and unemployed people and, second, adjusting for the number of hours actually worked. Thus, our final measure of TFP growth is given by,

$$TFP\ Growth3 = GdpGrowth - S_K * CapGrowthAdj - (1 - S_K) * (LaborGrowthAdj + SchoolGrowth)$$

where *CapGrowthAdj* is the utilization-adjusted growth rate of capital, and *LaborGrowthAdj* is the employment- and hours-adjusted growth rate of labor.

Figure I.2 shows the results of growth decompositions performed with the third approach for the median Latin American and Caribbean countries of our sample for each decade of the 1961–2000 period. Table 1.4 presents growth accounting results by decades for each of 20 countries with available data. We present the average annual GDP growth rate, followed by the components of growth due to labor, capital and TFP. The contributions of the factors of production are calculated as their rates of growth multiplied by the corresponding shares in income.

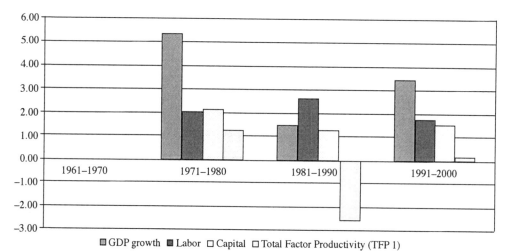

☐ GDP growth ▓ Labor ☐ Capital ☐ Total Factor Productivity (TFP 1)

Figure I.2   Growth Decomposition Adj. for Human Capital and Input Utilization – Median Country by Decade

Since educational attainment has increased in almost every period and country, the effect of adjusting for the quality of labor is that of lowering the component of GDP growth that is attributable to the growth of TFP. As for the adjustments for factor utilization, during recessions they have the effect of reducing the measured growth provided by labor and capital, thus increasing measured TFP growth. During recoveries, those adjustments have the opposite effect, which is to reduce the estimated rate of TFP growth. Given that our units of observation consist of decade averages per country, the adjustment for cyclical factor utilization is found to be small in general, although not negligible for some countries. At the decade frequency, the

Table 1.4 *Growth Accounting Adjusting for Human Capital and Input Utilization,*
1961–2000
Variable of interest: Annual GDP growth rates and contributions from production inputs and TFP

Country	Growth Components	Period		
		1971–1980	1981–1990	1991–2000
Argentina	GDP	2.95	−1.50	4.57
	Labor	1.41	1.08	0.80
	Capital	2.02	−0.18	0.09
	TFP3	−0.47	−2.40	3.69
Bolivia	GDP	4.15	0.10	3.83
	Labor	−	1.41	1.76
	Capital	−	−0.31	0.45
	TFP3	−	−1.00	1.62
Brazil	GDP	8.46	1.55	2.71
	Labor	1.80	2.70	1.67
	Capital	3.12	1.38	0.77
	TFP3	3.53	−2.53	0.26
Chile	GDP	2.86	3.77	6.60
	Labor	2.07	2.19	1.19
	Capital	0.65	1.27	2.73
	TFP3	0.15	0.30	2.67
Colombia	GDP	5.51	3.38	2.68
	Labor	4.68	4.03	1.09
	Capital	1.84	1.51	1.09
	TFP3	−1.01	−2.15	0.50
Costa Rica	GDP	5.64	2.41	5.25
	Labor	−	3.19	2.55
	Capital	−	1.06	1.46
	TFP3	−	−1.84	1.24
Dominican Republic	GDP	6.93	2.55	5.91
	Labor	−	−	2.28
	Capital	−	−	1.74
	TFP3	−	−	1.90
Ecuador	GDP	8.90	2.09	1.76
	Labor	−	2.67	1.79
	Capital	−	1.06	0.43
	TFP3	−	−1.64	−0.46
El Salvador	GDP	2.27	−0.39	4.56
	Labor	−	2.26	2.81
	Capital	−	0.87	2.20
	TFP3	−	−3.51	−0.45
Guatemala	GDP	5.65	0.87	4.06
	Labor	−	0.79	1.73
	Capital	−	0.55	1.41
	TFP3	−	−0.46	0.92

Table I.4 (continued)

Country	Growth Components	Period		
		1971–1980	1981–1990	1991–2000
Honduras	GDP	5.39	2.43	3.21
	Labor	2.05	2.98	5.30
	Capital	2.12	1.14	1.87
	TFP3	1.22	−1.70	−3.95
Jamaica	GDP	−0.79	2.46	0.31
	Labor	1.27	2.26	1.03
	Capital	0.38	0.70	1.91
	TFP3	−2.44	−0.50	−2.63
Mexico	GDP	6.68	1.81	3.50
	Labor	−	3.30	1.79
	Capital	−	1.77	1.59
	TFP3	−	−3.27	0.11
Nicaragua	GDP	0.35	−1.36	3.28
	Labor	1.51	4.10	3.54
	Capital	1.72	0.75	0.61
	TFP3	−2.87	−6.19	−0.87
Panama	GDP	4.13	1.37	4.46
	Labor	2.42	4.08	2.53
	Capital	2.16	0.47	1.79
	TFP3	−0.45	−3.18	0.14
Paraguay	GDP	8.87	2.77	1.97
	Labor	−	2.66	1.26
	Capital	−	2.82	1.48
	TFP3	−	−1.73	−0.17
Peru	GDP	3.63	−0.80	4.10
	Labor	2.38	3.92	3.48
	Capital	1.85	0.91	1.11
	TFP3	−0.60	−5.62	−0.50
Trinidad and Tobago	GDP	6.41	−0.04	3.08
	Labor	2.49	−0.20	2.38
	Capital	2.71	0.76	1.79
	TFP3	1.22	−0.59	−1.09
Uruguay	GDP	3.01	−0.03	3.01
	Labor	0.32	2.62	2.61
	Capital	1.07	0.05	0.50
	TFP3	1.62	−2.70	−0.11
Venezuela	GDP	2.70	0.82	2.02
	Labor	4.80	1.14	3.08
	Capital	2.93	0.76	0.69
	TFP3	−5.03	−1.08	−1.75

Notes: See Appendix A for sources and details of calculations.

Source: Authors' calculations

adjustment for the quality of human capital turns out to produce major changes in the measurement of TFP contribution. Taken together, these adjustments render for the median country even more negative rates of TFP growth during the 1980s and smaller although still positive rates during the 1990s.

As argued by Barro (1999b), the negative rates of TFP growth observed in many countries in Latin America and the Caribbean for long periods in the last 40 years are 'hard to understand as technical regress in the sense of literal forgetting of technology'. Rather, they could reflect a loss in efficiency of the private and public sectors due to misguided policies and weak institutions.

Comparing the 1980s with 1990s, the results obtained with the most complete method indicate an increase of about 2.1% in the rate of TFP growth of the average LAC country, which amounts to about 90% of the average increase of 2.3% in GDP growth between those two decades. The countries with the most notable performance in terms of productivity growth during the 1990s are Argentina, Bolivia, Chile, Costa Rica, and the Dominican Republic, all of which experienced TFP growth rates above 1% per year in average during this decade. For these countries, TFP growth in the 1990s was higher not only with respect to the 1980s but also the previous two decades. A second group comprises eleven countries that also experienced significant increases in their rates of TFP growth with respect to the 1980s. On average, those increases were of 2.9%, which amounts to 130% of the average increase in their rate of GDP growth. However, although in this group the 1990s were characterized by much higher TFP growth than the 1980s, average productivity growth was still close to zero during the past decade. This group includes Brazil, Colombia, Ecuador, El Salvador, Guatemala, Mexico, Nicaragua, Panama, Paraguay, Peru, and Uruguay. In a final, small group, Honduras, Jamaica, Trinidad and Tobago, and Venezuela, the growth rate of TFP actually decreased from the 1980s to the 1990s.

All in all, the main conclusion from the growth accounting exercise is that the recovery in output growth experienced by the vast majority of the countries in the region during the 1990s was driven, in eighty percent of the cases, by large increases in their rates of TFP growth. This result is consistent with the international evidence presented in Easterly and Levine (2001) to the effect that changes in growth are mostly driven by total factor productivity and less so by factor accumulation. Moreover, the large role of TFP in the swings in the growth rate from the 1970s to the 1980s and then to the 1990s confirms that the growth drop of the 1980s and recovery of the 1990s is not the exclusive result of a cyclical turnaround; rather, the large changes in the rates of TFP growth indicate an important role of structural changes in the workings of the region's economies.

3. Summary

After two decades of solid growth, most countries in Latin America and the Caribbean suffered a sharp drop in output per capita in the 1980s. However, the region recovered and restarted growth in the 1990s, with remarkable upturns in some countries. Although the drop of the 1980s and recovery of the 1990s had some elements of cyclical reversion, it was mostly a trend phenomenon, to be thus explained with structural factors. What is behind these trend changes? Growth accounting reveals that it is productivity growth and not capital accumulation what lies behind the major shifts in per capita output growth in the last decades in Latin America and the Caribbean. Therefore, in order to understand the patterns of growth in the region, we need to address the policies, institutions, and reforms that drive the economy's productivity. To this purpose, we turn next.

II. Determinants of Growth

In this section, we attempt to explain the economic growth performance of individual LAC countries using regression analysis. This econometric analysis is applied to data consisting of a multi-country and multi-period sample. We follow the largest strand of the empirical endogenous-growth literature, which seeks to link a country's economic growth rate to economic, political, and social variables using a large sample of countries and time periods. The estimated model is used to project the change in growth rate for each country and then examine whether its performance has been close to expected values.

1. Setup

In the majority of growth studies, the estimated regression equation is of the following form:

$$y_{i,t} - y_{i,t-i} = \alpha y_{i,t-i} + \beta' X_{i,t} + \varepsilon_{i,t}$$

where y is log of output per capita, X is a set variables postulated as growth determinants, and ε is the regression residual. The subscripts i and t refer to country and time period, respectively. For simplicity, the length of the time period is normalized to 1; then, the expression on the left-hand side of the equation is the growth rate of output per capita in a given period. On the right-hand side, the regression equation includes the (log) level of output per capita at the start of the period (to account for transitional convergence) and a set of explanatory variables measured during the same period.

We estimate the following variation of the standard growth regression:

$$y_{i,t} - y_{i,t-1} = \alpha y_{i,t-1} + \alpha_c (y_{i,t-1} - y_{i,t-1}^T) + \beta' X_{i,t} + \mu_t + \eta_i + \varepsilon_{i,t} \tag{1}$$

where y^T represents the trend component of output per capita, $(y_{i,t-1} - y_{i,t-1}^T)$ is the output gap at the start of the period, μ_t is a period-specific effect, and η_i represents unobserved country-specific factors. The inclusion of the output gap as an explanatory variable allows us to control for cyclical output movements and, thus, differentiate between transitional convergence and cyclical reversion. Accounting for cyclical factors is important in our case because we work with relatively short time periods (i.e., 5-year and 10-year averages). The time-specific effect, μ_t, allows to control for international conditions that change over time and affect the growth performance of countries in the sample. The term η_i accounts for unobserved country-specific factors that both drive growth and are potentially correlated with the explanatory variables.

2. Growth Determinants

There are a large variety of economic and social variables that can be proposed as determinants of economic growth. We focus on the variables that have received most attention in the academic literature and policy circles. These variables can be divided into five groups: transitional convergence, cyclical reversion, structural policies and institutions, stabilization policies, and external conditions (for details on definitions and sources see the full version of the paper, Loayza, Fajnzylber, Calderon, 2005, Appendix B).

Transitional Convergence. One of the main implications of the neoclassical growth model, and indeed of all models that exhibit transitional dynamics, is that the growth rate depends on the initial position of the economy. The 'conditional convergence' hypothesis maintains that, *ceteris paribus*, poor countries should grow faster than rich ones because of decreasing returns to accumulable factors of production. We control for the initial position of the economy by including the (log of the) **initial level of real GDP per capita** in the set of explanatory variables.

Cyclical Reversion. Although our main objective is to account for long-run trends in economic growth, in practice – both for econometric estimation and forecasts – we work with relatively short-time periods (5- or 10-year averages). At these frequencies, cyclical effects are bound to play a role. We include some explanatory variables that are not standard in the long-run growth literature but capture important elements of the business cycle. One of them deals with cyclical reversion to the long-run trend. (Other cyclical factors are included under the category of stabilization policies, introduced below.) We account for cyclical reversion, by including the **output gap** at the start of the period as a growth determinant. Apart from improving the regression fit, by controlling for the initial output gap we avoid overestimating the speed of transitional convergence (which is derived from the coefficient on initial output per capita).

The output gap used in the regression is given by the difference between (the log of) potential and actual GDP per capita around the start of the period. We use the Baxter-King filter to decompose the (log) of GDP per capita and estimate annual series of potential (trend) and cyclical output for each country in the sample.

Structural Policies and Institutions. The underlying theme of all the endogenous growth literature is that the rate of economic growth can be affected by public policies and institutions. Although there may be disagreement on what policies are most conducive to growth or the sequence in which policy changes must be undertaken, there is no doubt that governments can and do influence long-run growth in their countries. While theoretical work has usually studied one or the combination of a few policies, empirical work has tended to be comprehensive in the sense of considering a wide array of policy and institutional determinants of growth. Given our empirical objective, we also take a comprehensive approach to explaining economic growth performance. Thus, we consider explanatory variables representing all major categories of public policies. In this subsection, we focus on structural policies and institutions. In the next one, we consider stabilization policies. We recognize that to some extent the separation between structural and stabilization policies is arbitrary. However, the division helps us examine the trends and roles of policies directed to growth in the long run from those related also to cyclical fluctuations.

The first area of structural policies is **education**, and human capital in general. One of the founding papers of the endogenous growth literature, Lucas (1988), focused on the crucial role of human capital in long-run growth. It showed how the effects of human capital could counteract the forces of diminishing returns in other accumulable factors of production – such as physical capital – to render long-run growth. Obviously it was not the first study to highlight the role of education, but it promoted a wide search for the channels through which human capital drive long-run growth. Apart from the direct role of human capital as a factor of production, education and human capital can serve as a complement to other factors such as physical capital and natural resources (see De Gregorio and Bravo-Ortega, 2002), determine the rate of technological innovations in countries that produce technology, and facilitate technological absorption in countries that imitate it (see Borensztein *et al.*, 1998, and Olofsdotter, 1998).

We measure the policies directed to increase education and human capital in general with the rate of gross secondary school enrollment. This 'flow' measure captures more closely current policies on schooling and human capital investment than 'stock' measures related with educational attainment of the adult population or life expectancy.

The second policy area is related to **financial depth**. Well-functioning financial systems promote long-run growth. They influence economic efficiency and economic growth through different channels. Financial markets facilitate risk diversification by trading, pooling, and hedging financial instruments. They can help identify profitable investment projects and mobilize savings to them. Moreover, financial systems can help monitor firm managers and exert corporate controls, thus reducing the principal–agent problems that lead to inefficient investment. There is ample evidence from firm-level, industry-level, and cross-country studies that financial development leads to higher growth.

Our measure of financial depth is the ratio of private domestic credit supplied by private financial institutions to GDP. We concentrate on credit from and to the private sector because the incentives to perform efficiently are clearer and stronger for private agents. For this reason and the relatively wide availability of data for this variable, this is the preferred proxy for the size and activity of financial markets in recent empirical studies. It is also significantly correlated with other proxies such as M2/GDP, the traditional measure of financial depth, and indicators of other aspects of financial markets, such as the size and activity of stock markets.

The next area of economic policy is **international trade openness**. The literature points out five channels through which trade affects economic growth. First, trade leads to higher specialization and, thus, gains in total factor productivity (TFP) by allowing countries to exploit their areas of comparative advantage. Second, it expands potential markets, which allows domestic firms to take advantage of economies of scales and increase their productivity. Third, trade diffuses both technological innovations and improved managerial practices through stronger interactions with foreign firms and markets. Fourth, freer trade tends to lessen anti-competitive practices of domestic firms. Finally, trade liberalization reduces the incentives for firms to conduct rent-seeking activities that are mostly unproductive. The bulk of the empirical evidence indicates that the relationship between economic growth and international openness is indeed positive, and that it reflects a 'virtuous cycle' by which higher openness leads to growth improvement and this in turn generates larger trade.

Our measure of openness is the volume of trade (real exports plus imports) over GDP, adjusted for the size (area and population) of the country, for whether it is landlocked, and for whether it is an oil exporter. For us, this structure-adjusted volume of trade is preferable to the common, unadjusted measure because some of our econometric estimates and projections are based on cross-country comparisons. Without the adjustment, we would be unfairly attributing to trade policy what is merely the result of structural country characteristics (for instance, small countries are more dependent on international trade than large ones; oil exporters can have quite large volumes of trade and at the same time impose high import tariffs; and landlocked countries tend to face larger transport and trading costs and, thus, trade less than other countries).

The next area is related to the **government burden**, and it focuses on the drain that government may represent for private activity. Although government can play a beneficial role for the economy (as discussed below), it can be a heavy burden if it imposes high taxes, uses this revenue to maintain ineffective public programs and a bloated bureaucracy, distorts markets incentives, and interferes negatively in the economy by assuming roles most appropriate for the private sector.

To account for the burden of government we use as proxy the ratio of government consumption to GDP. The rational for this choice is that much of current (or consumption) expenditures by government do not have a clear social return and, in fact, are mostly devoted to cover the bureaucracy's wage bill. Of course, there are exceptions and one could argue that we should subtract from government consumption, expenditures on health, education, and the police, which are not wasteful but may promote growth. However, we do not make this adjustment because we lack consistent data for a large sample of countries on these expenditure categories. Moreover, some of the other explanatory variables (namely, GDP per capita and the measures of governance discussed below) can help control for the fact that not all government consumption can be regarded as an obstacle to growth.

Another important area of policy involves the availability of **public services and infrastructure**. The importance of productive public services in generating long-run growth has been highlighted in the analytical work of Barro (1990) and Barro and Sala-i-Martin (1992), among others. These have underscored the channels through which public services and infrastructure affect economic growth. Whether they are treated as classic public goods or subject to congestion, public services and infrastructure can affect growth by entering directly as inputs of the production function, by serving to improve total factor productivity, and by encouraging private investment through property rights protection. In any case, their theoretical importance has been well established, and recent empirical studies confirm this conclusion.

There are a few alternative measures of public services and infrastructure. Among them, the variables with the largest cross-country and time-series coverage focus on the provision of infrastructure. Due to data considerations, we work with telecommunications capacity, measured by the number of main telephone lines per capita. There are a few alternative proxies of public infrastructure, such as energy generation capacity (e.g., megawatts of electricity produced per capita) and transport facilities (e.g., kilometers of paved roads per capita). However, these measures are highly correlated with each other, and we expect the results to be qualitatively similar for any of them.

The last area is related to **governance**. This large area comprises several aspects of the institutional quality of government, including the respect for civil and political rights, bureaucratic efficiency, absence of corruption, enforcement of contractual agreements, and prevalence of law and order. After the seminal work by Mauro (1995) and Knack and Keefer (1995), governance has received increasing attention as a determinant of economic growth.

The recent empirical cross-country literature has used various subjective indices to measure different aspects of governance and compare them across countries and over time. In general these indices are highly mutually correlated, which suggests that the underlying processes they measure are quite interdependent. In our regression analysis, we use the first principal component of four indicators reported by Political Risk Services in their publication *International Country Risk Guide* (ICRG). They are the indicators on the prevalence of law and order, quality of the bureaucracy, absence of corruption, and accountability of public officials. All of them enter with almost identical weights in their first principal component.

Stabilization Policies. As argued above, the fact that we work with relatively short-time periods (5- or 10-year averages) for econometric estimation and forecasts forces us to consider policies that are normally associated with economic stabilization and crises. By controlling for them, we avoid producing biased estimates for the effects related to conditional convergence and structural policies. Also, by including stabilization policy variables, the regression fit and forecasting power increases significantly over horizons that are relevant to economic policy (again, 5 to 10 years). A possibly more important reason for including stabilization policies in a growth regression is that they not only affect cyclical fluctuations but also long-run growth. In fact an argument can be made that cyclical and trend growth are interrelated processes (see Fatás, 2000a and 2000b), which implies that macroeconomic stabilization and crisis-related variables have an impact not only over short horizons but also on the long-run performance of the economy (see Fischer, 1993).

Fiscal, monetary, and financial policies that contribute to a stable macroeconomic environment and avoid financial and balance-of-payments crises are important for long-run growth. By reducing uncertainty, they encourage firm investment, reduce societal disputes for the distribution of ex-post rents (for instance between firm owners and employees in the face of high unexpected inflation), and allow economic agents to concentrate on productive activities (rather than trying to manage high risk).

The first area in this category is related to macroeconomic stabilization policies. This is a vast subject, and we consider two interrelated effects of fiscal and monetary policies. The first is the **lack of price stability** and is measured by the average inflation rate for the corresponding country and time period. This is a good summary measure of the quality of fiscal and monetary policies and is positively correlated with other indicators of poor macroeconomic policies such as fiscal deficits and the black-market premium on foreign exchange. The inflation rate is the indicator of macroeconomic stability in many cross-country growth studies, including Fischer (1993), Easterly, Loayza, and Montiel (1997), and Barro (2001b), Bekaert, Harvey, and Lundblad (2001). The second aspect is the **cyclical volatility of GDP** and reflects the lack of output stability. It is measured by the standard deviation of the output gap for the corresponding country and period.

The second area is related to **external imbalances and the risk of balance-of-payments crises** and is measured by an index of real exchange rate overvaluation. This index is constructed following the methodology in Dollar (1992) and Easterly (2001). RER overvaluation captures the impact of monetary and exchange-rate policies that distort the allocation of resources between the exporting and domestic sectors. This misallocation leads to large external imbalances, whose correction is frequently accompanied by balance-of-payments crises and followed by sharp recessions.

The third area concerns the occurrence of **systemic banking crises** and serves to account for the deleterious effect of financial turmoil on economic activity, particularly over short and medium horizons. Banking crises may be the product of an inadequate regulatory framework for financial transactions, which leads to over-lending and unsustainable consumption booms. They can also result from monetary and fiscal policies that put undue burden on creditors and financial institutions. This is the case of, for instance, monetary policies that are overly contractionary or fiscal policies that tap excessively on scarce domestic financial resources only to default on debt repayment later on. The occurrence of banking crises is measured by the fraction of years that a country undergoes a systemic banking crisis in the corresponding period, as identified in Caprio and Klingebiel (1999).

External Conditions. The economic activity and growth of a country is not only shaped by internal factors but also by external conditions. These have an influence on the domestic economy both in the short and long runs. There is ample evidence of transmission of cycles across countries via international trade, external financial flows, and investors' perceptions about the expected profitability of the global economy. Moreover, changes in long-run trends can also be spread across countries. This is achieved through, for example, the demonstration effect of economic reforms and the diffusion of technological progress.

We take into account external conditions by including two additional variables in the growth regression. They are the **terms of trade shocks** affecting each country individually and a **period-specific shift** affecting all countries in the sample. Terms of trade shocks capture changes in both the international demand for a country's exports and the cost of production and consumption inputs. The period-specific shifts (or time 'dummy' variables) summarize the prevalent global conditions at a given period of time and reflect worldwide recessions and booms, changes in the allocation and cost of international capital flows, and technological innovations. Easterly (2001) finds that worldwide factors – such as the increase in international interest rates, the growth slowdown of industrial countries, the rise in the debt burden of developing economies, and the development of skill-biased technical innovations – explain the marked decrease in developing countries' growth rates in the 1980s and 1990s with respect to the previous two decades.

3.   Sample and Descriptive Statistics

As said above, we estimate a dynamic model of per capita GDP growth rates using (cross-country, time-series) panel data. Our sample is dictated by data availability and contains countries representing all major world regions. Most of the regression analysis is conducted using averages of 5-year periods. However, for comparison purposes and to check the robustness of the main results, we also estimate the econometric model with observations consisting of decade and full-period averages. See the full version of the paper (Loayza, Fajnzylber, Calderon, 2005), Appendix C, for a complete list of countries in the sample.

The main sample contains 78 countries and, for each of them, a minimum of three and a maximum of eight non-overlapping five-year observations spanning the years 1961–99 (evidently, the panel is unbalanced). A minimum of three observations per country is required to run the instrumental-variable methodology outlined below. Since one observation must be reserved for instrumentation, the first period *in the regression* corresponds to the years 1966–70. The total number of observations in the five-year sample is 350.

The sample based on 10-year averages consists of an unbalanced panel of 65 countries and 175 observations. The observations correspond to the years 1961–70, 1971–80, 1981–90, and 1991–99. Finally, the sample based on full-period averages consists of one observation for 70 countries. A country is included in the sample only if it has complete information for at least 30 years during the period 1966–99. The economic growth rate in this case is calculated as the log difference between the averages corresponding to 1996–99 and 1966–70, divided by 30.

Descriptive Statistics of Economic Growth and Its Determinants. Table II.1 presents descriptive statistics for the data in the samples of 5- and 10-year averages. The first panel shows univariate statistics, including the mean, standard deviation, minimum, and maximum of all variables. The dependent variable, the rate of growth of GDP per capita, shows considerable dispersion, with a range of almost 20 percentage points in the 5-year data. The variables that represent various aspects of economic development, such as the initial GDP per capita, secondary enrollment, private domestic credit, and phone lines per capita, show a skewed distribution with a long and thin lower tail (which reveals the presence of a few very underdeveloped countries in the sample). The inflation rate, the index of RER overvaluation, and the frequency of banking crises also present a skewed distribution, but in their case it reflects a few instances of extreme macroeconomic mismanagement and crisis. The remaining variables show a symmetric distribution, with almost no outliers. In general, the 10-year data have similar means but lower standard deviation and range than the 5-year data do.

The second panel shows correlations between pairs of variables. The correlation between the rate of economic growth and the initial level of GDP per capita is positive, a finding known as 'absolute divergence' (that is, richer countries tend to grow faster than poorer ones). The correlation between economic growth and the remaining explanatory variables have the expected signs: positive with indicators of economic, policy, and institutional development, and negative with measures of economic mismanagement and crisis. The only exception is the correlation with government consumption, which is nearly zero. Regarding the correlations between explanatory variables, two basic facts can be observed: First, the indicators of development (such as income per capita, secondary school enrollment, financial depth, phone lines per capita, and governance) are all highly mutually correlated. Second, variables that denote policy mismanagement and crisis (such as inflation, RER overvaluation, banking crisis, and output volatility) are positively correlated with each other and, in general, negatively correlated with the indicators of development.

4. Estimation Methodology

The proposed growth regression poses some challenges for estimation. The first is the presence of unobserved period- and country-specific effects. While the inclusion of period-specific dummy variables can account for the time effects, the common methods to deal with country-specific effects ('within' or 'difference' estimators) are inappropriate given the dynamic nature of the regression. The second challenge is that most explanatory variables are likely to be jointly endogenous with economic growth, and, thus, we need to control for the biases resulting

Table II.1   Descriptive Statistics of Economic Growth and Its Determinants

(A) Univariate

	Data in 5-Year Periods 78 Countries, 350 Observations				Data in 10-Year Periods 65 Countries, 175 Observations			
	Mean	Std. Dev.	Min.	Max.	Mean	Std. Dev.	Min.	Max.
Growth rate of GDP per capita	0.0148	0.0263	-0.1073	0.0857	0.0142	0.0224	-0.0784	0.0749
Initial GDP per capita (in logs)	8.1553	0.9871	5.9225	9.8279	8.1058	0.9431	6.1592	9.7251
Initial output gap (in logs)	-0.0007	0.0247	-0.1246	0.0668	-0.0034	0.0297	-0.1650	0.0528
Secondary enrollment (in logs)	3.9255	0.6734	1.2042	5.0294	3.9076	0.6753	1.0869	4.9289
Private domestic credit/GDP (in logs)	-1.1631	0.9104	-5.6893	0.7345	-1.1528	0.8454	-4.1289	0.7090
Structure-adjusted trade volume/GDP (in logs)	0.0369	0.4455	-1.6896	1.3629	0.0278	0.4472	-1.5450	1.2887
Government consumption/GDP (in logs)	-1.9355	0.3703	-3.1305	-0.9681	-1.9374	0.3708	-3.1781	-0.9722
Main telephone lines per capita (in logs)	3.8887	1.8291	-0.1576	6.5271	3.8287	1.8167	-0.2070	6.5244
1st principal component of ICRG indicators	0.5529	1.8510	-3.2562	3.4684	0.5201	1.8291	-3.2562	3.4684
Inflation (in log [100+inf. rate])	4.7905	0.4047	4.5749	8.7974	4.8142	0.4218	4.6151	7.8395
Std. Dev. of output gap	0.0196	0.0140	0.0023	0.0674	0.0222	0.0121	0.0038	0.0682
Index of real exchange rate overvaluation (in logs)	4.6400	0.4049	3.4627	7.2101	4.6563	0.3783	3.5838	6.6124
Frequency of years under banking crisis	0.1289	0.2772	0.0000	1.0000	0.1185	0.2144	0.0000	1.0000
Growth rate of terms of trade	-0.0068	0.0434	-0.1955	0.1876	-0.0049	0.0286	-0.0835	0.1351

(B) Bivariate Correlations

Lower triangle for data in 5-year periods. Upper triangle for data in 10-year periods

	Growth rate of GDP per capita	Initial GDP per capita	Secondary enrollment	Private domestic credit/GDP	Structure-adjusted trade volume/GDP	Inflation rate	Government consumption /GDP	Telephone lines per capita	1st p.c. of ICRG indicators	Initial output gap	Std. Dev. of output gap	RER over-valuation	Frequency of banking crisis	Growth of TOT
Growth rate of GDP per capita	1	0.26	0.37	0.35	0.08	-0.35	0.05	0.34	0.33	-0.05	-0.23	-0.25	-0.29	0.24
Initial GDP per capita (in logs)	0.24	1	0.81	0.7	-0.2	-0.09	0.42	0.95	0.8	0.77	-0.33	-0.03	-0.13	0.03
Secondary enrollment (in logs)	0.26	0.83	1	0.58	-0.77	-0.04	0.32	0.85	0.59	0.18	-0.39	-0.7	-0.02	-0.01
Private domestic credit/GDP (in logs)	0.31	0.71	0.58	1	0.03	-0.29	0.38	0.72	0.77	0.27	-0.37	-0.07	-0.73	0.05
Structure-adjusted trade volume/GDP (in logs)	0.05	-0.16	-0.07	0.02	1	-0.28	0.27	-0.2	0.01	0.03	-0.08	-0.09	0.02	0.09
Inflation (in log [100+inf. rate])	-0.35	-0.17	-0.08	-0.4	-0.17	1	-0.04	-0.1	-0.23	-0.26	0.2	0.3	0.24	-0.08
Government consumption/GDP (in logs)	0.01	0.46	0.35	0.35	0.2	-0.04	1	0.44	0.5	-0.03	-0.27	0.26	-0.21	-0.03
Main telephone lines per capita (in logs)	0.27	0.95	0.85	0.71	-0.16	-0.16	0.44	1	0.78	0.22	-0.39	-0.06	-0.14	0.04
1st principal component of ICRG indicators	0.27	0.8	0.61	0.69	0.01	-0.22	0.54	0.79	1	0.17	-0.4	-0.02	-0.17	0.02
Initial output gap	-0.23	0.16	0.18	0.13	0.05	0.03	0.07	0.18	0.13	1	-0.25	-0.3	0.11	-0.07
Std. Dev. of output gap	-0.26	-0.23	-0.28	-0.22	-0.06	0.21	-0.16	-0.27	-0.31	-0.14	1	0.12	0.09	-0.01
Index of real exchange rate overvaluation (in logs)	-0.2	0.02	-0.02	0	-0.09	0.19	0.26	0.02	0.03	-0.01	0.08	1	0.05	-0.12
Frequency of years under banking crisis	-0.33	-0.18	-0.07	-0.15	0.06	0.27	-0.13	-0.19	-0.19	0	0.11	0.05	1	-0.18
Growth rate of trade	0.2	0.08	0.04	0.11	0.05	-0.11	-0.05	0.08	0.06	0.08	-0.03	-0.14	-0.12	1

Source: Authors' calculations.

484

from simultaneous or reverse causation. In the following paragraphs we outline the econometric methodology we use to control for country-specific effects and joint endogeneity in a dynamic model of panel data.

We use the Generalized-Method-of-Moments (GMM) estimators developed for dynamic models of panel data that were introduced by Holtz-Eakin, Newey, and Rosen (1990), Arellano and Bond (1991), and Arellano and Bover (1995). Taking advantage of the data's panel nature, these estimators are based on, first, differencing regressions and/or instruments to control for unobserved effects, and, second, using previous observations of explanatory and lagged-dependent variables as instruments (which are called 'internal' instruments).

After accounting for time-specific effects and including the output gap in the set of explanatory variables X, we can rewrite equation (1) as follows,

$$y_{i,t} = \alpha y_{i,t-1} + \beta' X_{i,t} + \eta_i + \varepsilon_{i,t} \tag{2}$$

In order to eliminate the country-specific effect, we take first-differences of equation (2),

$$y_{i,t} - y_{i,t-1} = \alpha(y_{i,t-1} - y_{i,t-2}) + \beta'(X_{i,t} - X_{i,t-1}) + (\varepsilon_{i,t} - \varepsilon_{i,t-1}) \tag{3}$$

The use of instruments is required to deal with, first, the likely endogeneity of the explanatory variables, and, second, the problem that, by construction, the new error term, $\varepsilon_{i,t} - \varepsilon_{i,t-1}$, is correlated with the lagged dependent variable, $y_{i,t-1} - y_{i,t-2}$. Taking advantage of the panel nature of the data set, the instruments consist of previous observations of the explanatory and lagged dependent variables. Given that it relies on past values as instruments, this method only allows current and future values of the explanatory variables to be affected by the error term. Therefore, while relaxing the common assumption of strict exogeneity, our instrumental-variable method does not allow the X variables to be fully endogenous.

Under the assumptions that (a) the error term, ε, is not serially correlated, and (b) the explanatory variables, X, are weakly exogenous (i.e., the explanatory variables are assumed to be uncorrelated with future realizations of the error term), the GMM dynamic panel estimator uses the following moment conditions.

$$E[y_{i,t-s} \cdot (\varepsilon_{i,t} - \varepsilon_{i,t-1})] = 0 \quad \text{for } s \geq 2; t = 3,\dots, T \tag{4}$$

$$E[X_{i,t-s} \cdot (\varepsilon_{i,t} - \varepsilon_{i,t-1})] = 0 \quad \text{for } s \geq 2; t = 3,\dots, T \tag{5}$$

The GMM estimator based on these conditions is known as the *difference* estimator. Notwithstanding its advantages with respect to simpler panel data estimators, there are important statistical shortcomings with the difference estimator. Alonso-Borrego and Arellano (1996) and Blundell and Bond (1997) show that when the explanatory variables are persistent over time, lagged levels of these variables are weak instruments for the regression equation in differences. Instrument weakness influences the asymptotic and small-sample performance of the difference estimator. Asymptotically, the variance of the coefficients rises. In small samples, Monte Carlo experiments show that the weakness of the instruments can produce biased coefficients.

To reduce the potential biases and imprecision associated with the usual difference estimator, we use a new estimator that combines in a *system* the regression in differences with the regression in levels (developed in Arellano and Bover, 1995, and Blundell and Bond, 1997). The instruments for the regression in differences are the same as above. The instruments for the regression in levels are the lagged *differences* of the corresponding variables. These are appropriate instruments under the following additional assumption: although there may be correlation between the levels of the right-hand side variables and the country-specific effect in equation (2), there is no correlation between the *differences* of these variables and the country-specific effect. This assumption results from the following stationarity property,

$$E[y_{i,t+p} \cdot \eta_i] = E[y_{i,t+q} \cdot \eta_i] \text{ and}$$
$$E[X_{i,t+p} \cdot \eta_i] = E[X_{i,t+q} \cdot \eta_i] \text{ for all } p \text{ and } q \tag{6}$$

The additional moment conditions for the second part of the system (the regression in levels) are:

$$E[(y_{i,t-1} - y_{i,t-2}) \cdot (\eta_i + \varepsilon_{i,t})] = 0 \tag{7}$$

$$E[(X_{i,t-1} - X_{i,t-2}) \cdot (\eta_i + \varepsilon_{i,t})] = 0 \tag{8}$$

Thus, we use the moment conditions presented in equations (4), (5), (7), and (8) and employ a GMM procedure to generate consistent and efficient parameter estimates.

Using the moment conditions presented in equations (4), (5), (7), and (8), we employ a Generalized Method of Moments (GMM) procedure to generate consistent estimates of the parameters of interest and their asymptotic variance–covariance (Arellano and Bond, 1991, and Arellano and Bover, 1995). These are given by the following formulas:

$$\hat{\theta} = (\bar{X}'Z\hat{\Omega}^{-1}Z'X)^{-1} \bar{X}'Z\hat{\Omega}^{-1}Z'\bar{y} \tag{9}$$

$$AVAR(\hat{\theta}) = (\bar{X}'Z\hat{\Omega}^{-1}Z'\bar{X})^{-1} \tag{10}$$

where θ is the vector of parameters of interest (α, β), $\bar{y}$ is the dependent variable stacked first in differences and then in levels, $\bar{X}$ is the explanatory-variable matrix including the lagged dependent variable (y_{t-1}, X) stacked first in differences and then in levels, Z is the matrix of instruments derived from the moment conditions, and $\hat{\Omega}$ is a consistent estimate of the variance–covariance matrix of the moment conditions.

The consistency of the GMM estimators depends on whether lagged values of the explanatory variables are valid instruments in the growth regression. We address this issue by considering two specification tests suggested by Arellano and Bond (1991) and Arellano and Bover (1995). The first is a Sargan test of over-identifying restrictions, which tests the overall validity of the instruments by analyzing the sample analog of the moment conditions used in the estimation process. Failure to reject the null hypothesis gives support to the model. The second test examines the null hypothesis that the error term $\varepsilon_{i,t}$ is not serially correlated. As in the case of the Sargan test, the model specification is supported when the null hypothesis is not rejected. In the *system* specification we test whether the differenced error term (that is, the residual of the regression in differences) is second-order serially correlated. First-order serial correlation of the differenced error term is expected even if the original error term (in levels) is uncorrelated, unless the latter follows a random walk. Second-order serial correlation of the differenced residual indicates that the original error term is serially correlated and follows a moving average process at least of order one. This would reject the appropriateness of the proposed instruments (and would call for higher-order lags to be used as instruments).

5. Estimation Results

Tables II.2 and II.3 present the model estimation results. In Table II.2, we report the results obtained with various estimation methods on the sample based on 5-year averages. In Table II.3, we present the results corresponding to the regressions on different horizons; that is, using the samples based on 5-year, 10-year, and 30-year averages. The last column of each table shows our main results, that is, those obtained with the GMM system estimator on the 5-year sample. We first discuss the main results and then compare them with the rest in Tables II.2 and II.3. Before proceeding, we should remark that the employed specification tests support the GMM-system estimation of our model. That is, the Sargan and serial correlation tests cannot reject the null hypothesis of correct specification of the main model.

Transitional Convergence. The coefficient on the initial level of GDP per capita is negative and statistically significant. In contrast to the 'absolute divergence' result observed above, the negative coefficient on initial income indicates that there is 'conditional convergence'; that is, holding constant other growth determinants, poorer countries grow faster than richer ones. Given the estimated coefficient, the implied speed of convergence is 1.84% per year, with a corresponding half-life of about 38 years (this is the time it takes for half the income difference between two growing countries to disappear solely due to convergence). It is interesting to note that this estimate for the speed of convergence is almost identical to that estimated in the early cross-country growth regressions (e.g., Barro, 1991). Previous panel regressions estimated faster speeds of convergence, claiming that this was due to their correction of the downward bias produced by unobserved country-specific effects (see Knight, Loayza, and Villanueva, 1993, and Caselli, Esquivel, and Lefort, 1996). However, by working with shorter time periods, these panel studies introduced an upward bias due to cyclical reversion to the trend; for instance, a post-recession recovery was confused with faster convergence. In this study we control for both country-specific effects and cyclical factors, and we find that their corresponding biases on the speed of convergence nearly cancel each other.

Cyclical Reversion. The estimated coefficient on the initial output gap is negative and significant. This indicates that the economies in the sample follow a trend-reverting process. That is, if an economy is undergoing a recession at the start of the period, it is expected that its growth rate be higher than otherwise in the following years so as to close the output gap. Likewise, it is expected that a cyclical boom be followed by lower growth rates. The cyclical reversion effect is sizable – according to the point estimate, if initial output is, say, 5% below potential output, the economy is expected to grow about 1.2 percentage points higher in the following years.

Table II.2　Economic Growth Regressions: Various Estimation Methods
Dependent Variable: Growth Rate of GDP per capita
(t-Statistics are presented below the corresponding coefficient)

Regression Period: Time Horizon: Type of Model: Estimation Technique: Instruments:		1966–99 5-year periods		
	Pooled OLS –	Within OLS –	Levels – IV GMM Lagged Levels	System – IV GMM Lagged Levels/Difference
	[1]	[2]	[3]	[4]
Transitional Convergence:				
Initial GDP Per Capita	−0.0139	−0.0516	−0.0169	−0.0176
(in logs)	−3.49	−7.51	−5.37	−3.80
Cyclical Reversion:				
Initial Output Gap	−0.2834	−0.1614	−0.2528	−0.2371
(log[actual GDP/potential GDP])	−6.13	−4.33	−7.90	−8.52
Structural Policies and Institutions:				
Education	0.0085	0.0036	0.0043	0.0172
(secondary enrollment, in logs)	2.52	0.63	1.42	6.70
Financial Depth	0.0031	0.0050	0.0025	0.0066
(private domestic credit/GDP, in logs)	1.57	1.69	1.91	4.28
Trade Openness	0.0083	0.0215	0.0115	0.0096
(structure-adjusted trade volume/GDP, in logs)	2.67	4.16	3.45	3.14
Government Burden	−0.0125	−0.0210	−0.0077	−0.0154
(government consumption/GDP, in logs)	−3.16	−3.37	−2.33	−3.18
Public Infrastructure	0.0073	0.0067	0.0151	0.0071
(Main telephone lines per capita, in logs)	3.08	1.60	5.65	2.71
Governance	0.0012	0.0017	−0.0052	−0.0012
(1st principal component of ICRG indicators)	1.02	0.93	−3.27	−0.68
Stabilization Policies:				
Lack of Price Stability	−0.0085	−0.0083	−0.0097	−0.0048
(inflation rate, in log [100+ inf. rate])	−2.61	−2.64	−2.88	−1.89
Cyclical Volatility	−0.3069	−0.1904	−0.5290	−0.2771
(Std. Dev. of output gap)	−3.58	−2.46	−4.55	−3.76
Real Exchange Rate Overvaluation	−0.0080	−0.0070	−0.0076	−0.0061
(in logs; index is proportional, overvaluation if > 100)	−2.71	−2.01	−2.82	−3.90
Systemic Banking Crises	−0.0171	−0.0201	−0.0142	−0.0289
(frequency of years under crisis: 0–1	−3.96	−4.95	−2.73	−7.42
External Conditions:				
Terms of Trade Shocks	0.0619	0.0498	0.0533	0.0720
(growth rate of TOT)	2.34	2.27	4.26	4.98

Period Shifts					
(benchmark for Cols. 1 and 3: 1971–75;	71–75:				−0.0090
benchmark for Cols. 4: 1966–70;	76–80:	0.0017	0.0010	−0.0008	−0.0092**
benchmark for Col. 2: average 1971–99)	81–85:	−0.0147**	0.0072*	−0.0188**	−0.0238**
	86–90:	−0.0110**	−0.0031	−0.0160**	−0.0194**
	91–95:	−0.0158**	0.0038	−0.0226**	−0.0258**
	96–99:	−0.0168**	0.0002	−0.0222**	−0.0270**

Intercept	0.1418	0.0007	0.1756	0.1216
	4.12	0.15	4.91	2.79
No. Countries/No. Observations	78/350	78/350	78/350	78/350
Specification Tests (*P*-Values)				
(a) Sargan Test:			0.374	0.996
(b) Serial Correlation:				
First-Order	0.000	0.000	0.000	0.000
Second-Order	0.021	0.617	0.002	0.461

Notes:　For period shifts: ** means significant at 5% and * means significant at 10%.

Source:　Authors' estimations.

Table II.3   *Economic Growth Regressions: Various Time Horizons*
Dependent Variable: Growth Rate of GDP per capita
(t-Statistics are presented below the corresponding coefficient)

Regression Period:	1966/70–1996/99	1961–1999	1966–99
Time Horizon:	30-year period	10-year periods	5-year periods
Type of Model:	Cross-Section	System – IV	System – IV
Estimation Technique:	OLS	GMM	GMM
Instruments:	–	Lagged Levels/Differences	Lagged Levels/Differences
	[1]	[2]	[3]
Convergence Factors:			
Initial GDP Per Capita	0.0240	–0.0332	–0.0176
(in logs)	–6.34	–4.88	–3.80
Cyclical Reversion:			
Initial Output Gap		–0.1673	–0.2371
(log[actual GDP/potential GDP])		–5.57	–8.52
Structural Policies and Institutions:			
Education	0.0082	0.0059	0.0172
(secondary enrollment, in logs)	2.14	0.73	6.70
Financial Depth	0.0045	0.0056	0.0066
(private domestic credit/GDP, in logs)	1.56	1.92	4.28
Trade Openness	0.0048	0.0247	0.0096
(structure-adjusted trade volume/GDP, in logs)	1.24	5.02	3.14
Government Burden	–0.0145	–0.0167	–0.0154
(government consumption/GDP, in logs)	–2.82	–2.44	–3.18
Public Infrastructure	0.0116	0.0243	0.0071
(Main telephone lines per capita, in logs)	4.46	5.28	2.71
Governance	0.0018	–0.0056	–0.0012
(1st principal component of ICRG indicators)	1.15	–2.27	–0.68
Stabilization Policies:			
Lack of Price Stability	–0.0060	–0.0207	–0.0048
(inflation rate, in log [100+ inf. rate])	–2.11	–5.36	–1.89
Cyclical Volatility		–0.5079	–0.2771
(Std. Dev. of output gap)		–3.48	–3.76
Real Exchange Rate Overvaluation		–0.0007	–0.0061
(in logs; index is proportional, overvaluation if > 100)		–0.17	–3.90
Systemic Banking Crises		–0.0057	–0.0289
(frequency of years under crisis: 0–1		–0.60	–7.42
External Conditions:			
Terms of Trade Shocks		0.0000	0.0720
(growth rate of TOT)		2.40	4.98

Period Shifts	70s:	–0.0091**	71–75:		–0.0090**
(benchmark for Col. 2: 1960s	80s:	–0.0257**	76–80:		–0.0092**
benchmark for Col. 3: 1966–70)	90s:	–0.0398**	81–85:		–0.0238**
			86–90:		–0.0194**
			91–95:		–0.0258**
			96–99:		–0.0270**

	[1]	[2]	[3]
Intercept	0.2150	0.2816	0.1216
	6.09	4.33	2.79
No. Countries/No. Observations	70/70	65/175	78/350
Specification Tests (*P*-Values)			
(a) Sargan Test		0.9	0.996
(b) Serial Correlation			
First-Order		0.002	0.000
Second-Order		0.93	0.461

Notes: For period shifts: ** means significant at 5% and * means significant at 10%.

Source: Authors' estimation.

Structural Policies and Institutions. All variables related to structural policies present coefficients with expected signs and statistical significance. Economic growth increases with improvements in education, financial depth, trade openness, and public infrastructure. It decreases when governments apply an excessive burden on the private sector. These results are broadly supported by a vast empirical literature on endogenous growth, including Barro (1991) on the role of education, trade, and government burden, among other variables; Dollar (1992) on trade openness; Canning, Fay, and Perotti (1994) on public infrastructure; and Levine, Loayza, and Beck (2000) on financial depth. Apart from the sign and statistical significance of the coefficients, there is important information in their actual estimated size. However, we leave the analysis of the economic significance of these variables for the next section. There, we discuss the explanatory variables' role in explaining and forecasting the growth performance of Latin American and Caribbean countries.

Perhaps surprisingly, we find that governance does not have a statistically significant impact on economic growth, and the corresponding coefficient even presents a negative sign. This is so despite the fact that the governance index has the second largest positive correlation with the growth rate of GDP per capita. To check the robustness of this result, we replaced the ICRG index with each of its components in turn, namely, the indicators on bureaucratic efficiency, corruption, law and order, and accountability. We also replaced it with Gastil's index on civil rights. The estimated coefficients were never statistically significant, although for some governance proxies (law and order and bureaucratic efficiency) the coefficient sign became positive. Dollar and Kraay (2003) obtain a similar result – when they control for trade openness, various measures of governance have a relatively weak effect on growth, particularly over medium-term horizons (i.e., decadal growth). We interpret these results as saying that the effect of governance on economic growth works through the actual economic policies that governments implement. In a sense our results contrast with those in Easterly and Levine (2002), who find that governance and not specific policies matter for explaining cross-country differences in *income levels*.

Stabilization Policies. For the variables in these categories, all estimated coefficients carry the expected signs and statistical significance. In general, economic growth decreases when governments do not carry out policies conducive to macroeconomic stability, including the absence of financial and external crises. Similarly to Fischer (1993), we find that an increase in the inflation rate leads to a reduction in economic growth. Likewise, the volatility of the cyclical component of GDP has a negative impact on the growth rate of GDP per capita. This reveals an important connection between business-cycle factors and economic growth, a subject seldom explored in the endogenous growth literature. Our results in this regard are consistent with the theoretical and empirical work by Fatás (2000a and 2000b) and Hnatkovska and Loayza (2004).

The overvaluation of the real exchange rate also has a negative impact on economic growth. This effect is likely to work through a combination of mechanisms. An overvalued exchange rate produces a misallocation of resources away from export-oriented sectors, not so much for commodities (which tend to be price inelastic) as for manufactured goods (which have stronger links with the overall economy). Moreover, real exchange rate overvaluation generates a strong risk of balance-of-payments crises, which if severe are followed by a sharp and lasting decline of real economic activity. Similarly, we find that the frequency of systemic banking crises has a negative and large effect on economic growth: countries that experience a continuous banking crisis over, say, a five-year period suffer a slowdown in their annual growth rate of almost three percentage points.

External Conditions. Negative terms-of-trade shocks have the effect of slowing down the economy's growth rate. This result is consistent with previous studies. In one of them, Easterly, Kremer, Pritchett, and Summers (1993) find that 'good luck' in the form of favorable TOT shocks are as important as 'good policies' in explaining growth performance over medium-term horizons (e.g., decades).

Regarding the period shifts (or time dummies), we find that world growth conditions experienced a gradual change for the worse from the 1960s, with the biggest downward break occurring at the beginning of the 1980s. Broadly speaking, the deterioration of world growth conditions between the 1970s and 1980s leads to a decrease in a country's growth rate of about 1.5 percentage points. Considering only world growth conditions, our results indicate that any country in the sample is expected to grow almost three percentage points more slowly in the 1990s than in the 1960s. This is a considerable effect. After noting the world growth slowdown after 1980, Easterly (2001) concludes that worldwide factors are partly responsible for the stagnation of developing countries in the last two decades in spite of policy reforms.

Comparison with Results under Other Estimation Methods and Time Horizons

Table II.2 presents the estimation results obtained with four different methods applied on the same sample and explanatory variables. The first (Col. 1) is the pooled OLS estimator, which ignores the presence of country-specific effects and treats all variables as exogenous. The second (Col. 2) is the within OLS estimator, which demeans all variables using corresponding country means prior to OLS estimation. Thus, this method eliminates country-specific effects but ignores the joint endogeneity of the explanatory variables (including the initial level of income). The third method (Col. 3) is the GMM *levels* estimator, which uses instruments to control for joint endogeneity but ignores country-specific effects. The fourth (Col. 4) is the GMM *system* estimator, which as explained above, accounts for country-specific effects and joint endogeneity.

It is interesting to note that, with the exception of governance, all explanatory variables carry coefficients of the same sign under the four estimation methods. The statistical significance and estimated size of most variables are also remarkably similar across estimation methods. The sign of the coefficient associated with governance changes from positive to negative once joint endogeneity is taken into account, but in three of the four cases this coefficient is not statistically significant.

Table II.3 shows the estimation results obtained under various time horizons. Col. 1 presents the growth regression for a single cross-section of countries, where each observation corresponds to a country average over the period from the late 1960s to the late 1990s (about 30 years). Here we include all variables in the categories of convergence factors and structural policies and institutions, and one variable in the category of stabilization policies (the inflation rate). According to the received literature, these are the most pertinent for growth over a long time span. We estimate the model with OLS, given that the cross-sectional nature of the sample does not allow the use of internal instruments or the correction for time- and country-specific effects. Our cross-sectional OLS exercise is the one that most closely resembles those in the empirical growth literature. Col. 2 presents the growth regression using observations consisting in decade averages for each country. Given the panel nature of this sample, we can use the same model specification (that is, explanatory variables and estimation method) as in our main regression (presented in Col. 3).

All variables carry coefficients of the same sign in the regressions over different time horizons (except for governance). The statistical significance and size of the estimated coefficients are similar with a few exceptions. In the case of the cross-sectional regression financial depth and trade openness are not statistically significant. In view of their significance under different estimation methods, we can conjecture that their lack of statistical significance in the cross-sectional regression is due to the omission of variables such as banking crisis and terms-of-trade shocks, which control for some negative aspects of financial depth (credit booms) and trade openness (external vulnerability). In the case of the decades regression, RER overvaluation, banking crises, and education do not appear to be statistically significant. The lack of significance of the educational variable in some specifications (within OLS, GMM *levels*, and GMM *system* on decades) should serve to alert us concerning the pitfalls of educational measures as proxies for human capital, as discussed in Pritchett (2001).

6. Growth Explanations

We now employ the estimated econometric model to explain (or project) the growth rate of individual countries for various time periods. For this, we use both the main regression estimated coefficients and the actual values of the explanatory variables for the periods under consideration. Our objectives are, first, assessing the contribution of each category of explanatory variables to a country's expected growth and, second, examining whether the country's actual performance is close to expected values. We use the model to explain the *changes* over time in economic growth for a single country. As explained below, this comparative exercise does not require an estimate of unobserved country-specific effects.

Explaining Changes in Growth Rates over Time

Derivation of Projection Formulas. Making explicit that our basic regression uses periods of five years, the regression equation is given by,

$$\frac{(y_{i,t} - y_{i,t-5})}{5} = \alpha y_{i,t-5} + \beta' X_{i,t} + \mu_t + \eta_i + \varepsilon_{i,t} \qquad (11)$$

Then, the change in the growth rate between two periods for the same country is,

$$\frac{(y_{i,t} - y_{i,t-5})}{5} \frac{(y_{i,t-s} - y_{i,t-s-5})}{5} = \alpha(y_{i,t-5} - y_{i,t-s-5}) + \beta'(X_{i,t} - Xi,t-s) + (\mu_t - \mu_{t-s}) + (\varepsilon_{i,t} - \varepsilon_{i,t-s})$$

where *s* is the distance in years between the corresponding end (or start) points of the two periods under comparison. Since we work with non-overlapping periods, *s* can take the values of 5, 10, 15, etc. in the 5-year comparisons. Note that the country-specific effect disappears from the expression on growth changes given that it is constant over time. The projected change in growth is obtained by taking expectations of both sides of the equation:

$$E\left[\frac{(y_{i,t}-y_{i,t-5})}{5}-\frac{(y_{i,t-s}-y_{i,t-s-5})}{5}\right]=\hat{\alpha}(y_{i,t-5}-y_{i,t-s-5})+\hat{\beta}'(X_{i,t}-X_{i,t-s})+(\hat{\mu}_t-\hat{\mu}_{t-s}) \quad (12)$$

where hatted coefficients represent estimated values.

Equation (12) provides the formula to calculate the projected changes in growth rates between two 5-year periods, as well as the corresponding contribution of each explanatory variable (or groups of variables) to the projection. We are also interested in explaining the changes in growth between two 10-year periods. In order to be consistent with the 5-year comparisons, we must use the same data and estimated model (i.e., coefficients and period shifts). After a few lines of algebra, we can get from equation (12) and expression for the projected change in growth rates between two 10-year periods, based on 5-year information:

$$E\left[\frac{(y_{i,t}-y_{i,t-10})}{10}-\frac{(y_{i,t-s}-y_{i,t-s-10})}{10}\right]=\hat{\alpha}\left(\frac{(y_{i,t-5}-y_{i,t-s-10})}{2}-\frac{(y_{i,t-s-5}-y_{i,t-s-10})}{2}\right)$$
$$+\hat{\beta}'\left(\frac{(X_{i,t}+X_{i,t-5})}{2}-\frac{(X_{i,t-s}+X_{i,t-s-5})}{2}\right)$$
$$+\left(\frac{(\hat{\mu}_t-\hat{\mu}_{t-s})}{2}-\frac{(\hat{\mu}_{t-s}-\hat{\mu}_{t-s-5})}{2}\right) \quad (13)$$

Given that we work with non-overlapping periods, in the 10-year comparisons s can take the values of 10, 20, etc.

Discussion. Table II.4 presents the projections for the change in growth rates between decades for each available country in Latin America and the Caribbean (see also Figure II.1). Table II.5 presents the projections for growth changes between consecutive 5-year periods. We also present the contribution to the projected change from our major categories of explanatory variables, namely, transitional convergence, cyclical reversion, structural policies, stabilization policies, and external conditions. In the full version of the paper (Loayza, Fajnzylber, Calderon, 2005), Appendix D, presents a table per country where the contribution of each explanatory variable is presented separately.

It is particularly interesting to study the change between the 1990s and 1980s. The reason is that during the last decade, many countries in Latin America and the Caribbean – such as Argentina, Bolivia, El Salvador, and Peru – underwent strong market-oriented reforms (see Burki and Perry, 1997, and Loayza and Palacios, 1997). These were partly motivated by the belief that the reforms would generate high economic growth. Consequently, the success of the reforms has been judged by the ensuing growth improvement in the country (see Easterly, Loayza, and Montiel, 1997). Our methodology allows us to reassess this question as it gauges what growth improvement could have been expected from policy changes and other developments from the 1980s to the 1990s. We organize the discussion on the projections around the contribution of the reform process, extending the analysis not only to between the last two decades but also to developments since the 1970s.

As we can see in Table II.4, Panel A, for all 20 LAC countries under consideration the growth contribution from structural policies was positive in the 1990s with respect to the

Table II.4   *Explaining Changes in Growth Between Decades*
Variable of interest: Change in the growth rate of GDP per capita

(a) 1990s vs. 1980s

Countries	Actual Change	Projected Change	Transitional Convergence	Cyclical Reversion	Structural Reforms	Stabilization Policies	External Conditions
Argentina	6.71	4.45	0.15	1.70	1.07	1.71	-0.17
Bolivia	3.49	2.54	0.11	-0.02	1.34	1.70	-0.59
Brazil	1.49	1.00	-0.03	0.89	0.88	-0.53	-0.21
Chile	2.91	2.59	-0.66	0.65	1.67	1.33	-0.40
Colombia	-0.55	2.11	-0.32	0.15	1.15	1.47	-0.34
Costa Rica	3.80	1.13	-0.19	0.36	1.11	0.15	-0.31
Dominican Republic	3.44	2.42	-0.14	0.46	1.28	0.48	0.34
Ecuador	0.04	0.73	0.01	0.20	0.83	0.03	-0.35
El Salvador	4.14	2.09	-0.05	-0.10	2.21	0.41	-0.38
Haiti	-0.59	2.34	0.49	0.54	2.24	-0.56	-0.37
Honduras	0.84	0.82	0.04	0.25	0.71	0.16	-0.35
Jamaica	-1.86	-1.73	-0.30	-0.88	1.45	-1.30	-0.70
Mexico	1.72	1.80	0.05	0.19	1.51	0.24	-0.19
Nicaragua	4.40	1.84	0.67	-0.97	2.56	0.18	-0.60
Panama	3.51	1.87	0.04	-0.24	0.83	1.66	-0.43
Paraguay	-0.30	0.73	-0.02	0.47	1.79	-0.86	-0.65
Peru	5.32	3.84	0.30	0.28	1.29	2.42	-0.46
Trinidad and Tobago	3.28	0.68	0.21	0.01	0.91	0.37	-0.82
Uruguay	3.36	3.03	-0.20	0.76	1.05	1.78	-0.35
Venezuela	1.45	-0.39	0.11	0.20	0.67	-0.94	-0.44

(b) 1980s vs. 1970s

Countries	Actual Change	Projected Change	Transitional Convergence	Cyclical Reversion	Structural Reforms	Stabilization Policies	External Conditions
Argentina	-4.31	-3.27	0.01	-0.78	0.60	-1.59	-1.50
Bolivia	-3.62	-2.77	0.02	-0.56	0.38	-1.53	-1.09
Brazil	-6.17	-3.11	-0.64	-1.21	0.74	-0.73	-1.28
Chile	0.87	0.64	-0.32	-1.10	2.43	0.51	-0.88
Colombia	-1.78	-2.92	-0.40	-0.29	0.66	-1.39	-1.49
Costa Rica	-3.07	-1.69	-0.22	-0.60	0.32	0.05	-1.25
Dominican Republic	-3.87	-1.42	-0.47	-0.05	1.07	-0.26	-1.71
Ecuador	-6.12	-2.56	-0.63	-0.89	0.94	-0.39	-1.60
El Salvador	-1.29	-1.45	0.27	-0.28	0.30	-0.46	-1.28
Haiti	-4.84	-	-0.27	-1.21	-	0.43	-1.18
Honduras	-2.78	-0.36	-0.27	-0.34	1.30	0.27	-1.31
Jamaica	3.36	1.03	0.45	0.43	0.81	0.39	-1.05
Mexico	-3.87	-2.61	-0.49	-0.39	1.08	-0.98	-1.84
Nicaragua	-1.23	-3.62	0.68	-0.29	-1.18	-1.97	-0.86
Panama	-2.18	-	-0.23	0.19	-0.07	-1.24	-
Paraguay	-5.99	-2.24	-0.77	-0.99	1.07	-0.22	-1.34
Peru	-3.83	-4.05	0.03	-0.01	0.74	-3.36	-1.47
Trinidad and Tobago	-6.33	-1.92	-0.77	-0.38	1.54	-0.05	-2.26
Uruguay	-3.26	-1.69	-0.20	-0.48	1.43	-1.50	-0.93
Venezuela	-0.99	-1.79	0.26	0.33	-0.05	-0.31	-2.03

Source: Authors' calculations.

Table II.5   *Explaining Changes in Growth Between Five–Year Periods*
Variable of interest. Change in the growth rate of GDP per capita

(a) 1996–99 vs. 1991–95

Countries	Actual Change	Projected Change	Transitional Convergence	Cyclical Reversion	Structural Reforms	Stabilization Policies	External Conditions
Argentina	-2.91	-0.87	-0.44	-1.77	0.89	0.87	-0.41
Bolivia	-0.17	0.53	-0.14	0.03	0.60	-0.07	0.12
Brazil	-1.21	1.91	-0.14	-0.80	1.29	1.69	-0.12
Chile	-3.84	-1.76	-0.59	-0.95	0.74	-0.17	-0.79
Colombia	-3.97	-1.43	-0.22	-0.37	-0.08	-0.43	-0.33
Costa Rica	0.44	-0.83	-0.29	-0.52	0.55	-0.29	-0.28
Dominican Republic	3.50	-1.01	-0.19	-0.44	0.11	0.31	-0.81
Ecuador	-3.64	-3.94	-0.10	-0.33	0.25	-3.66	-0.10
El Salvador	-2.80	-0.01	-0.35	-0.81	1.48	0.25	-0.57
Haiti	5.59	2.17	0.47	0.15	0.84	0.94	-0.24
Honduras	-0.93	-0.32	-0.05	-0.20	0.41	-0.06	-0.43
Jamaica	-2.26	-1.93	-0.03	0.28	0.30	-1.81	-0.66
Mexico	3.88	2.29	0.03	1.23	0.66	0.31	0.06
Nicaragua	3.99	3.00	0.13	0.02	0.82	3.04	-1.00
Panama	-1.57	-0.30	-0.31	-0.60	0.43	0.17	0.01
Paraguay	-2.45	-2.46	-0.04	-0.19	0.58	-2.32	-0.48
Peru	-2.85	-1.11	-0.32	-2.49	1.05	0.95	-0.31
Trinidad and Tobago	3.28	1.73	-0.05	-0.01	0.42	0.30	1.08
Uruguay	-1.03	-0.09	-0.28	-0.18	0.47	0.13	-0.23
Venezuela	-3.20	0.66	-0.10	-1.05	0.35	1.27	0.19

(b) 1991–95 vs. 1986–90

Countries	Actual Change	Projected Change	Transitional Convergence	Cyclical Reversion	Structural Reforms	Stabilization Policies	External Conditions
Argentina	6.90	2.99	0.17	0.73	0.50	1.84	-0.25
Bolivia	1.60	0.95	0.00	-0.16	0.78	1.47	-1.15
Brazil	1.41	-0.76	-0.02	0.36	0.48	-1.24	-0.35
Chile	1.86	0.07	-0.43	0.35	0.90	-0.16	-0.60
Colombia	0.03	0.72	-0.22	-0.52	1.04	0.85	-0.43
Costa Rica	1.30	0.19	-0.17	-0.29	0.86	0.15	-0.37
Dominican Republic	1.58	1.81	-0.05	0.03	0.73	0.44	0.66
Ecuador	1.57	1.31	0.03	0.47	0.54	0.78	-0.51
El Salvador	3.26	1.14	-0.06	0.28	1.34	0.27	-0.68
Haiti	-3.58	-0.30	0.16	-0.25	1.39	-1.05	-0.55
Honduras	0.51	0.46	0.00	0.51	0.43	0.17	-0.66
Jamaica	-3.60	-2.52	-0.35	-1.86	0.84	-0.51	-0.63
Mexico	0.00	-0.17	0.03	0.45	1.02	-1.11	-0.56
Nicaragua	4.26	5.14	0.50	-0.40	2.86	1.42	0.76
Panama	6.19	3.52	0.24	0.70	0.70	2.53	-0.64
Paraguay	-0.20	-0.10	-0.06	-0.05	1.35	-0.30	-1.04
Peru	7.53	4.32	0.35	0.02	0.90	3.75	-0.70
Trinidad and Tobago	3.51	-1.44	0.25	0.24	0.00	-0.09	-1.84
Uruguay	-0.01	-1.23	-0.28	-0.73	0.61	-0.19	-0.64
Venezuela	1.15	-1.61	0.00	-0.04	0.03	-1.20	-0.39

Source: Authors' calculations.

Table II.5 (continued)

(c) 1986–90 vs. 1981–85

Countries	Actual Change	Projected Change	Transitional Convergence	Cyclical Reversion	Structural Reforms	Stabilization Policies	External Conditions
Argentina	2.20	2.86	0.36	2.67	0.35	−1.03	0.52
Bolivia	3.93	2.47	0.35	0.12	0.61	0.52	0.88
Brazil	1.23	1.46	0.09	1.43	−0.36	−0.09	0.40
Chile	5.51	6.12	0.06	0.94	0.88	3.14	1.10
Colombia	2.37	3.20	−0.01	0.81	0.29	1.62	0.48
Costa Rica	4.61	1.87	0.23	1.01	0.01	0.24	0.37
Dominican Republic	0.60	1.76	0.00	0.89	1.00	−0.21	0.09
Ecuador	0.18	2.52	0.05	−0.07	0.37	1.76	0.41
El Salvador	4.26	1.46	0.32	−0.47	0.44	0.06	1.11
Haiti	1.00	3.23	0.25	1.33	0.95	0.15	0.56
Honduras	1.49	1.34	0.13	−0.01	0.20	0.03	1.00
Jamaica	5.49	1.68	0.13	0.10	0.95	0.05	0.45
Mexico	−0.01	3.45	0.03	−0.07	0.40	2.44	0.67
Nicaragua	−3.28	−9.67	0.21	−1.53	−1.32	−5.20	−1.83
Panama	−3.97	−2.87	−0.11	−1.19	−0.11	−1.88	0.42
Paraguay	1.99	3.62	0.11	0.99	0.37	0.94	1.21
Peru	−1.91	−2.17	0.18	0.55	−0.15	−3.50	0.76
Trinidad and Tobago	−3.38	2.92	−0.04	−0.22	1.45	0.66	1.08
Uruguay	7.66	7.70	0.40	2.24	0.45	3.82	0.78
Venezuela	3.45	0.87	0.31	0.45	0.98	−0.61	−0.26

(d) 1981–85 vs. 1976–80

Countries	Actual Change	Projected Change	Transitional Convergence	Cyclical Reversion	Structural Reforms	Stabilization Policies	External Conditions
Argentina	−5.34	−3.50	−0.11	−1.47	0.09	−0.17	−1.85
Bolivia	−4.04	−3.40	−0.01	−0.07	0.05	−1.80	−1.57
Brazil	−5.14	−3.57	−0.36	−1.79	0.51	−0.51	−1.42
Chile	−6.17	−5.88	−0.48	−3.40	1.23	−1.14	−2.08
Colombia	−2.87	−5.02	−0.26	−0.69	−0.10	−2.06	−1.92
Costa Rica	−4.76	−3.20	−0.19	−1.33	0.00	0.01	−1.70
Dominican Republic	−2.34	−2.17	−0.21	−0.29	−0.09	−0.15	−1.44
Ecuador	−4.02	−4.56	−0.30	−0.59	0.46	−1.74	−2.38
El Salvador	−1.43	−2.54	0.19	−0.51	−0.05	−0.04	−2.12
Haiti	−6.67	–	−0.34	−2.39	–	0.53	−1.74
Honduras	−5.03	−3.00	−0.31	−1.60	0.83	0.15	−2.06
Jamaica	2.91	0.96	0.39	1.16	0.43	0.06	−1.09
Mexico	−4.48	−4.67	−0.37	−0.58	0.68	−2.05	−2.36
Nicaragua	4.96	0.82	0.65	−0.47	−0.69	1.30	0.03
Panama	0.23	–	−0.09	0.54	−0.31	−0.11	–
Paraguay	−8.64	−4.63	−0.65	−1.83	0.39	−0.24	−2.30
Peru	−1.63	−3.01	0.04	0.49	0.55	−1.69	−2.40
Trinidad and Tobago	−6.21	−4.25	−0.59	−1.16	0.41	−0.55	−2.37
Uruguay	−8.35	−5.85	−0.34	−1.18	0.65	−3.50	−1.48
Venezuela	−2.50	−2.84	0.09	−0.41	−0.68	0.04	−1.89

Source: Authors' calculations.

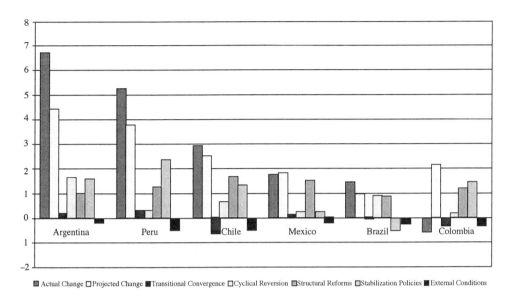

■ Actual Change □ Projected Change ■ Transitional Convergence □ Cyclical Reversion ▨ Structural Reforms □ Stabilization Policies ■ External Conditions

Source: Authors' calculations.

Figure II.1 Explaining Changes in Growth between the 1980s–1990s (Selected Latin American Countries)

1980s. For 15 of them, the contribution from stabilization policies was also positive. In the case of the star reformer, Peru, the estimated growth impact of structural and stabilization reforms reached about 3.75 percentage points. For the rest, however, the gains were more modest. In fact for most reforming countries (Argentina, Bolivia, Chile, Colombia, El Salvador, Nicaragua, Panama, and Uruguay), the estimated growth contribution from improvements in structural and stabilization policies ranged between 2.5 and 3 percentage points. This gain in growth is considerable but not as large as it was initially expected. At the beginning of the 1990s, many reform advocates envisaged that the market-oriented reforms would generate growth rates in Latin America and the Caribbean comparable to those of the East Asian tigers. These expectations proved to be overly optimistic and may have laid the ground for subsequent complaints against the reforms.

Cyclical recovery is also important to explain the higher growth of the 1990s *vis-à-vis* the 1980s. By the end of the 1980s most countries were experiencing a deep recession, the recovery from which led them to higher growth in the 1990s. This is the case for 15 out of 20 countries in LAC. In the case of Argentina, the contribution from cyclical recovery explains more than 25% of the large increase in its growth rate in the 1990s. For Brazil, cyclical recovery was also a strong force for growth in the 1990s, explaining more than 50% of the growth acceleration. The long-run counterpart of cyclical reversion, transitional convergence, also led to higher growth in the 1990s than 1980s for about half of the countries. Even when the convergence effect was negative, its size was rather small. As explained above, the usual effect of transitional convergence is to produce lower growth rates over time. The effect is opposite in many LAC countries because trend output (and not only cyclical output) fell during the 1980s. The only exception was Chile, for which the 1980s was not a 'lost decade'.

External conditions played against growth in the 1990s *vis-à-vis* the 1980s for all countries in LAC, except one (the Dominican Republic, who had strong positive terms-of-trade shocks at the beginning of the 1990s). In most cases, however, the negative effect did not surpass half a percentage point of the growth rate.

Has Latin America and the Caribbean's growth performance in the aftermath of the reform process been disappointing? In general no, but there are exceptions and some worrisome trends. Sixteen out of 20 countries in LAC grew more in the 1990s than in the previous decade. In some cases the growth improvement was quite remarkable – it surpassed four percentage points in Argentina, El Salvador, Nicaragua, and Peru. Moreover, for 80% of the LAC countries, the actual growth improvement between the 1980s and 1990s was virtually equal or greater than the projected change in the growth rate according to the regression analysis. This leads to the conclusion that for the majority of countries in LAC, the realized growth rate in the aftermath of the market-oriented reforms has not been disappointing: Controlling for non-policy factors, countries that reformed their economies the most experienced a correspondingly larger growth improvement in the 1990s.

There are, however, some countries whose actual growth change from the 1980s to the 1990s was significantly below what could be projected. The clearest cases are Colombia and Haiti, whose actual decline in growth rates contrasted sharply with the projected improvement: for them, the difference between actual and projected rates exceeded three percentage points. It is doubtful, however, whether these disappointing cases can be used as evidence of policy reform failure. It is more likely that the inability to explain Colombia and Haiti's growth deterioration resides on our empirical model's failure to consider the negative effects of criminal violence and political instability. The experience of Colombia and Haiti can be regarded as the flipside of what happened in El Salvador and Nicaragua in the 1990s. These Central American countries were able to resolve the civil war and political strife that afflicted them in the 1980s and their growth improvement in the 1990s was well above what our model could project. Falling into civil war impairs a country's growth performance in ways that are not captured by standard determinants, and, conversely, recovering from civil conflict and political trouble is bound to have a beneficial impact on growth.

What was the extent of the growth decline in the 'lost decade' of the 1980s and what factors may explain it? The comparison of the growth experience between the 1980s and 1970s offers some interesting insights to answer this question (see Table II.4, panel B). In 18 out of 20 LAC countries the growth rate fell in the 1980s. The exceptions were Chile and Jamaica. For the majority of countries, there was modest progress in structural policies, but this was vastly overshadowed by the worsening in stabilization policies. For about half of the countries in LAC, the combined effect of changes in structural and stabilization policies was negative, and just in four countries the positive growth effect went beyond one percentage point. The only clear case of policy improvement in the 1980s is Chile, for which the combined contribution of structural and stabilization reforms rendered about three percentage points of growth expansion. For the majority of countries, transitional convergence and cyclical reversion played against growth in the 1980s *vis-à-vis* the 1970s. The cyclical-reversion effect was sizable in some countries, particularly, Argentina, Brazil, Chile, Ecuador, Haiti, and Paraguay. For these countries, the expansion of the late 1970s proved to be a transitory phenomenon.

External factors also played against growth in the 1980s with respect to the 1970s. As observed above, the beginning of the 1980s represented a downward break for world growth conditions, and this shows in the large and negative effect that external conditions had on growth in all LAC countries.

Can the empirical model explain the 'lost decade' of the 1980s and the recovery of the 1990s? Qualitatively, the answer is yes. In all cases where the actual growth rate fell in the 1980s *vis-à-vis* the 1970s, the model projected a decline. Likewise, the model projected a growth increase in those countries where growth actually accelerated in the 1990s. Quantitatively, the extent of the fit between actual and projected changes varies across countries. In some countries the fit is quite acceptable for at least one of the comparisons, for example, Argentina, Bolivia, Brazil, Chile, Honduras, Jamaica, Mexico, Peru, and Uruguay. However, in general the model is unable to explain the full extent of the fall in growth rates from the 1970s to the 1980s and the complete extent of the rise from the 1980s to the 1990s. We can conjecture that this may be due to the following two factors, or a combination of both. The first is that for countries in LAC, the initial output gap may have a larger effect on subsequent growth than what is the case for the average country in the sample. This possibility is consistent with the relatively high volatility of cyclical output exhibited by countries in LAC (see section I.2). In fact if we double the size of the output gap coefficient – thus doubling the size of the cyclical reversion effect – the fit between actual and projected changes in growth rates between the 1970s, 1980s, and 1990s improves quite remarkably. The second possibility is that external conditions may impact on countries in LAC differently than on other countries in the world. If we consider that international conditions were less favorable for growth in LAC than in other regions during the 1980s – possibly because the debt crisis and consequent drainage of international capital flows hurt LAC disproportionately–, then the model can explain more closely the growth decline from the 1970s to the 1980s and the increase from the 1980s to the 1970s.

The questions on the sources of growth and the role of policy reform can also be addressed from comparisons between consecutive five-year periods (see Table II.5). The comparison between 1991–95 and 1986–90 resembles that between the 1990s and 1980s, that is, during and before the reforms. The contributions from all categories of growth determinants are qualitatively alike those in the comparison between the 1980s and 1990s. Also similarly, in 80% of LAC countries, the actual change in the growth rate was greater than or within half a percentage point from the projected change. However, in most reforming countries – most notably Argentina, Panama, and Peru – actual improvements in growth rates between the early 1990s and late 1980s far surpassed our projections. Thus, from the perspective of the mid-1990s, the growth payoff from reform appeared to be well beyond projections. As discussed below, the growth behavior of the second-half of the 1990s showed, however, that part of the growth gains were only temporary in nature.

The comparison between the first and second halves of the 1990s show a rather worrisome trend. The growth rate declined in the latter part of the 1990s in 14 out of the 20 countries in LAC. In 11 of those, the model correctly projected a decline in growth rates. However, in almost all cases of growth slowdowns, the actual decline far exceeded the projected one. In the comparisons between five-year periods, our model's inability to account for the *extent*, though not the direction, of changes in growth is evident, maybe more so than in the comparisons between decades. As we indicated above, this shortcoming of the model may be due to the differential response of LAC countries to cyclical effects and external conditions, *vis-à-vis* other countries. An optimistic implication from this possibility is that a large portion of the recent growth decline should be viewed as a business-cycle phenomenon and not as a permanent change.

III.   Growth in the Future

What can be realistically expected for economic growth in Latin America and the Caribbean in the next decade? And, if Latin America and the Caribbean make significant progress in economic reforms, what is the region's growth potential? A proper answer to these questions calls for a comprehensive, multifaceted approach. In this section, we address the issue of LAC's future growth from the perspective of cross-national empirical results. That is, we use the estimates obtained in our cross-country, panel regressions to forecast economic growth for the majority of countries in Latin America and the Caribbean for the following decade. To do so, we work under alternative assumptions for the behavior of the variables that drive growth.

To answer the question concerning realistic growth expectations, we project growth under the assumption that the explanatory variables continue their recent past trends into the next decade. To address the issue regarding the region's growth potential under a scenario of sharp reform, we consider the possibility that the policy determinants of growth in each country move to the top 25% of the LAC region and the world.

1.   Future Growth under Realistic Expectations

Forecasting any economic variable is a difficult and ungrateful task. This is particularly so in the case of economic growth because of its dependence on a host of factors difficult to control and predict. With this warning, we proceed with the forecasting exercise based on the estimated cross-country model presented in the previous section. We assume that the estimated quantitative relationship between the growth rate of GDP per capita and its proposed determinants is correct and stable across countries and over time. We then use the corresponding estimated coefficients to calculate the growth effects of future changes in the model's explanatory variables. Therefore, the quality of the forecasting exercise depends on three factors: first, the correct specification of the regression model; second, the accuracy and future stability of the estimated regression coefficients; and third, the prediction precision for all explanatory variables.

Forecasting Period. The forecasting period corresponds to the first decade of the 21st century, specifically the years 2000–10. That is, the projection period starts immediately after the regression period, examined in the previous section, ends (1999). Since we complete this report at the beginning of 2004, we have the advantage of knowing the major characteristics and trends on economic growth in LAC at the beginning of the forecasting period.

Projections for Growth Determinants. In practical terms, we need two ingredients to generate a growth forecast. The first are the estimated regression coefficients, which we take from the previous sections. The second are projections for the future behavior of the proposed growth determinants. Given that our intention is to provide 'realistic' forecasts, we use recent trends in each variable to project their behavior into the next decade. In practice this means that for the majority of variables, we use univariate regression models to formulate the predictions. In these models, the explanatory variables consist of linear, logarithmic, and/or quadratic trends, as well as autoregressive terms. Table III. 1 describes the methods to generate the prediction for each explanatory variable in the growth model.

We now comment on the predictions for variables that are treated in a somewhat different way. First, to account for transitional convergence, we use the actual level of GDP per capita at the start of the period (2000) and a model-consistent forecast for GDP per capita at the middle of the period (2005). We do this for consistency with the within-sample decade projections presented in the previous section. Second, for systemic banking crises, we use a panel data model to estimate the probability of crisis based on an index of real exchange rate overvaluation and the previous occurrence of crisis. For the first years of the forecasting period (2000–2003), we update the series on systemic banking crises using the criteria in Caprio and Klingebiel (1999). In general, we estimate low probabilities of new banking crises in countries that did not have one in the 1990s or early 2000s, and for those that did we estimate a gradually decreasing probability of reoccurrence. This is consistent with the belief that Latin American and Caribbean countries can learn how to successfully minimize the risk of banking crises in the future (hopefully, this assumption does not mean a departure from the 'realistic' scenario). Third, for inflation, the output gap, and cyclical volatility, we use the projections supplied by Consensus Economics Inc. (2002) and the World Economic Outlook (2002) for the initial years of the forecasting period, along with our own projections. Finally, regarding world growth conditions that determine the period shift (or period dummy), we assume that they will remain approximately the same in the next decade as in the 1990s. This may be a controversial assumption given that world growth conditions have differed notably between decades in the past. We base this assumption on the fact that the declining trend in world growth rates observed since the beginning of the 1980s appears to be tapering off over time. Our assumption is on the conservative side, considering that the World Bank's Global *Economic Prospects* (2002) actually predict an increase in world per capita income growth from 1.2% in 1991–2000 to 1.8% in 2001–10, and in industrial countries from 1.8% to 2.2%. We should note, however, that if world growth conditions shifted in the next decade, the region's growth performance would be considerably affected.

Forecasts for the Average Country in Latin America and the Caribbean. The forecasting results are presented in Table III.2. The average LAC country in the sample grew by 1.44% in terms of output per capita during the 1990s. According to our projections the average increase in the period 2000–10 would be about 0.56 percentage point, rendering a projected average growth rate of about 2% for the next decade. The region's projected average is not the result of outlying observations, as evidenced by the fact that the mean and median projections are quite similar.

The projected increase in growth would occur despite the negative growth effects of transitional convergence and cyclical reversion, which jointly would produce a decrease in the growth rate of per capita GDP by about 0.4 percentage points. These negative effects are explained by the fact that for the average (and typical) country in LAC, both trend and cyclical output were higher at the end of the 1990s than at the beginning of the same decade.

Table III.1   Procedures to Compute Projections for the 'Continuing Trend' Scenario

Variable	Procedure
Education	Projected for 2001–2010 using OLS regression models incorporating (linear or quadratic) trends and a convergence effect. The inclusion criterion was (i) to increase the fit of equation and (ii) to generate plausible values for the projected variable.
Financial Depth	Projected for 2001–2010 using OLS regression models incorporating (linear or quadratic) trends, a convergence effect, and ARMA terms. The inclusion criterion was (i) to increase the fit of equation and (ii) to generate plausible values for the projected variable.
Trade Openness	Projected for 2001–2010 using OLS regression models incorporating (linear or quadratic) trends, a convergence effect, and ARMA terms. The inclusion criterion was (i) to increase the fit of equation and (ii) to generate plausible values for the projected variable.
Inflation	For countries with inflation targets, central bank targets were used as the projections for the 2006–2010, private forecasts from *Consensus Forecasts* or the 2004–2005 period, and actual values for the 2000–2003 period. Projected for 2006–2010 (2005–2010) for countries with available *Consensus Forecasts* or IMF forecasts for 2004–2005 (2004) using OLS regression models incorporating (linear or quadratic) trends, a convergence term to annual inflation of 3%, and ARMA terms. The inclusion criterion was (i) to increase the fit of equation and (ii) to generate plausible values for the projected variable.
Government Burden	Projected for 2000–2010 using OLS regression models incorporating (linear or quadratic) trends and ARMA terms. The inclusion criterion was (i) to increase the fit of equation and (ii) to generate plausible values for the projected variable.
Public Infrastructure	Projected for 2003–2010 using OLS regression models incorporating (linear or quadratic) trends, a convergence effect, and ARMA terms. The inclusion criterion was (i) to increase the fit of equation and (ii) to generate plausible values for the projected variable.
Initial Per Capita GDP	Ratio of total GDP to total population in 2000 from the *World Development Indicators*. For 2005, projected value using the estimated growth rate during 2001–2005 and the initial per capita GDP in 2000. Estimated growth rates come from the projections of growth determinants for 2001–2005 and the panel data models previously presented.
Initial Output Gap and Cyclical Volatility	Initial output gap computed using the Baxter-King filter. Cyclical volatility computed from actual values and forecasts of output gap estimates for 2001–2005. Output gap for the 2003–2005 period projected using *Consensus Forecasts* or IMF forecasts for GDP growth and applying the Baxter-King filter to those forecasts. For 2006–2010 projected using a panel data estimation considering the first lag of the variable and fixed effects for each country.
Real Exchange Rate Overvaluation	Projected for 2000–2010 using OLS regression models incorporating (linear or quadratic) trends, the lagged difference between the index and the equilibrium level, and ARMA terms. The inclusion criterion was (i) to increase the fit of equation and (ii) to generate plausible values for the projected variable.
Systemic Banking Crises	Computed for 2000–2003 using the criterion defined in Caprio and Klingebiel (1999), and Kaminsky and Reinhart (1998). For 2004–2010 projected using a panel data model including the level of real exchange rate overvaluation and lagged presence of crisis as explanatory variables. The inclusion criterion was (i) to increase the fit of equation and (ii) to generate plausible values for the projected variable.
Terms of Trade Shocks	Computed using the projected of the level of terms of trade for 2000–2010 using OLS regression models incorporating ARMA terms. The inclusion criterion was (i) to increase the fit of equation and (ii) to generate plausible values for the projected variable.

Table III.2 Growth Forecasts under a 'Continuous Trend' Scenario

Countries	Growth Rate 1991–99	Projected Change 2000–10	Projected Growth Rate 2000–10	Transitional Convergence: Initial GDP per capita	Cyclical Recovery: Initial Output Gap	Structural Policies: Education	Financial Depth	Trade Openness	Government Burden	Public Infrastructure	Stabilization Policies: Inflation	Cyclical Volatility	Real Exchange Rate Overvaluation	Systemic Banking Crises	External Conditions: Terms of Trade Shocks	Period Shift
Argentina	3.72%	-2.29%	1.52%	-0.42%	-1.40%	0.18%	-0.10%	0.14%	0.20%	0.20%	-0.03%	-0.17%	0.38%	-0.97%	-0.20%	0.00%
Bolivia	1.53%	0.05%	1.58%	-0.28%	0.19%	0.19%	0.20%	-0.09%	0.05%	0.30%	-0.01%	-0.06%	-0.13%	-0.55%	0.22%	0.00%
Brazil	1.07%	2.65%	3.72%	-0.33%	-0.23%	0.39%	0.09%	0.29%	-0.08%	0.32%	0.31%	0.23%	0.30%	1.51%	-0.14%	0.00%
Chile	5.00%	-1.00%	4.00%	-0.78%	-0.12%	0.11%	0.06%	0.20%	-0.24%	0.40%	0.02%	-0.24%	-0.13%	-0.06%	-0.22%	0.00%
Colombia	0.72%	1.01%	1.73%	-0.14%	0.29%	0.01%	-0.05%	0.12%	0.21%	0.33%	0.05%	0.36%	-0.05%	-0.19%	0.08%	0.00%
Costa Rica	3.48%	0.57%	4.05%	-0.56%	-0.09%	0.29%	0.30%	0.31%	-0.14%	0.24%	0.03%	0.34%	-0.15%	0.00%	0.00%	0.00%
Dominican Republic	3.75%	-3.20%	0.54%	-0.53%	-0.59%	0.27%	0.22%	-0.01%	-1.19%	0.36%	-0.04%	0.09%	-0.06%	-1.73%	0.03%	0.00%
Ecuador	-0.43%	2.56%	2.13%	0.00%	0.44%	0.61%	0.22%	-0.01%	-0.29%	0.45%	0.10%	0.59%	0.30%	0.01%	0.15%	0.00%
El Salvador	2.67%	0.64%	3.31%	-0.39%	0.02%	0.13%	0.02%	0.55%	-0.20%	0.44%	0.01%	0.24%	-0.19%	0.00%	-0.03%	0.00%
Haiti	-2.97%	2.32%	-0.59%	-0.09%	0.11%	0.47%	0.06%	-0.15%	-0.26%	0.29%	-0.02%	0.91%	0.26%	-0.01%	0.39%	0.00%
Honduras	0.12%	0.82%	0.93%	-0.09%	0.02%	0.01%	0.19%	0.32%	-0.29%	0.28%	0.05%	0.48%	-0.19%	0.00%	0.08%	0.00%
Jamaica	-0.62%	2.73%	2.11%	0.01%	0.37%	0.24%	0.05%	0.05%	-0.23%	0.27%	0.05%	0.15%	-0.16%	1.74%	0.20%	0.00%
Mexico	1.42%	1.63%	3.05%	-0.34%	-0.25%	0.22%	-0.29%	0.60%	-0.12%	0.25%	0.05%	0.53%	-0.04%	1.11%	-0.10%	0.00%
Nicaragua	0.33%	2.52%	2.84%	-0.25%	-0.14%	0.25%	0.02%	0.42%	-0.07%	0.41%	0.46%	0.38%	-0.02%	1.25%	-0.19%	0.00%
Panama	2.80%	-0.46%	2.33%	-0.43%	-0.38%	-0.04%	0.29%	0.02%	-0.14%	0.14%	0.00%	0.12%	-0.04%	0.00%	0.00%	0.00%
Paraguay	-0.60%	1.40%	0.80%	0.02%	0.39%	0.12%	-0.08%	-0.42%	-0.17%	0.22%	-0.01%	0.10%	0.02%	1.24%	-0.04%	0.00%
Peru	2.32%	-0.11%	2.21%	-0.36%	-0.61%	0.12%	0.15%	0.05%	-0.19%	0.10%	0.06%	0.51%	0.08%	-0.27%	0.26%	0.00%
Trinidad and Tobago	2.08%	0.98%	3.06%	0.25%	-0.23%	0.01%	0.02%	0.23%	-0.08%	0.22%	0.00%	0.34%	-0.01%	0.00%	0.23%	0.00%
Uruguay	2.70%	-1.24%	1.46%	-0.33%	-0.31%	0.00%	0.49%	0.28%	-0.12%	0.20%	0.05%	-0.20%	0.20%	-1.35%	-0.13%	0.00%
Venezuela, RB	-0.30%	-0.52%	-0.82%	0.01%	-0.59%	0.54%	-0.28%	0.09%	-0.17%	0.04%	0.02%	-0.36%	-0.02%	0.30%	-0.12%	0.00%
Average	**1.44%**	**0.56%**	**2.00%**	**-0.23%**	**-0.15%**	**0.21%**	**0.08%**	**0.15%**	**-0.18%**	**0.27%**	**0.06%**	**0.22%**	**0.02%**	**0.10%**	**0.02%**	**0.00%**
Median	**1.48%**	**0.73%**	**2.12%**	**-0.30%**	**-0.13%**	**0.19%**	**0.06%**	**0.13%**	**-0.15%**	**0.27%**	**0.02%**	**0.24%**	**-0.03%**	**0.00%**	**0.00%**	**0.00%**

Notes: Forecasts for changes in determinants of growth are obtained using univariate regressions for most variables. Explanatory variables include linear/quadratic trends, and autoregressive terms. Projections for 2004–2005 of Consensus Forecasts or World Economic Outlook complement output-gap and inflation.

Source: Authors' calculations.

Both structural and stabilization policies would play a role in supporting an increase in growth in the next ten years. Developments in education and public infrastructure would contribute 0.21 and 0.27 percentage points, respectively, to the growth rate of per capita GDP. Increased trade openness would contribute 0.15 percentage points to the growth rate, and financial deepening about half that amount. Reflecting the trend towards larger governments in LAC, the only structural factor producing a decline in the growth rate would be the government burden on the economy, which would account to a reduction of 0.18 percentage points.

Regarding stabilization policies, the further reduction of inflation and real exchange rate overvaluation would jointly contribute a little below 0.1 percentage points to the growth rate, while lower cyclical volatility would increase growth by 0.22 percentage points. Avoiding banking crises has a lot of potential for growth improvement, and a few countries benefit from this by resolving the banking crises experienced in the 1990s (e.g., Brazil, Jamaica, and Mexico). However, for the average country this will not have a large effect (0.1) as many countries in the region continue or even start to suffer from systemic banking crises at the beginning of the decade (e.g., Argentina, Dominican Republic, and Uruguay).

External conditions are particularly difficult to predict. Our projections take a safe route and give external conditions a minor role for growth in the next decade. The average country in the region would receive a mild growth boost from the projected favorable improvement in the terms of trade (about 0.04 percentage points). Given the assumption that world growth conditions would remain the same in the next decade as they were during the 1990s, their contribution to growth acceleration in LAC is nil.

Country Forecasts. Individual country forecasts reveal some interesting features and departures from the region's average. Chile would continue to be among the region leaders although suffering a decrease of 1 percentage point with respect to the 1990s (with 4% of annual growth of GDP per capita). In Chile, further improvements in structural policies (particularly in trade and public infrastructure) are not enough to counter the negative growth impact of transitional convergence and larger macroeconomic volatility. Other regional leaders would be Costa Rica (improving slightly its 1990s performance) and Brazil (increasing its growth rate by over 2.5 percentage points). El Salvador, Mexico, and Trinidad and Tobago would also grow at over 3% during the next decade.

Among the large countries, Brazil would have the highest growth increase, due to a strong expansion in education, trade openness, and public infrastructure, as well as the solution of its inflationary process and balance of payments and banking crises. Also among the large countries, Argentina would suffer the largest drop in economic growth; the reason would be that the positive impact of improvements in education, trade openness, and public infrastructure would be far overshadowed by a combination of deterioration in stabilization policies (particularly regarding systemic banking crisis) and the negative growth effects corresponding to transitional convergence and, especially, the adjustment from the temporary upturn of the 1990s.

According to the projections, the lowest growth rates in the region during the next decade would belong to Venezuela, Haiti, Dominican Republic, and Paraguay. For Haiti, however, the projected growth rate of −0.6% would represent a large improvement with respect to its experience in the 1990s, as educational policies and diminished cyclical volatility begin to render beneficial effects. Venezuela's stagnation would occur in spite of strong gains in education given the concurrent worsening of financial depth and cyclical volatility.

2. Future Growth under Sharp Reform

We now address the question of what the growth potential is for countries in Latin America and the Caribbean. In the previous sub-section, we adopted a 'realistic' scenario. In this one, we consider the optimistic scenario of quick and sharp progress in the conditions that drive growth. In practical terms, we consider the possibility that the policy determinants of growth in each country move to the top 25% of their corresponding distribution in LAC and the world. We also assume that these improvements occur at current levels of per capita income. This is clearly an unrealistic assumption, particularly because improvements in education, financial depth, and public infrastructure normally accompany income expansion. However, we perform this exercise because it may be useful in establishing some upper bounds for what can be expected for growth in the region under a strong process of development and economic reforms.

Table III.3 presents the potential growth improvement if each policy explanatory variable jumped to the 75th percentile of its distribution in LAC. Table III.4 presents more ambitious projections, as each explanatory variable is made to jump to the 75th percentile of the corresponding world distribution. In every case, the potential growth contribution from a given variable is larger the more backward the country is with respect to the variable's region and world distribution. A country's overall potential improvement would be given by the sum of contributions from each growth determinant. Thus, countries that have already achieved substantial progress in the policy determinants of growth – such as Chile and to a lower extent Mexico – have less to gain from policy reform than relatively backward countries – such as Haiti and Bolivia.

For the average country in LAC, advancing its structural and stabilization policies to the top 25% of the region would represent a gain of nearly 2.5 percentage points in output growth per capita for the next decade with respect to the 1990s, even after discounting the negative impact of transitional convergence and cyclical reversion. Improvements in public infrastructure and education, as well as the avoidance of banking crises would render the largest contribution, each by around 0.5 percentage points to economic growth. Reduction in the burden of government, increased financial depth, expansion of trade openness, and reduction of cyclical volatility would each represent a growth improvement of roughly 0.25 percentage points. Lagging behind with a combined growth contribution of 0.1 percentage points are reductions in inflation and real exchange rate overvaluation.

As expected, advancing to the top 25% of the world would bring about a larger growth improvement, which for the average LAC country would amount to almost 4 percentage points (an additional gain of 1.5 p.p.). The potential growth contribution from all variables (except government burden) increases, and, more interestingly, their relative importance changes somewhat with respect to the previous exercise. Improvements in education and public infrastructure would be the most important sources of growth, providing close to 1 percentage point each. Financial deepening, larger trade openness, and absence of banking crises would provide contributions of somewhat over 0.5 percentage points. Following in the list of potential growth sources would be, in order of importance, reduction in cyclical volatility, government burden, inflation, and real exchange rate overvaluation.

It is interesting to note the contrast regarding financial depth and government burden between the two exercises. The region as a whole is relatively backward in financial depth

Table III.3   Growth Forecasts under a 'Sharp Progress' Scenario – to Top 25% of Latin America and the Caribbean

Countries	Growth Rate 1991–1999	Potential Change	Transitional Convergence — Initial GDP Capita	Cyclical Recovery — Initial Output Gap	Structural Policies — Education	Financial Depth	Trade Openness	Government Burden	Public Infrastructure	Stabilization Policies — Inflation	Cyclical Volatility	Real Exchange Rate	Systemic Banking Crises	External Conditions — Terms of Trade Shocks	Period Shift
Argentina	3.72%	0.20%	-0.53%	-1.40%	0.00%	0.38%	0.69%	0.23%	0.00%	0.00%	0.46%	0.29%	0.29%	-0.20%	0.00%
Bolivia	1.53%	3.98%	-0.45%	0.19%	0.52%	0.00%	0.20%	0.56%	0.72%	0.00%	0.00%	-0.01%	2.02%	0.22%	0.00%
Brazil	1.07%	3.64%	-0.37%	-0.23%	0.31%	0.08%	0.62%	1.03%	0.11%	0.30%	0.11%	0.09%	1.73%	-0.14%	0.00%
Chile	5.00%	-0.73%	-0.77%	-0.12%	0.00%	0.00%	0.01%	0.14%	0.00%	0.00%	0.20%	0.02%	0.00%	-0.22%	0.00%
Colombia	0.72%	1.67%	-0.18%	0.29%	0.11%	0.06%	0.37%	0.83%	0.00%	0.04%	0.18%	-0.11%	0.00%	0.08%	0.00%
Costa Rica	3.48%	1.46%	-0.62%	-0.09%	0.64%	0.59%	0.02%	0.51%	0.00%	0.03%	0.26%	0.10%	0.00%	0.00%	0.00%
Dominican Republic	3.75%	-0.16%	-0.66%	-0.59%	0.49%	0.25%	0.18%	0.00%	0.00%	0.00%	0.13%	0.02%	0.00%	0.03%	0.00%
Ecuador	-0.43%	4.39%	-0.15%	0.44%	0.45%	0.13%	0.21%	0.12%	1.03%	0.11%	0.43%	0.03%	1.45%	0.15%	0.00%
El Salvador	2.67%	1.86%	-0.47%	0.02%	1.08%	0.02%	0.44%	0.00%	0.84%	0.00%	0.00%	-0.04%	0.00%	-0.03%	0.00%
Haiti	-2.91%	6.02%	0.10%	0.11%	1.67%	0.57%	0.73%	0.00%	1.77%	0.04%	0.69%	-0.07%	0.00%	0.39%	0.00%
Honduras	0.12%	3.06%	-0.19%	0.02%	1.32%	0.12%	0.00%	0.17%	1.35%	0.03%	0.21%	-0.06%	0.00%	0.08%	0.00%
Jamaica	-0.62%	5.67%	-0.11%	0.37%	0.00%	0.19%	0.00%	0.53%	2.16%	0.05%	0.00%	0.26%	2.02%	0.20%	0.00%
Mexico	1.42%	2.23%	-0.38%	-0.25%	0.17%	0.27%	0.00%	0.15%	0.43%	0.03%	0.36%	0.09%	1.45%	-0.10%	0.00%
Nicaragua	0.33%	5.06%	-0.35%	-0.14%	0.60%	0.00%	0.00%	0.97%	1.84%	0.46%	0.26%	-0.13%	1.73%	-0.19%	0.00%
Panama	2.80%	0.31%	-0.44%	-0.38%	0.08%	0.00%	0.14%	0.66%	0.20%	0.00%	0.00%	0.05%	0.00%	0.00%	0.00%
Paraguay	-0.60%	3.46%	-0.05%	0.39%	0.81%	0.26%	0.00%	0.00%	0.74%	0.01%	0.00%	-0.12%	1.45%	-0.04%	0.00%
Peru	2.32%	0.68%	-0.41%	-0.61%	0.01%	0.46%	0.58%	0.01%	0.18%	0.06%	0.00%	0.14%	0.00%	0.26%	0.00%
Trinidad and Tobago	2.08%	2.72%	0.14%	-0.23%	0.00%	0.00%	0.81%	0.35%	1.44%	0.00%	0.10%	-0.12%	0.00%	0.23%	0.00%
Uruguay	2.70%	1.13%	-0.44%	-0.31%	0.00%	0.11%	0.68%	0.41%	0.33%	0.08%	0.29%	0.11%	0.00%	-0.13%	0.00%
Venezuela, RB	-0.30%	2.32%	-0.08%	-0.59%	0.83%	0.64%	0.41%	0.00%	0.00%	0.11%	0.42%	0.12%	0.58%	-0.12%	0.00%
Average	**1.44%**	**2.45%**	**-0.32%**	**-0.15%**	**0.46%**	**0.21%**	**0.31%**	**0.33%**	**0.66%**	**0.07%**	**0.21%**	**0.03%**	**0.64%**	**0.02%**	**0.00%**
Median	**1.48%**	**2.28%**	**-0.37%**	**-0.13%**	**0.38%**	**0.12%**	**0.21%**	**0.20%**	**0.38%**	**0.03%**	**0.19%**	**0.03%**	**0.00%**	**0.00%**	**0.00%**

Notes: The total potential change corresponds to the sum of the effects of each variable if it were to advance to the 75th percentile of Latin America and the Caribbean.

Source: Authors' calculations.

Table III.4 Growth Forecasts under a 'Sharp Progress' Scenario – to Top 25% of the World

Countries	Growth Rate 1991–1999	Potential Change	Transitional Convergence — Initial GDP Capita	Cyclical Recovery — Initial Output Gap	Structural Policies — Education	Financial Depth	Trade Openness	Government Burden	Public Infrastructure	Stabilization Policies — Inflation	Cyclical Volatility	Real Exchange Rate	Systemic Banking Crises	External Conditions — Terms of Trade Shocks	Period Shift
Argentina	3.72%	1.29%	-0.63%	-1.40%	0.18%	0.77%	0.93%	0.01%	0.39%	0.03%	0.65%	0.29%	0.29%	-0.20%	0.00%
Bolivia	1.53%	5.31%	-0.50%	0.19%	0.90%	0.18%	0.45%	0.34%	1.32%	0.03%	0.16%	0.00%	2.02%	0.22%	0.00%
Brazil	1.07%	5.18%	-0.43%	-0.23%	0.69%	0.47%	0.86%	0.80%	0.71%	0.33%	0.29%	0.09%	1.73%	-0.14%	0.00%
Chile	5.00%	0.36%	-0.82%	-0.12%	0.36%	0.00%	0.26%	0.00%	0.44%	0.03%	0.39%	0.02%	0.00%	-0.22%	0.00%
Colombia	0.72%	3.32%	-0.25%	0.29%	0.50%	0.45%	0.61%	0.60%	0.60%	0.07%	0.36%	0.00%	0.00%	0.08%	0.00%
Costa Rica	3.48%	2.80%	-0.67%	-0.09%	1.03%	0.98%	0.26%	0.28%	0.40%	0.05%	0.45%	0.10%	0.00%	0.00%	0.00%
Dominican Republic	3.75%	1.57%	-0.75%	-0.59%	0.88%	0.64%	0.42%	0.00%	0.59%	0.02%	0.31%	0.02%	0.00%	0.03%	0.00%
Ecuador	-0.43%	6.03%	-0.22%	0.44%	0.83%	0.52%	0.45%	0.00%	1.63%	0.14%	0.62%	0.03%	1.45%	0.15%	0.00%
El Salvador	2.67%	3.65%	-0.53%	0.02%	1.46%	0.41%	0.69%	0.00%	1.44%	0.02%	0.17%	0.00%	0.00%	-0.03%	0.00%
Haiti	-2.91%	7.84%	0.03%	0.11%	2.05%	0.96%	0.98%	0.00%	2.37%	0.07%	0.88%	0.00%	0.00%	0.39%	0.00%
Honduras	0.12%	4.54%	-0.24%	0.02%	1.71%	0.51%	0.07%	0.00%	1.95%	0.06%	0.40%	0.00%	0.00%	0.08%	0.00%
Jamaica	-0.62%	7.04%	-0.17%	0.37%	0.35%	0.58%	0.20%	0.30%	2.76%	0.08%	0.10%	0.26%	2.02%	0.20%	0.00%
Mexico	1.42%	3.61%	-0.43%	-0.25%	0.56%	0.66%	0.00%	0.00%	1.04%	0.06%	0.54%	0.09%	1.45%	-0.10%	0.00%
Nicaragua	0.33%	6.45%	-0.40%	-0.14%	0.99%	0.35%	0.00%	0.75%	2.44%	0.48%	0.44%	0.00%	1.73%	-0.19%	0.00%
Panama	2.80%	1.44%	-0.49%	-0.38%	0.46%	0.00%	0.38%	0.43%	0.80%	0.00%	0.17%	0.05%	0.00%	0.00%	0.00%
Paraguay	-0.60%	5.19%	-0.12%	0.39%	1.20%	0.65%	0.09%	0.00%	1.34%	0.04%	0.19%	0.00%	1.45%	-0.04%	0.00%
Peru	2.32%	2.23%	-0.50%	-0.61%	0.39%	0.85%	0.82%	0.00%	0.78%	0.08%	0.00%	0.14%	0.00%	0.26%	0.00%
Trinidad and Tobago	2.08%	3.28%	-0.53%	-0.23%	0.22%	0.07%	1.06%	0.13%	2.04%	0.01%	0.28%	0.00%	0.90%	0.23%	0.00%
Uruguay	2.70%	2.30%	-0.53%	-0.31%	0.03%	0.50%	0.92%	0.19%	0.94%	0.10%	0.47%	0.11%	0.00%	-0.13%	0.00%
Venezuela, RB	-0.30%	4.08%	-0.14%	-0.59%	1.21%	1.03%	0.65%	0.00%	0.60%	0.13%	0.61%	0.12%	0.58%	-0.12%	0.00%
Average	**1.44%**	**3.87%**	**-0.42%**	**-0.15%**	**0.80%**	**0.53%**	**0.50%**	**0.19%**	**1.23%**	**0.09%**	**0.37%**	**0.07%**	**0.64%**	**0.02%**	**0.00%**
Median	**1.48%**	**3.63%**	**-0.46%**	**-0.13%**	**0.76%**	**0.51%**	**0.45%**	**0.00%**	**0.99%**	**0.06%**	**0.37%**	**0.03%**	**0.00%**	**0.00%**	**0.00%**

Notes: The total potential change corresponds to the sum of the effects of each variable if it were to advance to the 75th percentile of the world.

Source: Authors' calculations.

507

and, thus, would gain significantly more if it were to advance according to world standards in this respect. On the other hand, the region is relatively well-advanced regarding government burden and, thus, would be better off progressing according to regional standards in this area.

Finally, we should consider a cautionary note. The above description of potential contributions from sharp reform in various areas usually places stabilization policies – such as the control of inflation, cyclical volatility, and real exchange rate overvaluation – as lagging behind structural policies. This could create the mistaken impression that stabilization policies are not essential for economic growth. As shown in the section II, improvement in stabilization policies account for much of the growth, expansion in the 1990s, and disregarding their importance could bring Latin America and the Caribbean down to the disastrous performance of the 1980s.

IV. Conclusions

The Major Patterns of Growth in the Region. For Latin America and the Caribbean as a whole, the 1960s and 1970s were decades of solid growth rates. This changed in the 1980s, when the growth rate of output per capita fell to negative values and its volatility increased notably. Indeed for most of Latin America, the 1980s represented a 'lost decade', an unfortunate experience shared by many countries in Africa and the Middle East. However, while some of these countries, particularly in Sub-Saharan Africa, continued its downward spiral in the 1990s, Latin America's economic growth became positive again in the 1990s, with truly remarkable turnarounds in Argentina, Costa Rica, El Salvador, Nicaragua, and Peru. Chile was the regional leader in economic growth during the 1980s and remained so through the 1990s. Although during the first half of the 1980s it appeared that Chile would follow the regional downward path, the country found its way to recovery and sustained growth.

Capital Accumulation or Productivity Growth? Solow-style growth-accounting exercises reveal that it is productivity growth and not capital accumulation what lies behind the major shifts in per capita output growth in the last decades in Latin America and the Caribbean. Specifically, the recovery in output growth experienced by the vast majority of countries in the region during the 1990s was driven in most cases by large increases in the growth of total factor productivity. This result suggests what regression analysis later confirms, that is, the growth recovery experienced by most countries in the region during the past decade was largely driven by structural and stabilization reforms that positively affected the economy's overall productivity.

What Factors May Explain the 'Lost Decade' of the 1980s? Cross-country regression analysis can allow the identification of the individual effects of the sources of growth. We can distinguish five major categories of growth determinants: transitional convergence (due to diminishing returns), cyclical reversion (from temporary recessions or booms), structural policies (including those on education, financial depth, trade openness, government burden, and public infrastructure), stabilization policies (including policies to control inflation, cyclical volatility, real exchange rate overvaluation, and banking crises), and external conditions (that is, terms of trade shocks and prevailing growth conditions in the world). Considering these growth determinants, we can attempt to understand the reasons for the fall in growth rates in the 1980s with respect to the 1970s. Generally in the region, there was modest progress in structural policies, which by itself would have encouraged growth. However, this was vastly overshadowed by the deterioration of stabilization policies. For about half of the countries in Latin America and the Caribbean, the combined growth effect of changes in structural and stabilization policies was negative, and just in four countries the positive effect went beyond 1 percentage-point increase in the growth rate. The only clear case of policy improvement in the 1980s is Chile, for which the combined contribution of structural and stabilization reforms rendered about 3 percentage points of growth expansion. Apart from bad policies, the drop in growth rates during the 1980s was also caused by diminishing returns and, specially, cyclical reversion. This negative effect was sizable (up to 2.5 percentage points of the growth rate) in countries such as Argentina and Brazil, where the expansion of the late 1970s proved to be a transitory phenomenon. To make matters worse, external factors played strongly against growth in the 1980s with respect to the 1970s. The beginning of the 1980s represented a downward break for world growth conditions, and this shows in the large and negative effect that external factors had on growth in all LAC countries (from 1 to 2 percentage-point drop in the growth rate).

Has Latin America's Growth Performance in the Aftermath of the Reform Process Been Disappointing? During the last decade, many countries in Latin America – such as Argentina, Bolivia, El Salvador, and Peru – underwent strong market-oriented reforms. These were partly motivated by the belief that the reforms would generate high economic growth. Consequently, the success of the reforms has been judged by the ensuing growth improvement in reforming economies. Our methodology allows us to assess this question as it gauges what growth improvement could have been expected from policy changes and other developments from the 1980s to the 1990s. For all 20 Latin American and Caribbean countries in our sample, the contribution from structural policies to growth was positive in the 1990s with respect to the 1980s. For 15 of them, the contribution from stabilization policies was also positive. For most reforming countries, the estimated growth contribution from improvements in structural and stabilization policies ranged between 2.5 and 3 percentage points. This gain in growth is considerable but not as large as it was initially expected. At the beginning of the 1990s, many reform advocates envisaged that the market-oriented reforms would generate growth rates in Latin America comparable to those of the East Asian tigers. These expectations proved to be overly optimistic and may have laid the ground for subsequent complaints against the reforms.

Cyclical recovery is also important to explain the higher growth of the 1990s *vis-à-vis* the 1980s. By the end of the 1980s most countries were experiencing a deep recession, the recovery from which led them to higher growth in the 1990s. This is the case for 15 out of 20 countries in Latin America. In the cases of Argentina and Brazil, the contribution from cyclical recovery explains more than 25% and 50%, respectively, of their increase in the growth rate in the 1990s. External conditions played against growth in the 1990s *vis-à-vis* the 1980s for almost all countries in Latin America and the Caribbean. In most cases, however, the negative effect from external conditions did not surpass half a percentage point of the growth rate.

Now we can come back to the question as to whether Latin America's post-reform growth has been disappointing. In general, the answer is no. For 80% of the countries in Latin America and the Caribbean, the actual growth improvement between the 1980s and 1990s was virtually equal or greater than the projected change in the growth rate according to regression analysis. Post-reform growth has not been disappointing because, controlling for non-policy factors, countries that reformed their economies the most experienced a correspondingly larger growth improvement in the 1990s.

What Can Be Realistically Expected for Growth in the Future? The average country in Latin America and the Caribbean grew by close to 1.5% in terms of output per capita during the 1990s. If we assume that recent trends in the determinants of growth continue into the next decade, the average increase in the growth rate for the period 2000–10 would be about ½ of a percentage point, rendering a projected average per capita GDP growth rate of about 2% for the next decade. This small projected increase would occur despite the negative effects of transitional convergence and cyclical reversion, which jointly would decrease the growth rate by about ⅓ percentage points. The major forces supporting an increase in growth in the next ten years would be improvements in structural policies. Developments in education and public infrastructure would each contribute around ¼ percentage points to the growth rate of per capita GDP. Increased trade openness would contribute 0.15 percentage points to the growth rate, and financial deepening about half that amount. The only structural policy that would diminish growth is a heavier burden of government consumption, with a negative effect of almost 0.2 percentage points.

For the average country in Latin America and the Caribbean, stabilization policies would also play a role in the next decade mainly through the reduction of macroeconomic volatility, which would render a little over 0.2 percentage points of higher growth. The resolution of the banking crises suffered in the 1990s had the potential of raising growth significantly in many countries in the region. However, the financial crises experienced at the start of the current decade indicate that Latin America has yet to learn the lessons on crisis avoidance. The relatively minor role of other stabilization policies for the average country, such as those on inflation and real exchange rate misalignment, does not imply that they are no longer important. Although at this time only small growth gains can be expected from *further* macro reform in these areas, there are potentially big losses if stabilization reforms are abandoned. Finally, given the difficulty in predicting external conditions, our projections take a conservative route by giving them only a small positive effect in the next decade, thus discounting the possibility of a substantial growth recovery in the world.

Blame Only the Guilty. Growth is a process caused by several factors. It does not only depend on structural and stabilization policies. In assessing whether a country's reforms have been beneficial to economic growth, we need to account for other determinants of growth. This will allow us to put the blame where it belongs in cases of disappointing growth and make the necessary corrections. In some cases poor growth will be due to insufficient structural reforms (e.g., low trade openness), in others to inappropriate stabilization policies (e.g., exchange rate overvaluation), and still in others to negative international conditions (e.g., growth slowdown in industrial countries). It is obvious but still correct to say that identifying the problem is the first step towards the solution.

Chile provides an interesting example of the admonition to blame only the guilty. Chile started its process of structural reforms in the mid-1970s. However, it made two crucial mistakes along the way. The first was related to stabilization policies and consisted of choosing a fixed exchange-rate regime that led to a sharp overvaluation of the peso in the early 1980s. The second one, on structural policies, was to liberalize the financial system without proper banking supervision. This combination proved to be fatal. The ensuing macro adjustment and the related banking crisis produced a sharp fall in output in 1983–84. Fortunately, the authorities resisted the demands to revert the whole program of structural reforms, which could not be jointly blamed for the recession. Separating the good from the bad, the government proceeded to both modify the exchange-rate regime (to a managed float) and institute proper banking regulation. Since then, Chile started to grow quite strongly and became the region's leading performer in the rest of the 1980s and all through the 1990s. Around 1998, the Chilean economy suffered again a downturn (although of much smaller magnitude than in the 1980s). The authorities correctly identified external conditions and some aspects of monetary and exchange-rate policy as the main causes for the downturn. There was never talk of reverting the structural reforms. There was never serious talk of blaming the whole reform program for the recession. Instead, the discussion focused on how to deal with external shocks and how to deepen market reforms. This is why Chile continues to have the best outlook for growth in the region.

References

Alonso-Borrego, C. and Arellano, M. (1996), 'Symmetrically Normalised Instrumental Variable Estimation Using Panel Data', CEMFI Working Paper No. 9612.

Arellano, M. and S. Bond (1991), 'Some Tests of Specification for Panel Data: Montecarlo Evidence and an Application to Employment Equations', *Review of Economic Studies*, **58**(2): 277–97.

Arellano, M. and O. Bover (1995), 'Another Look at the Instrumental-Variable Estimation of Error-Components Models', *Journal of Econometrics*, **68**(1): 29–52.

Barro, R.J. (1990), 'Government Spending in a Simple Model of Endogenous Growth', *Journal of Political Economy*, **98**(5) part II: S103–S125.

Barro, R.J. (1991), 'Economic Growth in a Cross Section of Countries', *Quarterly Journal of Economics*, **56**(2): 407–43.

Barro, R.J. (1999a), 'Determinants of Economic Growth: Implications of the Global Experience for Chile', *Cuadernos de Economía*, **36**(107), 443–78.

Barro, R.J. (1999b), 'Notes on Growth Accounting', *Journal of Economic Growth*, **4**(2): 119–37.

Barro, R.J. (2001b), 'Economic Growth in East Asia Before and After the Financial Crises', National Bureau of Economic Research Working Paper No. W8330.

Barro, R.J. and J.W. Lee (1994), 'Sources of Economic Growth', *Carnegie-Rochester Series on Public Policy*, **40**: 1–57.

Barro, R.J. and X. Sala-i-Martín (1992), 'Public Finance in Models of Economic Growth', *Review of Economic Studies*, **59**(4): 645–61.

Bekaert, G., C. Harvey and C. Lundblad (2001), 'Does Financial Liberalization Spur Growth?' National Bureau of Economic Research Working Paper No. W8245.

Bernanke, B. and R. Gurkaynak (2001), 'Is Growth Exogenous? Taking Mankiw, Romer, and Weil Seriously', National Bureau of Economic Research Working Paper No. W8365.

Blundell, R. and S. Bond (1997), 'Initial Conditions and Moment Restrictions in Dynamic Panel Data Models', University College London Discussion Papers in Economics 97/07, July.

Borensztein, E., J. De Gregorio and J. Whalee (1998), 'How Does Foreign Direct Investment Affect Economic Growth?' *Journal of International Economics*, **45**(1): 115–35.

Burki, S.J. and G.E. Perry (1997), *The Long March: A Reform Agenda for Latin America and the Caribbean in the Next Decade*. Washington, DC: World Bank.

Campbell, J. (1987), 'Does Saving Anticipate Declining Labor Income? An Alternative Test of the Permanent Income Hypothesis', *Econometrica*, **55**: 1249–73.

Canning, D., M. Fay and R. Perotti (1994), *International Differences in Growth Rates: Market Globalization and Economic Areas*, Central Issues in Contemporary Economic Theory and Policy Series: 113–47.

Caprio, G. and D. Klingebiel (1999), *Episodes of Systemic and Borderline Financial Crises*. Washington, DC: World Bank; mimeo.

Carroll, C.D. and D. Weil (1994), 'Saving and Growth: A Reinterpretation', *Carnegie-Rochester Conference Series on Public Policy*, **40**: 133–92.

Caselli, F., G. Esquivel and F. LeFort (1996), 'Reopening the Convergence Debate: A New Look at Cross-Country Growth Empirics', *Journal of Economic Growth*, **1**: 363–89.

Collins, Susan M. and B. Bosworth (1996), 'Economic Growth in East Asia: Accumulation versus Assimilation', *Brooking Papers on Economic Activity*, **2**(135): 91.

Consensus Economics, Inc. (2002), *Latin American Consensus Forecasts*, May.

De Gregorio, J. (1992), 'Economic Growth in Latin America', *Journal of Development Economics*, **39**(1): 59–84.

De Gregorio, J. and C. Bravo-Ortega (2002), *The Relative Richness of the Poor? Natural Resources, Human Capital and Economic Growth*. Central Bank of Chile Working Paper Series No. 139.

Dollar, D. (1992), 'Outward-oriented Developing Economies Really Do Grow More Rapidly: Evidence from 95 LDCs, 1976–1985', *Economic Development and Cultural Change*, **40**: 523–44.

Dollar D. and A. Kraay (2003), 'Institutions, Trade, and Growth', *Journal of Monetary Economics*, **50**(1): 133–62.

Easterly, W. (2001), *Growth Implosions, Debt Explosions, and My Aunt Marilyn: Do Growth Slowdowns Cause Public Debt Crises?* World Bank Policy Research Working Paper No. 2531.

Easterly, W., M. Kremer, L. Pritchett and L. Summers (1993), 'Good Policy or Good Luck? Country Growth Performance and Temporary Shocks', *Journal of Monetary Economics*, **32**(3): 459–83.

Easterly, W. and R. Levine (2001), 'It's Not Factor Accumulation: Stylized Facts and Growth Models', *World Bank Economic Review*, **15**(2): 177–219.

Easterly, W. and R. Levine (2002), *Tropics, Germs, and Crops: How Endowments Influence Economic Development*. Minneapolis, MN: University of Minnesota Press, mimeo.

Easterly, W., N. Loayza and P. Montiel (1997), 'Has Latin America's Post Reform Growth Been Disappointing?' *Journal of International Economics*, **43**: 287–311.

Elias. V. (1992), *Sources of Growth: A Study of Seven Latin American Economies*. San Francisco, CA: ICS Press.

Fatás, A. (2000a), 'Endogenous Growth and Stochastic Trends', *Journal of Monetary Economics*, **45**: 107–28.

Fatás, A. (2000b), 'Do Business Cycles Cast Long Shadows? Short-run Persistence and Economic Growth', *Journal of Economic Growth*, **5**: 147–62.

Fischer, S. (1993), 'The Role of Macroeconomic Factors in Growth', *Journal of Monetary Economics*, **32**(3): 485–511.

Hnatkovska, V. and N. Loayza (2004), *Volatility and Growth*. World Bank Policy Research Working Paper No. 3184.

Holtz-Eakin, D., W. Newey and H.S. Rosen (1988), 'Estimating Vector Autoregression with Panel Data', *Econometrica*, **56**(6): 1371–95.

Klenow, P. J. and A. Rodriguez-Clare (1997), 'The Neoclassical Revival in Growth Economics: Has It Gone too Far?' *NBER Macroeconomics Annual 1997*: 93–103.

Knack, S. and P. Keefer (1995), 'Institutions and Economic Performance: Cross-Country Tests Using Alternative Institutional Measures', *Economics and Politics*, **7**(3): 207–27.

Knight, M., N. Loayza and D. Villanueva (1993), 'Testing the Neoclassical Theory of Economic Growth: A Panel Data Approach', *International Monetary Fund Staff Papers*, **40**: 512–41.

Levine, R., N. Loayza and T. Beck (2000), 'Financial Intermediation and Growth: Causality and Causes', *Journal of Monetary Economics*, **46**(1): 31–77.

Lipsey, R. and I. Kravis (1987), *Saving and Economic Growth: Is the United States Really Falling Behind?* New York: The Conference Board.

Loayza, N. and L. Palacios (1997), 'Economic Reform and Progress in Latin America and the Caribbean' (World Bank Policy Research Working Paper No. 1829). Washington, DC: World Bank.

Loyaza, N., P. Fajnzylber and César Calderón (2005), *Economic Growth in Latin America and the Caribbean: Stylized Facts, Explanations and Forecasts*. Washington, DC: World Bank.

Lucas, R. (1988), 'On the Mechanics of Economic Development', *Journal of Monetary Economics*, **22**(1): 3–42.

Mauro, P. (1995), 'Corruption and Growth', *Quarterly Journal of Economics*, **110**: 681–712.

Olofsdotter, K. (1998), 'Foreign Direct Investment, Country Capabilities and Economic Growth', *Weltwirtschaftliches Archiv*, **134** (3): 525–47.

Pritchett, L. (2001), 'Where Has all the Education Gone?' *World Bank Economic Review*, **15**(3): 367–91.

Przeworski, A. and F. Limongi (1993), 'Political Regimes and Economic Growth', *Journal of Economic Perspectives*, **7**(3): 51–69.

Psacharopoulos, G. (1994), 'Returns to Investment in Education: A Global Update', *World Development*, **22**(9): 1325–43.

[19]

Journal of Economic Perspectives—Volume 13, Number 3—Summer 1999—Pages 3–22

Why Has Africa Grown Slowly?

Paul Collier and Jan Willem Gunning

I n the 1960s, Africa's future looked bright. On the basis of Maddison's (1995) estimates of per capita GDP for a sample of countries, during the first half of the century Africa had grown considerably more rapidly than Asia; by 1950, the African sample had overtaken the Asian sample. In the 1950s there were uncertainties of political transition, but after 1960 Africa was increasingly free of colonialism, with the potential for governments that would be more responsive to domestic needs. During the period 1960–73, growth in Africa was more rapid than in the first half of the century. Indeed, for this period, African growth and its composition were indistinguishable from the geographically very different circumstances of south Asia (Collins and Bosworth, 1996). Political self-determination in Africa and economic growth seemed to be proceeding hand-in-hand.

However, during the 1970s both political and economic matters in Africa deteriorated. The leadership of many African nations hardened into autocracy and dictatorship. Africa's economies first faltered and then started to decline. While Africa experienced a growth collapse, nations of south Asia modestly improved their economic performance. A good example of this divergence is the comparison of Nigeria and Indonesia. Until around 1970, the economic performance of Nigeria was broadly superior to that of Indonesia, but over the next quarter-century outcomes diverged markedly, despite the common experience for both countries of an oil boom in a predominantly agricultural economy. Since 1980, aggregate per capita GDP in sub-Saharan Africa has declined at almost 1 percent per annum. The decline has been widespread: 32 countries are poorer now than in 1980. Today,

■ *Paul Collier is Director of the Development Research Group at the World Bank, Washington, D.C. Jan Willem Gunning is Director, Centre for the Study of African Economies, University of Oxford, Oxford, United Kingdom. Their e-mail addresses are ⟨PCollier@worldbank.org⟩ and ⟨Jan.Gunning@economics.oxford.ac.uk⟩, respectively.*

4   *Journal of Economic Perspectives*

Figure 1
The Political Geography of Africa

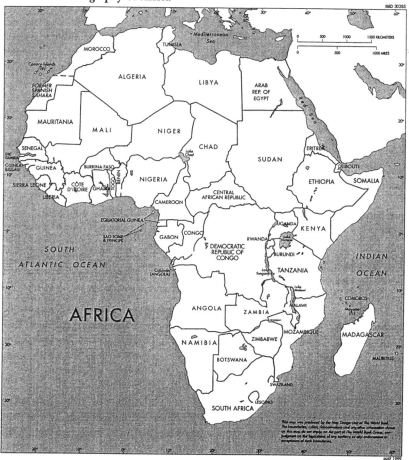

sub-Saharan Africa is the lowest-income region in the world. Figure 1 and Table 1, taken together, offer a snapshot of Africa today. Figure 1 is a map of the continent. Table 1 gives some basic information on population, GDP, standard of living, and growth rates for countries of sub-Saharan Africa. We focus on the sub-Saharan countries, setting aside the north African countries of Algeria, Egypt, Libya, Morocco and Tunisia. This is conventional for the studies of this area, since the north African countries are part of a different regional economy—the Middle East—with its own distinctive set of economic issues. It is clear that Africa has suffered a chronic failure of economic growth. The problem for analysis is to determine its causes.

Table 1
The Economies of Sub-Saharan Africa

Country	Population (Millions) 1997	GDP US$m at 1990 Prices 1997	GNP per Capita (PPP $) 1997	GNP Average Annual % Growth per Capita 1965–97	Life Expectancy at Birth (years) 1995	% of Population below $1 a Day (early 1990s)	Trade as % of GDP (in PPP) 1997
Angola	11.6	9,886	728	. . .	48	. . .	77
Benin	5.7	2,540	1,240		48	. . .	17
Botswana	1.5	4,458	7,440	7.7	66	33	. . .
Burkina Faso	11.1	3,643	936	0.9	47	. . .	7
Burundi	6.4	939	661	1.1	51	. . .	5
Cameroon	13.9	11,254	1,739	1.4	57	. . .	13
Cape Verde	0.4	393	. . .	. . .	66	. . .	. . .
Central African Republic	3.4	1,420	1,254	−1.2	50	. . .	10
Chad	6.7	1,492	978	0.1	49	. . .	4
Comoros	0.7	251	. . .	. . .	57	. . .	. . .
Congo	2.7	2,433	1,275	1.7	53	. . .	80
Congo, Dem. Rep.	48.0	6,094	698	−3.7	. . .	. . .	7
Côte d'Ivoire	14.3	13,320	1,676	−0.9	50	18	30
Djibouti	0.4	384	. . .	. . .	49	. . .	. . .
Equatorial Guinea	0.4	541	. . .	. . .	49	. . .	. . .
Eritrea	3.4	1,010	990	. . .	52	. . .	. . .
Ethiopia	60.1	11,327	493	−0.5	49	46	7
Gabon	1.1	7,280	6,480	0.4	55	. . .	58
Gambia	1.0	332	1,372	0.5	46	. . .	30
Ghana	18.3	7,892	1,492	−0.9	57	. . .	19
Guinea	7.6	3,699	1,763	. . .	46	26	14
Guinea Bissau	1.1	306	1,041	0.1	45	88	13
Kenya	28.4	9,879	1,150	1.3	55	50	16
Lesotho	2.1	998	2,422	3.2	62	49	. . .
Liberia	2.5	. . .	. . .	. . .	57	. . .	. . .
Madagascar	15.8	3,187	892	−1.9	58	72	11
Malawi	10.1	2,480	688	0.5	45	. . .	21
Mali	11.5	3,132	715	0.5	47	. . .	19
Mauritania	2.4	1,346	1,654	−0.2	53	31	28
Mauritius	1.1	3,755	9,147	3.8	71	. . .	37
Mozambique	18.3	2,144	541	−0.1	47	. . .	15
Namibia	1.6	3,141	4,999	0.7	60	. . .	. . .
Niger	9.8	2,776	824	−2.5	48	62	9
Nigeria	118.4	34,418	854	0.0	51	31	23
Rwanda	5.9	1,979	643	0.1	47	46	9
Sao Tome & Principe	0.1	56	. . .	. . .	. . .	. . .	. . .
Senegal	8.8	6,708	1,670	−0.5	50	54	11
Seychelles	0.1	435	. . .	. . .	. . .	. . .	. . .
Sierra Leone	4.4	. . .	401	−1.4	40	. . .	24
Somalia	10.4	. . .	. . .	. . .	48	. . .	. . .
South Africa	43.3	117,089	7,152	0.1	64	24	23
Sudan	27.9	13,119	. . .	−0.2	54	. . .	. . .
Swaziland	0.9	1,031	. . .	. . .	59	. . .	. . .
Tanzania	31.5	4,956	608	. . .	52	11	14
Togo	4.3	1,726	1,408	−0.6	56	. . .	24
Uganda	20.8	6,822	1,131	. . .	44	69	6
Zambia	8.5	3,564	900	−2.0	48	85	26
Zimbabwe	11.7	7,904	2,207	0.5	52	41	21

Sources: *African Development Report* (1998); and *World Development Indicators* (1999).

The debate on the causes of slow African growth has offered many different explanations. These can be usefully grouped into a two-by-two matrix, distinguishing on the one hand between policy and exogenous "destiny" and, on the other, between domestic and external factors. Table 2 compares Africa to other developing regions, using this grouping. Until recently it has largely been accepted that the main causes of Africa's slow growth were external, with the debate focusing upon whether external problems were policy-induced or exogenous. Especially during the 1980s, the World Bank, the International Monetary Fund and bilateral donors came to identify exchange rate and trade policies as the primary causes of slow growth in Africa. Table 2 offers some evidence that official exchange rates in sub-Saharan Africa have been more overvalued relative to (often illegal) market rates than is common for other less developed economies of Asia and Latin America. Tariffs and quantitative trade restrictions have also been higher in Africa than elsewhere. The rival thesis, often favored by African governments, was that the crisis was due to deteriorating and volatile terms of trade, and as Table 2 shows, terms of trade have indeed been more volatile for Africa than for other less developed economies. Jeffrey Sachs and his co-authors have emphasized a further adverse external "destiny" factor: Africa's population is atypically landlocked. As shown in Table 2, a high proportion of the population is remote from the coast or navigable waters.

Recently, attention has shifted to possible domestic causes of slow growth within African nations, but the debate as to the relative importance of policy-induced and exogenous problems has continued. Sachs and his co-authors have attributed slow growth to "the curse of the tropics." Africa's adverse climate causes poor health, and so reduces life expectancy below that in other regions, which puts it at a disadvantage in development. The adverse climate also leads to leached soils and unreliable rainfall, which constrains African agriculture. African nations also appear to have more ethnic diversity than other poor nations of the world, which may make it harder to develop an interconnected economy. In contrast to the domestic destiny argument, Collier and Gunning (1999) have emphasized domestic policy factors such as poor public service delivery. African governments have typically been less democratic and more bureaucratic than their Asian and Latin American counterparts.

Of course, once the conditions for slow growth are established by any combination of these reasons, they can become self-reinforcing in an endogenous process. Weak economic growth helps explain a lower saving rate and a higher proportion of flight capital for Africa compared to the less developed nations of Asia and Africa. Richer countries tend to see their population growth rates drop off, so the poverty of Africa has helped to keep its birth rates high, even as compared to the world's other less developed economies. Similarly, poverty may have increased the incidence of Africa's numerous civil wars, as well as being a consequence of them.

In the discussion that follows, we assess the policy/destiny and domestic/ external distinctions in various combinations. During the mid-1990s, African per-

Table 2
Africa Compared With Other Developing Regions
(figures are unweighted country averages)

	Sub-Saharan Africa	Other LDCs
Domestic-Destiny		
Life expectancy in 1970 (years)	45.2	57.3
Income in 1960 (1985 $ PPP-adjusted)	835.5	1855.2
Ethnic Fractionalization	67.6	32.7
Domestic-Policy		
Political Rights, 1973–90	6.0	4.0
Bureaucracy	1.38	1.72
External-Destiny		
Population <100 km from the sea or river (%)	21.0	52.0
Terms of trade volatility	16.4	12.8
External-Policy		
Parallel market exchange rate premium	40.0	26.0
Average tariffs 1996–98 (%)	21.0	13.0
Quantitative Restrictions, 1988–90 (%)	46.0	21.0
Endogenous		
Growth of GDP per capita, 1965–90	0.5	1.7
Investment rate in 1997 (%)	18.0	25.0
Population growth rate, 1980–97 (%)	2.8	1.8
Capital flight/private wealth, 1990 (%)	39.0	14.0

Sources: Life expectancy, World Development Indicators, 1998. Income and growth: Penn World Tables 5.6. The index of ethno-linguistic diversity is on the scale 0–100 with 0 being homogenous (Mauro, 1995). The Gastil index of political rights is on the range 1–7 with 1 being fully democratic.
The index of bureaucracy is on the scale 0–6 with high score indicating better quality (Knack and Keefer, 1995). Population living less than 100 km from the sea or a navigable river, from Bloom and Sachs (1999), Table 2, (other LDCs is the weighted average for Asia and Latin America). Terms of trade volatility is the standard deviation of annual log changes 1965–92, (Collins and Bosworth, 1996). Parallel exchange rate premium (%), (Easterly and Levine, 1997).
Average tariff: simple average, computed by IMF, we would like to thank Robert Sharer for these numbers. QRs: weighted average incidence of non-tariff measures over product lines; other LDCs is simple average of Latin America and East Asia; from Rodrik (1999, Table 12).
Investment rate and population growth rate, World Development Indicators, 1999 Capital flight/private wealth as of 1990 (Collier and Pattillo, 1999).

formance started to improve, with a few countries growing quite rapidly. We conclude by assessing these different explanations as guides to whether this improvement is likely to be transient or persistent.

Four Types of Explanation

Domestic-Destiny

Africa has several geographic and demographic characteristics which may predispose it to slow growth. First, much of the continent is tropical and this may handicap the economy, partly due to diseases such as malaria and partly due to hostile conditions for livestock and agriculture. Life expectancy has historically been low, with the population in a high-fertility, high infant-mortality equilibrium. With the advent of basic public health measures, population growth became very high. In particular, Africa has not been through the demographic transition whereby fertility rates decline which occurred in Asia and Latin America over the past 40 years. On one estimate, Africa's low life expectancy and high population growth account for almost all of Africa's slow growth (Bloom and Sachs, 1998). The argument is not clear-cut, however. Low life expectancy and high fertility are consequences of low income as well as causes, so the estimates are likely to be biased upwards. The household-level evidence suggests that the effects of poor health on income are small, although these in turn will be biased downwards by the omission of large-scale changes in economic activity which cannot be detected at the household level.

Whether or not Africa's past demographic characteristics have contributed to its slow growth, some African countries seem certain to go through a distinctive and disastrous demographic transition during the next two decades. As a result of AIDS, adult mortality rates will rise dramatically. In Africa, AIDS is a heterosexual disease. During the 1980s in parts of Africa it spread rapidly across the population before the risks became apparent, with up to 20-25 percent of adults now HIV-positive in some countries (World Bank, 1997). This human tragedy will have substantial economic effects during the next decade, especially since infection rates appear to be higher among the more educated, but it does not account for historically slow growth.

A second key characteristic of Africa which may predispose it to slow growth is that soil quality is poor and much of the continent is semi-arid, with rainfall subject to long cycles and unpredictable failure. Soils derive disproportionately from a very old type of rock ("Basement Complex"), which is low in micronutrients and varies considerably between localities. The application of additional macronutrients, which is the fertilizer package associated with the Green Revolution, is generally ineffective with low levels of micronutrients. Africa probably has scope for its own agricultural revolution, but it will depend upon locality-specific packages of micronutrients (Voortman et al., 1999). Since the 1960s, the semi-arid areas of Africa have been in a phase of declining rainfall (Grove, 1991). While there are no estimates of the output consequences of this decline, it may be significant, since agriculture is typically about one-quarter of GDP in this region. Given the lack of irrigation, the unpredictability of rainfall implies high risks in agriculture. With incomplete insurance and a high rate of time preference, households have to use assets for purposes of consumption-smoothing rather than investment. Households can thus become trapped in low-income, high-liquidity equilibria (Dercon, 1997).

A third relevant characteristic of Africa's economies, which can be seen as a result of these semi-arid conditions, is that the continent has very low population density. One by-product is high costs of transport which in turn have added to risk: poor market integration has hampered the use of trade for risk sharing. Another consequence of low population density is that Africa has relatively high natural resource endowments per capita (Wood and Mayer, 1998). High levels of natural resources can cause several problems. High levels of exported natural resources may lead to an appreciation of the exchange rate, which in turn makes manufacturing less competitive. Yet manufacturing may offer larger growth externalities, such as learning, than natural resource extraction. Natural resources may also increase "loot-seeking" activities. Collier and Hoeffler (1998) find that a dependence on natural resources strongly increases the risk of civil war, which has been a widespread phenomenon in Africa.

A further consequence of low population density is that African countries have much higher ethno-linguistic diversity than other regions; when groups come together less, there is less mingling and merging. Easterly and Levine (1997) find that this high level of diversity is the most important single cause of Africa's slow growth. There are various interpretations of this result. A common perception is that Africa's high ethnic diversity accounts for its high incidence of civil war. This turns out to be false: high levels of ethnic and religious diversity actually make societies significantly safer (Collier and Hoeffler, 1999). The effects of ethnic diversity on growth turn out to be contingent upon the political system; diversity has deleterious effects only when it occurs in the context of governments which are undemocratic. Collier (1999) finds that in democratic societies, ethnic diversity has no effect on either growth or the quality of public projects, but that in dictatorships, high levels of diversity reduce growth rates by 3 percentage points and double the rate of project failure relative to homogeneity. Dictatorships tend not to transcend the ethnic group of the dictator, so that the more ethnically fragmented the society, the more narrowly based a dictatorship will be, whereas democratic governments in such societies must be ethnically cross-cutting. In turn, the more narrowly based the government, the greater the payoff to predation relative to the inducement of generalized growth. Africa's problem was thus not its ethnic diversity but its lack of democracy in the context of diversity.

A fourth characteristic of Africa that may hinder its growth prospects is that because of its colonial heritage, Africa has much smaller countries in terms of population than other regions. Sub-Saharan Africa has a population about half that of India, divided into 48 states. These many states, combined with low levels of income, make Africa's national economies radically smaller than those of other regions. Very small states might be economically disadvantaged for several reasons. If government has some fixed costs, either in its administrative role or as a provider of services, then it may be hard for a small state to perform at minimum cost. Moreover, the society may forfeit much more extensive scale economies if it combines small scale with isolation. Some domestic markets will be too small even for the minimum efficient scale of production of a single producer; all domestic markets taken alone will be less competitive than in larger economies. Small economies are also perceived by investors as significantly more risky (Collier and Dollar, 1999a). Finally, they may have a slower rate of technological innovation; Kremer (1993) argues the incidence of discoveries may be broadly proportional to the population, so that if discoveries cannot readily spread between societies, low-population societies will have less innovation. However, in aggregate these effects cannot be large, because growth regressions generally find that state size does not affect a nation's rate of economic growth.

Domestic-Policy

For much of the post-colonial period, most African governments have been undemocratic. The median African government during the 1970s and 1980s was close to autocracy, and far less democratic than the median non-African developing country (as measured by the Gastil scale of political rights shown in Table 2). A typical pattern was that governments were captured by the educated, urban-resident population, with few agricultural or commercial interests. They expanded the public sector while imposing wide-ranging controls on private activity. These choices have been economically costly.

Public employment was expanded, often as an end in itself. For example, in Ghana by the late 1970s the public sector accounted for three-quarters of formal wage employment (Ghana Central Bureau of Statistics, 1988), and even in a more market-oriented economy like Kenya, the figure was 50 percent as of 1990 (Kenya Central Bureau of Statistics, 1996). Indeed, economic decline may have increased pressure for public sector employment. The large number of public sector employ-ees was reconciled with limited tax revenue by reducing wage rates and non-wage expenditures. The ratio of wage to non-wage expenditures in African governments is double that in Asia, and this has lowered the quality of public services; for example, in education, teaching materials are often lacking. The large, ill-paid public sector became the arena in which ethnic groups struggled for resources. For example, in the Ghanaian public sector, the locally dominant ethnic group re-ceived a wage premium of 25 percent over other groups after controlling for worker characteristics, and cognitive skills were completely unrewarded (Collier and Garg, 1999). The combination of low wage levels and payment structures, which rewarded social connections rather than skill, made it difficult for managers to motivate staff, and the difficulties of service delivery were compounded by the low ratio of non-wage to wage expenditures.

Since public sector employment was the main priority, managers were not under severe pressure for actual delivery of services from their political masters. Because of the lack of democracy, neither were they accountable to the broader public. As a result, Africa experienced a paradox of poor public services despite relatively high public expenditure (Pradhan, 1996). Poor service delivery handi-capped firms through unreliable transport and power, inadequate telecommuni-cations networks, and unreliable courts. For example, manufacturing firms in Zimbabwe need to hold high levels of inventories, despite high interest rates, due to unreliable delivery of inputs tied to poor transportation infrastructure (Faf-champs et al., 1998). A survey of Ugandan firms found that shortage of electricity was identified as the single most important constraint upon firm growth; indeed, the provision of electricity by firms for their own use was almost as large as the public supply of electricity (Reinikka and Svensson, 1998). A study in Nigeria found that own generators accounted for three-quarters of the capital equipment of small manufacturers (Lee and Anas, 1991). The poor state of African telecommunications was estimated to reduce African growth rates by 1 percentage point, according to Easterly and Levine (1997). (However, since telecommunications was the main infrastructure variable which they could quantify, and since lack of different kinds of infrastructure is probably highly correlated, their estimate is probably a proxy for a wider range of infrastructural deficiencies.) African commercial courts are more corrupt than those in other regions (Widner, 1999). As a result, firms face greater problems of contract enforcement. Some firms can overcome these by relying upon their social networks to screen potential clients, but it is common to restrict business to long-standing clients (Bigsten et al., 1999). Ethnic minorities, such as Asians in East Africa and Lebanese in West Africa, tend to have more specialized social networks and so are better able than African firms to screen new clients (Biggs et al., 1996). The problem of contract enforcement thus makes markets less competitive and reduces the potential gains from trade, while tending to perpetuate the dominant position of minorities in business.

Poor public service delivery also handicapped households through inefficient education, health and extension services. A survey of primary education expenditures in Uganda found that, of the non-wage money released by the Ministry of Finance, on average, less than 30 percent actually reached the schools (Ablo and Reinikka, 1998). The expansion of the public sector has reduced private initiative. Since major areas of economic activity were reserved for the public sector—often including transport, marketing and banking—and African elites looked to the public sector rather than the private sector for advancement, Africa was slow to develop indigenous entrepreneurs.

African governments built various economic control regimes. A few nations, such as Ethiopia, Angola and Tanzania, had wide-ranging price controls under which private agents had an incentive to reduce production—at least officially marketed production. These governments often attempted to counterbalance these incentives with coercive production targets, but the net effect was usually dramatic declines in economic activity. More commonly, firms were subject to considerable regulation. For example, for many years manufacturing firms wishing to set up in Kenya had to acquire letters of no objection from existing producers, which resulted in a predictably low level of competition. In Uganda, when the government removed the requirement that coffee could only be transported by rail, the market for road haulage expanded sufficiently to induce new entry, which in turn broke an existing cartel, nearly halving haulage rates. Similarly, in Tanzania during the long period when agricultural marketing was heavily regulated, marketing margins for grain were double what they were both before regulation and after deregulation (Bevan et al., 1993). In this period, food prices became much more volatile: between 1964 and 1980 the coefficient of variation (that is, the ratio of the standard deviation to the mean) of maize prices at regional centers doubled, falling again sharply when markets were liberalized.

Government interventions undermined the functioning of product markets in many countries. Private trading, which was often associated with ethnic minorities such as the Indians in East Africa and the Lebanese in West Africa, was sometimes banned. A particularly damaging intervention, practiced even in relatively market-friendly economies such as Kenya, was to ban private inter-district trade in food. Where government marketing monopolies were focused on ensuring the food supply to urban areas, this provision discouraged farmers from specializing in non-food export crops, since they could not rely on being able to buy food locally.

Since the political base of governments was urban, agriculture was heavily taxed and the public agronomic research needed to promote an African green revolution, based on locally-specific packages of micronutrients, was neglected. The main source of agricultural growth has been the gradual adoption of cash crops by smallholders, a process slowed down by government pricing policies (Bevan et al., 1993). While governments favored manufacturing, the basis for industrial growth in this area was also undermined, since trade and exchange rate policies induced industrial firms to produce under uncompetitive conditions and only for small and captive domestic markets.

The same urban bias initially led governments to favor the urban wage labor force. In the immediate post-colonial period, minimum wages rose and unions acquired influence, so that wages increased substantially. However, post-independence inflation has usually eroded minimum wages, so that in most of Africa, wage rigidities in the labor market are not currently a significant impediment to the growth process. The exceptions are South Africa, where the labor market may just be going through such a real wage adjustment now, and the low inflation environments of Ethiopia and the countries in the "franc zone," the 13 former colonies of France in west and central Africa which had currencies pegged to the French franc. While high wage levels are not normally a hindrance to African economies, the job matching process appears to be inefficient, so that job mobility offers unusually high returns (Mengistae, 1998). This is an instance of the high costs of market information; for example, newspapers are expensive and have low circulation.

Financial markets were heavily regulated, with bank lending directed to the government, public enterprises or "strategic" sectors, very limited financial intermediation and virtually no competition between financial institutions. A common proxy for the extent of financial intermediation, known as "financial depth," is the broad money supply, M2, relative to GDP. But although Africa has even less financial depth than other developing areas, currently available evidence suggests that this may have had only a modest impact on its growth. For example, Easterly and Levine (1997) estimate that lack of financial depth reduced the annual growth rate by only 0.3 percentage points. Similarly, microeconomic survey evidence on manufacturing firms indicates that the lack of external finance is not currently the binding constraint on industrial investment (Bigsten et al., 1999).

External-Destiny

Africa is better located than Asia for most developed economy markets. However, most Africans live much further from the coast or navigable rivers than in other regions and so face intrinsically higher transport costs for exports (as shown in Table 2). Further, much of the population lives in countries which are land-locked, so that problems of distance are compounded by political barriers. Even a relatively open border like the one between Canada and the United States appears to be a substantial impediment to trade, in the sense that trade across Canadian provinces or across U.S. states is far greater than trade of equal distance between Canada and the United States (McCallum, 1995). Landlocked countries face national borders on all sides, which may constitute an irreducible barrier to trade even if they have good relations with their neighbors. Typically, growth regressions find that being landlocked reduces a nation's annual growth rate by around half of 1 percent.

A further aspect of external destiny is that Africa's exports are concentrated in a narrow range of commodities, with volatile prices that have declined since the 1960s. The deterioration in the terms of trade for such commodities has undoubt-edly contributed to Africa's growth slowdown. However, there is controversy over whether its atypical exposure to terms of trade volatility has been damaging. Deaton and Miller (1996) find little evidence of detrimental effects in the short run. However, case study evidence suggests that shocks have often had longer-run deleterious effects. Investment has been concertinaed into short periods, during which construction booms have raised the unit cost of capital, and government budgets have been destabilized, with spending rising during booms but being difficult to reduce subsequently (Schuknecht, 1999; Collier and Gunning, 1999b).

Africa has attracted much more aid per capita than other regions. Donor allocation rules have typically favored countries which have small populations and low incomes, and were recent colonies—and African countries met all three criteria. There has been a long debate as to whether aid has been detrimental or beneficial for the growth process (for recent overviews, see Gwin and Nelson, 1997; World Bank, 1998). Early critics claimed that aid reduced the incentive for good governance (for example, Bauer, 1982). Since the 1980s, the World Bank and the International Monetary Fund have attempted to make policy improvement a con-dition for the receipt of aid. Econometric work does not find that aid has had a significant effect on policy: to the extent that aid encourages or discourages policy changes, the two effects apparently offset each other. However, the effect of aid on growth has been shown to be policy-dependent. Where policies are good, aid substantially raises growth rates, where they are poor, diminishing returns rapidly set in so that aid cannot significantly contribute to growth. This result holds whether the measure of policy is objective indicators of the fiscal and exchange rate stance (Burnside and Dollar, 1997), or subjective but standardized ratings of a broader range of policies done by the World Bank (Collier and Dollar, 1999). Until recently, many African policy environments were not good enough for aid to raise growth substantially. Hence, the evidence does not support Bauer's (1982) claim that Africa's large aid receipts were a cause of its slow growth, but does suggest that Africa largely missed the opportunity for enhanced growth which aid provided.

Excluding South Africa and the oil exporters (whose terms of trade have improved), the net aid inflows since 1970 have been around 50 percent greater than the income losses from terms of trade deterioration. The combination was thus somewhat analogous to an increase in export taxation: the terms of trade losses taking money from exporters, while the aid provided money to governments.

External-Policy

In recent decades, African governments adopted exchange rate and trade policies which were atypically anti-export and accumulated large foreign debts. On a range of indicators, Africa has had much higher trade barriers and more misaligned exchange rates than other regions (Dollar, 1992; Sachs and Warner, 1997). Exchange rates were commonly highly overvalued, reflecting the interest of the political elite in cheap imports. Tariffs and export taxes were higher in Africa than in other regions of the world, partly because of the lack of other sources of tax revenue to finance the expansion of the public sector. Exports were sharply reduced as a result of export crop taxation. For example, Dercon (1993) shows that Tanzanian cotton exports would have been 50 percent higher in the absence of taxation. Quantitative restrictions on imports were also used much more extensively, despite yielding no revenue. They often arose because of the difficulties of fine-tuning import demand in a situation where government was attempting to keep exchange rates fixed with few reserves. They probably persisted because they generated large opportunities for corruption, since someone could often be bribed to circumvent the quantitative limits.

The international growth literature has reached a consensus that exchange rate overvaluation and tight trade restrictions are damaging, but controversy continues over the effects of more moderate trade restrictions (Rodrik, 1999). However, there are reasons why Africa's poor export performance may have been particularly damaging. Since 1980, African export revenue per capita has sharply declined, which in turn has induced severe import compression of both capital goods and intermediate inputs. Moreover, because African economies are so much smaller than other economies, external barriers of a given height have been significantly more damaging (Collier and Gunning, 1999).

By the 1990s, several African economies had accumulated unsustainable international debts, largely from public agencies. Clearly, this is one way in which poor decisions of the past become embedded in the present. There is a good theoretical argument that high indebtedness discourages private investment due to the fear of the future tax liability. There is some supporting evidence for this claim, although since poor policies lower GDP, using high debt/GDP as an explanatory variable may simply be a proxy for poor policies more broadly (Elbadawi et al., 1997).

Policy or Destiny?

The dichotomy between policy and destiny is of course an oversimplification: some apparently exogenous features of Africa have often been induced by policy, and conversely, African policies may reflect exogenous factors.

Consider, first, some of the "exogenous" factors that we have discussed under destiny. For example, the claim by Sachs and Warner (1997) that geography and demography almost fully account for Africa's slow growth rests largely upon the lack of a demographic transition to lower fertility rates in Africa, as has happened in most of Latin America and Asia. However, it is more plausible to regard these continuing high fertility rates as a consequence of slow growth than a cause. The lack of employment opportunities for young women has prevented the opportunity cost of children from rising, and the low returns to education in an environment where many of the "good" jobs are allocated by political criteria have reduced the incentive for parents to educate their children.

Similarly, the argument that the concentration of Africa's population in the interior is an external force holding down growth can also be seen as an endogenous outcome; specifically, the population has remained in the interior because of the failure of Africa's coastal cities to grow. In turn, this is partly because the failure to industrialize has slowed urbanization, and partly because policy has often been biased against coastal cities; for example, in both Nigeria and Tanzania the capital was relocated from the coast to the interior. Where policy was less biased, as in the Côte d'Ivoire during the 1970s, the coastal population grew so rapidly that it supported massive emigration from the landlocked economy of Burkina Faso: at its peak, around 40 percent of the Ivorien population were immigrants.

Further, being landlocked need not be an economic disadvantage. Developed landlocked economies, such as Switzerland, have atypically low international transport costs because they have oriented their trade towards their neighbors. By contrast, Africa's landlocked economies trade with Europe, so that neighboring countries are an obstacle rather than a market. These patterns of trade are partly a legacy of the colonial economy, but they also reflect the high trade barriers within Africa erected by post-independence governments, and the slow rate of growth. Ultimately, landlocked economies were faced with neighboring markets that were both inaccessible and unattractive, which did not make it desirable to reorient the economy to trade with them. Finally, Africa's continued export concentration in a narrow range of primary commodities, which we discussed earlier as reflecting the destiny of resource endowments, probably also reflects a number of public policy decisions. Other export activities have been handicapped either directly through overvalued exchange rates, or indirectly, through high transactions costs. Poor policy has given Africa a comparative disadvantage in "transaction-intensive" activities such as manufacturing.

Now consider the reverse situation; that is, how some of the dysfunctional policies that we have discussed can also be considered the outcome of exogenous forces. The anti-export policies which we argue hindered growth can be viewed as a consequence of the fact that most of the population lives far from the coast (Gallup and Sachs, 1999). In such societies, it might be argued that the elasticity of growth with respect to openness is lower and so the incentive for openness is reduced. However, at present Africa offers little evidence for this hypothesis. According to the World Bank's standardized ratings of policy (currently confidential), all five of the worst-rated countries on the continent are coastal whereas many of the best-rated countries are landlocked. As another example, it is possible that restrictive import policies are adopted, at least initially, in response to trade shocks like those created by an external dependence on commodity exports (Collier and Gunning, 1999b). The prevalence of natural resources may bring forth a variety of other policy errors, as well. For example, it may worsen policy by turning politics into a contest for rents or, through crowding out manufactured exports, prevent the emergence of potentially the most potent lobby for openness.

Along with being endogenous to fixed effects like geography, policies are also affected by experience. Societies which have experienced high levels of economic risk may place a higher priority on income-sharing arrangements such as expanded opportunities of public employment, rather than focusing on income generation. Societies also learn from past failure. The African nations which have recently implemented the strongest economic reforms, such as Ghana and Uganda, tended to be those which had earlier experienced the worst economic crises. However, African countries facing the challenge of reversing economic failure have lacked significant role models within the continent. In east Asia, Hong Kong, Singapore, Taiwan and Korea provided early role models, as did Chile since the late 1970s in Latin America. Within-continent models may be important because the information is both closer to hand and more evidently pertinent. Once Africa develops examples of success, the scope for societal learning across the continent will make it unlikely that Africa is "destined" to poor policies by its geography: although its geographic characteristics may have given it some weak tendencies towards poor policies in the initial post-independence period.

Sorting out the policy effects from the destiny effects is a difficult econometric problem. In the ordinary least squares regressions common in the analysis of African growth, the dependent variable is typically the average growth rate over a long period, and a variety of policy and destiny variables enter as the explanatory variables. Depending upon the specification, either policy or destiny can appear important.

An alternative approach is to consider the extent to which African slow growth has been persistent, to take advantage of the insight that policies have varied, whereas destiny-like geographic disadvantages remain constant over time. Along these lines, Diamond (1998) provides a convincing explanation from a historical perspective of why geographic reasons, such as the north-south axis of the continent, caused African agriculture to develop only slowly prior to European colonization, due to a combination of technological isolation and small scale. However, since colonization gradually relaxed some of these constraints (while introducing others), pre-20th century experience is of limited pertinence for explaining patterns of growth in the last few decades.

More recent experience tends to argue that destiny plays less of a role than policy. After all, the economies of Africa did grow relatively quickly through the first half of the 20th century, and up until the early 1970s, which tends to argue that they were not obviously destined for lower growth. The arrival of slow economic growth in the 1970s coincides with a phase in which African economic policy became both statist and biased against exports. Moreover, the main exception to African economic collapse, Botswana, experienced the most rapid growth in the world despite the seeming exogenous disadvantages of being landlocked and having very low population density.

The most sophisticated econometric test of whether something about Africa seems intrinsically connected to slow growth is the study by Hoeffler (1999). She searches for a continental fixed effect using panel regressions of five-year periods over 1965–90. She first estimates a simple growth model in which the explanatory variables are initial income, investment, population growth, and schooling. She then uses the coefficients on these variables to compute the residuals, and regresses the residuals on regional dummies. The Africa dummy is small and insignificant, that is, there is no continental fixed effect to explain. However, she does find that both being landlocked and being tropical significantly reduce growth, and these are indeed locational characteristics of much of Africa. Between them they would reduce the African growth rate by around 0.4 percentage points relative to that of other developing regions.

Whereas in the distant past the economies of Africa may well have been intrinsically disadvantaged by factors like less easy access to water transportation or the geography of the continent, the thesis that this has persisted into recent decades is less plausible. Remember that by 1950 Africa had a higher per capita income than south Asia and its subsequent performance was indistinguishable from that region until the mid-1970s. Coastal Africa is not intrinsically markedly worse-endowed in any geographical sense than much of coastal Asia or Brazil, although its soil types pose distinct challenges for agronomic research.

By contrast, it is easy to point to policies which until very recently have been dysfunctional. Even as of 1998, Africa had the worst policy environment in the world according to the World Bank ratings. Microeconomic evidence shows how these policies damaged the growth of firms. Poor infrastructure, poor contract enforcement and volatile policies all make the supply of inputs unreliable. Firms have responded to this risky environment partly by reducing risks: they hold large inventories, invest in electricity generators, and restrict their business relations to known enterprises. They have also responded by reducing investment. A striking implication is the conjunction of a high marginal return on capital and a very low rate of investment, even for firms that are not liquidity constrained. In Africa, the elasticity of investment with respect to profits may be as low as 0.07 (Bigsten et al., 1999). Some of the effects of poor policy are highly persistent. Most notably, the colonial governments of Africa provided little education, especially at the secondary level. Although independent governments rapidly changed these priorities, for the past 30 years Africa has had a markedly lower stock of human capital than other continents. The rapid growth in education has, however, gradually narrowed the gap with other regions.

Even if one disagrees with this view that policy is more important in explaining Africa's slow rate of growth and finds the "destiny" explanations more persuasive, this by no means condemns Africa to growing more slowly than other regions. Some of the economic disadvantages of being tropical may be overcome, for example, by the discovery of vaccines or new strains of crops. Moreover, Africa has two potential growth advantages over other regions which should offset against any locational disadvantage. It has lower per capita income and so could benefit from a convergence effect with richer countries, and it has higher aid inflows and so could benefit from aid-induced growth. If public policies were as good as in other regions, aid and convergence should enable even those countries which are land-locked and tropical to grow more rapidly than other developing regions for several decades. Although the growth regressions would imply that in the long term such countries would converge on a lower steady-state income than more favorably located countries, even this is doubtful. If the coastal African nations grew, then being landlocked would cease to be disadvantageous, since the gains from trading with close neighbors would expand.

Domestic or External?

Until recently, there was broad agreement that Africa's problems were predominantly associated with its external relations, although some analysts emphasized the policy-induced lack of openness and markets, while others attributed poor performance to over-dependence on a few commodities, the prices of which were declining and volatile. In our view, the argument that Africa's poor performance originates in its overdependence on commodities has looked weaker in recent years: Africa has lost global market share in its major exports, often spectacularly. The focus of the discussion has consequently shifted to underlying reasons for poor domestic performance, and in turn to domestic factors. The domestic factors, as we have argued, can be divided into those that smack of destiny, like the fact that much of Africa has a tropical climate, and those that are related to policy. Indeed, we believe that domestic policies largely unrelated to trade may now be the main obstacles to growth in much of Africa.

To illustrate our argument, we focus on Africa's failure to industrialize. It might appear that Africa is intrinsically uncompetitive in manufactures because of its high natural resource endowments give it a comparative advantage in that area (Wood and Mayer, 1998). But while Africa may have a comparative advantage in natural resources in the long run, at present African wages are often so low that were African manufacturing to have similar levels of productivity to other regions, it would be competitive. Hence, it is low productivity which needs to be explained.

African manufacturing has been in a low-productivity trap. Because African firms are oriented to small domestic markets, they are not able to exploit economies of scale, nor are they exposed to significant competition, and their technology gap with the rest of the world is unusually wide—yielding large opportunities for learning. This suggests that African manufacturing might have atypically large potential to raise productivity through exporting. However, most African firms fail to step onto this productivity escalator. This is because they face high costs for other reasons. As discussed already, transactions costs are unusually high. With transport unreliable, firms typically need to carry very large stocks of inputs to maintain continuity of production, despite higher interest rates than elsewhere. Telecommunications are much worse than other regions. Malfunctioning of the courts makes contract enforcement unreliable, so that firms are reluctant to enter into deals with new partners, in turn making markets less competitive.

These high transactions costs have a relatively large impact on manufacturing. Compared with natural resource extraction, manufacturing tends to have a high share of intermediate inputs and a low share of value-added to final price. Consequently, transactions costs tend to be much larger relative to value-added. Africa's intrinsic comparative advantage in natural resource exports may thus have been reinforced by public policies which have made manufacturing uncompetitive relative to resource extraction. African policies may have given the region a comparative disadvantage in transactions-intensive activities.

Conclusion: Will Africa Grow?

During the mid-1990s, average African growth accelerated and performance became more dispersed. A few countries such as Uganda, Côte d'Ivoire, Ethiopia and Mozambique started to grow very fast, whereas others such as the Democratic Republic of the Congo and Sierra Leone descended into social disorder. "Africa" became less meaningful as a category. Both the improvement in the average performance and the greater dispersion among countries were consistent with what had happened to policy. During the 1990s many of the most egregious exchange rate, fiscal and trade policies were improved. By 1998, although Africa still ranked as the region with the worst policies on the World Bank ratings, it was also the region with by far the greatest policy dispersion.

However, the faster growth coincided not only with better policies but with improvements in the terms of trade. Further, investment in Africa as a share of GDP is currently only 18 percent. This is much lower than other regions: for example, 23 percent in South Asia and 29 percent on average in lower middle-income countries. Even these figures may understate Africa's true investment shortfall. Capital goods are more expensive in Africa than the international average, so that once the investment share is recalculated at international relative prices it approximately halves. Although it is not possible to disaggregate investment into its public and private components with complete accuracy, estimates suggest that the shortfall in African investment is due to low private investment. Thus, growth may be unsustainable unless there is a substantial increase in private investment.

On an optimistic interpretation of the evidence, Africa's slow growth from the early 1970s into the 1990s has been due to policies which reduced its openness to foreign trade. Since these policies have largely been reversed during the last decade, if this is correct then Africa should be well-placed for continued growth.

The pessimistic interpretation is that Africa's problems are intrinsic, often rooted in geography. This view implies that economic progress in Africa will be dependent upon international efforts to make its environment more favorable, such as research to eradicate tropical diseases, and finance to create transport arteries from the coast to the interior. The thesis that Africa's economic problems are caused by ethno-linguistic fractionalization has similarly intractable implications.

Our own interpretation lies between these extremes. We suggest that while the binding constraint upon Africa's growth may have been externally-oriented policies in the past, those policies have now been softened. Today, the chief problem is those policies which are ostensibly domestically-oriented, notably poor delivery of public services. These problems are much more difficult to correct than exchange rate and trade policies, and so the policy reform effort needs to be intensified. However, even widespread policy reforms in this area might not be sufficient to induce a recovery in private investment, since recent economic reforms are never fully credible. Investment rating services list Africa as the riskiest region in the world. Indeed, there is some evidence that Africa suffers from being perceived by investors as a "bad neighborhood." Analysis of the global risk ratings shows that while they are largely explicable in terms of economic fundamentals, Africa as a whole is rated as significantly more risky than is warranted by these fundamentals (Haque et al., 1999). Similarly, private investment appears to be significantly lower in Africa than is explicable in terms of economic fundamentals (Jaspersen et al., 1999). "Africa" thus seems to be treated as a meaningful category by investors.

The perception of high risk for investing in Africa may partly be corrected by the passage of time, but reforming African governments can also take certain steps to commit themselves to defend economic reforms. Internationally, governments may increasingly make use of rules within the World Trade Organization, and shift their economic relations with the European Union from unreciprocated trade preferences to a wider range of reciprocated commitments. Domestically, there is a trend to freedom of the press, and the creation of independent centers of authority in central banks and revenue authorities, all of which should generally help to reinforce a climate of openness and democracy, which is likely to be supportive of economic reform.

■ We would like to thank Alan Gelb and Satya Yalamanchili for the calculations on terms of trade losses compared with aid inflows. Earlier drafts of these papers were presented at a symposium sponsored by the Andrew Mellon Foundation and held at Princeton University, Princeton, New Jersey, on January 7, 1999. The paper has benefited from comments both by participants at the symposium and by the editors. The findings, interpretations, and conclusions expressed in this paper are entirely those of the authors. They do not necessarily represent the views of the World Bank, its Executive Directors, or the countries they represent.

References

Ablo, Emanuel and Ritva Reinikka. 1998. "Do Budgets Really Matter? Evidence from Public Spending on Education and Health in Uganda." Policy Research Working Paper No. 1926, World Bank.

African Development Bank. 1998. *African Development Report.* Oxford: Oxford University Press.

Bates, Robert, H. 1983. *Essays in the Political Economy of Rural Africa.* Cambridge: Cambridge University Press.

Bauer, Peter, T. 1982. "The Effects of Aid." *Encounter.* November.

Bevan, David. L., Paul Collier and Jan Willem Gunning. 1993. *Agriculture and the policy environment: Tanzania and Kenya.* Paris: OECD.

Biggs, T., M. Raturi and P. Srivastava. 1996. "Enforcement of Contracts in an African Credit Market: Working Capital Financing in Kenyan Manufacturing." RPED Discussion Paper, Africa Region, World Bank.

Bigsten, Arne, P. Collier, S. Dercon, B. Gauthier, J.W. Gunning, A. Isaksson, A. Oduro, R. Oostendorp, C. Pattillo, M. Soderbom, M. Sylvain, F. Teal and A. Zeufack. 1999, forthcoming. "Investment by Manufacturing Firms in Africa: a Four-Country Panel Data Analysis." *Oxford Bulletin of Economics and Statistics.*

Bloom, John and Jeffrey Sachs. 1998. "Geography, Demography and Economic Growth in Africa." *Brookings Papers in Economic Activity.* 2, 207–95.

Burnside Craig and David Dollar. 1997. "Aid, Policies and Growth." Policy Research Working Paper No. 1777, World Bank.

Collier, Paul. 1999. "The Political Economy of Ethnicity," in *Proceedings of the Annual Bank Conference on Development Economics.* Pleskovic, Boris and Joseph E. Stiglitz, eds. World Bank, Washington, D.C.

Collier, Paul and David Dollar. 1999. "Aid Allocation and Poverty Reduction." Policy Research Working Paper 2041, World Bank, Washington DC.

Collier, Paul and David Dollar. 1999a. "Aid, Risk and the Special Concerns of Small States." Mimeo, Policy Research Department, World Bank, Washington DC.

Collier, Paul and Ashish Garg. 1999, forthcoming. "On Kin Groups and Wages in the Ghanaian Labour Market." *Oxford Bulletin of Economics and Statistics,* 61:2, pp. 131–51.

Collier, P. and J.W. Gunning. 1999. "Explaining African Economic Performance." *Journal of Economic Literature.* March, 37:1, 64–111.

Collier, P. and J.W. Gunning. 1999a, forthcoming. "The IMF's Role in Structural Adjustment." *Economic Journal.* World Bank, Washington, DC.

Collier, P. and J.W. Gunning with associates. 1999b. *Trade Shocks in Developing Countries: Theory and Evidence.* Oxford: Oxford University Press (Clarendon).

Collier, Paul and Anke Hoeffler. 1998. "On the Economic Causes of Civil War." *Oxford Economic Papers.* 50, pp. 563–73.

Collier, Paul and Anke Hoeffler. 1999. "Loot-Seeking and Justice-Seeking in Civil War." Mimeo, Development Research Department, World Bank, Washington DC.

Collier, Paul and Catherine Pattillo, eds. 1999. *Investment and Risk in Africa.* Macmillan: London.

Collins, S. and B.P. Bosworth. 1996. "Economic Growth in East Asia: Accumulation versus Assimilation." *Brookings Papers in Economic Activity,* 2, pp.135–203.

Deaton, A. and R. Miller. 1996. "International Commodity Prices, Macroeconomic Performance and Politics in Sub-Saharan Africa." *Journal of African Economies.* 5 (Supp.), pp. 99–191.

Dercon, Stefan. 1997. "Wealth, Risk and Activity Choice: Cattle in Western Tanzania." *Journal of Development Economics.* 55:1, pp. 1–42.

Dercon, Stefan. 1993. "Peasant supply response and macroeconomic policies: cotton in Tanzania." *Journal of African Economies.* 2, pp. 157–94.

Diamond, Jared. 1998. *Guns, Germs, and Steel: The Fates of Human Societies.* New York: W.W. Norton & Co.

Dollar, David. 1992. "Outward-Oriented Developing Economies Really do Grow More Rapidly: Evidence from 95 LDCs 1976–85." *Economic Development and Cultural Change.* 40, pp. 523–44.

Easterly, William and Ross Levine. 1997. "Africa's Growth Tragedy: Policies and Ethnic Divisions." *Quarterly Journal of Economics.* CXII, pp. 1203–1250.

Elbadawi, Ibrahim A., Benno J. Ndulu, and Njuguna Ndung'u. 1997. "Debt Overhang and Economic Growth in Sub-Saharan Africa," in *External Finance for Low-Income Countries.* Iqbal, Zubair and Ravi Kanbur, eds. IMF Institute, Washington, DC.

Fafchamps, Marcel, Jan Willem Gunning and Remco Oostendorp. 1998. "Inventories, Liquidity and Contractual Risk in African Manufacturing." Department of Economics, Stanford University, mimeo.

Gallup, John L. and Jeffrey D. Sachs. 1999. "Geography and Economic Growth," in *Proceedings of the Annual World Bank Conference on Development Economics.* Pleskovic, Boris and Joseph E. Stiglitz, eds. World Bank, Washington, DC.

Ghana Central Bureau of Statistics. 1988. *Quarterly Digest of Statistics.* Accra.

Grove, A.T. 1991. "The African Environment," in *Africa 30 Years On.* Rimmer, Douglas, ed. London: James Currey.

Gwin, Catherine and Joan Nelson. 1997. *Perspectives on Aid and Development.* Johns Hopkins for Overseas Development Council, Washington DC.

Haque, Nadeem U., Nelson Mark and Donald J. Mathieson. 1999. "Risk in Africa: its Causes and its Effects on Investment," in *Investment and Risk in Africa.* Collier, Paul and Catherine Pattillo, eds. London: Macmillan.

Hoeffler, Anke A. 1999. "Econometric Studies of Growth, Convergence and Conflicts." D. Phil. Thesis, Oxford University.

Jaspersen, Frederick, Anthony H. Aylward and A. David Cox. 1999. "Risk and Private Investment: Africa Compared with Other Developing Areas," in *Investment and Risk in Africa.* Collier, Paul and Catherine Pattillo, eds. London: Macmillan.

Stephen Knack and Philip Keefer. 1995. Institutions and Economic Performance: Cross-Country Tests Using Alternative Institutional Measures." *Economics and Politics.* 7:3, pp. 207–28.

Kenya Central Bureau of Statistics. 1996. *Statistical Abstract.* Nairobi.

Kremer, Michael. 1993. "Population Growth and Technological Change: One Million B.C. to 1990." *Quarterly Journal of Economics.* 108:3, pp. 681–716.

Lee, K.S. and A. Anas. 1991. "Manufacturers' Responses to Infrastructure Deficiencies in Nigeria: Private Alternatives and Policy Options," in *Economic Reform in Africa.* Chibber, A. and S. Fischer, eds. World Bank, Washington DC.

Maddison, Angus. 1995. *Monitoring the World Economy.* Paris: OECD.

Mauro, P. 1995. "Corruption and Growth." *Quarterly Journal of Economics.* 110, pp. 681–712.

McCallum, J. 1995. "National Borders Matter: Canada-U.S. Regional Trade Patterns." *American Economic Review.* 85, pp. 615–23.

Mengistae, Taye. 1998. "Ethiopia's Urban Economy: Empirical Essays on Enterprise Development and the Labour Market." D.Phil. Thesis, University of Oxford.

Pradhan, Sanjay. 1996. "Evaluating Public Spending." World Bank Discussion Paper 323, Washington DC.

Reinikka, Ritva and Jakob Svensson. 1998. "Investment Response to Structural Reforms and Remaining Constraints: Firm Survey Evidence from Uganda." Mimeo, Africa Region, World Bank.

Rodrik, Dani. 1999. *Making Openness Work: The New Global Economy and the Developing Countries.* Overseas Development Council, Washington DC.

Sachs, J.D. and Mark Warner. 1997. "Sources of Slow Growth in African Economies." *Journal of African Economies.* 6, pp. 335–76.

Schuknecht, Ludger. 1999. "Tying Governments' Hands in Commodity Taxation." *Journal of African Economies.* 8:2, 152–81.

Voortman, R.L., B.G.J.S. Sonneveld and M.A. Keyzer. 1999. "African Land Ecology: Opportunities and Constraints for Agricultural Development." Mimeo, Centre for World Food Studies, Free University, Amsterdam.

Widner, Jennifer, A. 1999. "The Courts as Restraints," in *Investment and Risk in Africa.* Collier, Paul and Catherine Pattillo, eds. London: Macmillan.

Wood, Adrian and J. Mayer. 1998. "Africa's Export Structure in Comparative Perspective," forthcoming in the UNCTAD series *Economic Development and Regional Dynamics in Africa: Lessons from the East Asian Experience.*

World Bank. 1997. *Confronting Aids,* Policy Research Report. Oxford University Press.

World Bank. 1998. *Assessing Aid: What Works, What Doesn't, and Why,* Policy Research Report. Oxford University Press.

World Bank. 1999. *World Development Indicators.* Development Data Center, Washington, D.C.

Name Index

Aaberge, R. 375, 376
Ablo, E. 522
Abramovitz, M. 255, 256, 469
Acemoglu, D. 49, 50
Achdut, L. 215
Adelman, I. 107
Ades, A. 73, 85, 367
Agell, J. 49
Agenor, P.-R. 327
Aghion, P. 335
Ahluwalia, I. 423, 424, 457
Ahmad, S. 169
Aitchinson, J. 326
Akerlof, G. 133
Alesina, A. 307, 340
Ali, A.G.A. 325
Allen, R.C. 31, 32
Alonso-Borrego, C. 485
Amiel, Y. 142
Anas, A. 522
Anderson, E. 355
Araar, A. 233
Aranson, J.R. 229, 242
Arellano, M. 326, 485, 486
Artecona, R. 367
Atinc, T.M. 30, 31
Atkinson, A.B. 93, 122, 126, 138, 170, 231, 326, 336
Aurbach, A.J. 138

Babu, M. 426
Bagwell, K. 52
Baier, S.J. 23
Bairoch, P. 201, 205
Balakrishnan, N. 326
Balakrishnan, P. 423, 424, 426
Balassa, B. 256
Baldwin, R. 282, 359
Banerjee, A.V. 158, 220, 326, 336, 340
Bardhan, P. 454, 457
Barro, R.J. 12, 131, 266, 303, 307, 318, 336, 360, 466, 471, 476, 480, 487
Bauer, P.T. 524
Baumol, W.J. 108, 255, 256
Beck, T. 490
Becker, G.S. 12, 358

Bekaert, G. 481
Bénabou, R. 210, 335
Ben-David, D. 206, 266, 268, 273, 282
Bergstrand, J.H. 23
Berik, G. 367
Berman, E. 356, 365, 366
Bernanke, 471
Bernard, A.B. 257
Berry, A. 20, 107, 109, 115, 213, 214, 245
Betancourt, R. 156
Bevan, D.L. 522, 523
Beyer, H. 365
Bhagwati, J. 27, 396, 397, 398, 400, 418, 423, 438, 446
Bhalla, S. 332, 456
Bidani, B. 327
Biggs, T. 522
Bigsten, A. 522, 523, 528
Bils, M. 322
Birdsall, N. 337, 340
Blackman, S.A.B. 255
Blattman, C. 34, 51, 52
Bloom, J. 518, 519
Blundell, R. 326, 485
Bohara, A. 268
Boltho, A. 26
Bond, S. 326, 485, 486
Borensztein 479
Bossert, W. 142
Bosworth, B. 422, 423, 457, 469, 471, 514, 518
Bourdot, Y. 259
Bourguignon, F. 20, 25, 85, 93, 113, 122, 129, 132, 133, 170, 214, 245
Bover, O. 326, 485, 486
Brandolini, A. 326, 336
Braun, M. 150
Bravo-Ortega, C. 479, 479
Brown, J.A.C. 326
Bruno, M. 128, 334, 340, 341
Bulmer-Thomas, V. 52
Burki, S.J. 493
Burniaux, J.-M. 29
Burnside, C. 524

Cairncross 68
Calderón, C. 360, 471

Cannadine 61
Canning, D. 490
Capie, F. 52
Caprio, G. 482, 501
Caroli, E. 335
Caselli, F. 487
Cass, D. 255
Chadha, R. 416, 417, 450, 456
Chand, S. 424–5, 427, 453
Chen, J. 380
Chen, S. 52, 86, 107, 113, 127, 128, 129, 131,
    140, 145, 164, 165, 168, 169, 170, 171, 176,
    189, 200, 214, 248, 303, 304, 325, 326, 331,
    332, 334, 335, 340, 375, 376
Chiswick, B.R. 24
Chong, A. 360
Chotikapanich, D. 212, 213
Christensen, L. 469
Chua, A. 139
Clark, C. 201
Clark, X. 45, 46
Clarke, G.R.G. 340
Clemens, M.A. 24, 34, 41, 42, 43, 51, 52
Cline, W. 29, 48
Coatsworth, J.H. 34, 43, 50
Collier, P. 51, 71, 74, 76, 517, 518, 520, 521, 524,
    525, 527
Collins, D. 256
Collins, S.M. 157, 158, 422, 423, 469, 471, 514,
    518
Concialdi, P. 224
Cooper, R. 354
Couper, M.P. 332
Cowell, F. 126, 132, 142
Culpepper, R. 93
Cummings, D. 469
Cunningham, W. 367

Das, D.K. 426
Dasgupta, P. 126
Datt, G. 166, 189, 200, 327, 332, 337, 340
Daveri, F. 456
Davies, J.B. 221
Davis, D. 67
De Gregorio, J. 469, 479
Deaton, A. 163, 171, 189, 340, 524
Deininger, K. 83, 212, 304, 337, 340, 359, 360
DeLong, B. 20, 51, 198, 256, 420, 422
Denison, E. 469
Dercon, S. 519, 525
Desai, P. 396, 397, 398
Devereaux, M. 368
Dholakia, B.H. 424
Dholakia, R.H. 424

Diakosavvas, D. 35
Diamond, J. 527
Dickerson, A. 365
Dinopoulos, E. 369
Dollar, D. 28, 47, 68, 72, 73, 78, 83, 127, 136,
    256, 330, 332, 333, 337, 340, 343–5, 347–53,
    360, 481, 490, 520, 524, 525
Dowrick, S. 20, 51, 255
Duclos, J.-Y. 138, 233
Duflo, E. 220, 326, 336, 340
Durlaf, S.N. 257
Dutta Roy, S. 455
Duttagupta, R. 416

Easterly, W. 303, 307, 313, 326, 327, 340, 466,
    470, 481, 482, 490, 491, 518, 520, 522
Eastwood, R. 367
Edmonds, E. 48
Edwards, S. 28, 318
Eichengreen, B. 455
Eken, S. 283
El-Agraa, A.M. 256
Elbadawi, I. 325, 525
Elias, V. 469
Esquivel, G. 487
Evans, P. 197

Fafchamps, M. 521
Fan, S. 375, 383, 389
Fang, C. 375, 377, 383
Fatás, A. 481, 490
Fay, M. 490
Feenstra, R.C. 28, 356, 359, 365, 366
Fei, J. 369
Fernandez, R. 157
Fields, G.S. 128, 129, 145, 340
Filmer, D. 327
Findlay, R. 22, 25, 35, 50
Fink, C. 445
Firebaugh, G. 26, 214
Fischer, S. 327, 340, 360, 481, 490
Flam, H. 25
Flanders, M.J. 25
Fleisher, B.M. 380
Flemming, J.S. 30
Fontana, M. 358
Forbes, K.J. 307, 315, 316, 336
Forsyth, J. 125
Fortin, C. 233
Foster, J. 138, 170, 303, 325, 327, 350
Frankel, J.A. 72, 313, 327
Fujita, M. 64, 358, 385

Gallup, J.L. 303, 366, 526

Galor, O. 325, 326
Garcia-Penalosa, C. 335
Garg, A. 521
Gerschenkron, A. 206
Gibson, J. 166
Gilbert, C. 93
Gindling, T.H. 30, 365, 366
Glaeser, E. 73, 85, 367
Goldin, C. 24, 29
Gordon, J. 428
Gorg, H. 365, 366
Gouyette, C. 327
Graham, C. 157, 159
Gray 61
Green, F. 365
Greer, J. 138
Griffin, K. 30, 31
Griliches, Z. 469
Grosch, M.E. 107, 213
Grove, A.T. 519
Groves, R.M. 332
Gunning, J.W. 51, 71, 74, 517, 524, 525, 527
Gupta, P. 428
Gurkaynak 471
Gwin, C. 524

Hadass, Y.S. 35, 36, 37, 51
Hanson, G.H. 28, 31, 356, 365, 366, 367, 385
Hanson, J.R. 205, 359, 365
Haque, N. 531
Harrison, A.E. 30, 365, 385
Harvey, C. 481
Hassett, K.A. 138
Hatton, T.J. 24, 45, 46, 51, 79, 81
Hausmann, R. 151
Heckscher, E. 25
Helpman, E. 255
Hertel, T. 37
Heston, A. 4, 257
Higgins, M. 360
Hilgert, M. 216
Hill, K. 201
Hirschmann, A.O. 158
Hirst, P.Q. 22
Hnatkovska, V. 490
Hoeffler, A.A. 76, 520, 528
Hoekman, B.M. 37
Hoffman, P.T. 32, 47
Holtz-Eakin, D. 485
Huber, J.R. 35
Huberman, M. 49
Hulton, C.R. 423, 424, 427
Hume, D. 207

Hussain, B. 375, 376

Irwin, D.A. 33

Jalan, J. 340
Jaspersen, F. 531
Jenkins, R.S. 366, 455
Jenkins, S.P. 136, 142
Jensen, F.B. 256, 259
Jian, T. 385
Joekes, S. 358
Johnson, S. 50
Johnston, N. 326
Jones, C. 198
Jonsson, B. 26
Jorgenson, D.W. 469
Joshi, V. 398, 457
Jovanovic, B. 256

Kakwani, N. 221
Kanbur, R. 93, 135, 141, 211, 341, 375, 380, 389, 390
Katz, L.F. 29
Kaufmann, D. 313
Keefer, P. 313, 480, 518
Kehoe, T.J. 416, 419, 443
Kelkar, U.R. 228
Kelkar, V. 417, 448, 453, 457
Kemp, M. 284
Kendrick, J. 469
Khan, A.R. 375, 376
Khang, K.H. 385
Kim, J.-I. 422, 423
Kirman, A.P. 107
Klenow, P.J. 322, 470
Klingebiel, D. 482, 501
Knack, S. 313, 480, 518
Knight, M. 487
Knowles, S. 336
Kolm, S. 142
Konow, J. 138
Koopmans, T.C. 255
Korzeniewick, R.P. 213, 214
Kotz, S. 326
Kraay, A. 28, 47, 73, 78, 83, 127, 136, 325, 330, 332, 333, 337, 340, 343–5, 347–53, 360, 490
Kranton, R. 135
Kravis, I.B. 222
Kremer, M. 490
Krishna, B. 426, 427
Krishnan, P. 284
Krueger, A.O. 27
Krugman, P.R. 64, 255, 284, 358, 359, 422
Kuo, S. 369

Kuznets, S. 200, 204, 312
Kwiatkowski, D. 387

Lach, S. 256
Lambert, P.J. 136, 142, 229, 242
Lau, L. 422, 423
Leamer, E. 303, 319, 356
Lee, J.W. 466, 471
Lee, K.S. 522
Lefort, F. 487
Lerman, S.I. 228, 229
Levine, R. 313, 327, 397, 470, 482, 490, 518, 520, 522, 523
Levy, P.I. 285
Lewchuk, W. 49
Li, H. 210, 220, 303, 307, 326, 336
Li, X.-M. 375, 376, 386
Liang, E. 389
Limão 74
Lin, J.Y. 375, 380, 383, 384, 386, 391
Lindbeck, A. 224
Lindert, P.H. 19, 23, 25, 29, 60, 61, 71, 109
Lipton, M. 367
Little, I.M.D. 398
Livi-Baski, M. 201
Lloyd, P.J. 284
Loayza, N. 466, 471, 478, 481, 487, 490, 493
Lockwood, B. 368
Londono, J.L. 337, 360
Lucas, R.E., Jr. 5, 204, 478
Lunati, M. 354
Lundberg, M. 131, 210, 303, 304, 318, 360
Lundblad, C. 481
Lustig, N. 211, 389
Lyons, T.P. 375, 377

Ma, J. 380
Machin, S. 356, 365, 366
MacMillan, J. 375
Maddison, A. 20, 22, 58, 60, 62, 78, 108, 109, 115, 136, 158, 195, 196, 199, 201, 204, 263, 264, 278, 513
Manasse, P. 456
Martin, W. 37
Masika, S. 358
Mattoo, A. 445
Mauro, P. 480, 518
Mayer, J. 367, 520, 529
Mayes, D.G. 256
Mazumdar, J. 365, 366
Mazur, J. 299
McAskie, C. 93
McCallum, J. 524
Meade, J.E. 284

Mehra, R. 457
Melchior, A. 26, 50, 51, 243
Meng, L. 136
Mengistae, T. 523
Mezzetti, C. 369
Micklewright, J. 30
Milanovic, B. 50, 107, 108, 112, 129, 133, 134, 135, 149, 150, 157, 158, 225, 238, 340
Miller, R. 524
Mitra, D. 426, 427
Moav, O. 326
Mody, A. 368
Montiel, P. 466, 481, 493
Mookerjee, D. 115, 228
Moran, T. 213, 214
Morrison, K. 93, 245
Morrissey, O. 365
Morrisson, C. 20, 25, 85, 109, 129, 132, 133, 214
Mukerji, P. 419–20
Mundell 61
Musgrave, R. 369

Nadiri, I. 422, 423
Nafziger, E.W. 107, 213
Nagaraj, R. 455
Nelson, J. 524
Newey, W. 485
Nguyen, D.-T. 255
Nishimizu, M. 423

O'Connor, D. 354
O'Rourke, K.H. 21, 22, 23, 25, 35, 42, 47, 50, 51, 132
Oates, W. 369
Obstfeld, M. 24, 25, 41
Ohlin, B. 25
Olinto, P. 337, 340
Olofsdotter, K. 479
Oostendorp, R. 367
Ostry, A. 158
Ouliaris, S. 387, 388
Ozmucur, S. 31

Panagariya, A. 282, 416, 422, 434, 438, 443, 446, 454, 455, 457
Palacios, L. 493
Pamuk, S. 31
Papell, D. 206
Pattillo, C. 76, 518
Pavcnik, N. 48
Perotti, R. 307, 340, 490
Perry, G.E. 493
Persson, T. 307, 340
Pestieau, P. 327

Pfingsten, A. 142
Phillips, P.C.B. 387, 388
Piazza, A. 389
Pigou, A.C. 138
Pissarides, C. 356, 365
Podder, N. 212
Pogge, T.W. 189
Pomeranz, K. 31
Pradhan, S. 521
Prasad, H.A.C. 412
Preeg, E.H. 271
Pritchett, L. 20, 51, 108, 114, 117, 133, 151, 152, 155, 158, 159, 201, 327, 491
Prud'homme, R. 383
Psacharopoulos, G. 471
Pursell, G. 399, 400, 417, 418
Pushpangandan, K. 423, 424, 426
Pyatt, G. 226, 238

Qian, Y. 380
Quah, D.T. 119, 120
Quispie-Agnoli, M. 365, 366

Radetzki, M. 26
Rama, M. 354, 367
Ranis, G. 369
Rao, J.M. 423, 424
Rao, M.G. 452
Ravallion, M. 52, 83, 86, 107, 113, 125, 127, 128, 129, 130, 131, 137, 138, 140, 145, 148, 149, 154, 157, 159, 165, 166, 168, 169, 170, 171, 176, 189, 200, 214, 248, 303, 304, 325, 326, 327, 331, 332, 334, 335, 336, 337, 340, 353, 375, 376, 389
Rebelo, S.T. 313
Reddy, S.G. 189
Reinikka, R. 521, 522
Ricardo, D. 3
Richardson, D.J. 211
Ridao-Cano, C. 366
Riskin, C. 375
Robbins, D.J. 30, 365, 366
Robertson, R. 31, 48, 51, 365, 366
Robinson, J. 49, 50
Rodgers, Y. 367
Rodoano, M. 368
Rodríguez, F. 52, 72, 327, 344, 348, 369
Rodriguez-Clare, A. 470, 521, 522
Rodrik, D. 49, 52, 72, 155, 157, 307, 327, 340, 344, 347–8, 353, 359, 368, 369, 370, 394, 420, 422, 434, 518, 525
Rojas, P. 365
Roland, G. 380
Romer, P.M. 72, 255, 313, 327, 418

Rosen, H.S. 485
Ross, D. 340
Rostow, W.W. 196, 207
Rozelle, S. 376
Ruhl, K. 419

Sabot, R. 340
Sachs, J.D. 28, 71, 72, 83, 517, 518, 519, 525, 526
Sala-í-Martin, X. 26, 52, 129, 133, 135, 149, 266, 480
Samuelson, P.A. 255
Sandler, T. 93
Sandstrom, A. 231
Sastry, D. 228
Scandizzo, P.L. 35
Schuknecht, L. 524
Schultz, T.P. 26, 107, 132, 133, 135, 212
Seale, J.L., Jr. 107, 212
Seguino, S. 367
Selden, M. 383
Sen, A. 166
Sen, K. 366, 424–5, 427, 453
Serra, D. 456
Shah, A. 367
Shorrocks, A.F. 112, 113, 115, 221, 228, 234, 377
Silber, J. 228
Sivadasan, J. 426, 427, 450
Slaughter, M. 368
Smith, A. 3, 64
Sokoloff 64
Solinger, D. 383
Solow, R.M. 12, 255, 469
Son, W. 422, 423
Spilimbergo, A. 284, 285, 294, 303, 318, 360
Sprout, R.V.A. 107
Squire, L. 83, 128, 131, 210, 212, 303, 304, 318, 340, 341, 359, 360
Srinivasan, S. 423, 424, 427
Staiger, R.W. 52
Stein, E. 284, 285, 294
Stokey, N.L. 17
Strobl, E. 365, 366
Sudaram, K. 166
Summers, L.H. 201, 491
Summers, R. 4, 107, 257, 278
Sutton 64
Svensson, J. 521
Székely, M. 216, 303, 325, 327, 350, 360

Tabellini, G. 307, 340
Tachibanaki, T. 215
Taylor, A.M. 24, 25, 39, 41
te Velde, D.W. 365, 366

Teal, F. 366
Telle, K. 26, 50, 51
Tendulkar, S.D. 166
Thompson, G. 22
Thorbecke, E. 138, 148
Tomasini, L.M. 107
Toniolo, G. 26
Topalova, P. 426
Trimmer, A. 24
Tsui, K. 375, 376, 377, 380, 383, 391
Tzannatos, Z. 367

Unel, B. 426

Van de Walle, D. 140, 141, 200, 341
Van Ypersele, T. 359
Van Zanden, J.L. 31
Venables, A. 64, 68, 74, 282, 289, 358
Vergara, R. 365
Villaneuva, D. 487
Vines, D. 93
Voortman, R.L. 519

Wade, R.H. 189
Walter, I. 256, 259
Wan, H. 284
Wang, S. 389
Wang, X. 136
Warner, A. 28, 71, 72, 83

Warner, M. 525, 526
Weaver, J.H. 107
Weinstein, D. 51, 67
Whalley, J. 367
Wheeler, D. 368
White, H. 355
Widner, J.A. 522
Williamson, J.G. 19, 21, 23, 24, 25, 29, 32, 33, 34, 36, 37, 38, 39, 42, 43, 45, 46, 50, 51, 52, 60, 61, 71, 79, 81, 132, 211, 360, 456
Willig, H. 26, 50, 51
Wolff, E.N. 255, 256
Wood, A. 28, 30, 211, 354, 356, 357, 358, 359, 360, 365, 366, 367, 369, 370, 385, 520, 529

Yagi, T. 215
Yang, D.T. 375, 376, 377, 383, 390
Yao, S. 380
Yasuba, Y. 35
Yatopoulos, P.A. 107
Yitzhaki, S. 228, 229, 238
Young, A. 422

Zeira, J. 325
Zhang, T. 383
Zhang, X. 375, 380, 383, 390
Zhao, R. 30, 31
Zoido-Lobatón 71
Zou, H. 307, 336, 383, 390
Zveglich, J. 367